Books by Malcolm McConnell

Fiction
MATATA
CLINTON IS ASSIGNED
JUST CAUSES

Nonfiction
STEPPING OVER
INTO THE MOUTH OF THE CAT
INCIDENT AT BIG SKY
THE ESSENCE OF FICTION
CHALLENGER: A MAJOR MALFUNCTION
MEN FROM EARTH (with Buzz Aldrin)

With Carol McConnell:
FIRST CROSSING
MIDDLE SEA AUTUMN
THE MEDITERRANEAN DIET

HAZARDOUS
DUTY

☆ ☆

*An American Soldier
in the Twentieth Century*

MAJOR GENERAL
JOHN K. SINGLAUB

U.S. ARMY (RET.)

with

MALCOLM McCONNELL

SUMMIT BOOKS

NEW YORK   LONDON   TORONTO   SYDNEY   TOKYO   SINGAPORE

SUMMIT BOOKS
Simon & Schuster Building
Rockefeller Center
1230 Avenue of the Americas
New York, New York 10020

Designed by Irving Perkins Associates
Manufactured in the United States of America

1 3 5 7 9 10 8 6 4 2

Library of Congress Cataloging-in-Publication Data
Singlaub, John K.
Hazardous duty : an American soldier in the twentieth century /
John K. Singlaub with Malcolm McConnell.
p.   cm.
Includes bibliographical references and index.
1. Singlaub, John K.   2. Generals—United States—Biography.
3. United States.   Army—Biography.   I. McConnell, Malcolm.
II. Title
U53.S56A3   1991
355′.0092—dc20
[B]   91-14572   CIP

ISBN 0-671-70516-4

Editorial cartoon of Major General John K. Singlaub (U.S. Army, Ret.) reprinted courtesy of
Bob Englehart, *The Journal-Herald* (Dayton, Ohio).

MAPS BY RAFAEL PALACIOS

The authors gratefully acknowledge the following for permission to reprint photographs:

Leonard Wood: photo 5
OSS: photos 2, 6
Department of Defense/Office of the Secretary of Defense: photo 25
U. S. Army: photos 1, 14, 15, 16, 20, 21, 22, 23, 24, 26, 28, 29

This book is dedicated to my children, Elisabeth, John, and Mary Ann, in the hope they will better understand why their father was always "gone" . . . and to their mother, Mary, who took my place when I was.

Acknowledgments

☆　　　☆

Writing an accurate memoir that spans five of this century's most historic and tumultuous decades would have been an impossible task without the help of many individuals and institutions.

I wish to thank the staff of the Center of Military History, Department of the Army—particularly for the access they provided to unpublished manuscripts treating the deployment of combat troops to Vietnam in 1965. Research professionals at the National Archives, Military Branch, provided significant assistance in locating original unit records. The reference departments of the Pentagon Library and the U.S. Naval Academy's Nimitz Library were helpful in tracking down both original and secondary sources. Members of the National Security Council provided information on the Carter administration's plans to withdraw American combat forces from Korea. The Defense Intelligence College located certain key documents cited in the book.

Walter Pforzheimer, former legislative counsel of the Central Intelligence Agency, gave me the fascinating quote from General George Washington that appears as an epigraph. Mr. Pforzheimer was also generous with his time, briefing me on the role of the CIA during the first months of the Korean War.

Kevin A. Mahoney, consultant in twentieth-century military history, proved to be an energetic and insightful researcher, diligent in tracking down often obscure OSS records, including the Jedburgh Team James After-Action Report and the report of POW Rescue Team Pigeon.

5

Major Wyman W. Irwin, USA, shared with me much of his research on the Jedburgh program.

Jacques Le Bel de Penguilly demonstrated that his memory and perceptions are just as sharp today as they were during those exciting months of 1944 when he was my teammate in Jedburgh Team James. Daphne Mundinger Friele, a former British FANY, kept me honest in recreating my Jedburgh service.

In reconstructing the events of my OSS assignments in the Far East and the POW rescue mission to Hainan island, I am indebted to E. Howard Hunt, William McAfee, Ralph Yempuku, John B. Bradley, James McGuire, and Benjamin T. Muller. Former POW Merritt Eugene Lewis kindly shared with me his vivid unpublished memoir of his captivity on Hainan.

I was able to verify key facts about my CIA service in Manchuria and Korea with the help of Colonels David Longacre, John F. "Skip" Sadler, Fitzhugh H. Chandler, and John W. Collins III, USA (ret.), and Scott Miler, Carlton Swift, and Harold B. Leith.

Colonel Robert Channon, USA (ret.), kindly provided official studies and original unpublished manuscripts on the Rangers in Korea. Colonels George A. Meighen and John D. "Dan" Foldberg, USA (ret.), then first lieutenants in the 2nd Battalion, 15th Infantry Regiment, 3rd Infantry Division, as well as Colonel James Harvey Short, USA (ret.), were of particular help with the chapter on the Korean War.

Lieutenant General John H. Hay, USA (ret.), provided key insights into the discussion of my service at the U.S. Army's Command and General Staff College.

A number of my former colleagues in MACV/SOG, including Brigadier General Thomas Bowen, USA (ret.), George W. Gaspard, former ARVN Colonel Tran Van Ho, and Lieutenant Colonel Fred Caristo, USA (ret.), provided vivid and detailed information for this section of the book. My former embassy liaison officer in Saigon, Bill Donnett, refreshed my memory on several key points. Douglas Pike, Director, Indochina Studies Archive, Institute of East Asian Studies, University of California at Berkeley, shared his expertise on the Indochina war with me. Lieutenant General Harold G. Moore, USA (ret.), shared with me his memories of the battle of the Ia Drang valley. Lieutenant General Phillip B. Davidson, USA (ret.), provided insights on North Vietnamese methods and tactics, as did Colonel Harry G. Summers, Jr., USA (ret.). Lieutenant General Roy Manor, USAF (ret.), verified facts concerning the release of American POWs in 1973.

In writing about my Cold War service in Europe, I drew upon the recollections of Dr. Gene L. Curtis, Colonel Robert J. Pinkerton, USA (ret.), Powell A. Moore, Charles R. MacCrone, Colonel Edgar B. Colladay, USA (ret.), Brigadier General James K. Terry, USA (ret.), and Lieutenant General Robert C. Taber, USA (ret.).

Arthur R. Woods gave me useful background documents and information on Project MASSTER. Lieutenant General E. M. "Fly" Flanagan, Jr., USA (ret.), reminded me of the difficulties a fifty-year-old brigadier general encountered learning to fly the Huey helicopter. Colonel E. K. Johnson, USA (ret.), reminded me that managing a large Army readiness region was almost as difficult a task.

Thomas M. Ryan, Command Historian, U.S. Forces, Korea, provided declassified original documents and reports on the North Korean Army buildup of the 1970s, the ax murders in the JSA, and Operation PAUL BUNYAN. Colonel James Young, USA (ret.), detailed for me the intricate communications system we established for that operation. Intelligence analyst John Armstrong generously shared his unique insights and knowledge on the North Korean military. Ambassador Philip Habib provided similar assistance from the political perspective. James H. Hausman opened his files to provide details on the ill-fated John Saar background briefing.

General Frederick J. Kroesen, USA (ret.), reminded me of the intricate arrangements he made to shield my arrival at his command at Fort McPherson, Georgia, from the press.

Staff members of the congressional committees investigating the Iran-Contra Affair provided important insights on the testimony of several key witnesses. Former and serving American civilian intelligence officers also assisted me in writing my account of the Iran-Contra Affair. I respect these persons' desires to remain anonymous but nevertheless wish to acknowledge their invaluable assistance.

Several people graciously agreed to critique the book's long manuscript. In so doing, they provided vital information and corrected many inadvertent errors. These people include General Richard G. Stilwell, USA (ret.), Edward Luttwak, Constantine Menges, Adolfo Calero, Daphne Mundinger Friele, and Professor Geir Finne.

Despite the diligence of these unofficial editors and a rigorous effort by Summit Books' professional editors, a few inadvertent factual errors may remain in the text. I take full responsibility for these, and for the interpretation of historical persons and events in the book.

Contents

☆　　☆

PART IV
HAZARDOUS DUTY

LIST OF ABBREVIATIONS

ACofs—Assistant Chief of Staff

ACSFOR—Assistant Chief of Staff, Force Development

ACSI—Assistant Chief of Staff, Intelligence

AGL—Above Ground Level

AK—Automat Kalashnikov (series of Soviet-designed assault rifles: AK-47, AK-74, AKM, etc.)

ALG—Army Liaison Group

APACL—Asian People's Anti-Communist League. Later changed to Asian Pacific Anti-Communist League

ARDE—Nicaraguan Democratic Revolutionary Alliance (Spanish): Contra's southern front

ASC—American Security Council

AW—Automatic Weapons

BCRA—Bureau Central de Renseignements et Action (Free French Intelligence Bureau, World War II)

BOQ—Bachelor Officers' Quarters

CBI—China, Burma, India (Theater of Operations)

CCF—Chinese Communist Forces

CCRAK—Combined Command, Reconnaissance Activities, Korea

CG—Commanding General

CIDG—Civilian Irregular Defense Group

CINCFE—Commander in Chief, Far East

CINCPAC—Commander in Chief, Pacific

CINCSHAEF—Commander in Chief, Supreme Headquarters Allied Expeditionary Force

CINCUNC—Commander in Chief, United Nations command

CO—Commanding Officer

Co—Company

CP—Command Post

CSS—Coastal Survey Service (Part of SOG)

CW—Continuous Wave (Morse Code)

DCSLOG—Deputy Chief of Staff, Logistics

DCSOPS—Deputy Chief of Staff, Operations

DCSPER—Deputy Chief of Staff, Personnel

DGI—Cuban Directorate General of Intelligence (Spanish)

ESD-USN—External Survey Detachment–U.S. Navy

ETA—Basque Terrorist Group (Spanish)

FANY—First Aid Nursing Yeomanry (British, World War II)

FDN—Nicaraguan Democratic Front (Spanish): Contras

FDP—Force Development Plan

FEC—Far East Command

FFI—French Forces of the Interior

FMLN—El Salvador, Farabundo Marti National Liberation Front (Spanish)

FOB—Forward Operating Base

FORSCOM—U.S. Army Forces Command

FPAO—Force Planning and Analysis Office

FRS—Sandino Revolutionary Front (Spanish): Eden Pastora's Contra group

FSLN—Nicaraguan Sandinista National Liberation Front (Spanish)

FSSB—Fire Support Surveillance Base

FTP—Francs-Tireurs et Partisans

GCI—Ground Controlled Intercept (radar)

GRU—Soviet military intelligence

HALO—High Altitude, Low Opening (a technique of free-fall parachuting)

IDF—Israeli Defense Forces

JACK—Joint Assistance Command, Korea

JPRC—Joint Personnel Recovery Center (Part of the SOG)

JSA—Joint Security Area

KATUSA—Korean Augmentation to the U.S. Army

KMAG—U.S. Military Advisory Group to the Republic of Korea

KSC—Korean Service Corps

MAC—Military Airlift Command

MAC—Military Armistice Commission (Korea)

MACTHAI—Military Assistance Command, Thailand

MACV/SOG—Military Assistance Command, Vietnam, Studies and Observation Group

MAD—Mutually Assured Destruction

MDL—Military Demarcation Line

MINT—Nicaraguan Sandinista Ministry of Interior

MIRV—Multiple Independently Targeted Re-entry Vehicle

MISURA—Nicaraguan Miskito, Suma, and Rama Indian Contra resistance group

MLR—Main Line of Resistance

MOS—Military Occupational Specialty

MPLA—Popular Movement for the Liberation of Angola (Portugese)

NAD—Naval Advisory Detachment (Part of SOG)

NECC—North East China Command

NKPA—North Korean People's Army

NVA—North Vietnamese Army

OD—Officer of the Day

OD—Olive drab (color)

OP—Observation Post

OPLAN—Operations Plan

OSD—Office of the Secretary of Defense

PIAT—Projectile, Infantry, Anti-Tank

PIR—Parachute Infantry Regiment

POL—Petroleum, oil, lubricants

PPBS—Planning, Programming, and Budget System

PRC—People's Republic of China (Communist Government on mainland)

PRM—Presidential Review Memorandum

ROC—Republic of China

ROC—Republic of China (Nationalist Government on Taiwan)

ROKA—Republic of Korea Army

RPG—Rocket Propelled Grenade (Soviet design)

RPK—Soviet design light machinegun, 7.62 mm

SACSA—Special Assistant for Counterinsurgency and Special Activities

SGS—Secretary of the General Staff

SHAPE—Supreme Headquarters, Allied Powers Europe

SOE—Special Operations Executive (British, World War II)

SOG—Studies and Observation Group

SSU—Strategic Services Unit (of the War Department)

STABO—Harness worn by Special Operations personnel to permit helicopter extraction through jungle canopy; initials of five men who invented the system.

STANO—Surveillance, Target Acquisition and Night Observation

STASI—East German Ministry for State Security—Intelligence Service

STD—South Vietnamese Strategic and Technical Directorate

STRAC—Strategic Army Corps (colloquial: sharp military appearance)

STRATA—Short-Term Reconn and Tactical Teams (Part of SOG)

"TNT"—Tunnel Neutralization Team (Korea, circa 1976)

TO&E—Table of Organization and Equipment

TOW—Tube-launched, Optically Tracked, and Wire Guided (U.S. Army Anti-tank missile)

TTPPS—Transients, Trainees, Patients, Prisoners, and Students

UNITA—National Union for Total Independence of Angola (Portuguese)

UNO—United Nicaraguan Opposition: Contras' united front

USALG—U.S. Army Liaison Group

USASG—U.S. Army Support Group (Korea, circa 1970s)

USCWF—U.S. Council for World Freedom

USFK—United States Forces, Korea

VNAF—Vietnamese Air Force

VT—Variable Time (a type of radar-activated proximity fuse for artillery)

The necessity of procuring good Intelligence is apparent + the need not to be further urged— All that remains for me to add, is that you keep the whole matter as secret as possible. For upon Secrecy, Success depends in most Enterprizes of the kind, and for want of it, they are generally defeated, however well planned + promising a favourable issue.

—Letter from General George Washington to Colonel Elias Dayton, July 26, 1777 (original in the Walter Pforzheimer Collection on Intelligence Service, Washington, D.C.)

INTRODUCTION

U.S. District Court, Washington, D.C.

March 1, 1989

☆ ☆

OLLIE NORTH WAS the first person I noticed on entering the courtroom. He was hunched over a pile of documents at the defense table, next to his attorney, Brendan Sullivan.

This was the third day of testimony in the most celebrated Washington trial of the decade, and the benches of the gallery were jammed with news media, kibitzing lawyers, and diplomatic observers. Sullivan looked up and nodded, a precise, neutral gesture of recognition. His features were sharp, his hands well manicured, and the black-framed glasses intensified the intelligence of his blue gaze. Perched there like a hungry falcon, he would not have easily been mistaken for a potted plant.

Then Ollie nodded, his face still creased in concentration, a hint of a smile around his mouth, but wariness in his dark eyes. We had worked together closely, trying to support the armed democratic resistance to the Communist Sandinistas in Nicaragua during the two-year congressional ban on aid mandated by the Boland Amendment. But it had been many months since we'd had any substantive contact, a period of chaotic political upheaval during which Ollie had been dragged from obscurity on the National Security Council to become one of the best-known people in the Western world.

Judge Gerhard Gesell was seated on the bench, and the jury was in the box. Gesell had a round, ruddy face, thoughtful eyes, and fine white hair; he certainly *looked* eminently qualified to be a federal judge trying an important case.

15

But the members of the jury were another matter. After being sworn, I took the stand and faced them. They were almost all women. To qualify as jurors, they had to be citizens who voted, paid their taxes, and had no legal problems. But, even though the District of Columbia had the highest proportion of black professionals of any city in the world, these jurors were all working class, some without even a high school education. In order to serve on this panel, they'd had to convince the attorneys and Judge Gesell that they had not watched the television coverage of the Iran-Contra hearings, or formed any opinion about Ollie North's guilt or innocence.

They looked like decent people who worked hard, went to church, and cared for their families. But they also looked out of their depth.

Judge Gesell reminded me that my testimony had to be based on my personal recollection of actual events, and not on any of the depositions or testimony I had read or heard during the congressional Iran-Contra hearings. Every trial is governed by elaborate rules of evidence, but this procedure had attained almost metaphysical complexity. And I felt frustrated because these restrictions would prevent me from telling the jury all I knew of the whole sordid Iran-Contra fiasco. In theory, at least, the prosecution was under the same restraints.

The three attorneys at the government table were led by John Keker, a lanky ex-Marine with a Vietnam combat record as good as North's. Michael Bromwich was bearded and looked more scholarly. As David Zornow, the third government attorney, rose to begin my examination, he moved with the precision and control shared by veteran actors and trial lawyers. He spoke with exaggerated clarity, a slight echo of New York City's outer boroughs overlaid by Ivy League.

Zornow immediately established that I was a retired Army major general with more than thirty-five years' active duty.

Asked to outline my service in World War II, I noted that I had served in a parachute infantry regiment, then volunteered for "an organization known as OSS, the Office of Strategic Services." I faced the jury, trying to speak directly to them. "I was sent to Europe, where I joined a group of other Allied officers. We trained as teams of three, and I parachuted into Nazi-occupied France with a French officer and an American radio operator." I wanted to avoid military jargon, to speak plainly without condescension. "The three of us then organized, trained, and led the French Resistance in preparation for the Allied landings that were to take place on the southern coast of France."

I'd specifically used the word "Nazi" instead of "German." For a decade I'd been smeared as a right-wing fanatic, even a crypto-fascist, by some members of the media. I'd always found this ironic, considering the fact that I was one of a handful of American soldiers who had risked torture and execution by both German and Japanese fascists, while serving behind enemy lines in Europe and the Far East.

"During that duty," Zornow asked, "who did you report to? Who was your superior?"

My case officer, I said, "was a man by the name of William Casey." I stared at the jury. They gazed back with no sign of recognition.

"Is that the same William Casey, General Singlaub," Zornow asked, "who later became the director of Central Intelligence?"

I replied that it was.

Zornow then had me explain my OSS service leading Chinese guerrillas against the Japanese and my duty during the Korean War, working with the CIA, managing clandestine operations against the North Koreans, and later as the commander of a frontline infantry battalion. He asked about my service in Vietnam. "I went to Vietnam in early 1966, and served there until August of 1968. During that time I was the commander of what was called a joint unconventional-warfare task force. I had the responsibility for running covert and clandestine operations into North Vietnam, Laos, and Cambodia."

A lady in the front row of the jury box frowned. She looked like a person who didn't approve of men who ran clandestine operations.

I next sketched my service as a chief of staff of American forces in Korea in the mid-seventies.

"Under what circumstances did you leave that post?" Zornow asked, his tone still friendly.

"I had an unfortunate confrontation with Mr. Carter. I had—"

"Is that President Carter?"

"President Jimmy Carter," I answered. The President, I explained, had been planning to withdraw all American ground forces from Korea and I gave a reporter an off-the-record briefing, commenting that such a withdrawal "would lead to war just as surely as it did in 1950 when we withdrew our forces." Carter, I added, did not appreciate reading my comments on the front page of the *Washington Post*.

Apparently Zornow wanted to make it clear that I was a man of independent, outspoken temperament. And I certainly intended to be just as forthright here today. At no time during the laborious congressional and grand jury inquires into the Iran-Contra affair had I ever been the subject of criminal investigation myself. Because I hadn't broken any law, I had nothing to hide. So I'd gladly testified to the independent counsel's grand jury and to the congressional committee without requesting any immunity whatsoever from prosecution.

Honesty and openness were the personal traits I valued most highly. My dad had told me, "Jack, if you always tell the truth, you don't have to *remember* anything." And that had been my watchword during a long military career. On my second *Nightline* appearance two years before, Ted Koppel had noted, "General Singlaub, it's always so refreshing talking to you because you say things just as they are."

I guess he'd meant honesty was a rare commodity in Washington.

Zornow asked about my efforts to secure private aid for anti-Communist resistance groups around the world through the United States Council for World Freedom, a group I'd helped establish in 1981. Defense counsel Brendan Sullivan popped up to object on several occasions when Zornow's questions stretched a minor rule of testimony procedure.

Finally, Sullivan took his seat, having again demonstrated that he was not there merely for decoration. But he obviously had another motive: establishing a record of objection to be used in a post-conviction appeal. I gazed at Ollie North, who looked troubled now. Although the major criminal conspiracy charges against him had been dropped just before the trial began, he still faced a possible fifty-year sentence and huge fines.

I realized he had good reason to be worried. This jury might not be sophisticated, Ollie's true "peers," but they obviously had enough common sense to recognize fraud and outright theft when they saw it. Even though they supposedly had not watched the televised Iran-Contra hearings, they must have seen the famous media image of Lieutenant Colonel Oliver North standing at attention before the Iran-Contra congressional inquisitors in bemedaled uniform, his right hand stiffly raised as he swore to tell the truth. That was the Ollie North whom President Reagan had proclaimed "an American hero."

And I suppose in contrast to some of the hypocritical politicians on the dais in the Senate caucus room, North was heroic. But he certainly had not told the truth. It seemed to me that there had been at least two realities at work during the Iran-Contra affair: One involved the ongoing East-West struggle, the other domestic politics.

People often forget that 1984, when the Boland Amendment suspended all American aid to the Contras, was an election year. There was a popular Republican president in the White House and a Republican majority in the Senate. Congressional Democrats were frustrated. One of the few ways they could get to Ronald Reagan was to limit his constitutionally mandated responsibility for conducting foreign affairs. People also forget that Congress— both Democrats and Republicans—had come to its senses and American aid to the Contras had been resumed by the time the "Irangate" hearings took place in 1987. But many Democrats—especially presidential candidates—had hoped the criminal trials resulting from the affair would take place in 1988, another election year, and serve to open a chink in the armor of the Reagan White House.

But that had not happened. Independent counsel Lawrence Walsh had been outmaneuvered. George Bush was now in the White House, untarred by the brush of scandal. Ollie North's trial was an anticlimax.

The irony here was that neither the congressional joint committee, which took twenty-seven volumes of depositions, nor the independent counsel, who spent millions investigating the matter, had revealed the truth to the American people.

To people all over the world Ollie North was a hero. But I knew better. There was a wide gap between the media image of Ollie North, the honest, loyal Marine, and the sordid reality of his true character and performance.

Most people ignored North's ill-advised connection to a disreputable fund-raiser named Carl "Spitz" Channell and his gang of crooks whom the intelligence community disparaged as "the Fruit Loop." They'd skillfully exploited Ollie, using him as a front man for their tax-exempt National Endowment for the Preservation of Liberty, which raised several million dollars in private contributions for the Contras. Most of that money went directly into the silk-lined pockets of Channell and his colleagues. They had already bartered damaging testimony against North to plea-bargain their way to suspended sentences and, in the process, had left him facing the felony charge of defrauding the Internal Revenue Service. But the Iran-Contra congressional hearings had downplayed this nasty episode.

In their effort to drag Ronald Reagan and George Bush into the morass of the Iran-Contra scandal, the congressional committee had not exhaustively investigated North's association with Richard Secord, a former Air Force general, and Albert Hakim, his Iranian-born partner. North apparently either had not known or hadn't cared that Secord had been involved with Ed Wilson, the renegade former CIA officer. Wilson was among the worst rogue agents in the history of American intelligence, having made a fortune running a sabotage school for international terrorists in Khaddafi's Libya before being lured back and arrested in America. Without doubt, Wilson's direct support of Middle Eastern terrorists had eventually resulted in the deaths of hundreds of innocent victims, many of them Americans. And Richard Secord had narrowly escaped prosecution for his part in Wilson's crooked dealings by testifying against Wilson. But, incredibly, it was this same former General Secord whom North chose to handle the clandestine resupply of the Contras during the two-year Boland prohibition on government aid.

Far from being an astute master of intrigue (the image he reveled in), North had been a gullible dupe whom Secord and Hakim had easily manipulated. From my reading of the committee's voluminous depositions, it was obvious that it had been Secord, Hakim, and some of their Middle East contacts who had manipulated Ollie during the tragicomic fiasco of bartering weapons for American hostages. And their motive had been profit, not patriotism.

With North's blessing, they had diverted $12 million of Contra support money contributed by foreign donors to bank accounts under their control. When the tragically flawed decision to ransom American hostages was reached, Secord and Hakim had used $6 million to secretly purchase American Hawk missiles, which they sold for four times that amount to Iran, netting a profit of $18 million. Secord and Hakim had kept the bulk of the profits, and returned a mere token of the original contribution to the Nicaraguan resistance. But the committee never revealed the true nature of this diversion of funds. To compound this theft, North gave Secord and Hakim the exclusive contract to resupply the growing Nicaraguan resistance with arms and ammunition. They continued to exploit this opportunity to reap obscene profits.

During the period the Boland Amendment was in effect, my own group had been able to buy high-quality Soviet-bloc weapons on the international market at bargain rates and efficiently deliver them to the Contras in Honduras. I never made one penny of profit from this operation; I donated my time and money. But once Secord's company controlled the resupply effort, North and Secord forced the resistance to pay twice this price for inferior arms and equipment, so that Secord and Hakim could pocket the profits.

In early 1986, Contra director Adolfo Calero met with me to bitterly complain that the corrupt and inefficient Secord resupply system was rapidly eating up the Contras' funds and was clearly not capable of providing the arms needed to train and equip the thousands of disgruntled anti-Sandinista peasants flooding into their camps in Honduras. Worse, the Contra units already operating deep inside Nicaragua were short of ammunition, and the North-Secord airdrop supply system (which relied on expensive, but obsolete, aircraft) wasn't capable of meeting their desperate needs. Brave men, Calero told me, were dying in the jungle because of Secord's greed and incompetence. Ironically, during this period, the news media were savaging the Contras for their inability to carry the fight to the Sandinistas.

Calero implored me to meet with North, so that I could again arrange the supply of high-quality weapons at wholesale prices. When I did, North implied that the CIA would probably soon resume the resupply effort and sent me on a wild goose chase to see Director of Central Intelligence Bill Casey. During the period of the Boland Amendment, Casey had always adamantly refused to discuss Nicaragua with me. Once he'd said, "Jack, if you even mention the word 'Nicaragua' again, I'll throw your ass out of my office." Now North wanted me to take the Contras' case back to Casey. It was then that I began to realize that North perhaps had another agenda, and that the well-being of the Nicaraguan democratic resistance might not be his primary concern. Only later did I learn that he was already preoccupied with the ill-fated hostage-barter fiasco.

And while this whole corrupt process unfolded, the Iranians simply ordered the kidnapping of more American hostages, and the Soviets redoubled their already massive aid to their Sandinista surrogates. By the end of the second Reagan administration, there were more Americans held hostage in Lebanon than before the Iran-Contra debacle, and the Communist Sandinistas had built one of the largest armies in the Western Hemisphere.

Colonel North had betrayed the Nicaraguan resistance he had claimed so passionately to defend.

I gazed across the courtroom at North, whose head was bent as he studied a detailed chronology. As an officer who had spent much of his military career in covert operations, I might have been able to sympathize with a young Marine colonel caught up in the clandestine world for the first time, who'd been manipulated by skillful operators like Secord and Hakim. But Ollie North had broken a cardinal principle of military ethics. He had lied to his colleagues. In the covert world, there was a clear distinction between a cover story and deceiving your own men. Not only had he lied to me and others who had struggled to keep the Nicaraguan resistance alive and in the field, Ollie North had also lied about me to the congressional committee.

When asked during the hearings why he had chosen Secord's company to supply the Contras over the Washington-based firm with which I was involved, North had stated under oath that my group had illegally delivered sensitive technology to the Eastern Bloc and was thus unsuitable. A senator pressed North about this slanderous accusation. But Ollie North backpedaled, now claiming it had been one of the firm's unnamed European agents who had been involved with the fabricated illegal technology transfer. He conveniently cited Bill Casey as his source; Casey had died two months before.

North had made much of his combat record before the committee. However, one fact about combat officers I'd learned during three wars was that they never lied about operational matters. If a man called in to report he had seized an objective on Hill 804, you never doubted his word. The same principle applied to clandestine operations. But North had broken the rules.

Watching Ollie North across the stuffy courtroom, I realized that three aspects of our careers had been similar. We had both commanded troops in combat as young officers. We had both held positions of unusual responsibility in the murky world of covert operations. And, of course, we had both worked with Bill Casey. But I think that I had survived with my integrity intact and North had not.

The integrity of two military officers, however, was a minor consideration compared to the fundamental issue of who would conduct our nation's foreign and defense policies. At the height of World War II in 1944, I'd worked for Casey, a young civilian holding a temporary Navy commission. He, in turn, reported to General "Wild Bill" Donovan, the commander of the OSS. And, in his own right, Donovan took his orders directly from the president, Franklin Delano Roosevelt. In retrospect, Casey had enjoyed extraordinary authority for a junior officer. But we were at war with ruthless, totalitarian enemies, and extraordinary measures were needed to achieve victory. Most important, America had been united in a national purpose, and was dedicated to defeating fascism whatever sacrifices were required.

When Ollie North became involved with Secord and company and seemed to lose interest in the Contra guerrillas marooned in their jungle camps, America was also at war—albeit through surrogates on both sides—with an equally ruthless totalitarian enemy. Sadly, our nation was anything *but* united.

As the testimony dragged on, my thoughts returned to my early career. An image rose in my mind of two young officers in an oak-paneled room of an English manor house, standing beside a map of central France. One wore gray tweed that matched his cool gray eyes. It was William Casey. The other was a wind-burned young first lieutenant named Jack Singlaub, receiving the final briefing from his case officer a few days before dropping behind Nazi lines.

On that rainy afternoon in England in 1944, I obviously could not imagine the hazardous and complex events that would spin like a fateful web during the five turbulent decades that lay between that map room and this witness stand, to eventually entangle Bill Casey, Ollie North, and me. But now I began to see the connection.

PART I
☆   ☆

World War

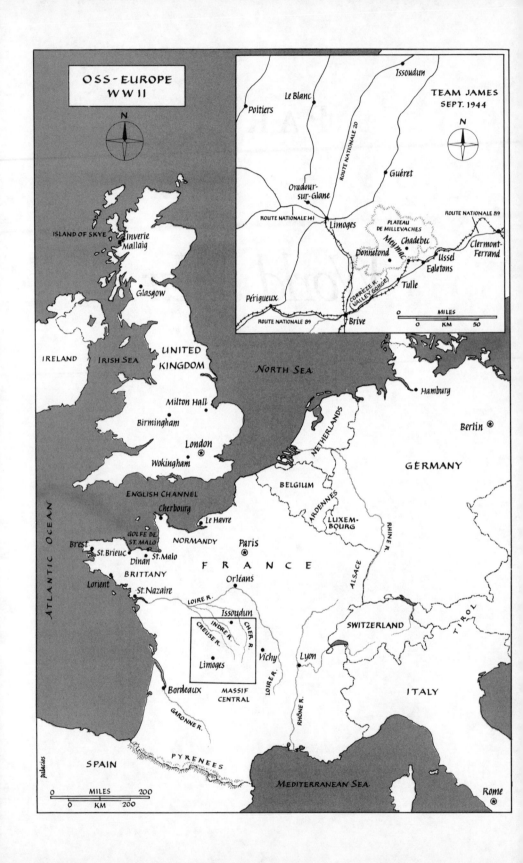

OSS-EUROPE
WW II

N

TEAM JAMES
SEPT. 1944

N

Issoudun

Poitiers   Le Blanc

Guéret

Oradour-
sur-Glane

ROUTE NATIONALE 20

ROUTE NATIONALE 141   Limoges

PLATEAU
DE MILLEVACHES

ROUTE NATIONALE 89

Chadebec

Meymac

Donnetond   Ussel

Eyletons   Clermont-
Ferrand

Périgueux

CORRÈZE R.
(VALLEY GORGE)

Tulle

ROUTE NATIONALE 89   Brive

MILES

KM   50

ISLAND OF SKYE   Inverie
Mallaig

IRELAND   IRISH SEA   UNITED
KINGDOM

NORTH SEA

Glasgow

Hamburg

Berlin ⊛

Milton Hall

Birmingham   GERMANY

London ⊛

NETHERLANDS

Wokingham

BELGIUM

ENGLISH CHANNEL

Cherbourg

ARDENNES

LUXEM-
BOURG

RHINE R.

Le Havre

GOLFE DE
ST. MALO   NORMANDY

Paris ⊛

Brest

St. Brieuc   St. Malo

ALSACE

Dinan

BRITTANY

F R A N C E

Lorient

Orléans

St. Nazaire

SWITZERLAND

TIROL

LOIRE R.

Issoudun

INDRE R.

CREUSE R.

CHER R.

Vichy

Lyon

ITALY

Limoges

LOIRE R.

ATLANTIC OCEAN

Bordeaux   MASSIF
CENTRAL

RHÔNE R.

GARONNE R.

palacios

SPAIN   PYRENEES

MEDITERRANEAN SEA

Rome ⊛

MILES   200

KM   200

CHAPTER ONE

OSS: The Jedburghs

1943–1944

☆   ☆

It was hard to stay calm as I strode down the Washington Mall on that bright October morning in 1943. A few weeks before, I'd been just another young rifle platoon leader in the 515th Parachute Infantry Regiment training at Fort Benning, Georgia. Then I answered a call for volunteers with foreign-language ability willing to accept "hazardous duty" behind enemy lines. Now I had classified War Department orders to report for an interview with an organization called the Office of Strategic Services, the OSS. I hadn't even heard of the OSS until my regimental adjutant, Captain Elvy Roberts, had told me the outfit was involved with secret intelligence and sabotage operations overseas and commanded by the fabled General "Wild Bill" Donovan. That had been good enough for me.

I entered a cluttered office in the Munitions Building, one of several *temporary,* concrete-slab World War I structures that had blighted the west end of the Mall since 1917. Placing my orders on the desk, I saluted a middle-age major who seemed uncomfortable in his rumpled uniform. There were bulging cardboard boxes of personnel files and teetering stacks of mimeographed orders scattered on his desk and nearby cabinets. He looked like a kindly professor and hardly seemed the proper gatekeeper for a supposedly crack cloak-and-dagger unit.

I felt suddenly uneasy. Maybe I'd made a bad mistake leaving the regiment. Maybe I was headed for some dead-end desk job. Since high school I'd had one ambition: to become a career Army officer. Because my dad was a Democrat in a heavily Republican district of southern California, I'd missed an appointment to West Point. At UCLA, I'd majored in Military

Science and was ROTC Cadet Colonel, hoping to earn a regular commission as Honor Graduate, but that program was canceled after Pearl Harbor. One of the reasons I'd gone Airborne was to serve in combat with an elite outfit and better my chances for a regular commission after the war. At twenty-two, of course, I had boundless confidence that I would survive the war.

After casually verifying my dates of commission and previous assignments, the major took off his gold-framed glasses and spoke with the cool, inquisitorial tone of a district attorney. "Lieutenant," he asked, "just what makes you think you are qualified for hazardous duty behind enemy lines?"

His sudden shift in manner caught me off balance, which, of course, was his design. In my very first exposure to the OSS I was learning an important lesson: Don't judge people by appearance, and maintain a proper degree of wariness when dealing with anyone.

"Sir," I began, "I'm a parachute infantry platoon leader, trained to lead men in small-unit action."

The major frowned and feigned impatience. "I *have* read your file, Lieutenant. That's why you're here. What else have you got to say for yourself?"

This interview was sure different from those I'd had in the regular Army. "I believe I'm resourceful, sir. I broke my ankle after my second jump, so I volunteered to go to demolition school while my leg was healing. Then I finished parachute training with an extra qualification." This was harder than I had thought. Obviously, they weren't looking for someone to sit behind a desk. "Sir," I continued, "I guess you'd say I've got initiative." I had been about to add that I was working on my private pilot's license and that I was serving as the regimental demolition officer, a post normally held by a captain, which gave me additional qualification for duty on sabotage missions. But, as the major had made clear, he was intimately familiar with my personnel file.

He stared at me, again the prosecuting attorney. "Do you understand a mission behind enemy lines involves unusual risk?"

"Yes, sir, I do." I knew I looked young, but I hoped I appeared tough enough for the challenge. "Sir, my old regiment is losing men as replacements for outfits already overseas. It's just possible the 515th might spend the war training replacements. I don't want that, sir."

He pursed his lips and wrote on a notepad, then filled out a printed chit, using a pen from a handsome desk set. "Our headquarters is in the old Public Health Service buildings on Twenty-fifth and E." He clipped the chit to my orders and handed them across his desk. "Report to Building Q over there at I P.M. tomorrow . . . ah, 1300, I mean." He grinned at his faux pas, an admission of fallibility by a desk-bound Washington warrior, whose job it was to do the initial sorting of wheat from chaff among earnest young men who would be asked to fight and perhaps die in desperate, isolated battles on the other side of the planet, while he held his ground in this untidy little office.

☆ ☆

IN THE headquarters parking lot the next afternoon, I found a group of nine young officers, mostly lieutenants with a couple of captains thrown in, already assembled on the sidewalk. Five of us were parachute infantry, and there were a couple of armored cavalry men, and even one Marine. After we piled into the back of a deuce-and-a-half Army truck, a corporal pulled the tarpaulin across the tailgate. We were then driven past the marble-pillared administration building and the sentry gates of the walled compound.

"You gotta keep the tarp closed," the driver called back as we rumbled up Pennsylvania Avenue toward Georgetown.

"Where're we headed?" a captain asked the driver.

"The Congressional Country Club, sir," the kid called over his shoulder, nervously wheeling the truck on the cobblestones and streetcar tracks.

The captain shook his head. "Hell," he muttered, "you ask a simple question . . ."

But the driver was not just another wiseacre GI. Half an hour later we rolled up a crescent drive and stopped before an impressive redbrick colonial structure. This was not a typical requisitioned civilian hotel stripped of its peacetime splendor. There were still handsome leather furniture, crystal chandeliers, and oil paintings in gilded frames. After the sweltering huts and fly-blown outdoor latrines of Fort Benning, this place was real luxury.

At our orientation the next day, we saw the unmistakable influence of General Donovan on the OSS. The officers who briefed us were wealthy, influential civilians who had traded Brooks Brothers gabardine for well-tailored uniforms, not West Pointers who had served between the wars in the dusty outposts of the peacetime Army. Donovan was intimate with the most successful corporate and Wall Street lawyers in New York, as well as the luminaries of the Ivy League. It was from these institutions that he drew the inner circle of his organization.

Many of the young junior volunteers were also from the wealthy East Coast milieu. They seemed to know one another, or at least recognized the subtle signs of breeding and privilege, which most of us didn't display. By the end of the war, the OSS was being called the "*Oh So Social.*" Glancing around the Club ballroom, however, I saw other tough-looking young Airborne lieutenants who bore more of the rough-edged stamp of ROTC or Officer Candidate School than recent Ivy League graduates.[1]

The welcoming colonel was quick to impress on us the secret and sensitive nature of the assembly.

"You've been brought here," he told us, "to evaluate your suitability for combat duty with resistance groups in enemy-occupied areas." He stared over his half-frame glasses at the rows of folding chairs filled with eager young officers. "I'm talking about guerrilla warfare, espionage, and sabotage. Obviously, no one doubts your courage, but we have to make certain you possess the qualities needed for a type of operation never before attempted on the scale we envision."[2]

Guerrillas, the colonel said, move fast and operate mainly at night, then disperse into the countryside, only to reassemble miles away. The skills required of a guerrilla leader would be the same as those shown by legendary backwoods fighters and Indian scouts. I smiled now. Since early childhood, I'd preferred outdoor sports, camping, hunting, and fishing, to the regimentation of playground games and team sports. All during high school and college, I had trekked the wilderness of the High Sierras, and knew from firsthand experience how to stalk mule deer in deep timber and climb miles of canyon and rock slide to find an untouched trout stream. I felt quite confident that I'd do well in the training.

But the colonel suddenly deflated this premature confidence. "We aren't looking for individual heroes," he stressed, "although your courage will certainly be tested in coming weeks. We want mature officers who can train foreign resistance troops, quickly and efficiently, then lead them aggressively. If we are not completely satisfied with your potential, you *will* be reassigned to normal duties."

☆   ☆

OVER the next several weeks I grew to respect my fellow volunteers. One quiet-looking type, Frank Coolidge, for example, had served five years in the French Foreign Legion and had survived hand-to-hand combat in the mountains of North Africa. Bill Colby was an Army brat with a scholarship degree from Princeton, who'd qualified in the Airborne despite poor eyesight. Hod Fuller, an easygoing, sandy-haired Marine captain, had fought with the First Division on Guadalcanal. Before the war, he'd sailed a small boat around the world, so this adventure was nothing new. And Bernie Knox, an older scholarly guy, had fought on the Republican side in the Spanish Civil War. These men knew infinitely more about combat than I did.

More important, Bernie's experience in Spain had given him a level of political sophistication far beyond my own. I knew enough military history to understand Clausewitz's axiom that war was merely an extension of politics. But I was only beginning to grasp the dimensions of the totalitarian systems then struggling for world domination. The war in Spain had been described as a dress rehearsal for World War II, not just a conflict between fascism and democracy, but also as a ruthless struggle between the two dominant brands of totalitarianism: European fascism and Soviet communism. When idealistic young volunteers like Knox had trooped off to fight for "liberty" in the hills of Catalonia, they had not expected to be cynically manipulated and even betrayed by Moscow-trained political commissars.

They learned through harsh experience that neither Communist nor Fascist gave a good damn about the kind of individual freedom we in the Western democracies regarded so highly that we would risk our lives for it. Now battle-hardened young men like them were prepared for the intrigue and potential betrayals inherent to a guerrilla war in occupied Europe, where Moscow-controlled Communist resistance groups had taken the early initiative against the Nazi occupiers. It would be months before I would gain bitter experience from these same political complexities.

Our initial training emphasized the skills of guerrilla warfare and, we were told, was designed to test us both physically and psychologically. The famous Club golf course had been transformed into a night-stalking area, with sentry posts, simulated railway trestles, power transformers, and other target paraphernalia. Not only were we required to crawl through the wet grass undetected, and spring from the manicured boxwood hedges on supposedly unsuspecting sentries (who were usually unarmed combat instructors), but we were also required to do this in teams. Often one of the team members was a ringer from the training staff, put there to rattle us through incompetence or overaggression. How we handled this *subordinate* was more important than our clandestinely placing a token demolition charge at a rail switch.

As the training progressed, the intrusions by psychologists became blatant. We were interviewed by gentlemen in tweed jackets who would gaze thoughtfully across the brims of their briar pipes as we struggled to answer their hypothetical questions about our potential reactions to danger and betrayal behind enemy lines. Rorschach inkblot tests were routine, as were bizarre word-association exercises. Again, however, the overt testing was often a facade for hidden methods of assessment. The Irish-American officers would be approached by a friendly instructor after an orientation lecture on the British unconventional warfare units with which we might eventually work. The instructor might begin a subtle anti-British patter, hoping to elicit a similar response. If this didn't work, the Irish guy might be asked outright how he could morally justify serving with the same British troops that had brutally suppressed his "homeland." One of these officers, a tough ex–regular Army sergeant named Jack Gildee, quickly saw through this probing. "I don't give a damn if I fight with 'em or against 'em," he said. "I just want to get over there and fight."

By mid-November the several dozen captains and lieutenants who had been briefed in the ballroom numbered fewer than fifty. But there was still one major hurdle to pass, a personal interview with Wild Bill Donovan himself.

I approached my own interview with the General gripped by the same kind of pleasant apprehension I always felt before a parachute jump. Everything about Donovan was somehow larger than we average mortals. In World War I Donovan took command of the first battalion of the New York National Guard's 69th Infantry Regiment, an outfit commonly known as the Fighting Irish. His own battalion, whom he called his "Micks," were tough, working-class guys whom you didn't lead into the frontline trenches of France by bromide and homily, but rather through example. On October 15, 1918, his battalion was one of the point units of the Rainbow Division that broke through the enemy trenches during the Meuse-Argonne offensive. They then repulsed a savage German counterattack, which practically decimated Donovan's unit. Although his right knee was shattered from a machine-gun bullet, Donovan called for volunteers to carry him on a bloody blanket through the trenches and over barbed-wire entanglements on the parapets. He skillfully rallied his defense, directing a mortar barrage and machine-gun fire against the waves of German attackers. Near unconsciousness from pain and blood loss, he refused evacuation until his own wounded were removed.

Donovan received America's three highest decorations for valor, the Congressional Medal of Honor, the Distinguished Service Cross, and the Distinguished Service Medal, as well as the Purple Heart with two oak-leaf clusters, making him one of the most decorated American soldiers of the war.

After the war, he pursued his law career with equal vigor, serving as the head of the Justice Department's Antitrust Division in the mid-1920s. He became one of the best legal strategists in the country and later dabbled in New York State politics before establishing a successful international law firm in New York.

In 1940, when President Roosevelt wanted a personal emissary to assess the war situation in Europe, he sent Donovan. When Pearl Harbor came, he chose Donovan to organize and lead America's wartime central intelligence organization (which became the Office of Strategic Services in 1942). To Roosevelt, Donovan was the logical choice. "When in serious trouble," FDR told an aide, "it's a good idea to send for Bill Donovan."

My interview with Donovan was in his second-floor office in the old Public Health Service Building. A colonel stood beside his desk, noting my military qualifications from my personnel file. Donovan listened politely, for he was a man of great personal charm, then nodded to the officer to desist. My eyes were fixed on the rows of ribbons on the General's chest, in particular on the tiny star-flecked blue rectangle of the Medal of Honor.

"Lieutenant," he said, smiling, "you have an excellent training record. And you know how I feel about thorough training."

"Yes, sir," I answered. We had been snaking on our bellies along the golf course fairways most of the night trying to evade K-9 teams.

General Donovan held me with his bright, probing gaze. "Well," he said, "I just want you to know that the kind of combat we'll be in is a lot rougher than any training." His blue eyes did not blink. "You do understand that, don't you?"

"Yes, sir."

He nodded and smiled again. "I believe you do," was all he said. The interview was over. I had passed the hurdle.

☆   ☆

THE survivors in my group moved to Area B-1, the former boys' camp in the mountains of western Maryland that had become FDR's weekend retreat, "Shangri-La," and would later be known as Camp David. Here the emphasis was practical "tradecraft," not ink blots.

Although the accommodations were still comfortable—pine-paneled cabins with indoor plumbing—the classroom and exercise schedule ran from early morning to late at night. Our principal weapons and unarmed combat instructor was British Major William Ewart Fairbairn of the legendary Fairbairn-Sykes team, who had invented the double-edged fighting knife that bore their name, and had developed the hand-to-hand combat training course for the Commandos.

Fairbairn was a tough former colonial police officer with years of service in China, and was known as the "Shanghai Buster." Once you felt his callused grip on your throat when he trip-tossed you savagely to the ground during your first feeble attempt at a knife lunge, you realized you had a lot to learn from "the old man."

The Major's fighting credo was simple: A well-trained man had nothing to fear from close combat. Rather, if this man was properly armed, all nearby adversaries had *everything* to fear. We would become so proficient with a variety of Allied and enemy weapons over the coming months, he promised, that using them would become "instinctive."

"You chaps have been trained to *aim* a weapon," he told us during our first session with him on the pistol range. He stood upright, hefting a standard

Army .45 automatic, then pointed it toward a target. "That's all proper and good on the range." He turned away and slid the pistol into his belt. "The only problem is that your average Hun or Nip rarely stands still with a bull's-eye on his nose."

Three spring-loaded silhouettes of enemy soldiers—the first such targets we'd seen—clanged up in the thornbushes twenty yards away. The Major spun in a crouch, his right arm cocked with the pistol just forward of his hips, his left arm also cocked as a balancing boom, and his knees slightly bent. The six shots came in three quick groups of two. Squinting into the low November sun, we saw the tight pattern of bullets in the center of each silhouette. Major Fairbairn had not aimed his pistol. He and the gun were simply not separate units; the man and the pistol had become a single weapon.

☆　　　☆

WHEN the training schedule permitted, I'd head into Washington to see Mary Osborne, a Wave officer working on a highly classified project for Naval Intelligence. We'd been introduced by my sister Anita, a petty officer on the same project. Anita was only eighteen months younger than I, and we'd always been close. But I couldn't reveal the nature of my OSS assignment, and she and Mary certainly could not discuss theirs, beyond the unusual comment that the work was "ultra" secret. I hadn't heard that classification level before and had no way of guessing that they were assigned to the Ultra code-breaking program that did so much to shorten the war.

Mary was a quiet, thoughtful, and extremely attractive blond who could have had her pick of the large Washington officer corps. I was never quite certain what she saw in me. Usually, I was so exhausted from training that I'd snore through the latest Bing Crosby movie. But we certainly did click. After a few weeks in Washington, we were planning on marriage. Provided, of course, that I made it back from overseas.

☆　　　☆

BY THE end of November, our training at Area B-1 had become a grueling marathon. We fired American, British, and German weapons almost every day. We crawled through rain-soaked oak forests at night to plant live demolition charges on floodlit sheds. We were introduced to clandestine radio procedure and practiced tapping out code and encrypting messages in our few spare moments. Many mornings began with a run, followed by a passage of an increasingly sophisticated and dangerous obstacle course. The

explosive charges under the rope bridges and wire catwalks no longer exploded to one side as exciting stage effects. Now they blasted directly below,
a moment before or after we had passed.

Once the word was out that Wild Bill Donovan was training a batch of
educated cutthroats up in the Maryland mountains, Area B-1 became an
obligatory stop on the make-work schedules of VIP staff officers who
crowded wartime Washington. The city was a mecca for men with political
connections, who pranced like show horses in their handsomely tailored
uniforms in the drawing rooms of Embassy Row and Kalorama Circle. For
them, the war was a splendid entertainment after the drab years of the
depression and the drudgery of the New Deal bureaucracy. What made this
adventure even more exciting was their secure knowledge that they wouldn't
see actual combat, even during their carefully orchestrated inspection tours
overseas, where they netted a respectable clutch of campaign ribbons. Sometimes after an exhausting day in the classroom and on the firing range, we'd
be ordered to assemble in Class A uniform and forced to listen to some
sleek brigadier from the War Department proclaim how proud the country
was to have produced fine young fellows like us who would soon have Hitler
by the throat. We knew full well we would be involved in throat slashing
in a matter of months, while this gentleman waxed eloquent over dry martinis
at the Army-Navy Club. But we couldn't be certain whose throat would be
cut, ours or the enemy's.

On one memorable occasion we were visited by William F. Stephenson,
the British Secret Intelligence Service officer (code name Intrepid) who had
been handpicked by Churchill not only to establish a Washington office in
1940 to help bring America into the war, but also to steer attorney William
Donovan toward the helm of America's own clandestine intelligence service.
Stephenson was a man of great experience and intellect who normally would
have received our utmost attention and respect. Unfortunately, his visit was
the last of a series of pep talks by sleek noncombatants. We'd had enough.

As Stephenson spoke of the great pride our British counterparts felt in
shepherding us toward our glorious destinies, a bizarre chant rose in the
rear ranks of our formation. "Forty-eight," a man called. "Forty-nine," two
more replied. Guys like Bill Colby, Bill Pietsch, and me, who'd gone through
parachute school at Fort Benning, used this form of hazing to deflate official
pomposity. Stephenson looked surprised, then chagrined, as he realized what
was happening. "Fifty!" A dozen of us now chanted. "Some shit!" the
formation shouted in unison.

The Man Named Intrepid shook his head sadly and turned to his mortified
American escort officer for a full explanation. The patriotic formation was
dissolved, and we could get on to more important things like practicing our
codes or cleaning weapons.

☆   ☆

THE *Queen Elizabeth* arrived at the Clydeside port of Gourock on the fifth day out of New York. It was a cold December afternoon, and the estuary was burnished by the weak sun. But the sprawling port of Glasgow was gray with coal smoke. Standing with my friends on the midship's boat deck, I watched the hooting tugs maneuver the huge liner alongside the pilings. The redbrick warehouses and rusty cranes had a decrepit quality to them. Further up the Clyde heaps of sooty rubble marked the destruction of the Blitz. The troops and stevedores on the dock moved purposefully in the cold sunshine. Even though Great Britain was in its fifth year of war, its people had not lost their determination to win.

Several thousand American soldiers crowded the decks, jostling and laughing, happy to be safely in port. I gazed across the Clyde at the camouflaged destroyers and corvettes getting up steam to go to sea. We had crossed the Atlantic alone on a flank-speed zigzag course, faster than any U-boat could track us. But the bulk of men and matériel for the invasion of Europe still came by slow convoy from east coast ports in America and Canada. And these convoys were still the prey of U-boat wolf packs. A line of rusty transports and Liberty ships was unloading on nearby docks, the survivors of an Atlantic convoy. I watched the columns of British troops tromp down the gangways to form up at dockside: Canadians with black berets, Sikhs in khaki turbans, tough little Gurkhas with flat, impassive faces. The term "World War" acquired a new reality. Men were, indeed, converging from all across the planet to prepare for the impending invasion of Europe. The anonymous columns of disembarking troops and the grimness of the war-battered port reminded me we had come a long way from the linen napkins and chandeliers of the Congressional Country Club.

British soldiers took my group to a warehouse where we waited until darkness fell. Then two battered lorries drove us through the blacked-out city to the railway station. The waiting rooms were smoky and dim. People moved through the shadows like phantoms, trailing the scent of cheap tobacco and wet wool. The train north was crowded with troops, stuffy and dimly lit.

It had taken us just five days to cross the Atlantic, but the trip from Glasgow to Mallaig lasted almost thirty hours and involved three such trains—the last a narrow-gauge line in the Northwest Highlands. The dry weather of our arrival gave way to a chill, wet gale that swept Loch Nevis as a motor launch carried us toward a bold ridge of heather and lichened stone. This was the old estate called Inverie House, our first training site in Britain.

The establishment was run by the Special Operations Executive (SOE), the godfather of the various British unconventional-warfare groups that had arisen during the war. In 1940, Churchill had created the SOE as one of his first official acts as prime minister, giving the organization the typically Churchillian edict, "Now, go out and set Europe ablaze!" He understood that the very success of the Nazis' Blitzkrieg contained the seeds of its downfall. By occupying all of Europe, from the Barent Sea to the Pyrenees and east to the Aegean, the German forces were stretched terribly thin over the ground.

So Western Europe was ripe for aggressive actions by resistance groups. The brief of the SOE was to help organize, train, and supply these groups. By the time we arrived in Britain, the organization had become huge. Fittingly, the SOE's headquarters was on London's Baker Street, not far from Sherlock Holmes's imaginary digs.[3] The SOE now had clandestine training sites around the world, including a number like Inverie House in the isolated moors of Scotland and the northern English shires. In addition, the SOE controlled squadrons of airdrop and reconnaissance planes, speedboats, and a couple of submarines, and managed a regular cottage industry of forgers and mapmakers.

SOE officers had established espionage and sabotage networks throughout occupied Europe. Now, as 1943 ended and the year of the invasion began, America was ready to shoulder its share of the unconventional warfare burden in Europe. There were already a few OSS teams in France transmitting good intelligence, and a couple of advance American liaison teams to the French Maquis were in place. Our group, we learned, would be part of an eventual major guerrilla offensive.

Inverie House was a twenty-room manor, small by British standards, but it certainly seemed palatial after the cramped quarters aboard ship. The grounds were overgrown, and nearby hedges and outbuildings had been adapted as weapons and demolition training areas. That night we feasted on a dinner of roast venison. As we bedded down, we wondered how the lean young British officers on the training staff stayed so fit with such an ample mess.

☆　　　☆

OUR SOE training staff quickly demonstrated how they maintained their fighting trim, despite the establishment's well-stocked larder. The emphasis here in the Highlands would be on grueling outdoor exercises designed to build our stamina and test our courage. We were sent on twenty-mile "jaunts" across the windswept moors, lugging a heavy rucksack, a shoulder weapon, and ammunition. On the crests of the ridges, the chill northeast wind would slice in from the burnished Hebrides Sea beyond the Isle of Skye.

One freezing morning we were sloshing through a half-frozen bog between two bare ridges when our British host announced that this would be a dicey place to be caught in a mortar barrage. Then, like Mephistopheles, the captain waved a handkerchief, and live two-inch mortar rounds began to smack into the hillside above, a walking barrage that was definitely headed toward us. "Well, chaps," he said, "I shouldn't stooge around here, if I were you."

We dashed toward the shelter of the opposite slope, but the mortars continued to fall behind us. I flopped into the wet heather beside a lichened boulder, my chest heaving and my mouth parched from exertion. Even as I did so, I knew this was too obvious a place to take cover. I saw the mortar rounds had been switched from high explosive to smoke, a sure sign they were going to bracket this boulder field. Bill Pietsch, a West Pointer my age, was behind a rock to my right. He had reached the same conclusion. "Let's get the hell out of here, Jack," he called. I rolled onto my stomach and slid sideways to center the rucksack, pushing free of a boulder as I did so. At that moment, a mortar round exploded with an incandescent shock wave, *exactly* where I had been lying. I was on my feet and running low toward the ridge line, my heart thudding in my ears like a jackhammer. Bill had been a cross-country star at West Point, and was probably the fastest runner in our group. But he sure as hell couldn't catch me that morning.

☆   ☆

Two weeks later our group had moved to a manor house near Wokingham in the green Berkshire countryside west of London. Here the hazards were psychological, not physical. We were joined by a group of British, Dutch, and Belgian officers. Our training focused on "schemes" involving clandestine tradecraft, including the demanding skill of living a cover story. We would be issued a packet of personal documents to memorize, and then were interrogated about our backgrounds. Next we were driven to a station in Hampshire (yet another requisitioned country manor) to spend a few days among strange officers, all the while maintaining our false identity. We were ordered to hold the cover from departure to our return. One fellow did well during the two days at the other site and was complimented roundly by the British staff. Afterward, over a drink in the manor house library, his British escort got chummy and asked who the man "really" was. Our guy made the mistake of revealing his true identity. This cost him his job; the next morning he was sent back to a Parachute regiment.[4]

☆   ☆

IN February, we went in small teams to the RAF parachute school at Ring-way in the Midlands. Even though many of us were parachute-qualified, the Brits had their own way of doing things. And the SOE in particular insisted on all its covert personnel completing the Ringway agent's course, which involved three jumps, one a night drop from a tethered balloon.

The British Airborne parachute was different from ours in that its canopy was packed in a bag and didn't deploy until the suspension lines were pulled taut. This was a much safer system than the American chute. U.S. T-7 parachutes burst open as soon as the static line went tight and could mal-function easily; hence we carried a small reserve parachute on our chests. The British did not. If their chute didn't deploy, you were dead.

The SOE used bombers to drop agents. Not only did these planes have a greater range than standard transports, their true advantage lay in their stealth. Almost every night RAF Bomber Command struck targets in Ger-many, deploying a long "stream" of aircraft from British bases. German radar operators often saw individual bombers aborting the mission and loop-ing back west toward England. These lame ducks were not worthy tar-gets. What they never realized was that many of these *aborted* missions were actually SOE Halifax or Stirling bombers with teams of agents on board. When the plane dropped below the German radar horizon, it would turn back east and fly to a Maquis drop zone in the French country-side.

In SOE parlance, an agent was "Joe." And the hatch in the bomber's belly was called the Joe hole. On most planes, you sat with your legs dangling into the hole and the RAF dispatcher tapped you on the helmet when it was your turn to jump. But on the Stirling, a rectangular section of the aft deck was removed, and you simply moved toward the tail and stepped into the slipstream.

The British chute worked well on an aircraft drop, where the prop blast would quickly deploy the bagged canopy. But jumping from a tethered balloon was another matter. When I slid through the narrow Joe hole of the balloon's wicker basket and into the darkness, I was braced for the twanging jolt and pendulum swing I'd experienced on plane drops. Instead, I felt only the silent drop as the night fog swallowed me, washing out the horizon. The balloon was tethered at 800 feet, and I had already fallen a good 300 without the lurch of a canopy opening. My hand went for the ripcord of my reserve, but there was no reserve parachute there.

Then the chute deployed with a gentle, rubbery pop. I looked up to see symmetrical suspension lines rising into the wet cotton fog. I grinned. In typical SOE manner, the instructors had not warned us about the slow, quiet opening on a balloon drop.

☆   ☆

OUR final move in England was to yet another stately home, Milton Hall near Peterborough in Cambridgeshire north of London. The manor was an imposing gray limestone manor house, the ancestral home of the Earl of Fitzwilliam. When the American contingent arrived we were joined by a hundred British and French officers who'd been training elsewhere, and by forty American radio operator sergeants. The oak-paneled bedrooms had been divided into small dormitories, and British, French, and American fellows were mixed up through "random" room assignments.

From this international combination, it was obvious that we were being prepared for a major joint operation. At our briefing the next morning, a British lieutenant colonel confirmed our speculation. A secret unconventional warfare plan had been approved by Supreme Allied Headquarters (after much heated debate on both sides of the Atlantic, we later learned), which involved the British, Americans, Free French, Belgians, and Dutch in an attempt at multinational military cooperation unique in the war.

For the first operations in France, three-man teams, composed of a British or American officer, his French counterpart, and an enlisted radio operator, would be parachuted into France to help organize, train, and eventually lead Maquis resistance groups. The principal goal of this operation was the arming of tens of thousands of resistance volunteers with air-dropped and captured weapons, their rapid training with these arms, and their deployment against German garrisons and lines of communication. The purpose of this resistance offensive was to support the Allied invasion of Nazi-occupied Europe. It was hoped that the Nazi occupation army would find itself simultaneously attacked by regular Allied troops on the invasion front and by thousands of well-equipped and well-led *maquisards* in the rear. But to maximize impact, and minimize Nazi reprisals, it was vital that the big resistance offensive not come until the cross-Channel invasion. The mission bore the name JEDBURGH, and the individual units would be called Jedburgh Teams.

☆   ☆

As THE spring of 1944 ground inexorably toward invasion summer, we trained in the East Midlands countryside, and the military traffic on the rail lines and roads seemed to swell daily, most of it headed south. We knew D-Day was coming, but we didn't know when. In the meantime, our SOE mentors stepped up the pressure. Now we worked eleven straight days, and had three days off to unwind in London. The emphasis was on small-unit combat. We fired a variety of Allied and German weapons every day, on courses with pop-up targets. For my personal weapons I chose a Spanish Llama, which was a 9mm version of the U.S. Army .45, and the UDT 9mm submachine gun. Both could fire German 9mm parabellum ammo. Our close-combat instructor was now Major Bill Sykes, Fairbairn's partner. Sykes's method of instinctive firing training involved creeping around a blacked-out cellar and shooting at moving targets illuminated by the muzzle flash of our first shot. Once we could consistently hit the targets with absolutely no hesitation, Major Sykes pronounced us "improving."

I was impressed by the British Jeds. Several were former Commandos or Special Air Service (SAS) officers with combat experience. Captain Tommy MacPherson, for example, had led the raid on Rommel's desert headquarters, was wounded and captured by the Germans, and later escaped from his prison camp and made it to neutral Sweden. He could have sat out the war there, but returned to Britain and joined the SOE. Captain Joseph Coombe-Tennant, formerly of the Welsh Guards, was another escaped POW who served with great distinction as a Jed.[5] One of my British roommates, Captain Adrian Wise, had been on the costly but successful Commando attack in Norway that had destroyed the German atom bomb program's sole heavy-water plant, thus thwarting the Nazi effort to build a nuclear weapon.

By now the American Jeds had instructed their allies in the fine art of deflating Colonel Blimps. Our Airborne hazing had evolved into the continental *"quarante-huit, quarante-neuf, cinquante . . . quelle merde!"*

☆　　　☆

On my first trip into London, my friends and I stopped by the OSS office just off Grosvenor Square ("Eisenhower Platz" according to Whitehall wags) and down the street from Supreme Allied Headquarters. But first we shared a taxi from King's Cross with another Jed, Prince Michel de Bourbon Parme (nom de guerre: Maurice Bourdon), a descendant of the French royal family. He politely asked to be dropped at Buckingham Palace to visit his friend Princess Elizabeth. The cockney driver almost blew a gasket when the young French officer got out of the taxi and strode smartly past the Grenadier Guards at the gate.

We met the Jedburgh case officer, a soft-spoken, shuffling Irish bear of a Navy lieutenant named William Casey. Like many of Donovan's key subordinates, Casey was a New York attorney in civilian life. His slow, unflappable manner disguised a quick intellect and tenacity. He questioned us closely on our training progress, especially on our relationship with the French officers.

Before coming to Milton Hall, he explained, our Free French officers had been politically divided among a variety of factions ranging from royalists like Prince Michel to followers of General Charles de Gaulle to men loyal to de Gaulle's archrival, General Henri Giraud. They had harbored suspicion and bitterness toward those they felt responsible for the military capitulation of 1940. But once they'd been assigned to the Jeds, they suspended their rivalries and prepared for combat. Casey was ten years older than we young paratroop officers, and had the sophistication to recognize the problems inherent in this French discord.

I listened to him closely that afternoon and vowed that I would avoid entanglement in the internecine French struggle.

☆   ☆

THAT spring the training evolved into realistic "schemes." We were dropped at night from low-flying RAF bombers into the coastal plains of Lincolnshire or far up into Scotland. To increase the realism of these operations, the SOE would inform the local Home Guard and Scotland Yard Special Branch that "foreign parachutists" had been reported in the area. Our task was to make it back to our pickup point by a prescribed date without detection.

I teamed up with my French partner and our American radio operator in May. One afternoon following a rigorous Bren-gun exercise, a tall young Breton aristocrat, whose nom de guerre was Lieutenant Dominique Leb, approached me. He said he'd been watching me in training and hoped we could become teammates. His English was much better than my French, and he was determined to improve it. (His real name was Jacques Le Bel de Penguilly, but he didn't reveal it for several weeks; Nazi reprisals against the families of Free French officers were commonplace.) Jacques's invitation was fortuitous; the two areas in which I felt weak were my spoken French and my knowledge of the current French political scene. He was a Gaullist who had escaped occupied France and been recruited for the General's Bureau Central de Renseignements et Action (BCRA) in North Africa, the fiefdom of General Giraud himself. Obviously, he understood French factional intrigue as well as anyone.

We both were enthusiastic about Technical Sergeant Tony Denneau, a scrappy kid from Green Bay, who was among the best radio operators at Milton Hall. Although he weighed only about 120 pounds, Tony relished the night parachute drops and the long treks. He was also a damned good shot.

☆   ☆

WHEN D-Day finally came, I was in a U.S. Army hospital, recovering from an emergency appendectomy. (General Donovan defied the War Department to personally inspect the beachhead.) I listened to General Eisenhower's invasion proclamation over a scratchy loudspeaker in the ward. I was afraid I'd lost my chance to be a part of the greatest adventure of the war. But Jacques came to see me on his next pass and explained that only a few teams had been dispatched. Supreme Headquarters was still deeply concerned about provoking a premature Maquis uprising. The chances were, Jacques explained, that the Jedburgh teams would not be dropped in until— and *if*—Allied forces broke out of Normandy. Then, the Jeds would be badly needed.

"And also, Jack," he said, "we have decided, Tony and me, to stay together with you as a team. We will wait, *c'est tout.*"

I gripped his hand. My teammates thought enough of me to wait until the medics pronounced me fit.

☆   ☆

BILL Casey came to Milton Hall in early August and assembled four American team leaders in the oak-paneled library. He wore his anonymous gray civilian suit, a subtle clue that he was on a confidential mission. Casey paced slowly before us, speaking softly, an attorney preparing an important summation.

"You'll be going on alert soon," he said. "I don't have to tell you the importance of your missions. But I'm sure you've guessed something big is going to happen."

We'd heard rumors about a second invasion of France, this one through the Mediterranean, to relieve pressure on the Allied armies still bottled up in Normandy. Casey was not confirming this, but he still got across the import of his message.

"I can't go into details," he added, "but let me simply say that enemy resistance to our operations has been fierce." He gazed at us with his gray, assessing stare, then looked away. "Unfortunately, there have also been some terrible reprisals against civilians in your areas of operation."

I exchanged glances with my friend Stewart Alsop. Casey was leading up to something.

"You've all been drilled on escape and evasion," he said, staring at us once more, "and resisting interrogation. I just want to emphasize that things are getting rough over there."

The men around me nodded grimly.

"There's something else I have to tell you," he continued with his typically soft, unemotional tone. "A couple of weeks ago Wehrmacht headquarters in Berlin ordered all German units in France to execute anyone, captured outside what they call the 'zone of legal combat,' who's taking part in resistance operations." He fixed us all once more with his cool gray eyes. "They emphasize this applies to all parachutists no matter what nationality or uniform."

Casey didn't have to state the obvious: If the enemy were going to execute you anyway, they'd probably torture you first to obtain whatever tactical information they could.

"If any of you want to be issued an L-tablet," Casey said, "now's the time to ask for it."

The L-tablet was a cyanide capsule in a tough gelatin shell. You put it in your mouth and bit down hard. Three seconds later you were dead.

"Jack," he said, standing beside me, "do you want one?"

"No, sir," I answered as firmly as I could. "I don't intend to get captured."

☆   ☆

MY TEAM was placed on alert on August 9. We were taken to the Joe house at Fairford RAF station for our final briefing . The SOE intelligence officer was a low-key young French lieutenant named André Wastrin. The team, he explained, was code-named "James." Our destination was the Department of Corrèze, in the rugged, wooded hills of the Massif Central.

The Maquis had been active there for over a year, taking advantage of the forests and isolated farms for cover. But the Germans, Wastrin said, had swept up many resistance units with specially trained anti-Maquis troops, which worked closely with the hated Vichy militia, the Milice. Nevertheless, Maquis pressure had grown steadily, especially after D-Day. There were already almost 8,000 *maquisards* of the Forces Françaises de l'Interieur (FFI) divided into eighty companies in the region. Unfortunately, they were further divided along political lines. Resistance fighters of de Gaulle's Armée Secrète totaled about 5,000 men, well armed and well disciplined. The Communist Franc Tireurs et Partisans (FTP) had almost as many men under arms, but had so far resisted close cooperation with the Gaullists. On July 14, many of these units had been armed through an audacious daylight airdrop that delivered over fifty tons of munitions. An SOE liaison team, code-named Tilleul, had also been dropped in July, and they confirmed that the area was ready for a major Maquis uprising.

Lieutenant Wastrin went to the map easel and traced a major highway, Route Nationale 89, northeast from Bordeaux through the Department of Corrèze to the city of Clermont-Ferrand and on to Lyons. "This is the main Hun escape route from southwestern France," he said. "Both the road and the rail lines run through narrow valleys in Corrèze, especially here." He tapped the map three times, touching the towns of Brive, Tulle, and Egletons. "Naturally, there are numerous bridges, viaducts, and culverts in this area." Once the Allied armies broke out of Normandy, the German garrisons south of the Loire would be cut off. If a second Allied invasion swept up the Rhône valley from the Mediterranean coast, these enemy units would be trapped.

Jacques and I smiled. Our months of ambush and demolition training were about to bear fruit.

"Your mission has two objectives," Wastrin continued, "training these Maquis units in the use of the weapons they've received, as well as sabotage and ambush operations. You will also be the official liaison between the Maquis and London as concerns further weapons drops." He came back to the table. "Oh, yes," he added with a smile, "you'll be expected to lead these troops against the Germans."

He opened a blue pasteboard file with a crimson SECRET label. The German order of battle in Corrèze was impressive, over 2,000 veteran troops, equipped with artillery and armor, divided among four heavily fortified garrisons along Highway 89. The Germans obviously intended to keep the road open. Our job would be to close it.

Finally, Wastrin addressed the issue of our cover story. We would not be given one, he said with flat finality. If captured, we were to demand treatment as Allied officers, under the terms of the Geneva Convention. Jacques and I looked at each other again. This time we did not smile.

☆   ☆

I WAS bent like a hunchback in my parachute harness, wedged against the rattling forward bulkhead of the Stirling bomber. It was almost two in the morning on Friday, August 11, 1944. The bomber's narrow fuselage was jammed with cargo pods, our three-man team, and a ten-man reconnaissance party of French SAS troops. We had been flying for three hours, first in the bomber stream across northern France, then back toward the Channel on a bogus abort, now southeast over the Massif Central.

After so many night training drops in England, I felt perfectly normal in my British para helmet and baggy camouflage smock. But this was not another exercise. The musette bag on my chest held our codebooks and 100,000 French francs. My leg bag was heavy with extra ammunition and grenades. In the dim green light from the cockpit instrument panel, I saw Jacques and Tony hunched close beside me. Further aft, Captain Wauthier's tough French SAS troopers were grouped around the open rectangular jump hatch. The engine tone changed, and I felt the aircraft slow. Faint shouts reached me through the howling slipstream. The cramped cabin seemed to lighten as the dark shapes of the SAS troops tumbled through the hatch. A crewman pushed free their cargo pods.

Now it was our turn. We shuffled along the vibrating deck until we reached the cold, whistling maw of the hatch.

"About three minutes," the RAF dispatcher shouted in my ear, the fleece of his collar rubbing my face.

We hooked up our static lines, and each man checked his teammates' snap-clip on the deck ring, then double-checked his own. I could just distinguish dark blocks of forest and lighter open fields. There were few roads visible and no lights. Then three flaring orange signal fires swept by through the darkness below, the characteristic drop-zone light pattern of the Maquis. Although I couldn't see it, I knew someone on the ground was flashing a prearranged code letter to the pilot. If the code was correct, we would go out in a moment.

"Get ready," I shouted to Jacques and Tony.

The dispatcher smacked my helmet. "Go!"

I dropped feet first, ankles and knees together, hands tight against my thighs, grasping the wool of my trousers, a soldier snapping to attention 800 feet above the dark forest of the Massif Central. The chute opened with the familiar elastic boom. I checked my canopy against the cold stars above, and looked below at the gently rocking landscape. The fires on the drop zone seemed much too large, a brazen taunt sure to attract German units. But I didn't have time to worry. Above me, two more chutes snapped open, Tony and Jacques. Then the four smaller canopies of our cargo pods. The Stirling droned away into the darkness.

I hit hard in waist-high brush and rolled onto my side. After dragging my parachute into a clumsy bundle, I snatched out my heavy Llama pistol. If this drop zone was a German trap, I didn't intend to surrender.

Jacques and Tony thudded down fifty yards behind me. I saw dark forms loping from the tree line. They called softly in French, dashing now to intercept the cargo chutes. A figure appeared near me. In the starlight I saw he wore a para smock like my own.

"Well done," the man called in a clipped regimental accent. "You blokes are smack on schedule."

His name was Flight Lieutenant André Simon, a veteran SOE officer. We had landed in a forest clearing three kilometers from Bonnefond and about twenty kilometers from the nearest Nazi garrison in Egletons. I was finally in occupied France. The long months of training were over.

CHAPTER TWO
Team James
August–September 1944

☆　　☆

As FLIGHT LIEUTENANT Simon helped me jam my chute into a sack, men dashed into the weedy meadow to smother the signal fires. Several cargo pods had drifted into the hardwood forest to the left, but squads of *maquisards* were after them.

Once I was free of my harness and had pulled on my rucksack, Jacques and Tony trotted up. Simon welcomed them. Jacques grinned in the starlight, clearly pleased to be back in France after almost four years in exile. I helped Tony load the clumsy Jed radio valise into his rucksack, then slid a magazine into our team submachine gun and shouldered the weapon. We were ready to move out.

Simon had been in the area with the SOE Tilleul mission since July, and he led the way along a dark forest trail that climbed away from a steep escarpment above the Corrèze River.[1] So far we'd only exchanged brief but warm greetings with the Maquis soldiers. It wasn't a good idea to hang around a drop zone drinking toasts to de Gaulle, Roosevelt, and the King. But I noted that these troops were well armed and trained. They kept a good interval in their column along the trail and were wary enough to send out flankers right and left and push a point squad ahead.

On our first break, Simon took us down a path to a limestone outcropping that overlooked the valley.[2] The sky had cleared and a lopsided setting moon lit the landscape.

"There's the road," he said, pointing toward the faint ribbon of Route Nationale 89 curving away from the river below. "Tulle and Brive are on the river, beyond that ridge, and Egletons is on another ridge beyond the head of the valley."

"What's the nearest enemy position?" I was well aware that this was not another realistic training scheme in the Highlands.

"Egletons," he answered. "Twenty kilometers from here. But all the local German garrisons are surrounded. They won't come out at night for fear of ambush. Egletons is a tough nut, though, Lieutenant. A reinforced company of Hun infantry, with at least a platoon of SS. The proper lot of machine guns, several anti-tank guns, and maybe some mortars. They've also got a wireless, so they're in contact with their division HQ in Clermont-Ferrand."

Jacques crouched beside me, frowning with concentration. Clermont-Ferrand was the headquarters of the Wehrmacht's specially trained anti-Maquis unit in the Massif Central. They had light armor, trucks, and even their own spotter planes. His initial joy at returning to France gave way to the serious and unforgiving business of guerrilla warfare.

Simon pointed southwest down the valley. "The German garrisons at Brive and Tulle are larger, but we also have more Maquis companies surrounding them." He grinned in the moonlight. "They don't have a wireless, either, and we've cut all the phone and telegraph lines. Poor buggers don't know what we're up to."

That would explain the size of the signal fires at the drop zone. But we were only fifty kilometers from a large, well-equipped German anti-guerrilla force. Here in the Corrèze, the enemy was temporarily held at bay, but not yet defeated. As team leader, I couldn't be lulled into the dangerous fallacy common in guerrilla outfits: Because the enemy has not yet reacted, it doesn't follow that he *will* not.

☆   ☆

On Simon's suggestion, we set up our first "PC" (*poste de commandement* in Maquis parlance)[3] in an old fieldstone farmhouse near the forest hamlet of Chadebec, on the edge of the thinly populated Plateau de Millevaches. As the name implied, the region was rugged upland pasture, with thick stands of oak—an excellent terrain for the Maquis. The Tilleul mission had been rotating its own PC through neighboring villages and hadn't used this farm for two weeks, so we felt relatively secure.

Just after dawn, Captain Wauthier's SAS party came out of the nearby woods and joined us in the milking room of the whitewashed stone barn for a tactical conference. His team had landed without injury on a narrow drop zone across a steep ridge and had marched for hours to get here. Unfortunately, three of their cargo pods had burst and one had drifted to the other side of the valley. They'd lost valuable weapons and ammunition. We spread our maps on a rough-planked cheese table and, with Simon's help, drew up an estimate of the local enemy order of battle.

Outside, Wauthier's troopers and several squads of Maquis kept perimeter guard. The Maquis soldiers were from the group that had met us, a Gaullist Armée Secrète (AS) unit called the Corps Franc de Tulle. There were about 3,000 men in this outfit, under the command of an energetic former French regular army officer whose nom de guerre was Captain Hubert.

He arrived in a battered Renault soon after Wauthier. Our escort party, Hubert said, were his best-armed and most disciplined troops. They carried captured German Mauser rifles, Schmeisser submachine guns, and a few British Sten guns and pistols. Some wore tattered wool uniform jackets, several had military caps, and all wore tricolor armbands emblazoned with the Cross of Lorraine, the symbol of the FFI.

Unfortunately, Hubert said, only about a third of his men had weapons. The best-armed local Maquis unit, Simon explained, was commanded by Patrick, chief of the AS in Corrèze. On July 14, Bastille Day, the Americans had conducted a massive daylight supply drop to the Maquis in central France. Here in Corrèze, over seventy B-17s had roared across the high plateau, just above the treetops, dropping hundreds of cargo canisters.[4] Patrick had exercised the commander's prerogative by equipping his own unit first. His men were now fully armed with rifles, Sten and Bren guns, grenades, and pistols, even a few bazookas and British Piat anti-tank weapons. With 2,000 men so well equipped, Hubert said, Patrick had blocked Route Nationale 89 with permanent ambushes in three places. He had Brive completely ringed, and had sealed the southwest entrance of the Corrèze valley. The smaller Duret AS group—almost as well armed as Patrick's troops—had closed the northeastern approach to the valley near Ussel.

Hubert made his first direct appeal for weapons. He understood that, as team leader, I'd choose the drop zone for the next weapons delivery, so he took Simon, Jacques, and me aside and spoke slowly, hoping I would understand every word. "*Monsieur le Lieutenant,*" he began formally, "my men have waited patiently. All the other units are now very well armed." To emphasize the merit of his case, he added that many of his troops had been languishing in these forests for three years, because they had been among the first Maquis who had formed among escapees from the Nazi Blitzkrieg, seeking refuge in this remote area of then Vichy France. But they were among the last to be armed. "My men are ready to fight the Boches. But we cannot do this with naked hands." He spread his callused fingers wide.

"We must make a detailed list of your requirements," Jacques assured him, "then contact London."

☆   ☆

HUBERT opened his tattered leather map case, a relic of his army service before the Capitulation. "*La voilà.*" His arms and equipment needs were neatly typed on rough notepaper and stamped with the official seal of the Corps Franc de Tulle, FFI, which appropriately bore the crowned image of Liberty.

Jacques and I were impressed. Hubert was a serious, professional soldier.

"There is another matter," Hubert said, choosing his words carefully. "The Franc Tireurs et Partisans is now here in force, especially south of the highway, in the hills around Egletons, the area which had been mine." These FTPs, he added, were commanded by a former schoolteacher and army corporal who used the decidedly unproletarian nom de guerre of "Colonel" Antoine. He had 5,000 troops, and most were as well armed as Patrick's troops, having received massive American airdrops on Bastille Day, when they'd been operating in the Department of Lot-et-Garonne to the south. "Antoine is not at all interested in cooperative operations," Hubert said, not hiding his distaste. "He is very *politique*. . . . He wants a public victory over the Boches. But he certainly does not want to share that victory with us."

Hubert's warning was clear. Unless his group was brought up to the armed strength of the FTP, the Communists might gain all the credit for liberating the central Corrèze, which they would no doubt use to further their postwar political agenda. The FTP, of course, had been willing to fight hard and take casualties when their leaders felt confident they could inflict a public defeat on the Germans. And there was no doubting the bravery of individual FTP soldiers. Since the German invasion of the Soviet Union in June 1941, the French Communists had thrown their support wholeheartedly into the anti-Nazi resistance. The alliance between Communists and Gaullists, however, was strained.[5]

But there was more to Hubert's anxiety than political concerns. The night before, Colonel Rivier, the FFI military commander for Region 5, had issued an order from his secret headquarters near Limoges. Major action by the Maquis in the region was imminent. The American Third Army under General George Patton had finally broken out of Normandy and was racing east between the Loire and the Seine. Patton's right flank was already badly exposed and the situation would only grow worse as the American armored columns plunged ahead. (General Patton, however, wasn't overly concerned; in typical fashion, he told an aide: "Let the other son of a bitch worry about flanks.") The FFI had been given the important task of protecting Patton's right flank by blockading the German forces south of the Loire and west of the Massif Central. But that would require carefully coordinated action. If independent, politically motivated groups like Antoine's FTP refused to cooperate, Hubert warned, the Germans could squash each pocket of resistance in turn, and also decimate the civilian population through savage reprisals.

"You know about Oradour and Tulle?" he asked, searching our faces.

Before leaving England I'd read reports of massacres in central France, but I wasn't sure of the details. Flight Lieutenant Simon now provided them, speaking in his typically understated regimental manner.

"Just after D-Day," he began, "some of the local lads got a bit too eager. They attacked the German garrison in Tulle. It was a fair botch-up, I'm afraid. But at the end of the day, they captured the barracks and seized a good supply of weapons."

Hubert's English was good enough for him to follow, and he continued in French. "The *salles Boches* fought hard." He shrugged, a gesture of muted Gallic respect. "There were casualties. When the Germans surrendered, many of the men found Milice and Wehrmacht security police among them." He looked away from us. "There were executions . . ."

Simon assured us that Hubert's unit had not been involved. "It was the FTP," he finally said. "Antoine's men."

Hubert nodded and continued in French. The SS Das Reich Panzer Division was transiting the Corrèze en route to Normandy, two days later. But the Maquis were harassing them with ambush and sabotage. The Germans were very frustrated because the rail lines had been cut and they couldn't transport their tanks by train. They unleashed a series of reprisals. The day after the Maquis attack, the Germans sealed the town with their armor. They were going to shell Tulle to rubble, with the population in the buildings, but the *préfet* intervened, pointing out that many local people had tended the German wounded. Hubert's eyes grew moist. "So *les salles Boches* showed their gratitude . . ."

Simon was looking away as he recounted the details of the retribution. They rounded up all the men in the yard of the arms factory. The SS had already decided to execute 120 hostages, but they had trouble deciding who should be hanged. Some of the men were skilled workers from the factory, and others were actually pro Vichy. But they finally sorted out their victims, and began hanging them from lampposts and balconies in the town square. By the end of the day, there were almost 100 men hanging like bullocks around the square.

As Simon spoke, Jacques grew silent and pale, then a ruddy anger spread across his face and his eyes, normally lively, became chilly and distant.

"Oradour-sur-Glane was even worse," Simon continued. Units of the same division, he explained, transited Limoges toward Normandy. An SS major commanding a battalion was abducted from his staff car on a highway near Limoges by the Maquis. The Germans were frantic to recover him, but he had disappeared. Someone implicated the small town of Oradour-sur-Glane as the home base of the *maquisards* who'd seized the German officer. It was June 10 and the village was full of people from Limoges buying food from the weekly market. There were also hundreds of school-children there, some evacuees from Lorraine, and others assembled for their summer physical examinations. "The SS jammed all the men into garages and barns, and the women and children into the town church. They locked the church door."

Hubert's face was wet with tears now.

"They machine-gunned the men in the barns, then burnt the buildings, with the wounded still alive," Simon related flatly. "They used some kind of incendiary device on the church. It was covered with flames quite quickly. Any women or children trying to escape were machine-gunned. Then they looted the town, and winkled out a number of people hiding in cellars and attics. When they left, the town was dead."

"How many were killed?" I asked.

Simon shook his head.

Hubert finally said, "Hundreds."[6]

☆   ☆

LATER that morning, messengers arrived from Maquis units to the north. An American OSS Operational Group had blown the rail bridge near Salon La Tour between Brive and Limoges. Other Allied saboteurs had knocked out the hydroelectric plant at the Marege dam, cutting off power to the arms factory in Tulle and to the electrified rail system all the way to Bordeaux. Maquis company commanders from various units were requesting explosives to blow the bridges on Route Nationale 89 in the Corrèze valley.

I hadn't slept in almost forty hours, and cups of bitter ersatz coffee had little effect. But I was able to keep tactical considerations foremost. If we blew those bridges, German troops retreating from southwest France—or offensive units headed toward Patton's exposed flank—would be funneled toward the more open country north of the Massif Central. But if Route 89 were kept open, enemy units would be attracted to the narrow Corrèze valley. From what I had seen, this was excellent ambush country. By drawing the Germans into this trap, we'd simultaneously achieve two objectives. I consulted with Jacques and we issued our first orders of the campaign. The Maquis were to maintain their pressure on the German garrisons, but to leave the highway bridges intact.

That still left the problem of balancing the strength of Antoine's FTP forces with well-armed, better disciplined AS units. Fighting drowsiness, Jacques and I conferred with Captain Wauthier, compiling a detailed list of weapons and munitions needed to beef up the SAS team and equip Hubert's companies. Wauthier's plans were to move across the Massif Central to the Department of Haut Vienne to reconnoiter the area and carry out additional sabotage and harassment, thus helping funnel German units into our killing zone. A regular officer trained at St. Cyr, Wauthier seemed a little too prone to do things by the numbers; Jacques told me later he found the captain too traditional for effective guerrilla action. Wauthier said he needed light mortars, command-detonated road mines, and more Bren guns for the job. We decided to piggyback our initial Maquis arms request on his first resupply airdrop.

Working doggedly with Jacques and Tony, I wrote out our long message and encrypted it from page two of my one-time-only code pad. I'd used page one of the flimsy little "Bingo" book for our first message to London, announcing our safe arrival. These pages were supposedly edible paper which would quickly dissolve in your stomach, and they burned with sudden smokeless flame.

Sometime around noon I looked up from my maps to see Jacques and Tony staring toward the nearby farmhouse kitchen. A tantalizing, strangely familiar aroma filled the warm afternoon: hot butter and eggs. Monsieur Etien, our local host, arrived with a copper skillet heaped with the largest, fluffiest omelet I'd ever seen. He set the skillet on the map table, and proceeded to cut wedges from a thick, dark loaf of bread. In England, our food ration had included one "egg" a week, but it was often in powdered form. We fell on the food like refugees and washed down the meal with harsh *vin ordinaire*.

Well wined and dined, I crawled into my sleeping bag late that afternoon for a few hours of rest. Jacques and Hubert were still deep in discussion, and Tony was diligently tapping out our long, coded message, the Morse dots and dashes sounding like distant birds through my stupor. But as tired as I was, sleep did not come quickly. The horrible images of refugee women and children trapped in a burning church and of young men hanging like sides of beef in a village square could not be swept away by a few enamel cups of red wine. This limestone barn was less than a hundred kilometers from similar barns where the Nazis had burned those poor people alive.

At twenty-three, I was at war with a cruel and dangerous enemy from whom I could expect no mercy.

☆   ☆

OVER the next two days, Jacques and I reconnoitered the area. As Simon had told us, the German units in Brive, Tulle, Egletons, and Ussel were holed up in heavily defended barracks, with sandbagged windows, barbed-wire entanglements, and machine-gun emplacements. Maquis units were set up behind roadblocks and barricades around each town. The French tricolor flew from many liberated buildings, but the civilian population was subdued and wary, despite the bright August sunshine and the promise of imminent liberation. Obviously the ghosts of Tulle and Oradour haunted the region.

Hubert's people informed us he had gone up to Egletons to meet with his two company commanders, who had joined an uneasy alliance with seven of Antoine's FTP companies that were tightening their grip on the town.

Jacques and I decided to go there ourselves the next day, once we had sorted out the SAS airdrop and had a final tactical conference with Wauthier. So far we had not met Antoine personally, only his rather surly company commanders, who seemed to relish speaking in fast, slurred, barracks patois that Jacques had almost as much trouble following as I did. Clearly, these men did not appreciate taking orders from a Gaullist officer and an American lieutenant. But they were openly curious about the possibility of an airdrop.

Hubert's local commander, Laurence, warned us not to discuss this in any detail. "The FTP are treacherous," he said. "They have set up their own false drop zones for *parachutages* in the past, tricking the RAF into dropping them arms destined for *l'Armée Secrète*."

I thought about the inevitable confrontation with "Colonel" Antoine. Jacques, Tony, and I each carried a Supreme Headquarters Allied Expeditionary Force (SHAEF) identity tag printed in English and French and signed by General Eisenhower and de Gaulle's intelligence deputy, General Marie-Pierre Koenig, which gave us freedom of movement in occupied France and authority over FFI units when we were relaying Koenig's orders. In theory, the FTP was a willing partner in the FFI alliance. But I knew alliances were often matters of convenience for the Communists. Bouncing along the rutted lanes on a wheezing *gazogene* farm truck toward the drop zone, I recalled my first encounters with Communists, when I was an ROTC cadet at UCLA. As a freshman in 1939, I was denounced as a "militarist" by the Communist student organization. That was during the weird two-year period of the Hitler-Stalin nonaggression pact, when the American Communist Party followed Moscow's orders to propagandize for strict American neutrality. In effect, the Communists on campus harangued everyone who would listen about the evils of aiding the British imperialists (who, they neglected to add, stood alone against Nazi Germany, Russia's erstwhile ally). Then, in 1941, Hitler invaded the Soviet Union and the student Communists suddenly did an about-face, proclaiming the guys in ROTC heroes in the sacred global struggle against fascism.

Casey had warned us that the Soviet embassy in Switzerland, not de Gaulle's headquarters in London, had secret military command over FTP units in France.[7] I intended to test Antoine's loyalty to the FFI as soon as possible.

☆   ☆

I HAD just bedded down after dawn in our new command post when Jacques shook me awake. After hiking all night from another drop zone near the village of Chamberet, I was stiff and groggy. The SAS airdrop had been late, and the cargo pods were again scattered into the surrounding forest. Wauthier complained his men weren't yet fully equipped for their mission. Beyond that, my team had received none of the weapons I'd requested for Hubert. Now we had a visitor, Lieutenant François Sarre-Demichel, Patrick's regional intelligence officer, whose nom de guerre was Coriolan. He was an anti-Nazi Austrian who had been active in central France for several years, working under commercial cover and traveling widely through occupied Europe. His German, of course, was native; his French and English were fluent. Moreover, Coriolan had a sharp intellect and the requisite shrewdness and audacity to be a first-class clandestine operative.

As I tried to wake up over a tepid cup of ersatz coffee, Coriolan briefed us on two important new developments. At five that morning, the BBC had broadcast an order from General Koenig to all active FFI units. They were to "attack between the Loire and the Garonne all German garrisons, however important they may be." Koenig had given a similar order just before D-Day in Normandy; London would not have risked another major uprising unless the second invasion were imminent.

But Koenig's order was not the only news. Coriolan had people inside the FTP units. They had just alerted him that Antoine had moved forward in the night to attack Egletons, without warning Hubert of this operation, even though two of Hubert's companies held down a sector of the encirclement. This uncoordinated advance had backfired. The Germans had fallen back to a fortified position in the Ecole Professionelle, a three-story complex of reinforced concrete and stone standing on a ridge on the eastern edge of the town. Hubert added that the well-disciplined AS troops in the other garrison towns were conducting coordinated attacks on the isolated German units. Only in Egletons was the enemy able to seek refuge in an almost impregnable position. Worse, this garrison had radio contact with the regional German HQ.

Our next move was obvious. We had to get to Egletons to coordinate the attack, and to prepare to ambush the inevitable German relief column. Coriolan, Jacques, and I studied the map while Tony took down our long-wire antenna from the nearby apple trees and packed up his radio. Coriolan was needed in Tulle and would use his ancient motorbike to get there over backcountry lanes and trails. He stressed that there were collaborators and Milice spies in the hills. So the three of us would have to hike all the way to Egletons, twenty-five kilometers as the crow flies, but more like fifty using Maquis trails to avoid detection.

We marched all day, up and down the rocky limestone ridges above the Corrèze. Hubert provided a ten-man Maquis escort, who once again showed their training and discipline. The most dangerous part of the march was crossing the river on a stone bridge near a ruined Romanesque church, five kilometers northwest of Egletons. The burly Maquis sergeant in charge of our escort dashed across the span first, his Sten gun at high port, heavy German potato-masher grenades swinging from his belt. After checking the roadside for ambushers, he signaled us to cross.

Slogging through the steep fields of hay stubble toward the town, we heard the unmistakable clatter of Bren guns, answered by the deeper pounding of German machine guns. On the edge of town, we passed through one flimsy FTP roadblock, more a token than a serious deterrent to the Germans. The men at the barricade were sullen and suspicious of our team.

It was dark when we entered the district of the school. The firing had fallen off, but occasional orange tracers looped down the dark streets to ricochet wildly off the steep slate roofs. Hubert had his PC on the ground floor of a solid fieldstone house with a walled garden, about 500 meters down the wide road from the northwest corner of the school. His two companies held positions in neighboring houses and along a sunken road to the left. Antoine's troops were concentrated in pockets facing the other three corners of the school compound.

Jacques and I checked Hubert's perimeter, then set out in opposite directions to link up with the FTP. But we both decided independently this was a risky maneuver, after being challenged and shouted back by Antoine's sentries hidden in nearby gardens.

☆   ☆

DAYLIGHT came, windless and clear, and with it the predictable fusillade of uncoordinated fire from the FTP. Their Bren guns were chewing up the school's stone facade, but causing no real damage. Once more we set off to conduct the type of reconnaissance needed for a proper attack plan. As we moved cautiously from garden to garden, Hubert's troops left their positions to shake our hands and embrace us. Their eyes gleamed with pride as they reached out to touch the Cross of Lorraine patch on Jacques's uniform. I was glad now that I'd insisted the team keep their uniforms as clean as possible, that we wash, shave, and brush our hair—in short, that we look like soldiers.

Hubert's men appreciated our presence, but, as we sprinted across the street and under the dusty plane trees, it became clear that Antoine's troops resented us.

"Qui passe là?" they shouted—"who goes there?"—challenging our passage into their sector.

"Two officers of the FFI," Jacques responded, glaring at a bearded fellow who brandished a Sten gun and blocked the path around a garden shed. "Where is your commander?"

The man scowled, then deigned to nod toward a bullet-pocked house nearer the school.

Keeping low, we dashed from one garden wall to the next, aware that this end of the street was visible from the top floor of the Ecole Professionelle. Now the houses were pitted from the heavy machine-gun fire of the previous afternoon, and the pavement was littered with glass shards and splintered stone. We tried to be as quiet as possible, but our boots crunched on the debris. To make matters worse, the FTP troops in the surrounding houses were yelling out the shattered windows, once more challenging our right to pass through their sector. Jacques said it was better to just ignore them.

We crept through a cabbage garden and dashed for the back door of the tall house closest to the school. There was an attic window in the peaked slate roof that overlooked the school courtyard, 200 meters away. I left Jacques to guard the ground floor, while I crept up the narrow stairs like a burglar.

The attic was low under the dusty roof beams. The small square window opened easily. I lay to one side and carefully raised my face to look outside. We'd been trained at Milton Hall to make quick, accurate recons, and I tried my best to do so now. The trick was to focus your gaze like a camera lens, to clear your mind of conscious thought, to allow the image to engrave itself on your brain as if it were photographic film. I scanned the school's walls and courtyard across the road, noting the timber barricades, the upturned concrete slabs, and the heavy furniture blocking the windows. Shadows moved in the shrubbery, probably a machine-gun crew. I was about to look again when angry shouts erupted from below. Men were arguing loudly in French, and I heard Jacques's distinct *"merde, alors."* Then I saw movement from the corner of the attic window. Antoine's ill-disciplined men were stupidly pointing up here, as if to spot for the German gunners. I was stunned; this was like the "bungler" training exercise at the Congressional Country Club all over again. But those shadows across the road were not blasé Ivy League psychologists, waiting to see how I'd react to this unexpected nuisance.

I rolled away from the window and scuttled crablike toward the attic stairs. Just as my boots hit the second-floor landing, the Germans opened up on the attic window with at least two machine guns. The bursts of steel-jacketed rounds smacking the slate roof sounded like the house was being slammed by giant hammers. I was down the stairs and out the back door before the enemy gunners lowered their aim and swept the front windows.

Jacques was crouched near the back step, gripping a Sten gun, his face a mask of frustrated anger.[8]

I clapped him on the shoulder. "Let's get the hell out of here in case the Krauts've got a mortar over there."

With a flat crack and a monstrous crowbar clang, a 37mm anti-tank gun cut loose from the school and blasted a hole clear through the slate roof above. We were showered with fragments of slate tiles, but otherwise unhurt. I'd been crouched up there less than a minute before. I gazed at the splinters spiraling away in the early morning light. My first combat action was not going to be an easy fight.

☆   ☆

HUBERT, Jacques, and I waited more than thirty minutes for Antoine to join our tactical conference. We were well protected in a small fieldstone barn on the other side of the sunken road. There were a row of masonry houses, two lines of thick chestnut trees, and these heavy barn walls between us and that anti-tank gun. We'd come to the logical conclusion that taking the school would be impossible with the weapons on hand—Bren and Sten guns, rifles and pistols, and a few hand grenades.

We could see only two alternatives: a long siege, or a quick, perfectly coordinated attack, supported with mortars and bazookas.

Antoine's chief of staff appeared around eight. *Le Colonel,* he explained, had been called away on urgent military matters. But Antoine had left orders for the siege to continue indefinitely. After all, "there's SS inside!" the man proclaimed, grinning like a pirate. The idea of pinning down a company of despised Nazi SS troops was appealing to Antoine. This was the type of grand gesture that would reap political fruit.

He wouldn't listen to our arguments that a siege of several days was bound to provoke a violent response from the strong German garrison in Clermont-Ferrand. He had his orders, and that was good enough. After sponging some American cigarettes "for his *camarades,*" he left.

But Jacques and I wouldn't accept this stupidity. Captain Wauthier had received a second airdrop of men and munitions during the night; we'd heard the drone of low-flying Liberators over the plateau around 0300. His SAS unit probably now numbered thirty, and they had Piats and mortars. They could help us break this siege in a few hours and, in the process, pick up some badly needed anti-tank guns and some heavy machine guns for their ambushes farther north. Jacques wrote out our request for support to Wauthier, and Hubert dispatched a runner.

Maybe we could steal an hour's sleep while waiting. But that proved impossible. With Germanic precision, the first Luftwaffe planes arrived at exactly 0900. There were three of them, Heinkel III medium bombers—

fast, lean, twin-engined planes with gracefully tapered wings. They clattered right over the rooftops, then banked out above the valley and lined up for their bomb run. Hubert's men shouted the warning, and we dashed to the edge of the sunken road. The first plane dropped a stick of heavy bombs, probably a 200-kilo high explosive, which blasted a smoking furrow through the line of stone houses facing the school. We were deafened by the shock waves and shaken like rag dolls by the concussion. Shrapnel whined and crackled across the roofs. As the Heinkel passed overhead, we saw the flickering orange flame from its tail gun, and tracers glided into the street.

We clambered into the relative shelter of the sunken road and up the opposite bank. The second Heinkel was leveling off at about 200 feet, lining up on the houses in Antoine's sector. To our amazement, we saw several FTP troops run into the center of the road and blaze away with Sten guns and rifles at the approaching bomber. As they did so, they came under machine-gun fire from both the school and the plane's nose gunner. But they held their ground. You certainly couldn't fault their courage. Their judgment, maybe, but not their guts. Three men fell, either hit or finally taking cover. The bomber swept over them and unloaded two heavy tan bombs that tumbled into a garden beyond a cross lane. A moment later, they exploded with a shimmering blast that blew leaves off the trees above us.

Jacques and I saw what was happening. "Delayed-action fuses," I shouted. The Luftwaffe was using about a two-second delay on bomb detonation, so that the low-flying planes could escape the blast. If we could coordinate the ground fire against the planes, the bombardier's aim might be thrown off, and we just might be able to protect these frontline positions.

Jacques rounded up four FTP Bren gunners and I recruited four from Hubert's sector. Once we got them assembled in the sunken road, I gave the instructions while Jacques shouted the translation. The bombers were making slow, single-bomb passes now, working from a lazy orbit above the valley. This road was parallel to the school, and the planes passed directly overhead. Jacques's gun team would take the far end; mine was near the junction of the sunken road and the lane to the PC barn. As a Heinkel approached, we would judge its altitude and speed and hold up our fingers to signal the gunners the number of plane-length "leads" to give the aircraft before firing: Two fingers equaled two leads, and so on. A clenched fist meant no lead at all.

The next Heinkel lined up right above the sunken road, flying below 200 feet. I watched the sun glint on the plane's greenhouse nose. I could see the two pilots in their leather helmets. The Bren gunners crouched beside me. I stepped into the middle of the road and held up my index finger. "Fire!" I shouted.

The gunners raised their heavy Brens and fired quick five-round bursts.

As the plane blasted by overhead, I saw dark clumps of rounds strike the left wingtip. The pilot had banked right at the last moment and most of our fire had thrown left. We sprang for cover as the German tail gunner swept the sunken road.

The next plane was not so lucky. It roared straight toward us, even lower than the last. I could clearly see the bombardier's face in the glass nose. Jacques was on his feet, his clenched fist waving. "No lead!" I yelled. My men pounded the Heinkel with accurate, coordinated fire. The Bren fired a .303 round, the same as the Spitfire. In effect, we'd ambushed the plane with the firepower of an RAF fighter, shooting at point-blank range. Glass flew from the nose. Holes tore open in the plane's green belly. The right engine nacelle was pocked with Bren rounds, and dark oil streamed across the wing root.

Banking sharply left, the German pilot aborted his bomb run and gave his plane full throttle. Only the left engine responded. Smoke trailed in a thick, oily stream from the right wing. The men cheered.

I climbed to the crest of the sunken road and watched the Heinkel limp north above the Corrèze valley, slowly losing altitude. The men were still howling their wild pleasure. My heart thudded in my throat and temples. My breath was ragged. I was caught up in the savage rage of battle.

☆   ☆

CAPTAIN Wauthier's SAS platoon arrived around 1300, sprinting the last kilometer into town under strafing from three Focke-Wulf 190 fighter-bombers that had suddenly rolled out of the blinding midday sun. Wauthier brought word from Coriolan that the Heinkel we'd hit had crashed and burned near Ussel. But these Luftwaffe pilots did not make the same mistake as their colleagues.

While the fighters strafed our forward positions, we held a quick war council in Hubert's narrow barn. It was agreed that Antoine's plan for a prolonged siege was dangerous folly—the Germans wanted to hold Egletons because of the town's commanding position above the Corrèze valley; otherwise they wouldn't have continued to expend so much air support to protect the school. We could soon expect an armored relief column from Clermont-Ferrand. Therefore, we had to either strike fast, using the SAS heavy weapons to prepare the assault, or regroup to ambush positions along Route 89 northeast of town in order to intercept the threatened German column.

Wauthier had trained his men to precision. Even Antoine's independent troops were awed by these French SAS in their red berets, who moved like a pack of hunting cats, indifferent to the strafing and fragmentation bombs from the Focke-Wulfs. Wauthier's NCOs now took charge. They'd received two-inch British mortars in the airdrop, but only had about a hundred rounds of ammunition for them. We decided to lay down a mortar barrage on the school courtyard, to drive the enemy indoors, so that we could move our Bren-gun positions forward and dig them in. While Wauthier prepared his mortar pits behind the first row of houses, Jacques left to find the elusive Antoine. He would try again to convince him to work with us on a coordinated attack, or, failing that, to get his agreement to lend us troops for the ambush positions north of town.

Tony set up a radio in my forward command post, a house one street in from the school. I then moved up to the steep-roofed house that had taken the anti-tank fire that morning. This time the FTP soldiers in the garden included the Bren gunners from the sunken road, and they greeted me with warm smiles, not surly threats. Their sergeant, a tough young kid who enjoyed flourishing the Communist clenched-fist salute, would be my relay to Wauthier's mortar men. I crept up the attic stairs gingerly and slid onto the floor, keeping as low as I could. The planks were thick with broken slate and splintered wood from the 37mm round.

Wauthier's first mortar round dropped cleanly into the center of the courtyard, and I saw German soldiers scurry for cover from shallow rifle pits in a hedgerow. I shouted down the staircase to correct fire twenty meters right and then forward. The next round exploded on a timber barricade near the school's long administration wing. More enemy troops dashed for cover. I was enjoying myself, getting even for the pounding we'd taken from the planes that morning. And the Focke-Wulfs overhead were actually muffling the sharp chug of the mortars. Ten rounds later, the mortars were dropping devastating fire on the outside positions, just as we'd hoped. Now I directed them to hit the slate-and-timber roof of the school to drive the German machine gunners down from the upper floors. Wauthier sent several phosphorus rounds after the high explosive, starting fires in the smashed roof timbers. That would give the bastards something to think about.

But I got overconfident and forgot the Germans would be searching for the mortars' forward observer. I also forgot that I was silhouetted against the 37mm exit hole as I stooped to peek out the circular entrance hole on the front of the roof. The Germans reminded me of my negligence. Machine-gun rounds bracketed the shell hole, smashing the slate tiles and ricocheting loudly through the attic. I was hit. One moment I was crouching at the hole, the next I was sprawled on my back, my skull ringing like a gong. It was as if someone had thrown a bucketful of rocks in my face. I felt the blood, warm and salty, on my right cheek, then saw thick, dark drops raining on the floor. My hand went to my ear and came away sticky red. There was blood all down the front of my para smock now. The pain began after the initial shock, hot and persistent. I got control of my breathing and took stock. My head moved all right on my neck, and there was no spurting arterial blood. So I must have been superficially gouged by slate and bullet fragments.

The machine gun had shifted to a lower floor and I stole one last glance toward the school. It was then I saw the snout of the 37mm anti-tank gun moving beneath a camouflage net in the hedgerow only seventy meters away. The crew wore floppy camouflage jackets and had leaves on their helmets. But they were clearly exposed. Without seriously considering my actions, I dropped down the stairs and sprinted to the back garden.

The FTP soldiers were shocked at my appearance and came forward to provide aid. But I had other things in mind. I snatched up their Bren gun and a spare thirty-round magazine. Too dazed to get out the proper French, I mumbled something about "*le cannon Boche*" and jogged away to the side of the garden. From there I sprinted to the cover of a wide, bomb-blasted plane tree thirty meters down the street. I caught my breath and hefted the heavy Bren gun. When I came out from the cover of the trunk, I knew I'd have the enemy gun crew in easy range. The worst of the bleeding had stopped, and I could breathe through my nose to steady my chest.

There was no sense waiting. I slid around the trunk and leveled the gun's long barrel, sighting on the hedgerow sixty meters away. Even with their camouflage, the German gun crew were visible. I fired four long bursts, shucked out the empty magazine and jammed in the fresh one. Men were falling around the gun as they struggled to turn it toward me. One tall German raised his rifle, then flew backwards, his arms extended. I fired until the second magazine was empty. I don't know who shot at me as I dashed back for the cover of the house. But I wasn't hit. In the garden, the FTP troops took back their Bren gun and washed my bloody face with water from a bucket. They stared at me with wide, nervous eyes. I sat with my back against the cool stone wall, gazing at the billowy clouds in the afternoon sky, feeling my heart slow in my chest.

☆   ☆

AT sunset, we met again in Hubert's command post. Wauthier had stopped firing after I was wounded, but he only had around twenty mortar rounds left. Jacques had not found Antoine, but his company commanders had agreed to follow Wauthier's command. Now he laid out his attack plan. The SAS Bren teams had moved well forward along the school's left flank during the mortar barrage. Unfortunately, they'd lost one experienced trooper, shot through the head, and another had been seriously wounded. But these gun teams were now in place to sweep the school courtyard. Wauthier had written a formal request for an RAF bomber strike on the school to come the next afternoon at 1700 hours, and Tony was now transmitting the message to London. Just before the air strike, we would drop back two streets. Then the SAS would open up with their mortars and Piat anti-tank weapons, to drive any Germans from their foxholes back into the school. RAF Mosquito bombers would then dive-bomb the buildings. As soon as they were gone, Jacques and I would each lead a company of *maquisards* into the rubble to finish off the enemy garrison.

Wauthier had more faith in London than Jacques or I had. The munitions we'd requested for Hubert had still not arrived on the second SAS drop. And London hadn't even acknowledged our request. Obviously, they were preoccupied with other operations. While we met in the barn, the BBC announced exactly what those preoccupations were. Allied armies under General Alexander Patch had invaded the south of France at dawn that day. And Maquis units "cooperating with Free French, British, and American advisers" were conducting widespread offensive action in south and central France to support the invasion. We were only one of a hundred such units.

I took a handful of aspirin and drank two cups of wine to ease the pain of my torn ear and cheek, then gratefully crawled into my sleeping bag. Maybe I'd have an easy night. I certainly needed the rest.

But the night was not restful. German spotter planes dropped flares over the town. Enemy machine guns traded fire with the SAS Brens, as the Germans tried to push out new positions on the edges of the school grounds. I dozed as best I could with tracers smacking the barn roof and men pounding by in the lane shouting. Finally, I got up before dawn, washed my wounds and shaved around the bandage, then put on a clean shirt. I was just cutting a wedge of cheese for breakfast when the barn was rocked by a massive explosion. The Luftwaffe was back, this time with more Focke-Wulf fighter-bombers.

With the sun well up, the planes used it to full advantage, climbing high and dropping straight down, their engines screaming. They alternated hitting our positions with small fragmentation bombs, incendiaries, and walloping 100-kilo high-explosive bombs. Sometimes they'd roar in at treetop level, strafing with 20mm cannons. This air support was perfectly coordinated with the enemy garrison in the school, who used the attacks to shift their heavy machine-gun positions.

The day ground on with no sense of actual time, only noise, heart-pounding exchanges of fire, and stolen moments of rest in smoky cellars. Fires were burning on several streets. The FFI aid station on the edge of town was filled with moaning, wounded soldiers. During lulls in the bombing, the shocked civilians retreated further to the outskirts, but were afraid to risk crossing the open fields to the shelter of the surrounding forest in daylight.

At the appointed hour that afternoon, Antoine's and Hubert's companies fell back two streets. Wauthier's mortars opened up, and his courageous troopers moved forward to fire their Piats. As planned, the enemy retreated into the school. But the only planes overhead were German. The Heinkels were back, protected by Focke-Wulfs. There was little we could do but keep down and wait for darkness. We met in the barn again at sunset. I was groggy, my head pounded, and I was almost deaf from bomb concussions. The situation in Egletons was a stalemate.

But there was some good news. Coriolan had sent us a runner who announced that Duret's group in Ussel had breached the enemy's defenses and the Germans there had surrendered. Even better, the larger enemy garrisons at Brive and Tulle had agreed to unconditional surrender, after being surrounded by Patrick's troops and Hubert's other companies. Actually, the man added, there was *one* condition: Coriolan had promised the Germans an American officer would accept their surrender, an assurance against Maquis reprisals. I was the only American officer in the Department of Corrèze, so the job fell to me. While Wauthier and Jacques planned the next day's action, Hubert and I drove south in his shaky little Renault.

☆   ☆

My memory of that night is a splintered mixture of pain and jubilation. Somehow I managed to doze while the rickety little car bore south along the river. On the outskirts of Tulle, we got out and hiked around the town center, wary of snipers in the moonlight. The German commander had agreed to surrender at dawn, but there were rumors of dissenters in his ranks, poised for a breakout from the besieged garrison. A *gazogene* farm truck took us to Brive, where again we got out at the first Maquis roadblock. I arrived in the town square just as the German infantry *Hauptmann* ordered his three companies to stack their weapons before the beaming ranks of Patrick's AS troops. I signed an ornate document in French and German, which I was told guaranteed the prisoners the protection of Supreme Allied Headquarters. As soon as I did so, the tense ranks of German troops visibly relaxed. They were actually joking as the Maquis led them away to the improvised POW camps in the surrounding hills.

I awoke in the cab of the *gazogene* at dawn, blinking at another pastel summer morning. Hubert found some reasonably palatable ersatz coffee in a cafe on the edge of Tulle. I drank it and changed my bandage, then followed him through the narrow medieval streets to the village square. As we waited for the German commander to appear, Hubert pointed out the overhanging balconies where the SS had hung their hostages two months before. Once more, I signed for SHAEF. Once more, the Germans smiled with relief that their war was over. Hubert grinned for other reasons. The weapons of the

Tulle garrison went directly to his men—rifles, machine guns, a 75mm field gun, and cases of grenades.

On the road back to Egletons around noon it became clear that this part of the operation was still not going well. A Maquis road watcher flagged us down, warning that the Luftwaffe was strafing anything that moved along the highway. Hubert and I wearily hiked the rest of the way to town, keeping to the trees for cover.

We entered town just as the Focke-Wulfs swept past on another run, plastering the streets with fragmentation bombs and 20mm cannon. For the next twenty minutes we inched forward from house to house until we reached the site of Hubert's headquarters. The barn was a smoking heap of rubble. I found Tony with Wauthier in a nearby house, whose flaming roof beams had collapsed. All the windows were blown out and there were cracks in the walls you could see through. Tony was crouched in a corner with his earphones perched atop his head, patiently tapping out another message from Wauthier to London.

"Il est formidable," Wauthier said, pointing at Tony. He explained that the young American sergeant had remained faithfully at his radio post, transmitting important messages, even as the house took direct hits from German bombs. I looked around the walls above Tony's head. The plaster was scarred with deep shrapnel gouges. Tony tapped his Morse key, a cigarette dangling from his lips, his eyes rimmed with fatigue.

I found Jacques at Antoine's command post down the street. The FTP commander himself was now present, a stocky little guy with a loud voice and intelligent dark eyes. Something extraordinary had happened in my absence. One of Antoine's runners had arrived from Tulle with a shocking intelligence report: Instead of surrendering, he announced, the German garrison there had supposedly broken free and were now en route to relieve the siege of Egletons, threatening to take our positions from the rear.

I sat down hard on a German ammunition box. "That's not true, *Chef Antoine,*" I said. The rumored dissenters among the Tulle Germans, I explained, had indeed surrendered with the rest of the garrison at dawn. I myself had seen them disarmed and marched away. But Antoine was not convinced. He insisted there were "others," who had escaped in the night and infiltrated the forest behind us. Further, Antoine was now thinning out his companies to establish ambush positions above the highway between Egletons and Tulle, in order to intercept these phantom Germans.

To compound the confusion, Lieutenant Coriolan arrived on his crackling little motorbike. He had valid intelligence that the German relief column from Clermont-Ferrand was finally en route: a force of 2,000 heavily armed men in 150 trucks, and two armored cars with automatic cannons.

Wauthier, Jacques, and I immediately saw the danger. But Jacques and

I also saw the opportunity. The captain wasn't convinced, but my partner and I were sure there was time to establish ambushes on the twisting, forested curves of the highway between Ussel and Egletons. But someone had to maintain pressure on the Germans here. We needed Antoine's well-armed men both to beef up our ambushes and to hold the line around the school. Antoine sat impassively, smoking a hand-rolled cigarette of black tobacco as we frantically studied our maps. He had already given his orders, and he wouldn't back down.

☆ ☆

TONY and I remained in the forward positions near the school after Jacques and Wauthier moved up the road to set their ambushes. With darkness, the Luftwaffe finally gave up. The town hall was ablaze several blocks away, and shattered houses smoldered around us, exuding the acrid stench of the incendiaries. But there were no civilians left in town to fight the fires. They'd taken the Maquis wounded with them as they fled to the hills. Even the Germans inside the school were quiet. They'd obviously received radio messages that relief was en route. I had great faith in Wauthier and Jacques, but I knew they alone couldn't stop such a heavy column. When the last of the civilians were reported gone, I ordered the few remaining FTP troops and Hubert's walking wounded to fall back to the cover of the forest.

Tony and I sorted through our gear to lighten our load. We took the radio, our codebooks, some emergency rations, and our tightly wrapped bundles of hundred-franc notes. At the last minute, I jammed several extra Sten-gun magazines in the deep pockets of my smock. A *maquisard* led the way through the burning streets. We marched up steep pastures, through stands of hardwood, along dark forest trails. We avoided hamlets and farmhouses. We walked all night. I was a zombie, lifting one heavy boot before the other, my mind floating free of my aching body. Several times Tony shook me awake as I stumbled on the path, actually marching in my sleep.

Away to the northeast, we heard the now-familiar rattle of heavy machine guns and the dull rumble of land mines. Jacques and Wauthier were giving them hell up there. Sometime before dawn, our Maquis guide led us off a farm lane to a stone barn. He told us to hide in the hay, then disappeared into the darkness. I did not need a formal invitation. I burrowed into the musty stack, and pulled hay behind me like a mole going to ground. That's the last thing I remember about that long night.

☆ ☆

TONY woke me late the next morning. Birds were singing in the sunshine. My back and legs ached, but I was rested.

He grinned. "We had visitors last night," he said, munching a chunk of hardtack. "The Krauts pounded on the farmhouse up the way, yelling about escaped Maquis. The farmer told 'em there were no Maquis in the area. They didn't come down here."

While I'd slept, a German patrol from the relief column had swept the countryside. But Tony kept guard, his Sten gun cocked, grenades lined up before him. He swore he would have woken me had the situation been serious.

☆   ☆

As planned, we joined Wauthier and Jacques at a ruined forest church on the western side of the Corrèze valley. They were exhausted but quite pleased with themselves. It had taken all of Jacques's persuasive powers to convince the cautious Wauthier to split his unit into small ambush teams. But once he did, their ambushes between Ussel and Egletons had destroyed one armored car and knocked out six trucks. They counted at least twenty-five enemy dead and many wounded on the highway. The German relief column had not reached Egletons until dawn. Coriolan's agents reported that the enemy garrison in the school had loaded thirty casualties onto the convoy before the trucks departed for Tulle. The fortress we had struggled to take was now empty. But Hubert's troops had linked up with Antoine's ambush positions and together they continued to harass the German column. On last report, the battered relief force was moving back north, having reached Tulle at least one day too late.

Hiking along a forest ridge that afternoon to outflank the German column and establish more ambushes, we heard the deep drone of aircraft engines over the valley. A line of eight sleek, camouflaged RAF Mosquito bombers roared by above and wheeled with sharp precision toward the smoking town of Egletons. Each twin-engined bomber banked sharply and unloaded its bombs on the school. We sat wearily as the planes wheeled back again, pulverizing the now empty German redoubt. We couldn't help but admire their technique. But their timing was lousy.

☆   ☆

THE siege of Egletons and the surrender of the German garrisons in the valley together with the aggressive ambushing by the FFI and SAS along Route Nationale 89 had combined to take the fight out of the enemy in the region. Moreover, the Maquis had captured the weapons of over 2,000 German troops and were dug in strongly in all the former German-held towns. Corrèze was liberated.

But we kept Route 89 open as an enticement for the German First Army

Group, still in garrison in southwest France. Over the next ten days, Jacques and I trained Antoine's and Hubert's troops in the use of the captured weapons and dispatched demolition teams to blow the bridges on the side roads above the highway. If the Germans retreated this way, they'd have to use the Route Nationale, and the Maquis were waiting for them.

Hubert still had six unarmed companies of troops. Day after day we radioed London, begging for an airdrop to equip these eager Maquis soldiers. Being a veteran regular officer, Hubert understood the importance of harassing the Germans farther north, of keeping them below the Loire and away from Patton's flank. Hubert had taken over a fleet of captured German trucks and scout cars, and he proposed equipping a highly mobile *Battalion de Marche* to hit the retreating German columns in the valleys of Creuse, Indre, and Cher to the north of Limoges.

Hearing nothing from London on this matter, I took the team up to Limoges to confer with Colonel Rivier, the regional FFI commander. He immediately saw the value of Hubert's plan and authorized the operation to begin as soon as possible. The only problem was arms. Hubert needed bazookas, machine guns, and mines to do the job well. Again, we badgered London for these weapons, but to no avail. The OSS/SOE bureaucracy was obviously overwhelmed by the Maquis uprising and the related arms requests from Jedburgh Teams and Operational Groups supporting the resistance. In the end, Hubert had to disarm six of his ambush companies to equip the mobile battalion. This was a sad commentary on Allied responsiveness. I knew full well there were thousands of tons of munitions earmarked for the Maquis in depots in England. But the bureaucrats couldn't see clear to get them aboard planes.

(Nevertheless, Hubert's battalion was able to harass the German retreat for weeks, and even captured the key road junction of Issoudun. Decades later, when I was involved with supporting guerrilla fighters in other parts of the world, I remembered this bitter lesson: It isn't so much what you promise the men in the field that's important, it's what you deliver. And I learned to act first, then inform headquarters.)

☆   ☆

WE linked up with an SOE operations team, led by a dashing French major whose nom de guerre was "Popeye" Revez (Jacques Robert). His team had been betrayed twice by collaborator Gestapo informants and had narrowly escaped capture. Their last escape was late one night when they fled a farmhouse in their underwear as the Milice were kicking down the front door. While Revez's local Maquis helped train Hubert's mobile group in a forest camp near Guéret, Revez, Jacques, and I took off on a series of breakneck reconnaissance missions, scouting the highways and side roads of the Creuse, Indre, and Cher valleys for Hubert. We had a fast, 1939 Citröen *traction-avante*, which we used to great advantage.

Paris had been liberated ten days before, and the German units in central France were streaming east on every open road to escape encirclement by Patton north of the Loire and by Patch in the Rhône valley. We never knew when we'd encounter a German column, even on rutted back lanes. However, we quickly learned that the Wehrmacht maintained its predictability, even in retreat. To minimize Allied air attack on their convoys, the vehicles were staggered by time intervals—"serials" in military language. The convoys all move west to east, so we'd enter a village on the north-south road and watch for the German convoy. Once we got the timing of their serials down, we'd simply slip our Citröen into the interval and cruise along unscathed, marking our maps with the best ambush positions.

After being strafed by P-47 Thunderbolts, however, I decided to paint a large U.S. Army white star on the Citröen's roof. This didn't deter the Air Corps very much, but it gave the local French people a real thrill. As tough as he was, Revez never got used to my yelling, "Hey, honey, how're you doing?" to the local ladies as we rolled through their villages in the middle of the German convoys.

☆   ☆

BACK at Guéret we found Hubert's road companies at the peak of training and efficiency. They had managed to scrounge more weapons too, so Revez dispatched them into the Indre and Cher with orders to hit the major German convoys from the ambush positions we'd scouted. Coriolan arrived, as always energetic. True to form, he saw beyond the immediate tactical situation and proposed a fascinating new operation. He was in contact with large numbers of French *resistants* in Austria, French who had escaped forced labor in the Reich and had taken to the Tyrol Mountains. He proposed forming a new Jed team (or teams) to drop into these mountains and organize the unarmed Frenchmen into the type of Maquis we'd developed in the Corrèze. Alternatively, he suggested forming a column of fast, lightly armored vehicles to actually enter and harass the German retreat convoys using our audacious "serial" techniques.

☆   ☆

THESE proposals interested London and I found myself flying out of le Blanc, a captured Maquis airstrip north of Limoges, aboard a blacked-out RAF Hudson after dark on September 10. That night I actually slept between clean sheets in a Mayfair hotel room. Unfortunately, the air raid sirens interrupted my well-earned rest. London was in the middle of the buzz bomb and V-2 Blitz. The echoing explosions and pounding of the anti-aircraft guns made me feel right at home.

The next day on Grosvenor Street, Casey and British colonel Carleton-Smith listened with considerable interest to Coriolan and my proposals. The light-armored column, they said, was a splendid idea, but such an operation would have to be approved by the Free French, so that idea disappeared into the bureaucracy of the Allied command.

OSS headquarters was, however, intrigued by the Austrian-resistance Jed Team concept. I was told to find another Jed officer and return to France as soon as possible to recruit candidates for the program.

My good friend Adrian Wise, now a major, was back at Milton Hall, debriefing from his two months inside Nazi-occupied Brittany with Team Frederick, one of the bravest, most effective Jed outfits in France. As I expected, Adrian loved the idea of the Austrian operation. He took charge of logistics, organizing a Hudson flight back to le Blanc in three days' time.

Meanwhile, we decided to unwind in London. We had plenty of cash in our pockets, and there was only so much champagne you could drink, so one afternoon we found ourselves on the second floor of his Savile Row tailor, being fitted for dress uniforms. The air raid sirens droned for the tenth time since lunch, announcing the arrival of yet another buzz bomb. The staid, elderly tailor raised his gray eyebrows wearily, displeased with the interruption.

"Carry on, Mr. Maxwell," Adrian said. "I shouldn't think they're aiming at us."

"Quite, Major Wise," the old man said.

But the German robot bomb in question was, in fact, headed our way. As we stood at the large windows, the rasping, putt-putt of the buzz bomb grew louder, followed by the smacking AA guns in Green Park. We listened to the drone of the buzz bomb until the engine cut off. When the silence reaches you, you know that the bomb has gone into its dive. The blast finally came from across the park, rattling the windows.

The tailor never missed a beat as he marked the rich dark wool of Adrian's uniform blouse with his fine chalk.

Late that same night, Adrian and I were in Mayfair as the pubs were closing, strolling through the warm late-summer blackout toward Oxford Street. I was just saying something amusing about the Maquis when the whole world blazed with a giant welder's torch. We both hit the greasy pavement. A glowing shock wave swept past, followed by a double blast-furnace roar. We got to our feet. Two blocks away, flames swept from a shattered pub. The front of a taxi was wedged into second-floor rubble. A

V-2 warhead had exploded, just south of Hyde Park, followed immediately by a second blast that rocked us like a thunderclap, the sonic boom from the descending missile.

☆   ☆

WHILE Adrian and Coriolan recruited candidates from the local Maquis, I drove the Citröen back to Corrèze to check on the ambush positions we'd established. I found Hubert's people in good order, but Antoine's FTP seemed to have quit the military fight to concentrate on the political struggle. They'd taken over Tulle and had the arms factory running again, having actually resorted to armed threats to force the engineers and technicians to work for them. Antoine himself was not interested in the tactical picture. He had orders from elsewhere to produce armaments for use after the war.

☆   ☆

TEAM James returned to Milton Hall for debriefing on September 26. We'd been in the occupied zone only seven weeks. On our first morning back, I was told of the unit's casualties. Among my friends, Larry Swank had been killed in an operational accident in Haute Savoie; Major John Bonsall's entire team had been wiped out; at least three British-led Jed Teams had been ambushed and killed soon after landing. Cy Manierre was known to have been captured in eastern France, and to have been savagely tortured by the Gestapo. The SOE actually had agents inside Cy's prison in Alsace, trying to stage his escape, but he was too weak from torture to respond to their signals.[9]

As I sat down on my old cot that afternoon and began opening my mail from home, I felt as if a weary old man had taken the place of the eager boy who'd once slept here.

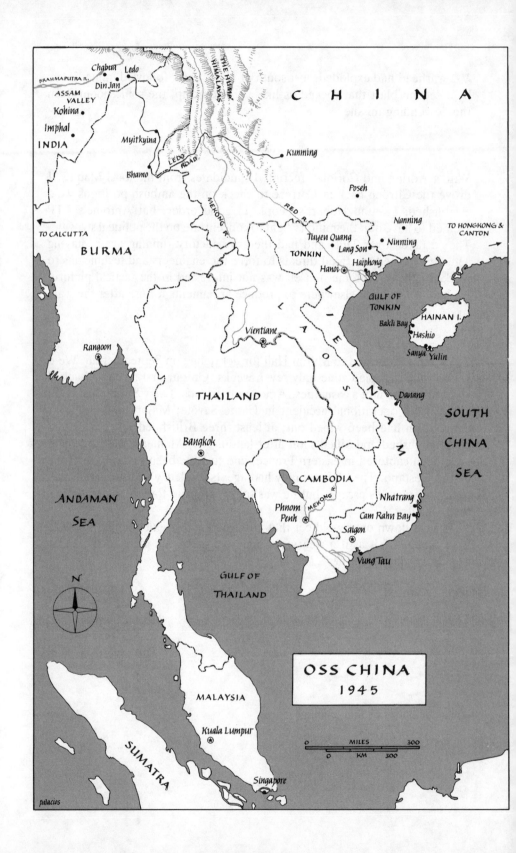

CHAPTER THREE

OSS China

1945

☆   ☆

By the time Casey's people finished debriefing our team at a safe house in London, I learned that approval for Lieutenant Coriolan's Austrian Tyrol operation was running into trouble. The problem was that the Allies had already decided to partition Austria into four occupation zones, to be administered after the Nazi defeat by the Americans, British, French, and Soviets. The zone boundaries would meet in the Tyrol. So London headquarters had to get authorization from all four powers before starting an American-led resistance movement in the southern mountains. Casey told me the plan had merit and would probably be okayed—"eventually"—but admitted he didn't know how long this would take.

Back at Milton Hall, we got word that the OSS China station was looking for volunteers among combat-tested American Jeds to conduct similar operations in the Far East. I wasn't surprised that guys like Mac Austin, Lou Conein, and Aaron Bank immediately signed up. Despite their weeks of intense Maquis fighting that summer, they wanted more action. All of us who'd worked behind enemy lines in France knew the tactical value of well-organized resistance operations. And we were confident we could use our hard-won experience to good advantage against the Japanese.

But I was frustrated. Jacques and Coriolan were counting on the Austrian operation, and were in the middle of intensive planning with the SOE and the French BCRA. We were still a team, and they wanted Tony and me with them. It's hard to explain the mutual respect—indeed, mutual dependence—of men who've fought together in a guerrilla unit. One of the main reasons they were enthusiastic about going into the Tyrol was that we

71

each possessed skills and attributes that complemented those of our team-mates. In a way, we were a very successful, highly specialized military *firm*, a partnership. I owed those men a lot, and I hated the thought of abandoning them.

On the other hand, I realized we simply might not get authorization. The way Patton was rolling east and the Soviets were pushing west, the war in Europe might well be over by Christmas, as some optimists in SHAEF were predicting. If I stooged around England, waiting, I could easily miss my chance to fight in the Far East.

My dilemma was alleviated somewhat by a quick combat mission back to occupied France, which Adrian Wise organized in early October. His Jed team had helped seal off the major Nazi garrisons on the Brittany peninsula after D-Day, and Maquis units he'd trained still laid siege to the strong German fortress cities of Lorient and St. Nazaire. As the Allied armies sped east toward the Rhine, their vulnerable "Red Ball Express" supply route (a single highway, reserved for military traffic) stretched behind them all the way to the battered Normandy ports of Cherbourg and Le Havre; we still hadn't captured France's major channel port, Brest, on the tip of Brittany.

Headquarters was worried that the well-equipped and relatively un-blooded Wehrmacht garrisons in Brittany might escape to cut this supply line to the front, possibly in concert with a German counterattack. Our job was to establish an effective combat intelligence network inside the German fortresses cut off on the peninsula, which would give HQ ample warning of an attempted enemy breakout.

We landed by rubber boat near the fishing port of St. Brieuc on the north Brittany coast just before dawn on October 2. The trip across the channel on a Royal Navy torpedo boat had been rough, and landing our black, two-man dinghy loaded with arms, munitions, and radio gear in a rocky cove had not been easy. Adrian and I both appreciated the small-boat training we'd suffered through the previous winter in Scotland.

Adrian had good local contacts, and within five hours we linked up with the regional *Armée Secrète* commander in a hamlet near Lorient. The situation on the peninsula was bizarre, even by the standards of wartime France. Allied bombers regularly hit the German positions, but refrained from striking inland roads and villages. In effect, there were pockets of intense combat side by side almost idyllic pastoral enclaves of harvest-time Brittany. This situation was further confused when heavily armed German foraging parties, often led by light tanks, raided market towns when food stocks grew low in the besieged garrisons. The Maquis sniped and ambushed; the Germans conducted their brutal reprisals; the FFI tried to exert legitimate government control in an area supposedly "liberated," only to have the Wehrmacht reappear to terrorize the civilians.

We procured a fast car and a trustworthy AS driver, then conducted a quick reconnaissance of the peninsula's Atlantic coast. Within three days, we'd established our intelligence networks, giving considerable authority to local Maquis commanders. We also identified key road and rail bridges to be blown, should the Germans attempt a breakout. Finally, we surveyed special drop zones, where French SAS troops and munitions could be dropped to beef up the Maquis, should the situation require reinforcements. Our only real adventures on the operation were a couple of close encounters with large German foraging patrols. But we used the techniques we'd evolved along the Indre and Cher to evade them. This brief but demanding mission had required only a few days, an accomplishment neither of us would have believed possible during our Jedburgh training. This was my first clear understanding that there is no replacement for combat experience in building a soldier's competence.

Before leaving Brittany, we kept a promise to Jacques and called at his family's large estate near Dinan up on the Golfe de St. Malo. The fighting had been savage in this region and burnt-out tanks and trucks littered the narrow farm lanes. There were temporary German and Allied cemeteries in abandoned pastures, the rows of graves marked by simple wooden stakes. Some of the villages had been bombed into mounds of blackened rubble. But Jacques's farm had escaped major damage. We met his family and were given a real feast of roast goose and turnips. Jacques's sister, Louise, decided to come with us to Paris. Early the next morning, we crossed an old humpbacked stone bridge and were back in Normandy, the region officially liberated by Patton's Third Army. I showed my SHAEF pass and priority orders to a skeptical MP sergeant, and he reluctantly issued us a vehicle pass to drive the Red Ball Express.

For the next two days we rolled along, wedged among long convoys of olive-drab semi-trailer trucks and lumbering tank carriers, all heading east toward the front. But the narrow roads sometimes became clogged with empty convoys speeding back to the Normandy ports, so our eastbound lane was flagged down to wait out a long line of westbound vehicles. Most of the drivers were black GIs who gladly shared their rations with us as we waited out the traffic jams in shell-blasted village squares. Paris was full of staff rats, and even some of the bemedaled military bureaucrats from Washington had found their way to comfortable billets in Right Bank hotels. We didn't waste much time there swapping war stories.

Back in England that bitterly cold autumn, the Austrian Maquis operation seemed hopelessly stalled in the Allies' Byzantine negotiations. Adrian and I killed some time in additional parachute training, then I volunteered for duty in the Far East. I received orders routing me through the States—with priority transportation status and a thirty-day leave to get married thrown in.

On a frigid December morning almost exactly one year from our arrival in Gourock, I was back in the battered Clydeside port, about to board the *Ile de France* for New York. My travel orders made me a Top Secret SHAEF courier, in charge of a large shipment of classified documents, stored in dozens of locked bags weighing several tons. Since I could not be physically separated from the sacks until they were safely stored in the ship's vault, I chose to ride with them in the cargo net, which swayed precariously over the water before clanking down through a hatch.

This vantage point allowed me to survey the harbor as I had the year before from the deck of the *Queen Elizabeth*. More convoys were unloading. More fresh troops disembarked, en route to the fighting in Europe. One day after leaving the port of Glasgow, the Germans unleashed their massive counteroffensive in the Ardennes Forest, the epic bloody campaign that soon became known as the Battle of the Bulge. I felt a definite twinge of regret, and a stab of guilt, as the ship began its zigzag course through the Irish Sea, north toward the open Atlantic. While we sat down to dine on starched linen in the officers' mess, hundreds of thousands of young Americans were fighting for their lives in the frozen mud and snowdrifts of Belgium. If the Nazi advance did manage to cut the Allied armies in half, Hitler had a chance of capturing the Channel ports, and expanding the V-2 rocket bombardment of British supply ports. The European campaign had reached a critical point, yet I was sailing west. I was a Jed, and the idea of retreat did not sit well.

☆   ☆

MARY and I were married on January 6, 1945, in Elizabeth, New Jersey. The news from Europe was still not good. Although the brunt of the Ardennes attack had been broken, the cost was horrendous. Worse, optimistic projection of a sudden German capitulation had been shattered. There were months of bloody combat ahead as the Allies advanced into Germany. In the Pacific, there was still savage fighting in the Philippines and more ahead for the Marines and Army as we prepared to capture the heavily defended inner circle of Japanese islands, including Okinawa and Iwo Jima, in preparation for the actual invasion of the Home Islands. Massive armies still faced each other on mainland China. The situation in Burma had improved greatly, and Allied armies were beginning to push, reversing the final savage Japanese offensive that had penetrated the Assam valley of India in 1944 and besieged British garrisons at Imphal and Kohina.

I was now paused halfway between the fighting in Europe and the upcoming climactic battles in Asia. Once more, I realized this was truly a global war. But America was relatively untouched. Mary and I made the rounds of her friends and relatives, driving a comfortable borrowed car with generous gasoline rations down brightly lit streets. Although civilians griped about shortages, they had no concept of the deprivations in England or the widespread suffering in Europe. And from what I'd heard, conditions in the Far East made the ETO seem like a Scout jamboree.

In preparation for my new orders, I was given a temporary duty assignment in Washington, getting "read in" on the OSS Far East mission. Mary returned to her regular code-breaking duties in Naval Intelligence. We rented an apartment in Georgetown, but Mary was on the midnight-to-eight graveyard shift, and we would often meet on cold mornings walking toward each other on N Street, she returning from work and me just leaving. The same ground rules about secrecy applied: She couldn't discuss her Ultra work, and I could not detail the Jedburgh operation, although I now wore two French *Croix de Guerre* and had an Invasion Arrowhead on my ETO campaign ribbon. It was as if we were in some kind of isolation chamber, shielded from the cruel reality of total war, pretending to lead a normal life as a newly married couple. Then the phone would ring, and the landlady would say there was a call for "Lieutenant Singlaub." We always had to ask, "John or Mary?"

One day Mary got a call from OSS headquarters from an officer who was familiar with this telephone confusion. "There won't be any more calls for Lieutenant John Singlaub," he explained. "He just made captain."

☆   ☆

I SHIPPED out for the Far East aboard a crowded Navy transport from Long Beach, en route to India in early April. For the passage, I'd been made officer-in-charge of a large, eclectic group of OSS personnel—officers, enlisted ranks, and civilians—all bound for the Far East via Calcutta. I was happy to see that Tony Denneau, now a first sergeant, was with us. Although I didn't have specific orders, it was probable I'd be forming a Jedburgh-type resistance team in southern China, and I certainly intended to have Tony as my radio operator. The transport sped along at about fifteen knots, easily breasting the endless blue Pacific swells, cutting a wide arc south and west, away from the war zone. Our relatively good speed made convoy travel unnecessary, and our zigzag course supposedly made us invulnerable to Japanese submarines. But after witnessing the Keystone Kops gun drills of the merchant crew, I increased my prayers for a safe crossing.

Several of the OSS men on board were Yugoslav-Americans who'd fought in the Balkans. Some had served with Tito's Communist partisans and others with General Draza Mihailovich's Chetnik guerrillas. They had hair-raising stories to tell of the desperate, three-way conflict in the mountains of Serbia. During the long and boring passage, one of these officers, Eli Popovich, came close to "killing" a colleague, George Wuchanich, an open Communist sympathizer with the somewhat nebulous assignment as an intelligence officer. Prior to World War II, he had been a radical "labor organizer," and he continued this after the war.

I was shocked to see that these men truly hated each other; moreover, I was beginning to realize that the Office of War Information's simplistic "Four Freedoms" rationale for America's involvement in the war did not encompass the harsh political realities that lay beneath the surface of military operations. As in France where the Communist FTP was more interested in the political struggle after liberation, and as in Yugoslavia where a similar hidden conflict raged, I came to realize that my guerrilla warfare assignment in China would be anything but straightforward. In China there was a situation analogous to the FTP-AS French conflict, but on an infinitely vaster scale. Generalissimo Chiang Kai-shek's Nationalist forces maintained an uneasy (and clearly temporary) truce with Mao Tse-tung's Communist Red Army. As in Europe, both factions were eager for Allied war matériel, so they kept up pressure on the Japanese occupation forces. But, again mirroring the situation in Europe, the Communist and anti-Communist forces in China seemed to be preparing for another struggle once the Japanese were defeated.

To exacerbate this complexity, the future of Indochina might also be at stake. The Japanese had occupied the French colonies with the cooperation of the Vichy government in 1940. Although these forces had recently come under air attack from American bases in the Philippines, a large, well-equipped enemy army group was still in the field. A few Free French guerrilla outfits harassed them, but the major opposition to the Japanese in Indochina came from guerrilla troops loyal to a fiery Communist leader whose nom de guerre was Ho Chi Minh, "He Who Leads." Like Mao, Ho viewed fighting the Japanese as a necessary precursor to the inevitable battle against French colonial power. In my Washington briefings I'd learned that American policy under Roosevelt had been to aid the Communist guerrillas in their effort to pin down the Japanese; in exchange for this alliance, America was to help establish decolonized "protectorates" following the Japanese defeat, which, it was hoped, would somehow evolve into independent democratic nations. But Roosevelt was dead now, and President Truman had reversed this policy, throwing American support behind France's efforts to regain its overseas colonies. Naturally, this muddled political and military situation would make my eventual combat assignment "très intéressant," as we used to say in Corrèze.[1]

☆ ☆

CALCUTTA was a stifling ant heap of humanity. The premonsoon heat shimmered in glaring waves across the dusty plain of the Ganges delta. Luckily, we moved through the ramshackle metropolis quickly, and the unit I was in charge of (now shed of various exotic civilians) was sent north to the cooler Assam valley. As the narrow, varnished teak passenger cars of the train rattled across the dry rice paddies and climbed the terraced watershed of the Brahmaputra River, the ancient stench of India—a mixture of human and animal excrement, dust, and charcoal smoke—was washed away by the cool breezes from the white bastion of the Himalayas.

We got off the train at Chabua air base, near Dinjan in the upper Assam valley, where Colonel Ray Peers had established the headquarters of OSS Detachment 101 for his operations in Burma two years before. Chabua was one of the termini of the air bridge "over the Hump" to China. A few miles away, the town of Ledo was the land bridge terminus. All day and most of the night, dusty American transport planes— workhorse C-47s and C-46s, as well as converted Liberators—landed and took off, hauling supplies to Kunming in China and returning for more.

I learned that OSS Special Operations personnel with orders for China duty might have to wait as long as two weeks for air transportation across the Hump to Kunming. The men in my unit were used to action, and they'd been cooped up aboard ship for a month, so I was afraid they might get into trouble in this comfortable backwater, where the virtue of the local tea planters' wives and daughters might indeed be in jeopardy. As Colonel Peers was about to move his headquarters down the Ledo Road to a forward position at Bhamo in Burma, I volunteered my unit to assist. Packing up Detachment 101's well-stocked supply huts provided unexpected bounty. A couple of the ex-Jed NCOs "liberated" a good selection of jungle knives, survival equipment, and light automatic weapons, all of which we'd heard were hard to find in China.

Jolting south down the Ledo Road in our convoy of deuce-and-a-half trucks was an interesting experience. Six months before I'd helped organize Maquis ambushes of German truck convoys south of the Loire. Now I was in charge of a similar convoy, albeit on a much more primitive "road." These cool green foothills with jungle-clad ridges and long grassy streambeds had ostensibly been cleared of Japanese the year before. But enemy straggler units regularly ambushed the road to replenish their food and ammunition. The area had also been a bastion of Chinese bandits for several decades. So I didn't get much of a chance to enjoy the splendid scenery of the tropical highlands because I was too busy scanning likely ambush sites with my glasses, and searching for easily defended bivouac spots each night.

In Bhamo I found a scene straight out of Kipling. The officers' club was in a *basha* stilt house with a thick roof of palm thatch, the home to foot-long lizards and fruit bats with amazing wing spans. Many of the troops staging through the town were veterans of irregular units that had distinguished themselves in Burma: British officers from Wingate's Raiders and American guys from Merrill's Marauders. You could spot them immediately—their faces, hands, and forearms were burnt ocher from months in the sun, but their chests and backs were yellow from months of taking the malaria-suppressant Atabrine. The true field soldiers were laced with leech welts and fungus. Even in this camp they moved quietly on rubber-soled boots and instinctively scanned the tree lines of the surrounding jungle. Over rusty cans of warm Schlitz we swapped tales of guerrilla warfare in central France and the jungles of Burma.

For me, this was invaluable training because you can learn a lot more about your enemy from men who have actually fought him in the field than you ever could in a formal intelligence briefing. What I learned in Bhamo about the Japanese was that they were tenacious, brave in combat, cruel in occupation, and potentially vulnerable in their overly rigid military hierarchy. One captain from Merrill's Marauders recounted a Japanese banzai charge in the Mangin Mountains the year before, in which an entire enemy company had been "stacked up like railroad ties" as they attacked a small American unit in wave after wave, not attempting to outflank two well-placed machine guns. I remembered the stubborn and resourceful SS defenders at Egletons, and realized I was now facing a much different enemy.

☆   ☆

THE OSS China Special Operations compound was in a pleasantly green rice paddy camp two miles west of Kunming. As in India, there was a definite, all-pervasive stench to southern China, which here was heavy on the human manure used to fertilize the paddies. The surrounding area, however, was strikingly beautiful, with turquoise lakes and dramatic, freestanding limestone towers crowned by stands of bamboo and hardwood. On early summer mornings, the mist rose slowly from the paddies and swirled around these white stone towers. Peasants in conical coolie hats padded along the dikes. Ducks and geese cackled in the paddies, and water buffalo chewed dripping fodder. If you ignored the drone of aircraft and truck engines, you felt you were in the mysterious Cathay of Marco Polo.

But we weren't tourists in China. We had a war to finish, and it looked as if the final battles against Japan might prove the bloodiest of the entire

Second World War. Japanese resistance on Iwo Jima and Okinawa had shocked the War Department, which was already drawing up staff plans for the invasion of the Home Islands. If the enemy fought so hard for these outlying possessions—and was willing to squander the lives of thousands of young pilots in kamikaze attacks—it was feared that the actual invasion of Japan might cost the lives of several hundred thousand Americans. Therefore, Allied strategists were determined to use every ploy and deception available to reduce casualties.

In our area of operations, the main concern was the large, unblooded Japanese occupation army in French Indochina, particularly the 21st Infantry Division stationed around Hanoi in Tonkin, as North Vietnam was then known. Although we weren't made privy to strategic details, it was generally accepted that there would be an American amphibious landing in southern China in the fall, which would serve two functions: a diversion that would hopefully draw Japanese forces from the Home Islands (to be subject to air and submarine attack en route to China), and establishment of advance American bomber bases closer to Tokyo than our B-29 fields in the Mariannas and western China. This China diversion could be threatened by a counterattack from the Japanese forces in Indochina. So our job was to keep them bottled up in the former French colony.

My assignment was to equip and train a thirty-man Operational Group guerrilla unit composed of "Annamites"—young Vietnamese volunteers from Ho Chi Minh's Viet Minh forces—led by American officers and NCOs, with the help of several Vietnamese veterans of the French Foreign Legion. Once I got this unit into fighting shape we were to parachute into the rugged highlands north of the Red River delta, northwest of Hanoi and Haiphong. There were only three passable military lines of communication north from Tonkin to China proper. One was a French-built road connecting Hanoi and Ninming and passing through the Tonkinese border town of Lang Son. The second was a railroad, which paralleled the road and threaded through a steep limestone gorge south of Lang Son, crossing numerous bridges and culverts. Our job would be to blow the bridges on these two routes, then to harass the Japanese, preventing repairs. That would close two routes out of Tonkin. Other Operational Groups would conduct similar attacks on the other roads and railroads connecting Vietnam with southern China.

After my initial intelligence briefings and first contacts among the French and Annamite volunteers, I decided not to use any French officers in order to prevent possible friction between them and the intensely nationalist Viet Minh. I should add here that Ho Chi Minh and his close colleagues disguised their Communist affiliation to better recruit volunteers among the heavily Roman Catholic Tonkinese. Also, careful scrutiny of the map showed that my operation was going to be dicey; the Japanese would not be pleased to have their road and railroad blown and their engineers ambushed. They would no doubt beat the bush searching for us. So it was better to keep the number of Caucasians in the team to a minimum. In those jungle mountains, we just couldn't throw on a French peasant's blue smock and black beret and fade into the background.

For my team NCOs, I chose Tony Denneau as my radio man, Corporal Jim Healy, a young Boston Irishman, as medic, and another Irishman, Sergeant Bill Cavanaugh, as weapons and demolition instructor. We moved south to the small mountain town of Poseh, where the OSS maintained an advance training camp. Conditions here were relatively primitive—you reached our camp by crossing a river on a crude, hand-hauled ferry—but the climate was not bad.[2] This ferry, by the way, caused an interesting incident later that summer. The local peasants knew we had explosives and begged us incessantly to explode charges in the water to stun fish for them. One day, Sergeant Cavanaugh and I were crossing on the ferry when he got tired of the peasants' singsong harangue. He grabbed a one-kilo block of C-4, primed it, lit the fuse, and then tossed it in the river. Unfortunately, he threw it *upstream*. To my horror, the block of plastic explosive, its fuse smoking like a toy steamer, floated back down under the planks of the ferry and detonated with a thunderclap and a geyser of muddy water. The raft-like ferry immediately began to sink. But the peasants on the banks jumped with glee as they scooped up basketloads of dead and stunned fish. We barely made it to the wet clay bank before the ferry settled to the bottom.

There was a decent steel-mat-runway airstrip at Poseh, so our supply and reconnaissance capabilities were quite good. While Sergeant Cavanaugh trained our volunteers in the mysteries of the M-1 carbine, hand grenades, land mines, and C-4 plastic explosives, I made my first aerial reconnaissance of the territory south of Lang Son.

I flew on C-47 supply drops to OSS teams already in the field, some with Ho Chi Minh's headquarters group in the mountains above the Red River. Either coming or going, I'd convince the pilots to drop low enough for me to snap pictures out the open cargo door. This was real seat-of-the-pants flying, and the young 14th Air Force crews obviously took their Terry and the Pirates role seriously. There were no navigational aids, of course, and our charts and maps were badly out of date, so we'd often get lost. Sometimes we'd be barreling up a steep gorge of limestone cliffs and scrub jungle only to have monsoon clouds spill over the ridges like an avalanche of cotton, eradicating visibility. The only recourse was to firewall the throttles and climb, sweating blood until you broke through on top. On other trips I'd argue with the pilot and co-pilot about our position, as we descended south from the mountains onto the delta, only to have our discussion interrupted by a string of tracers from a Japanese ack-ack site. That was *one* sure way of pinpointing enemy positions.

As our training advanced that summer, the Japanese forces learned through their spies that American-led guerrilla units were forming in the region. The enemy began aggressive forays by company- and battalion-size units, which raided along the roads north of the Chinese border. Although the larger towns like Nanning were held by strong Nationalist Chinese garrisons, the countryside was a no-man's-land. We never knew as we hiked the hillsides of scrub jungle, or drove our jeeps along the muddy lanes between bamboo groves, if we would encounter a Japanese ambush or roadblock. But this confused tactical situation made for excellent training. By July, I had my people worked up to peak combat efficiency. We could hike twenty miles up and down the ridges with heavy loads, skirt heavily defended Japanese bivouacs undetected, and even infiltrate their supply dumps to steal ammunition and provisions.

My fellow Jed, Captain Lucien Conein, had a larger composite Operational Group. His job was to move south from the Chinese border town of Ninming and occupy Lang Son just across the Indochina frontier. It was hoped he could defend the town by arming local volunteers to supplement his own troops, and protect the highway bridge there. His outfit was already en route when I took off on a recon flight after four days of thick overcast. We flew southwest to a place called Tuyen Quang and dropped a heavy load of rice and munitions into a jungle clearing. As we passed low overhead, I saw a couple of American guys in sweat-soaked fatigues talking to a thin, elderly Annamite in a pith helmet. The plane banked steeply above the clearing, and the native guerrilla leader waved his thin hand languidly, as if to dismiss a loyal subordinate.

"Who's that guy?" I shouted to the young crew chief as we clung to the static line anchor cable like straphangers in a crazy subway.

"That's old Ho, sir," the kid shouted back. "Ho Chi Minh, the honcho himself."[3]

Flying back to Poseh, I again prevailed on the crew to drop low above the Hanoi–Lang Son highway. As we climbed to breast the ridge above Lang Son, I was shocked to see the unmistakable signs of fresh fortifications—bunkers, mortar pits, and machine-gun posts—cut in the red laterite soil. We flew a low orbit of the town and I spotted fresh field telephone lines and a camouflaged truck park. Without doubt, the Japanese had occupied the town with at least a battalion and were now well dug in. Lou Conein's group was probably only a day's hike away, and they were marching into a trap. As soon as we landed, I told the Poseh tower to alert our headquarters in Kunming to stand by for an emergency operational message.

Tony and I sweated through the hot afternoon encoding a detailed report on the unexpected enemy occupation of Lang Son and requesting a thorough aerial photo reconnaissance of the region. Further, I suggested that the photos themselves be airdropped to Conein and he be given discretion whether to continue the advance or to pull back.

As often happens in the field, a compromise was reached. Lou's outfit was ordered back, but he wasn't told the reason for the withdrawal.

☆   ☆

I GOT back to our small compound in Poseh one rainy night in August after a tough patrol, dodging truck-borne enemy raiding parties. One of my Annamite NCOs was quite excited. He'd heard a radio report of *"une bombe très puissante"*—a very powerful bomb—that had been dropped on Japan. Within a week we got news of the second atomic bomb, and then, a few days later, word reached us that Emperor Hirohito had spoken to the Japanese people, urging them to accept the inevitability of defeat. Our local combat intelligence nets, however, reported no stand-down by the Japanese troops in the area. Until I heard better, I kept my outfit on combat readiness.

Then I got priority orders to report to Kunming with my American teammates for a special operation. We landed on the morning of August 25, in the middle of a monsoon downpour that had been going on for a week. As I dashed through the rain to the Ops hut, a driver from Colonel Paul Helliwell, our intelligence officer, saluted and told me to hop in his jeep. The Colonel, he said, had urgent business with me.

Helliwell didn't waste time with small talk. He had several map easels of southern China and northern Indochina arrayed in his office. As I shook the rain off my poncho, he handed me a Secret Theater Directive dated August 15, concerning "Prisoner of War Humanitarian Teams."[4]

"As you can see from that document, OSS has the mission of rescuing Allied POWs in this theater. There's a prison camp on the west coast of Hainan Island." He went to the map. "We would like you to volunteer to lead the mission to Hainan, Captain," Helliwell said, tapping the south China map with his pointer to indicate the large oval island that hung like a pear from the Canton coast southwest of Hong Kong. "We think the camp's near an ore-loading wharf here." Again, he tapped the map. "That's Bakli Bay."

"How do I get there, sir?"

"You jump in." Helliwell stared at me for a moment. "Tomorrow night."

"Tomorrow, sir?" I couldn't help shaking my head. "How many men?"

Helliwell said that was up to me, but I had to consider that the plane would be heavily laden with medical supplies and food. "I'll need a good medic and a good commo man," I said, then began ticking off the other positions on my fingers. "Japanese interpreter, Chinese interpreter . . ."

"That's up to you, Captain," Helliwell said, handing me another Secret document. "The Japs have been executing Allied prisoners for several months now, supposedly in retaliation for our air raids. We have good reason to believe they'll try to massacre the POWs in remote areas to prevent them from being witnesses to earlier atrocities."

I studied the intelligence report. Agents in Singapore, Thailand, Formosa (now Taiwan), and Japan proper had noted increased atrocities against Allied POWs, including public executions.[5]

"In some parts of China," Helliwell continued, "the Japanese forces have apparently received no news on the surrender. Or at least the local commanders haven't told their subordinates. It's a tricky situation, kind of a limbo. Once their troops find out the Emperor has called for surrender, there's no telling how they'll react."

I looked at the map again. Hainan certainly was remote, a good five-hour plane ride from Kunming. "Any indication the Japs on the island want to surrender?"

Helliwell shook his head. "Well, they shot at our recon plane yesterday, if that's any indication." He rose and reached across the desk to shake my hand. "My staff will brief you. Better get going. Good luck."

"Thanks, sir." I knew I was going to need it.

☆   ☆

THE next forty hours were probably the busiest I've ever spent, outside of an actual combat zone. In my first briefing from Helliwell's staff, it became clear that I wouldn't be leaving for Hainan the next day. There were a total of eight OSS Mercy Mission POW rescue groups being formed to jump into known Japanese prison camps. They bore the code names of birds: Magpie (Peking), Sparrow (Shanghai), Quail (Hanoi), etc. I would lead Mission Pigeon to Hainan.[6] Our orders were to make contact with Allied POWs in our respective areas, take the prisoners under our protection, and render all possible medical and humanitarian assistance to them. Next, we were to secure a suitable nearby airfield for their evacuation, and if that was impossible, to prepare a large drop zone for additional personnel and medical supplies. We were also charged with intelligence responsibilities, including locating any downed Allied airmen who had escaped or evaded capture. In the process, we were to draw up a detailed order of battle of the Japanese forces we encountered. Headquarters was worried some regional Japanese commanders might simply continue the fight of their own volition. Therefore, it was vital we learn as much as possible about enemy strength on Hainan, as quickly as possible.

The military situation on Hainan, I learned from Helliwell's intel briefers, was dangerously confused. According to Nationalist agents on the island, there were at least five hostile groups fighting one another in various combinations. The Japanese forces included naval defense garrisons, the naval air wing, and a large contingent of so-called Hokaido Marines, crack Japanese troops who had fought in the Pacific campaign. There were also Communist and Nationalist guerrillas in the central mountain jungles, as well as Chinese bandits loyal to local outlaw leaders, and fierce indigenous tribesmen known as the Li.

Allied POWs were known to include Australian army troops and Dutch army and naval forces plus some civilians captured in the Netherland East Indies in 1942, as well as Sikhs from the Hong Kong–Singapore Royal Artillery, and an unknown number of American airmen shot down on the island in the past eight months, the period during which Hainan came in range of our Philippine-based bombers. The intelligence reports also noted a large number of Chinese civilian prisoners from Hong Kong, whom the Japanese had enslaved to work the island's rich iron and copper deposits near Bakli Bay.

My final OSS briefing officer was a specialist on Japanese military operations. He stressed that the Emperor's "surrender" speech of the previous week had been enigmatic at best, delivered in obscure and highly indirect court phrasing that served to avoid the dishonor of defeat. Therefore, he said, local commanders on Hainan might still consider themselves bound by their oaths of loyalty to resist the enemy at all costs.

"You're just going to have to take charge," he said. "But they might not want to listen to a captain."

He explained that a field-grade officer—major and above—in the Japanese Imperial Army literally had power of life and death over his men. It was unlikely that the commandant of the POW guards would be a field-grade officer, so we agreed I would have the temporary rank of major for this operation.

When my briefing was completed, I knew I'd need a highly skilled and resourceful team to carry out the mission. The POWs themselves were thought to be suffering badly from malnutrition, disease, and the systematic cruelty of their guards. Therefore, I'd need a good medic. Jim Healy had shown himself to be well qualified, resourceful, and damned near fearless on the Indochina border. Tony Denneau, of course, would be my commo man. We'd been through a lot together, and each felt good to have the other on the team.

I'd also need a brave, intelligent Japanese interpreter. Our first minutes on the ground would be crucial. If the Japanese had not gotten word of the pending surrender, I would be the first to bring them the news. It might be hard for them to resist the old habit of executing the bearer of bad tidings. So I would have to psychologically dominate the enemy, cowing them into cooperation. We certainly couldn't physically subdue them. Given weight restrictions and fuel requirements, I'd be limited to a team of fewer than ten.

That afternoon, I met Captain Leonard Woods of the Air Ground Aid Service (AGAS), the outfit responsible for preparing our air crews for escape and evasion (E&E), and eventual rescue if they were downed behind enemy lines. AGAS was also preparing for POW evacuation, so Woods had stock-piled medical supplies in his compound. I was impressed by Woods's enthusiasm. Even though he'd never jumped before, he was eager to parachute into Hainan. I named him my executive officer. Helliwell suggested I take a well-trained intelligence officer, and recommended First Lieutenant Charles Walker, whom I had not known previously. This was a key position because of our requirements to locate Allied airmen evaders among the guerrillas. Lieutenant Arnold Breakey would be the supply officer to co-ordinate the supply drops and take care of other logistic functions. Marine First Lieutenant John C. Bradley had been with me on the Indochina border. I knew him to be a damn good weapons man. I hoped I wouldn't need his skills on this mission, but he was anxious to go with us, so I made him the team adjutant to take care of team and POW administration.

Late that night, our chief OSS interpreter, Harrison Hsia, finally located a parachute-qualified Chinese Nationalist officer, Lieutenant Peter Fong, who spoke Mandarin as well as several of the island dialects. That still left the problem of a Japanese interpreter. In addition, Breakey and Woods had not yet been able to round up adequate quantities of medical supplies, particularly the B vitamins needed to combat acute beriberi and Atabrine for malaria treatment.

All these problems, however, were minor irritants compared to the local weather. The rain had not yet stopped, and the streams and rivers had burst their banks. Our compound was soon flooded by several feet of evil-smelling muddy water. Later that night, as I tried to steal a couple hours of sleep, the mud-baked walls of our team house collapsed and the room was flooded waist deep. The next morning I actually used an Air Force rubber raft to move equipment from the warehouse. Still the rain fell from a thick low overcast the consistency of wet cement. No planes were flying that afternoon.

By dark that night, I got word that Helliwell's office had finally found a qualified Japanese interpreter, Army First Lieutenant Ralph Yempuku, a wiry young Nisei from Honolulu, who'd fought with OSS Detachment 101 in Burma. Ralph joined us at the Kunming airfield around midnight. Like Woods, he'd never jumped before, but did not hesitate to volunteer.

☆   ☆

AT dawn on August 27, the overcast at Kunming lifted enough for our C-47 to take off. It was crowded in the rattling, drafty fuselage, the nine of us grouped around several tons of bundled parachute cargo. We all wore jump boots and jungle fatigues, with each officer's jacket bearing a large American flag on the left sleeve. I'd decided that each man would carry a .45 automatic pistol and two extra magazines, but no shoulder weapons. As with the Jed Team, we had one Thompson submachine gun for the whole group. Obviously, nine men didn't stand much chance of shooting it out with a Japanese marine division, should the enemy oppose us. If we were going to survive the next few hours, it would be thanks to our wits, not physical bravery.

After takeoff, I pinned major's oak leaves to my green jungle fatigues, to which I'd already sewn a large American flag. I felt something like a kid going to a masquerade party, but I was willing to try anything that would improve the success of the operation and ensure my team's survival.

To an outsider we would have appeared to be a crack parachute outfit. But in reality, only four of us had jumped before, and only Tony and I in actual combat. As the plane droned southeast into the hot eye of the morning sun, I delivered a shouted, highly abbreviated refresher course of the parachute instruction I had given in the hour before takeoff. We were using new static-line main parachutes with a circular quick-release buckle that connected the harness in the center of the chest. I showed the men how to hook up, exit the door, and check to make sure their main canopy had deployed properly. I also went through the motions of explaining the reserve chute. But I had already decided to jump from below 800 feet, to increase the element of surprise and minimize the chance of being shot at in our chutes. Probably only Tony and I realized that the reserves were mere ornaments when you jump from that low an altitude.

We crossed over the South China Sea above the myriad limestone islands near Haiphong. I went up to the cockpit and convinced the young pilot to keep the plane just above the wave tops as we crossed the Gulf of Tonkin. Despite his age, he was a veteran Carpetbagger—the 14th Air Force special ops squadron that supported the OSS behind enemy lines. He knew the advantage of coming in under enemy radar. There was nothing more for me to do, so I lay down on the deck with my head on a cargo chute and managed to snatch almost an hour's sleep, the first I'd had in thirty hours.

The monsoon cloud deck boiled away as we neared Hainan, and the inland mountains shimmered in the mid-morning heat mirage. We made landfall north of Bakli Bay, and banked right, roaring along only a hundred feet above the arid coastal plain of brown scrub brush and prickly pear. Each summer the prevailing southeast monsoon was absorbed by the mountains, making this side of the island a bleak semi-desert, reminiscent of Baja California. We crossed the red scar of a railroad embankment leading from the foothills to the coast. Ahead a large wooden trestle wharf jutted out into the warm blue sea. I leaned over the pilot's shoulders and squinted through the cockpit windows, trying to identify landmarks on my map. A jumble of low buildings connected by dirt tracks appeared on the sun-blasted flatlands. Inland about a mile from these structures I saw larger, more substantial buildings surrounded by power lines and telephone poles.

"That's it," I yelled to the pilot, pointing over his shoulder harness at the first clump of buildings.

He banked sharply right again and took us down to wave-top level. Our plan was to circle out of sight, a few miles out to sea, then head straight in and climb just before reaching the drop zone on the empty plain between the camp and the Japanese garrison.

"Get ready!" I yelled, swinging back into the fuselage.

The team got to their feet and hooked their static-line snaps to the overhead anchor cable. I was jumping number one and hooked up last. I swung back along the stick, checking each man's static line and patting his shoulder for encouragement. Ralph Yempuku stood near the windy maw of the door, an expression of determined resignation on his face, his short, wiry frame bent beneath the weight of the chute. I heard the engine tone change as we climbed. A line of white foam and a rocky beach swept by the door. The red standby light blinked. I hooked up and double-checked my static line. Tin-roofed sheds flashed by 500 feet below. We were still climbing.

The green light came on, indicating that the pilot considered conditions safe to jump. When we reached the open field I had selected from the aerial photos, I shouted "Go!" and was out the door. Suddenly I was aware the pilot had not throttled back the engines. The chute opened unusually hard, and I swung violently in the hot sunlight. But I didn't have time to worry about my canopy. The next swing drove me into the gravel and stubbly grass. We'd probably jumped at between 500 to 600 feet. I hit my quick release and dragged off the harness, just as Ralph Yempuku thudded down twenty yards away. There were gouts of crimson blood streaming from his face. My first reaction was that he had been hit. He struggled to his feet cursing and I helped him with his harness.

"Damn thing's too big," he said, pointing to the quick-release buckle. Ralph was only five foot three and, even at its tightest setting, the parachute harness was too loose. Jumping fast and low as we had, the buckle had split his chin on opening shock. Luckily, he wasn't badly hurt, but the blood was certainly impressive.

The rest of the team landed close by. A couple were shaken up, but there were apparently no life-threatening injuries. Len Woods, however, got up slowly, his head wobbling on his shoulders, his eyes almost blank. He'd been hit across the jaw and temple by the metal riser links when his chute opened, giving him a concussion. So Jim Healy had two casualties to worry about even before we found the prisoners. He worked quickly, putting a butterfly bandage to Ralph's chin and convincing Len Woods to sit down and rest.

I had other worries. The C-47 made a lazy orbit of the field, then banked toward us, losing altitude as it approached. The crew were obviously worried about Japanese ack-ack and they weren't about to make an easy target of themselves. By the time they crossed the field again on the cargo run they weren't much higher than 200 feet. The colored cargo chutes snapped open just as the bundles hit the ground. The medical supplies were fairly well padded, but our tommy gun and Tony's radio equipment were not so well packed. When Tony found his set, the bundle had burst open, spreading the equipment through a stand of prickly pear.

I was about to take stock of the loss when Charlie Walker pointed inland across the barren field. Two Japanese army trucks barreled toward us, raising a plume of orange dust. From down the coast a mob of Chinese civilians in black pajamas and coolie hats trotted in our direction. We stood in the blazing midday sun among our shattered cargo watching both groups approach.

"Everybody just take it easy," I said. "Keep your hands off your weapons." Ralph Yempuku was right beside me, watching the Japanese troops.

The trucks stopped about 500 yards away, and I heard the shrill commands of the Japanese officer forming his men into a skirmish line. They advanced toward us at a fast walk, their bayonets leveled in our direction.

"Okay," I told Ralph. "You just translate."

When the enemy soldiers were less than a hundred yards away, I gave their officer what I hoped was an aloof, scornful glare, folded my hands behind my back, and turned on my heel to gaze away in the opposite direction. Their officer was a first lieutenant in pressed khaki with a polished Sam Browne belt, pistol, and long samurai sword. He was shouting something now, but I resisted the urge to look at him.

"He wants to know who we are," Ralph whispered. "He's asking why we're here."

Still not facing the Japanese officer, I took a deep breath and shouted. "Stop right there."

Ralph translated, fortunately (I learned that night), prefacing the order with the formal Japanese military edict, "the Major commands . . ."[7]

Again the enemy lieutenant screamed his query. Again I gave my order and Ralph translated, this time matching my own outraged tone. When I turned to face the Japanese soldiers, they were standing motionless thirty yards away. "Turn those troops around," I yelled. "Face the Chinese civilians. You will protect these supplies from them."

Once more Ralph relayed the order, again with the edict "the Major commands."

This was the crucial test. If the Japanese officer obeyed a sequence of orders, we had him in our pocket. The sun beat down. There was silence. Finally, the enemy lieutenant growled an order, which a burly sergeant echoed. The troops turned away from us and swung into a protective arc, now leveling their bayonets at the advancing throng of Chinese. The lieutenant approached warily. I glared at him. "We are here to help the Allied prisoners," I said. "The war is over. Send your soldiers across the field and establish a perimeter. Then bring your trucks here to load our supplies."

The officer spoke again, a quieter tone, but still angry.

"He's asking about your authority," Ralph said, his voice grave.

"I'll discuss all this with his commander, once these supplies are loaded." I turned away the instant I had spoken, the essence of the haughty, conquering officer. Sweat rolled down inside my shirt. My heart was pumping in my throat.

Once more, Ralph relayed my words with suitable invective. The Japanese trotted their skirmish line back across the field now, forcing the civilians to retreat. The sun was like a jackhammer. I licked my cracked lips, gazing at the sea. After a long while, I heard the trucks approach to load our supplies. We had won our first engagement of this strange campaign.

☆   ☆

THE Japanese were garrisoned in the more substantive group of buildings I'd seen from the air, about two miles inland. We were escorted to their company headquarters in a long, brick building with an overhanging tiled roof and introduced to a tall naval infantry captain named Yamasaki. I waited until he bowed before offering a perfunctory salute. Our orders prohibited "fraternization with the enemy" and called for all contacts with the Japanese to be "official, courteous, and impersonal." So I avoided niceties and stood silently waiting for the captain to explain the local situation. He said he was number two in command of the Hashio naval fortifications which had control of the prisoner compound. His superior, Colonel Aoyama, was absent, but the captain would contact him at once.

We were escorted to the officers' dayroom beside the headquarters office and offered green tea from a thermos. There was a sink and a bar of soap, so I had the men wash off the sweaty dust from the drop zone and brush their uniforms. I stood close to the office door, eavesdropping on the captain's phone call while Ralph whispered a running translation.

"Colonel," Yamasaki shouted into the phone, "the American major jumped near the camp in broad daylight. He says the war is over . . ." I could hear a tinny harangue on the other end of the phone line. "But, sir . . . the Americans landed in the middle of the day . . . the Major insists the war has ended . . ."

The Captain returned. Again, I waited for his bow. "The Colonel will arrive in early morning," he said. The Colonel, he added, was seeking permission from General Goga for us to visit the prison compound. "Until then, you must wait."

He led us to a nearby building, which was the unused hospital of the Mitsui Corporation, the contractor for the nearby iron and copper mines. There were a latrine and shower and a row of short cots. Outside, the troops who'd carried our cargo bundles inside had now taken up positions around the building. They still had fixed bayonets. I decided not to argue.

By now, it was almost sunset and none of us had had much sleep in the past two days, what with the flood in Kunming and the frantic preparations. A shy Chinese cook brought several aluminum pots of food—soup and a spicy stirfry of prawns and vegetables. A porcelain basin was heaped with steaming rice.

When he'd gone, Len Woods stuck a fingertip into each pot to taste. "You think they'd try to poison us?"

I looked out the open shutters. The guard had been reinforced by three burly NCOs with stubby submachine guns. Obviously, if they wanted to kill us, they had plenty of firepower for the job. Poison seemed unlikely.

"Hell," Tony said. "I'm hungry." He grabbed a rice bowl and dug in with his GI spoon.

The food was delicious. With darkness, I assigned a guard roster, then rolled out a blanket on a cot and lay down to sleep. I was almost as exhausted as I'd been in the haystack in Corrèze. Just before slipping into sleep, I heard the quiet murmur of the guards outside. Maybe, I thought, this operation won't be so tough after all.

☆ ☆

AT exactly 0900, Colonel Aoyama and his staff arrived in a polished Ford sedan with a right-hand steering wheel. I'd already staked claim to the small headquarters office and had taken chairs on the far side of the conference table with Ralph, Len Woods, and my other staff officers, John Bradley and Charlie Walker. I knew that this side of the table, which faced the door, was the place of authority and honor in Oriental protocol. I wanted to make it clear that we, not the Japanese, were running this meeting.

The Colonel bristled and actually hissed when he saw the arrangements. Again, I was slow in returning the enemy salute. Then I began firing a series of quick practical questions at Aoyama, cutting through their attempts at polite chitchat. I wanted to know about transportation and medical capabilities, food supplies, and the condition of the local airstrip. He tried to deflect my questions by claiming he had "just received word" of the pending surrender—which he called the "unexpected end of the war." He also claimed that his headquarters in Haikou on the north coast had advised him the *we,* the Allies, would provide medical supplies for any "unfortunately ill" prisoners.

After a frustrating hour, I called a halt and demanded to speak directly with the POWs' senior officers. This delegation arrived in the same Ford sedan twenty minutes later. Len and I went to the porch to greet them. We had trouble containing our emotions.

The men who tottered up the three brick steps were little more than skeletons. Lieutenant Colonel W. J. R. Scott, the senior Australian, was a tall, balding man in a ragged, mildewed uniform. When I shook his hand, I felt the tendons roll over bone. There was simply no flesh, no muscle tone to his limbs. Commander Jager and Lieutenant Colonel Kapitz, the Dutch officers, were even more skeletal. Jager's face was a scarred skull, his milky blue eyes wide and unfocused. The Dutch colonel's neck and arms were ripply with old overlapping scar tissue, an indication that he'd been repeatedly beaten with a whip or wooden baton. As they entered the office, I became aware of a faint, sweet-sour odor, something like fermentation, which I soon recognized as the stench of starvation.[8]

I brusquely ordered Aoyama and his staff to a row of chairs and gave the table to the Allied officers. Again, Aoyama hissed, but didn't voice his outrage. Ignoring the Japanese, I turned my attention to Scott and the Dutch officers.

They had come prepared. Scott presented a detailed troop roster, printed with pencil on a scrap from a paper cement sack. There were, he said, a total of 260 Australian prisoners, of whom 80 were in the camp hospital, plus 267 Dutch, of whom 91 were hospitalized. Sixty-seven Australian soldiers and over 100 Dutch had died in captivity since their group arrived on Hainan from the Netherlands East Indies in November 1942, he said. Most had died in the previous nine months from malnutrition and beriberi. Nine had been killed when their work party was ambushed by Chinese bandits, and ten had escaped and were thought to be held by guerrillas in the mountains.

The gaunt Australian officer spoke slowly, with exaggerated clarity, as he relished an American cigarette. "We observed your parachute drop," he said. "Fine show. Three days ago, the Japs told us to prepare for the arrival of an Allied medical team. They neglected to mention Japan had surrendered." He cast a disdainful glance toward Colonel Aoyama. "We waited for you last night . . ."

Aoyama started to speak, but Ralph ordered him silent.

"This morning," Scott continued, "they ripped down the electric fence around the prison cage. I expect that's why you were detained here."

"What electric fence?" I was having trouble containing my mounting rage.

"Four-forty volts," Scott said. "Quite deadly. They put it up in March. That's when they stopped the work parties and cut our rice ration to four ounces a day."

Charlie Walker was jotting notes. "Four ounces cooked or dry, sir?" he asked.

Again, Colonel Scott gazed at his Japanese counterpart before answering. "Cooked, if you can call it that. We were given the sweepings from their gristmill. Not the hulls themselves, mind you, but the broken polished kernels. The hulls would have had some nutrition at least. As it is . . ." His voice trailed off in midsentence. Over the days that followed I recognized this speech pattern among many prisoners, a natural survival mechanism that prevented them from detailing everyday horrible experiences.

"What were the work parties?" I asked.

Scott smiled, a death's-head grimace. He lit another cigarette and tried to compose himself. "Major," he began, "you have to realize we were brought here from Ambon Island as *convalescent* patients. Most of the men already had malaria and dysentery. The work details were heavy labor, seven days a week, dawn to sunset . . . forest clearing, road construction, building the coastal artillery batteries. When the men didn't work fast enough, they were beaten." All three Allied officers stared at the row of Japanese now. "They were beaten with pick handles, bamboo clubs, and steel pipes. The majority of my blokes have broken limbs. It's worse among the Dutch."

Charlie Walker was writing fast. Scott noticed this and withdrew a packet of stained paper scraps from his tunic pocket. "We've tried to keep a record of the brutality," he said, handing across the papers. "We'd like those back, of course."

"What are your immediate needs?" I was unable to even look at the Japanese now for fear of attacking them.

"Two of our lads died last night." Scott shook his head. "The beriberi cases are quite far gone. And some of the lads' dysentery is severe . . ."

I had heard enough. Standing up, I faced Colonel Aoyama squarely and pointed my finger at his face, a gross insult in Japanese etiquette. Ralph translated as I issued my orders. "Lieutenant Walker and our medical corpsman will return to the camp immediately with Colonel Scott. They will carry food and medical supplies from our present quarters. By 1400 hours, the Japanese will have delivered additional food and medical supplies for three days." Aoyama showed signs of protesting, but I waved him silent. "The Japanese guards at the camp will leave the gates. From now on, no prisoner will bow or salute to a guard." I turned away from the Japanese. "That's it." Charlie and John Bradley were already on their feet. "Let's get moving."

We filed past the Japanese and onto the shady porch. In the distance, the corrugated iron roofs of the prison compound rippled in the heat. I waited for Aoyama to issue his first order. Finally, I heard his voice behind me, subdued, almost stricken. The war was over, and he had lost.

☆　　　☆

WHILE my advance party went to the prison cage, Ralph and I consulted a map of the island with Colonel Aoyama, trying to locate the most practical evacuation point. He said the naval air station at Sanya, near the southern port of Yulin, had suitable "rest facilities" for the prisoners, as well as an airfield which could be made operational with minimum repairs. The port also had a passenger wharf. The train between Bakli Bay and Sanya was the safest means of transport, he said, the roads being subject to guerrilla attack. I ordered him to send word to Sanya to prepare the facilities and to arrange for the prisoners' rail transport there.

Then I took the rest of the team to the Hashio prison camp. A hot, sandy wind blew across the barren plain as we approached. We parked the truck near the crude pine-plank guardhouse and dragged open the barbed-wire gate. Despite the Japanese efforts to conceal their electric fence, they'd neglected to fill the post holes or remove the white porcelain insulators. Len Woods photographed this evidence. Just inside the gate we encountered an elaborate log-frame punishment rack, one of the few well-made structures in the entire camp. Here prisoners had been hung from a cross member and beaten to provide entertainment for the guards. Again, Len documented this evidence of brutality with his camera. The prison barracks were in three long, low sheds of rough, unpainted pine planks roofed with uneven sheets of rusty corrugated iron, riddled with holes. There were no windows or screens, but crude plank shutters could be raised for ventilation.

As we approached the huts, a cloying sweet stench met us. Flies rose in lazy clots. Colonel Scott had mustered his Australian officers near their shed, and several dozen enlisted men stood wavering in the shade waiting for us. None of them weighed more than a hundred pounds. All had deeply sunken eyes. Most had festering sores on their limbs and torsos. As I shook their hands, I was again aware of the brittle bones just beneath the skin. I walked the length of their hut, greeting men too weak to muster outside. They lay on stained jute sacking piled on a crude plank sleeping platform. In the flyblown shadows they stared up at me with streaming, luminous eyes. Charlie had distributed cigarettes and K-rations, but most of the men inside were too stunned to eat or smoke. Away from the Japanese, Scott confirmed the earlier fears of the OSS: that the Japanese had originally planned to massacre the prisoners in the event of an American amphibious landing on Hainan.[9]

Colonel Scott led me to the hospital shed. Here the stench of dysentery and festering wounds was nearly overpowering. The patients lay on primitive bunks fashioned from crates and scraps of plywood, segregated by their affliction—the beriberi cases to one side, the men with dysentery isolated at the far end. Jim Healy and Tony Denneau were here, cleansing wounds and administering vitamin B_1 injections. The worst of the beriberi cases were grotesque. The men's bellies and limbs were swollen to elephantine proportions, their scrotums distended like terrible orange melons.

Outside, Colonel Scott gave me another folded scrap-paper document, this containing the evidence against the local Japanese "chief surgeon," Captain Ichiro Kikuchi, the prison's medical officer. He had systematically withheld treatment from the prisoners, diverting the vitamin B tablets he received for his own uses. Further, he saw himself as a nutritional expert who could calculate the absolute *minimum* amount of food necessary to prevent complete starvation, while maintaining enough strength in the prisoners to keep them working. On several occasions he visited the camp with colleagues and toured the barracks, jabbing their distended, fluid-heavy limbs and noting that Caucasians were more prone to malnutrition than their Chinese counterparts in the slave labor camp up the coast. Kikuchi took pleasure in taunting the sick prisoners who were too weak to join the forced labor parties. "*Shigoto nai, taberu nai,*" he told them (no work, no eat).

In July 1943, Scott told me, Captain Doctor Kikuchi took part in a massacre of over 120 hapless Chinese laborers, who were bayoneted and beheaded to provide a diversion for the Japanese officers.

I had been en route to Burma when the Allied armies overran the German concentration camps in Nazi-occupied Europe. But the newsreels of these hellish places caught up to us in Kunming. Now I stood on the hard-packed mud of a camp every bit as cruel as Buchenwald or Dachau. The flies whined incessantly. Inside the huts, men moaned and babbled. Outside the wire, Japanese soldiers stared at us with fear and distaste. I swore that I would do my best to get these men out of this hellhole alive. I also vowed that I would do my best to see the Japanese responsible for this atrocity brought to justice.

☆　　　　☆

THE next morning, we had fifty Dutch prisoners strong enough to be moved, fifteen unconscious on makeshift litters, loaded aboard the three-car narrow-gauge train for Sanya. I had Ralph Yempuku, John Bradley, and Tony Denneau with me. Len Woods would be in charge of the rest of the team in my absence. The little potbellied steam engine chugged out of the Bakli siding at 10:30 that morning. Half an hour later we had climbed from the dusty coastal plain to a cooler spur of jungled hills. As the train swayed along, I printed out a message for Kunming, which I hoped Tony could transmit from a radio in the Japanese naval headquarters at Sanya.

I was rereading the message when the engine's brakes shrieked and the train jumped from the tracks, lurching savagely to the right in a shower of gravel and steam. The sick prisoners moaned as they fell across the floor. We clambered from the cars to find a curved section of track detached at the lip of a small rise. I had ambushed enough trains in France to recognize the procedure. The Japanese engine crew pointed fearfully to the surrounding palm groves.

"Guerrillas," Ralph translated. "They're afraid of an attack."

We were easy targets, if there was an ambush team in the surrounding brush. And the only thing I could do to prevent an attack was to make it obvious we were Europeans. So I led several Dutch prisoners around the train, as if inspecting for damage. No shots came from the scrub jungle above the tracks.

It took hours for the repair engine to reach us, and we didn't arrive in Sanya until well after dark. But the Japanese were waiting for us with ambulances. The hospital facility on the naval base was crude by Western standards, but a paradise compared to the Hashio camp. Once we gave our orders to the Japanese medics, we met with the island's senior medical officer, a colonel named Miyao. He was eager to sit us down to a formal dinner, replete with gin and scotch—booty from Hong Kong. But I insisted my men eat at their own table and that the discussion be limited to official business.

At this point, a Major Arai, who served on General Goga's staff, came forward and bowed deeply. When, he asked, would I be able to discuss with the General arrangements for the formal surrender of Japanese forces on Hainan? When would American naval units arrive in Yulin?

I stared at this stocky marine major, carefully considering my response. There were only nine armed Americans on the island, and our security depended on the Japanese assumption that Allied forces were en route. It would have been wise to give the impression that a larger American unit would soon arrive to take charge. But I was still disgusted and furious at the Japanese treatment of their prisoners, particularly the reported massacres of interned Chinese civilian slaves.

"Representatives of the Chinese First Army," I said slowly, "will be here soon to take command. They will accept your surrender." I probably should have kept this information to myself. The prospect of surrendering to the Chinese might have driven the Japanese to further resistance.

It was as if I had hit the man with a club. He bowed once more and hurried away to make his report. After five years of brutal occupation of Hainan, the Japanese had much to answer for to the Chinese authorities. Maybe, I thought, the prospect of surrendering to the Chinese might alleviate the condition of those poor civilians still in custody.

☆　　　☆

THE next morning, the second trainload of sick Dutch POWs arrived with Jim Healy in attendance. While John Bradley worked with Healy getting them settled in the makeshift hospital, Tony and I sweated in the Japanese radio room, trying to use our crystal in their equipment. Around noon, Tony finally managed to jury-rig a set and contact Kunming on our emergency frequency. The Japanese equipment was so powerful, however, that the operators in Kunming refused to believe it was us. We had to go through our elaborate challenge-and-response procedure before they would agree to copy our coded message.

That afternoon we were taken to the Japanese naval hospital near the port to interview three American airmen who had been prisoners since March: Captain Merritt Lawlis, Lieutenant Jim McGuire, and Sergeant Ben Muller. The Japanese had them in a clean, comfortable ward with new mosquito nets and a thermos of tea at each bedside. There were even flowers in the room. A brief interview, however, revealed that this treatment was a sham. They'd each been injured badly when their planes were shot down, and the Japanese had refused to treat their wounds and burns. They had also been subjected to systematic beatings with clubs and pipes, "punishment" for Allied air attacks on Japan.[10] After being moved to the naval compound at Sanya, they had been subjected to the same systematic starvation as the prisoners at Hashio. Two of the men downed with them had died of this treatment.[11] After satisfying myself they were now receiving decent medical care, I left to inspect the improvised POW hospital across the base.

Corporal Healy had taken charge of everyone, and even had Japanese NCOs sweeping the floors and emptying bedpans. He took me aside on a delicate matter. The senior Dutch doctor, Major Peiffer, had hoarded the medical supplies Healy had given him to administer to the sick Dutch patients. Apparently, the doctor couldn't believe they'd actually been freed. When I confronted him, he was incoherent. Obviously, the strain of captivity had driven him to irrational behavior. I had Healy give him a morphine shot and ordered that the doctor be relieved of his responsibilities. That night a full trainload of Australians arrived. Unfortunately, I got word that things were not going as planned up at Hashio. Two more prisoners had died of malnutrition. The guerrillas were still sabotaging the train tracks, and the Japanese quartermaster, a Lieutenant Hirata, was blocking Len Woods's efforts in providing adequate food to the remainder of the prisoners, who were now housed in the Mitsui Corporation barracks.

I knew that I would have to return there soon. But I had problems here. Our radio schedule with Kunming the next morning was jammed. Tony suspected the jammer was in the Japanese radar installation in the building next door. Clearly, the enemy was beginning to chafe at the realities of defeat. A little after noon a Carpetbagger C-46 buzzed the airfield, flying a prearranged query pattern. We were supposed to reply with signal panels on the ground if the field was usable. But our Japanese liaison officer, Lieutenant Matsuoko, couldn't "locate" our car. By the time we got to the airfield, an American Army doctor, Lieutenant Tom Mitchell, had parachuted from the plane. Unfortunately, he was no jumper and dislocated his shoulder on landing. Almost as bad, two huge cargo nets of canned rations and shoes for the prisoners burst open in midair and the contents were splattered across the runway. Tony and I quickly signaled the pilot and he made a steep, fast approach and landed. Now we had another injured American on our hands. But Dr. Mitchell was tough. After Healy helped him pop his shoulder back in place, Mitchell refused a painkiller and got to work with the sick prisoners.

In my last message from Len Woods, I'd learned that the Japanese at Hashio were now openly defying his orders, refusing to allow the team access to the nearby compound for Chinese prisoners. At one meeting, Aoyama claimed the Chinese were well-paid "volunteers," with whom the Japanese mixed well. Colonel Scott confronted him on this point, demanding he account for the Chinese slave laborers whom Scott had personally seen the Japanese massacre. Aoyama refused to answer. More ominous, the Japanese refused Woods's repeated demands to inspect their supply dumps. The enemy was still armed and our control up there was tenuous at best.

I waited for the last POW train from Hashio all next morning, only to be informed that it had been derailed once more by guerrillas and forced to return to Bakli Bay. That afternoon, two C-47s landed at the airstrip and unloaded a Recovery Team of nineteen Americans, led by a Service of Supply lieutenant colonel named Charles Andrus. He was an elderly, graying, rear-echelon type with the prissy manner common to his organization. My first meeting with him didn't go well. Why, he demanded, hadn't I had vehicles waiting for them at the strip? He wouldn't accept my explanation that Kunming had never announced their arrival.

While Andrus and his staff wasted hours setting up their personal quarters,

I toured the naval port to determine the kinds of vessels it could handle for the eventual POW evacuation. When I got back to the hospital I discovered Andrus was further annoyed because I had been operating on my own without his authorization. I saw that it was going to be hard working with this officious noncombatant.

Another C-47 arrived with supplies from Kunming, and we convinced the crew to remain overnight due to the late hour. If the train track to Bakli Bay was not repaired by morning, I was determined to bum a lift on the returning plane and jump into Hashio alone to confront Aoyama. Ralph Yempuku asked if he would have to parachute with me, brave as ever, but clearly not thrilled with the prospect. He mentioned that one of Colonel Aoyama's Formosan aides spoke enough English to translate simple orders, so I told Ralph to stay at Sanya and work with Colonel Andrus, who had neglected to include an interpreter in his entourage.

The next morning, the track was still blocked, so I jury-rigged a parachute, using an Air Force seat pack worn over my original static-line chute harness, to which I attached my reserve. We reached Bakli Bay around 0800 and I had the pilot throttle back about 1,500 feet above Japanese headquarters. I jumped in a tucked-up position, counted one-thousand, two-thousand, then jerked the ripcord. The chute opened hard and I managed to steer the canopy to the edge of the enemy headquarters compound.

Len Woods was there to meet me. An hour later, we had Colonel Aoyama's full attention. I simply told him we would shoot any Japanese soldier or officer who blocked our passage in any way whatsoever. He tried to imply that Len Woods had made "impossible" demands and had conducted himself improperly, drunkenly consorting with local Chinese women. This was absolute slander. I told him as much. End of discussion.

Two more Australian prisoners had died in the night, despite the treatment Healy had arranged. It was imperative to get the remaining survivors down to Sanya.

But first, Peter Fong suggested we tour the Chinese prisoners' compound, so that I could see their conditions with my own eyes. If the makeshift hospital at the Hashio camp had been some kind of purgatory, the Chinese "hospital" was absolute hell. Dead and dying patients lay on platforms, covered with flies and excrement. There was no running water and little food, yet several emaciated nurses did what they could. But the night before, three drunken Japanese soldiers had broken in, severely beating prisoners with clubs and rifle butts, and torturing one dying man with lit cigarettes held to the soles of his feet.[12]

When I returned to Hashio, I left a written order for Aoyama stating he would be held personally responsible by Allied headquarters for any additional outrage. I didn't add that his name was already high on the list of war criminals to be indicted as soon as possible. Of the 100,000 civilian internees from Hong Kong who had been enslaved on the Hainan mining project, fewer than 20,000 were still alive. I was confident the Chinese authorities would find a suitable punishment for him.

☆   ☆

WE made it back by train to Sanya late that night. John Bradley took me aside to report that Colonel Andrus had ordered all American officers to attend a formal dinner given by the senior Japanese staff the night before, an affair that clearly transcended the bounds of "fraternization" as outlined in our orders. During this banquet, Andrus—who had never heard a shot fired in anger—toasted the enemy and announced that the Japanese had proved to be "a worthy foe," and that the Americans were "deeply grateful for the cooperation" we'd received on Hainan, which was better, he added, than that he'd received from the Chinese, who were supposed to be our allies. He also announced that Colonel Miyao would remain in charge of the hospital, even if other American medical personnel arrived. Finally, Andrus brought a bottle of whiskey from his own comfortable quarters and personally served drinks to the Japanese officers. As the liquor flowed, Andrus told the enemy that, had they followed their attack on Pearl Harbor with an invasion of California, it would be the Japanese, not the Americans, who had won the war.

I was outraged.[13] I demanded an immediate meeting with Andrus and the senior Japanese staff. When we were assembled I detailed the atrocities I had seen at Hashio and told Colonel Sato, the Japanese adjutant, that Aoyama should be removed from his command. Andrus was furious, but kept silent. After the meeting, he wanted to know my date of rank and I admitted that my major's commission was a temporary operational expedient. He grinned like a shark, obviously hatching some plan.

☆   ☆

OVER the next few days we got definite word of several Allied evaders in the mountains. With Peter Fong's help, I drew up some handbills in English and Chinese, requesting contact with Allied personnel still in hiding. We tied these handbills to bottles of Atabrine, and each bottle was attached to a twelve-inch pilot parachute. Then we took a C-47 ride around the island, dropping the messages into the village markets in the highlands, where we knew the guerrillas were located.

When I got back from this mission, Andrus dropped his own bombshell. He'd issued written instructions to the Japanese to no longer obey orders from me or my officers. Further, he said he was taking control of all OSS supplies and equipment. When he explained this, he made a point of addressing me as "Captain."

I got my men together and suggested we prepare to leave whenever there was room on a plane out. The next afternoon, however, Andrus had to backpedal. We received word that a large group of Indian, Dutch, and Australian prisoners, as well as one American airman, had been located in a mountain camp of Chinese Nationalist guerrillas. The guerrillas did not trust the Japs and would release the evaders only to an American officer. Andrus came to ask my advice on this matter, noting that the Japanese would not provide an armed escort along the booby-trapped trails through the bandit country. I suggested Andrus take a car and a truck and go up there himself, the map references being easy enough to read. Andrus fussed, then turned to me. "I really don't have sufficient personnel on hand to do the job," he said lamely.

Sufficient personnel! His staff had swollen with each C-47 from the mainland. But if I was going to pull his chestnuts out of the fire, I'd do it in style. Andrus's personal jeep had arrived by plane the day before. I told him I'd need that vehicle for the trip. He had no choice but to comply.

☆   ☆

THE trip up to the guerrilla camp proved tense but uneventful. When we got there, the well-armed Nationalist guerrillas expressed surprise that we'd made it through the Chinese Communist-held territory without ambush. That night we attended a banquet with appropriate military fanfare in a thatched-roof longhouse. Outside, squat Li tribesmen beat on hollow logs and danced beside a bonfire. The guerrilla leader, General Wong Yee, insisted we toast all twenty-odd Allied powers with coconut-shell cups of some kind of moonshine. The next day, there were very hungover Allied personnel jolting down the mountainside toward Sanya.

When I got back, the British destroyer *Queenborough* stood off Yulin harbor. The first contingent of Dutch and Australian POWs were loaded aboard for evacuation to Hong Kong. I told Len Woods to get the team ready to move out. But I still had business in the hills. We'd gotten a note from another downed American pilot, Lieutenant Walter Wyatt, who was holed up with the Communist guerrillas on this side of the island. They'd seen our passage the day before and wanted an escort for the American. After several hours of palaver in the Chinese market, it was agreed Peter Fong would fetch Wyatt back with a car.

My final business on the island involved Lieutenant Jim McGuire, the B-25 pilot recuperating from his brutal treatment in Sanya naval hospital.

McGuire told us one of his captors, Major Arai, had threatened him with execution earlier that year, adding that McGuire was to be publicly beheaded, the same fate meted out to five of his squadron mates who'd been among nine airmen captured that winter. Ralph, Peter Fong, and I found several Chinese who confirmed that Americans had been publicly executed after being paraded through the streets of bombed-out towns. When we confronted Major Arai with this evidence, he at first denied all knowledge of any such incident, then claimed any talk of execution was a lie and that mention of "nine American airmen" had simply been propaganda printed in a local newspaper. We demanded copies of the newspaper, which he reluctantly produced. They contained no mention of American prisoners. Arai then changed his story, claiming he'd been away from the island when the incident occurred. We turned his name over to the officer in charge of war crimes investigations.

☆   ☆

ON the evening of September 16, Ralph Yempuku, Len Woods, John Bradley, Arnold Breakey, Charlie Walker, and I sat on wicker chairs on the terrace of the Peninsula Hotel, overlooking the broad, twilight panorama of Hong Kong harbor. For the first time in almost five years, all the city's lights were lit. The British Pacific Fleet had gathered to celebrate victory. As far as we could see, aircraft carriers, battle wagons, cruisers, and destroyers stood in gray ranks against the green hills of Hong Kong island. At 9 P.M. the fireworks display began. For an hour illumination rounds, star shells, and parachute flares lit the night sky. We sat sipping our icy drinks, not flinching at the explosions, as we had at so many other, less benevolent pyrotechnics for so many years. The long war was finally over. I gazed past the candy-pink glare of the flares into the somber darkness of the South China Sea, wondering what road lay ahead.

1943. Lt. Singlaub, static line hooked up, becoming airborne qualified at Fort Benning, Ga.

1944. Jedburgh team is briefed before being parachuted into France. This "team," typical in its international makeup, was a composite of members of other teams and was being photographed for a documentary. Lt. Singlaub is second from right.

1944. OSS Jedburgh team in France. Lt. Singlaub (left, with hand on hip) is interrogating a German captured by his Maquis troops.

1945. With wife Mary, in her Wave uniform.

1945. On the DZ on Hainan Island. OSS POW rescue team has just landed and is collecting supplies. Singlaub (on right) refused to negotiate with Japanese lieutenant sent out to capture the team.

1945. OSS headquarters, Kunming, China. Col. Hefner decorating Capt. Singlaub. Note the picture of Gen. Wedemeyer on the table.

7

OSS, Kunming. Singlaub observes Nationalist forces during aborted rebellion.

CIA, Manchuria. Capt. Singlaub with the trusty L-5 spotter plane, flown by Sgt. Clayton Pond. Note the improvised extra fuel tank on the strut.

8

CIA, Manchuria. Singlaub in village with German residents of the area.

Korea, 1953. Maj. Singlaub at his battalion command post, using a handy tree branch as a cane while his broken ankle is in a cast.

11

Outpost Harry, 1953. Maj. Singlaub (left), Gen. Dunkleberg (center), and Lt. Dan Foldberg (right).

Korea, 1953. Maj. Singlaub receives the Silver Star from Gen. George Smythe for leading the counterattack on Outpost Harry.

12

Korea, Feb. 1953, Main Line of Resistance. Maj. Singlaub (left), Col. Richard Stilwell (center), Lt. Dillard, Lt. Foldberg, Sgt. Arney discuss the artillery support for Outpost Harry.

PART II

☆   ☆

Cold War

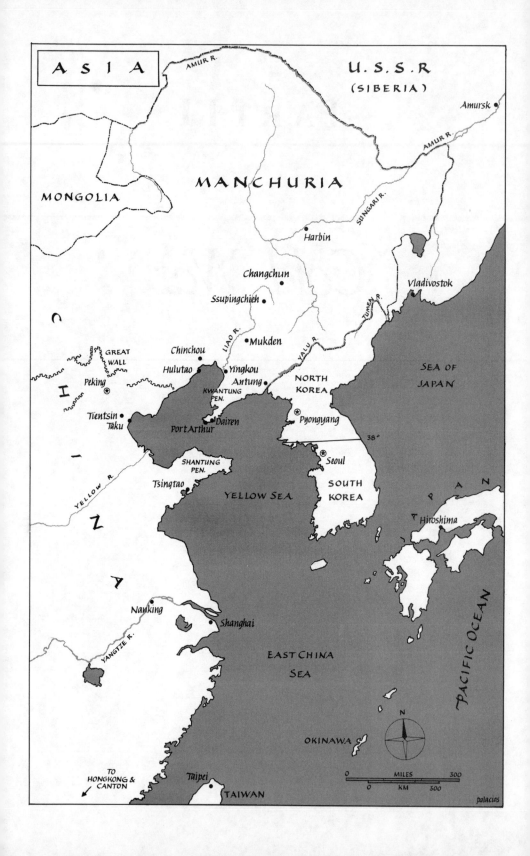

CHAPTER FOUR
CIA Manchuria
1946–1948

☆   ☆

THE SITUATION BACK at Kunming was an odd combination of hectic confusion and deeply felt relief. The war was over. The Japanese had surrendered, and we would not be facing more combat. At least not immediately.

In the Special Operations compound in Kunming most of my buddies were preoccupied with finding priority passage to the States for discharge. I had other concerns. My application for a Regular Army commission was under consideration in Washington, and I hoped the matter would be quickly resolved. That summer the Purple Heart and the Bronze Star from my combat in France finally came down through channels. Superior officers assured me that these decorations would help my chances of winning a regular commission, as would the POW rescue mission to Hainan. But I'd heard there were a lot more wartime officers seeking such commissions than there were slots available.

Meanwhile, the task of winding down OSS operations in China, including turning over supplies and equipment to the Nationalist army, dragged along at a predictably slow pace. I was given a low rotation priority because I hadn't been very long in the China theater compared to many of the guys who'd been out there more than three years. But at least waking up each morning without a loaded weapon beside me, without the wariness of ambush or attack, was a simple pleasure bordering on luxury.

That luxury didn't last long. I'd just climbed into my bunk one humid September night when a mortar round slammed into the compound, and machine-gun tracers slashed past my window. I was on the floor, pulling on my boots with one hand and loading my carbine with the other when the firing swelled to a real crescendo. The rear-echelon types in my billet were running around, waving flashlights, and yelling—making themselves damned good targets. You could tell the field soldiers among us; we kept low and quiet, and followed the course of the action by the pattern of fire.

A runner arrived with news. The local Nationalist governor, a warlord named General Lung Yun, had decided to rebel against Generalissimo Chiang Kai-shek's Kuomintang (KMT) Nationalist government. Loyal Nationalist troops under General Tu Yu-ming surrounded our compound, supposedly to "guard" us. Lung's men were attacking them. As the senior combat arms officer with field experience, I was ordered to organize the defense of the compound. Throughout that night and the next day I put together ad hoc rifle squads and machine-gun teams, sometimes assigning a veteran corporal to command several nervous rear-echelon majors and captains who weren't quite sure how to cock their weapons.

While the firefight ebbed and flowed around the camp, a young technical sergeant from *Stars and Stripes,* named John Roderick, tried to sneak into town to file a story at the local telegraph office. It seemed he had elected to take his discharge in China, and already had a job offer from the Associated Press. Roderick appeared to favor Mao Tse-tung's Communists, and was eager to report on this obvious example of disunity in the KMT. He was indignant to the point of insubordination when I ordered him to stay in camp. Over the coming years, Roderick's reports from China consistently reflected his anti-Nationalist bias.

By the next afternoon, General Lung's men had had enough and the siege was lifted. While the headquarters types considered the "attack" an exciting punctuation to their China service, I found the incident more troubling. The Japanese collapse had unleashed China's centrifugal divisiveness, suppressed during the wartime alliance, among the Nationalist forces and between the Nationalists and their erstwhile Communist allies. As I finally boarded my flight over the Hump to Calcutta, it was clear to me that the war in China had not ended, but had simply entered a new, more dangerous phase.

☆   ☆

My friend Lieutenant Howard Hunt (later a major player in the Watergate affair) and I ended up in so-called black-market lodgings in Calcutta, waiting for a troop ship home. The U.S. Navy transport *General M. B. Stewart* was virtually packed to the gunnels with troops and civilians returning from the Far East. And the accommodations were a far cry from the *Queen Elizabeth* or the transport out from California. Howie and I were assigned to a stifling four-tier officer's compartment on an airless lower deck that stank of bilges and stale kitchen grease. We took advantage of the mild Indian Ocean weather to stake out a patch of deck just aft of the bridge that had daytime shade and plenty of breeze. Our army blanket on the deck became private territory, which we jealously guarded around the clock, never leaving it unattended.

Naturally, there was a certain amount of fraternization among the men and the nurses and the female civilians on board. One night my OSS colleague Bob North and a young lady were caught in flagrante delicto on the top deck by the burly master-at-arms. Their brazenness was probably related to the bottles of scotch that lay empty beside them. This probably also accounts for Bob's unusual response to the situation. By this time the girl had passed out. He dumped her clothing and most of his down an air vent, slung her over his shoulder, and carried her down the steep ladders to the women's quarters. But the entry to her cabin was blocked by a stern young OSS secretary from Kunming named Julia Child. In her characteristic, forthright voice, Miss Child announced, "I'll take her from here."[1]

Although Howie and my open-air "cabin" were better than a shared bunk in the dungeon below decks, I was furious to discover that my Communist OSS colleague Captain George Wuchinich (who'd almost had his throat cut by his American-Yugoslav buddies on the passage out) was now residing in a well-ventilated private cabin. In China he had managed to wangle orders to the north, where he'd promptly broken those orders to cross lines to a Communist "liberated area" and had disappeared for several months. This period with Mao Tse-tung's troops was now officially considered captivity, which entitled him to prisoner-of-war status, including those comfortable accommodations.

Howie was a former journalist and a talented writer, who had relished his OSS experience in the "exotic" Orient. Like me, he was uncomfortable with the idea of returning to a tame civilian existence. We spent hours drinking tepid coffee from canteen cups and talking about the future as the ship rolled through the blue tropics toward Africa. Now that Nazi Germany and its Japanese ally had been crushed, the Soviet Union possessed the largest military force in the world. True, they didn't have the atomic bomb, nor was their navy or air force any match for those of the Western Allies. But the Red Army was firmly in control of much of the Eurasian land mass, with well-armed garrisons stretching from the Elbe River in Germany all the way to the 38th parallel in Korea.

The men around us talked longingly of normal peacetime lives, of college, families, of the dream homes they would build in the suburbs and the cars they would drive to them. But Hunt and I were convinced that the world we were entering would be anything but peaceful.

☆   ☆

THE Pentagon was also concerned about future Soviet intentions. Apparently, the Army's postwar officer corps would be larger than expected. I had no trouble passing my interviews for a regular commission. On my recuperation leave in California, Mary and I had plenty of time to discuss our own future. She fully supported my plans for an Army career, despite the danger and separations inherent in the profession. But when my orders came to report to the Infantry Replacement Training Center in Camp McClellan, Alabama, we both felt let down. After London, Paris, and China, the rural South was a disappointment.

We drove to Alabama to get a look at our future home before heading up to New Jersey to visit Mary's family. Camp McClellan was a desolate stretch of piney hills in the red clay Appalachian piedmont, halfway between Birmingham and Atlanta. By the time we paid our first visit, almost all the off-base quarters were rented. We spent two fruitless days searching. Finally, we were shown a newly renovated "apartment" on a dusty road several miles north of Anniston in some chigger-infested woods. The whitewashed shed was obviously a converted chicken coop. But the farmer renting it was anything but a gullible yokel.

I checked the tarpaper roof and the reasonably new screen door. "What are you asking for it?"

The man looked at Mary's well-cut tweed skirt and my sportcoat. "What did you say your rank was?"

So much for patriotism. Down here, the rent on a chicken coop depended on your pay grade. "I didn't say," I answered. Mary got in the car and I followed. There had to be something better than this.

☆   ☆

I WAS more or less resigned to a couple of years training draftee recruits in Alabama when my dad called. There'd been a telegram sent to me in California requesting an immediate interview in Washington to discuss a possible "overseas assignment."

I reported to the Strategic Services Unit (SSU) of the War Department in the old OSS headquarters at 25th and E streets. In September 1945, President Truman had disbanded the OSS and turned over its intelligence collection responsibilities to the State Department. But it soon became clear that State could not handle the far-flung intelligence collection and operations duties of the OSS. These had now devolved to the War Department's SSU, but this temporary organization, I learned, was about to become the Central Intelligence Group (CIG).

The tall colonel and stocky civilian who interviewed me were both Far East veterans of the OSS Secret Intelligence branch. They got right to the point.

"How much do you know about Manchuria?" the Colonel asked.

Not much, I had to admit.

For the next hour, they gave me an intense briefing, drawing on the latest secret intelligence reports. Under the terms of the Yalta Accords, the Soviet Union had agreed to enter the Pacific war against Japan and engage the much-touted Japanese Kwantung Army in occupied Manchuria. Prior to the dropping of the atom bombs, the potential of the Kwantung Army had been a knotty strategic problem for the United States. We had almost no independent military intelligence in Manchuria, and had to depend on our Soviet allies for information on Japanese troop strength in the region. The Soviets—who were not then at war with Japan—had an active intelligence network in Manchuria. Based on their reports, the Pentagon had estimated that Japanese forces from the puppet Manchukuo state (established by the Japanese in 1932) posed a major threat to our invasion of the Japanese Home Islands.[2]

So the Soviets were given the responsibility of neutralizing this powerful enemy formation by invading Manchuria overland from Mongolia and Siberia. In return, they'd receive the naval harbor of Port Arthur and joint custody of the major Manchurian railroads. (The fact that these Yalta concessions to the Soviets were made secretly, *without* the knowledge of the Chinese Nationalist government, was to prove a continued source of strained relations between America and Chiang Kai-shek in the immediate postwar years.[3]) But when the Soviet columns swept into Manchuria in August 1945, the Japanese immediately capitulated. As the Soviets knew, these Manchurian forces had been bled piecemeal for replacements during the three years of the Pacific war; the army was now made up of boys and old men. The Soviet Red Army under Marshal Rodion Malinovski quickly occupied all of Manchuria and the Korean peninsula north of the 38th parallel. There had been perhaps a week of fighting, and Soviet casualties were light. The Soviet price for entering the Pacific war had been low. But few at the time recognized their deception.

"Around here," the wry civilian said, "we started calling it the *Sham*tung Army."

The Soviet occupation, of course—like that of Eastern Europe—was meant to be temporary. Officially, Manchuria comprised the three northeastern provinces of China. The legitimate government of China was headed by Chiang Kai-shek's Kuomintang, with its capital in Nanking, over a thousand miles south of the Manchurian border. The Allies had agreed that the Nationalists were to accept the surrender of Japanese forces and take possession of their arms and industrial assets throughout China, except for the three northeast provinces: those of Manchuria, where the Soviets would take the enemy surrender and "safeguard" Japanese industry. But the uneasy truce between Mao Tse-tung's Chinese Communist Party and the Nationalists had not survived the Japanese surrender. Throughout the Communists' "liberated areas" Mao's growing armies took the Japanese surrender and seized enemy war matériel. In Manchuria, the Soviets were required by treaty to perform this function only as representatives of the Nanking government. However, American intelligence now feared the Soviets had stockpiled the Japanese munitions in Manchuria for delivery to their Communist Chinese allies.

By early in 1946, these fears had not been confirmed because the Soviets had simply not allowed Chinese government or American observers into Manchuria. The prescribed ninety-day Soviet occupation period had expired two months before, but the Russians had blackmailed Chiang into asking for an extension of it. If he didn't agree, the Russians threatened to simply pull out, creating a power vacuum that would suck in Mao's army.

"Under the Japanese," the Colonel noted, "there were no Communists in Manchuria. Chiang Kai-shek is gambling that he can occupy the area before Mao."

Clearly China was on the verge of a civil war, a cataclysmic struggle involving millions of troops. Estimates of the conflicting armies' sizes varied, but the Communists probably had a million armed regulars with 2 million militia "volunteers." Chiang Kai-shek's Nationalist armies numbered over 3 million, but his best trained and best equipped forces were several thousand miles away from Manchuria in western China, Burma, and even in training bases in India. The Communist forces were on the march from their bases in northern China to Manchuria. To counter this move, the American military was transporting tens of thousands of Nationalist troops north and east in a massive air and sea lift. Unfortunately, the Soviets—well ensconced in their newly mandated sovereign enclave at Dairen and Port Arthur at the tip of the Kwantung Peninsula—were steadfastly blocking the entry of Nationalist troops into Manchuria.

President Truman was so concerned about this explosive situation—which threatened to involve America and the Soviet Union in direct military conflict—that he'd dispatched General George C. Marshall, his wartime chief of staff, to China to act as his personal peace mediator. Marshall's mission was to somehow knock together a viable coalition government, with a division of civil and military power agreeable to both Chiang's KMT and Mao's Communists. His first order of business was to effect a cease-fire between the Nationalists and Communists, whose forces had already begun skirmishes in northern China. General Marshall was personally determined to accomplish this daunting task, I was told, but his chances of success were slim.[4]

"Mao and Generalissimo Chiang have been at each other's throats for over twenty years," the civilian officer said. "It's going to take more than George Marshall to keep them apart."

Marshall's limited stock of negotiating tools included the carrot of continued American economic and military support and the stick of suspending that aid. But this pressure only worked with the Nationalists; Mao had never depended on the Americans, but rather on the Soviets. On the other hand, America had carefully courted the Nationalist government during World War II, rebuilding the ragtag KMT army into a powerful force equipped with modern American weapons and trained in conventional tactics. We had hoped to use China's armed might in the final offensive against the Japanese. To this end, the Allies had led Chiang Kai-shek to believe he was an equal partner, including him in the major wartime conferences. The net result of this alliance was a Nationalist military machine utterly dependent on the United States. Chiang's army fired American-caliber ammunition from U.S. weapons, rode in American trucks, and flew in American aircraft. If we cut aid and logistical support, the KMT army would collapse.

But Mao's Communist forces relied almost exclusively on captured Japanese munitions for their hordes of light infantry organized on guerrilla-style formations. Their heavy weapons were Soviet, and their few armored units depended on Soviet equipment and advisers.

This was the grim situation in the early spring of 1946. Most of America had happily turned its back on the dark days of the war. But one of the epic military contests of the century was smoldering toward explosion in China. If there was going to be a Chinese civil war, the pivotal battles would no doubt be fought in Manchuria. And America, I was told, needed an effective intelligence presence on the scene. The two officers formally asked me to volunteer to join and eventually lead this intelligence mission.[5] They wanted me to become Chief of Station in southern Manchuria. My cover would be commanding officer of the "U.S. Army Liaison Group" in Mukden, Manchuria, a liaison and observer team to the Nationalist forces, which the United States hoped were about to replace the Soviet Red Army on the ground.

Because of the confused situation, wives and dependents were not authorized to join us, and they couldn't tell me how long I'd be out there. I'd been married a little over a year, and Mary and I had spent maybe two months of that time together. Now the Army wanted me back on the other side of the planet again, more hazardous duty in a muddled and complex situation. But the alternative was training recruits in the Alabama foothills.

I looked around the neat, well-appointed office. Like most professional intelligence establishments, there was a conspicuous absence of paperwork and documents, but the filing cabinets were secured with thick combination-lock drawers, each bearing a white cardboard "CLOSED" tag. I suddenly recalled the cluttered office of the OSS reception major in the Munitions Building in 1943; the organization had matured considerably in the thirty months since. For that matter, so had I. Then, I'd been a relatively naive, untested infantry lieutenant, the type of "eager" young officer that General Donovan sought to mold to his organization's wartime needs.

But a lot had happened to me in those two and a half years. I'd spent that time with the Special Operations branch, the ruffians of the outfit, the dagger branch of the cloak-and-dagger service. Now I was being asked to work in SI, Secret Intelligence, the murky world of espionage and counterespionage, where nothing was direct or straightforward, where layers of deception concealed reality, where a man survived not by physical courage but by cunning. I was twenty-five, a mere captain, but these two experienced officers now offered me responsibilities far beyond those I could find in a Regular Army unit. I'd be a fool to pass up this opportunity. But the decision was not mine alone to make.

"We'd like you to talk to your wife about this, Captain," the Colonel said. "Depending on the military situation out there, you could be separated quite a while."

When I broke the news to Mary that afternoon, she listened intently. "How dangerous will it be?" She assumed I'd already made up my mind. Other young wives across America were buying cribs and washing machines for their new suburban homes. She was sending her husband off to another distant conflict.

"I don't know," I answered, "probably not as bad as the war."

"Well," she said, "it certainly sounds more interesting than training recruits down in Alabama."

☆   ☆

THE U.S. military facility in the southern Manchurian town of Chinchou was in a large brick house requisitioned from a Japanese official by the Chinese army. My group arrived at the tail end of the bitter Manchurian winter, when the first green shoots appeared in the mud and cackling geese and mallards swarmed across the Yellow Sea on their long migration back north to Siberia. I was immediately struck by the contrast between Manchuria and the lush rice paddies and jungles of Yunnan Province, thousands of miles to the southwest, where I'd trained Annamite guerrillas the year before.

Most of the Manchurian coast was flat grasslands, with a rocky spine of mountains rising from the sea near the Great Wall and another stretching down the Kwantung Peninsula. The town itself was a sprawling collection of dusty, brick-walled compounds, some of recent Japanese construction, others centuries old with peaked roofs of russet, patched tiles. Tropical Yunnan Province had open village markets bounded by lichee hedges and bamboo, plodding water buffalo, and peasants with conical straw hats. But these Manchurian towns had a closed, cloistered atmosphere, protection against both the harsh winter and the procession of marauding armies that had swept across the natural invasion routes of the broad plains throughout the millennia. Clomping one-horse *drashki* carriages were the ubiquitous transport for goods and people. The Manchurians were taller and more raw-boned than the round-faced southerners I'd known in Kunming. When my group arrived in Chinchou, the milling crowds were still dressed for winter in thick, padded coats and trousers and fur hats with dangling earflaps. The town's narrow lanes were choked with coal smoke and the warm stench of stabled horses. Up here above the Great Wall (built so many centuries before to keep back the Manchu hordes), I felt much closer to the cold plateaus of the Mongol interior than to the emerald paddies of the south.

There was a reinforced U.S. Marine division garrisoned along the coast of China to the south of the Great Wall; the mood was one of optimistic permanence, as if America was solidly supporting its Chinese ally. Ostensibly, the American presence was merely a continuation of our wartime assistance program. But now our official responsibilities included repatriating thousands of Japanese and also logistical support for the Nationalist government's rehabilitation efforts. While I had nothing to do with either the repatriation or the logistical support efforts, occasional American presence in the area gave credibility to my cover as being a part of the Navy's External Survey Detachment 44, with headquarters in Shanghai. The civil war had already begun, and America was providing somewhat grudging military support to the Nationalists.

Through the Yalta concessions the Soviets had gained control of Manchuria's principal naval base at Port Arthur (annexed as sovereign Soviet territory) and the principal land transport, the South Manchurian and Chinese Eastern Railroads. They also occupied the nearby commercial port of Dairen. Legally, the Soviets should have allowed the Nationalists access to the "open" port facilities of Dairen in order for Chiang to move his armies into Manchuria. Moreover, the smaller port of Yingkou was clearly beyond the well-defined Port Arthur Naval Zone given the Russians at Yalta. But the Soviets stubbornly rejected the Nationalists' requests for access to their own territory during the crucial months following the Japanese collapse. By doing so, the Soviets effectively sealed off the Nationalists' practical routes of entry into Manchuria.

China's ancient emperors knew what they were doing when they built the Great Wall; the highlands north of Peking and the mountains of the Kwantung Peninsula formed a natural bottleneck, funneling access to the plains of Manchuria to a narrow coastal choke point: the delta of the Liao River where the dusty town of Chinchou now stood. Chiang Kai-shek wanted desperately to move his best, American-trained "new armies" into Manchuria, but the way was blocked by the Soviets.

The Russians were too politically astute to refuse outright Nationalist rightful demands for access to Manchuria. Instead, the Soviets claimed that unsubdued Japanese forces, renegade Manchurian puppet troops, and otherwise unspecified "bandits" had disrupted rail and road communication.[6] With Soviet assistance, the Chinese Communists occupied Yingkou, thereby denying the use of that most logical entry port into Manchuria to the Nationalists.[7] The initial ninety-day Soviet occupation specified by the Yalta Accords and ratified in the Sino-Soviet Treaty of August 1945 was now in its third extension.

Cease-fire supervision teams organized by General Marshall's mission in Peking—the Executive Headquarters—which were destined for Manchuria, were now stalled in Tientsin and Chinchou awaiting Soviet permission to enter. These teams each had tripartite leadership, with an American, Nationalist, and Communist officer sharing command. In practice, this meant the Communist could side with the Russians and prevent the team's deployment in "dangerous" areas, specifically Manchuria north of the Sungari River, where the Soviets were equipping the Red armies of General Lin Piao.

Brigadier General Henry Byroade, Marshall's chief American deputy in the Executive Headquarters, came to Chinchou in early March 1946 to discuss the deployment of the cease-fire teams with our unit.

Never one to hold back, I spoke my mind. "Sir, the Japanese never tolerated any Communist forces in Manchuria. It isn't as if there already were KMT and Communist troops in cease-fire positions that needed supervision." He was frowning, but I pressed on. "Every day we hold the Nationalist forces back, more Red troops pour in from North China."

"Captain," he said coldly, emphasizing my junior rank, "I don't think we can prove that. The Communists deny that they are moving troops into Manchuria. We have not seen any evidence of this from our aerial reconnaissance of the area."

"Sir," I continued, "our agents who have recently come from Jehol Province report that the Communists are moving at night by the thousands into Manchuria. They hide out in villages during daylight. If we continue to immobilize the Nationalists, the Communists will be able to shift their entire force into Manchuria where they can make contact with the Soviets."

The General glared, then simply said, "Thanks for your opinion, Captain." His mind was already made up; more to the point, General Marshall,

Byroade's superior, was determined to exert his will on Chiang Kai-shek.

But my unit commander (and the officer I was scheduled to replace), an Army full colonel named Fitzhugh Chandler, echoed my assessment. Byroade didn't seem impressed by either of us. He returned to Peking later that day, convinced the Executive Headquarters could end the fighting.

Hugh Chandler was an old OSS hand whom I'd met in England, where he ran the clandestine OSS airdrop supply center at an RAF base in East Anglia. He hadn't been home since 1942, and was long overdue for rotation. While we were delayed in Chinchou, Chandler gave me a cram course in running an intelligence station. The prospect of taking the place of this experienced senior officer was both daunting and exciting.

The more I studied the situation, the more obvious it became that the Allies' decision at Yalta to invite Soviet participation in the Pacific war through their invasion of Manchuria was a blunder of epic proportions, which stemmed from faulty intelligence. Had we known the true state of the Kwantung Army, we could have dispatched American-trained Nationalist divisions to handle the occupation. Now we were stuck with a permanent Soviet presence in the region. Establishing a professional, clandestine intelligence station in Manchuria was therefore of vital national importance. In the future, I vowed, any strategic decisions about Manchuria made by America's leaders would at least be based on accurate information. While the Soviet stall tactics dragged on, our station's complement of specialist officers grew. Some were military intelligence officers; others had expertise in counterintelligence and security; some had been recruited to run agent networks. I felt reasonably confident I could manage their activities effectively.

In Hulatao, the port of Chinchou, as well as in ports along the Yellow Sea, large numbers of Nationalist troops en route to Manchuria were arriving daily aboard U.S. Navy transports. If the Soviets did not lift their occupation of Manchuria soon, there was bound to be an open military clash between the Nationalists and Russian forces. Already, small Nationalist units had moved up the railroad against Soviet objections, clearing token Communist resistance along the way. In the garrison outside of town, the KMT troops were being prepared for the coming struggle. Above their camp gate hung a huge banner with bold yellow characters: "China will survive or perish with the Northeast!"[8]

During one of these forays, the Mukden-Dairen rail line was cut and a Soviet military train was stalled north of the Russian enclave. An enterprising Soviet army artillery major decided to hike around the rail cut and was promptly captured by Nationalist troops, who delivered him to us. The Russian officer was a gregarious guy with a wrestler's build and a frost-nipped face. He had wide Slavic eyes of pale blue and he smiled frequently, revealing a couple of stainless-steel teeth. He was obviously relieved to be in American custody, and spoke frankly over a bowl of hot, meaty soup.

Once he learned we were both combat veterans, he scornfully condemned the troops the Red Army had used for the initial invasion of Manchuria. "They were penal battalions," he said, shaking his head. "They suffered more losses brawling with each other when they looted the shops and hotels than they did fighting the Japanese."

Moreover, the Major added, the Soviet troops had been told by their political commissars that Manchuria was ripe for socialist liberation, the region having suffered for decades under the exploitive yoke of the fascist Japanese. But his men had been stunned to find modern cities such as Harbin and Mukden, replete with broad boulevards and public utilities, including sewage and water systems. The factory workers' apartment blocks, the well-appointed cinemas and sports complexes, surpassed anything he'd seen in the Soviet Union. Asked about the Japanese factories themselves, the Major went silent, again shaking his head. "Very modern," was all he said.

☆   ☆

THE Soviet occupation troops finally were pressured into evacuating Manchuria in mid-March.[9] But then there were immediate sharp clashes between the first Nationalist troops airlifted into Mukden and Soviet-supported Chinese Communist guerrilla units. For the next two weeks the fighting around the city was so intense that our team was advised to wait before proceeding north. The first week in April, Colonel Hugh Chandler and I led the advance party of the Army Liaison Group (ALG) into Mukden, arriving on two-man, single-engine L-5 spotter planes, the rugged little aircraft that would become our main means of transport around Manchuria. Flying up the alluvial valley of the Liao River, I watched the constricting mountains curve away both east and west and the broad expanse of low Manchurian hills and plains rise before me. Even though the Yellow Sea was only sixty miles behind us, I felt as if we were entering into the ancient heart of Asia.

The city of Mukden was anything but ancient. It sprawled across the flood plain of the Liao like a redbrick factory town transported from the Midwest. The first landmarks I sighted from the window of the L-5 were factory chimneys, grain elevators, and the angular steel geometry of blast furnaces and chemical plants. Unlike the old border towns to the south, Mukden was crisscrossed by wide boulevards and dotted by parks. The huge industrial complexes of Japanese conglomerates like Mitsubishi dominated the outskirts.

On this first aerial inspection, I saw considerable damage to the factories: blown-out windows, sections of roof missing, odd rectangular holes in walls. But strangely, there were no bomb craters in the factory yards. I knew that even American B-29s couldn't have bombed *that* accurately.

Once on the ground, we discovered the true cause of this damage. The first Nationalist military teams allowed in Manchuria by the Soviets had reported widespread looting of the industrial areas. Now we saw firsthand just how systematic the Soviet pillage had been. For three days we visited factories in and around Mukden. The pattern was the same wherever we went: From a distance the factories appeared nearly normal; on entering the compound, however, we discovered mere shells of buildings. Most walls and roofs were intact, but the factory interiors had been gutted.

When we drove into the vast Toyo Rubber Tire Company, for example, the factory yard seemed to have been swept clean for our inspection. But when Hugh Chandler and I entered the long building itself, we realized the absence of normal industrial grime was not the work of janitors. The place had been literally picked clean. The main factory hall, which once held hundreds of fiber-spinning and vulcanizing machines, was absolutely empty, although the concrete floor revealed the anchor bolts of the stolen machinery.

That afternoon, we found the interiors of the Mitsubishi Heavy Industry factories more chaotic. Here the looting had been quite selective. Only new lathes, drills, and milling machines had been taken, but the electric motors from older equipment were also stolen, as were all the overhead cranes. In some factory sheds we found machinery that bore orange chalk indications in Cyrillic, "Nyet," indicating older equipment to be left behind. Machines destined for pillage, we learned, had been inspected by Russian engineers, who chalked "Da" on each piece to be taken. The Red Army troops doing the work then simply blasted holes in the factory walls to drag the machines outside.

But our Chinese escort had more to show. "Come to see, please, the houses for workmen."

He led us outside the factory gates. The workers' housing blocks were severely damaged, with entire roofs removed along with windows, doors, and plumbing. The devastation was the same at each factory. This damage, KMT officials told us (corroborated by Japanese we interviewed), was caused by mobs of Chinese looters, whom the Soviets had encouraged to pillage, once the official Soviet looting of valuable equipment had been completed by the Red Army.[10]

☆   ☆

THE Nationalist forces controlled the city, but the Communists had left behind saboteurs and propaganda teams. Mukden's rail station and government buildings were guarded by huge sandbagged pillboxes. Overall, the atmosphere was tense and unsettled.

But I didn't feel personally threatened. That changed one night in April as I was returning to my temporary quarters after conferring with American civilian officials in the Shenyang Railway Hotel, which stood on a wide traffic circle in the city's center. Because of power cuts, the street lighting was sporadic at best, and the voltage was so low that the few working lights gave a weak yellow glow. I drove my open jeep slowly around the wide circle, aware of the empty streets. It was well past curfew, but I felt secure because the police headquarters, a tall, imposing building, stood directly across the circle.

The crack of the sniper's rifle and the whiplash of the bullet past my face were almost simultaneous. The bullet slashed only inches from my forehead and shattered the asphalt just below the scooped entry sill on the passenger side. I'd been shot at enough in France to recognize a near miss. Grabbing the wheel with outstretched arms, I swung below the dashboard and floored the gas pedal. My first thought was that the sniper had fired from police headquarters. Then I saw he'd probably been in the bank building next door. I turned onto a wide boulevard and zigzagged, the tires squealing. If there was another shot, I didn't hear it.

Roaring along through the semi-blackout, I collected my thoughts. The sniper had undoubtedly used a telescopic sight; therefore, the attack was probably a planned assassination attempt, not a spontaneous action. This meant the Communists knew my real mission in Manchuria, probably through a local employee agent in my office. From now on, I could never feel completely secure in these supposedly government-controlled areas.

☆   ☆

ONE of our first tasks in Mukden was to get the team settled in permanent quarters. There was a large prewar American compound in the diplomatic quarter not far from the American consulate. Originally intended as a residential and office district for American business and consular personnel, the compound had been only partially occupied by the Socony Vacuum Company before Pearl Harbor. An OSS prisoner-of-war rescue team used it in August 1945, but the Soviet army gave them only twenty-four hours to evacuate. Now I intended to return the favor. Even though the Soviet army had officially withdrawn, there were still Russian troops in the city, including a number of their GRU military intelligence types. They'd simply removed their hammer-and-sickle tunic buttons and replaced them with the wrench-and-hammer insignia of Soviet rail workers.

Despite the sniper incident, I now made a point of flying an American flag on my jeep, as an effort to show American support for the struggling local government officials. I rolled up to the compound gates, shouldered my way past the sentries whose tommy guns hardly resembled railroad tools, and demanded an audience with the Red Army colonel. He was disinclined to meet me, so I told his executive officer I was officially reclaiming the American compound and that they had twenty-four hours to vacate it.

The Russians immediately protested to the American consul general, a career Foreign Service officer named O. Edmund Clubb. Ed Clubb was a typical old-school State Department man—cautious, circumspect, and extremely wary of confrontations of any kind. He called me to his office that afternoon.

"Now, Jack," he began, "you simply can't do this. The Soviets claim you're throwing them out on the street. They need time to pack their files and personal effects."

I stared at him for a moment without answering. He knew perfectly well the Soviets had unceremoniously booted out our OSS team eight months before. He also knew these Red Army soldiers were serving as a Chinese Communist listening post in the heart of the city. "The compound's ours," I said. "We need quarters and office space as soon as possible. Unless we're firm, the Russians will find one excuse after another not to leave."

But Clubb was not convinced. "They've got women and children in there. It's cruel to just evict them."

"Mr. Clubb," I said, carefully choosing my words, "I don't have to remind you that everything we do here is watched closely by the Communists and the Nationalists. They try to read our actions like tea leaves. Booting the Russians out on their ass will demonstrate our support for the KMT. It'll show the Communists we've got some backbone."

He frowned. "I don't think it's wise to bully the Soviets . . . or to lean too far toward the Nationalists."

"Well," I said, swallowing my frustration, "the Chinese Reds have been making fools of our truce teams for months . . ."

"Do you really think that's a fair assessment, Jack?"

I did not answer immediately. I was going to have to work with this man in the coming difficult months, and already I sensed an inherent anti-Nationalist, possibly pro-Communist attitude.

Clubb broke the silence. "Well, perhaps you could find them some trucks." Like the good diplomat he was, he offered a compromise.

I was hesitant to accept it because I still wanted to exert my team's authority as early as possible with the Soviets. But I realized my relationship with Clubb was probably more important than any impression I might make on the Russians or their Red Chinese allies. But trucks and fuel were scarce in Mukden, and the transport was vitally needed to beef up the government defense of the city. I told Mr. Clubb that the Russians could scrounge their own transport, but that they could have an additional twenty-four hours to vacate American property.

The incident in itself was hardly important, but it exemplified the attitude of many American diplomats in China, Clubb included. Their careers had evolved during the years between the two wars when appeasement of totalitarian governments through supposedly effective restraining treaties and toothless international bodies like the League of Nations had been the hallmark of diplomacy. When this policy failed in both Asia and Europe, the career diplomats were forced to spend the war years in impotent frustration. The conduct of the war, of course, was controlled by military men, not the Foreign Service. Now that we had entered an ostensibly peaceful period, the diplomats were eager to settle Chinese problems through negotiation, not military operations. Career State Department officers equated war, or even the display of military power, with the failure of diplomacy.

This inclination was partly motivated, in my opinion, by a disdain for the military by men like Ed Clubb. He viewed us as brash and unsophisticated, lacking the language skills and deep knowledge of Asian culture that were the hallmarks of "Old China Hands" in the State Department.

He was probably right. But the situation in Manchuria involved fundamental military issues, not the nuances of treaty interpretation. The Nationalist government led by Generalissimo Chiang Kai-shek was the sole legitimate government of China. Manchuria was an integral part of China. The Communist forces in Manchuria under General Lin Piao were in open rebellion, aided and abetted by the Soviet Union. You didn't have to be an Asian scholar to recognize this. Any soldier experienced enough to follow troop movements on a map and recognize geographical choke points and natural lines of defense, such as mountains or the Sungari River, could see the Communist strategy. They were perfectly willing to be legalistic—especially manipulating the cease-fire teams to their benefit—but were equally capable of striking hard military blows when it suited their purposes. This was a prime example of Mao's "Talk-Fight, Fight-Talk" strategy, which he boldly explained to General George Marshall in 1947, as an example of Communist resolve. In Mandarin, this phrase can be romanized as "*Da-Da, Tan-Tan.*" Mao openly used this approach in the long struggle with the Nationalists, which was one reason Chiang Kai-shek never had much faith in negotiations during the civil war. As with many of Mao's aphorisms, this expression lent itself to popular dissemination in an army of illiterate peasants.[11] But in all my service in Manchuria I was never able to convince State Department men that you couldn't successfully negotiate with the Communists. Such a philosophy was anathema to old-school diplomats.

There was more to their attitude, however, than an ingrained love of negotiation. Most State Department professionals in China were thoroughly anti-Nationalist. They viewed Chiang Kai-shek's government as corrupt, inefficient, untrustworthy, and repressive. It cannot be denied that there was some substance to these charges. Chiang Kai-shek's Kuomintang was certainly not perfect. And relations between his government and the United States had often been rocky during the war. But in my opinion, State Department policy reflected a simplistically moralistic animosity toward the Nationalists.

Chiang's task had never been easy. When he inherited the Sun Yat-sen mantle in the late 1920s, Chiang was immediately challenged by the Communists on one side and a host of powerful, independent warlord generals on the other. A few years later he had to contend with a full-scale Japanese invasion. In effect, the Nationalists were attempting the task of what we now call "nation building," while simultaneously fighting a civil insurrection and foreign military aggression.

The Nationalists' strategy focused on winning the support of the educated urban classes during the first phase of their revolution. To establish a viable economic system to fill the void of the collapsed empire, Chiang had to confront the foreign powers who controlled the modern economy through their extraterritorial concessions along the coast. He allied himself with important Chinese bankers in Shanghai who conducted business in the Asian manner and who certainly weren't above making a profit from organized vice, including gambling, prostitution, money lending, and narcotics.

This pragmatic Nationalist approach to government ran counter to the attitude of moral superiority among the Western missionaries and educators who had labored in the heathen vineyards for a century. The fact that many of America's China experts in both the Foreign Service and the State Department bureaucracy sprang from missionary roots helped explain their paternalistic, anti-Nationalist attitude. Chiang's supporters were secular and educated. Although many were Christians, they did not kowtow to Western missionaries. Chiang himself was a titular Christian, but—to the chagrin of the missionaries—he advocated a return to traditional Confucian morals through his New Life Movement. Also, he never learned English and his wife, Soong Mei-ling, was the type of independent Chinese woman whom missionaries instinctively distrusted.

The Nationalists' emphasis on building a modern urban country bypassed the masses of rural peasants among whom the missionaries often worked. Thus, Chiang was seen as indifferent to the suffering of the common people.

During the war these American attitudes hardened. President Roosevelt viewed Chiang as a subordinate, not an equal partner in the Big Four alliance. The Nationalists' refusal to accept Communists into an anti-Japanese coalition government was thus viewed as insubordination. America's chief military man in China, General Joseph Stilwell, never accepted Chiang's premise that admitting Communists to a coalition government and giving them Western military aid was tantamount to national suicide. Stilwell's key political advisers, including State Department officers John P. Davies and John Stewart Service, were vehemently anti-Nationalist.[12]

It was much easier, of course, for Americans to document the Nationalists' shortcomings than those of the Communists. Mao kept foreign observers at a distance, and only allowed visiting American delegations to his northern sanctuary on a few occasions. But the daily problems caused by venal and inefficient Nationalist civil and military officials grated on Americans eager to press on with the war against Japan. These diplomats seem to have forgotten our own country's checkered history of inefficiency and corruption during our protracted "nation building." Certainly, the Nationalists were no worse than the carpetbaggers and robber barons of the nineteenth century, and were far less corrupt than those responsible for recent scandals such as Teapot Dome. But the American political advisers chose to judge Chiang's government by unrealistic standards.

Parallel to this ingrained anti-Nationalist sentiment was the vague but pervasive belief that the Chinese Communist Party and People's Liberation Army led by Mao Tse-tung were somehow not "true Communists," that they were simply agrarian reformers who had been forced to the left of the political spectrum by the corrupt and repressive Nationalist regime. Above all, it was believed, Mao would never blindly do Moscow's bidding. Once there was a substantial American military and political presence in China during the war, Mao and his astute deputies such as Chou En-lai carefully cultivated this image. Their combined civil-military operations in areas "liberated" from the Japanese—in reality, regions of marginal tactical and strategic value which the Japanese High Command had bypassed—favorably impressed many Americans, including the military diplomat Major General Patrick Hurley, who served as ambassador in 1944 and 1945. From all appearances, the Communists had established egalitarian, grass-roots democracy in the areas they controlled. Considerable emphasis was placed on mass participation, on land redistribution, on village-level public works, and on agit-prop mass demonstrations to vigorously fight the Japanese.[13]

Their activities also made a strong impression on key career American diplomats. Urging the State Department to abandon the Nationalists and "declare ourselves for the Communists," John Davies wrote in a wartime dispatch that such a policy would mean "we shall have aligned ourselves behind the most coherent, progressive and powerful force in China."[14]

☆   ☆

THE Soviets' crippling of Manchuria's hydroelectric plants had greatly reduced power available, causing the shutdown of Mukden's sewage treatment
system. With refugees crowding the city, lack of sanitation quickly spread
disease, including plague. During its industrial heyday, the population of
Mukden had been 2 million. Now there were at least that many in the city,
but there was no work for them and little food. And the overall economic
situation was not promising. The Soviets had raided Manchuria's banks of
gold bullion and 600 million Manchukuo yuan, the Japanese-backed currency. They then flooded the market with almost 10 billion worthless Occupation yuan, which they knew the Nationalist government could not
redeem. The gutting of the local economy was near complete. Commenting
on this situation, Ambassador Edwin Pauley noted, "If the Soviets plan to
delay the economic recovery of the Orient a full generation, and to sow the
seeds of violent social unrest, their plans have been successful." The combined Soviet and Communist Chinese pillage, he stated, "left a population
hungry, cold, and full of unrest."[15]

The human face of Mukden was both exotic and pitiful. Stateless and
displaced Europeans, including several hundred Germans and a thousand
White Russians, formed the top stratum of the refugee community. Hapless
Japanese peasants, many barefoot in the harsh Manchurian spring, were at
the bottom of the heap. In between came Koreans, Mongolians, Japanese
industrial workers, businessmen and engineers, and tens of thousands of
Manchurians formerly employed in the factories. Luckily, Manchuria was
a bountiful agricultural area and there were sufficient food stocks available
to stave off widespread famine. But the United Nations relief workers had
their hands full keeping food and medical supplies moving up the railroad,
which was under attack by the Communists.

As I had learned in Kunming, however, the Chinese people were energetic
and resourceful when it came to making a living under difficult conditions.
The various Mukden black markets thrived in this near anarchy. Strolling
the teeming side streets near the main railway station with Harold Leith,
who'd been on the OSS prisoner rescue mission to Mukden, I found kids
as young as ten and wizened old grandfathers squatting on the pavement
selling a truly bewildering variety of items, many looted from the homes of
wealthy Japanese. I bought two Japanese telephone sets in excellent condition for two U.S. dollars each. In Shanghai they would have fetched fifty.

One old woman offered an excellent selection of golf clubs (then, as now,
the Japanese were enraptured by the game). On the next street over, Harold
Leith bought a Leica camera for fifteen dollars. We stood in the crowded
lane watching the lively commerce, a bedlam of Asian languages, Mongolian,
Mandarin, Korean, and Japanese, sweeping over us. Little boys in peaked
Japanese military caps jostled past with trays of sweetened rice cakes, which

they quickly traded for Russian or Shanghai cigarettes, the price being two cakes for a cigarette. Under the Japanese, Manchurians were forbidden to eat rice, and were forced to make do with sorghum and millet. These young entrepreneurs were the salesmen of a cottage industry that probably supported an entire extended family. In their own small way, they embodied the irrepressible Chinese affinity for commerce.

Local art dealers were more cunning. They'd gone north on horse caravans to Changchun, the capital of the Manchukuo puppet state, when the Japanese surrendered. Mobs had looted the palace of P'u-yi, the "last Emperor" of China, and art treasures dating back to ancient dynasties were available for a pittance. Now the Mukden dealers sold Ming vases and jade for U.S. greenbacks.

☆   ☆

WE were soon contacted by members of Mukden's White Russian community. There were about a thousand of these anti-Soviet refugees in the city, some veterans of the White Army defeated by the Bolsheviks in the civil war, others their children who had been born as stateless exiles in Manchuria. They had been tolerated by the Japanese, and some had attained responsible positions in local industry. When the Soviet Army swept in, in August 1945, the White Russians had been engulfed by the totalitarian state they had fled more than twenty years before.

But the Soviet authorities had not simply rounded up the White Russians and shipped them to labor camps, as many refugees had feared. Instead, the White Russians were made to register their families with the Soviet authorities and then were issued Soviet passports, and encouraged to return to help rebuild the "Motherland."

One day that summer I was visited by a Russian doctor named "Ivanov" (a pseudonym; his family is still in the Soviet Union). When he entered my office in the old Socony Vacuum compound, he looked nervously around the room before taking his chair, apparently searching for microphones or hidden cameras. The doctor was middle-aged, thin with bristly white hair and a certain aristocratic hauteur. He didn't waste time.

"You are with the *Renseignements,*" he stated directly, using the French term for intelligence service. "I will work with you, but you must help my family."

I shook my head. "We are an Army Liaison Group to the Kuomintang military," I said.

"As you wish," the doctor answered. "I have been asked to return to Soviet territory, to Amursk in Siberia. It's a military zone."

I listened intently, aware the man might well be a Soviet intelligence officer, but also aware he had a rich potential as an agent. Such "walk-ins" were often valuable resources.

"My mother and my brothers survived the war," he continued, unperturbed by my silence. "The Soviet authorities have given me . . . letters from them. I have agreed to return."

"I see." He was being pressured by a family held hostage, a well-tested Soviet tactic.

"And also," the doctor said, sighing with resignation, "I'm tired of being stateless."

"How can we help you?" I hadn't committed myself, but I'd given him the opportunity to do so.

"My son Sergei is twenty-four years old. He has a wife and a child. If you take them safely from Manchuria, I will work for you."

The recruitment of an agent is more like a courtship than a business transaction. And this courtship had reached a delicate moment. If the doctor was a Soviet counterintelligence specialist, my proceeding too quickly would confirm Communist suspicions that my liaison group was really an intelligence team. Then my teammates and I would become the immediate targets of organized counterespionage operations. But if I "lived" my cover story too convincingly, the doctor might simply disappear.

"Would it be possible to meet your son?" The chances were the Soviets had not recruited an entire family here in Mukden and already trained them as convincing double agents.

The doctor rose and shook my hand warmly. "We will return this afternoon."

When Dr. Ivanov and his son came that afternoon, I introduced them to my three best professional case officers, Scott Miler, Rutherford "Pinky" Walsh, and Phil Potter. Pinky and Phil were ex-OSS (Pinky had been a Jed until he tried to outsmart the SOE psychologists in training). They had already established safe houses in Mukden and secure nearby villages where the Russian agents could be trained in tradecraft. Scott Miler's specialty was counterintelligence, so he would conduct the initial screening. By now, we had access to Japanese intelligence files and had the full cooperation of the Nationalist intelligence service. It was unlikely Soviet double agents would escape our scrutiny.

Dr. Ivanov was the first White Russian agent in what was to become a moderately successful network in Siberia and European Russia. The Soviets had pressured a number of refugees of his generation to return. Like him, they were weary of statelessness, resigned to their fate, but deeply concerned for the future of their children who had been born in exile. We were able to negotiate safe conduct for these children through the Nationalist lines and on to American-occupied Japan. Some settled in the United States, others in Western Europe. Many eventually worked in private and governmental anti-Soviet organizations, such as Radio Liberty. Their parents kept the bargain. Within six months, American intelligence began receiving a sporadic flow of economic and political intelligence from parts of Siberia completely off-limits to foreigners.

One of the first tasks this group performed was informing the large un-committed group of Russian exiles about true conditions inside the Soviet Union. Walsh and Potter had arranged simple word codes for the Russians before they returned. For example, "Uncle Vanya is feeling better" meant the conditions of daily life were acceptable. A phrase such as "Aunt Natasha is suffering from arthritis" meant severe repression and hardship. The correspondence from the returned exiles reported epidemics of arthritis and rheumatism among their elderly relatives.

☆   ☆

ATHOUGH our workload mounted steadily, there were some diversions. The marshes west of the city where the Liu and the Liao rivers formed an inland delta were thick with mallards, snipe, and Siberian geese. The new British consul general, Walter Graham, and I were both avid hunters. So we converted an Army ambulance, which I'd swapped for a jeep, into a mobile hunting lodge. Whenever we could, Walter and I would drive out the rutted, muddy farm lanes to the wetlands and shoot.

The only problem with this sport was that the area was often infiltrated at night by Communist troops. This was a classic guerrilla-versus-conventional-force situation. Government soldiers controlled the area during the day, but fell back to fortified camps at night. As long as we got into the marshes after dawn and out before sunset, we had excellent hunting.

But one chilly afternoon, our ambulance bogged down in a stream and we were stuck after dark. A local village headman took us in and insisted we bed down on his family's sleeping mats in his smoky little mud-brick house. Walter spoke good Chinese and asked the headman if Communist troops and armed propaganda teams ever occupied this village.

The old man's face was typically impassive. "Oh, yes," he answered, "many times. They were here two nights ago."

Walter and I exchanged uneasy glances. Government artillery flares cast a chalky glow in the distance, indicating just how far we were from Nationalist lines. If the Communists entered this village tonight, we would be captured. There was no way out. The headman had promised to bring oxen in the morning to tow our ambulance from the stream. But the morning was ten hours away. In the meantime, we waited.

Amazingly, we both fell asleep. But I woke up around three, the darkest hour in that cold night. On the opposite sleeping platform, one of the headman's sons sat on his haunches, gazing at the two huge foreign devils on his bed. The boy's father had been obliged by traditional Confucian ethics to offer us hospitality, despite the certain knowledge that this gesture put his entire family at risk of execution, should the Communists discover us. The boy was old enough to recognize and to stoically accept this harsh dilemma. I gazed back at him in the chill, diffused moonlight. Although his face was almost empty, there was a mixture of compassion and fear in his dark young eyes. Time passed. We continued to silently watch each other. Finally, I slept.

The next morning when we got back to the city, we found both our staffs almost frantic with worry. On our future hunting trips we avoided that stream. I never saw the village headman or his son again.

☆   ☆

BUT hunting was only a hobby. Accurate reporting on the progress of the civil war was my main concern. Normally this duty would fall to a military attaché from the embassy in Nanking, and, indeed, we did have just such an officer on TDY in Mukden, Major Robert B. Rigg. He was an armor officer, originally from the Black Horse Troop, an Illinois National Guard cavalry outfit that specialized in stunt riding: medieval jousting and cossack charges in the thirties. Rigg had sat out the war in Tehran far from the combat zones, overseeing lend-lease shipments to the Soviets. He was one of the most arrogant and obnoxious officers I'd encountered. Bob Rigg seemed obsessed with self-aggrandizement and was given to well-publicized feats of derring-do, after which he'd inevitably assemble the foreign press corps at the bar of the Shenyang Railway Hotel and regale them with dramatic tales of his narrow escapes "behind Commie lines." He reminded me of certain OSS *field* officers in Paris (actually staff rats assigned to the headquarters of regular outfits) who'd muddy their combat boots in the Bois de Boulogne, strap fighting knives to their web belts, then tell war stories about the Maquis at the bar of the Ritz Hotel. Over the years I've learned that every army has such phonies; it's just unfortunate when they land responsible assignments.

This would have been tolerable if Rigg's intelligence was accurate. But it wasn't. The Nationalists distrusted him because his secretary, Tanya Krupenin, was an attractive White Russian woman born in exile. Nationalist intelligence suspected her (unjustly) of being a Soviet agent. Interestingly enough, Amos D. Moscrip, the head of all covert CIA operations in China, was also associated with a White Russian woman—in this case, his girlfriend.[16] Moscrip ran a large operation from a compound in the French concession in Shanghai. He was a heavy drinker and cut a wide swath in Shanghai social circles. But his deputy, Bob Delany, made up for this. Bob had been the second-in-command of OSS in Kunming; he knew China well and was trusted by the Nationalists.

This trust spilled over to my office in Mukden. Harvey Yu, a Chinese-born American Marine officer, was my military intelligence specialist. The Nationalists' North East China Command gave him free access to their war room, where he obtained accurate daily situation reports. But I also had to rely on personal observation conducted by me or my staff. Often this took the form of flying over combat zones in our flimsy little L-5 aircraft. The plane had the virtue of flying low and slow, which made for good observation. Unfortunately, this made the L-5 an excellent target. I encountered this problem one afternoon flying over the trenches around Ssupingchieh, a vital crossroads town midway between Mukden and Changchun. The Soviets had delivered the town to the Communists that spring; now a strong Nationalist force, supported by armor and artillery, had the Red garrison under siege.

My best pilot, Sergeant Clayton Pond, handled the L-5 with considerable skill. He'd flown in the mountains of Burma during the war and knew how to avoid ack-ack. Pond kept down at treetop level as we overflew the Nationalist rear areas, which spread from the Mukden-Changchun highway through the newly green sorghum fields and orchards to the northeast. Ahead of these positions the Nationalist artillery batteries were dug in around shattered farm villages. I got a good look at the artillery, American-supplied 105mm howitzers and heavy mortars. These troops were part of the New First Army, which had been trained and equipped by the United States for the final offensive against Japan. The trenches and bunker systems began forward of the artillery, and snaked in a muddy scar across a range of low hills. The Communist forces were entrenched on the shell-pocked opposite slope.

I was astounded by the magnitude of the engagement. This was fighting on a densely packed front reminiscent of the trench warfare of the First World War. From what I saw, the Nationalists' earlier training was paying off. They had the Communists pinned down southwest of the town, and were in the process of turning the enemy flank, using light and medium artillery to great effect.

The L-5 was a handy little spotter plane, but it was cramped. My observer seat was wedged directly behind Sergeant Pond's. We hardly had headroom beneath the wing, the center of which was the main fuel tank. Just behind me was an even narrower compartment for radio equipment, but we had removed the set to lighten the load and increase our range. In a pinch, we could put a third person back there, hopefully someone who didn't suffer from claustrophobia.

We climbed up to a thousand feet to get a better look at the Red positions. Unlike the Nationalist side of the line, there was no evidence of truck parks, or vehicle tracks, or radio antennas and field telephone lines for that matter. These massed Communist forces were lightly armed compared to the KMT troops. The local Red commanders, Kao Kang, Ting Hua, and Chou Pao-chung, were veteran guerrilla leaders, in reality warlords from north China who had sided with the Communists after the Japanese invasion. They were fighting their first fixed engagement against disciplined, well-equipped Nationalist troops. And they seemed to be losing.

But they hadn't yet lost their will to fight. As we droned along above the trenches, a stream of orange tracers erupted from the enemy hills. Immediately, a second, then a third heavy machine gun opened fire on us. The tracers seemed slow and lazy in the warm afternoon, like aimless insects. Then the fire converged. Pond dragged back the throttle, chopping power, and slammed the control stick hard right. The little plane stood on its wing, stalled, and slipped into an abrupt dive. I was about to yell at Pond to take it easy when I heard a sound like a screwdriver puncturing a cardboard box. Craning my neck, I saw a line of bullet holes in the fabric-covered left wing. The holes stopped inches from the overhead gas tank. I was fascinated by the shreds of fabric flapping in the slipstream. They reminded me of wing feathers on a falling duck. But this wasn't mallard hunting. It was war.

Sergeant Pond centered the stick and kicked hard left rudder, preventing a spin. At about 200 feet he firewalled the throttle, and we regained a positive rate of climb just above the Nationalist lines. Pond had saved our lives. Had we stayed on that heading, we'd have flown into a converging stream of machine-gun fire.

He leaned out to check the left wing. "Hope they didn't hit a spar or something, sir."

"Me too," I shouted back.

☆   ☆

In late April, Major Bob Rigg prevailed on me to borrow Sergeant Pond and his L-5 to go to Changchun. The Communists had besieged the Nationalist troops flown in after the Soviet evacuation. I told him flat out I didn't want to risk the aircraft or pilot up there. But Rigg said he had direct orders from Consul General Ed Clubb to get a "firsthand look" at the situation. Some American reporters had made their way to Changchun and Rigg apparently couldn't resist the opportunity to get some publicity. Sure as hell, he landed all right and they went into town without any problem, but the Reds then cut the road between the city and the airfield, stranding them.

I learned of this from the local Nationalist headquarters and went to see Clubb before filing my report to Shanghai. Clubb was with Sabin Chase, the consul general designate to Harbin, who was temporarily assigned to Mukden. Chase was an "Old China Hand" Foreign Service officer. He spoke Chinese well, but was ponderously slow and cautious to a fault. When I raised even the most mundane matter with him, Chase always considered every possible ramification before venturing an opinion. In this regard, he and Clubb were similar. So they were virtually stunned speechless when I broke the news about Rigg.

"Major Rigg and Sergeant Pond have been captured in Changchun," I announced. "I just got word from North East China Command."

Clubb and Chase stared at me gravely.

"Mr. Clubb," I continued, "I just wanted to confirm that Bob Rigg was acting on your orders before I report the incident to my headquarters."

Clubb pursed his lips. "Major Rigg . . . Rigg, well." He shook his head. "The name is familiar, certainly, but . . ." Now he turned to Sabin Chase. "Isn't Major Rigg assigned to *you*, Sabe?"

Chase smoothed his fine white hair. "Oh, no, no . . . I'm sure he's not." Clubb was passing the buck, but Chase was dodging it.[17]

This could go on all afternoon. But I didn't have time to waste with these jellyfish. I filed my report, noting Rigg claimed to have been acting on Clubb's orders. Later that day I received a real rocket from Shanghai. According to headquarters, I had been "totally irresponsible" in giving Rigg an aircraft and pilot. This was my first formal reprimand, and I was mad, both at Rigg for conning me and at myself for letting him. I was also worried about Pond; he was a fine young soldier who deserved better. As for Rigg, he might have actually backed into a dangerous situation for the first time in his life.

But they got back to the airstrip a few days later. They found their plane had been drained of gas, the radio stolen, and even their seat belts were missing. Luckily, there was still about nine gallons of fuel in each of two improvised wing tanks we'd installed on the struts. Pond scrounged some old Japanese "aviation" gas that was syrupy from months of evaporation. They used their regular fuel for takeoff, then switched to the gas Pond had found. The engine lost power so fast they couldn't maintain altitude. So they had a hundred-mile roller-coaster ride back to Mukden, with Pond switching tanks to gain altitude as needed. Rigg found the whole adventure quite thrilling.

Sergeant Pond took it all in stride. Once when flying back with him from Changchun we had a five-pound can of coffee stowed behind my seat. We came under ground fire, and bullets pierced the can, filling the cramped L-5 with the tantalizing aroma of freshly brewed coffee.

"Hey, Captain," Pond yelled over his shoulder, "pour me a cup."

☆   ☆

THE fighting in Manchuria that spring and summer was savage. But the Nationalists proved they could defeat the Reds in set-piece engagements. If this pattern continued, I realized, the KMT might push the Communists all the way up to the Siberian border before winter. The Nationalists had fought to open the railroad to Jehol Province to the south, and were steadily moving supplies into Manchuria by both train and airlift. In the face of this pressure the Communists wisely disengaged and abandoned Ssupingchieh. However, the fact that 70,000 Communist troops had literally slipped out of the Nationalists' encirclement overnight did not augur well for the future conduct of the war. Whereas Chiang Kai-shek had ordered his generals to capture and occupy territory as if in a conventional campaign, Lin Piao's forces were fighting a classic guerrilla war. The Communists realized their immediate goal was not to capture real estate—especially cities with large, hungry populations—but to annihilate the Nationalist army.

After the Nationalists took Ssupingchieh, they continued north to engage the Communists at Changchun. There the fighting was bitter, and initially indecisive. But again they routed the Communists. The Reds switched tactics, the bulk of their troops retreating north of the Sungari River, while stay-behind guerrilla units harassed the Nationalists' extended lines of communication.

Now they opened an offensive on the political front. The cease-fire teams of General Marshall's Executive Headquarters flew in from Peking. Communist team members no longer dragged their feet, but spurred the truce teams to energetically inspect the newly captured Nationalist positions. This cease-fire activity naturally drew the attention of foreign correspondents. So the Nationalist North East China Command was obliged to cooperate. By midsummer the government forces were formally constrained from further advances, and had little choice but to dig in and fortify the positions they already held. North of the Sungari River in Communist territory, however, the cease-fire teams did not have things so easy. Once more the Communists reported widespread attacks by "bandits" and unsubdued Japanese forces. In late June a U.S. truce team finally managed to visit Communist-occupied Harbin, with the mission of inspecting Red forces there. After a gala banquet, the Communists refused the team's request to inspect the garrison. The Reds next announced there would be no truce teams from the Executive Headquarters permitted in their territory until an overall settlement in the civil war was reached.[18]

Incredibly, the American officers from the Executive Headquarters accepted this outrage without undue protest. Nationalist military leaders in Mukden were aghast. They had never had much confidence in Marshall's cease-fire teams, and now their suspicions were confirmed. When George Marshall assembled his unit, he reportedly sought out mature staff officers, mainly colonels too old to have seen combat in the war. The Nationalists scornfully referred to their Peking headquarters as "The House of Ten Thousand Sleeping Colonels." Their languor was due in no small part, I'd heard, to the frequent banquets they attended, usually hosted by their erstwhile Communist teammates.

Marshall's officers had been completely outmaneuvered in Manchuria. They petitioned the Communists for permission to travel north of the Sungari, but Lin Piao's generals held them at bay. Meanwhile the Communist army regrouped and was reequipped by Soviet advisers who turned over the remaining stocks of captured Japanese weapons and equipment. In effect, the Communists had consolidated their position quite efficiently, shortening their lines of communication to supply bases in north China and Siberia. When the Red Army staged its next offensive, it would be well supplied with artillery and ammunition. While this consolidation was under way, Mao Tse-tung traveled to Moscow to consult with Stalin and Molotov about the next phase of operations in Manchuria.[19]

As if to highlight the Soviet involvement in Manchuria, the Communist leader most closely associated with the Russians, Li Li-san, was the political adviser to General Lin Piao. Li had spent the war in the Soviet Union, preparing for the Soviet role in the inevitable civil war. I hosted a dinner for the Executive Headquarters attended by the senior military officers of the U.S., Nationalist, and Communist delegations. The junior officers and some civilian advisers ended up sitting in an anteroom, well separated from the rest of us. After the dinner, one of my interpreters took me aside, his manner unusually solemn.

The thin man who called himself Li Min-jen, the interpreter told me, "was no other than Li Li-san."

Apparently, Li had come to personally take the measure of the "sleeping colonels."

He wasn't disappointed. In southern Manchuria the cease-fire team was quick to cite the Nationalists for "violations" when government forces moved out of their fixed positions to pursue Communist guerrilla units. Nationalist frustration with the Americans was growing daily. Naturally, relations became strained, although my personal contacts with North East China Command remained cordial.

(I kept their trust in part by treating them as true colleagues, not Asian subordinates. To emphasize this, I jumped with their Airborne regiment stationed at the main military air base and was the only American to do so. I also took part in a couple of drinking contests with NECC officers. One KMT officer was carried half-conscious from a party muttering, "Major

Singlaub . . . Major Singlaub," after I'd somehow managed to better him downing the fiery local Kaoliang sorghum liquor.)

In Nanking and Peking, General Marshall was himself showing frustrated impatience. He had come to China fully confident that he would succeed, just as he had with all of his major assignments in World War II. And Marshall was known to have little tolerance for those who stood between him and success. "I am going to accomplish my mission and you are going to help me," Marshall angrily told General Al Wedemeyer, who had warned Marshall that Communist intransigence might jeopardize his mission.[20]

☆   ☆

OVER the following months, the Communists deftly manipulated both the political and military situation. They controlled the Manchurian heartland above the Sungari River and kept guerrilla pressure on the Nationalist garrisons in the south. When Executive Headquarters interference became blatant, the Nationalists finally reacted by restricting their movements. This further angered General Marshall. In the spring of 1947, he withdrew the last of the U.S. cease-fire teams from Manchuria, citing Nationalist interference—not Communist intrigue—as the reason.[21] (Marshall had become secretary of state in January 1947, and made no secret of his distaste for the Nationalist cause.)

The Communists reacted almost immediately with a massive offensive across the frozen Sungari River. One hundred thousand re-armed Red troops cut the road and rail link between Mukden and Changchun. Within weeks, the area was engulfed in massive, large-unit operations, with well-equipped Communist forces engaging the best Nationalist units. In the midst of this fighting, Major Bob Rigg managed to get himself captured again. This escapade caused an international incident that diverted attention from the fighting. Rigg and his assistant, Captain Rip Collins, were inspecting a Communist bridgehead south of the Sungari. When they reached the final Nationalist outpost, they were ordered not to proceed, but Rigg pushed on, as if he were back jousting in Chicago, not in the middle of a savage civil war. He and Collins were captured, taken to Harbin, and held for several weeks, where they were interrogated by none other than Li Li-san.[22]

☆   ☆

DURING Lin Piao's major conventional offensive from the redoubt north of the Sungari, his forces recaptured Ssupingchieh and the Nationalists were obliged to counterattack. This time the Communists did not withdraw. The fighting in the city was savage and prolonged, a street-to-street, sometimes room-to-room struggle, reminiscent of Stalingrad. The Nationalist New First Army led the attack and finally overran the Communists, inflicting heavy losses.

I visited the city at the end of the battle. While it had become popular in some American circles to discredit the Nationalists' fighting spirit and resolve, I saw firsthand just how disciplined and effective their attack had been. The rifle companies that had borne the brunt of the counterattack had suffered losses as high as fifty percent. I shared a victory meal of pickled carp and rice in the rubble with the survivors of a machine-gun squad whose leader had been killed on the last day of street fighting. It was hard to eat with the stench of death and burnt-out buildings so heavy. These young troops had been trained and equipped by American advisers in India eighteen months before. Now they had faced and passed their first major combat test. They were tired and bloodied, but their morale was obviously high. When I showed them my field map, they were eager to regroup and press the attack north of the Sungari.

In the barbed-wire POW compounds, it was the Communist troops who were shocked and dejected. I realized that the Nationalists stood a good chance of victory, if Chiang's generals used these crack units correctly, and if his American ally continued supporting the Nationalist cause. Tragically, however, Chiang did not follow up on this victory, and American disillusionment with the Nationalists was spreading.

The situation in the south grew worse. Communist forces were alternating their pressure between conventional attacks and guerrilla forays. By June 1947, it was clear the Nationalists were on the defensive throughout southern Manchuria.[23]

☆ ☆

MARY had come out to join me earlier that year, and as the situation deteriorated I began to seriously question the wisdom of having her here. She was teaching English at the university, and determined not to let the military situation interfere with the semblance of family life we were able to maintain in our compound. We were friends with Scott Miler, whose wife, Nell, was my secretary. One Sunday we took a picnic lunch out to the beautiful pine groves of the Tung Ling Tombs, the ancient burial site of a Manchu emperor. The only reason the forest was intact was that cutting one of the sacred trees carried the death penalty during the Japanese occupation. We were joined by General Tao Huang, a senior officer in the 52nd Army, which was guarding the Mukden sector. The General had been educated in the States and had absorbed our natural optimism. As we sat in the mottled shade of the pine grove, drinking beer and chatting about the future, General

Tao told us how eager he was to complete these operations, so he could return south to visit his young wife and children.

A few days later, the General's command post was overrun and he was captured. The Communists condemned him to death. The sentence was carried out in a typically sadistic manner. He was dragged to a platform before the assembled Red troops and skinned alive.

☆   ☆

GENERALISSIMO Chiang Kai-shek took the military situation seriously enough to fly into Mukden. He understood that the loss of Manchuria would be catastrophic. But Chiang was never one to delegate authority well, which was probably his greatest fault. In an operational theater, he normally made the right decisions and, in fact, rallied his troops well to break up the Communists' spring offensive. But he did not leave behind effective military leadership in Mukden. As elsewhere in China, the Nationalist command was fractured along political and military lines. The North East China Command conducted purely military operations. But the parallel President's Headquarters in Mukden held overall responsibility for Nationalist policy. The Communists avoided this bifurcated system by melding political and military authority in all their field commanders. Eventually, the Nationalists adopted this pattern. It wasn't until September 1947, however, that General Chen Cheng, who had Chiang's full confidence, took over the President's Headquarters. By that time, the Communists had regained the initiative.

☆   ☆

ANTUNG was a strategic city on the Yalu River, the border between Manchuria and Soviet-occupied North Korea. The government had taken it in late 1946, despite a show of force by the Soviet army, massed across the Yalu bridge. My unit was now officially part of the newly formed Central Intelligence Group, which had taken over from the SSU. I had been promoted to major and my staff had grown considerably with the addition of several civilian intelligence officers. John Chrislaw was one of them, a resourceful, energetic young man who worked hard and kept a low profile, as befits the profession. I named him to open the small station in Antung.

The Koreans represented an unknown factor in the Manchurian equation. Their country had been colonized by the Japanese for decades, and many had suffered during the long Japanese occupation of Manchuria. Most of those we encountered distrusted the Soviets' motives in their country, but were nevertheless eager to return home. They represented a promising group of potential agents. A Korean named Kim Hong Il, who was a major general in the Chinese Nationalist Army, gave us entrée into the Korean community in Manchuria.

With his help we contacted a number of bright, patriotic young Koreans willing to accept some hazardous assignments if it would benefit their country. My officer Scott Miler groomed them in tradecraft and brought them down to Antung to build their cover stories before insertion into Soviet-occupied Korea. He encouraged them to enter the military and civil government and to advance as quickly as possible. Their reporting channels would be through dead-letter drops to be established at a later time, once we had a better network support system inside Korea. In an emergency, they could move south across the 38th-parallel truce line into the American zone, where we would receive them at safe houses in Seoul.

The only problem with this system was that I hadn't been able to establish the safe houses. My initial request to Far East Command in Tokyo to do this was rebuffed. General Douglas MacArthur, the American viceroy in that part of Asia, despised the OSS and its various successor agencies, including the CIA. He had never allowed OSS operations in the Pacific theater during the war. This animosity stemmed from the jealousy he had long harbored for General Bill Donovan, who had come out of the First World War more highly decorated than MacArthur. Major General Charles Willoughby, MacArthur's intelligence chief, shared his master's distaste for our organization. And when "Sir Charles," as he was disparagingly known in the Agency, showed his contempt, you felt it.

So the only way I could set up safe houses in Seoul was by subterfuge. Drawing on lessons hard-earned with the Jedburghs, I dispatched a young officer named Tom McAnn to Seoul "on leave," with enough money to secure safe houses and a trustworthy agent staff to monitor them.

While these operations were under way, I often flew down to Antung in an L-5 to check their progress. It was always an interesting trip. The approach to the racecourse we used as an airstrip took us to the middle of the Yalu, near the steel-trestle bridge connecting China and Korea. On several occasions, as we were setting up for final approach, our little plane would be violently buffeted by Soviet P-39 fighters that buzzed us, sometimes only inches from our wingtips. The Russians didn't like our being there.

I once complained of this to a Soviet "railway" captain, noting that America had given the P-39s to the Soviets in the first place during the war.

The man was adamant. "*Nyet, nyet,*" he insisted, these planes were a product of "Soviet science." This same officer believed that the Studebaker nameplates on his unit's deuce-and-a-half trucks denoted a famous Soviet engineer of Baltic-German extraction. The prowess of Soviet science was almost an article of religious dogma among the Russians in Manchuria. One local NKVD boaster named Chicherin would bore us for hours in hotel bars,

claiming the Russians had invented everything from penicillin to prophy-
lactics, not to mention the radio and the steam engine. My officers joked
that anyone using a Russian prophylactic would damn well end up needing
penicillin.[24]

☆   ☆

DURING the fall of 1947, the combined military and political situations continued to deteriorate. The almost nonstop seesaw battles had bled both
armies horribly. But whereas the Nationalists were throwing their best units
piecemeal into Manchuria in a last-ditch effort to push back the Communists,
the Reds often resorted to human-wave attacks with massed, lightly armed
infantry. These attacks were usually in conjunction with well-coordinated
assaults on government rail lines and isolated garrisons by crack Communist
units. The net result was a steady hemorrhage of Nationalist resources.

With Marshall now secretary of state, his personal animosity toward
Chiang Kai-shek and his frustration with the situation in China combined
to sour the Truman administration on the Nationalist cause. I began to
receive increasingly alarmed reports from North East China Command about
a steady decrease in U.S. supplies and replacement equipment. As the
record-cold winter of 1947–1948 slowly moved toward a bleak spring, I
sensed a palpable decay of Nationalist morale. Twenty enemy divisions were
operating between Changchun and the coast, striking government positions
with impunity. Many of these Communist troops were supplied with brand-
new Soviet equipment and munitions, including field artillery with calibers
unique to the Soviet army. But when the Nationalist government complained
of this blatant foreign aggression in the United Nations, its American *ally*
was hesitant to back the claim.[25]

In Mukden, the population was again swollen with refugees, and the food
and fuel situations were perilous. Tragically, the splintered Nationalist po-
litical-military command could not agree on a practical rationing system.
The Communists were quick to exploit this situation with propaganda teams
who promised fair food distribution as soon as the city was "liberated."

☆   ☆

ELSEWHERE in China, Mao's armies probed and feinted, keeping Chiang's
high command off-guard. But it was obvious that Manchuria was the crucial
theater of operations. Chiang visited Mukden on several occasions to rally
his troops' flagging morale. But his charismatic leadership was no longer
sufficient to carry the day. He assigned his best field commander, General
Wei Li-huang, as overall commander of all Nationalist operations in Man-

churia. "One Hundred Victory" Wei, as the general was known from his brilliant record against the Japanese, was decisive. He arrested several corrupt division commanders, promoted brave and effective young colonels to command entire corps, and withdrew several badly exposed divisions to better defense positions. Wei then launched a series of sharp counterattacks that temporarily upset the Communist juggernaut.

But he quickly discovered how desperate the Nationalist supply situation was. Although the Nationalists had most of their air force in Manchuria, the American-supplied P-51 fighters were short of fuel, spare parts, and ordnance. Government artillery forces were in even worse straits. One rainy afternoon that spring, General Wei called me to his home to discuss this matter. His beautiful young wife, a graduate of the University of Hawaii, acted as interpreter, a situation I found strange until I learned the nature of our discussion.

"Major," he said, coming right to the point, as was his manner, "we know you have a direct line into the White House in Washington."

I swallowed hard. The Nationalists apparently knew my radio reports were sent directly to EDS-44 HQ in Shanghai and sometimes tagged directly for Washington, but always bypassing the embassy in Nanking. But I didn't want to acknowledge this, so I answered with a noncommittal, "Please continue, sir."

General Wei smiled briefly. "We do not trust your embassy," he said. "I have a very sensitive matter to raise directly with your president."

I'd been in Asia long enough not to show my hand in this kind of poker game. Wei wanted to use my communications to Washington to avoid his normal chain of command. "Please continue, sir."

"On the island of Okinawa," Wei said, tapping a map on his desk, "there is a very large American supply depot. It contains matériel from your many Pacific operations during the Japanese war." He put on a pair of frameless glasses and consulted a notebook. "There are wing tanks for our aircraft, shells for our light and medium artillery, ammunition for our small arms . . . batteries for our radios . . . repair parts for our vehicles." He raised his glasses and sighed. "I think you understand, Major."

"Yes, sir. I do."

Wei reminded me that the U.S. Congress had appropriated a grant of 125 million dollars for emergency military aid to the Nationalists. But Secretary of State George Marshall was blocking that aid. "If my troops do not receive ammunition soon," he stated flatly, "we will be defeated here in two months." He looked at his map once more. "If we are defeated here, all of China is lost."

General Wei rose from his desk and stood close beside me. His wife approached my other shoulder. When he spoke again, his voice was a strained whisper. "You have my permission to visit *any* of my units, day or night, unannounced. Go where you will. You are a soldier, use your own eyes. All I ask, is you report what you see directly to President Truman."

For the next three days I did just as he requested, visiting the army units defending Mukden and the principal railheads and army supply depots. Every outfit I inspected was short on small arms and especially U.S.-caliber artillery ammunition. Their troops were half-starved. I returned to Mukden and sent my report, Eyes Only Moscrip, For The President. I requested no lateral dissemination of the message in China.

Within days, I received word that President Truman had been briefed, that he was "concerned" about the situation. But the urgently requested supplies never arrived.

☆   ☆

In August 1948, the Communists began shelling Mukden nightly. Mary was six months pregnant and couldn't sleep through the barrages. I flew her out to Shanghai, where she boarded a Navy transport for California. This time when we said goodbye, Mary had more than a vague sense of the dangers I faced in the war zone. And she knew I intended to stay in Mukden as long as possible before evacuating. But I did not intend to be captured. The Reds knew my real job there. The brutal murder of General Tao was on both our minds.

"Well," she said, looking over the ship rail at the bustling Shanghai docks, "we could have been living in that chicken coop in Alabama."

☆   ☆

By October the situation had become desperate. Now the Communist gunners who had dragged their artillery units forward each night to shell Mukden no longer bothered to retreat with daylight. The government air force and artillery did not have the munitions to challenge them. The siege ring tightened around the city. There was widespread panic and terrible scenes as civilian mobs swarmed the airfield seeking flights out of the isolated city. In the outer defenses far to the south, some government units simply succumbed to low morale and surrendered en masse to the enemy, hoping for clemency. Ever practical, the Communists turned these troops against their former comrades.

I evacuated my entire staff, and gave evacuation orders to the few American officers I had in other provincial cities. John Chrislaw escaped from the south, clinging to the underside of a flatcar. But his cook and houseboy weren't so lucky. When the People's Liberation Army took Antung, the Reds butchered the innocent servants.[26]

In Mukden, the best Nationalist units held the perimeter. I'd often see truck convoys from the crack units careening through the city, speeding from the southern front to the northern lines to prevent a Communist break-through. These soldiers had been abandoned by their superiors in Nanking and by their American supporters, but they still fought on bravely. We all realized, however, that the city was about to fall.

Angus Ward, the consul general who replaced Ed Clubb, was a different kind of Foreign Service officer altogether. He courageously volunteered to remain in Mukden after the inevitable Communist occupation. Ward had served in Tehran and spoke good Russian. His wife, a burly Finn named Irmgarde, was disdainful of all Communists, whatever their ethnic back-ground. Ward shared her politics. One dreary morning, when the geese were again honking their way south to central China amid sporadic Communist barrages, I trekked across the empty boulevard to Ward's office. I had been burning Secret documents all morning in oil drums in the weed-strewn com-pound garden. I had evacuated my primary radio transceiver, retaining only my small emergency radio transmitter and one codebook. I needed to use the consulate radio to arrange my evacuation.

In Ward's stuffy little code room, I composed my final message from Mukden, which I addressed Eyes Only to Admiral Oscar Badger, the Amer-ican naval commander in Tsingtao: "MUKDEN SITUATION PRECARIOUS. I CON-SIDER IT IMPERATIVE I NOT BE CAPTURED. REQUEST IMMEDIATE RESPONSE MYTEL OF 9/10/48. SINGLAUB."

Three days before, I'd asked for two air evacuation flights. Yesterday's flight removed the last of my people and other priority passengers, many of whom worked for the American consul general. I remained the extra day to activate some stay-behind agents and to turn over to Angus Ward some assets he might find useful in the weeks ahead. On this particular day, I learned through consular communications that the U.S. Air Force plane scheduled to pick me up had refused to fly into the Mukden airport, because it was now under long-range Communist artillery fire.

Two hours later, Admiral Badger replied. The crew of a C-46 from the First Marine Air Wing had volunteered to land at Mukden that afternoon. It was my ticket out of the city. If I missed it, there would be no other.

I cleaned and loaded my .45 automatic and my carbine, checked the office once more for stray classified documents, then put the leash on my cocker spaniel, Blackie. He loved to ride in the jeep, but would often jump out, so the leash was a precaution, considering we would transit the pathetic starvation zones of the refugee camps on the way to the airport. Blackie was not pleased with the midday shelling. He cowered at my feet, and I had to push his head aside with my boots to shift gears.

There were no more refugees crowding the shell-pocked airport terminal, because the field was under combined infantry and artillery attack. I parked my jeep near the Nationalists' command bunker and was met by an amazingly cheerful young lieutenant colonel friend who commanded a battalion of horse-drawn Japanese artillery. In the previous year, during less hectic times, he and I had ridden his fine horses just for the exercise and recreation. He was a graduate of an artillery officers course at Fort Sill, Oklahoma, and we frequently exercised the infantry versus artillery rivalry about which was the real combat arm. He was amused by the fact that the infantry man was withdrawing from the field of battle which was being defended by the field artillery. His troops had saved back a supply of 150mm ammunition so they wouldn't be overrun without a fight. I told him an American transport was about to land and asked him to instruct his soldiers not to shoot at it. I also suggested that some counter-battery fire against the Red artillery would be helpful while I was loading and taking off.

Before I left, the Colonel gave me a packet of important personal papers, including his farewell letter to his children, which he politely asked me to send to his family in the South. I gave him my jeep.

The C-46 dropped out of the sky with alarming speed. Because the north end of the runway was obscured by shellfire, the pilot had landed downwind. I grabbed Blackie and ran to the edge of the tarmac. The battered old transport roared toward me, spun on one engine in a cloud of yellow dust, and stopped. We were inside in seconds and the plane was rolling again straight down the runway. I didn't think we had enough room to take off, but at the last second the pilot hauled back and we cleared the old Japanese hangars by at least a foot.

As we clawed for altitude over the government-held sections of the city, a few halfhearted tracers looped toward us. We spiraled up tightly, trying to stay within Nationalist lines until we had enough altitude. Finally, we were above the effective range of small arms, and headed south. Behind us, the Mukden airfield was now half hidden by the dust and smoke of exploding artillery. But out ahead I saw a Soviet transport plane circling low on a reconnaissance flight for the Communists. The plane's Red Star insignia were vivid in the autumn twilight.

I leaned against the oily window, Blackie panting at my knee. It was finished. This war was lost.

"Over to you, Ivan," was all I said. Blackie didn't understand my words.

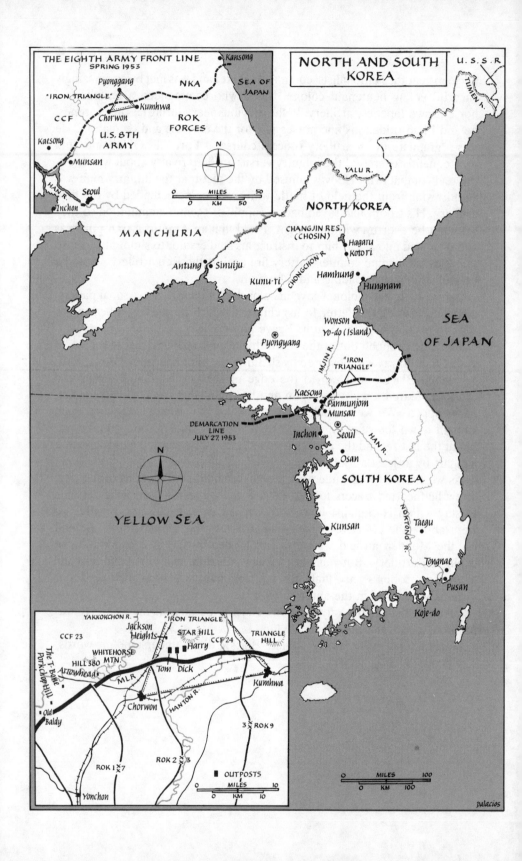

NORTH AND SOUTH KOREA

THE EIGHTH ARMY FRONT LINE
SPRING 1953

Pyonggang

"IRON TRIANGLE"

Kumhwa

Chorwon

NKA

SEA OF JAPAN

CCF

U.S. 8TH ARMY

ROK FORCES

Kaesong

Munsan

N

0   MILES   50

0   KM   50

Seoul

Inchon

HAN R.

Kansong

U.S.S.R.

TUMEN R.

YALU R.

NORTH KOREA

MANCHURIA

CHANGJIN RES.
(CHOSIN)

Hagaru

Kotori

Antung

Sinuiju

Kunu-ri

CHONGCHON R.

Hamhung

Hungnam

SEA OF JAPAN

Wonson

Yo-do (Island)

Pyongyang

IMJIN R.

"IRON TRIANGLE"

Kaesong

Panmunjom

Munsan

DEMARCATION LINE
JULY 27, 1953

Inchon

Seoul

HAN R.

N

Osan

SOUTH KOREA

YELLOW SEA

Kunsan

NOKTONG R.

Taegu

Tongnae

Pusan

Koje-do

YAKKOKCHON R.

"IRON TRIANGLE"

CCF 23

Jackson Heights

STAR HILL

CCF 24

TRIANGLE HILL

The T-Bone

Porkchop Hill

WHITEHORSE MTN.

HILL 380

Arrowhead

MLR

Tom

Harry

Dick

HAN TON R.

Kumhwa

Old Baldy

Chorwon

3 × ROK 9

ROK 1 × 7

ROK 2 × 3

OUTPOSTS

MILES

0   MILES   10

0   KM   10

Yonchon

0   MILES   100

0   KM   100

palacios

CHAPTER FIVE

CIA and U.S. Army, China and Korea

1948–1952

☆ ☆

I WAS IN Tientsin, trying to reassemble my station personnel, when Mukden finally fell. The confirmation came late in the day, and we soon received a report that Nationalist bombers were attacking Communist forces in the city. It wasn't hard to picture what conditions must have been like, Mukden being swollen with hungry refugees. I remember going outside the American military compound that cold November afternoon to stare at the flaring sunset over the brown inland plains. There was the familiar smell of northern China in the air—coal smoke, horse dung, dust. Geese were honking south again across the coastal marshes. Anonymous clots of refugees in padded tan coats squatted around straw cook fires in nearby fields. The trudging files of troops along the roads looked either very young or very old.

I knew the situation was grave. With Nationalist forces defeated in Manchuria, Mao Tse-tung now had almost a million combat-tested troops free to attack down the narrow coastal invasion route from the north. And Chiang Kai-shek did not really have much to oppose them. He'd squandered his best forces piecemeal in Manchuria. As a military leader he had been guilty of several cardinal sins: He had underestimated his enemy's resources and abilities, and he had overestimated the resolve of his ally, America.

A few days later, I received a call at the compound from the wife of General Wei Li-huang. She and General Wei had gotten out of Mukden just before me. The General, she said, had urgent business to discuss. Could I be in front of the government telegraph office at three that afternoon? It was an odd request. Normally, I would have driven my jeep to the General's headquarters for an appointment. But these were not normal times. The ramifications of the Manchurian debacle were now being felt. The Nationalist government's elite "New" armies, the cream of their American-trained and -equipped forces, had been destroyed. And relations between Generalissimo Chiang Kai-shek and the American government—particularly with Secretary of State George Marshall—were at a low ebb. For the first time, the Kuomintang had to face the specter of defeat, not just in the northeast, but throughout the vast country. It would not be long before scapegoats wearing generals' stars would be offered up in sacrifice.

I wore a plain GI overcoat devoid of rank or unit patch to my street-corner rendezvous, hoping to blend in with the rear-echelon American Marines still in Tientsin. At exactly three, a Chevrolet sedan with dark curtains on the rear windows slid to a stop and the door opened. Madame Wei was there, stylish as ever. General "One Hundred Victory" Wei sat beside her in a dress uniform, replete with decorations. As I sat down between them, General Wei pulled the side curtains more tightly shut and issued a curt order to his driver.

The chauffeurs of Chinese generals often negotiated crowded streets at full speed, with a blaring horn. But the General's driver proceeded with unusual caution, past the teeming railway market streets, out along the airport road toward the junction of the main route to Peking. I couldn't see much, and the KMT military police along the route certainly couldn't see me. Finally, we pulled onto a dusty farm road and through the gates of a mud-walled compound. The establishment appeared to have been the home of a once prosperous minor landlord; there were the usual granaries, stables, and a large, tile-roofed kitchen. But, judging from the tangles of field telephone wires and radio antennas, the buildings had been taken over by a military headquarters, probably that of at least a corps commander.

We were ushered into the largest room, in which folding tables and map boards had replaced the traditional sleeping mats. A rugged, middle-aged officer with smooth Han features and close-cropped iron-gray hair rose to meet us. He wore a simple military tunic adorned only with the collar tabs of a full general. It was Fu Tso-yi, a legendary Nationalist commander in northern China, a former warlord who had thrown in his lot with Chiang even before the Japanese invasion in the 1930s. General Fu was known to have a huge and loyal following in the mountains of Shanhsi and Ninghsia provinces, the region the Nationalists called the Twelfth War Area. He had come to this isolated headquarters of a subordinate without his usual entourage of staff.

The General greeted us and called for tea. In deference to his American guest, however, his servant also offered a rusty tin of rather petrified powdered coffee, probably a relic of the war. I chose tea. Being a trained intelligence officer, I couldn't help observing that General Fu's situation maps were not draped for my visit. A quick glance showed the disposition of at least six army corps stretching from the coast to positions along the Great Wall in the mountains northwest of Peking. These troops, I knew, had been engaged against Communist guerrilla forces, but had so far avoided the huge meat-grinder battles that had decimated the armies in Manchuria. I was beginning to understand why I had been summoned here.

As in the past, Madame Wei translated smoothly, her English flawless, without a trace of accent. Her husband stood beside her, but seldom spoke in deference to his senior colleague. General Fu walked stiffly to his maps. One of his legs was badly arthritic, a legacy of a lifetime of war and wounds.

"General Wei's surviving forces are regrouping inside my lines, here." He indicated several garrisons along the coast between Chinchou and Tientsin. "More troops have escaped than your newspapers report," the old general added wryly.

I nodded agreement. My intelligence reports indicated whole battalions had escaped from Manchuria through the ineffective Communist encirclement.

"But these forces," General Fu continued, "have not retained all of their American equipment and weapons."

Again, I nodded. The stragglers coming out of Manchuria had abandoned their vehicles, heavy automatic weapons, and artillery. Their vehicles had run out of fuel, and the artillery was worthless without ammunition.

"My own forces," Fu said, turning back to the map, "were never as well equipped as General Wei's." He smiled bleakly, a classic Chinese gesture, the neutral acceptance of impersonal fate. "We relied on Japanese weapons after the surrender. And, of course, we have seized some Soviet equipment from the Reds."

Now General Wei spoke his piece. Between the two commanders, he said, there were at least 400,000 veteran soldiers in the region. They were in garrisons and assembly areas astride the only practical invasion route from Manchuria. Wei went to the map and swept his two open hands back and forth along the coast. "As you know, this area controls the marching route into and from the northeast."

General Fu returned to his desk. "We understand your government's feelings about the Kuomintang," he said bluntly. "President Truman and General Marshall distrust Chiang."

I was about to add the traditional denial usually expected in such discussions, but I realized they were being remarkably blunt by Oriental standards. "Please continue," was all I said.

General Fu noted that Wei Li-huang had briefed him in detail about the

huge supply dumps of surplus American munitions and equipment on Okinawa. "With some of these supplies," he said flatly, "General Wei and I
can equip five field armies. We have the men, but we do not have enough
guns, trucks, and ammunition." He nodded for me and Wei to sit beside
his desk, a subtle conspiratorial gesture.

Wei concisely outlined their plans. They hoped to create a "Third Force,"
a democratic, anti-Communist option to Chiang's Nationalists. This force,
he said, would form an impenetrable buffer between the Communist armies
in Manchuria and the KMT forces in the south. They would hold the old
capital of Peking, the city of Tientsin, and the port of Taku. With their field
armies supplied with modern American equipment, neither the Nationalists
nor the Communists could dislodge them. Wei asked me if America's goal
in China was still to establish an effective cease-fire in the civil war and to
somehow hammer out a coalition government, including the Reds and the
KMT.

As far as I knew, this was still the goal of U.S. policy.

"We trust you will inform your government of our offer," General Fu
said, rising painfully on his bad leg to say goodbye.

"Yes, sir," I answered, shaking his hand. "I will transmit your message."

By noon the next day I was aboard Admiral Oscar Badger's command
ship in Tsingtao harbor. Badger was excited by the prospect of a viable third
force in China. He got quick confirmation from MacArthur's Far East Command (FECOM) that the mountain of supplies on Okinawa could be readily
transported to northeast China. Badger's secure communications room
transmitted my Top Secret cable to CIA headquarters in Washington. I had
done all I could to help Generals Fu and Wei.[1] From my discussions with
Admiral Badger, I believed their offer represented the only viable option
to preventing a complete Communist victory in China. Clearly, America's
lack of confidence in Chiang after the Manchurian defeat augured poorly
for our support of his government in the inevitable battles to be fought in
the south. If General Fu's armies could physically separate the two forces,
a partition of China between the three political elements might be possible.
It was a desperate alternative. But no one could deny these were desperate
times.

☆   ☆

My own orders home arrived soon after the clandestine meeting. Just
after New Year's, 1949, I was debriefed at CIA headquarters in the old
OSS compound on 25th and E streets. Although the rooms were familiar, the images of that fresh-faced young paratroop lieutenant who had
marched down these same halls six years before to face his interview with

General Donovan seemed far removed, like a faded daguerreotype from the Civil War. I'd seen too much betrayal and intrigue, too many mass graves and shell-blasted, smoldering ruins, to ever again view my profession as a straightforward test of courage and dedication. Without question, soldiers still needed these attributes. But I'd learned in the "postwar" world that they weren't sufficient. An officer in my line of work had to combine a certain degree of animal cunning with the traditional military virtues.

As I had feared, General Fu's audacious solution to the China impasse was rejected out of hand by the U.S. government. In fact, I was told, my cable had "sent the State Department into shock." That was the second time in a few weeks I had achieved that dubious distinction.

The first was in early November when I'd cabled from Tsingtao suggesting America send a relief flight to Mukden to reestablish communications with our beleaguered consulate staff under Angus Ward, whom the Communists had placed under house arrest. Ward was a brave and dedicated Foreign Service officer who had experienced communism firsthand when he had served as a political officer under Ambassador William C. Bullitt in Moscow before World War II. Since arriving in Mukden he had often locked horns with his superiors in Nanking and Washington. While they had maintained the naive "agrarian reformer" character of the Chinese Communists, Ward had consistently reported that the Reds were ruthlessly totalitarian in their Manchurian operations. Recalled for consultations in Washington, Ward told me he had confronted an "Alice in Wonderland" situation, in which senior State Department officials consistently *told him* what the situation was in Manchuria, rather than listen to his firsthand reports. The only person who gave him a fair hearing, he said, was Secretary of Defense James Forrestal.

Now Ward, his small staff, and their families were being held at gunpoint in several buildings in Mukden, incommunicado after Red troops had confiscated his consulate radio. I had proposed dispatching an unarmed American transport plane (with a fighter escort) to Mukden ostensibly to "repair" the consulate's radio equipment. Given the unsettled situation, I had added, a squad of Marine guards would be an appropriate addition to the consulate staff. I knew from my own experience that the Red Chinese at that point had no sophisticated anti-aircraft weapons and appeared reluctant to murder U.S. officials in broad daylight. Such a show of force, I'd argued, would let the Reds know we planned to insist on a minimum level of civilized behavior in their areas of occupation.

Unfortunately, such "aggressive" actions were anathema to the striped-pants set surrounding Secretary Marshall. Ward and his people languished under cruel conditions for many months after the capture of Mukden, and were only expelled after the State Department kowtowed to Mao. I had learned from several years in Asia that a clear demonstration of force by a powerful entity—be it a military unit or an entire country—was often a necessary counterpart to traditional diplomacy. But Washington was not interested in the opinion of Army majors or dedicated officers like Angus Ward.

I was assigned as the Agency's China desk officer that spring of 1949. From this interesting vantage point, I witnessed the total collapse of the Nationalist forces in the south, their withdrawal down the coast, and the evacuation to Taiwan. Mao Tse-tung had won the civil war. The world's most populous country was now controlled by a ruthless Communist government.

From the perspective of the recently created CIA, this disaster was especially troubling. The Agency had evolved from the wartime OSS and its immediate postwar successors. The China/Burma/India theater of operations had made extensive use of the OSS during the war, but General Douglas MacArthur had rejected General Donovan's every attempt to establish an OSS presence in the Pacific theater. MacArthur's FECOM, based in the Dai Ichi building in Tokyo, was more an imperial court than the headquarters of a military occupation force.

With the defeat of Chiang, the CIA's China stations had been rolled up. The logical course of action would have been to regroup our assets in Japan and to base our Far East operations from this secure rear area. And I can attest that this was exactly what Admiral Roscoe Hillenkoetter, the CIA director, intended. After all, under the National Defense Act of 1947, the Director of Central Intelligence (DCI) was responsible for coordinating *all* intelligence from around the world and presenting it to the President and his cabinet. With China now under Red control, and the Soviet Union fomenting and supporting "anti-imperialist" struggles throughout Asia, Hillenkoetter could hardly be expected to supply serious intelligence on Communist intentions without an adequate Asian base.

But General of the Army Douglas MacArthur rejected with typically disdainful hauteur the DCI's request to reestablish its Asian headquarters in Japan. Hillenkoetter was only a rear admiral, a pay grade that MacArthur viewed as just slightly higher than the MP sergeants in polished helmets he stationed throughout the Dai Ichi building day and night as a kind of centurion guard. MacArthur informed Truman that FECOM's own organic intelligence organization under his trusted aide, Major General Charles Willoughby, was more than sufficient to meet America's requirements. He considered the Agency's officers rank amateurs in Asia and let it be known that he and Willoughby combined decades of Far East experience. Any political or military intelligence President Truman might need, they could supply. It is interesting to note that MacArthur's stature was elevated so far beyond that of a normal general that he was able to prevail on this vital matter without encountering serious opposition in Washington.[2]

While these matters were being settled in Tokyo and Washington, I was involved in the more pedestrian daily operations of intelligence. The official American policy in China was for our diplomatic and even some of our military offices to hunker down and remain open, as the Nationalist collapse spread south and the Red forces took over cities such as Peking and Shanghai. The Agency, however, was less naively sanguine than the State Department (or the U.S. Army, for that matter). The main CIA station in Shanghai was disbanded and the regular personnel—American, Chinese, and "third country"—evacuated.

But there were some exceptions. The need for so-called stay-behind agents was vital. Once the Communists had overrun the country, it would not be long before our diplomatic missions were completely neutralized. And my section was predicting that Mao's government would unleash a complete clampdown on foreign contacts. Therefore, one of the final acts of the Shanghai station was to recruit what it hoped were reliable agents among Chinese and resident Europeans, including those White Russians stranded there. In the process of this recruitment, however, an especially troubling case was revealed.

While station chief in Mukden, one of my civilian staff had been a young former OSS enlisted man named Hugh Redmond. He was a likable guy, but not terribly effective. I'd put him to work as a positive intelligence case officer, attempting to recruit Mongolian agent networks. But his language skills and general tradecraft were below average. He returned to other duties at the Shanghai station. When I was there just before the fall of China, I learned Hugh had married a White Russian girl and planned to remain in Shanghai, documented as a European businessman, and planned to serve as a stay-behind agent. I immediately went to Barney Fielden, the head of counterespionage, and expressed the view that Hugh was far too well known in Manchuria to survive very long as a stay-behind agent. As often happens in compartmentalized intelligence matters, I was thanked for my information, but not told how it would be used.

In May, I learned that Hugh and his wife had been arrested almost immediately after the Communists took Shanghai. Theirs was one of the first Communist show trials of foreigners. They both received life prison sentences. To me, this was tantamount to a slaughter of innocents. The Agency had simply underestimated the sophistication of the Communist counterespionage capabilities. "Big-nose" foreigners, be they American or European, were too visible in China to escape close scrutiny. It was the height of folly to believe an amiable young amateur like Hugh Redmond, no matter how dedicated, could function well against a ruthless totalitarian foe that relied heavily on clandestine intelligence and operations.[3]

Equally naive was the U.S. Army's attempt to retain its language school in Peking after the Reds occupied the city. The school was commanded by Colonel Morris E. DePasse, an independent-minded officer who felt confident his long experience in China prepared him for dealing with the Communists. His administrative officer was Captain Homer B. Hinckley, an enormous guy, well over six foot three and weighing around 250 pounds. He was one of the most visible Americans in Peking. I'd had many dealings with Homer during my time in Manchuria. Whenever I needed American Army supplies, such as uniforms or rations, Homer would bypass the red tape and fill my request, making sure the load reached Mukden on the next flight. His connection to my station in Manchuria was no doubt observed by Red intelligence agents. He and the entire school staff were expelled in the spring of 1949.

This pattern was repeated not only with American government and business operations in China, but also with most journalists and other foreign commercial and diplomatic establishments. Mao was sealing China off from foreign observation, even the relatively benign perspective of legitimate business people. The reason for this crackdown became obvious that spring. For almost thirty years, the Chinese Communists had been unable to win what later became known as the "hearts and minds" of the Chinese people, even among the most benighted peasants. When they parlayed their Manchurian military success into an overall victory, the Communists set about systematically to *reeducate* hundreds of millions of their new subjects.

Their chief weapon in this campaign was terror. Even in the smallest village, a cadre of leaders dominated by Communists oversaw the cleansing of the population. The Party's principal enemies were the "landlords," often only peasants who had husbanded family income for generations to buy a small plot of land. Throughout the spring and summer of 1949, and on into the following years, millions of these *exploiters* were murdered in public executions that, for sheer magnitude, rivaled the genocides of the Nazis and Stalin's Soviet Communists.[4] This was the agrarian reform many American diplomats had hailed as such a progressive force.

That spring in Peking, I learned, another trial of foreign spies had taken place, during which a particularly dastardly "German-American" major identified only as Hseng Lo-pu was condemned to death in absentia. *New York Times* reporter Hank Lieberman, who attended the trial, obligingly informed the world that this person was "undoubtedly" U.S. Army Major John K. Singlaub.

☆   ☆

THAT summer I was assigned back to the Regular Army. I could have stayed with the Agency, but I'd already been away from normal postwar Army assignments for almost four years.[5] And, from what I saw of thwarted "Company" operations in the Far East, I could do more for my country as an infantry officer. The Army obviously thought so as well. I was ordered to attend the Advanced Course of the Infantry School at Fort Benning, Georgia, a kind of graduate course for potential battalion commanders. This is one of the mandatory courses every career officer had to take as a normal activity in the profession of arms. Even though going back to the sweltering classrooms of a southern Army base was anticlimactic after my unusual duties and intrigues in Manchuria, I realized the assignment augured well for my advancement in the Army.

By a strange quirk of fate, one of the first guys I ran into at the Infantry School was none other than the friendly giant, Homer Hinckley, now a major fresh back from Peking. As the course progressed I got a chance to repay Homer's kindness. He had kept us supplied with long johns and space-heater wicks in the numbing Manchurian winters. I labored for hours after classes at night and early in the morning to teach him the fundamentals of map reading. The ability to take advantage of terrain, to move troops safely, avoiding ambush and artillery barrage, was an absolutely basic skill of an infantry officer. This was something every second lieutenant had to learn before he took over a platoon. Somehow, Homer never had. And he wouldn't graduate from the Infantry School until he could master the complexities of contour lines, compass azimuths and variations, and generally use an Army topographic map with the efficiency of a first-class Boy Scout.

It wasn't easy, but, with help from me and other combat infantry veterans, Homer managed.

Most of the officers in the course had seen combat in World War II, and several had been seriously wounded. I became close to three or four men with whom I later served in different parts of the world. Major Harvey Short, for example, was West Point, 1943. He had almost been killed by Japanese artillery in the bitter fighting on Okinawa in 1945. I often saw him gazing with an expression of slightly bemused impatience as the eager young instructors went from blackboard to sand table, proclaiming how a "standard" battalion assault against fortified positions evolved like clockwork from the opening artillery barrage to the final evacuation of wounded. On the bloody ridges of Okinawa, American battalions had hardly "maneuvered," and the Japanese defense was slightly more than *standard*. Combat in those muddy foxholes and shell craters had more in common with Neanderthal warfare than the classrooms of Fort Benning.

But still we listened attentively, asked the proper questions, took notes, and sweated out our exams. Our future as officers depended on good performance here because there was no real war to otherwise test our mettle.

Not that there wasn't fighting in the world. The Greek civil war was still going strong, and the French army was up to its neck in the mud of Indochina. But the advent of nuclear weapons had brought about a tense stalemate between the world's two major military powers, the United States and the Soviet Union.

In Europe, the allies of World War II now faced each other across the tense 400-mile Armistice Line separating their occupation zones, the line Winston Churchill had christened the Iron Curtain. If, or more likely *when,* the balloon went up in Europe, my classmates and I might well command battalions in "standard" infantry battles.

But I couldn't forget what I had seen in Manchuria. The Chinese Communists simply did not employ conventional tactics. They had defeated Chiang's armies by a war of mobility, involving relatively lightly armed small units that foraged for rations, carried their own ammunition and mortars on their backs, and relied on sturdy battalions of peasant porters and ox carts to move their heavier supplies. The Red Chinese had evaded Nationalist air force interdiction by perfecting night movement and attack. They made skillful use of deception tactics and psychological warfare to confuse their enemy. In effect, the Chinese Red Army was a hybrid combination of guerrilla forces and conventional light infantry. What made this combination so devastating was the sheer number of troops.

What we were being taught that winter at Fort Benning might well do some good fighting the Russians. But I couldn't help wonder how these tactics—which were basically what the United States had drilled into Chiang Kai-shek's best "New Armies"—would stand up in a war against Mao Tse-tung.

Another aspect of the U.S. Army's conventional organization that I found troubling was racial segregation. Negro units, as they were then known, made up a fair percentage of the Army. During the war, black support troops, including the resourceful truckers of the Red Ball Express in the ETO, had been vital to the Allied victory. But there had been relatively few black combat units. Many black soldiers elected to stay in the Army after the war, seeing the armed forces as a means of advancement. But with an official policy of racial segregation, the career opportunities for a black officer or NCO were truncated. A kind of sealed, dead-end mentality often took hold among them, by which they maintained a wary truce with their white counterparts, and often with their white officers. Because of the stigma of segregation, their loyalties sometimes followed racial lines, not the traditional chain of command.

As if this was not bad enough from a human perspective, segregation was downright impractical and terribly wasteful of limited resources. For example, every base with Negro units had to maintain "separate-but-equal" (hardly the latter) facilities such as barracks, mess halls, latrines, hospital wards, service clubs, and so on. From an operational standpoint, black units rarely functioned efficiently during training maneuvers. The all-important bond of human contact between line troops, noncoms, and higher-ranking officers simply wasn't there. Negro units were therefore unjustly castigated as being lazy and inefficient.

I was from southern California and had gone through UCLA with black students, including outstanding young men like Kenny Washington and Jackie Robinson, who broke the segregation barrier in professional sports. Therefore, I had little patience with the military's antiquated racial status quo.

When I voiced my opinion on this during classroom discussions at the Infantry School, however, most of my colleagues parroted the same lame defense of segregation: "You never served with them," they said. "They're just not like us."

☆　　　☆

ONE of the many demonstrations at the Infantry School that I'll always remember was the so-called "Mad Minute." Our class was assembled on bleachers behind a battalion defensive position where troops were deployed with a variety of small arms and automatic weapons. As an instructor lectured over an echoing public-address system, the troops began to fire toward the sandy wasteland ahead. First came the M-1 rifles, Browning automatic rifles (BARs), and light machine guns—well supplied with bright tracers—then came heavy machine guns and mortars. The purpose of the exercise was to demonstrate to future battalion commanders the effects of the fire support available to their units. As the crackling small arms and chugging mortars continued, 105mm and 155mm howitzers began firing behind us, their shells rumbling overhead like trolley cars on a bad track. The artillery was joined by 4.2-inch mortars; then came the big 8-inch self-propelled guns. M-26 tanks that had been hidden beneath floppy camouflage nets in a pine woods on our left now cut loose with their 90mm guns. The whiplash crack of these tank weapons shook the bleacher seats. Out ahead, the overgrown approaches to the sandbagged trenches became a chaos of boiling dust and smoke, illuminated by dazzling orange flashes. The instructor announced the addition of "VT," variable-time, airburst artillery rounds, which employed a tiny radar altimeter fuse, set to explode a shower of shrapnel at a predetermined height above the ground. Finally, Air Force F-80 Shooting Star jets roared by, lacing the battalion defenses with rockets and smoky red napalm.

"Gentlemen," the instructor proclaimed, "you have just witnessed the unsurpassed firepower available to an infantry battalion."

I gazed into the churning smoke. Without question, an enemy force advancing across that open ground would have been slaughtered. Unlike many of my colleagues who had served in regular infantry outfits in Europe and the Pacific, I hadn't seen the effects of massed artillery firsthand in France or China. But I quickly recognized that this impressive demonstration represented optimal fire-support efficiency. I decided then and there to learn as much as I could about artillery and air support, particularly the problems of coordination between a battalion headquarters and the artillery and Air Force units assigned to support it. The firing ranges of Fort Benning were a long way from the real world, where I might have to lead a battalion in combat.

☆   ☆

MOST of us began informal maneuvering for assignments in March 1950, when it was clear we'd graduate that summer. I wanted back in the Airborne. But so did a lot of other guys. From a wartime strength of five divisions, our Airborne forces had been reduced to two divisions, the 82nd Airborne at Fort Bragg, North Carolina, and the 11th at Fort Campbell, Kentucky. That spring, my old Jedburgh friend Mac Austin visited Fort Benning, en route to Bragg where he'd been assigned as a battalion executive officer in the 504th Parachute Infantry Regiment. We got together with another ex-OSS officer, Major Dow Grones, whom I had met in Detachment 101 at Bhamo in Burma. Dow was going to the 82nd as well, but to take command of the 3rd Battalion of the 505th Regiment, the only Negro parachute infantry outfit in the Army. Over drinks at the officers' club I kidded him about the assignment, offering to lend him my lecture notes covering the greater efficiency of racially integrated units.

A month later, Dow gave me a chance to test my theories. I was to report to the 82nd Airborne Division at Fort Bragg following completion of the Infantry School at the end of June 1950. He arranged to have me assigned as his executive officer. When I broke the news to Mary, she chuckled. Being number-two man in a Negro battalion lacked the prestige of regular duties in the 82nd. In effect, I could anticipate two years of worthwhile but officially thankless drudgery in the peacetime Army, as a reward for my outspoken liberal views on race relations.

"One of these days, Jack," she said, shaking her head, "you're going to learn to keep your opinions to yourself."

As things turned out, however, there wasn't much peacetime duty for anyone in the U.S. Army to enjoy for the next three years.

☆   ☆

JUST before a rainy dawn on Sunday, June 25, 1950, almost 100,000 troops of the North Korean People's Army (NKPA) swept across the 38th parallel dividing the Communist North from the Republic of Korea. The invasion was opposed by fewer than three, under-strength South Korean divisions. Korea had been administratively partitioned between North and South by the Allies in 1945, so that Soviet forces could accept the Japanese surrender north of that line and U.S. troops to its south.

This arbitrary boundary became the border between a Communist puppet state and a fledgling, U.S.-sponsored democracy during the five years of Cold War that followed. North Korea's government was a dictatorship under Premier Kim Il-Sung, an ex-major in the Soviet army, whom the Russians handpicked as the leader of their client state. The leader of the South was President Syngman Rhee, an elderly, American-trained educator who had organized early resistance to Japanese occupation.

The Soviets invested heavily in the buildup of North Korea's armed forces, equipping the NKPA with tanks and heavy artillery. When the Russian Red Army officially departed North Korea in 1948, it left behind thousands of advisers. Just as important, the Soviet Union continued its massive buildup of war matériel in the North. At the time of the invasion, North Korea's army had grown to 135,000 men, and many of its officer corps had been trained in Soviet military academies and had seen combat under Soviet sponsorship with the Chinese Communist army in Manchuria.[6]

The Republic of Korea's army (ROKA) numbered fewer than 100,000. It was trained, advised, and equipped by the United States. Regular U.S. occupation troops of the 24th Corps had officially withdrawn from Korea in May 1949, leaving behind the U.S. Military Advisory Group to the Republic of Korea (KMAG), a training cadre and logistical unit of 500 officers and men. South Korean forces had no tanks, little artillery, and few qualified officers. The small KMAG operation was directed from Washington, not FECOM. To communicate with MacArthur's headquarters, they had to route their radio traffic through roundabout relay stations.

The rout of South Korea's forces that began that Sunday morning was one of the most unequal contests in the history of modern warfare.

On June 25, 1950, there existed FECOM contingency plans for the use of U.S. forces in the defense of South Korea. But these plans never anticipated a massive, coordinated surprise assault, spearheaded by modern Soviet-built tanks, across the entire breadth of the 38th parallel.[7] American advisers were really training a paramilitary constabulary to repel minor border skirmishes and guerrilla forays from the North. The Soviets had other goals.[8]

Within forty-eight hours of the Communist invasion, ROK resistance had crumbled. The road lay open for the North Koreans to sweep the peninsula.

☆   ☆

MY class graduated from the Infantry School on Saturday, June 24, 1950. The next day, a typically muggy Sunday, I was packing up our quarters near Fort Benning when the baseball game on the radio was interrupted with the news of the invasion. My first reaction was anger, followed by grudging professional admiration. To strike simultaneously with so many divisions was not an easy feat for any army, especially one that had been only recently organized.

My next reaction was frustrated curiosity. Why hadn't American intelligence predicted the invasion? All that spring there had been minor probes and feints by the North Koreans along the 38th parallel. Surely the CIA and FECOM's G-2 (military intelligence) under Major General Willoughby had been on an increased state of alert. But ROK forces had been literally caught in bed in some cases, and trapped inside their ill-defended garrisons in others. There had been a grand total of *one* American military adviser with the ROK troops on the 38th parallel that Sunday morning.[9] It was almost inconceivable that the North Koreans had achieved such total surprise.

The more I considered the situation, the more difficult it became to accept a complete absence of intelligence information about the Communists' intentions. If they had been able to strike totally without warning, they had pulled off a feat as great as the attack on Pearl Harbor. But I knew from my own work forming intelligence networks in North Korea (the task led by my case officers Scott Miler and John Chrislaw) that the CIA had dispatched dozens of well-trained young agents across the Yalu from Manchuria from 1946 to 1948. Despite the resistance of MacArthur and Major General Willoughby, we had inserted enough dedicated anti-Communists into North Korea with the *specific* mission of invasion early warning that at least one of them would have sounded the alarm. Moreover, the CIA had finally established a small station in South Korea's capital, Seoul, in 1949, when U.S. occupation forces had withdrawn. I'd been on the Agency's China desk when the station was set up, and knew the office to be staffed by reliable officers. In mid-1949, the Korea station had been receiving a good flow of intelligence from these agents. It was not likely they'd all simply dried up before the invasion. If they had, *that* would have been a clear warning in itself.

Over the ensuing years, while serving again with the CIA, on military assignments to Korea, and discussing the issue in detail with men who'd been key members of the civilian and military intelligence establishment at the time, I have managed to unravel the mystery of the great "intelligence failure" of June 1950.[10]

That spring Kim Il-Sung's Communist government had unleashed a virulent propaganda campaign against the South, condemning the elections there and threatening unspecified military action. This campaign had been for public consumption, to eventually mollify fears through hyperbole. Meanwhile, Kim's Soviet-backed army undertook specific steps to prepare for invasion, steps which did, in fact, raise the alarm with American-trained agents in North Korea. These brave young men had done as they were ordered: They'd worked their way into influential positions in the North Korean civil and military administration, including jobs in the transportation system.

By June, several of these agents either had sent specific reports of North Korean preparations or had actually slipped across the 38th parallel and reported to CIA officers in South Korea for debriefing. An important Intelligence Estimate dated June 19, 1950, compiled from "CIA Field Agency reports," described in detail "extensive troop movements," reinforcement of roads north of the border to carry heavy equipment and armor, and repairs to railroad lines leading south, which had been ripped up by the Soviets in 1945. Even more ominously, the Estimate cited agents' reports that civilian traffic had been halted on North Korean railroads linking major military centers with the border. This document concluded that a North Korean invasion was pending, that Kim had positioned his forces to strike whenever he wanted to.[11]

A full five days before the invasion, CIA director Admiral Roscoe Hillenkoetter had made sure that this Estimate was delivered to the White House and President Truman's key military and foreign policy advisers, including Secretary of State Dean Acheson, Secretary of Defense Louis Johnson, and Chairman of the Joint Chiefs of Staff General Omar Bradley. A summary of the Estimate was also telegraphically dispatched to Generals MacArthur and Willoughby at FECOM in Tokyo.

America's key military and civilian policy-makers had ample evidence of North Korean intentions before the invasion. And this evidence was based on reports by well-trained agents. The logical question is: Why didn't America's leaders react? Why didn't they put North Korea on formal notice that any military action would be met with massive force? Why, at least, didn't American Air Force reconnaissance planes make themselves conspicuous over the only three invasion routes from the tangled mountains of the north?

CIA field officers serving in the Pacific at the time later gave me answers to these questions. They explained that FECOM's G-2, the imperious Major General Charles Willoughby, had reviewed a stream of such reports from the Seoul CIA station that spring and had labeled them all with the negative designation "F-6": Untried Source, Reliability Unknown. In the intelligence profession, an F-6 evaluation was very low, not quite as bad as an E-5— Unreliable Source, Improbable Information—but certainly tainted. Because

U.S. operations in Korea were no longer under the personal command of MacArthur, his chief intelligence officer deigned the reports unworthy of serious consideration. So labeled, this growing stream of information was never taken seriously outside the CIA in Washington. General Bradley, in fact, let it be known in the intelligence community that the increasingly alarming reports from the field were like someone "crying wolf" (which was probably the goal of the North Koreans' shrill propaganda offensive that spring).

But Admiral Hillenkoetter had stuck to his guns. It was not his job to make policy based on intelligence, but rather to provide the policy-makers with the most reliable information available. Hence, his last estimate on June 20 continued to warn that a North Korean invasion was pending.

On Monday, June 26, 1950, of course, speculation about the possible attack and the warnings of our field agents were moot points. Most of the Congress had adjourned, it being an election year. But the Senate Appropriations Committee, chaired by a near-senile Democratic curmudgeon from Tennessee named Kenneth McKeller, was still sitting on the Hill. Republican senator Stiles Bridges (never one to avoid the hot lights of the newsreels or a radio microphone) called for a closed session in which America's key foreign policy and intelligence leaders would be forced to explain why the North Korean surprise attack had caught us flat-footed.

Dean Acheson and Defense Secretary Johnson testified during the morning session. By lunchtime, unnamed senators had leaked the news that the North Korean attack represented a shocking "failure" of American intelligence.

Walter Pforzheimer was Admiral Hillenkoetter's legislative counsel, the man who prepared him for congressional testimony. The Director and Pforzheimer conferred that morning at CIA headquarters, while Acheson and Johnson testified. Secretary Acheson telephoned after his testimony to tell Hillenkoetter he had "done his best" to defend the intelligence community in the face of savage attacks by the outraged senators. Acheson, apparently still defending the Director, had made an appointment for Hillenkoetter to brief President Truman at three that afternoon; unfortunately, the meeting conflicted with the Director's scheduled testimony before the Senate committee.

Admiral Hillenkoetter had been blown out of the water aboard the battleship *West Virginia* at Pearl Harbor, and had been our naval attaché to the Vichy government during the war; he had learned a few things about danger and palace intrigues. He told Pforzheimer to assemble all the agents' reports from North Korea and the latest Intelligence Estimates, which had already been sent to key policy-makers. They drove together to the White House; if Hillenkoetter was delayed very long with the President, Pforzheimer was to continue on to testify on the Hill.

As the Admiral later reported to Pforzheimer, the meeting with President Truman was cordial, brief, and straightforward. Hillenkoetter showed the President the documents he intended to present to the senators. Truman was a bit surprised that the Director still intended to testify. "Admiral," Truman said, "do you really want to go up there?"

"Mr. President," Hillenkoetter answered, hefting the stack of documents, "I believe we have a good story to tell."

Truman gazed at him a moment through his rimless glasses. "I believe you do. Go ahead."

When Hillenkoetter and Pforzheimer reached the committee room they discovered the reason Acheson had tried to stall them at the White House. During his testimony that morning, the Secretary of State had tried to shift the blame for the Korean debacle onto the CIA. This was the true source of the outraged reports on "intelligence failures" that had been already leaked to the press. Hillenkoetter was angry, but maintained his composure as he patiently read from the Estimates and agents' reports, which clearly cited specific evidence of the North Koreans' invasion plans.

At one point, Senator McKeller demanded to know why these Estimates had not been disseminated to the secretaries of State and Defense.

"Senator," Admiral Hillenkoetter stated, "every Estimate was circulated to the key cabinet officials."

McKeller looked skeptical; that very morning, Secretary Acheson had sworn he had received no such warning. McKeller demanded proof. The Director promised to deliver signed receipts, proving these cabinet officers had received the Estimates, including the critical June 20 document containing the specific warnings.

By the end of the closed hearing, the senators, both Democrats and Republicans, understood that the CIA had done its job. They also realized that the "intelligence" failure did not occur among America's intelligence professionals. That afternoon, several senators spoke to the press to affirm their confidence in the Central Intelligence Agency. Stiles Bridges grudgingly allowed that the CIA "was doing a good job," although he had not thought so before the hearing. Republican senator William Knowland of California, who had previously thought the administration had been caught flat-footed, declared, "I am satisfied that the CIA is and was performing its function."[12]

But Senator McKeller was not mollified. He demanded that Walter Pforzheimer appear the next day with the actual signed receipts, showing the Estimates had been received by Acheson and other cabinet members. When Pforzheimer produced these receipts on Tuesday morning, the old senator took one look at them and threw them on the committee room table. "These are forgeries!" he shouted. "Get out of here."

Pforzheimer held his ground, politely indicating that the signatures were authentic.

Senator McKeller examined each signature, comparing the handwriting with other authenticated documents. Still fuming about forgeries, he gradually was forced to acknowledge the validity of the receipts. But he never shared this information with the press.

At least, however, the courageous work of the young Korean agents we had trained in Manchuria had not been completely in vain. They had faced torture and lonely execution to bring us warning of the Communist attack. The CIA had forwarded this warning. Although the politicians had refused to act, on the ground in South Korea, the Agency was better prepared for the invasion than the ROK military.

The official Communist propaganda line, originated in Moscow and parroted by Party organs around the world, held that there had been no invasion at all. Rather, the North Koreans were simply counterattacking the South Korean "Quislings," who had infiltrated north of the 38th parallel to ambush the hapless border guards of the North Korean People's Army. Now the "people's peace movement" had pursued the fascist aggressors south of the 38th parallel, in an effort to punish the "Wall Street puppet regime."[13]

☆   ☆

IN July, I took over as executive officer, 3rd Battalion, 505th Parachute Infantry Regiment. Fort Bragg was beginning to feel the confusion of another wartime buildup. In an incredible ten-day period, President Truman had committed American military forces to repel the North Korean invasion, the United Nations had voted to support the South Koreans, and the first American Army units had been dispatched to Korea.

But the news from Korea was not good. Within three days, Seoul was overrun. Units from the American 24th Infantry Division were arriving piecemeal in Korea from their occupation duty in Japan. They were lightly armed and clearly no match for the tank-supported NKPA units. By mid-July, some regiments of the 24th Infantry Division had lost half their men, and the combined ROK-U.S. force was being squeezed to the bottom of the peninsula. The light armor of the 1st U.S. Cavalry Division was arriving slowly in the south, and the 25th Infantry Division was en route from Hawaii. But it was uncertain whether the "United Nations" forces under the command of American Army General Walton Walker could hold out against the North Korean juggernaut.

At Fort Bragg, the mood was one of excited anticipation, melded with frustration. The 82nd Airborne Division had become the repository of most of America's battle-tested professional paratroop officers and NCOs. We wanted to get into the fight, but we also recognized that repulsing the well-organized Communist aggression in Korea would require a massive buildup of U.S. forces. The country had virtually turned its back on Asia, lulled by the grandiosity of MacArthur's imperial reign in Tokyo. MacArthur was a five-star general, as was Chairman of the Joint Chiefs of Staff Omar Bradley. But MacArthur definitely viewed himself as first among equals. Therefore, the important responsibility of defending Asia had fallen exclusively to FECOM.

In Europe, American forces were involved in the integration of the new NATO command. If the country was going to meet the aggression in Korea, the troops would have to come from elsewhere. I was heartened when President Truman ordered the mobilization of Air Force, Army, and Marine Corps reserve and National Guard units. This was not a politically popular move, but it was absolutely vital from both a military and foreign policy standpoint. We couldn't expect U.N. allies to send combat troops if we ourselves were unwilling to make sacrifices.

At meetings of regimental and division staff officers, I learned that the 82nd was scrambling hard to get its component units up to combat strength, to fill the Table of Organization and Equipment, the all-important "TO&E." What was especially frustrating for me was the fact that my battalion, the only Negro paratroop outfit in the U.S. Army, was practically double strength, with almost 1,600 men. This meant we had surpluses of everything, including fairly well-trained personnel. While the other battalions needed 4.2-inch mortar platoons, medics, radio men, and so on, we had them in abundance.

But our soldiers' skins happened to be black. That meant they could not serve alongside their white counterparts, the severity of the national emergency notwithstanding. Never one to passively accept the status quo, I made a real pain of myself in the regiment and division that summer, proposing the transfer of mortar platoons, commo sections, and other specialized troops from the 3rd Battalion for assignment elsewhere in the division. My efforts at unofficial integration were thwarted. At that point, racial segregation was the official policy in the U.S. military, and the law of most southern states, including North Carolina. It would be several more months before President Truman took the politically bold but absolutely logical step of desegregating the armed services.

Meanwhile, we had a battalion to prepare for combat. And that was not an easy job. Our unit was both physically and psychologically separated from the rest of the regiment. I spent a fair amount of my time in the battalion as Summary Court Officer. In that capacity I was subjected to some truly exceptional and innovative stories from black troopers explaining why they were three days late returning from passes. Going AWOL was not considered a normal part of soldiering in this outfit, but trying to outwit the Summary Court Officer was considered a legitimate exercise in creative expression. Because of segregation, the loyalty of the men ran horizontally along racial lines, not vertically up and down the chain of command. In the past, their white officers had been viewed as aloof and patronizing, more like detached schoolmasters than combat leaders. Major Dow Grones and I set about to change that attitude.

By tradition, Airborne troops are supposed to be tough, and parachute infantry the cream of the lot. But our outfit had gotten fat and sluggish. The other battalions all ran two miles before breakfast. When I joined the battalion, the men were used to trotting a few blocks around the company area after some limited calisthenics, then settling in for a slow, high-calorie mess-hall breakfast. We got them running—not trotting—a full six miles around the entire regimental area every morning. At first, the dropout rate was scandalous. But Dow asked me to take several bright young lieutenants to police up the stragglers. These slackers were assembled each afternoon for a little additional physical training, an exercise which I personally led. The word went out. Either you ran six miles behind Major Grones in the cool of the morning, or you ran six with Major Singlaub in the humid heat of the afternoon.

Within a month, the men were back in what I considered fighting shape. Equally important, they were beginning to take pride in themselves as soldiers. As we ran each morning through the company streets of the white battalions, the men of our outfit now chanted a steady, almost defiant cadence. It was as if they were challenging the rest of the 82nd to be as "Airborne" as they were. This newfound sense of pride spilled over to the serious business of combat training. On night jumps, our five companies landed with few injuries and assembled quickly on the drop zone, a clear indication the individual soldiers were working hard. By September, I was confident that we could lead these men into combat and they would account for themselves well on the battlefield. So much for the myth of the lazy, ineffective black soldier.

But I never got the chance to test them. I was on the rifle range with my troops one blazing September morning when a runner arrived with priority orders. I was to report at once to Fort Benning, Georgia, where the Army had established a new Ranger Training Center.

☆   ☆

THE Rangers have a venerable history in the U.S. Army. Independent companies of scouts and irregulars—practitioners of what we now call unconventional warfare—fought in all of our wars, starting with Rogers' Rangers in the French and Indian Wars.[14] In World War II, the Rangers served with distinction, particularly in the D-Day invasion, where the First Ranger Battalion stormed the formidable cliffs of Pointe du Hoc above Omaha Beach and neutralized the German batteries there. By August of 1950, Eighth Army recognized the need for a long-range patrol capability within the units fighting in Korea. A provisional company was established from volunteers in Eighth Army and another in X Corps. The Army General Staff decided to authorize a small special Ranger company to be assigned to each infantry division. They would act as the division commander's long-range patrollers, serving far behind enemy lines, conducting thorough, reliable reconnaissance missions and, when necessary, disrupting enemy lines of communication. In effect, the new Ranger companies would be a combination of an OSS Operational Group and a World War II Ranger battalion.

So it wasn't surprising that a former Jed like myself was summoned to Fort Benning to join World War II Ranger veterans like Major Bill Bond and Major "Bull" Simons. The commander of the new center, Colonel John Van Houten, gave us considerable latitude. Our job was to establish a training curriculum that would take already well-trained Airborne volunteers and mold them quickly into Ranger companies that would be physically and mentally tough enough to function well behind enemy lines.

The Army General Staff decided that we'd form the Ranger companies with volunteers from regular army Airborne units. That way, a man would be a triple volunteer by the time he arrived, a pretty good indication he was motivated for the job. The training itself relied heavily on Jedburgh and Ranger techniques, with an emphasis on instinctive firing, demolition, infiltration, and clandestine communications. The training cadre not only designed the separate courses, we also went through them ourselves to test their practicality.

I led the advanced Airborne training section, which specialized in low-altitude night drops. By this time, the American Airborne had already adopted British parachute landing techniques, and accidents were relatively rare. My job was to teach men to pinpoint small drop zones at night and to consistently dispatch sticks of jumpers and their equipment into these clearings or islands in the Georgia swamps. I found myself jumping almost every night, testing new equipment and drop techniques. While some of the other guys still considered leaping from an airplane an unusual experience, to me the task became simply part of my job. The guys around me began calling me "Jumping Jack," a nickname that has stuck with me.

One day I had a stick of young Ranger officers aboard an Air Force C-47 for some special jump-master training. The flight crew was new to my unorthodox drop techniques, and I went up to the cockpit to lead the pilot through a dry run across the drop zone. Colonel John Van Houten, who didn't jump very often, was along on this drop to make an administrative pay jump to keep his Airborne qualification active. He had an appointment the next morning at the Pentagon and was in a hurry to complete the drop and catch his flight to Washington. When I went up forward, he mistakenly assumed the drop was about to begin.

Turning to a young lieutenant named Jonathan Carney, the Colonel said, "Come on, son, tap me out."

He hooked up his static line and shuffled up to the door. Carney being pretty green acted as an impromptu jump master. He tapped the Colonel's helmet and Van Houten stepped into the prop blast.

When I came back from the cockpit I saw he was gone. "Where the hell's Colonel Van Houten?" I shouted over the engine roar.

Carney looked stricken. "He jumped, sir," Carney squawked. "Wasn't he supposed to?"

I shook my head. Colonel Van Houten had jumped with the aircraft flying at almost full throttle, a good 150 knots. He'd be damned lucky if his back wasn't broken by the opening shock. And he'd be equally lucky if his canopy survived intact. I signaled the crew to slow down and jumped myself as we crossed back over the drop zone.

On the ground, I found Major Dan Gallagher looking like he'd just been doused with ice water. "The Colonel's bleeding from his ears and mouth," he said. "He could hardly walk."

Van Houten somehow made it to his sedan, which was waiting to take him to the airport. As he started to leave the drop zone, he saw me running toward his car. The driver stopped and the Colonel rolled down his window and motioned for me to come to him. "Jack," he said, with typical Ranger humor, "let this be a lesson to you. Never leave me alone again in the back of an airplane."

I saluted smartly and rendered a relieved, "No, sir," as he rolled up his window and motioned to the driver to continue the trip to the airport.

☆   ☆

WHILE we were preparing to receive our first Ranger trainees, the situation in Korea shifted dramatically. United Nations forces had stabilized a perimeter around the port of Pusan in the southeast corner of the peninsula, and repelled repeated, savage North Korean attacks. Then, in mid-September, MacArthur unleashed the most brilliant operation of his career, the amphibious assault at Inchon, the port of Seoul. In one fell swoop, MacArthur's X Corps, composed of the Army's 7th Infantry Division and the U.S. Marines 1st Division, went ashore against light enemy opposition.

By the end of September, they had recaptured Seoul and were cutting across the narrow waist of the Korean peninsula. The Eighth Army under General Walker broke out of the Pusan perimeter and drove north to link up with X Corps. Now the NKPA divisions that had routed the ROK and American forces in July were themselves routed. By October, the situation on the battlefield was completely reversed. North Korean forces had been shattered and were retreating in total disarray as U.N. units pushed far north of the 38th parallel. America drew on its battlefield success to shepherd a resolution through the General Assembly that vaguely endorsed American-led U.N. military action north of the parallel, what was called "all appropriate steps" to create stability throughout the country, which would lead to a unified government elected under U.N. auspices.[15]

The Joint Chiefs of Staff under General Bradley (with the strong support of General George Marshall, who had replaced Louis Johnson as secretary of defense) cautioned MacArthur to avoid provoking intervention by either the Soviet Union or the Chinese Communists as U.N. forces drove north, pursuing the shattered NKPA. Despite his serene bravado, MacArthur was known to be initially concerned about such intervention. But as no Chinese or Soviet advisers were killed or captured, his confidence grew daily.[16]

MacArthur was an audacious strategist. Rather than pursue a mundane land advance up the mountainous peninsula, he packed up the X Corps once again aboard Navy transports and staged another massive amphibious landing, this one halfway up North Korea's east coast at Wonsan. The landing, however, did not go smoothly. Soviet submarines had sown the harbor thick with mines and it took two weeks to clear them. While the 1st Marine Division's invasion flotilla was stalled at sea, the ROK 3rd and Capital Divisions beat the Americans to Wonsan and were already many miles farther north when the Marines landed. "Even Bob Hope was there before them," military historian Max Hastings notes ironically. To their profound chagrin, "by a stroke that entered Marine legend, the entertainer staged a USO show in Wonsan the night before the division stormed ashore to take position."[17]

General of the Army Douglas MacArthur was apparently not amused.

A more ominous aspect of this operation was the splitting of the U.N. command into two unequal halves. The Eighth Army under General Walker became the junior partner in the drive north. X Corps commander Lieutenant General Edward M. Almond retained his position as MacArthur's FECOM chief of staff, an unorthodox arrangement to say the least. With this inside track to FECOM, Almond siphoned off the lion's share of men and matériel, leaving Walker's Eighth Army somewhat of an orphan.

Worse, Walker allowed the professional standards of some units to deteriorate on the march north toward the Yalu. Because there was little resistance from the NKPA, he and his subordinates (down to company level in some cases) made the fatal mistake of assuming the war was over. His principal ground-combat forces, the U.S. 2nd and 25th Infantry Divisions and the 1st Cavalry Division, were loaded with green replacements. The offensive up North Korea's west coast acquired a slapdash character. MacArthur himself did not help matters much in mid-October, when he announced that victory was at hand and that the men would be home by Christmas. It's hard to get a tired GI (especially a teenage kid new to combat) to dig in properly on a frozen ridge or to hump that heavy extra case of machine-gun ammunition up a steep Korean mountain if his Supreme Commander has proclaimed the fighting will be over in eight weeks.

Major General Charles Willoughby issued a detailed intelligence report in Tokyo on October 14, concerning the delicate question of possible Soviet or Communist Chinese intervention in support of their North Korean ally. He concluded that the Soviets would have already intervened if they intended to prop up the NKPA. As for Chinese Communist forces (CCF), Willoughby dismissed Chinese threats to enter North Korea as "diplomatic blackmail." He did note, however, that the Chinese had at least nine field armies with thirty-eight divisions garrisoned in Manchuria and that twenty-four of these divisions were poised along the Yalu River in a position to intervene. Nevertheless, he judged this Communist order of battle to be mere posturing.[18]

But within six weeks, the American military would succumb to another surprise hammer blow; this one would make the North Korean invasion seem like a Scout jamboree in comparison.

☆   ☆

I FLEW out to Korea the last week of November 1950 to confer with the division staffs of the Eighth Army and X Corps on the addition of Ranger companies to their units. When I arrived in Tokyo the mood was still euphoric. Advanced American units, I learned, were already dug in on the banks of the frozen Yalu River and MacArthur's final offensive was about to begin. But, as I went about my job, briefing FECOM staff officers on the planned deployment of Ranger units in Korea, disturbing reports began to circulate in FECOM about large-scale fighting both in the Eighth Army's area of operations and in the frozen mountains of the east coast where the X Corps was supposedly advancing unopposed toward the Chinese and Soviet borders.

By November 30, when I flew from Tokyo to X Corps headquarters at Hamhung, the rumors of a massive Chinese intervention had been confirmed. The Eighth Army's 2nd Infantry Division and a regiment of the 1st Cavalry had been overwhelmed along the Chongchon River in the west. In what became known as the Battle of Kunu-ri, the 2nd Division was smashed into small units by massively superior Chinese forces; in turn, either these units were cut off in the roadless wilderness of mountains and destroyed, or they were captured intact.[19] The survivors of the 2nd Division retreated in a disarray that rivaled the NKPA debacle of three months earlier. Other elements of the Eighth Army, whether in contact with the Chinese or not, were ordered to execute a withdrawal to the south to preserve the integrity of the Army.

I was saddened to learn that my good friend Homer Hinckley had been one of the casualties of this unequal meeting engagement. Homer's battalion had been strung out along the river when they were overrun by several Chinese regiments. Attempting to extract his headquarters company, he had stumbled into an enemy ambush and his entire headquarters unit was killed or captured. Homer was now listed as missing in action, a probable prisoner of the Chinese. I couldn't help wondering if Homer's notoriously bad map skills somehow led to his capture. I was worried because Homer's distinctive size was bound to be noticed, and with this attention his background in Peking would undoubtedly be revealed. The Chinese probably had him on their list of "spies," and this might well seal his fate in captivity.

The CCF attacks in the west were carried out by the Chinese 13th Army Group, which followed the classic tactics of its veteran leader, my old nemesis from Manchuria, General Lin Piao. The Chinese forces moved easily across the mountain wilderness, carrying what they needed on their backs. They marched at night to avoid American air attack. And they also attacked at night, usually before the American troops had a chance to properly dig in.

Intelligence reports of the Chinese offensive I read in Hamhung bordered on the unbelievable. Surviving GIs spoke of "human wave" attacks in which thousands of Chinese infantrymen in tan padded uniforms trotted doggedly up the snowy slopes, encouraged by blaring bugles. In some cases, American units were overrun when the GIs had simply expended all their ammunition killing Chinese who just kept advancing through the frozen night in the garish light of red signal flares. Some elements of the Eighth Army were surprised and defeated by the CCF, but the majority of the American troops were terribly confused by their sudden orders to execute a deep withdrawal to terrain south of Seoul. One day their commander promised them they'd be home by Christmas, and his lofty chief of intelligence dismissed rumors of Chinese intervention as propaganda. The next day the admitted presence of a vastly superior Chinese force caused all of the United Nations forces to abandon much of the territory they had recently seized from the North Koreans. In the first weeks of December, as the harsh Korean winter swept down from Siberia, the Eighth Army was able to avoid the enveloping maneuvers of the Chinese by a series of major withdrawals. The CCF never repeated the hammer blows of Kunu-ri because the Eighth Army was falling back on its supply lines, while the Chinese were stretching theirs to the limit; also, Chinese lines of communication were subjected to increasing attack by the U.S. Fifth Air Force.

On the eastern side of Korea's central mountain spine, the Chinese struck with equal savagery. However, geography and the nature of the American X Corps push north influenced a different outcome to this collision of the two armies. The 7th Division had been advancing on a broad front through valleys toward the Yalu. Most of these small units were separated from each other by steep ridges when the Chinese struck. Cut off from reinforcements and supplies, the American units fought desperate actions, often in the frigid darkness. When possible, battered battalions of the 7th Division coalesced into improvised task forces. One of the best known of these was Task Force Faith, composed of remnants of the 1st Battalion, 32nd Infantry and the 3rd Battalion, 31st Infantry, and commanded by Lieutenant Colonel Don Faith. We had been tent mates in a parachute regiment in 1943.

In the steep, almost roadless mountains around the frozen Chosin Reservoir (also known as the Changjin Reservoir), Don Faith's unit faced its most severe test and performed heroically. Already personally decorated by General Almond with a Silver Star, Colonel Faith led his forces in a desperate and skillful defense against an overwhelming Chinese division-strength attack. The unit suffered grave casualties as they broke out of the Chinese encirclement and fought their way toward larger units of the 1st Marine Division. Although less well publicized than subsequent Marine actions around the Reservoir, the conduct of Task Force Faith was exemplary. Despite horrendous cold, lack of food, and depleted ammunition, Faith's troops inflicted heavy casualties on the enemy, and in effect, blunted a major Chinese attack. Don Faith was mortally wounded in the action and was posthumously awarded the Medal of Honor.[20]

On the west side of the Reservoir, the 1st Marine Division under Major General O. P. Smith had not become as widely separated as the Army. In fact, Smith had argued with General Almond about over-extending the Marine division along the axis of advance. So the Marines were better prepared to meet the Chinese onslaught. But they still had to fight their way out of encirclement, moving down a single unpaved mountain track, between dominating snowy ridges. And on this high ground, the Chinese deployed no fewer than seven infantry divisions (almost 90,000 soldiers) to oppose their withdrawal. As General Smith told correspondents who flew into his surrounded headquarters at Hagaru at the bottom of the Reservoir, "Gentlemen, we are not retreating. We are merely advancing in another direction."[21]

X Corps headquarters was a sprawl of snowy tents around the old Japanese airfield on the edge of Hamhung. The town stood on a narrow coastal plain dominated by steep snowy mountains inland; the frigid Sea of Japan was a few miles east where the small fishing harbor of Hungnam had been designated the evacuation port for the beleaguered X Corps. I knew several of the Corps' staff officers, working for Lieutenant Colonel Jack Chiles, chief of operations; Major Salve Matheson, an ROTC colleague from UCLA; and my very close friend from Fort Benning, Major Harvey Short. The mood at Corps headquarters was serious, but not defeatist. Major Harvey Short told me one frozen afternoon as we watched C-47s disgorging frost-bitten and wounded Marines, "This is a new war. And we better get damn serious about it if we're going to win."[22]

I was one of the few American officers in Korea who had seen CCF tactics firsthand. I knew the enemy could be defeated if we fought him with flex-ibility and resolve. The Chinese moved at night in small units; they were thus vulnerable to ambush. Their mass-infantry attacks could be broken up with well-placed artillery support. The Marines had already changed their tactics to match the enemy's. But American forces in general still had many lessons to learn.

I felt a little useless, trying to brief officers about the future deployment of Ranger companies when they were naturally preoccupied with extracting their forces from Chinese encirclement in the icy mountains. Then a situation came up where my talents were suddenly put to good use. The Communists had destroyed one of the key bridges spanning a critical gap on the single road of the Marine retreat route south of Koto-ri. Unless that bridge was replaced, the 1st Marine Division would be forced to abandon its tanks, trucks, heavy weapons and supplies, and some of its wounded to the Chinese forces who were in close pursuit. There were Treadway bridge sections available to span the gap, but we just couldn't put them on semi-trailers and drive them through the Chinese encirclement to make the repair.

It was decided an air drop was required. But there were few qualified heavy-drop officers in Hamhung. So I was tapped to reconnoiter the job. I had been working on the problem of dropping large rubber boats and bridg-ing equipment to Ranger units, and I understood the complexities of finding a decent drop zone in mountainous terrain. Early one absolutely bone-chilling December morning, I flew up to the invasion route on an L-19, the metal-skinned version of the reliable old L-5s I'd used in Manchuria. The mountains of Korea's northeast coast were frightening, there's no other word for it. Snowy razor-back ridges and steep, icy gorges rose and tumbled in all directions. The only "road" was a narrow dirt track that zigzagged pain-fully through the high country, an absolutely perfect ambush route. Judging from the black smears of burnt-out tanks and trucks, the Chinese were using the terrain to good advantage. We found the gap easily enough, and noted the American foxholes scraped into the surrounding ridge line.

As we circled the American positions, I noticed an unusual feature of this campaign. Only a few yards behind some foxholes and machine-gun pits the Marines had hacked shallow depressions in the snow and erected warming tents. Black smoke spiraled from these tents' chimneys. It was as if the troops were fighting two equally deadly foes: the Chinese and the Korean winter. Elsewhere on the ridge, I saw small groups of Marines huddled around outdoor fires, like hobos.

Swooping low beneath the hills, I plotted the approach route for the drop aircraft, and noted the clearance to the pass ahead. The country around the gap was too steep for an airdrop, so we hopped over a snowy ridge and flew across a narrow plateau. The frozen, shell-torn village of Koto-ri was bordered by fields into which the Marines had scraped a landing strip. That would have to be the drop zone. It was not as close to the bridge site as desired, but the Marines' engineers had the trucks to move the bridge sections forward. This was not peacetime and everybody had to take their chances if X Corps was going to pull off this withdrawal.

We flew north up the valley to view the entire column. The Marines were in good formation, despite the almost constant Chinese harassment. At the very end of the column, Marine MPs kept a half-mile interval between the U.S. forces and a ragtag band of civilian refugees. Seen from the air, it was hard to tell the difference between the frozen troops and the frozen, starving refugees.

We turned back toward the coast. Dropping down off the icy mountains, we flew over the newly dug positions of an American relief column. This was Task Force Meade, from the 3rd Infantry Division. They had tanks and artillery dug in to guard the final third of the retreat route. If the Marines could make it across that bridge, they could fall back in good order.

When I got back to Hamhung, the shiny, twin-boomed C-119 Flying Boxcars had arrived from Japan. I helped the parachute riggers with the heavy cargo chutes on the icy metal bridge spans. The young Air Force crew seemed nervous, but grimly determined. They asked me all the right questions and I helped them plot their optimum route in for the drop. Finally, the captain of the lead plane said what was on everybody's mind. "Is there any flak up there, Major?"

I shook my head. "I never saw any." There was no sense painting too rosy a picture, however. "But that doesn't mean there won't be when you get there."

The young man nodded somberly. "Oh well," was all he said. "Let's get this show on the road."

That afternoon, the brave young Air Force crews dodged Chinese anti-aircraft fire to drop the spans. The road was bridged again, and the 1st Marines were able to execute an orderly withdrawal of their men and matériel, thanks to the combined and coordinated efforts of the U.S. Air Force and the U.S. Army.

I flew out of Hamhung the same afternoon and landed in Seoul a few hours later. The South Korean capital was in a state of panic, the roads clogged with refugees heading south. For the second time in six months, Seoul was about to be overrun by a Communist army. There were thousands of civilians fleeing the Chinese advance. I'd seen similar pathetic groups streaming down from the mountains toward Hungnam. The United Nations command had announced that any anti-Communist civilians seeking refuge in the South would be welcome. It was a magnanimous gesture, but as an experienced intelligence officer, I couldn't help but note that our Western compassion had the practical effect of stripping North Korea of potential resistance forces.

At a camp outside Seoul near Kimpo Airport, I found a group of American soldiers who were anything but defeated. They were members of the Eighth Army's Provisional Ranger Company. For several months they had fought in small teams in the Korean mountains. They were lean, tough, and, I noted, literally bloodied. One of their officers, Lieutenant Ralph Puckett, had been hit in the foot a few days before but refused evacuation. The Rangers spoke of ambushing Chinese headquarters' units, of observing primitive CCF field radio stations, and of eavesdropping on enemy bivouacs a few feet from the Chinese foxholes. Their confident attitude reminded me of the young Jedburghs I'd served with in England.

One of their best officers was a lieutenant named John Paul Vann. He had led small reconnaissance patrols deep into the mountains of North Korea, hiking by night—sometimes close beside Chinese columns—and hiding by day. They had lived off the land and depended on no one for logistical support. Vann had the unmistakable self-confidence and aggressive determination of a born soldier.

"Sir," he said, "if we get enough Rangers out here, we can beat these bastards at their own game."

☆ ☆

OVER the next six months, I worked practically nonstop at Fort Benning training Ranger companies. In Korea, the bloody seesaw fighting continued. General Walker was killed in a truck accident north of Seoul. The city again fell to the Communists on January 4, 1951. General Matthew Ridgway, one of America's distinguished Airborne leaders of World War II, took over the Eighth Army. The U.N. front was stabilized about sixty miles south of Seoul. Ridgway worked wonders with the Eighth Army. By the end of January 1951 the U.N. forces were on the offensive again. Seoul was recaptured in March.

But the biggest event of that spring was political, not military. President Harry Truman relieved General Douglas MacArthur on April 11. Ridgway was named to replace him at FECOM and General James Van Fleet took over the Eighth Army. Relieving MacArthur was an unfortunate necessity, tinged with anticlimax. In reality, his career had ended with the surprise Chinese intervention in North Korea. By April, MacArthur had lost touch with reality. The stated goals of American policy in Korea were to stabilize the military situation and rebuild the South. A soldier's job, whether he be a buck private or a five-star general like MacArthur, is to implement the legitimate orders of duly elected civilian authority.

MacArthur defied those orders. He tried to bypass the chain of command through allies in Congress. His goal, he said, was the defeat of Communist China. To accomplish this task, he called for air and ground attacks against the Chinese mainland, some of which would employ Nationalist forces from Taiwan. He also campaigned for the destruction of the bridges across the Yalu River and the Chinese airfields in southern Manchuria. This latter tactic made considerable sense. But MacArthur's erratic campaign of press conferences that spring demonstrated he was more interested in personal aggrandizement than strategy. He remained true to character to the very end. He had gambled and he had lost.

By that summer, Ridgway and Van Fleet's troops had repulsed a major Chinese counteroffensive and pushed the enemy back north of the 38th parallel. With the CCF in retreat, the Soviet Union finally proposed U.N.-sponsored truce talks. The preliminary cease-fire discussions began near the town of Kaesong, not far from the 38th parallel. American forces continued the offensive. Some of their fiercest battles were in the central mountains at Heartbreak and Bloody ridges. The battle lines now became static and a stalemate ensued. Three American and four ROK army corps were dug into the mountains above the old 38th-parallel border in the east, and just below it in the west. Five Chinese army groups faced them in similar positions on slightly higher ground to the north.

The trench lines, sandbagged outposts, and bunkers, supported by massed heavy artillery on both sides, were a throwback to the Western Front of World War I. America had accepted a strange new concept: limited war.

The truce talks had now become a complex political and propaganda show, a classic confrontation between dogmatic Asian communism and an uneasy alliance of Western forces. Predictably, the thorniest issue was not real estate, but ideology, and that intangible Oriental attribute we often simplistically disparage as "loss of face."

We had tens of thousands of North Korean and Chinese prisoners cooped up in POW compounds in the South, principally on the island of Koje-do, near Pusan. The Communists had several thousand U.N. POWs. Before the Chinese would accept any permanent cease-fire, they insisted that *all* prisoners be exchanged. But we knew many North Korean and Chinese prisoners were involuntary conscripts who, given the choice, would prefer to remain in the South. The issue of involuntary repatriation of prisoners became the proximate cause for the chronic failure of the peace talks. But the reality was a test of will. We could not return these hapless pawns to the Communists against their will. The Chinese and North Koreans could not publicly acknowledge that any of their soldiers preferred capitalist enslavement to the bountiful life in the People's Republics.

While the truce talks ground on, the war in the hills continued. Young American, British, French, Greek, and Turkish soldiers died every day. So did young Koreans and Chinese.

☆   ☆

IN December 1951 I was called to CIA headquarters in Washington. The Agency wanted my services again. I was interviewed by two Army colonels, Bill Depuy and Richard Stilwell. They didn't mince words. The U.S. government had decided to step up pressure on the Chinese Communists by supporting guerrilla movements on the mainland of China, especially along the lines of communication to the CCF forces in Korea. It would be a clandestine operation run out of the large new CIA station in Japan, and supported by a fleet of transport aircraft and surface vessels. They said I was an Army officer with some background in this type of operation. They emphasized that the Army was willing for me to take the job.

I thought about it. Another Agency assignment would put me even farther from the mainstream of the U.S. Army than I already was by training Rangers. What I wanted instead was a combat command, an infantry battalion in one of the U.S. divisions facing the Chinese.

"Jack," Bill Depuy said, "you take this job and we'll make sure you get your battalion. The war's not going anywhere."

I arrived back in Korea just after New Year's, 1952. Colonel Depuy was right. The war certainly showed no signs of winding down. The cease-fire talks were sporadic and vitriolic, still stalled over the thorny issue of prisoner repatriation. My first duty station was the old CIA headquarters at Tongnae, a sprawling compound in a spa village outside Pusan. The Agency's chief of station was Ben Vandervoort, a burly former battalion commander from the 82nd Airborne (later played rather convincingly by none other than John Wayne in the film *The Longest Day*). Ben had lost an eye fighting in Holland and had retired from the Army. In Korea, however, he went under U.S. Army cover, with the rank of colonel.

CIA operations had their own bland cover—Joint Advisory Commission, Korea ("JACK"). Soon after I arrived, the outfit moved back north to the new station in the renovated Traymore Hotel in Seoul. I quickly discovered that our archrival for personnel, funding, air support, and, above all, mission authorization was a hodgepodge intelligence operation managed by FECOM called Combined Command for Reconnaissance Activities, Korea (CCRAK), pronounced "sea-crack."[23]

Fairly early on, I also discovered that the Agency's plan to undercut the determination of the Chinese high command through a guerrilla offensive on the mainland was anything but an established policy. While the operation was pending, I became the CIA deputy station chief in Korea with the mission of deploying military intelligence, espionage, and resistance agents in North Korea. I found myself the deputy in a command which had several lieutenant colonels even though I was still a major, a bureaucratic hurdle that was overcome by officially tagging my position with the title "By Direction of the President."

We were near the end of the second year of the war and the Agency's operations had matured. JACK had a network of covert intelligence bases on offshore islands stretching up the west coast of North Korea, which were supported by a small flotilla of fast, heavily armed patrol boats. We also maintained a base on Yo-do Island at the mouth of Wonsan harbor. Our main mission was to collect military intelligence by dispatching Korean agents north, by either parachute drop or sea insertion from our island bases.[24]

There was no shortage of brave young Koreans with family ties to the North. We recruited many of them from the refugees who had volunteered for service in the ROK forces. The problem was not with them, but with the actual conditions in Communist North Korea. Our open invitation to every potential anti-Communist refugee to accompany the retreating U.N. forces the year before had literally stripped North Korea of potential resistance networks. An agent could not function well without such support. In World War II, our best successes had been in Nazi-occupied countries where the bulk of the population chafed under the yoke of an oppressive enemy force. There were plenty of anti-Communists in Korea; unfortunately, we'd invited almost every one of them to live in the South.

Nevertheless, we managed to insert a few successful small teams who still had family connections in the North and were able to deliver reliable intelligence on enemy troop movements. But we were never able to establish anything approaching a true Maquis-type resistance network.

CCRAK's work overlapped ours. Their biggest operation was in Hwanghae Province, along the coast northwest of Seoul, where the battle lines divided a traditionally united population of fishing villages. The people there had established armed resistance to Kim Il-Sung's Communist regime even before the North Korean invasion of June 1950. So it wasn't difficult to exploit the situation by adding a few American advisers and pouring in arms and equipment. But such grass-roots "partisan" resistance never spread elsewhere in North Korea. The main thrust of CCRAK's operations, therefore, became small-scale sabotage raids, most launched from secret bases on the west coast's scattered islands and wild peninsulas.[25]

One of the biggest obstacles I faced was the Pentagon's prohibition on using American unconventional-warfare troops in North Korea. The Pentagon was worried that these units might be captured, broken by physical and psychological torture—the new term for this was "brainwashing"—and turned against us for propaganda purposes. I certainly could have made good use of the Ranger companies we'd worked so hard to train at Fort Benning. Unfortunately, they were not available. As I'd feared, the traditional division commanders to whom we'd assigned these companies had a deep distrust for Special Operations and no appreciation for its potential. The Ranger companies were terribly misused, and many good soldiers were killed or wounded serving as assault troops, after the line was stabilized, rather than as Special Operations forces. The survivors were assigned to the 187th Airborne Regimental Combat Team in Japan, a kind of fire brigade held in reserve for combat emergencies.[26]

One of my most successful, and hitherto unpublicized, operations in Korea involved a tough Air Force master sergeant who ran a converted wooden junk out of our bases on the west coast islands. He lived with his crew, had a Korean "wife," and was bound and determined to raise hell with the enemy. The sergeant had learned from Korean seamen that there was a marine telephone-telegraph cable connecting the Shantung Peninsula in mainland China with Dairen in Manchuria. He realized this had to be one of the main telecomm links between CCF in Korea and Peking. The Yellow Sea is generally shallow; the sergeant was enterprising. Early one May morning, his trailing grapples fetched up the thick, weedy cable. While the barnacles popped from the cable to crunch beneath his boots on the swaying deck, the sergeant wielded a fire ax, whacking out a three-foot length of cable. He then ran to the wheelhouse, called for maximum speed, and hightailed it back across the Yellow Sea.

When I reported this, CIA headquarters was furious I'd unleashed an operation with potentially serious international ramifications. But the National Security Agency code busters who were my neighbors in Seoul were delighted. The CCF, deprived of a secure surface telecomm cable, had been forced to use radio teletype. Within weeks, our crypto specialists had busted the Chinese code and were reading their operational traffic. This gave us a definite advantage during the protracted bargaining of the later cease-fire negotiations. The Chinese negotiators had to report daily to Peking and follow the orders of the CCF high command there. With the cable knocked out, our intelligence was able to eavesdrop on this sensitive enemy communication.

Most of our naval operations were on the east coast, where we'd often land raiding parties ashore to ambush trains and truck convoys. I flew into Yo-do Island several times to brief our Korean crews on these missions. They were a cheerful lot, well pleased to be killing Chinese, who had been their masters for centuries before the Japanese occupation. Being up on an advanced base, within enemy artillery range, reminded me I was a soldier. But one of the immutable imperatives of war in Asia was that Westerners could never simply disappear behind enemy lines into the civilian population as we had in Nazi-occupied Europe.

Because I could not actually lead my agents in combat, I decided I would do my damnedest to make sure they were at least inserted correctly. The Chinese were well aware of our airdrop operations in the North and had long before learned to recognize a low-flying transport with an open door as a sign of an agent drop. Parachuting being my specialty, I set about to correct this problem. American B-26 light bombers prowled the skies of North Korea every night, and were hardly viewed as unusual. But we had never dropped agents from them.

JACK acquired a couple of B-26s and I personally modified them for agent drops. The key was to rig the bomb bay as a jump platform. I took care of this by installing a couple of parallel planks about three feet apart. On the first test jump near our training drop zone on the Han River sandbanks, I told the pilot to keep his airspeed close to normal for level flight. I crouched in the bomb bay facing aft, one boot on either plank. When the clamshell doors gaped open beneath me, I simply snapped my feet together, arms at my sides, assuming the same position I'd used jumping from Stirlings as a Jedburgh. Unfortunately, the American chutes did not open as gently as their British equivalents under these conditions. The opening shock that day damn near knocked my molars loose. But I proved we could use bombers for agent drops.

I still wasn't satisfied, however. Too many of our people were being caught near the drop zone. North Korea was so crowded with well-dispersed enemy forces that the sound of any low-flying aircraft raised an alarm. There was a way around this problem too: free-fall drops. I tested this system several times. Captain Skip Sadler, my Airborne specialist, rigged me a ripcord chute with a backpack and reserve. We took the door off an L-19, and I had the pilot climb to 8,000 feet above the drop zone. This was years before the advent of skydiving, so I had no concept of stable free-fall positions. I simply used some old high school physics formulas for an "object in free fall" and calculated the number of seconds I could wait before safely pulling the ripcord relatively close to the ground.

When I tumbled out the open door of the L-19, the cold blue horizon seemed to tumble with me. I found myself staring *up* at the muddy sandbanks that rocked gently back and forth. I was upside down. Slowly, the horizon slid back above me and I was seated on a springy, invisible column of air, watching the river rise toward me. Given this spectacular visual display, I had forgotten to count my seconds. But I knew that objects on the ground came into sharp focus within a thousand feet. So I watched a vehicle on the road resolve from a blurred speck to a child's toy, to an actual U.S. Army jeep with a clear white star stenciled on the hood. I pulled the ripcord. The chute twanged open, and I checked the pleasant white canopy. My feet hit the sand.

Skip Sadler came pounding across the puddles toward me. "God, Jack!" he shouted. "Why'd you wait so long?"

"Well," I replied, "I got here, didn't I?"

Neither of us realized it, of course, but we'd just invented the concept of "high altitude–low opening" (HALO) parachute drops, now the principal means of inserting special warfare teams deep behind enemy lines.[27]

☆   ☆

In December 1952, I got a call from Colonel Richard G. Stilwell, the officer who'd recruited me back into the CIA.[28] He now commanded the 15th Infantry Regiment of the 3rd Division, serving in IX Corps in the center of the U.N. command front, the region called the Iron Triangle.

"Jack," he said, "you still want that battalion, or have you found a home with the gumshoes?"

Several times in the past months I had made inquiries about getting a combat command. But the Agency was against the idea. They cited the death sentence handed down by the espionage court in Peking in 1949, as well as the sensitive nature of my present work. Exposing myself to possible capture on the front lines, they said, put me at an unfair risk. But risk is part of a soldier's daily life; it comes with the uniform and those pretty ribbons they put on your chest. Now Stilwell, who had gone from his own Agency assignment to commanding a frontline regiment, was offering me a job.

"I'd still like that battalion, sir."

"Pack your bags," he said. "I've got an outfit that certainly needs a good commanding officer."

I was on my way to the shooting war.

CHAPTER SIX

15th Infantry, Korea

1952–1953

☆   ☆

By December 1952, the Korean War was stalemated both on the front lines and at the truce negotiations in the neutral village of Panmunjom. In fact, the war had become more of a *place* than an event. The two opposing armies were static, facing each other from lines of elaborate fortifications that stretched across the mountains and valleys of the peninsula from the Yellow Sea to the Sea of Japan. The U.N. command's Main Line of Resistance (MLR) was a 160-mile battlefront that curved and bulged near the original border of the 38th parallel.

Both sides had abandoned the massive offensives, amphibious assaults, and fast-paced war of maneuver that had characterized the seesaw fighting of the conflict's first sixteen months. For a year now, neither the U.N. nor the Communists had captured or lost a major position. Both armies were dug in deep. Both now relied more on artillery than on ground assault to punish the enemy. And inflicting unacceptable casualties on the opposing army in order to win concessions at the truce negotiations had become the combatants' principal strategy.

This was the prevailing situation when Colonel Richard G. Stilwell asked me to take over the 2nd Battalion of the 15th Infantry Regiment, which he had commanded for two months. The 15th Infantry was one of three regiments of the 3rd Division, which in turn was one of four divisions assigned to the U.S. IX Corps holding the central sector of the U.N. lines. The area was known as the Iron Triangle. It included the Chorwon River valley, one of the few natural, north-south invasion routes through the mountains. Before the war, road networks and a rail line through the valley had linked the three corners of the Triangle at the towns of Pyonggang in the north with Kumhwa and Chorwon in the south. The sides of the Triangle were steep valleys; its center was a block of wild, roadless parallel ridges and free-standing mountains. As elsewhere along the battlefront, the country to the north was higher than the mountains to the south, which gave the Communists the military advantage of controlling the high ground.

Dick Stilwell invited me to visit the regiment in the line, while my orders were pending in early December. I drove north from Seoul, up through the sprawling rear areas with their supply depots, truck and armor parks, workshops, and field hospitals occupying all the reasonably flat ground available. Moving north, the refugees' cardboard and tarpaper squatter villages thinned out until I crossed the IX Corps' southern boundary near the shell-torn village of Yonchon. From here on, civilians were not officially permitted. Tent camps now had elaborate sandbagged bunker complexes dug into the reverse, southern side of the mountains. The farther north I drove, the fewer tents there were and the bigger the bunkers became. I knew I was near the fighting front from the concentrations of our artillery dug into sandbagged positions, all the howitzer tubes facing north through camouflage nets.

Dick Stilwell gave me a good briefing on the 2nd Battalion at his regimental command post. The unit was up to full strength, approximately 900 men, divided among three rifle companies, a heavy-weapons company, and the normal support elements, including some anti-aircraft teams and a platoon of engineers. But it seemed the battalion had lost its will to fight, what he called the "aggressive spirit." Most of the men were more concerned with the fundamental issue of survival than with performing well as soldiers. The outfit's problem, he explained, was not unusual at that time in the war. Everyone knew the conflict would be eventually settled through negotiation, not military operations. The average soldier's job consisted of guarding his own sector, patrolling the mile or so of no-man's-land between the lines, and pulling dangerous tours of duty on the isolated outposts forward of the MLR.

Given the limited nature of the war, a formal duty system had evolved by which all American troops in Korea earned "rotation points" toward their eventual transfer back to the States. The magic number was thirty-six points. An infantryman earned four points for every month he spent on a line. Artillerymen and tankers got three points a month, depending on their proximity to the MLR, and so on back toward the rear. On the average, a guy in a combat outfit could expect to serve nine months. The purpose of this system was to spread the risk of death or wounding fairly. In practice, the rotation-point policy often destroyed unit morale and esprit de corps by making each individual soldier acutely conscious of his time remaining in combat. It was only human nature to take fewer risks if you had just a few weeks left on the line. Loyalty to a particular unit—a company, battalion, or regiment—had no place in Assistant Secretary of Defense Anna Rosenberg's rotation policy.[1]

But the Chinese Communists on the opposing ridges were there for the duration. Those who survived were veterans, skilled in the local geography and the methods of their enemy. By contrast, Americans were rotated back to the States just when they had acquired these skills. The Chinese were often more aggressive than the American troops they faced. And by this time the CCF were very well equipped with Soviet-made medium and heavy artillery, which had been in short supply during their initial intervention. In the Iron Triangle, the Chinese had dug truly elaborate bunkers and tunnels, often cutting right through a mountainside from north to south, with the southern firing position carefully camouflaged. From these positions they could drop 76, 85, and 105mm howitzer rounds on our trenches and most of the approach roads from the rear. And they weren't short of ammunition. A quick glance at the regimental records showed our lines had been hit by dozens of artillery rounds daily. Some nights hundreds of Chinese howitzer and mortar shells struck the positions.

One effect of this shelling was to keep men down in the trenches, rather than out patrolling or working to improve their bunkers. The men had come as individual replacements and hoped to make it through their months on the line, to depart as individuals. This survival attitude, Stilwell said, was most prevalent in the 2nd Battalion. The men patrolled poorly, seldom making contact with the enemy. They were even reluctant to dig their trenches too deep or fortify the roofs of their bunkers for fear the improved positions might attract enemy artillery fire. Lieutenant Colonel Hughes Ash, the 2nd Battalion commander, had tried to win his men's loyalty through kindness, granting them unusual concessions. For example, men who were "short" (who had almost earned their thirty-six points) were excused from outpost duty or patrols. There was an insidious ripple effect to this leniency: By the time I took over, the least experienced men drew the most hazardous assignments. Naturally, this led to unnecessary casualties, which only compounded the men's aversion to aggressive combat.

And, interestingly enough, the CCF had somehow discovered the battalion's weakness, so they directed the brunt of their artillery and ground assaults—usually night attacks on outposts—against 2nd Battalion positions.

The disparate backgrounds of the men in the rifle companies exacerbated the morale situation. Every platoon had American GIs (almost all of them draftees) and Korean soldiers of the Korean Augmentation to the U.S. Army (KATUSA). The American soldiers were further divided by race and culture. The 3rd Division was one of the first Army units to be racially integrated the year before, but there was still a prevailing lack of confidence in the fighting ability of the black soldier. My regiment also had several hundred Spanish-speaking Puerto Ricans from the 65th Infantry Regiment (a National Guard unit), which had done badly in combat that fall and had been broken up as a wholly ethnic unit.[2] These Puerto Rican soldiers were further divided along racial lines; those with predominantly African ancestry were often shunned by their lighter-skinned compatriots. So a buck sergeant squad leader in this battalion (probably a draftee without benefit of an NCO academy background) found himself trying to lead twelve men with little in common, some who couldn't even understand his orders.

Noncommissioned officers are the backbone of any infantry unit. But in Korea at this time, almost all experienced career NCOs had served their combat tours and were gone. This meant a unit depended on the leadership of junior commissioned officers—who were often kids fresh out of ROTC, simply serving their four-year obligation. These lieutenants in turn depended on their regular army battalion staff officers for leadership. Unfortunately, Dick Stilwell told me, Lieutenant Colonel Hughes Ash was not up to providing the kind of leadership the troubled 2nd Battalion needed.

I took over the battalion from Ash three days before Christmas when the unit had been pulled out of the MLR and placed in the regimental reserve area for training. I had visited the outfit in the line a few days earlier and had drawn some preliminary conclusions about exactly the kind of training they needed.

The war along this front was fought at night. And the CCF had shown they were masters of the night assault. But the men of my new command had little experience moving quietly and efficiently up and down the steep, snow-packed mountains at night. This meant the battalion could rarely mount a successful counterattack, when the Chinese threatened an isolated outpost. Service at these outposts, therefore, was terrifying. A company on outpost duty simply hid in the trenches, hoping to get through their two- or three-day stint without a Chinese assault. They only improved the outpost bunkers and firing positions when absolutely necessary. The men also were so fearful of artillery that, when on patrol, they rarely radioed for friendly fire support. This aversion to calling in the "protective fires" of American mortars and artillery close to their position had reached the point that several of my companies were grossly ignorant of the actual fire support available to them.[3] But I remembered the "Mad Minute" demonstration of precision artillery support I'd witnessed at the Infantry School at Fort Benning. I was determined that all my men would become familiar with this firepower and gain confidence enough to depend on it.

Their fighting spirit and efficiency had deteriorated to the point where apathy was general. All each man wanted was to survive another day. The junior officers, noncoms, and individual soldiers simply did not understand that their chances for survival would increase if they learned to fight effectively as a unit. It was my job to teach them.

☆   ☆

I started the process by assembling my company commanders, mortar section officers, and the liaison officers from regimental artillery. We went back to the fundamentals. I wanted my men to know the exact capabilities of the mortars and big guns supporting them. When we went back into the line, I told them, I expected optimal coordination between infantry and artillery. If an outpost asked for a flare over its position at 0220 in the morning, I expected that flare to be *there* within thirty seconds, not five minutes later half a mile down the line. Equally, I expected every noncom (and every commissioned officer), be he in a rifle platoon or from the "clerks and cooks" support staff, to be skilled at the vital task of pinpointing his exact position by map coordinates, so that artillery support could be effectively used.

The men were not pleased with this rigorous assignment. Most of them had expected that their time in regimental reserve would be punctuated by "I&I"—Intoxication and Intercourse—in the shantytown beer halls and brothels that sprouted (between periodic MP sweeps) like mushrooms in the rear areas. But I let them know any NCO or officer unable to clearly demonstrate his map skills would be relieved. My job was not to make friends of these people through leniency; it was to keep them alive and fighting. There'd be time for friendship later. Mutual respect came first.

Once I had them working on improving fire support, I turned to another fundamental of infantry tactics: the night attack. Until I took over the battalion, most of the men saw the naked slopes north of the MLR as a threatening wilderness controlled by the enemy. Part of this feeling came from the geography. The Chinese did hold the distant highlands. But the forward slopes near our positions were *our* real estate. If we learned to move across this terrain silently and fast, beginning with squads, then increasing unit size to full companies, we could prevent the Chinese from capturing our outposts or sections of the MLR, which had occurred with unacceptable regularity in the preceding months. Most of our men Killed in Action (KIA) had died trying to recapture positions we never should have let the Chinese take in the first place.

So I let it be known that a sergeant's or lieutenant's job depended on his ability to move his men quickly and quietly in absolute darkness. The men simply had to learn that this darkness was their ally, that they could use it if they took the time to learn the basic skills of their jobs. But on the first demonstration of these "skills" I witnessed the spectacle of squads and platoons bungling through each other, cursing loudly as they did so, and I even saw NCOs and lieutenants shining flashlights—as if this could help them find their way in the frozen wilderness.

Over the next two weeks I had the battalion out each night in the icy gullies and snowy, boulder-strewn slopes of the reserve area, moving up and down the hills, from one prearranged coordinate to another. And I was out there with them, every night, not back at the cozy oil stove in my tent doing paperwork. I had an adjutant for that task. My job was to be with the troops. Once they learned they had an honest-to-God soldier in command, I knew they would respond. But you don't get that kind of respect from delivering pep talks or issuing idle threats.

I also worked closely with my Pioneer platoon and the engineers who supported us. When we went back into the line, I wanted them available to help the rifle companies improve the fortifications. From what I'd seen earlier, many men had been satisfied with a poorly shored trench and a firing bunker that couldn't take a near miss from a heavy mortar, let alone survive a direct hit from an artillery round. We built models of the kinds of bunkers I expected to see in the line. They were dug deep into the hillsides and had vertical supports of heavy, twelve-by-twelve-inch timbers. The fronts were thickly protected with sandbags. The machine-gun positions were carefully designed to protect the men inside but allow adequate defensive fire. Most important, the bunker roofs had to be carefully constructed with alternating timbers, sandbags, and a "burster" layer of stones, gravel, and brush, all capped by more sandbags. In bunkers like this, the men could survive fierce enemy artillery barrages. And they would feel confident about calling in their own artillery on those terrifying moonless nights when the Chinese bugles sounded and the dark forms of men in padded suits flitted through the shadows on the slopes below.

I also used the engineers to construct a combat firing range that employed the kind of pop-up silhouette targets I'd been introduced to by the indomitable team of British commando officers, Majors Fairbairn and Sykes, during my Jedburgh training. My troops in Korea had learned to fire their rifles on the range, not while charging up a snowy hill. I taught them the fine art of instinctive firing. After several cold nights on this range, the companies were consistently riddling the silhouettes as the men advanced smoothly up the hillside. Now was the time to introduce additional realism. I had the mortar sections fire walking barrages close enough ahead of the advancing columns to accustom the men to that vital form of fire support.

Three weeks after I took over the 2nd Battalion, I staged my first full-unit night exercise. The objective was to move a counterattack force of three companies, by platoons, to the crest of a hill, while the fourth company maneuvered along a ridge line and dug in as a force to block the enemy retreat. The exercise involved artillery flares and mortar support. By three in the morning all of the objectives had been secured ahead of schedule and the men were safely back off the mountain. There'd been no serious accidents or injuries, despite the use of live fire in darkness on an unfamiliar mountainside. The men had come a long way in a short time.

I'd identified several young officers with real leadership potential, including First Lieutenants Dick Atkinson and George Meighen, the commanders of G and E companies. Atkinson was an Airborne soldier who'd been fuming at the lax conditions in the battalion. Meighen's company had a large proportion of KATUSA and Puerto Rican troops, but he made them the top scorers on our combat firing range. Another promising lieutenant was Dan Foldberg, Meighen's executive officer. He was a former All American tackle from West Point who could have easily landed a job coaching football in Japan. I knew I could depend on them when we returned to the line.

After the company officers reported in to my jeep that night, I suggested we head over to the Headquarters Company mess for a cup of coffee to celebrate the successful maneuver. I'd been unnaturally antisocial with these young lieutenants until then, purposefully distancing myself. Now I felt it was time to get to know them a little better. It was still pitch dark outside, and probably well below zero. We headed for the mess tent by the shortest route, across a shallow stream where trucks and jeeps had broken the ice repeatedly that night. I didn't notice that the stream banks had frozen again into a sheet of pure glare ice. As soon as I fell and landed with my right ankle twisted beneath me I knew it was broken. Even through my thick rubber Mickey Mouse boot I heard the dull pop of the bone.

I sat down on the ice, shaking my head. "Somebody get my jeep," I said, "I just broke my damn ankle."

For the next three hours I was shuffled back through the regiment's medical facilities, exactly what I did not want to happen. I'd hoped to get my leg taped up at the battalion aid station or, failing that, at the regimental collecting station. But the medics there examined the angry blue-and-yellow swelling and dispatched me to the division clearing company. Now military bureaucracy took charge. Officially, I was a "casualty" who couldn't be cared for within my parent organization. That meant I was technically no longer in command of the battalion. After sunrise, I found myself at the corps MASH unit several ridge lines back from the division front. This hospital, incidentally, was the one on which the "4077th MASH" of television fame was modeled. But while I was there, no one offered me a martini.

I sat in a drafty tent with wounded GIs moaning around me on bloody stretchers while clerks filled out their multiple admission forms, in triplicate, of course. The X-rays showed a nasty full fracture. The cast went all the way up to my knee. By ten o'clock in the morning I was in a bed, wearing GI pajamas, a long way from the 2nd Battalion.

This was unacceptable. I hadn't worked so hard getting the unit back in condition to abandon them. I waited until the senior MASH officers had made their rounds, then scrounged a wheelchair and went to the office to call my executive officer, Frank Hewitt. I told him to send the battalion surgeon down to the MASH with my jeep and driver. When they arrived, I had the doc browbeat the young NCO at the admissions office to release my uniform, telling the kid he was "moving" Major Singlaub.

By early afternoon I was back at my battalion command post, using a handy tree branch as a cane. I called Colonel Stilwell to explain what had happened.

"I'm glad you called," he said. "I just heard from General Smythe. That MASH colonel down there has you listed as AWOL and has filed a complaint with the corps commander."

"Damn," I muttered. "What can we do, sir?"

Stilwell had told me we'd soon be back in the line, and I knew he didn't want to have to find another CO for the 2nd Battalion. "You sit tight, Jack," he said. "We'll work something out."

The compromise was acceptable. I went back to the division clearing company for a couple of days to make sure the cast hardened correctly, and they plastered on a walking iron so that I could hobble around my area. In my personal gear I found an old rubberized rice bag, a relic of OSS days in China, which protected the cast from the mud and slush. I even managed to secure a handwarmer under the bag, so my toes didn't freeze as I supervised each night's training. The men probably thought I was crazy to be out there, leaning on a cane as they stormed up the exercise hill. But they certainly knew I was serious.

☆   ☆

Two weeks later, the 15th Infantry moved back into the Iron Triangle MLR, relieving the 35th Infantry Regiment of the 25th Division. My battalion took up positions on the right center, the eastern side of our sector. One of the 35th's departing officers offered this advice:

"Major," he said, "this isn't a bad part of the line. I've found that if you don't mortar them"—he pointed across the barren hills toward the frozen high ground to the north—"they won't mortar you."

I thanked him for the suggestion. That was exactly the type of defeatist attitude I'd worked so hard to eliminate among my men. Predictably, the trench line we'd inherited needed a lot of work. I deployed Easy and Fox companies from left to right, and set each to work with an engineer team, strengthening their bunkers, deepening their trenches, and extending their barbed wire and mine fields.

Two thousand yards northeast of our MLR sector stood Outpost Harry, a shell-pocked knob of an isolated hill that was the most advanced American position in the Iron Triangle. Harry was a company outpost, which meant in practice that there was room for three platoons plus some support elements at one time (about 100 men), with one platoon rotating back to reserve behind the MLR. During their last tour on the line, the 2nd Battalion had occupied a similar, but less exposed outpost. The practice then had been that a given company would only pull outpost duty for two days at a time, three maximum. This had been another of Colonel Ash's concessions to the prevailing survival attitude.

But, again, the effect had been negative. An infantryman who believes he's only in a trench or bunker for forty-eight hours will do little to improve the position. I had other plans for my outpost.

I took Lieutenant Dick Atkinson aside and pointed across the slope to the outpost. "You've got it for the duration, Lieutenant," I said.

"Sir?" He didn't look especially troubled, just curious.

"George Company will occupy Outpost Harry," I said formally. "You will hold that position until relieved. I think you're going to want to make some improvements out there, so I've got the engineers standing by."

Atkinson pursed his lips and nodded. His expression was neither pleased nor disappointed. He certainly didn't look afraid. Without my saying so, he understood that I had chosen his company for the toughest assignment. They would hold that exposed outpost for as long as required. It was a job for real soldiers.

Over the next several days I spent as much time with Atkinson and his men as I could. The trek out there along the snaking communication trench was not easy with that heavy cast on my leg. But I knew the men would appreciate my coming. It's one thing to order troops to do a hard job; it's another to lead them in the task.

The Chinese had good observation of our positions and seemed to realize a new battalion was in the line. That made things interesting on Harry. They hit the outpost with 82 and 120mm mortar fire for three nights running. But luckily they didn't stage a ground attack. That gave Atkinson and his men time to dig. We moved a lot of timber and construction material forward along a communication trench, depending on the strong backs of our Korean Service Corps "Chiggies," civilians who stoically accepted their heavy loads, the cold, and enemy fire.[4]

As George Company's men dug in deeper, they found some shocking discoveries. In one shell-torn bunker they ripped up to rebuild, they came across the decomposed remains of three Chinese soldiers and two GIs. I couldn't help but wonder at the morale of the American outfit that had shoveled rocks and burst sandbags over the bodies of these soldiers. It was an indication of the prevailing survival obsession along the line.

Men who would do that had to have been too scared to function well as soldiers. The outpost itself was a moonscape of shell holes. I realized that massed enemy barrages, and the resulting casualties, could scare men into such action. But I was determined that Harry would stand up to the toughest assault. The Chinese were skilled at attacking *through,* not behind their own mortar fire. This tactic caused casualties, but usually overwhelmed the American defenders hiding in their bunkers as the mortar rounds burst in the trenches. Every trench and fighting hole on Outpost Harry, I ordered, would have timber and sandbag roofs, so that my soldiers would be protected from mortar barrages and could still fire their weapons as the enemy advanced.

While George Company improved the outpost, I made sure the other companies were dug in well. Our emphasis on night tactics now paid off. Each company dispatched listening posts and ambush patrols well forward of its trench lines. When the Chinese probed the slopes of our positions, they encountered GIs hidden in the shadows. To build the men's confidence in night fighting, I devised a system to help them find their way in the dark, and also locate enemy patrols in the no-man's-land between the lines. We had a twin-barreled 40mm anti-aircraft gun dug in on the right corner of our position. The gun could fire a single glowing tracer, due north up the shallow valley that was the main Chinese attack route. On a dark night the shimmering red glare from that tracer round gave just enough light to detect moving troops. Our patrols would call for this illumination by simply clicking the "transmit" button of their walkie-talkie on a prearranged Morse letter. Because the 40mm gun fired due north, the system also gave my patrols instant orientation. They quickly grew to depend on this illumination to ambush enemy patrols or to call in artillery on the advancing enemy. Gone were the days of waving flashlights and squads bungling into each other in the darkness. The night no longer belonged to the Chinese. Now it was their turn to fear the darkness.

There were a series of short, savage encounters between our ambush teams and their probing patrols. Obviously, they got the message that this section of the line was well defended, because they switched from ground probes to massed artillery within a few days of our taking over the sector.[5]

☆   ☆

ONE afternoon in early February, I was coming back from having lunch with the men at Outpost Harry when I heard enemy shelling falling behind the MLR ridge line into the battalion rear. There were two roads up from regimental headquarters, which, unfortunately, could be seen by Chinese artillery observers hidden in the highland to the north. They didn't usually fire during the day unless there was a tempting target because this could provoke an air attack on their own artillery. When I got back down the hill, I discovered the Chinese 85mm barrage had disabled one of our three-quarter-ton trucks, hauling a precious cargo, a water trailer. The vehicle was stalled about 300 yards down the road, in a shallow, bowl-shaped valley. My Korean porters were due to climb the back slope to the companies in a few hours, carrying a hot meal in insulated marmite cans as well as the next day's water supply. I needed that trailer.

The sergeant driver was not overly eager to go back out in that exposed position to see if he could start the truck engine. In a situation like this, the officer-in-charge had to show a little leadership.

"Let's go, Sergeant," I said. "The troops can't eat snow."

He looked dubiously at my cane and the muddy cast on my leg, but he led the way.

When we got to the truck, I saw immediately that shell fragments had pierced the hood and punctured the radiator. Hopefully, all we'd have to do was fill it with water and she'd crank over. But we didn't get a chance to test my theory. The sergeant and I were standing near the hood when we both heard the unmistakable ripping canvas sound of incoming artillery.

I debated for a second whether to dive under the truck and risk getting burned from the exploding gas tank or to take shelter beside the vehicle. The first 85mm round exploded thirty yards in front of us. The second round was about twenty yards behind us. The third, fourth, and fifth rounds were less than ten yards away. By this time we had taken cover in the slight depression beside the road. I had my right arm tight across my helmet, protecting my face when the next round struck. The shrapnel pierced my forearm and ricocheted off the lip of my helmet with a frightening clang. My arm felt numb for a moment, then began to burn as if someone had jabbed me with a glowing poker. Blood flowed warm and heavy through the torn sleeve of my field jacket.

Two more rounds exploded in the snow nearby. Shrapnel and frozen clods showered over us. By this time I could see that the truck had received a lot more shrapnel hits and would be unlikely to start regardless of what we did at this time.

"Sergeant," I said, rising to an unsteady crouch, "I think we better get the hell out of here."

☆   ☆

ARRIVING at the corps MASH this time, I was strapped down under a blanket to a stretcher. The surgeon in charge of the triage tent bent down to examine my wound tag. He'd obviously seen a lot of seriously hit men and could tell at once from my coloration and alertness that I was in no grave danger.

"SFW," he mumbled, noting I had a shell fragment wound in the right forearm. "We'll get this wound debrided, Major . . ." He glanced at the name tag on my field jacket. "Singlaub . . ." Recognition dawned. He gazed the length of the blanket and saw the bulge on my right leg. In a flash he had the blanket back and was stroking the cast. "Get the Colonel," he shouted to an orderly. "Tell him we got that Major Singlaub again."

I can attest that the colonel in charge of the real-life MASH was not as amicable as the various actors who played him on television. He had not been amused the month before when a field-grade officer went AWOL and got away with it. He was even less amused when this officer returned with a wounded arm to match the injured leg. The Colonel scrutinized my records and was pleased to discover I had enough time in Korea to merit rotation to the States. After my arm was treated, he ordered me dispatched to the 121st Evacuation Hospital south of the Han River, near Seoul. And he made sure I got there by shipping me to the railhead in one of his own ambulances, guarded by two husky orderlies.

As we drove away from the muddy MASH, I heard artillery thumping in the ridges to the north. My outfit might well be under attack and here I was being evacuated for a serious but nonthreatening flesh wound. I had other plans.

After the orderlies returned to the MASH, I managed to get hold of my old JACK pilot, Air Force Captain Bill Ford, who flew his L-19 up and landed at the railhead medevac strip. Bill delivered me back to Seoul where I took a room at JACK headquarters in the Traymore Hotel. From there I telephoned my old Jedburgh buddy Mac Austin, who was serving with CCRAK. "Mac," I said, "find Doug Lindsey and tell him I need his help."

Colonel Doug Lindsey was Eighth Army surgeon, the head medical honcho in Korea. Mac and I had gotten to know him the year before during a medical emergency when CCRAK had tragically dropped some ROK agents undergoing parachute training into the Han River. Mac and I had happened to be driving by and saw Doug Lindsey, buck naked, dragging drowning Koreans from the swirling waters. We'd helped him as best we could and a friendship developed from that sad incident.

When Lindsey called I explained my predicament and swore the wound was superficial. Lindsey somehow arranged to have my evacuation orders canceled. But he insisted I check into the Evacuation Hospital for treatment. I hated to do this because I knew the medics were itching to take away my uniform and get me into hospital pajamas. I never have been much on hospitals. When I was stationed in Manchuria, I had come down with jaundice and was hospitalized by the Navy at Tientsin. When their medics started clucking their tongues at my fever, I'd simply checked myself out and flown to Mukden in the back of an L-5. Now I planned the same type of escape.

I met Captain John Laurer, a medical officer from a supporting artillery battalion who'd broken his ankle playing Ping-Pong. John had a medical school buddy in the 121st Evac; within a day, I was free to go.

Once more I called Bill Ford. "Bill," I said, "I have a new mission for you."

Ford flew me back to the regimental airstrip in his L-19. As soon as I landed I hitched a ride to Dick Stilwell's headquarters to tell him I was back. He took one look at me and shook his head. I'm sure I appeared an unlikely combat leader with my right arm in a sling, and the muddy old cast still on my right leg.

"Well," he said, "at least you got here before the corps commander called to report you AWOL again." He picked up his field telephone. "This way I get to call him, instead."

The ground rules Dick worked out were better than I'd hoped for. I was allowed to keep my command as long as I stayed in the regimental area until the medics removed the drain from my wound and made sure it wasn't infected.

When I got back to the outfit five days later, I noticed men who had no proper business at the command post finding excuses to come by to get a look at their CO. I'm sure this time they realized I was serious.

☆   ☆

WHILE I'd been gone, the Chinese had stepped up the artillery assault of our lines. During one twenty-four-hour period over 500 shells had hit our trenches. But the newly fortified positions held up well to this barrage and casualties were relatively light.[6]

The Korean winter slowly thawed to a muddy spring. And with the warmer weather enemy pressure increased. The truce negotiations had resumed again in Panmunjom, and this time it appeared the Communists would compromise on the prisoner repatriation issue. But intelligence indicated they planned to follow Mao's well-known "Fight-Talk, Talk-Fight" strategy. They needed to gain face on the battlefield before compromising on the diplomatic front. To do this, they planned to capture exposed American positions and hold them until a cease-fire was effected. As military historian Walter G. Hermes described the situation: "If they could conclude the fighting with a successful assault upon the UNC lines, the general impression of a Communist military victory in the war might, in the eyes of the Asian community, be sustained."[7]

What this situation meant to us was continued enemy pressure, especially against Outpost Harry.

☆   ☆

ONE of the first places I went after returning from the hospital was the artillery observation post, a bunker at the crest of a conical mountain on my battalion right. The young lieutenant from corps artillery commanding the OP was a little surprised to see an infantry major with two casts hobble up there, but he soon understood the purpose of my visit. From this position we had good line-of-sight observation of the enemy hills. The Chinese artillery fire that had wounded me had to have been spotted from an enemy OP bunker hidden somewhere out there on those serrated ridges. I planned to have my engineers blast a narrow zigzag road up the reverse slope of this mountain to accommodate an M-26 tank. The tank had a flat-firing 90mm rifled gun that could put a shell straight out there several miles, hopefully right down the throats of those bastards in the Chinese OP. The lieutenant liked my plan.

Within a week we had the tank dug in. The Chinese made their mistake on a late afternoon a couple of days later. The setting sun glinted off their powerful artillery glasses, just long enough to give us a good fix on their OP. The tank began firing. Six rounds later, the enemy artillery spotter bunker was a smoking ruin. We kept up this pressure. They would build a new OP and we would shell it. Maybe this was a futile exercise, but it sure made me feel good.[8]

I also made a point of visiting Outpost Harry to make sure the reinforcing of the positions had continued unabated while I'd been gone. Lieutenant Dan Foldberg of Easy Company was helping with this important task. As I toured the trenches, noting the timber-and-sandbag roofs of the fighting positions, Foldberg walked behind me. He had obviously been startled to see me trudging up the communications trench to the outpost, my arm in a sling and my leg cast squelching in the mud. But he was too much the correct young West Point lieutenant to comment.

Years later, however, I discovered Foldberg employed an ingenious trick that day to test my sangfroid. One of his sergeants crept along the trench twenty yards behind us, tossing out hand grenades, which rolled down the slope to explode under the barbed-wire entanglement.

"Incoming mortars, sir," Foldberg had shouted when the grenades exploded.

The blast did sound like Chinese 60mm mortars, but the explosions didn't seem all that close. I carried on inspecting the new bunkers. There were more explosions. "You'd better get under cover, Lieutenant," I said. "It's too dangerous following me around. Wherever I go, the Chinese shoot at me."

Foldberg had apparently judged the purpose of my visit to Outpost Harry was serious business, not grandstanding. We continued the inspection with no further "mortars."[9]

☆   ☆

Unfortunately, Colonel Richard Stilwell was transferred in the middle of March. He'd done a fine job with the regiment, but his talents were needed farther east where ROK divisions held the line and had come under increased Chinese pressure. Stilwell had served as a division operations officer under General Van Fleet in Europe during the war and was a master at rebuilding battered units. He had his work cut out for him in the ROK 1st Corps on the east coast. His replacement as regimental commander was a different kind of officer altogether.

Colonel Russell F. Akers, Jr., had several undesirable attributes. The worst was his drinking. Although it's not generally known by the public, there's always been a lot of alcohol on America's battlefields. Some men use liquor to dull their fear in combat. Akers, I believe, drank to reduce the anxiety of command. Whatever his reasons, Akers drank a lot. Every day, as a matter of fact, beginning in early afternoon and extending well into the night. On many occasions I'd arrive back at regimental headquarters before sunset for a briefing on the night's operations and encounter Colonel Akers, red-faced and sweating in his command tent, the alcohol sweet and cloying on his breath.

What a man drank in the civilian world didn't matter that much. But in a combat zone a drunken commander—or drunken troops, for that matter—could be disastrous. For that reason, I had instituted a rule in the battalion that there'd be absolutely no drinking by any officer or man while we were in the line. I had the supply officer, Captain Guzzardo, stockpile our daily beer ration, to be consumed when we rotated back to reserve. The men grumbled about this, but eventually saw the logic of my order. Many of the young soldiers in the line were in their teens, unaccustomed to alcohol. Even a few beers made them sleepy. A sleepy soldier was dangerous to his buddies.

I ran afoul of Colonel Akers almost immediately because of this rule. When I attended his first dinner meeting for the regiment's battalion commanders, he was serving martinis he mixed himself in a well-loved sterling cocktail service. I asked for a cup of coffee instead, explaining it would be unfair to return to the MLR with liquor on my breath, when my troops were up there, denied their beer ration.

Akers refused to accept my explanation. "By God," he said harshly, thrusting a glass into my hand, "when I drink, everybody drinks."

"Sir," I protested.

"Drink, damn it," he snapped. "That's an order."

I was dumbfounded. If he insisted on his booze, why didn't he drink at lunchtime and sleep it off? I liked a beer or drink before dinner as much as anyone, but we weren't back at Fort Benning, enjoying happy hour. Everyone knew the hours of darkness were the critical period along the MLR. If the Communists were going to attack, they always came after midnight. By that time, Akers had probably gone through an entire bottle of gin. History tells us that General Ulysses S. Grant made some of his better decisions after a bottle or two of whiskey. That might have been the case with Grant. I don't think Akers was cut from the same cloth.

I tried to avoid his dinners, and when I couldn't, I always had a thermos of hot coffee in my jeep to drink on the way back to the line.

☆ ☆

ON March 30, Chinese foreign minister Chou En-lai indicated his country would accept an Indian-sponsored compromise on the prisoner repatriation issue, by which individual POWs would be questioned by neutral observers as to their preference for release. The truce talks at Panmunjom, which had been suspended yet again, resumed once more with considerable fanfare. While the world press heralded this "statesmanship," we on the battle line prepared for a fresh assault on our positions.

Our regiment had two other outposts besides Harry: Outpost Dick in the center, and Tom on our left. But these two positions were less of a threat to the enemy, and also easier for us to defend than Harry. When the CCF began extending their line of trenches and shelter bunkers from a spur of high ground we called Star Hill directly toward Outpost Harry, it was clear that this outpost would receive the brunt of the expected enemy attack.

I conferred with the unit on our right, a reinforced battalion of the Greek Expeditionary Force, an outfit made up of tough professional veterans of the Greek civil war who had volunteered for duty in Korea. They were commanded by a jaunty little colonel named Stergos Kaumanakous. The Greeks had fought this kind of battle against Communists on their Albanian border, and they were quite capable of defending their line. They were also in a good position to rake Star Hill with heavy machine-gun fire to help spoil a Chinese attack on Harry.

But Harry's best defense would be precise, massive artillery protective fires, up to and including the last desperate use of variable-time (VT) shrapnel airbursts directly above the outpost itself. I'd planned on this tactic when I'd ordered Lieutenant Atkinson and the engineers to completely overhaul Harry's bunkers and trenches. They had greatly improved the defenses, concentrating on building mortar-proof cover on all fighting positions.

With an enemy attack pending, I was glad I had George Company still defending Harry. They were damn good troops, and they accepted this hazardous duty without complaint. I made sure they had plenty of small arms and automatic weapons ammunition, as well as extra barrels for their machine guns. I also made sure their field telephone lines to the MLR were doubled off and shielded against mortar fire. But I knew the lines would not last through a concerted enemy attack, so I issued extra radios and batteries to the outpost. Finally, I had a long conference with Atkinson, his executive officer and first sergeant, and the battalion artillery coordinator. We plotted the protective fires for Harry in great detail and rehearsed a system of emergency procedures with a signal lamp. If he was being overrun, Atkinson could use either his radio or the lamp to call in VT on his own position—if all other means of communication were knocked out. As a final precaution, I got together with the regimental air support officer and arranged to have a C-47 flare plane standing by on alert should we need really strong illumination over the outpost. Our supporting artillery, of course, had plenty of flares and star shells, but I knew the smoke and dust raised by an intense enemy barrage might be so thick that we'd need the dazzling, one-million-candlepower aerial flares to pierce the aptly named "fog of battle."

☆   ☆

THE enemy assault on Harry began with some minor harassing mortar fire a few hours after dark on the night of April 2, 1953. These were sporadic 60mm rounds that did little damage. But by ten that night the mortar fire was dropping on Harry in regular rolling barrages, and the 60s had been augmented by 82mm and 120mm. I left my executive officer, Major Frank Hewitt, in charge of the artillery coordination at the command post and I climbed the slope to the trenches of our MLR. There was no word yet of an enemy ground attack, but I instinctively felt one coming. It was a clear, cool night with no moon, and the temperature was just above freezing. Good conditions for an attack. I talked to Atkinson by field telephone, offering to dispatch his regular rotating relief platoon early if he wanted them. This would give him a chance to have some fresh men, and, of course, to send back anyone he felt might not do well in an assault.

"Yes, sir," he said, sounding quite calm. "I think that's a good idea."

I briefed the platoon leader, and went through the trench at the men's jump-off position, making sure each soldier carried plenty of ammunition, grenades, and water.

No sooner had Atkinson acknowledged that the relief platoon had reached the outpost than we heard the distinctive thunderclaps and rumble of Chinese heavy artillery. I watched through binoculars as enemy 85mm and 105mm howitzer rounds began to walk across the outpost, but lost count after fifty. The orange shock waves and churning dust now completely obscured Harry. But our own artillery flares were still bright enough to give us good observation. In the chalky flare light, we could clearly see small groups of enemy soldiers moving down the slopes of Star Hill toward Harry. I called in a fire mission on their approach route, and requested the Greeks sweep the area with their heavy machine guns.

From our right, the Greek tracers soared and looped in gaudy red streams. American light and medium artillery was bursting all along the enemy approaches to Outpost Harry, churning up more smoke and dust. The enemy artillery barrage intensified now and they began heavy shelling of the units along our MLR to keep their heads down.

I called for the activation of the improvised battalion reserve. It consisted of G Company's relief platoon plus the Pioneer and Ammo platoon and another platoon made up of cooks and clerks from Headquarters Company. This composite company was under command of the HQ company commander, Lieutenant Lischak, who had rehearsed the assembly and movement of his reserve force only a few days earlier. Lieutenant Lischak was a damn good commander, but his improvised company lacked the strength, training, and firepower of a line company. While these men assembled in the vicinity of the battalion headquarters, the artillery barrage up front intensified to a level I had never seen before. The enemy rounds were falling without interruption on the outpost, which now resembled a smoking, molten volcano. When I tried to reach Atkinson on the field telephone, I discovered both lines had been severed.

Now we saw enemy flares, first a single white rocket. Then a double red and a green star cluster. I assumed that that was their attack signal. I got on the radio with Atkinson and warned him of the impending assault.

"I know, sir," he said through the crackling static. "They're right outside our wire now. We're getting grenades already." Atkinson then requested final protective fires. I relayed his order and all of the battalion mortars and division artillery behind us cut loose, laying down a carpet of carefully plotted barrages that struck all around Harry's trench line and wire. Now the volcano was hidden by its own smoke. I called for the Air Force flare ship. Within twenty minutes the droning C-47 was out there releasing the brilliant parachute flares. The shadowy night was replaced by a garish imitation daylight that somehow reminded me of an overexposed newsreel.

I told Lieutenant Lischak to move his reserve force into an assembly area near the F Company command post and await further orders.

Atkinson was back on the radio. "They're in the trenches," he shouted. "Request VT on position; repeat, VT on position. Acknowledge."

He sounded young and scared now. It was definitely his voice. There had been several Chinese attempts to trick us with English speakers on the radio in the past few weeks. But I knew the Lieutenant's voice too well to disregard his call. He had reached the critical point in the battle. As we had arranged, he would now pull his men under the covered fighting positions and into their reinforced bunkers. They would try to keep the Chinese exposed outside on the hilltop while the American artillery burst overhead. If the tactic worked, the enemy would be caught in the open and be either massacred or forced to withdraw. But if American soldiers were caught outside, they too would be slaughtered by the storm of shrapnel. It was a terrible risk. But losing the outpost and having to recapture it was an unacceptable alternative.

Lieutenant Colonel John Roddy, the artillery battalion commander supporting our regiment, answered my request personally. "VT right on them, Jack?" He wanted to be sure that was my intention.

"VT on Outpost Harry," I repeated. "Keep firing until George Company requests normal protective fires. I take full responsibility."

No sooner had I jammed the field telephone back in its case when the familiar freight-car rumble of outgoing howitzer rounds passed close overhead. It was as if a Fourth of July fireworks' crescendo from several small towns went off simultaneously out ahead of us. The barrages were constant now. The sky over Harry pulsed with red explosions and white-hot shrapnel. Even at this distance, the shock waves pounded our faces and throats.

It was time to move out the reserve force. I called Lischak at the Fox Company command post and told him, "Execute Counterattack Plan Baker." As the counterattacking force moved along the road in front of Fox Company's positions, the radio reports from Harry became more frantic. Most radios could not be heard because their antennas had been blown away by the intense artillery fire. The bunker closest to the MLR reported "many friendly KIA," and enemy troops between his position and the command post. I decided I had better go with the counterattacking force. As I passed through the MLR, I borrowed an M-I rifle and a bandoleer of ammunition. I placed two frag grenades in the pockets of my field jacket.

"Let's go," I told the men. "Move out." As we passed through the wire and filtered into the zigzag communication trench, I saw that the VT barrage on Harry was lifting, to be shifted back to the protective fires once again. We moved down the trench line to the bottom of our slope and started across the exposed flat.

So far the men had kept up a good pace, but here the trench had been battered by enemy mortars and the going was slow. Just as they began to bunch up and falter, I heard the shriek and snort of incoming artillery. Suddenly the ground around us erupted with 105mm bursts and heavy mortars. The enemy had this trench zeroed in, and they'd been waiting for this counterattack force to appear. I shouldered my way through the men, pushing them ahead, shouting to move out, to escape this trap. But either they couldn't hear me through the explosions, or they were immobilized by fear. It's almost impossible to convince men to leave the illusory shelter of a trench and strike across exposed ground.

There was only one way to get them out of there. I clambered out of the trench and ran along the edge, trying to keep low, but still be seen by the men beneath me.

"Come on, you sons of bitches," I shouted, breaking my cardinal rule never to swear at my troops. "They *need* us up there."

I've always said that if an officer has to swear at his men he isn't much of a leader, but I had to shock them out of their immobilizing fear.

They hesitated a moment, then rushed forward along the trench. I continued to trot beside them on the edge, shouting encouragement.

When we left the trench and stumbled up the muddy, blasted slopes of Outpost Harry, I ordered the men to halt and take cover in the shell holes. The final rounds of friendly protective fire were still striking above us around the remnants of Harry's barbed wire. I was amazed at the consistent accuracy of our fire control. The artillerymen behind the battalion lines were firing blind over two ridges, following the orders of a distant forward observer. But they had their howitzer tubes so well sighted in that they could place a round anywhere they wanted on Harry with absolute precision.

The barrage finally lifted and I led the men up the hill. We shouldered a narrow spur and there was sudden movement to our left. Less than thirty yards away several squads of Chinese soldiers in their distinctive tan quilted uniforms struggled to retrieve their dead, wounded, and weapons. I opened fire with the rifle and the men around me cut loose with carbines, rifles, and BARs. The enemy troops fell in the garish light of the flares. We struggled on up the hill. Near the crest we encountered another pocket of Chinese in the shattered trenches. Again, my men repelled them.

I shouted through the smoke and dust, trying to alert the men in the outpost that their relief had arrived. A distant voice shouted back. The scene on the hilltop was terrible. Dead enemy soldiers lay sprawled all around us, many sliced apart by the VT shrapnel. The shell holes overlapped in crazy patterns like a moonscape. The air hung with dust, cordite fumes, and the stench of burnt, mangled flesh. As I dropped into a trench, I encountered a horrible sight that I have never forgotten. A dead American soldier was hunched forward on the sandbags, his face inches from me in the flare light. A mortar round had struck close behind him, and the explosion had somehow burst his head, swelling his features grotesquely. But I recognized the man. He had been a cheerful young corporal from G Company's relief platoon who had joked with me only a few hours before in the MLR trenches. Now he had become this grotesque distortion.

The company first sergeant worked his way toward me through the broken sandbags and shattered timbers, probing dead Chinese soldiers with his bayonet. "Sir," he said, his voice breaking, "we're sure glad to see you." He pointed his rifle toward the shell-ripped bunker roofs behind him. "We bitched when you made us dig in so deep. But that cover saved our lives tonight."

We collected over fifty dead Chinese soldiers around the outpost. Our observation post on the MLR had seen the enemy withdraw, dragging maybe another fifty. Two of the fallen Chinese in Harry's trenches were still alive and we evacuated them with our own wounded. All told, the defense of Outpost Harry had cost Company G nine men killed and twenty-one wounded out of the 120 defenders.

When the last of the wounded had been evacuated and I was finally able to return to my command post after dawn, Frank Hewitt informed me that the battle for Outpost Harry had set a division record for artillery expended. Over 100 American mortar and howitzer tubes had supported us during the night, firing a total of almost 20,000 rounds. Enemy artillery fire had totaled over 8,000 shells.[10] This was fire on a scale far beyond anything American forces had ever encountered in Korea.

But our tactics had succeeded. Maybe, I thought, peeling off my bloody, mud-crusted flak jacket, the enemy will think twice before they try again.

☆   ☆

Two days later, Lieutenant Atkinson, sixteen of his officers, NCOs, and troops assembled with me in the regimental rear. Major General George Smythe, the division commander, presented us with decorations for valor. When it was my turn, General Smythe personally read from the citation, noting that I had taken command of the counterattack and deliberately exposed myself to enemy fire. For this "outstanding gallantry, initiative, and devotion to duty" I, too, was awarded the Silver Star. Naturally I was proud. But I couldn't help remembering that dead soldier's face.

Atkinson received the Silver Star, as did his first sergeant and several of his men. The others received the Bronze Star.

Late that night I was back in the line, checking the repairs to my companies' positions. Through the fine spring rain we heard the Chinese loudspeakers blaring their tinny music toward us. Then the familiar voice of their propaganda man sent greetings to the troops of the 2nd Battalion. "You are being punished for your aggression in Korea," he told us. "Korea is a hell of a place to die."

The grizzled first sergeant beside me in the trench shifted his cud of chewing tobacco and spat into the mud. "No shit, Dick Tracy," he said. "What else is new?"

There was more singsong Chinese music. Then the speaker resumed, again addressing the men of my battalion. "This war in Korea has been going on a long time," he informed us. "But now the fighting is really going to start."

The music echoed through the mist. After a while, American 155mm Long Tom rounds screeched through the clouds overhead and thumped into the unseen mountains to the north. The music stopped.

☆   ☆

THE Chinese pressure shifted west. For the next two weeks they assaulted Porkchop Hill, an exposed outpost similar to Harry on the 7th Division's front. The battle there was one of the most heroic of the Korean War. By the time the assault was over, the U.S. Army had held its position and the Chinese had wasted hundreds of their best troops.

The pressure moved back east again. On the night of April 24, Outpost Harry was suddenly hit with a devastating Time-on-Target heavy artillery barrage that totaled almost a thousand rounds. I had Fox Company on the outpost, and had briefed their commanding officer, platoon leaders, and first sergeant that afternoon to prepare for an assault.

This attack developed along the same pattern as the assault on Harry three weeks earlier. But now the enemy artillery barrages were even heavier. From the Chinese flare patterns it became obvious that the ground assault would be in several waves, involving almost a battalion of troops. Once more our artillery was accurate and devastating. The volcano of Outpost Harry erupted again. Just before midnight the company commander radioed his request: "VT on position. They're in my trenches." I was again leading the counterattack force of Fox Company's reserve platoon and a composite group of clerks, drivers, and engineers out of the MLR when my radio operator reported Fox Company's fire-support request. It took me a while to convince regimental artillery to fire the VT mission on our own position.

But Fox Company had other means to protect themselves. After the attack on April 3, Lieutenant Dan Foldberg of Easy Company and his West Point classmate Lieutenant Alan Lichtenberg, the commander of my battalion's engineer platoon, had booby-trapped the outpost's slopes with a crude, brutally effective weapon: "Fougasse." These were buried 55-gallon drums filled with a mixture of thickened gasoline and diesel fuel—homemade napalm, fused with a phosphorus grenade, that could be triggered from the outpost command bunker. When Fox Company lit off their Fougasse, the approach trenches swarming with Chinese troops were flooded with cascading liquid fire. The enemy survivors were then hit by the incoming VT.

But they kept coming. By the time I reached the outpost, several bunkers had been overrun, but Fox Company had rallied to repel the Chinese. The scene was worse than after the first attack. Enemy dead and wounded lay everywhere.

But our losses in the hand-to-hand fighting were severe. Nineteen Americans had been killed and almost fifty wounded. And a medic reported seeing one wounded GI being dragged away screaming when the enemy finally retreated.

The next night, the Chinese propaganda echoed again across the still-smoldering hills. Our soldiers were encouraged to lay down their weapons and come across to the Chinese lines where they would be "welcomed with arms wide open."

☆   ☆

THE first of the summer heat came in early May. Now the muddy roads behind the MLR were choked with dust from trucks and tanks. The enemy began to alternate battalion-size attacks on Eighth Army outposts with periods of absolute calm, during which their propaganda speakers worked overtime. I used the opportunity to improve the defenses of Outpost Harry. I knew the Chinese would be coming again, but I didn't know how large the attack would be. If they were willing to squander several hundred men in a multiple-battalion assault, they would undoubtedly capture Harry. My plan was to repulse every one of their probes so savagely that they would shift their attention elsewhere.

I was in my command bunker the warm starlit night of May 10, when I heard the familiar rumble of an enemy barrage smacking Harry. The field telephone whirred beside me and Frank Hewitt reported another Time-on-Target had just hit the outpost. I grabbed my helmet and flak jacket and dashed to the fire-control bunker beside my command post.

If a major ground assault against Harry was coming, I wanted to break it up as best I could with long-range fire missions against the enemy approach route. I took my time with the battalion artillery coordinator, carefully plotting the exact sequences of barrages I wanted laid down. We worked as calmly as we could plotting the azimuths and sequences of high-explosive, white-phosphorus, and VT rounds needed. But we were both aware of the mounting thunder of the enemy barrage. Obviously, the noise of the Chinese artillery was heard back at regiment. Frank Hewitt answered the field phone and called me across the bunker.

"It's Colonel Akers, Jack," Frank said. "He wants to know what the hell's going on." Frank was not paraphrasing the Colonel. That's the way Akers talked. "He wants to speak to you, personally."

But I was too busy with the artillery fire-support coordinator to explain my plans. At any rate, I had given Akers a detailed briefing on my latest outpost defense tactics only that morning. But this was late at night and I didn't know how much gin he'd swallowed.

"You brief him, Frank," I said. "Tell him I can't talk to him right now."

When I was certain the artillery officer understood my orders, I left Frank Hewitt in charge of the command post and dashed up the hill to the MLR with my radio operator. I had no sooner settled into the observation trench to spot the first barrages when the nearby field telephone rang.

The sergeant who answered yelled over the noise of the outgoing artillery. "Major Hewitt wants to talk to you, sir. He said it's absolutely urgent."

I was annoyed. Frank knew I'd be busier than a one-armed paper hanger up here, trying to get the counterattack force organized while simultaneously observing the supporting fires. As any infantry officer knew, the decision of when and how you commit your reserve was the critical one in the conduct of the battle. And this decision must not be delegated to a subordinate.

I impatiently grabbed the phone. "Major," Frank began, addressing me formally. "I hate to tell you this, but Colonel Akers called back . . ." I wondered what the hell was causing Frank Hewitt to talk this way. Then he told me. "Major," he continued, "Colonel Akers told me to inform you that you are relieved of your command as of right now. You are to leave the area immediately. He's bringing Major Fred Thomas from 1st Battalion to take over the command."

Frank might as well have hit me in the guts with a rifle butt. Being relieved of a command under fire was probably the worst thing that could happen to any combat officer. I was speechless. Finally, I found some words. "What on earth happened, Frank?" I asked. "Didn't you tell him I was up here trying to get things organized?"

"Jack," Frank said, "Akers is drunk. He wouldn't listen to anything I said. But he did make it clear you are relieved of command. He insisted I note it in the commo log."

That was the end of that. I told the company commander in the trench beside me to take over. An hour later, I was back at regiment. Akers refused to see me. I slept that night fitfully, listening to the distant slap and rumble of the artillery battle raging around Harry. Fortunately, the outpost again survived the enemy attack.

☆   ☆

WHEN I came out through division en route to Seoul, Colonel Ed Burba, the division Chief of Staff, took me aside. "Jack," he explained, "we don't want you worrying about this. General Smythe sent an officer up there to investigate the circumstances. He knows you were unfairly relieved, but he's got to uphold his regimental commanders."

I nodded grimly. That was the Army way.

But Burba saw I wasn't convinced. "By the way," he added, "Dick Stilwell was on the horn as soon as he heard. He let it be known that if anything disparaging went into your record there'd be hell to pay."

That *was* encouraging.

Stilwell's warning must have worked. Within a day, Akers had sobered up enough to sign a Meritorious Bronze Star medal citation, which cited my "aggressiveness and inspirational leadership" while molding my battalion into an extremely effective combat team. When I picked up my 201 personnel file from the division clerks, there was no indication I had been relieved of duty, only that I'd been temporarily reassigned to division headquarters. And my new permanent-change-of-station assignment as a student at the Command and General Staff College at Fort Leavenworth, Kansas, remained unchanged.

I got to Seoul the next day and headed for CCRAK to stay with Mac Austin until I got a flight to the States. When Mac picked me up, he had a big smile on his wind-burned face. I had just made the promotion list to lieutenant colonel, a good six months ahead of schedule. That was all the assurance I needed that Akers's drunken outburst had not affected my record. And I could rest easy that the battalion was in good hands because Fred Thomas and I shared the same command philosophy.

But Mac had some bad news as well. In the debriefing of the first sick and wounded American POWs to be exchanged, CCRAK had learned the fate of my friend Major Homer Hinckley. Apparently Homer had made the mistake of swearing at his captors in Chinese. He was singled out for special scrutiny. Then it was discovered he had served in Peking in a questionable capacity. The Chinese took Homer and a number of other American prisoners to a secret military jail near Peking. They tortured Homer daily for information, but he had none to give. Finally, they chained him naked in a cage like an animal and tortured him in front of the other assembled prisoners. Even a giant of a man like Homer could not survive such treatment. He died, a tormented, frozen skeleton at the end of that terrible winter.

I caught a plane from Kimpo field the next afternoon. I was leaving the blood-soaked shores of Asia. But part of me would always remain there.

Lt. Col. Singlaub on maneuvers with 101st Airborne Division, 1958.

Lt. Col. Singlaub with Gen. William Westmoreland, Commander of the 101st Airborne Division.

Germany, 1961. Col. Singlaub leads the staff of the 16th Infantry on a regimental visit to Luxembourg.

*Vietnam, 1968. Singlaub
recuperating from another
injury.*

*Long Thanh, Vietnam, 1967. Col. Jack Singlaub is the first person in Southeast
Asia to be lifted by the Fulton Recovery Rig.*

Vietnam, 1968. Col. Singlaub with Col. Tran Van Ho, his Vietnamese counterpart.

Project MASSTER, 1970. Lt. Gen. William Depuy (center) and Brig. Gen. Singlaub (to Depuy's left), inspect new Army sensors.

1970. Brig. Gen. Singlaub learns to fly the UH-1 Huey and qualifies as an Army helicopter pilot.

Singlaub parachutes with the U.S. Army Parachute Team.

23

Singlaub, left, with U.S. Army Parachute Team.

PART III

☆   ☆

No Parade

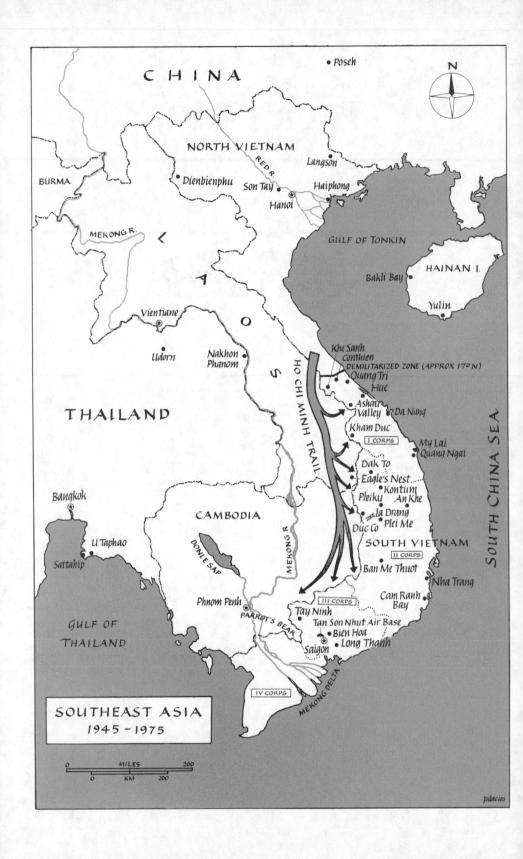

SOUTHEAST ASIA
1945 - 1975

CHAPTER SEVEN
The Profession of Arms
1953–1957

☆　　　　☆

Flying home from Korea was a strange experience. I was leaving the war zone while the battle still raged. During World War II, I'd moved from one theater to another in a global struggle against fascism, a war that rumbled inexorably toward victory. In the summer of 1953, however, military victory in Korea was no longer an option. The best we could hope for was an armistice that would leave both armies in place, and which would allow South Korea the chance to rebuild its shattered nation. But the farther I moved from the battle lines, the more remote this bitter struggle became.

When the Canadian Pacific Constellation finally landed in the warm drizzle of Vancouver, the comfortable prosperity of North America in the 1950s overwhelmed the intense alertness that grips every soldier in the combat zone. The bus down to Fort Lawton in Seattle was surrounded by shiny new cars, many with the candy bright colors that had suddenly replaced the ubiquitous black enamel of the 1940s. Along the summer highway, young families crowded the parks and softball fields. Prefab suburbia seemed a peaceful and secure civilization. As I repacked my bags for the flight to the East Coast, the dried red mud of Outpost Harry crumbled from my boots and sifted to the waxed tile floor of the BOQ. For me, the war was over.

I joined Mary at her parents' home in New Jersey. Little Elisabeth was shy at first. An absence of eighteen months is an immense gap to a child of four. But she did recognize her dad. When I'd left, John Jr. was hardly walking. Now he dashed about on sturdy legs. After I picked him up and gave him a big hug, he stood staring at me, then turned to Mary. "Who is that man?" he asked.

Neither child noticed the vivid red scar on my arm or that I walked with a slight limp. But Mary did. She'd known what to expect when she'd married a soldier, but I don't think she had understood the wars I had to fight would continue indefinitely. I suppose none of us had.

But I followed news reports of the fighting in Korea very closely. The 15th Infantry was still in the line, although the 2nd Battalion had been hit so hard that it had been put in reserve and its place taken by the Greek Expeditionary Force Battalion.

Although the Communists had accepted the Indian-sponsored compromise on the prisoner repatriation issue and had resumed regular peace talks at Panmunjom, they didn't really get serious until June. Then, in one week, they agreed to virtually every United Nations truce proposal. All that remained to be done before a cease-fire went into effect was to work out the technical details of the prisoner exchanges, as well as boundaries for the so-called Demilitarized Zone that was to be established along the fighting lines. It was logical to assume the Communists would scale down the level of fighting at this time.

But the Chinese and North Koreans did not operate by the principles of Western logic. Even with the cease-fire pending, they continued to fight. And the Iron Triangle took the brunt of some of their heaviest attacks. In mid-June the Greeks repelled a major Chinese assault on Outpost Harry. The Chinese had chosen a moonless night to send their assault troops down the valley and hit Harry after a massive artillery barrage. But the positions I'd helped fortify that spring protected the Greeks, who fought back with a frenzied determination. Even the massed assault of 4,000 Chinese troops, who swarmed in waves across the hilltop from all directions, couldn't capture the outpost. Once more the division's massed artillery delivered accurate VT fire on the position. When the Chinese finally pulled back before dawn, Harry's slopes were littered with 120 dead and almost 500 wounded Chinese.[1]

The attacks mounted in scale and intensity over the next several weeks, and by mid-July a full-scale, multidivision offensive was under way. Sixty thousand Chinese troops launched the biggest attack in two years and drove the ROK Capital Division back through its carefully constructed reserve lines and into the corps rear.[2] The line was stabilized on the south bank of the Kumsong with the help of the U.S. 3rd Division. The Chinese had succeeded in capturing a bulge several miles deep and almost twenty-five miles wide, but the cost had been horrendous. In effect, they had sacrificed their troops to massed artillery in a senseless slaughter reminiscent of the fruitless British Flanders Offensive in 1917. The Chinese had lost an estimated 72,000 men, including 25,000 killed in this final mindless assault.[3]

The United Nations resolve in stopping the final offensive eventually restored stability to the battle lines. The Chinese reluctantly agreed to end the bloodshed. But when the cease-fire finally came on July 27, and the thousands of artillery tubes and mortars stopped firing, I had to accept the fact that the armistice was simply that, a pause in the hostilities, not their cessation.

And, as the Korean War wound down, the war in French Indochina intensified. The French were making little progress suppressing Ho Chi Minh's Communist insurgents, the Viet Minh. Now the Chinese could shift resources from Korea to the south to assist Ho. As we drove through the calm midwestern countryside, I knew it was likely I would have to fight in another Asian war.

☆   ☆

THE Command and General Staff College at Fort Leavenworth, Kansas, was located at one of the Army's historic posts. In 1827, the War Department sent Colonel Henry Leavenworth west to the bend in the Missouri River that marked an informal border between the settlements of America's western frontier and the plains of the Indian nations. In this century the post grew, with many of its handsome buildings retaining the fort's traditional style of hewn gray limestone. The Army established its penitentiary there, officially the U.S. Army Disciplinary Barracks, a classic stone castle that looked like something out of a Jimmy Cagney movie.

In 1881, General William T. Sherman, the commanding general of the U.S. Army, added an educational role to the frontier support mission of Fort Leavenworth by establishing the School of Application of Infantry and Cavalry. The school activities were shut down during the Spanish American War, but in 1902 Secretary of War Elihu Root directed the establishment of the General Service and Staff College to help educate the Army's officer corps in the details of the general-staff system that Secretary Root had just introduced into the U.S. Army. Root was impressed by the French *Etat Major* system, which prepared senior officers for command through rigorous formal education.[4] The main teaching facility was in an imposing, high-roofed riding hall that dated from the turn of the century when equestrian proficiency was required of all Army officers, whatever their branch. The concept of formal courses of instruction for career officers reached the U.S. Army via the European general-staff system, which had evolved on the Continent in the nineteenth century.

Prior to World War I, our government considered the Army a relatively simple organization with a straightforward mission: waging war in the defense of the Republic. Then, the Army had been a small body of regulars composed of officers, noncommissioned officers, and enlisted men. The U.S. Military Academy at West Point provided most of the officers. A young

West Point graduate could choose a commission in a particular branch of the Army, such as the infantry, cavalry, or the engineers. He could expect to remain in that branch, advancing slowly in rank and responsibility. The heart of this system was the regiment, where an officer might serve his entire career. Building on his West Point education, he acquired the additional skills of command from personal experience.

But World War I made it clear that a small force of traditional regiments was insufficient. America faced global responsibilities that required a greatly expanded army. The draft and the reserve forces would provide most of the manpower. But we needed a larger pool of qualified officers. In 1917, for example, the Army ballooned from a few regiments to almost 100 divisions.

Commanding a division in peacetime garrison duty was demanding in itself; successfully leading a large unit in combat was infinitely more challenging. Most civilians view war as chaos, a cruel, formless anarchy in which victory or defeat is beyond human control. Career soldiers know differently. Success in war depends on effective leadership and well-motivated troops. And effective leadership means making correct decisions, one after another, in the proper sequence, throughout the confusion and turmoil of battle. Few men are born with the innate skills of such leadership. Most have to be taught.

This was the theory behind the Command and General Staff College. The "College," as we called it, represented one stage in a career officer's ongoing education, which began with his attending the basic school of his particular branch. In my own case, I'd gone through the equivalent of the Basic Infantry Officer's School at Fort Benning. I was trained to lead an Airborne rifle platoon in combat. The advanced infantry course, also at Fort Benning, had prepared me for battalion command in Korea. Now, as a lieutenant colonel, the one-year College course would give me the skills and knowledge needed to serve on a division or higher-level staff. Later, if I were fortunate, I might be selected to attend the Army War College, the final graduate school in the profession of arms, the alma mater of most of our general officers.

This system was a pyramid. Only the top half of the graduates of the Advanced Infantry School, for example, were chosen for Staff College. And only a small percentage of the College graduates eventually went on to the War College. Before World War II, the Command and General Staff College had been a two-year program with only the top half of the first-year's class continuing for the second term. Those who didn't make the grade had to face the fact that their chances for advancement were low indeed. Suicides were not uncommon among the unsuccessful first-year students. The Army was a meritocracy, not the aristocracy that critics of the military often accused it of being.

☆   ☆

THAT August I joined about 500 other field-grade officers—majors and lieutenant colonels—as students in the College class of 1954. How well we did in the ten-month course would shape the rest of our careers. Like many modern graduate schools, the College relied on a case-method curriculum. Whereas Harvard Business School students might study the financing and development of a particular industrial complex, we worked with battlefield scenarios called "problems." The vast teaching hall was divided by movable walls into twelve classrooms, each seating forty students at two-man tables. The instructors lectured from platforms, and relied heavily on maps, silk-screen charts, and Viewgraph slides.

Some of the problems were one-day exercises; others might take a week. We were expected to become experts not only in our own branch, but also in each of the other branches available to a division or corps commander. A typical problem might concern a classic battle of World War II, the German airborne invasion of Crete, for example. The instructor would lay out the overall situation, then his NCO assistant would "issue the tissue," distribute transparent map overlays with symbols representing the positions of the opposing forces. The instructor would then state his first "requirement."

"You're the division G-3," he'd say, referring to the division operations officer. "What are your actions and orders on receiving the first alert of the German airborne attack?"

Whoever was called on had to stand and recite as concisely and authoritatively as possible the procedures and orders required by the situation.

The day would proceed apace, with the "battle" unfolding as a map exercise. The instructors gave us minimum information and kept up the pressure, to simulate an actual command post atmosphere. In the final hour of instruction we might be asked to write a detailed critique of the enemy infantry commander or the commander of the friendly artillery. On another day, we might be given the job of organizing a task force to defend a river crossing in Burma; that requirement might be to write a formal order organizing the group, bearing in mind all the special needs of such a unit, possibly including bridging equipment, artillery forward observers, liaison aircraft, and so on. We were graded on such written work, and the instructors were no pushovers when it came to these grades.

As the semester advanced, we were increasingly required to make key decisions at the pivotal point in a particular operation, either a hypothetical or a historical battle that had been analyzed for the exercise. It was this decision-making ability—usually under rigorous time constraints, with less than adequate information—that would determine our eventual rank in the class.

Although most of the exercises involved standard-formation units waging conventional war (thus the emphasis on World War II), we were introduced to the concept of tactical nuclear weapons, and some of our problems covered anti-guerrilla warfare. Mainly, however, we learned to think like division or corps commanders. The idea was to become fully familiar with the concept of "combined arms"—infantry, armor, and artillery—supported by ordnance, signal, and engineers. Any man who couldn't keep all these mental balls juggling under pressure had no place on a division staff, and certainly was not destined for high command.

Most of us were fascinated by the intellectual challenge. This certainly didn't mean we were eager for war. There aren't many professional soldiers who actually find combat pleasurable. Critics of the military—especially liberal academics and journalists—mistakenly believe that soldiers enjoy war. That's as logical as assuming surgeons enjoy cancer. We study the profession of arms not to wage war, but to defend the values of our civilization. This is an uncomplicated patriotic notion that is hard for sophisticated civilians to swallow. But our dedication to professional excellence does not mean that career soldiers are especially cruel, or that we value human life less than our civilian counterparts. In fact, there is abundant proof to the contrary to be found in the thousands of citations for combat gallantry in actions to save lives.

Acquiring this expertise kept us at our desks or in the library late each night. But on weekends College tradition provided for general relaxation, focused on that hallowed Army institution the Friday-night happy hour. My family was quartered in a converted wartime barracks that had been divided into four reasonably comfortable apartments. The other three units were occupied by married majors in my class. As the senior man, it was up to me to host the happy hour. So on Fridays (and on other nights, schedule permitting) I would blow my duck call into the rattling old furnace vents and the noise would reverberate through the building. Within minutes my colleagues and their wives would be down and the first martini would be poured.

The Kansas plains are prime quail-hunting country. I like to eat quail, and I couldn't afford to buy them. I also liked bird shooting, for both the exercise and the practice it gave keeping my shooting eye sharp. But I needed a good bird dog. That's how I acquired Prince, a truly exceptional little Brittany spaniel, which another officer had to sell due to a sudden reassignment. He was a bright-eyed spotted pup when I got him, and I didn't know much about training bird dogs. Luckily, my friend Lieutenant Colonel John Hay, whom Mary called "the handsomest officer in the U.S. Army," was a former forest ranger from Montana who'd hunted quail with dogs his whole life. Within a few months we had Prince outperforming much more experienced dogs. What Prince had in his favor was absolutely boundless energy and a fiendish desire to hunt. He learned to point, search out birds in briar patches, and retrieve. Brittanys are not tall dogs, and prairie grass is over their heads. To follow my hand signals, Prince learned to leap up on all four legs like a jack-in-the-box, catch my signal, spin in the air, and hit the ground running in the right direction.

Several years later at Fort Campbell, Kentucky, I had to find a home for Prince when I got overseas orders. John Hay was fortunate enough to be stationed there at the time and snapped at my offer to adopt Prince. With that dog, John became the champion quail hunter on the post. He would often hunt with the governor of Kentucky, a genteel sportsman who came with dog handlers and a batch of six or eight expensive German shorthaired pointers.

Giving Prince a dubious look, the Governor asked John, "Colonel, will *that* little dog honor my dogs' point?"

"Yes, sir," John replied. "You just watch him." At the end of the morning, when the Governor's first three pointers were exhausted, Prince was literally doing back flips to get away from the lunch tent and out to the field again. The Governor never disparaged Brittany spaniels again.

A couple of years after the episode we'd returned to the States, and I made overtures to John about getting Prince back.

"Jack," he said in a convincing tone, "you've got a better chance of getting my *daughter* than my dog."

☆   ☆

HAPPY hours and quail hunting, of course, were diversions that broke the stress of our profession. By the time I completed my ten months as a student at the College, the Cold War with the Soviet Union was reaching an ominous level of intensity. In 1949, the Soviets had shocked the West by exploding their first atomic bomb, several years before our intelligence services estimated they would. It was reasonable to assume that this nuclear capability had given Stalin the confidence to unleash the Communist aggression in Korea, ten months later. And, while America came to grips with the reality of Soviet atom bombs, the Russians proceeded directly from fission weapons to the development of a fusion device, the so-called superbomb, the thermonuclear or hydrogen weapon, which was vastly more destructive than the bombs that flattened Hiroshima and Nagasaki.[5]

Harry Truman made the decision to follow suit and build an American hydrogen bomb in 1950, overcoming the reluctance of his science advisers who feared this development would start a spiraling arms race. The Soviets obviously had no such constraints. Under the leadership of physicist Andrei Sakharov, they were well on their way to producing the world's first true hydrogen bomb. Edward Teller led the American scientists at the Los Alamos National Laboratory in a desperate game of catch-up. In 1952, they had produced a thermonuclear weapon with a ten-megaton "yield," the explosive equivalent of 10 million tons of TNT. But the device was large and cumbersome, too heavy to be carried by our B-36, the world's biggest bomber.

The Soviet Union had already overcome this problem by eliminating the bulky refrigeration equipment needed to condense the weapon's hydrogen-isotope fuel, deuterium. They made a compact bomb fueled with lithium deuteride, a greasy solid the consistency of sea salt. This was the true stuff of H-bombs. In the summer of 1953, they overcame the humiliation of their failed Korean adventure by exploding a "small" hydrogen bomb at their Arctic test site. Again, the Americans scrambled to equal the feat. By 1954, we had our own H-bomb weighing less than five tons. It was tested at the Bikini atoll and vaporized the entire test island with a fifteen-megaton blast.[6]

Mankind now had the ability to unleash the power of the sun as a weapon.

With the reality of lightweight thermonuclear weapons, the technology to deliver them halfway around the planet by ballistic missile was quickly advancing. Once more, the United States reluctantly played catch-up with the Soviet Union, this time to develop the first intercontinental ballistic missile (ICBM).[7] Years later, I found it ironic that many leaders of the various peace movements always faulted the United States for "goading" the hapless, underdeveloped Soviet Union into the wasteful folly of the arms race.

Nikita Khrushchev, the Soviet leader who eventually replaced Stalin, was enamored of his country's growing nuclear arsenal. These weapons neutralized those of the West and provided an effective new saber to rattle whenever the Soviets' aggressive expansion was challenged. By the time of the Soviet-sponsored invasion in Korea, the Russians had brutally crushed all democratic resistance to their empire in Eastern Europe. Socialists, trade unionists, agrarian parties, and moderates of all persuasions were eliminated; thousands were murdered by the Soviet secret police, the NKVD. Tens of thousands of others disappeared into the labor camp Gulag. As Churchill had warned, a true Iron Curtain had descended across the continent, walling in the formerly independent nations of Poland, Czechoslovakia, Hungary, Romania, and Bulgaria. The Soviet occupation zone in Germany became a Communist puppet state.

In response, the Western powers relied on a system of global alliances. NATO armies faced the Soviets along a tense frontier that stretched from the Arctic Ocean all the way to eastern Turkey. An overlapping system of other military treaty "organizations" bolstered the frontier the rest of the way around the planet's northern hemisphere. Communist China was restrained on the Asian mainland. In effect, totalitarian communism was quarantined by the military power of the West. And the United States provided the bulk of the forces and bore the lion's share of the expense in this defensive system.

The West was unable to free the millions already under Communist domination, but we were determined to hold the line. To transform this determination into practical policy, President Eisenhower's secretary of state, John Foster Dulles, formalized the de facto containment policy into the flawed strategy of massive retaliation. If the Soviets or Chinese broke through our containment wall to expand their empires, we would respond "massively" with nuclear arms. It was an inflexible strategy; there would be either peace or nuclear holocaust.

This was the troubled geopolitical situation my colleagues and I faced as we prepared for the responsibilities of senior command. Because the Cold War eventually lasted so long, it's easy to forget how unsettling the new reality was at the time. As soon as both sides had practical nuclear arsenals, the haunting prospect of a third world war fought with hydrogen bombs— in which hundreds of millions of civilians would be incinerated along with their cities—had to be accepted as a practical possibility, not an insane nightmare. In the bizarre language of the period, military planners did indeed have to think the "unthinkable."

Within the Defense Department, it was the Air Force that benefited most from our massive retaliation policy. They had the planes and missiles to deliver the nuclear weapons on China or the Soviet Union. The more massive our threat, the Soviet (and later Chinese) counterthreat, and our own anti-counterthreat response became, the greater the Air Force's need for manned strategic bombers, fighter-bombers, and long-range missiles. By 1954, there were even rumblings that the Air Force could eventually replace the Army, which was viewed in some quarters as being on the verge of obsolescence. Conventional ground forces, it was argued, simply couldn't be defended against atom bombs. And nuclear weapons were, after all, cheaper than a huge standing army. Even though we had a peacetime draft, expanding the U.S. Army to the size needed to realistically counter the combined threats of the huge Soviet and Chinese ground forces would have completely altered our *peacetime* society. So for almost a dozen years—until the Cuban Missile Crisis of 1962—America relied increasingly on its nuclear strike force, to the detriment of the Army.[8]

That such a ludicrous argument could gain the credence it eventually did is a reflection of the dilemma we faced. Postwar American prosperity was fueled by a free-market consumer economy supported by the world's largest middle class, who enjoyed remarkably low taxes. On the other hand, meeting our global Cold War commitments required a steadily growing defense establishment, which each year absorbed a larger portion of our national wealth. The country wanted both guns and butter, but our political leaders feared the economic dislocation of such a policy. A nuclear arsenal was simply cheaper than a large conventional force. In one form or another, this dilemma has bedeviled us through all the decades of the Cold War.

Almost as soon as the massive retaliation doctrine was accepted, however, its shortcomings became obvious. The Soviet Union was constrained from a conventional assault on Western Europe for fear of nuclear retaliation. And the Chinese were equally discouraged from renewing the aggression in Korea or invading the Nationalist Republic of China on Taiwan. But fear of America's nuclear arsenal did not stop either the Chinese or the Soviets from supporting (and in some cases actually sponsoring) the so-called wars of national liberation that became one of the major military aspects of the Cold War.[9]

☆   ☆

THE first of these conflicts was the Greek civil war, a bitter struggle that dragged on for five years before the Soviet-backed forces were defeated. In the Far East, a different type of conflict evolved in Indochina. France's Asian war was in many ways a testing ground for the political and military strategies, the battlefield tactics, and the technology of similar struggles in the emerging post-colonial world over the coming decades.

The sweeping Japanese victories in the early years of World War II laid the ground for the anti-colonial struggle of the postwar years. The European imperial powers—France, the Netherlands, and Great Britain—had all been defeated by the Japanese. The myth of European racial superiority crumbled. In 1945, when the colonial powers returned to take up business as usual, nationalist leaders in Malaya, Indonesia, and French Indochina realized that their colonial masters were not invincible. In Tonkin, the northern region of Vietnam, it was Chiang Kai-shek's KMT, not the French, who took the Japanese surrender.[10]

The colony's best-organized anti-French resistance, the Communist Viet Minh, seized large amounts of French and Japanese munitions, overpowered lesser nationalist groups, and proclaimed the independence of the Democratic Republic of Vietnam in early September 1945.

When the French military finally arrived in force, they made the mistake of assuming that Ho's Viet Minh were a ragtag band of malcontents who could be either persuaded to accept the benefits of French rule or, alternatively, ruthlessly suppressed by superior arms. They were wrong on both counts. Ho Chi Minh was a nationalist in name only. Although he was fervently anti-colonialist, Ho saw himself as the leader of a revolutionary Communist "nation" that transcended traditional boundaries.[11]

Ho had founded the Indochina Communist Party in 1930; it evolved into the broader-based Viet Minh in 1941. He came from a poor family of rural Vietnamese Mandarin (Nguyen) scholars and was trained as a teacher by the French. But he left the colony as a young man before the First World War and spent almost twenty years abroad, much of it in France, where he became a militant founding member of the new French Communist Party in 1920. He was trained as an international agent in Moscow, where he spent a year, then served in various capacities in Asia as an official representative of Comintern, the Communist International. The wartime struggle against both the French and the Japanese drew him closer to a cadre of tough, like-minded younger lieutenants, particularly Vo Nguyen Giap and Pham Van Dong. They all were convinced that Mao's principles of revolutionary struggle would sweep the post-colonial world.[12]

The French military was the first European army to encounter such an enemy. Initially, they tried to reclaim their colony using conventional military forces. One of their chief strategists, General Jean de Lattre de Tassigny, devised an ambitious multiphase plan involving fortified urban zones free of the Viet Minh, which would serve as enclave garrisons to shelter the French forces and the quasi-independent local government headed by the loyalist emperor Bao Dai. Within the enclaves, the loyal Vietnamese were to train an anti-Communist army. And regiment-size *groupements mobiles* (mechanized mobile columns) were to stage forays from the enclaves, seeking out and destroying the Viet Minh in the jungle hinterland. America provided the weapons and matériel for these mobile groups: tanks, armored cars, half-tracks, trucks, and artillery.

But de Lattre's plan had fundamental defects. First, little progress was made building a loyal indigenous army. Also, the mobile groups were restricted to the colony's rudimentary "highways." And when a mobile group actually encountered a large enemy force, the Viet Minh dissolved into small guerrilla bands, just as Mao's troops did in Manchuria. Finally, when the French tried to "pacify" the countryside with small paramilitary units, the Viet Minh reverted to large-scale combat.

The French unleashed their air power on indiscriminate punitive raids, which only drove more alienated peasants into the arms of the Viet Minh. (The archetype of such counterproductive punitive actions was the French naval bombardment of Haiphong in November 1946, a senselessly brutal response to a Viet Minh provocation that killed 6,000 innocent civilians and became the stimulus Ho needed for broad-based support.[13])

By May 1954, as I was preparing to graduate from Command and General

Staff College, the French military effort in Indochina was about to end in defeat. The cream of their elite parachute regiments faced annihilation by the Viet Minh at Dienbienphu, a valley outpost near the Lao border. Contrary to accepted infantry doctrine (either conventional or guerrilla), the French had opted to hold a valley position, dominated by steep mountains. Despite ample experience, the French commander, Lieutenant General Henri Navarre, had been confident that Ho's *irregular* forces would not be able to oppose them in this remote area. The French forces in this trackless mountain valley were resupplied by airlift; the Viet Minh did not have that option.

But Ho's principal military leader, General Vo Nguyen Giap, confounded the French once again. That spring he deployed 35,000 troops, equipped with almost 200 artillery pieces and mortars (many recently transshipped from the Chinese lines in Korea), in a ring of steel above the French positions. Giap's supply lines to China were relatively short and protected from air attack by heavy jungle cover. And when the French air force tried to suppress the artillery and increase the resupply effort, they were met with devastating anti-aircraft fire from Soviet-provided 37mm and 57mm guns.[14] The battle dragged on for several months, as the French threw one unit after another into the cauldron. By May, it was over. Dienbienphu had been overrun. Two thousand sick and wounded survivors were marched away as dejected prisoners, long columns of gaunt Europeans guarded by wiry Asians in threadbare khaki, an image that haunted the Western world for years. Ho's Viet Minh (supported by the Chinese and Soviets) had defeated the best of the French empire.[15]

☆   ☆

ALL of us at the College with Airborne backgrounds watched the unfolding debacle of Dienbienphu very closely. As the French artillery blundered toward inevitable defeat, an intense debate over American intervention on the French side developed within the Eisenhower administration. Contingency plans ranged from a multidivision airborne and amphibious invasion of Tonkin to massive air raids with B-29s dropping conventional bombs, to the use of nuclear weapons against the Viet Minh. These plans anticipated Chinese support of their Communist allies in reaction to our support of the French. One plan even called for the airborne occupation of Hainan Island as part of an overall intervention in Indochina.

When it became clear that our European allies who had fought with us in Korea did not have the stomach to answer Secretary of State Dulles's call for a "united front to resist Communist aggression in southeast Asia," the U.S. Army led the resistance to unilateral American intervention.[16] It was Army Chief of Staff General Matt Ridgway—an Airborne leader not known for avoiding battle—who fought hardest against ill-advised half-measures and such panaceas as nuclear attacks against Viet Minh jungle bases.

As historian Ronald Spector has revealed, Ridgway cut to the heart of the matter. "If it was really vital to the United States to prevent the loss of Vietnam, the wisest course, in Ridgway's view, would be to strike directly at China, without whose aid the Viet Minh would be unable to persist."[17] But this action, Ridgway reminded the politicians, would require a full mobilization of the United States and the direct cooperation of our Western allies, who at least would have to take up the slack on the NATO front while we fought China. Ridgway was not guilty of alarmist fantasy. He was an experienced, realistic wartime leader who knew what was involved in Indochina. The French had been bled to death by half-measures. If America was going to fight there, he wanted the war to be on our terms.

But the war was avoided, or at least deferred. A peace conference in Geneva that summer involving the Soviet Union, Communist China, France, Great Britain, and the United States—as well as representatives of France's other Indochinese colonies and the Viet Minh—agreed on a face-saving independence formula. Vietnam would be "temporarily" divided at the 17th parallel between a Communist government in the north and a French-sponsored administration in the south, pending general elections two years later. Most experts privately dismissed this agreement as an impractical, face-saving political expedient from the beginning, one that merely allowed the French army a chance to regroup in the regions of Annam and Cochinchina. Laos and Cambodia would become self-governing during the same period. The French army would be allowed to withdraw with the tattered remnants of their honor intact. But the issue of "national" elections was moribund from the outset. North Vietnam had a much larger population than the South, and the Communist Viet Minh had already purged its ranks of non-Communists while simultaneously dispatching Communist agents south to infiltrate democratic (or at least anti-Communist) political parties. The deck was stacked in Ho's favor.

As my friends and I discussed the significance of these events to our futures, we were also naturally preoccupied with our next assignments. I had hoped to go from the College to become the operations or intelligence officer of one of our Airborne divisions, the 11th Airborne based in Germany or the 82nd Airborne at Fort Bragg. I was pleased when I got my graduation ranking, 75th in a class of over 500, which placed me in the top 15 percent. But, surprisingly, I was assigned as a faculty member at the College, a three-year position normally granted to the Army's most intellectual and promising field-grade officers.

When I got over my surprise, I realized the faculty assignment represented a real opportunity. Army doctrine—that formal body of plans and directives controlling strategy and tactics—was undergoing a convulsive evolution, given the rapidly changing nature of the Cold War. The advent of tactical nuclear weapons, atomic munitions fired from artillery or short-range missiles, would soon radically alter the doctrine of ground warfare. And it became obvious that the Army's new doctrines would be developed here by the College faculty.

I was assigned to Department IV, which was responsible for Airborne, Army Aviation, and amphibious operations. My immediate boss in the department was Lieutenant Colonel Norman Martin, an artilleryman who had served with the 11th Airborne Division in the Pacific in World War II. He was one of the most meticulous officers I'd ever met, not a nit-picking perfectionist, but rather a man who sincerely believed in giving every assignment his maximum effort. He expected such an effort from his subordinates.

Norm was not content repeating the same student exercises each semester, mainly rehashes of Allied and German airborne operations in World War II. More to the point, the introduction of battlefield nuclear weapons had a special impact on Airborne doctrine.[18] Unlike a standard infantry division, which might assemble for an attack from widely separated regimental or battalion base areas, Airborne units had always mustered at a single airfield complex and been flown to their drop zones in tight formations of aircraft. This doctrine made Airborne forces lucrative targets on the nuclear battlefield as they assembled before takeoff. And the tight formations of their airlift columns were equally vulnerable. But traditional doctrine held that parachute troops had to be delivered in a massed formation, not piecemeal, if they were to survive in the enemy rear, their normal area of operation.

Colonel Martin gave me the assignment of evolving a new doctrine for the Airborne, one which would permit a division to assemble at widely dispersed departure fields and fly to their objectives in multiple air columns, to land simultaneously on multiple drop zones, then quickly reassemble to carry out their mission. This was a logical, seemingly straightforward evolution of procedures. But, once I got into the exercise, I soon realized how complex this problem was.

The capability of our para-drop aircraft was only one of many knotty issues. During World War II, the twin-engine C-47 (the military version of the DC-3) was the standard Airborne plane. It carried twenty-four paratroopers and had a range of only a few hundred miles. Ten years later, we had advanced to the C-119 Flying Boxcar that had a larger payload and a greater range, but which was still severely limited. Neither of these aircraft was capable of the flexibility we envisioned for the Airborne. What was needed would be a large, fast transport that could operate from departure airfields separated by hundreds of miles, which had the speed and the reliability (hence, four engines) to operate in multiple air columns that arrived simultaneously on the objectives.

After several months of evolving these new requirements, I ran the exercises through my classes, and was delighted by the enthusiastic response of my students. Inventing new doctrine was far more exciting than studying the invasion of Sicily or the D-Day landings at Normandy. I was especially heartened when senior Army staff officers from outside the College began to send queries about our exercises. I realized that the work we were doing here stood a good chance of being adopted in the real world beyond our classrooms.

Given this stimulus, I didn't regret my faculty assignment. Besides, this was the first time that Mary and I had been able to enjoy a reasonably normal family life in ten years of marriage. When our third child, Mary Ann, was born in September 1954, I decided to stay in the delivery room. I'd missed out on the births of both our other children; Elisabeth was born while I was in China, and John came along while I was on my first temporary duty assignment in Korea. As a combat soldier, I'd seen my fair share of unusual sights, but the birth of one of my own children was a powerful experience.

Immediately after the delivery, the Army obstetrician took me aside. "Colonel," he said, "are you all right?"

"Of course," I muttered. "Why?"

"Well, he answered, "I've never seen anybody look quite that green."

So much for the tough soldier.

☆　　　　☆

ARMY Aviation was another of the Department's responsibilities in need of modernization. In Korea, Army pilots had flown artillery spotter planes and the buzzing little liaison helicopters that ferried senior officers around the corps areas behind the MLR. That was about the extent of Army Aviation in the mid-1950s.

The Aviation instructors in my department were all World War II liaison pilots who saw no use for Army aircraft beyond spotter planes and possibly medical evacuation helicopters—provided the vulnerable choppers did not venture too close to the actual fighting. Once more, however, under Norm Martin's creative direction, we began working on the problem of expanding the role of Army Aviation. Rapid troop mobility was the key to success on the nuclear battlefield; widely dispersed troops were less vulnerable to atomic attack, but to operate effectively a commander had to be able to bring these disparate units together quickly. Troop-carrying helicopters could accomplish this mission. Once you accepted this principle, the concept of *armed* helicopters serving as flying artillery support platforms was a logical development. We were beginning to hammer out the rough shape of a doctrine that eventually became known as airmobile warfare.[19]

☆   ☆

DURING my first two years on the faculty our work with modernized doctrine ran parallel to a major overhaul of the Army then being planned by none other than Chief of Staff General Maxwell Taylor. He had been deeply troubled by the congressional support the Air Force had garnered for the wrongheaded notion of drastically reducing the *obsolete* Army. This situation transcended traditional interservice rivalries. There were some in high government positions who believed the Army could be cut to a tiny fragment of its normal size and relieved of its traditional battlefield role, which would devolve to the panacea of our nuclear strike force.

Despite the pressure of our teaching loads, several of us on the faculty joined an informal group that met every other Sunday to discuss the major issues of our profession. Naturally, we were preoccupied by the debate over massive retaliation and the "obsolescent" Army. I worked with Lieutenant Colonel Winant Sidle, a gifted writer, and Lieutenant Colonel Raymond L. Shoemaker to write an article proposing a more logical national strategy of flexible response to Communist aggression. We argued that threatening the Soviets with Armageddon over every aggression was tantamount to crying wolf; America needed a more practical, appropriate doctrine of military reaction. To our surprise, the article was published in the *Military Review,* and won the annual award for best original contribution.[20] More important, our article served to expand the national debate on this vital issue.

General Taylor's response to the zealous advocates of massive retaliation was to put forward a radical concept he called the "Pentomic Army," a structural reorganization of traditional units, which allowed ground forces to be widely dispersed in much the same way we had proposed for Airborne units. To accomplish this, Taylor proposed abolishing the Army's traditional building blocks: the battalion and regiment. The heart of the reorganization would be the Pentomic division, made up of five battle groups of 1,400 men each. They would be composed of five rifle companies, plus support companies that were larger than traditional rifle companies. The battle group would be a third bigger than a normal battalion—hence, more powerful— but much smaller than a regiment. Battle groups were meant to have dispersed garrisons and greatly increased mobility. The Pentomic Army was designed to survive and fight on a battlefield dominated by tactical nuclear weapons. For the first time, ground forces would have their own nuclear arms, albeit relatively crude ones such as the Davey Crockett, Honest John, and Little John battlefield fission weapons. These were supplemented by long-range artillery capable of firing nuclear shells. This force was Taylor's method of implementing a policy of flexible response.[21]

General Taylor was known as a powerful personality of strong intellect and vast experience, who rarely lost a fight on or off the battlefield. When he decided on the Pentomic Army, his will prevailed. It was up to people like us to transform this new organization into meaningful doctrine. This was opposite of standard procedure. In World War II, for example, a new doctrine of armored warfare would be hammered out, then the armored units needed to implement that doctrine would be organized. Our responsibility was the reverse. General Taylor laid down the organization; the Army had to develop doctrine to make it work. And he wanted results fast.[22]

To exacerbate the situation, the College got a new commandant, Major General Lionel C. McGarr, a crusty, sawed-off West Pointer with a brilliant combat record in both World War II and Korea, where he had amassed an amazing total of seven Purple Hearts and several decorations for valor, including the Distinguished Service Cross. The General was the type of old-school officer who believed in authoritarian command.

When he took over the College, McGarr had been directed to modernize the curriculum in anticipation of the upcoming Pentomic reorganization. He understood his orders to mean the entire curriculum would be completely rewritten—every exercise, every problem, and all the vast panoply of supporting maps and audiovisual aids. Before any problem became part of the curriculum, the class material had to be carefully reviewed by faculty panels, modified, then critiqued again. We weren't training humanities undergraduates here, but the future leaders of the U.S. Army. Completely reorganizing the curriculum was a gargantuan project that would require thousands of hours of demanding staff work.

But General McGarr arbitrarily decreed that the revamped curriculum would be ready within a single academic year. Further, the faculty would accomplish this task while simultaneously teaching their regular class load. We normally worked over forty hours a week as it was, what with classroom preparation, counseling students, and supervising special projects. Suddenly our workload shot up to eighty, even ninety hours a week. Friends of mine like Harvey Short, now a lieutenant colonel, who had joined the faculty after a military adviser assignment in the Philippines, stood up reasonably well to the strain. Harvey was an intellectual soldier who combined brains with battlefield courage. But others, men who had fought some of the bitterest campaigns of World War II and Korea, virtually staggered under this punishing workload.

What made this especially difficult was the needless deadline and the total reorganization that McGarr had decreed. In Department IV, for example, we had already rewritten our curriculum to match the new Airborne doctrine we were evolving. This was true to a lesser degree in other departments. But McGarr refused to discuss retaining existing material. In fact, he rarely deigned to converse with anyone below the rank of general. He quickly became an archvillain. Because of his beer-barrel physique and a haircut that divided the top of his head into two waxy wings, he acquired the derisive nickname "Split-head Magoo."

Whereas the General's cartoon namesake, Mr. Magoo, was a benign dolt, McGarr displayed malevolent (even paranoid) cunning, not unlike the fictional Captain Queeg of *The Caine Mutiny*. The College's assistant commandant, Brigadier General Fred Zierath, tried to reason with him, but McGarr saw this as disloyalty. He appointed two personal advisers, Majors Dick Hallock and Jack Cushman, to oversee the reorganization. In effect, they were McGarr's spies.[23] Within weeks the normal atmosphere of professional camaraderie had been poisoned. Men who had felt honored to serve on the College faculty suddenly found their careers in jeopardy. Based on reports of disloyalty, McGarr began relieving hard-working officers. The stress was terrible. McGarr was undeterred, however. He accomplished his cherished modernization, but he left the blighted careers of several fine officers in his wake.[24]

(Those who appreciate poetic justice will be interested to learn what eventually happened to General McGarr. In 1960, he was assigned to command the trouble-plagued Military Assistance Advisory Group in South Vietnam, the precursor of our larger Military Assistance Command in Saigon. The security situation was deteriorating rapidly as the Communist Vietcong increased operations under orders from Hanoi. McGarr couldn't take the strain. He had a complete mental breakdown and had to be institutionalized at an Army hospital in the States. Like the men he had broken years before at the College, General McGarr was forced to retire with his career in shambles.)

☆　　　☆

WHILE the College faculty struggled to follow General McGarr's arbitrary orders, events in Europe and the Middle East exploded, dramatizing the dangerous and unpredictable state of international affairs.

The people of Hungary rose up against their Soviet masters in October 1956. This revolt was a stunning development, in that both the supposedly loyal puppet Communist government led by Premier Imre Nagy and the Soviet-sponsored Hungarian army joined the rebels. The Hungarian army opened its arsenals to the rebels, equipping civilians with light weapons and even armored vehicles. By the last week of October, Nagy had managed to create a genuine coalition government that was predominantly non-Communist. Even more surprising, Soviet troops had evacuated the country or retreated into garrisons, and Nagy predicted a complete Red Army pull-out. He announced that Hungary had withdrawn from the Warsaw Pact and requested the United Nations recognize his country as a neutral state. It appeared the Soviet empire was crumbling.

American reaction was cautious. We could give the brave Hungarians moral support, but their country lay behind a shield of dozens of Red Army divisions on full alert in East Germany and Czechoslovakia. On November 3, the world learned of the Soviet response. The Red Army reentered Hungary in strength. Within two weeks Soviet tanks had brutally suppressed the democratic rebels in bitter street fighting throughout the country. Thousands died; thousands more were rounded up and shipped in cattle cars to Siberian labor camps. Almost 200,000 refugees escaped to Austria and on to Western Europe. Imre Nagy and his advisers were kidnapped by the Soviet secret police and later executed.

While this drama unfolded in central Europe, another crisis exploded in the Middle East. Egyptian president Colonel Gamal Abdel Nasser nationalized the Anglo-French Suez Canal Company, and threatened to close the waterway to "imperialist" traffic. Nasser's action went beyond radical nationalism. The year before he had established close ties with the Soviet bloc and had become their unofficial proconsul in the Middle East, in exchange for massive economic and military aid. His seizure of the canal was ostensibly a reprisal against Great Britain and the United States for their refusal to fund the gargantuan construction project of a hydroelectric dam at Aswan.

Great Britain, France, and Israel reacted by launching a combined airborne, amphibious, and ground attack to seize the Suez Canal. The Soviets responded with ominous threats of nuclear retaliation. The United States policy was muddled—first bolstering our NATO allies, then condemning them. The Suez War sputtered to an inconclusive settlement with the eventual withdrawal of foreign troops from the canal.

These two crises, although disparate in nature, underscored the type of military situation the United States could expect to confront in the unstable world of the Cold War. The sad fact was that we had almost no means of influencing these events because we lacked the ability to project our military power quickly and decisively on a global scale. America had opted for the least expensive defense establishment in terms of financial and human sacrifice. Nuclear weapons were cheaper than a huge standing army, and the air and sea lifts needed to transport this army around the world. And this also meant that most of our skilled young citizens could be employed in productive civilian employment. But Hungary and Suez had demonstrated that the policy of massive retaliation was patently impractical. We couldn't simply threaten to incinerate the Soviet Union every time American and Soviet interests clashed. We needed a more flexible, practical response.

The Marine Corps was our primary intervention force, but Marine strength was below two divisions and the Navy lacked the fast amphibious capability to deliver Marine battalions overseas. This situation underscored the need for a modern, effective U.S. Army Airborne reaction force that could be quickly deployed to trouble spots throughout the world. General Taylor had already decided to reactivate his former World War II unit, the 101st Airborne Division, as the Army's first Pentomic division. This would bring Army Airborne strength to three full divisions. In theory, this was exactly the type of force the country could rely on in the so-called "brushfire" military situations breaking out across the world, especially where Western and Soviet interests conflicted in newly independent or developing countries.

The only problem with all this was that our Airborne forces simply did not have the airplanes—the "airlift capability"—to carry them into battle. The U.S. Air Force was responsible for transporting the Airborne. But Air Force leadership at the time was preoccupied with building manned bombers and developing a variety of nuclear ballistic missiles. They had devoted a piddling 5,000 tons of airlift to the Army, most of it in the form of lumbering piston-engine transport planes, C-47s, C-119s, and the clumsy C-123, which had actually been designed as a glider in World War II, and now, with two engines added as an afterthought, functioned as an incredibly slow airdrop plane. There were some bigger, four-engine C-124s, capable of dropping almost 300 paratroopers, but they were also slow and vulnerable to ground fire.

Even if the Army grudgingly accepted these obsolescent transport planes as a serious Air Force contribution to national security, the 5,000-ton total airlift capability was woefully inadequate. It took 20,000 tons of airlift to transport just one Airborne division into battle. We now had three divisions. General Taylor gave top priority to calculating the Army's true airlift requirement. He knew the current world situation augured well for congressional funding of a viable fast-reaction Army force. In effect, creating an Airborne force supported by a realistic airlift would give America a practical alternative to Dulles's unrealistic massive retaliation.

But before lobbying Congress to fund such a force, Taylor needed to know exactly what the Army required. To his chagrin, he could find no one in the Pentagon capable of calculating these requirements. He next turned to the Continental Army Command (CONARC) at Fort Monroe, Virginia. But they had no one qualified for this demanding task. Officers at CONARC recalled, however, that Department IV of the Command and General Staff

College had been active in devising modern Airborne doctrine. That summer I had led discussions on this new doctrine during Exercise Pine Cone, a large-scale Airborne maneuver at Fort Bragg, North Carolina.

So in late November 1954 I left Mary and the kids to have Thanksgiving dinner without me and boarded a plane to Fort Monroe. In typical Army fashion, the team I joined had been given all of twelve days to calculate the entire airlift requirement for the Airborne. The leader of this effort was Major General Harvey J. Jablonsky, known to his troops as "Jabo." He had been my regimental executive officer back in the 515th Parachute Infantry in 1943, and had commanded Airborne troops in combat in Europe. Jabo believed in assigning the right man to a job, whatever his rank, then letting him get on with it.

I ended up as team chief and, along with Lieutenant Colonel Jay W. Herrington of Jabo's staff and my friend Captain Bob Channon (a former Ranger officer I'd helped train for combat in Korea), we calculated the total airlift requirements to move every man and every piece of equipment in the entire division plus the necessary ammunition and supplies to enable it to fight. We worked practically around the clock, and had to repeatedly revise our painstaking calculations as more information became available.

The heart of the problem involved the unique nature of airborne warfare. In conventional ground operations an infantry division with a standard complement of men and equipment would attack an objective and be reinforced as needed with men and special weapons during the course of the offensive. Planning for such an operation was therefore a sequential responsibility that moved geographically *forward* from the assembly area toward the particular real estate to be occupied. An airborne operation was the reverse of this. Parachute troops arrived en masse at their objective; everything and everybody needed to accomplish the mission had to be calculated in advance. This meant the planner had to realistically calculate the *exact* number of 6omm mortar rounds, hand grenades, medical corpsmen, radio men, and all the other myriad requirements of men and matériel that composed an Airborne division in battle.

And we had twelve days to do this. Luckily, CONARC had computers, rudimentary as they were in 1956. These mysterious, humming machines were serviced by white-coated, almost priestly experts accustomed to conducting their abstract labors without the interference of impatient field soldiers like me. But I had a hunch their exotic computers could simplify our task. I was right. Once the computer experts understood the nature of our problem, they accepted the challenge enthusiastically.

To everyone's surprise, we completed our exercise a day ahead of schedule. For the first time in the history of the Airborne, the Army knew exactly how many and which type of aircraft were needed to transport its forces to a variety of objectives throughout the world. One of the major offshoots of this exercise was the realization by the Defense Department that America needed modern airlift equipment. We could no longer rely on planes of World War II vintage. Within a few years the Air Force had deployed a whole new class of fast, long-range transports, including the durable turboprop C-130 Hercules and the jet C-141.

One of the unexpected results of this exercise was to force the Army's leaders to assess realistically our country's global military responsibilities. We had passed through the roller-coaster cycles of postwar demobilization and the chaotic mobilization for the Korean War. It was now time to accept the harsh reality that we were locked in a protracted political and military competition with a powerful and intransigent foe. There was no end in sight to the Cold War, and we were in for the duration.

CHAPTER EIGHT

Cold War

1957–1963

☆   ☆

I COMPLETED MY final year on the College faculty in 1957. That winter I was sent to discuss airlift requirements with the newly activated 101st Airborne Division at Fort Campbell, Kentucky. Naturally, I lobbied for an assignment to the division. Being the Army's first Pentomic division, the 101st was bound to receive the close scrutiny of Chief of Staff General Maxwell Taylor. This was a double-edged deal. If an officer did well with the unit, his performance would be noted in high places; but if he "ripped his knickers," that might hurt his career.

The division operations officer, or G-3, was Lieutenant Colonel Bill Bond, whom I'd known in the Ranger Training Center during the Korean War and who had later been one of my students at the College. Bill had been in the First Ranger Battalion in World War II, the outfit that had stormed the German battery on Pointe du Hoc, the headland dominating Omaha Beach in Normandy. He was a colorful guy. Before coming to Leavenworth, Bill had left a NATO assignment to drive his personal jeep all the way from Paris to New Delhi, right through the hot spots of the Middle East.

On my temporary duty (TDY) to Fort Campbell that February, Bill told me he was recommending me to be his replacement. I had another good contact on division staff, Lieutenant Colonel Norm Martin, who had gone from the College faculty at Leavenworth to become the division G-4, the assistant chief of staff for logistics.

Their two recommendations, combined with my experience developing the new Airborne doctrine and my hard labor in the airlift-planning vineyards, convinced the commander, General Thomas Sherburne, I was the

241

guy for the job. He contacted me personally back at Leavenworth with the good news. But Bill Bond's assignment wouldn't be over until later that year, so I got the General's permission to take four months' administrative leave that fall to go back to UCLA. I was a few credits short of my degree requirement because of my wartime call-up.

Returning to a college campus as an undergraduate was a fascinating experience. I took a full course load of eighteen credits, heavy on international relations and diplomatic history, with a focus on the Far East. Several of my professors espoused the standard liberal position: Mao's Chinese Communists were doing well in their agrarian reforms and rooting out the last vestiges of Nationalist corruption.

Now that Mao had consolidated his power and had decreed the Hundred Flowers liberalization—soon followed by the disastrous but superficially attractive Great Leap Forward—my professors were confident peaceful progress would flourish in Asia. But I saw hypocrisy here. Democracy was apparently fine for Westerners, but the benighted races of Asia had to make do with the totalitarian repression in order to make progress.

They also portrayed Ho Chi Minh as a courageous Nationalist who had defeated his country's evil colonial masters. There wasn't much discussion of either Ho's or Mao's background as international Communists. But I did research on both leaders and cited solid documentary evidence to show they were Communist ideologues first and patriots second. Some of my instructors responded by ignoring me, but others joined in the spirit of honest discourse. I respected those who welcomed this debate, even though we were ideological rivals. One history professor in particular enlivened his discussions by often turning to me and announcing to the class, "Now, perhaps Mr. Singlaub has another view on this issue." I always did, and the students seemed to respond well to my alternative and, to my mind, more realistic description of the Communists' true motives and methods.

☆   ☆

MY job as the 101st Airborne's assistant chief of staff for operations was another of those demanding but utterly engrossing assignments that test an officer's mettle—and the long-suffering patience of his wife. Twelve-hour days became commonplace again. The 101st was literally writing the book for General Taylor's Pentomic Army. This meant our field-training exercises were closely scrutinized by ubiquitous senior officers from Washington.

The 101st Airborne had proud traditions. The division had jumped at Normandy and had withstood the massive German siege of Bastogne in the Battle of the Bulge. The division's "Screaming Eagle" shoulder patch was one of the proudest insignias in the U.S. Army. Interestingly enough, President Eisenhower had chosen troops from the 101st to guard Central High School in racially troubled Little Rock, Arkansas, the previous fall to demonstrate his support for school desegregation. In so doing, he had shown his confidence in the discipline and professionalism of the 101st.

The division was the first unit to use the new turboprop C-130 Hercules. This aircraft was a quantum improvement over the slow transports of World War II. The Hercules had four powerful engines and could cruise at 350 knots, almost three times the speed of the C-47. The C-130 carried sixty-four fully equipped paratroopers and several tons of their equipment. With its high tail and unique hydraulic cargo ramp, the C-130 could also drop jeeps, artillery, and even light armored vehicles. For the first time, the Army had the means to dispatch troops long distances on short notice, to extinguish "brushfire" conflicts before they spread. Given this capacity, the 101st proudly accepted the designation of the Fire Brigade.

The operations officer was responsible for organizing all troop movements, anything from a training exercise to a parade. And Airborne units had the reputation of presenting spectacular parades. To a civilian, the attention given such ceremonies might seem a waste of resources. But that intangible unit pride known as esprit de corps is fostered by such public displays. On the average, we trained twice as hard as ground units—which meant our officers and GIs were away from their families for long periods. And this training was often hazardous.

Therefore, Airborne troops—like other elite units from the Coldstream Guards to the Bengal Lancers—found pleasure in public displays of their military prowess. Soon after arriving at Fort Campbell, I was responsible for organizing General Sherburne's farewell parade. The General, a decorated World War II paratrooper, had been the officer most responsible for bringing the division quickly up to strength after its reactivation, and the men respected him. But this respect didn't necessarily mean the troops wouldn't try to cut up during the parade. Airborne soldiers were notorious for exotic flouting of "straight-leg" Army regulations. And individual units within the division maintained keen rivalries. Therefore, with 10,000 troops preparing for the parade, I could anticipate anything from a formation being led by a mascot goat equipped with his own parachute to an impromptu kazoo band.

But the assistant division commander, Brigadier General Reuben Tucker, let me know he wanted this parade "STRAC," by the book. Tucker was one of the crustiest old paratroopers in the Army, having served with the 504th Parachute Infantry in all of their World War II battles from North Africa to the Rhine. He spoke from the corner of his mouth in clipped phrases, liberally punctuated by epithets. He explained that the "goddamn press" would be watching this parade closely to assess the professional comportment of General Taylor's expensive new Pentomic division. "Jack, I want you to pull out all the stops, but no rinky-dink," Tucker ordered.

I planned the parade like a combat operation. The troops would pass in review from right to left, the opposite of the normal order, to display the Screaming Eagle patches on their left shoulders. The division's own bald eagle would stand proudly on its perch beside the reviewing stand. Just before the actual march-by, General Sherburne would parachute onto the parade ground from an L-20. Then wave after wave of Air Force transports would fly by, dropping multicolored cargo chutes. Toward the finale, division artillery would stage a mock firing of our Little John battlefield nuclear missile, replete with a simulated mushroom cloud in the distance. It would be a spectacle worthy of Cecil B. deMille.

Still, General Tucker repeatedly cautioned me to be alert for fancy dress and other irregularities among the troops. The day of the parade, I stationed my own men in the assembly area. They confiscated penny whistles, unauthorized scarves, and other offending accoutrements.

The parade passed with surprising precision. Until the end. The division medical battalion was the second-to-last unit. At the reviewing stand they broke into a quick step and chanted "Fire Brigade, Fire Brigade medics!"

I was standing beside General Tucker next to the reviewing stand. "Shit, Jack," he muttered, a mild enough reprimand from him.

I finally began to relax. The last troops in the long column were the parachute rigger company, an outfit particularly known for its unit pride. But just before leaving their position in the formation to pass in review, and without warning, they removed their authorized black helmet liners with by-the-numbers precision. Each man withdrew a bright red riggers' baseball cap and clamped it on his head just before the order "Column left, march."

General Sherburne was amused. But Reuben Tucker realized the men had gotten the best of him. "Damn it, Jack," he said, "how did you let them get away with *that?*"

During another parade on a hot summer afternoon, our division mascot got too much sun and toppled to hang ingloriously from the perch by his talon chain. The new assistant division commander, Brigadier General Andy McAnsch, was beside me. "The eagle just croaked," he muttered. "This time, Jack, you've gone too far."

☆   ☆

GENERAL William Westmoreland took over as division commander from General Sherburne. "Westy" came well recommended by all who had served with him. A graduate of West Point in the 1930s, where he'd been Cadet First Captain, he had served in the field artillery in North Africa and Europe during World War II, and ended up commanding an infantry regiment. He didn't go through parachute training until after the war. But he quickly became a staunch advocate of the Airborne. In Korea, he had commanded the 187th Airborne Regimental Combat Team during the fierce fighting of the final Chinese offensive in 1953. He was one of the hardest-working and most decisive officers I've ever met.

Those leadership qualities were put to a severe test only a few days after he took command. The division carried out a field training exercise called White Cloud, a mass parachute drop, with units arriving over the Fort Campbell drop zones from air bases in several surrounding states. Again, the press was watching our performance and we wanted to do our best. General Tucker, the most experienced paratrooper in the division, was on the Sukchon drop zone (named for a Korean War battle of the 187th RCT), acting as drop zone safety officer who certified jumping conditions were within safety margins. It was late spring in Kentucky, a period of unstable weather.

I was at Seward Air Force Base in Tennessee, supervising the movement of the multiple air columns. The C-130s carrying the first unit swept in from the north, and General Tucker authorized their drop. Now things suddenly went bad. Although the ground wind had been reported marginal, gusting around ten knots, the conditions were acceptable.

As several planeloads of the 502nd Parachute Infantry neared the ground, however, a freak wind came up, funneling the men toward two gullies at the edge of the drop zone. These gullies were a jumble of bulldozed timber, left over from the original clearing operation. Hundreds of troops were dragged along the ground and smashed into the pile of broken tree trunks. In a few moments, five men were dead and scores lay helpless among the pine logs with broken arms and legs.

I received word directly from General Tucker. There'd been some "injuries," he reported. But the wind conditions were still acceptable. General Westmoreland's element was approaching the drop zone. Tucker requested my advice. Should he release green smoke authorizing the General to drop? I had to make a quick decision. Men had been injured (neither Tucker nor I had yet received reports of deaths). If we canceled Westmoreland's drop, it might appear that the General had ordered men to jump in conditions he himself would not accept. But if the General were injured or killed, the officers authorizing the drop would be blamed. Making such hard decisions was what we were paid to do.

"I recommend we proceed, General," I radioed Tucker. By now, Westmoreland had learned of the earlier accidents. He could have canceled his own drop to prevent further injuries, but this would have looked as if he were willing to risk others in a dangerous situation that he himself refused to face. Westmoreland jumped and had a rough landing. He was dragged over a hundred yards before he could collapse his parachute, and was shaken up but not seriously injured.[1]

In the investigation following the accident, it became obvious that the standard T-10 parachute harness was unsuitable for such conditions. For years, the Airborne had been begging the Army to adopt quick-release shoulder connections that would separate the risers from the harness, allowing an immediate collapse of the canopy. But the Army had resisted this improvement because it was too expensive. General Westmoreland led the fight for the new equipment. Within a year, we were issued the improved harnesses.

☆   ☆

ONLY a few weeks after the White Cloud exercise, the division faced its first operational deployment. Vice President Richard Nixon was on a state visit to Caracas, Venezuela, when a huge anti-American crowd attacked his motorcade. He and Mrs. Nixon narrowly escaped and were barricaded in the U.S. embassy. Other American officials weren't so lucky; two military attachés were almost killed by the mob. The embassy itself was under siege by thousands of rioters, led by a well-organized cadre of Communist agitators.[2]

President Eisenhower ordered the Marines to dispatch an amphibious landing team to the Caribbean, and told General Maxwell Taylor to place his best unit on alert. Taylor called Westmoreland and asked him how soon he could send a task force from the 101st to Ramey Air Force Base in Puerto Rico, prepared to rescue the Vice President if necessary. The force should not exceed 600 men and should be commanded by an experienced full colonel. Westmoreland called me. He explained the mission.

"How soon can we get aircraft to start moving the alert force, Jack?" he asked.

We always had one battle group on alert with two of its companies ready to depart on four-hour notice. At the present time the alert force was the 502nd Airborne Battle Group, but its commander, Colonel Bill Kuhn, was away on emergency leave, which meant that it was temporarily commanded by a relatively inexperienced lieutenant colonel. I advised against sending them. However, at that very moment we did have the entire 506th Airborne Battle Group lined up with all of its equipment undergoing a command inspection by the assistant division commander, Brigadier General Charlie Rich, and the division staff. We also had six C-130s at the post, conducting parachute training. On Westmoreland's orders, we designated the commander of the 506th Battle Group, Colonel Robert Works, as task force commander. We had the first company of his task force aboard the refueled C-130s and en route to Puerto Rico less than three hours after the initial call from General Taylor. We established a schedule of one aircraft departure every fifteen minutes. Before the last of the six aircraft we had under our control took off, the Tactical Air Command (TAC) sent in others, so we could maintain our schedule.

I made sure the six C-130s were loaded to full capacity. We'd jammed communications jeeps, weapons carriers, and their drop pallets and cargo chutes aboard the planes. Once the task force landed in Puerto Rico, they could quickly rig the equipment for a drop in Venezuela. We'd even sent a light command helicopter with them.

Meanwhile, at the Pentagon, Taylor asked Air Force Chief of Staff General Curtis LeMay how long before he could divert airlift planes to Fort Campbell. General LeMay was told by the commander of the Military Airlift Command (MAC) that it would take a minimum of forty-eight hours. LeMay was furious. He was later pleased when he learned that we had worked out a local agreement and that six TAC aircraft were already carrying paratroopers south.

The only problem was that none of the staff en route to Puerto Rico had a detailed map of Caracas on which to locate drop zones and a march route to the besieged embassy. I contacted Lieutenant Colonel Bob Brugh, division intelligence officer, who had served in Caracas as Army attaché. "Jack," he told me, "the best damn map of Caracas is issued by the Esso Oil Company." He spent a frantic half hour telephoning Esso executives and finally tracked down the man who had a good supply of Caracas street maps. The Air Force dispatched a T-33 jet, which ferried the bundle of maps to our troops in Puerto Rico. Based upon Bob Brugh's intimate knowledge of Venezuela and its armed forces, I recommended and Colonel Works agreed that Bob Brugh be designated as the deputy task force commander. Within an hour, Lieutenant Colonel Brugh was on one of the aircraft en route to Ramey Air Force Base in Puerto Rico.

That evening, Eisenhower briefed the press on the crisis. The United States, he stated gravely, was strongly considering a military option.

"Where are the Marines?" a reporter asked.

"I don't know where the Marines are tonight," the former Army general replied. "But I can tell you an Airborne task force is already on the way."[3]

We later received word that the commandant of the Marine Corps had not been particularly amused by the President's comments.

The quick military response helped diffuse the crisis. The mob in Caracas dispersed that night. I suggested to General Westmoreland that we take advantage of the deployed task force to stage a realistic training exercise. The following day, the troops parachuted onto Fort Campbell's drop zones with a training mission similar to the real one they might have executed in Venezuela. It was one of the most realistic training exercises we had ever had. One offshoot of the Venezuela crisis was that we were able to reduce the reaction time of the readiness force from four to two hours, a standard that has lasted to the present day.

☆　　　☆

THAT summer U.S. Marines and paratroopers were dispatched to another trouble spot, Lebanon. For months, the unstable Middle Eastern country had been wracked by fighting between pro-Western Christian forces and their Muslim allies, who backed the elected government, and rebel Muslim army units. The rebels were supported by thousands of infiltrators from neighboring Syria, which had recently joined President Nasser's grandiose United Arab Republic. The UAR was the spearhead of a Soviet-supported pan-Arab movement whose stated goal was to sweep aside Western influence in the region. Blocked by Western Alliances from expanding militarily in Europe and Southwest Asia, the Soviets now supported surrogates to further their policies in the unstable regions of the Third World.

When the UAR-backed rebellion was unable to topple the Beirut government, a bloody stalemate ensued. Each side sought expanded outside support. The situation grew especially tense in midsummer when Secretary of State Dulles proclaimed America would send troops to protect Lebanon's independence. The Soviets countered by offering the rebels the support of Soviet military "volunteers."[4]

Then a Soviet-sponsored coup d'état toppled the pro-Western government in nearby Iraq, and Lebanon's president, Camille Chamoun, appealed directly to President Eisenhower for American military intervention. A battle group of the 11th Airborne Division had already been airlifted from Germany to U.S. bases in Turkey. Within twenty-four hours American paratroopers had secured Beirut's international airport and prepared landing sites for U.S. Marines. Eisenhower had called the bluff of the Soviet Union and its new Egyptian client. Any direct Soviet troop support for the rebels would pit Russian soldiers against the Americans, a risk the Russians wouldn't accept.

That September of 1958 I was ordered on temporary duty to Lebanon as part of a five-officer team representing the XVIII Airborne Corps and Continental Army Command. Our mission was to review the effectiveness of rapid deployment of airlifted troops in areas with no existing U.S. military support structure. After the inspection tour in Lebanon we were to report to concerned U.S. Army and NATO commanders in Europe.

I was surprised by the amount of destruction we encountered around

Beirut. I guess we'd been accustomed to assuming that Arab civil wars were more comic-opera posturing than full-scale battle. But both sides had been well supplied with armor, artillery, and heavy weapons. Beirut's elegant white terraces rising from the blue Mediterranean into the cedar-clad hills were badly pocked with shell holes. The shaded highways of the Corniche were littered with burned-out armored vehicles.

The biggest shock, however, was my encounter with the U.S. Marines. The Airborne guarded the main Damascus-Beirut highway from positions in the foothills behind the city. The Marines held similar positions in the Chouf Mountains to the south. But there was really no comparison between the two services' outposts.

The Army troops were well dug in, with sandbagged bunkers and an excellent network of observation posts. The Marines were bivouacked in a hodgepodge of shallow foxholes and tents, surrounded by barbed wire. They hadn't even dug in their mortars and ammunition or protected them with sandbags. And the Marines themselves looked worse than the ragged units of the local army. For some reason, these Marines equated a slovenly appearance with combat readiness. They'd been ashore for two months, but were still eating C-rations. Their fatigues were greasy; the men looked like they shaved once a week at most. Many of them suffered from diarrhea brought on by poor sanitation. It was as if they were playacting the battle of Guadalcanal.

Worse, they threw the empty ration cans into their barbed wire to become mosquito-breeding grounds and a haven for swarming rats. Some old salt had told them that tin cans in the barbed wire made good intruder alarms. Unfortunately, when the intruders were rats, the Marines kept everybody awake all night firing their rifles and machine guns.

The Marines I had seen in China and Korea had certainly been sharper troops than those in Lebanon. As a professional soldier, I couldn't help but wonder at the caliber of the career officers in the Marine Corps who would allow—or even encourage—their men to perpetuate the type of adolescent macho posturing I'd seen around Beirut.

☆   ☆

AFTER I briefed the NATO staff in Paris on my return trip, I contacted an old French resistance colleague whom I will call "Etienne." He was delighted to hear from me and graciously invited me to attend a dinner that night with another former French resistance leader, "Claude," with whom we'd campaigned in the Cher and Indre. It was great to see them again. Neither man seemed fourteen years older, and we reminisced, driving out the Orleans highway through the splendid autumn countryside. Our host that evening was a business colleague of Claude's who owned a jewel of a small stone château surrounded by an ancient chestnut grove. When we arrived there were already four or five other men enjoying cocktails in the company of their stylish wives. I noticed several of the men had the short hair and upright bearing of career military officers, although they all wore well-cut civilian suits.

I drank several glasses of wine, chatting with the French ladies. When I looked around for Etienne, I was surprised that all the men were gone. I had another glass of wine. Twenty minutes passed, then another twenty, but no men appeared. The ladies seemed to accept this without comment. Finally, when an hour had passed, one of them told me that the men had a little business to discuss.

This was a period of extreme political tension in France. The war in Algeria had reached a critical point. Three months before, General Charles de Gaulle had been granted almost dictatorial power by the National Assembly and given the responsibility of finding an honorable solution to the war while simultaneously reforming France's unstable political institutions. He had proposed a new constitution, which would be tested by referendum in a few days. If this reform was accepted, de Gaulle would then run for president of the new Fifth Republic. If de Gaulle was defeated, the country might degenerate into civil war.

I was vaguely familiar with all this, of course. But I didn't associate my old colleagues or their friends with the political crisis.

A little after nine that night, the gentlemen drifted back to the drawing room and we all sat down to a late dinner. I was in my hotel in Paris a little after midnight. Twenty-four hours later, I was eating a midnight supper of a cheese sandwich and black coffee at my desk at Fort Campbell. The château, roast venison, and the finer points of French political intrigue were long forgotten.

It wasn't until several years later when I saw Etienne again that I recalled the evening. "What *were* you fellows doing by yourselves for so long?" I asked.

Etienne shrugged with typical Gallic nonchalance. "Oh," he said, "we were planning a coup d'état. Several of those with us at the château were commanders from the parachute regiments. Had de Gaulle been rejected, we planned to seize the government."

I stared at him, absolutely speechless, half suspecting this was one of his elaborate jokes. But he was serious. While I had been sipping burgundy with the bejeweled ladies, the men in the billiard room had been planning a coup. What if the Deuxième Bureau had raided the party? I had been the operations officer of the 101st Airborne Division, America's elite Fire Brigade strike force. I doubt very much that I'd have been able to convince the French authorities that my presence there had been purely social.

☆   ☆

FOLLOWING the crises in Venezuela and Lebanon, we all realized the 101st might be ordered into some distant trouble spot on short notice. General Westmoreland stepped up the already hectic training schedule. He was a commander who always encouraged innovation, which is ironic considering the way he was pilloried in the press during the Vietnam War for supposedly being too inflexible.

We steadily increased the role of helicopters. The 101st Airborne was the Army's first unit to deploy significant numbers of the new UH-1 Huey troop transport chopper. Once they were available, we worked hard to increase their effectiveness. On one huge field exercise at Fort Bragg, we used helicopters to lay miles of field telephone wire, dropping it into the treetops from containers slung beneath the choppers. By doing this we beat our archrivals, the 82nd Airborne, in linking our positions by secure telephone line. Soon, we were using helicopters to resupply outposts and deploy long-range reconnaissance patrols.

Westmoreland also encouraged small-unit proficiency. The division might soon be asked to intervene in Vietnam, where Ho Chi Minh's Communists were stepping up their support for the Vietcong guerrillas in the south. Westmoreland established a special division training course called the RE-CONDO School (an anagram of "reconnaissance" and "commando"), in which the best young officers and NCOs in the division learned the demanding skills of irregular warfare. I was pleased when he chose Major Lew Millett to run the school. Millett had won a Medal of Honor leading a bayonet charge in Korea and then had gone through Ranger training at Fort Benning. The RECONDO School stressed courage tests, mental flexibility, and physical toughness. Following the Ranger training procedures we'd established, the men were grouped in small patrols, and patrol leadership was rotated to give each man confidence.

Sport parachuting had just been introduced in the States by Jacques Istel, the Frenchman who had pioneered the sport in Europe. Westmoreland asked me to organize a division skydiving team, which, we agreed, would enhance troop morale and give the men greater confidence in their regular jump duties. I sent two sergeants, Dick Fortenberry and Loy Brydon, over to Fort Bragg, where Istel was training Army skydiving instructors. When they returned, they trained me.

I was enthralled by the sport. In Korea, I'd made several free-fall jumps from moderate altitudes, but I hadn't understood the aerodynamic principles of "stable" skydiving. Now I learned to arch my back on exiting the aircraft and slide into a comfortable swimming position, face and chest parallel to the ground. After a few seconds, I reached terminal velocity and lost the falling sensation. I became a powerful bird, suspended in the sunlit wind, completely free of gravity. But a skydiver couldn't get too carried away and forget to pull his ripcord.

☆   ☆

IN the summer of 1959, I was one of ten Army officers selected to attend the Air War College at Maxwell Air Force Base, Alabama. I wasn't over-joyed, although I was certainly honored to have been chosen to represent the Army. The assignment was definitely made more attractive when I got word late that summer that I had been selected for full colonel, a promotion that came well ahead of schedule.

As the first semester at the Air War College advanced, I became more familiar with U.S. Air Force policies and institutions. I was surprised to discover that many of my fellow students had never attended formal Air Force service schools. The Air Force at that time placed little emphasis on a regular system of postgraduate education for its career officers. The paradigm for the Air Force officer in the 1950s was still the hard-drinking, hard-flying stick-and-rudder jet jockey that Tom Wolfe later immortalized in *The Right Stuff*. Men made rank in the Air Force by their prowess as aviators, not managers. And career officers fought hard to avoid duty as "desk ween-ies."

Above all, I learned, the Air Force was enamored of powerful jet aircraft, be they huge B-52 strategic bombers or tactical fighter-bombers like the F-100. As an Airborne infantry officer I found this troubling. Close air support should have been one of the infantry commander's greatest assets. In World War II, for example, Allied fighter-bombers had practically sealed off the vulnerable Normandy beachhead, protecting the invasion force from German armor and mechanized artillery. But those planes had been "slow movers," prop-driven P-47s and Hurricanes that could loiter over the battlefield and fly low above German Panzer columns.

In Korea, the Air Force had been in transition to an all-jet service. F-80 Shooting Stars and F-84 Thunderjets certainly *sounded* and looked powerful as they swept across the jumbled mountaintops. But the sad fact was that the U.S. Air Force and Navy fighter-bombers simply had not been able to interdict the Chinese lines of communication in Korea. When I pointed out to my colleagues at Maxwell that the Chinese had been able to launch their biggest artillery-supported offensive of the war in June 1953, after almost two straight years of intense aerial bombardment, the Air Force students and instructors practically considered me a heretic.

Air Force doctrine, I discovered, was much more vague than that of the Army. Air superiority was their first goal; so they designed their fighter-bombers for speed and range, in order to strike enemy airfields. Such aircraft had little value supporting infantry in mountains or jungle. But the massive retaliation mentality still prevailed. The Army was tolerated as an obsolescent service, in every way inferior to the nuclear might of SAC.

Although I couldn't then articulate my apprehension, I had the gut feeling that the Air Force's unrealistic love affair with their powerful, gleaming jets would one day blunt our military efforts in some distant trouble spot.

☆   ☆

I WAS definitely pleased when I was assigned as the commanding officer of the 1st Battle Group, 16th Infantry of the 8th Infantry Division stationed in West Germany. My orders called for me to report to Baumholder in the Rhineland in July 1960. It had been almost seven years since I had actually commanded troops.

Following the doctrine of the Pentomic Army, the 8th Division's five battle groups were dispersed among different base areas between the Rhine and the industrial Saarland. Division headquarters was at Bad Kreuznach, but our main battle areas were much further east. Baumholder was a former Wehrmacht barracks and training area in the pleasant forested countryside of the Rhineland-Pfalz. The nearby towns had been reconstructed in their handsome plaster-and-timber Rhineland style after the destruction of World War II.

When I took over the unit from Colonel David Daly, I found that a generally complacent garrison mentality prevailed among the officers and men. Colonel Daly was a tall, distinguished southerner with patrician manners. He placed considerable emphasis on military ceremony. The battle group participated fully in all the field exercises and was proficient in the mandatory combat skills tests, but there just wasn't much enthusiasm for the mission. Most of the troops and NCOs didn't seem to know why they were in Germany; most of the officers were too young to have served in combat and were generally ignorant of world politics in the previous turbulent decades.

The headquarters staff had been accustomed to straggling into their offices at a comfortable hour each morning and immersing themselves in mundane paperwork. They passed their days indoors, and knocked off in plenty of time for happy hour at the officers' club. There was a real gulf between the five rifle companies and my headquarters. This problem was definitely inherent to the Pentomic structure. Unlike a traditional battalion commanded by a young lieutenant colonel, my battle group suffered from a real generation gap in the command structure. The captains commanding the rifle companies were men in their mid-twenties with only a few years' service.

They saw me as a battle-scarred old veteran of almost forty with whom they shared few common experiences.

I knew from Korea that the personal style of a commanding officer greatly influenced unit spirit and efficiency. So I immediately set about to change the garrison mentality. One of my first orders was that *all* personnel would participate in regular morning runs. Getting the staff officers—myself included—out with the rifle platoons at dawn every day went a long way toward reestablishing command contact.[5] I also introduced sport parachuting to the unit and encouraged my officers to participate. Within a few months, the outfit became known as the "16th Almost Airborne Infantry."

One of my greatest challenges, however, was convincing the men that they actually were combat soldiers, that their duties were not simply the military equivalent of a civilian job. The garrison troops in Japan in June 1950 had been sorely unprepared to face combat in Korea. Not wanting my men afflicted with this type of "occupation" mentality, I began conducting unscheduled weekend alert exercises to shake up the troops. If the Soviets were ever going to attack West Germany, I knew they'd do it on a Friday evening, when the *Gasthauses* and service clubs were crowded with GIs, their bellies full of beer and sausage.

Unfortunately, several of my best young platoon officers were on the unit's football team, the Baumholder Spader Rangers. I told them that they couldn't play Saturday football and also lead their troops on maneuvers. But Major General Lloyd Moses, the division commander, loved his football. I lost that particular battle.

One battle I didn't lose, however, involved what was then known as the Command Information Program. I felt it was vital that the soldiers understand the nature of the Soviet threat, that they be educated in the history of the totalitarian Communist system and the brutal repression of Eastern Europe. Student draft deferments were still common then, and most of our enlisted men had no college; some lacked high school diplomas. It was hard to get them motivated to face a potential enemy they knew nothing of beyond vague animosity toward the "Commies." So I began a regular series of lectures, tracing the history of expansionist Soviet policies and subversion.

This type of education was particularly important then because the Soviets had embarked on a reckless policy of military confrontation. They had achieved parity with the West in nuclear missiles, and were determined to exploit this strength. Following the downing of the American U-2 spy plane flown by Gary Powers, Khrushchev canceled his proposed arms control summit meeting with Eisenhower and the Soviets launched a test program of increasingly larger warheads, a policy intended to intimidate our NATO allies. For the next several years, the Soviets repeatedly used their growing missile force and the dangerous tactic of atmospheric nuclear weapons tests in an attempt to wrest concessions from the West. They hoped to control our elected leaders by cynically manipulating the natural public revulsion for nuclear weapons tests.[6]

Major General Edwin A. Walker (whom I had known at the Ranger Training Center) was the commander of the 24th Infantry Division south of us in Bavaria. He conducted a similar troop-education series called the "Pro-Blue Program." Unfortunately for Walker, he included a few materials from the far-right John Birch Society in his lectures. Equally unfortunate, Ted Walker ran afoul of the *Overseas Weekly,* a muckraking private newspaper that aimed its sensationalism at lonely and disgrunted GIs. (The paper thrived on sex and scandal; most soldiers called it the "Oversexed Weekly.") After Walker banned one of the paper's reporters from the 24th Infantry Division's base because the man stole confidential court-martial records, the *Weekly* launched a crusade against Walker. They targeted his Pro-Blue Program, which exploded in a controversy led by headline-seeking congressional investigators. President Kennedy responded by relieving Walker—a distinguished soldier and certainly no crypto-fascist—of his command. Only after he was sacked was General Walker impartially investigated. He was found guiltless of actionable wrongdoing, but admonished in a vague manner for being "injudicious" in his comments about prominent Americans. Ted Walker then resigned from the Army in protest against the illegal procedures taken against him by President Kennedy and his secretary of defense, Robert McNamara.[7]

U.S. forces in Germany were closely watched by press vigilantes following the Walker debacle. Word filtered down unofficially from 8th Division headquarters that it might be prudent to suspend our own troop-indoctrination program until the dust settled. I refused to comply. The material I used in my program was a product of honest scholarship, not extremism. I had risked my life fighting fascism in two theaters of World War II. I had also fought the Communist equivalent of fascism in Korea. The mission of the U.S. forces in Europe was to support democracy and oppose totalitarianism. I intended to accomplish my mission.

Despite the recommendation of my staff officers that I back down on this sensitive matter, I refused to be intimidated. The lectures continued and we got no formal complaints from the Army.

☆   ☆

IN 1961, the Seventh Army's major field exercise, Winter Shield II, was conducted at the sprawling Graffenwoehr training ground in the empty forests near the East German frontier. I had made a point that fall of preparing the men by conducting night maneuvers at Baumholder, training they sorely needed. By the time Winter Shield came, they were proficient at night movement.

I was pleased when I read the classified maneuver orders, which pitted our V Corps against the heavy-armor "Aggressors" of VII Corps. To increase realism, we didn't get our alert order until the afternoon of Thursday, February 2, 1961. The battle group was ordered to deploy to a combat bivouac along the Vils River within twenty-four hours. Over 200 miles of German highway lay between Baumholder and the objective.

To make things interesting, it began to snow just as the lead reconnaissance vehicle of our long convoy pulled out of the base. The weather forecast was for intermittent snow and sleet. But the sky looked more threatening than that. I stopped the column where it was and gave the order, "All vehicles will put on chains." Several of my staff officers noted that this would slow down the column, possibly jeopardizing our on-time arrival, which in turn would threaten our overall performance rating on the exercise. They had a point, but so did I. As a compromise, I ordered each commander in the long convoy to add the necessary minutes to his complex march table to compensate for the slower speed, then deduct this from the planned rest stops.

Meanwhile, I set off in my command jeep and sped east in the failing winter twilight to reconnoiter the route. To my chagrin, I discovered most of the roads blocked by skidding German civilian cars that had been caught out in the unexpected blizzard. Other commanders later said this blizzard was not representative of the "real-world" problem we might encounter facing a Soviet offensive. To me, the weather presented *exactly* the conditions the Russians—like the Germans during the Ardennes offensive in 1944—would capitalize on to screen their attack. By mid-afternoon, the main highways had become impassable, so I diverted the columns onto secondary roads, and had each element led by reconnaissance vehicles. But even this precaution was not enough. At one point the next morning, I saw a tank from another unit poised on the crest of an icy hill. A moment later it was sliding sideways down the snowy road completely out of control. As it spun gracefully down the hill, the tank's long 90mm cannon clipped down telephone poles like a scythe.

But somehow the 16th Infantry arrived at its bivouac site on schedule, even though we had traveled the longest distance of any in the V Corps forces.

While the other units straggled in, I took advantage of our early arrival to dispatch reconnaissance patrols through the snowy woods to scout out the positions of our principal opponent, the 2nd Armor Division. Our first operation in the exercise called for the battle group to be the lead unit in a combined infantry-armor task force. We were to spearhead a night crossing of the Vils River. Luckily, I had rehearsed just such an operation with the unit several times that fall. Even luckier, the snow came again to mask our movement.

By the next morning we had infiltrated the 2nd Armor positions and passed in strength and undetected through their main defense area and into their rear, where we seized all the principal crossroads. As their fuel tanker and ammunition convoys approached, we simply diverted them into makeshift truck parks, and "captured" the truckers. The men now understood the importance of combat-readiness training. As a reward, Lieutenant General Frederick Brown, V Corps commander, excused the 16th Infantry from the Annual Army Training Test for that year. He considered that our maneuver performance had adequately demonstrated our combat proficiency.[8]

☆　　　☆

THAT spring and summer I increased the recruitment drive for the battle group sport parachute club and skydiving team. As the jump schedule intensified, we found ourselves running short of equipment, especially parachutes. One of my sergeants devised a method of modifying Air Force chutes for skydiving, which eliminated the cotton canopy sleeve normally used on a sport jump. I felt it was my responsibility to test this new chute.

I jumped from an Army U-1 Otter aircraft at 8,000 feet above the Ranger drop zone at Baumholder. It was a standard twenty-second delay, one of my favorite jumps. I watched the lush green pine forest gently rocking below me as the ground seemed to rise as if on some gigantic, unseen lift. A jump like this was pure pleasure. But when I pulled the ripcord I immediately knew something was wrong. The canopy exploded around my right arm and jerked me wildly to the right. Although the chute had deployed fully, I felt like I'd slammed into a brick wall.

Then I looked down and saw my right arm was not where it should be. It simply wasn't there, and neither was the sleeve of my coveralls. Craning my neck, I looked back to see my arm hanging helplessly behind me, next to the open parachute pack. My shoulder had been completely separated by the runaway canopy.

There was nothing I could do except reach back gingerly with my left hand and place my numb arm atop my reserve chute chest pack. I hooked one of the elastic opening bands over the little finger. It was like handling the limb of a store-window dummy.

This was a Sunday afternoon, and the small clinic at Baumholder had no doctor on duty. I had to be driven to a nearby field hospital. En route, the numbness gave way to searing pain. The doctor on duty at the field hospital took one look at me and grinned. "That's something straight out of the textbook," he said. "You don't often see such a *dramatic* separation." His casual attitude reminded me of Mary's obstetrician back at Fort Leavenworth.

The doctor had me lie on my left side on the examining table while he cradled my dangling right arm. Then, with a horrendous pop, he jammed the arm back into the shoulder socket. The next thing I knew I was sitting up and medics were applying a full-torso cast. "I don't think you'll be jumping for a while, Colonel," the doctor added.

When I got back to Baumholder later that evening, I called the duty officer, Lieutenant Powell Moore, to check for messages. Moore was an articulate young southerner of a literary bent, whom I had shanghaied from a rifle company to be my public information officer. I guess I tried too hard to impress the young man that I was still in command when I gruffly summoned him. He assured me that everything was normal.

"Nothing unusual?" I asked.

He paused. "Oh, yes, sir," he added. "There is. The battle group commander dislocated his shoulder while skydiving."[9]

☆ ☆

As in any other large oganization, a person who shows talent for a particular field in the Army is often precipitously reassigned to exploit his expertise. I was happily minding my business commanding the battle group that summer when I got orders to become the chief of training in the office of the assistant chief of staff (G-3) of the Seventh Army. This meant moving the family once again. Our new duty station was at Patch Barracks in Stuttgart.

I reluctantly relinquished command of the 16th Infantry and took up my new duties in Stuttgart. I had to admit, however, that this new staff assignment was fascinating. President John Kennedy had been in office for less than a year and had already weathered two crises involving Soviet expansionist policies. The Bay of Pigs fiasco that spring taught Kennedy that military half-measures didn't work against a determined, well-equipped Soviet surrogate like Fidel Castro. And the North Vietnamese attempt to overthrow the pro-Western government of Laos demonstrated the need for strong American conventional forces rather than the unusable nuclear juggernaut of massive retaliation.

Kennedy correctly assumed that our bankrupt policy would embolden the Soviets to take some aggressive action in Europe. In anticipation of this, he authorized the complete modernization of the U.S. Army in West Germany. I arrived as this modernization got under way. For several years the Soviet forces opposing us in East Germany and Czechoslovakia had built up their mechanized infantry and armored units. They now clearly had the potential to slash through the flatlands of the so-called Fulda Gap and cut our armies in half before NATO could properly react. Such a Blitzkrieg attack could only be repulsed with the wide use of tactical nuclear weapons.

But the Soviets understood well that America and her allies were deeply reluctant to resort to this drastic remedy. The only way to lower the nuclear threshold was to create a viable conventional force that offered a realistic defense against the Red Army. This meant that all U.S. combat ground troops in Germany would become mechanized in order to expand their maneuverability and survivability. When I'd arrived in Europe the year before, American troops moved on wheels. Now the Army decided all of its divisions in Europe would be deployed on tracked, armored personnel carriers and tanks. In effect, we were being transformed from a static occupation garrison army to a modern mechanized army.

This might sound like a straightforward task. In reality, the modernization program presented one of the toughest staff jobs in the peacetime Army. *Every* aspect of battle doctrine, and all the related training and combat proficiency testing, had to be overhauled. Once more, I dug in for a siege of twelve- and fourteen-hour days.

It didn't take the Soviets long to test Kennedy's resolve in Europe. On the night of August 12, 1961, Soviet and East German troops barricaded Communist East Berlin from the western half of the city. Within a week, a prefab concrete-and-block wall was rising as a permanent "anti-fascist" barrier, the notorious Berlin Wall. The purpose of the wall was to stop the hemorrhage of refugees fleeing communism. The Soviets followed this outrage by a general blockade of the city. That October, the Red Army began to restrict NATO and West German road access to West Berlin. They had completely closed the Autobahn to civilian traffic within a week. The next move in the well-orchestrated campaign was a direct military threat against the small U.S. Army garrison in West Berlin. Soviet tanks rolled to the city's East-West sector borders and leveled their cannons at the American barracks.

Kennedy's reaction was forceful. The 18th Infantry Battle Group under Colonel Glover Johns was beefed up with tanks and armored personnel carriers and sent to reinforce our Berlin garrison. When Johns's unit arrived at the western terminus of the auto route, the Soviets and East Germans tried to stall him. He negotiated with them patiently, then called his lead tanks forward. The moment of crisis had arrived. If the Soviets used force, Johns had orders to return fire. The Communists backed down. That night the 18th Infantry, in full combat gear, took up positions facing East Berlin.[10]

To underscore the gravity of the crisis, Kennedy began to airlift troops into West Germany, a demonstration of our new quick-response capability. More important, Kennedy called up Army Reserve and National Guard units. From the European perspective, mobilization was equated with serious resolve. Our augmented forces in West Berlin then confronted the Soviets in a series of dangerous face-offs that succeeded in calling the Russian bluff.[11] If Kennedy hadn't taken this politically risky step, the Soviets would probably not have backed down and would have imposed another blockade.

☆   ☆

OVER the next two years, I plugged away at the seemingly endless task of supervising the modernization, training, and testing of the two armored and three mechanized divisions now assigned to Seventh Army. Another, even more serious confrontation with the Soviets, the Cuban Missile Crisis of 1962, passed with the Russians again backing down in the face of firm American resolve. At the time many civilians did not realize how close to general war with the Soviet Union we actually were. Although American troops in Europe were ordered not to reveal our increased state of readiness, the U.S. Army was prepared to go into battle on a few hours' notice.[12]

The Berlin and Cuban crises blunted Soviet military adventurism in Europe and the Americas. They shifted their attention to a more promising arena, the Far East.

I had been asked by Seventh Army to extend my European assignment for a fourth year. The family was delighted with the prospect of another year in Germany when I received sudden orders back to the States. General Bill Depuy, the officer who, with Dick Stilwell, had recruited me out of the Ranger Training Command and back into the CIA during the Korean War, now wanted me to work for him in the Pentagon. Depuy led a directorate in the relatively new Army General Staff section called ACSFOR, the Assistant Chief of Staff for Force Development. Although I didn't know it at the time, the Army was already planning to counter a new aspect of Soviet military aggression.

Just as the situation in Europe seemed to have stabilized, a dangerous new confrontation between the Soviet Union and the United States was building in the jungles and rice paddies of Southeast Asia.

CHAPTER NINE

The Pentagon

1963–1965

☆　　　　☆

O UR FAMILY COMPENSATED for the disappointment of not staying in Europe by vacationing in the French château country en route to Le Havre to board the S.S. *United States*. It was strange to drive slowly along those quiet back roads in the shade of the plane trees. The last time I'd been on these roads was nineteen years before, clutching a Sten gun and watching each fieldstone barn and medieval steeple for possible ambush. On an absolutely splendid summer afternoon we stopped for a picnic on the banks of the Loire, just downstream from the ferry site over which Jacques and I had crossed the river to link up with Patton's armor columns. Muddy white ducks swam in the tranquil backwater, squabbling for the crusty scraps of baguette the children tossed. The burnt-out panzers were gone; no American fighter-bombers growled overhead. Mary and I split a nice bottle of wine, watching the clouds above the slate roofs of a château nearby. At a time like this, it was hard to remember I was a soldier in a dangerous world.

I looked forward to my new assignment in the Pentagon with a certain ambivalence. I had the temperament and skills of an effective staff officer, but I preferred command of a combat unit. Serving in the office of the Assistant Chief of Staff for Force Development (ACSFOR), however, would put me in direct contact with the Army's leadership. At this point in the Cold War, with the largest standing "peacetime" military establishment ever, a Pentagon tour was considered a part of the maturing process for senior officers. If we were going to be successful generals, we had to understand the methods and manners of the Defense Department's civilian leadership. I accepted this. But a Pentagon staff job lacked the kind of soldiering—

contact with the troops and field exercises—that I'd enjoyed in the 101st Airborne and the 16th Infantry.

So, I was prepared for three years of bureaucratic drudgery, during which, hopefully, I would "mature" and grow wise in the ways of the Washington power elite, all in preparation for a senior command position. But I had no way of knowing, when I went to work for General Bill Depuy in the summer of 1963, that two years later I would be at the vortex of the most critical and controversial series of decisions the U.S. military faced in the second half of the twentieth century.

☆   ☆

IN 1939, when the Pentagon was completed, the massive structure was considered an almost brazen political and architectural statement: the institutionalization of a large, permanent military establishment, something new in America. The miles of dun-colored corridors, radiating in concentric circles from an open courtyard in the five-sided building, provided offices and conference rooms for a giant military bureaucracy then known as the War Department. But twenty-five years later, the Pentagon where I reported to work was only one building of the American military's huge Washington headquarters complex. Various annexes and technical support centers had spread for miles across Washington's northern Virginia suburbs. Tens of thousands of career military personnel and civilians labored in this sprawling establishment, supporting a global military system that had become the single most expensive sector of the federal government.

The driving force behind this military juggernaut, of course, was America's Cold War commitment, specifically our containment policy. Like the Roman Empire of the first century, the Western world had cordoned off the barbarians and was obliged to guard the frontiers with a huge standing army. But now the relatively spartan legions of the Caesars had been replaced by aircraft carrier battle groups, nuclear-powered missile submarines, intercontinental ballistic missiles (ICBM), airborne and armored divisions equipped with tactical nuclear weapons, Special Forces groups, and far-flung teams of military advisers.

As the technical stakes increased, so did our expenditures. Unlike World War II, which had a finite (but horrendously challenging) strategic objective—the total defeat of fascism—our Cold War objectives were less defined. The arms race was a fact of life. The Soviets' development of an ICBM with a thermonuclear warhead provoked a crash program for the development of our own Atlas missile.[1] The deployment of a new British or American battle tank prompted a similar deployment by the Soviets. Battlefield and short-range tactical nuclear weapons proliferated with amazing speed on both sides of the Cold War frontier.[2] Communications and headquarters detachments had to be "hardened" to survive on the nuclear battlefield. Chemical and biological weapons also proliferated as adjuncts of tactical nuclear arms. And the list went on.

The high cost and complexity of this permanent global military confrontation became issues of major concern in the Kennedy White House. The young president had been taken aback by the awesome power (and escalating cost) of the American military. The aborted Bay of Pigs invasion of 1961 and the subsequent Cuban Missile Crisis of 1962 further impressed on Kennedy that the American military required much tighter civilian management than he had originally anticipated.[3] In certain ways, Kennedy felt the military had grown to a point of alarming autonomy, that it had to be reined in, subdued, and controlled. His chosen instrument for this task was Robert Strange McNamara, the secretary of defense.

In theory, McNamara was the perfect man for the job. He had spent World War II as a bright young Pentagon official who had used the methods of management science he had learned at the Harvard Business School to help organize America's global conflict. Specifically, McNamara and his colleagues had applied new statistical analysis systems to accomplish the challenging mission of controlling the flow of men and matériel on an unprecedentedly vast scale. At age thirty he joined a group of talented "whiz kids" who reorganized the Ford Motor Company after World War II. McNamara the Ford executive instituted a system of rigorous cost-accounting techniques, by which every aspect of the company's operations could be reduced to logical, quantifiable data. His cost-effectiveness techniques seemed to work—although many people forgot that the "logic" of this approach produced the Edsel, the most disastrous design failure in American industrial history. In 1960, he was the first man outside the Ford family (and the youngest) ever to become company president. But he only served as Ford president for a month before becoming Kennedy's secretary of defense.

Although distracted by the Berlin and Cuban crises of 1961 and 1962, McNamara never lost sight of his primary objective, the modernization of America's armed forces along logical, cost-effective lines. He was aided in this mission by a handpicked coterie of like-minded young civilian systems analysts, many recruited from academia. McNamara was absolutely confident that he could streamline and rationalize the cumbersome military juggernaut. And he was equally certain that the career officer corps, including the Joint Chiefs of Staff, represented an institutional obstacle to this rationalization process. The military, he believed, lacked the imagination and insight to modernize itself. McNamara dismissed the hard-earned, mature "military judgment" of the Joint Chiefs as imprecise and illogical. His key civilian subordinates, such as former academic Alain Enthoven, who headed the Pentagon's new Office of Systems Analysis, went so far as to proclaim that "the so-called 'principles of war' are really a set of platitudes that can be twisted to suit almost any situation."[4] McNamara and his disciples felt the military would have to be led kicking and screaming through the portals of the cost-effectiveness utopia.

Like all experienced managers, McNamara understood that the budgeting process was the key to authority. He who controlled the purse strings controlled the entire operation, be it a corporation or the Department of Defense. One of McNamara's first major steps at the Pentagon was to overhaul the traditional budget-request, procurement process, replacing it with an elaborate new management technique: the Planning, Programming, and Budgeting System (PPBS). The rationale for PPBS was in the logic of connecting precisely defined "Program Objectives" to the means and methods (including funding and procurement) to accomplish them. This technique evolved directly from McNamara's corporate management experience. It worked well solving stable, straightforward problems with clear solutions: conditions that rarely prevailed in wartime.

Before the advent of cost-effectiveness management techniques, American industry would often produce products, then try to develop a market for them. This was a wasteful, imprecise process McNamara abhorred. As a Ford executive, he reversed the process, striving to first clearly identify a market niche, then building a product to fill it. In effect, the marketplace became a *system* that could be *analyzed*. For example, if Ford analysts foresaw a market for a compact car (or fuel-efficient delivery van) five years in the future, producing such a vehicle became an obvious corporate objective. The organization would be mobilized to achieve that objective; budget would be allotted only to those corporate groups that could demonstrate—through elaborate statistical projections—that they could most effectively meet the objective. In essence, the PPBS approach connected tactics to strategy through the budget process. Above all, every phase of the process *appeared* rational. At any given stage of the design and marketing, every manager involved could demonstrate exactly why he was spending company funds.

McNamara was determined to impose this same level of rational accountability on the Pentagon. The Air Force might want to order a new tactical fighter-bomber because American industry could provide an aircraft superior to anything in their inventory. But now the Air Force chief of staff had to "quantify" exactly how this new plane cost-effectively met formal policy objectives. Before McNamara, technical innovation leading to tactical superiority was self-justifying. Under PPBS, this was no longer the case. Cost effectiveness became the watchword, indeed the shibboleth of the McNamara Pentagon.

The logical extension of all this was the principles of joint procurement and of minimum requirements. If, for example, the Marine Corps and the Army both wanted to buy an anti-tank missile, PPBS required that the two services match their requirements and jointly procure the weapon, thus eliminating waste. Such cost effectiveness worked well on Alain Enthoven's computer spreadsheets. In reality, however, things weren't so simple. The Marines' requirements might have included man-portability and resistance to saltwater, while the Army's ideal missile might have been vehicle-mounted and robust enough to survive airdrops. With cost effectiveness as the primary procurement criterion, such special requirements were often disregarded, resulting in weapons that didn't work.

The most flagrant example of this flawed process was the saga of the dual-purpose F-111, the "McNamara fighter." In 1961 both the Air Force and the Navy wanted an advanced tactical fighter-bomber. The Navy aircraft had to operate off aircraft carriers, while the Air Force plane was to fly low-level deep-penetration missions. In a protracted test of wills between the McNamara-Enthoven systems analysts and the Joint Chiefs of Staff, the civilian leadership prevailed, requiring the two services to develop a single aircraft to meet their needs. This was obviously impossible, at least to experienced Air Force generals and Navy admirals. Again, "military judgment" reared its ugly head to dispute the logic of cost effectiveness. The result was an Edsel aircraft of monumental proportions. Design compromises made the Air Force F-111 almost impossible to fly safely on low-level missions (many crashed in Indochina attempting to do so), while the Navy's F-111B weighed in at thirty-five tons, far too heavy for carrier operations. But to McNamara and his team the plane was a fine example of cost effectiveness.[5] In fact, the whole process was a monument to the efficient production of an unusable aircraft.

☆   ☆

AN atmosphere of confrontation between the military professionals and McNamara's cold-blooded analysts prevailed when I took over the Army's Force Development Plans Division, working for Brigadier General Bill Depuy, director of Plans and Programs. But even the staunchest opponents of McNamara's bean-counters had to admit that the armed services needed reorganization. Specifically, confusion as to the roles and missions—McNamara's almighty "Objectives"—had led to widespread waste and duplication. Under McNamara's armed forces reorganization policies each service had to reexamine and justify its force structure in terms of its actual mission. In addition, the individual services no longer procured their own equipment and supplies; this responsibility was given to a newly created branch of the defense department, which submitted all requests to PPBS analysis.

My division led the reorganization effort in the Army. Bill Depuy gave me my assignment and guidance, and then supported my efforts completely. He was no fan of McNamara, but he hoped a more efficient Army might evolve from the painful exercise. The Plans Division had the responsibility of analyzing the Army's long-term force structure. I had to dig deeply into each branch, unit by unit, to determine if the personnel and equipment met the Army's overall mission objectives.

The basic "War Plan" projected a possible conventional ground war in Europe between NATO and the Warsaw Pact, to which the Army would contribute active and reserve units adequate to repulse a Soviet-led invasion. In addition, the Plan foresaw various Third World contingency operations. My office had to analyze the future staffing and equipping of both active-duty and reserve units to meet these requirements. What I found was often shocking. My staff discovered that there were thousands of "TTPPS"—Transients, Trainees, Patients, Prisoners, and Students—the "horde of personnel who are always coming or going, but never seem to arrive," which the Army seemed to have forgotten.[6]

And when we analyzed the Transportation Corps, we found dozens of amphibious support companies equipped with Ducks, seagoing trucks designed to transport men and matériel from ships to an invasion beach. But the Army had not had an amphibious operations mission for years; that job had formally passed to the Marine Corps in the 1940s. Yet thousands of men and millions of dollars' worth of equipment were tied up in these companies. Even more shocking, I discovered that the Army's deputy chief of staff for logistics had equipped them with a great many amphibious vehicles because procuring them in great quantity had lowered the unit price. Without question, this was the type of bloated waste McNamara's reorganization was meant to abolish.

My investigation of the Transportation Corps led to the Corps of Engineers, where I discovered an all but forgotten Amphibious Support Brigade. This was a little empire unto itself, with both active and reserve units, including men who had served since World War II. Their sole purpose was to keep alive the skills of amphibious warfare, which the Army no longer needed according to current roles and missions statements.

I recommended abolishing the amphibious support units of both the Transportation Corps and the Engineers. As expected, howls of protest arose from their ranks. Depuy prepared me to take my case to General Creighton Abrams, the vice chief of staff of the Army, who handled purely Army matters for Army Chief of Staff General Harold K. Johnson. Abrams had been one of Patton's best tank commanders in Europe. He was known for his direct, sardonic manner. After I made my case against the amphibious units, Abrams gazed coolly over his smoking cigar at the representatives of the Engineers and Transportation Corps, who had also made presentations to support their positions. These branches had sent their big guns, a major general from Transportation and a lieutenant general from the Engineers, with a couple of brigadiers thrown in as spear holders. There were one hell of a lot of stars on the opposition's epaulets facing my lonely silver eagles. But I guess I had made my point well.

"Unless you gentlemen have something more to offer," Abrams said to the representatives of the Transportation Corps and to the Chief of Engineers, "I have to go with the ACSFOR."

We had won our first battle in the reorganization war.

Later, my office began a careful analysis of the Medical Corps, once more comparing requirements for personnel "spaces" and equipment with actual mission objectives. We discovered a pattern of overstaffing (and over-equipping) that made the Transportation Corps appear impoverished. There were literally hundreds of field hospital units, mostly in the reserves and National Guard. We found that most of the medical units had been added in the 1950s. The documentation justifying all these field hospitals cited the large number of projected casualties from a tactical nuclear war. In addition, the Medical Corps assumed that these casualties would be treated in the field, rather than evacuated to safe areas or to the United States. Both these assumptions were out of date. Army doctrine at the time foresaw a conventional, not a nuclear conflict; the combination of Army medical evacuation helicopters and Air Force jet aircraft was capable of the rapid transportation of casualties from the battlefield all the way to the States in a matter of hours.[7]

The Medical Corps was planning for a nuclear war using transportation of World War II vintage without regard to the intercontinental medical-evacuation role assigned the USAF. Once more, I recommended a deep reduction of personnel and equipment to eliminate waste. Once more, I was sent to General Abrams to argue the ACSFOR's position in the matter. But the Medical Corps did not give up easily. They were represented by the Surgeon General, who brought along a suave lieutenant colonel, equipped with an easel and charts in the best Pentagon dog-and-pony-show tradition. While the Surgeon General nodded gravely, the Colonel presented a graphic case for the continuation of the Medical Corps' existing staff level. He showed grisly photos of battlefield casualties, and reassuring pictures of the medics and nurses ministering to the wounded. Without all those field hospitals, he said, thousands of men would die needlessly.

"General Abrams," the Colonel said earnestly, tapping his easel with a pointer, "until you've actually treated a sucking belly wound in the field, you have no idea how important these units actually are."

Having been a frontline commander for General George "Blood and Guts" Patton, Abrams had undoubtedly seen his share of sucking belly wounds. He chomped on his cigar noncommittally and spoke from the corner of his mouth. "Well, Singlaub?"

I stated my case, emphasizing that the newly upgraded strategic airlift, equipped with C-141 jet transports, could quickly evacuate such seriously wounded soldiers to the Medical Corps' splendid facilities here in the States. I was about to make my follow-up arguments, when Abrams nodded brusquely.

Again, he chomped his cigar. "Well, I agree with the ACSFOR."

That was the end of the meeting.

That afternoon, when the decision to cut the field hospitals was made formal, I got a call from a Medical Corps friend, Dr. Stodard Parker, who worked in the office of the Surgeon General. It seemed I wasn't too popular among the medics. "Jack," Doc Parker said, "my only advice to you is don't get sick."

I didn't have time to worry about the medics' possible vengeance. I was ordered on TDY to assist Brigadier General Robert C. Taber on a special project. Bob Taber was an assistant division commander of the 82nd Airborne who had managed the airlift of our troops to the Dominican Republic. I'd worked with Bob during my airlift planning days, and he needed me to help analyze the entire U.S. military's strategic movement capabilities for both sealift and airlift over the next five years. As with all such complex assignments, the Army wanted the results yesterday. So I found myself shunted from a comfortable office in the Pentagon to a gritty, stuffy old World War II building at National Airport, where Bob had set up shop for STRATMOVE 69, as the project was called.

We were given three future requirement scenarios: the reinforcement of American forces in Europe, in Vietnam, and in Indochina outside of Vietnam.

Our initial analysis was so effective that it eventually spawned nineteen additional studies, which in turn reshaped America's global military mobility. We saw a requirement for a huge new strategic airlift transport capable of moving large armored vehicles and helicopters intercontinental distances. This ultimately became the massive C-5A transport. We also foresaw the need for a whole new class of roll-on/roll-off naval transports for the rapid deployment of mechanized divisions. And we started the planning for the biggest logistical operation since World War II: the pre-positioning of equipment and supplies in the Pacific and Far East aboard ships—"floating warehouses"—for entire American divisions that could be flown from their stateside bases within days of an alert.

Finally, we planned a realistic logistical system for American operations in Southeast Asia that was centered on our strongest ally in the region, Thailand. This would entail building a modern military port at Sattahip, south of Bangkok, and a large air base nearby at U Taphao. To me, these plans indicated America was becoming serious about stopping the advance of communism in Southeast Asia.[8]

☆   ☆

WHILE the civilian and military leaders at the Pentagon were grappling with reorganization of the armed forces, the political and military situation in Vietnam was steadily deteriorating. During the eleven years between the Geneva agreements ending the French-Indochina War and mid-1965 when the United States faced its most important policy decisions in the region, the non-Communist Republic of Vietnam had struggled against mounting direct military aggression from North Vietnam and Communist-sponsored insurgency. By 1965, a Communist military victory was imminent.[9]

To understand the evolution of this situation, it is necessary to recall the course of events following the Geneva agreements in 1954. Vietnam was divided at the 17th parallel, with French armed forces regrouping to the south and the Viet Minh occupying the north. A final political settlement was to be based on nationwide elections scheduled for July 1956. But the non-Communist provisional government of the South, headed by the former emperor Bao Dai, and its new ally, the United States, refused to sign the election-schedule provisions of the accord.[10] A year later, Ngo Dinh Diem, the president of the newly founded Republic of Vietnam, refused to even discuss elections with Communist officials of North Vietnam. He cited the Geneva accords and noted that the Communist Viet Minh had taken control of the North by force of arms, not through elections. What Diem did not enunciate, but what everyone understood, was that any "nationwide" election was sure to be won by the Communist leaders of the more populous North, who controlled their country through typical totalitarian methods, and who had left behind thousands of Viet Minh agents in the South.[11]

The 17th parallel became an international frontier, dividing the Communist north and the non-Communist south. After the French collapse hundreds of thousands of anti-Communist refugees, many Roman Catholic (including Diem and his large, wealthy family), fled to the south, where they soon dominated politics in Saigon. As the French reduced their military and economic aid to the South, the United States moved in to fill the vacuum. By 1960, South Vietnam was receiving more per-capita American aid than any country in the region. Under American pressure, the Diem government undertook a program of land reform intended to break the traditional grip of powerful Mandarin absentee landlords. The United States also set about training and equipping a new army of the Republic of Vietnam (ARVN). While Diem struggled to consolidate his power and accommodate his American sponsors, he had to face a series of bloody revolts by the militias of several indigenous religious sects. Suppressing these revolts earned Diem a reputation for brutality (particularly in the liberal European and American press), but in reality he used the traditional Asian methods of bribery and division of spoils more than wholesale repression.[12]

Ho Chi Minh and his advisers were taken aback by Diem's resiliency. They had not anticipated the successful formation of a non-Communist government in the South. Ho's goal of becoming the leader of a super-national Southeast Asian Communist "nation," however, was still paramount. But the North needed a breather from armed conflict in order to consolidate its control. Rather than initiate immediate armed aggression against the South, Ho summoned several thousand former Viet Minh soldiers and political cadres to the North for training in guerrilla warfare.

The Diem government responded with a vigorous anti-Communist campaign, which drove most of the Viet Minh cadres underground—often into refuges in the roadless jungles near the Cambodian border. But a year later the Communist guerrilla leaders, newly trained and reequipped in the North, were moving south along a system of footpaths in the jungle mountains of the Annamite Cordillera, an infiltration route that became known as the Ho Chi Minh Trail.

These political cadres and guerrillas spread out through the southern provinces of the Republic of Vietnam and unleashed a well-managed program of anti-government terror. The focus of this campaign was the so-called *tru gian*—"the extermination of traitors"—effort. This was a widespread assassination campaign, employing Communist death squads who targeted government officials and functionaries, ranging from rural health workers to village mayors, schoolteachers, and, of course, military officers. According to a former Communist cadre leader, the *tru gian* assassination campaign "tried to kill any government official who enjoyed the people's sympathy and left the bad officials unharmed in order to wage propaganda and sow hatred against the government."[13] It is not surprising, therefore, that the Diem government's efforts at "nation building" were less than spectacular.

Over the next several years, the Saigon government and its American ally worked with grim determination to counter the Communist guerrilla war. The derogatory epithet "Vietcong" (Vietnamese Communists) was applied to all the groups within the Communists' umbrella organization in the South, the National Liberation Front. American military and political advisers poured into the country. By 1963, there were over 23,000 American military advisers working with South Vietnamese armed forces. American Special Forces units were involved in active combat against the Vietcong. The terms "insurgency" and "counterinsurgency" became the new watchwords of the

Pentagon. Our strategy was to steadily increase our military, political, and economic support of the Diem government, just as the North increased their military aggression in the South.

But Buddhist and student resistance to Diem's increasingly authoritarian rule cost him the support of the Kennedy White House. Diem and his influential family became comparable to the ostensibly "corrupt" Chiang Kai-shek regime.[14] In August 1963, bloody raids by Vietnamese Special Forces under orders from Diem's brother Ngo Dinh Nhu against Buddhist pagodas outraged Western sensibilities. Pressure on the Kennedy White House to dump Diem in order to find more efficient leadership to prosecute the counterinsurgency aimed at winning the "hearts and minds" of South Vietnam's peasants became irresistible. Kennedy approved a coup against Diem.[15] President Diem and his brother were murdered by the junta that led the coup. Contrary to popular myth, the coup that toppled the Diem government was not engineered by the CIA. In fact, the Agency, as well as the Joint Chiefs of Staff, recommended continued American support for Diem. But Ambassador Henry Cabot Lodge relayed White House orders that Saigon CIA officers—including my old Jedburgh colleague Lucien Conein—serve as conduits between the junta and Washington.[16] The Saigon leadership disintegrated into anarchy. Over the next eighteen months there were five more military coups. Clearly, the ARVN leadership was preoccupied with political turmoil, not waging a vigorous war against the Communists.[17]

The U.S. military involvement intensified in August 1964, when the Johnson White House used the pretext of North Vietnamese torpedo boat attacks on American destroyers operating in international waters of the Tonkin Gulf to unleash air strikes against Communist base areas in North Vietnam. Johnson and his advisers concealed the fact that the destroyers *Maddox* and *Joy* were supporting South Vietnamese Special Operations forces along coastal North Vietnam. The Tonkin Gulf incident became the pretext for a congressional resolution giving Lyndon Johnson freer military options in the region. But rather than striking hard to truly punish Ho Chi Minh, Johnson acted timidly. He stated that the United States sought "no wider war," while personally approving the air raids against leftover French naval facilities. This pattern of North Vietnamese aggression against the American military, followed by limited reprisal raids against Communist military infrastructure, was to continue for years, and indeed became a cornerstone of our overall strategy.[18]

There were many obvious problems with this policy, which deeply troubled my colleagues in the Pentagon, especially those like me who had served in Indochina during World War II. To begin with, the White House made a false assumption that Ho and his Communist leadership truly valued the barracks and bases left behind by the French army. In reality, the North Vietnamese Army (NVA, which had evolved directly from the Viet Minh) was organized on the Red Chinese pattern: Units were usually billeted in villages or the jungle, and did not rely on rigid, Western-style large formations dependent on barracks. Equally important, such national assets hardly mattered to an international Communist. He intended to lead a revolution throughout Indochina, after which infrastructure could be rebuilt. Bombing old French bases might have made sense to McNamara and his eager neophytes like Assistant Secretary of Defense for International Security Affairs John McNaughton, who became one of the chief target selectors. But, as my friends in ACSFOR often put it, Ho didn't give a "rat's ass" for a bunch of old French barracks. The destruction of those buildings was simply not the way to pressure him.

What would have hurt North Vietnam, of course, was a maritime quarantine and the destruction of its rail and road links to Communist China. By 1965, North Vietnam was receiving massive military aid from the Soviet Union and its allies, most of which passed through the port of Haiphong. Aid from Communist China came on the same railroads and narrow highways that I had reconnoitered for sabotage as a young OSS officer in 1945. If we really wanted to hurt Ho's ability to make war in the South, we should have destroyed the port of Haiphong, mined the harbor, and taken out the vulnerable land transportation links to China. In fact, that is exactly what the Joint Chiefs of Staff proposed as the first step of any American escalation in Vietnam.[19]

In Saigon, America's uncertain policy was carried out by General William Westmoreland, the commander of the Military Assistance Command, Vietnam (MACV), and Ambassador Maxwell Taylor, the retired chairman of the Joint Chiefs of Staff. As Communist infiltration from the North increased and ARVN resolve weakened, Westmoreland and Taylor requested American ground combat troops in limited numbers. U.S. Marine battalion landing teams beefed up the defenses around the Danang air base in the north of the country and the 173rd Airborne Brigade arrived to carry out a similar mission around the air bases near Saigon. The presence of U.S. troops did thwart anticipated Communist assaults on these bases, but the ARVN was still being battered all across South Vietnam.

While Saigon's military leadership disintegrated into the internecine struggles of a banana republic, the North Vietnamese stepped up their infiltration of the South and shifted from guerrilla warfare to the next stage of Mao's revolutionary struggle blueprint: semi-conventional warfare. The Vietcong were now organized in regular "main-force" battalions, which could maneuver in groups of three as regiments. The North Vietnamese Army (NVA) had dispatched several such regiments (some in division-size formations) down the Ho Chi Minh Trail, where they either set up base camps in the Cambodian or Laotian forest or were shunted east through valleys into the lightly populated central highlands of South Vietnam. Under the cover of the southwest monsoon, the NVA besieged the American Special Forces camp at Duc Co and battered the ARVN units in the highlands. By the early summer of 1965, MACV intelligence gave Westmoreland the "gloomy" estimate that one NVA regular division was already operating in the highlands and that two more were en route south along the Trail.

Ironically, as the military situation in the countryside deteriorated, Saigon's generals finally thrashed out their political rivalries. A relatively stable military government emerged with General Nguyen Van Thieu as chairman and Air Vice-Marshal Nguyen Cao Ky as premier. Both officers understood the gravity of the situation, and were eager to put palace intrigues behind them and make the sacrifices necessary to block a Communist victory. But the situation was so desperate that MACV intelligence recognized that the ARVN alone was incapable of blunting the swelling Communist offensive.[20]

Westmoreland advised Washington that he would need much larger numbers of American combat troops to prevent the outright defeat of the ARVN. After consultations with McNamara and Lyndon Johnson's national security adviser, the former Harvard professor and Kennedy appointee McGeorge Bundy, Westmoreland and Taylor worked out a formula for direct American military intervention to save the ARVN. An international force was planned, including several army and marine battalions from the Republic of Korea, a token force from Australia, and a large new U.S. force totaling one division and three brigades. This would bring overall allied combat strength up to forty-four maneuver battalions.[21] With helicopter and other support units, American forces in Vietnam would total almost 130,000. This request galvanized the Pentagon and the White House into an intense examination of America's long-term strategy in Vietnam.

After intense consultation with the Joint Chiefs of Staff, McNamara was convinced that the United States could not delay any longer the decision on committing significant combat forces. He recommended to Lyndon Johnson that Westmoreland's request for combat troops be quickly implemented, and that those troops be allowed to go on the offensive, undertaking the "search and destruction of the main enemy units." Equally important, McNamara backed the JCS recommendation that a complete quarantine of war matériel be imposed on North Vietnam, using all available air and naval power. This would require mining North Vietnamese ports, bombing airfields and missile sites, and destroying rail and road links to China.[22]

In other words, Secretary of Defense Robert McNamara was properly forwarding to the President the only logical strategy, which had been developed after much consideration by the country's senior military leaders.

The JCS fully understood Ho's indifference to limited reprisal bombing of purely military targets. Ho Chi Minh was a dedicated, disciplined international Communist, with decades of revolutionary struggle behind him. It was ludicrous to hope a few bombing raids on old French barracks would suddenly change him. If America wanted to stop Communist aggression in the South, the obvious way to do that was to destroy North Vietnam's war-making capability, not try to "punish" Ho Chi Minh with a limited carrot-and-stick bombing campaign.

Even more important was the need to clearly and unequivocally demonstrate to the North Vietnamese—and their Soviet and Chinese Communist sponsors—that the United States intended to stand behind South Vietnam. Everyone knew the Saigon government was battered and undercut by venal generals on the one hand and widespread Communist insurgency (including the terror of the *tru gian* death squads) on the other. If America was going to intervene militarily to support this country through the long, bloody process of nation building, while simultaneously defeating aggression from the North, we had to demonstrate our determination, our stomach for the protracted battle.

In other words, we had to convince Ho Chi Minh we were serious. The JCS knew the best way to accomplish this was through the declaration of a national emergency, which would include extension of terms of service, as well as the mobilization of the armed forces reserves. The call-up of the reserves was a key element here, and served several purposes. First, mobilization would demonstrate exactly how serious we were, just as Kennedy's reserve call-up during the Berlin crisis of 1961 showed the Russians our true resolve. Both the Soviet and North Vietnamese leadership operated with a European internationalist mindset, in which mobilization was tantamount to a declaration of war. Conversely, a country that did not mobilize its reserves in a military emergency was obviously bluffing. Second, on a more practical level, a reserve call-up was needed—especially by the Army—in order to staff the planned force-structure expansion (what became the "Army Buildup Plan") with qualified personnel. Unless we called up the reserves, we would not have experienced officers and NCOs to lead the new units to be created to replace the forces deployed to Vietnam.

This mobilization was an integral part of the JCS war plan, which also included the maritime quarantine of North Vietnam and the destruction of vital lines of communication. The Joint Chiefs were unanimous in the recommendation of this plan to McNamara, and the strongest advocate was Army Chief of Staff General Harold K. Johnson. He had visited South Vietnam on several occasions during the building crisis and was convinced that only a massive U.S intervention (with a reserve mobilization) would succeed in defeating the Communist invasion and their will to continue the war.

Johnson had been a prisoner of war of the Japanese for almost four years. He commanded the 8th Cavalry Regiment that bore the brunt of the Chinese intervention in Korea. He understood that war in Asia was not an academic exercise in "counterinsurgency" that could be fine-tuned through the subtleties of target selection and alternating threats and promises. While President Johnson seemed to view the conflict in Indochina in terms of backroom political dealing, Chief of Staff General Harold Johnson saw the crisis in Vietnam in direct, brutal military terms.

The Army obviously would have the largest responsibility in the enlarged war. After McNamara's initial support for Westmoreland's intervention plan, General Johnson gave his ACSFOR, Lieutenant General Ben Harrell, the responsibility of creating a practical force-structure plan that would permit the Army to fight in Vietnam and continue to meet its other requirements, especially its NATO responsibilities. The job of writing this Army Buildup Plan (which went through several major modifications) fell to my colleague Colonel Lloyd "Chill" Wills, head of the Programs Division in the Plans and Programs Directorate. Wills was a crusty infantryman who had commanded a line battalion in the 3rd Division in the Iron Triangle during the savage fighting in the spring of 1953. He worked his Pentagon staff as if they were the headquarters of a combat outfit. Chill Wills understood that his division's task was to produce vital action documents that could make the difference between success or failure as the Army prepared for war in Southeast Asia. (The other division chief in our directorate was Colonel Fritz Kroesen, who went on to become a four-star general and commander of the U.S. Army in Europe in the 1970s, where he was almost blown up in a terrorist assassination attempt.)

Wills's task was further complicated by the sudden American military intervention in the Caribbean nation of the Dominican Republic. A revolt by leftist military units there threatened to destabilize the country and Lyndon Johnson decided to intervene to support pro-American government elements to prevent a pro-Castro coup d'état. From the perspective of ACSFOR, this complication meant one of our key strategic intervention forces, the 82nd Airborne Division, would not be available for fast deployment to Vietnam.[23] Nevertheless, Wills had to plan a buildup that would achieve quick results on the ground in South Vietnam, not just satisfy McNamara's clipboard professors.

Everybody had an opinion on accomplishing the complex buildup. But Wills did not need opinions, he needed a formal plan. As his officers worked almost around the clock in June and early July 1965, Wills repeatedly told them, "Don't get it *right;* get it written." McNamara began to modify the buildup plan by cutting back on the "round-out" reserve forces to be mobilized to augment regular units, so Chill Wills and his staff had to scrap one draft plan after another to match the new requirements.[24] It's important to recall that this demanding staff work was accomplished before the days of desktop computers and word processors. As McNamara's systems analysts pared down the reserve call-up to achieve their sacred cost effectiveness, Wills's people had to shuffle and readjust their plan. Their adding machines and electric typewriters clattered through many a late night. But Chill Wills stayed on top of this long, frustrating exercise. When things got really confused, he'd thump his desk and proclaim: "Get your pencils out. I don't need any more technical advice."

I watched my colleagues struggle with this intense effort through the first weeks of July. Wills and his staff kept us informed on their effort, both as a professional courtesy and also because the shape of the expanded Army had a direct bearing on our own work for the future force structure. In mid-July, McNamara, accompanied by Henry Cabot Lodge, the newly redesignated ambassador to Vietnam, left for Saigon to consult with Westmoreland and Ambassador Maxwell Taylor, who was about to leave the post. While there, McNamara got word that President Johnson had approved the basic intervention plan, including the Army buildup with its reserve call-up and, equally important, the extension of active-duty personnel tours. Simultaneously, Lyndon Johnson held a series of press conferences at which he also announced America was prepared for full mobilization. The President went so far as to proclaim that our "national honor" had been committed to the defense of South Vietnam.[25]

These were strong words. All of us in ACSFOR naturally assumed that the inevitable declaration of an emergency would automatically extend service terms. This was only common sense. If a brigade of the 101st Airborne, for example, was deployed to fight in Vietnam, *all* the officers and men who had trained together would be needed in combat, including those whose enlistments were due to expire. Even though some men might have only signed up for three years, the declaration of a national emergency and the mobilization of the reserves would mean for all practical purposes that America was at war, albeit a limited one. There would probably have to be some kind of rotation point system established, as there was in Korea, but at least outfits would go into combat at full strength.

When McNamara returned from South Vietnam, he presented President Johnson with a Top Secret memorandum summarizing the recommendations on the planned military intervention, which had been endorsed by the JCS, Westmoreland, and Ambassadors Taylor and Lodge. It is important to note the timing and content of this message. Military historian Walter Hermes has summarized it as follows: "He [McNamara] proposed that the U.S. strength in Vietnam be increased to 175,000 by October, including 34 maneuver battalions, with possibly another 100,000 men to be added in 1966. Congress should be asked to authorize the call-up of about 235,000 Reserve and National Guard troops, including 125,000 for the Army, 75,000 for the Marines, 25,000 for the Air Force, and 10,000 for the Navy. Although the call-up would be for two years, the reserves would probably be released after a year, when the increases in the regular forces would be trained and ready to replace them. The Army would expand by 270,000 men, the Marines by 75,000, and the Air Force and Navy would each add 25,000 to their regular personnel to provide for other contingencies in the interim, using the draft, recruitment, and extending tours of duty to fill these requirements."[26]

This was indeed a serious recommendation, which had the full endorsement of America's professional military leaders, as well as that of the Secretary of Defense. McNamara's memo sparked a high-level White House meeting on Vietnam that began on the morning of Thursday, July 22. The Joint Chiefs were present, as were McNamara and LBJ's national security adviser, McGeorge Bundy. The issue on the table was clear: Was America prepared to meet Communist military aggression in Vietnam with appropriate force? McGeorge Bundy led the argument against full mobilization and a proclamation of a national emergency. Calling up the reserves, he said, was tantamount to a declaration of war. McNamara concurred, but pointed out the seriousness of the crisis in Vietnam. Without a large-scale intervention by American combat troops, he said, South Vietnam would fall. The members of the JCS each spoke adamantly in favor of mobilization. Again, the strongest advocate was General Harold Johnson.

LBJ asked Johnson if he believed Ho Chi Minh's statement that his nation would fight for twenty years if need be.

"I believe him," General Johnson replied.

The President noted that Congress might oppose mobilizing the reserves, but McNamara was confident he could convince Congress of the need. Johnson adjourned the meeting, leaving the strong impression among the JCS that America was about to mobilize for war.[27]

Back at the Pentagon, Chill Wills's shop was churning out paper nonstop, fine-tuning the reserve call-up orders and augmentation of regular units. They worked through the weekend. General Johnson contacted Major General Harry Kinnard, the commander of the 1st Cavalry Division (Airmobile). The new Air Cav was the fruition of years of planning and represented the shift in doctrine that I had helped plan back at the Staff College at Fort Leavenworth. With the 82nd Airborne tied up in the Caribbean, the Air Cav would be our first major combat unit deployed from the States for offensive operations in Vietnam. Their area of operations would be the central highlands, that roadless, jumbled terrain where major NVA units were now poised to cut South Vietnam in half. Johnson told Kinnard his division would be the point unit of a major American mobilization.

"Get ready," the Chief of Staff told Kinnard. "You're going to Vietnam."
"When?" Harry Kinnard asked.
"Now."[28]

While the Army grappled with the complexities of a major combat deployment, President Johnson met once more with his close advisers, this time in the quiet atmosphere of Camp David. McNamara was joined by Johnson's longtime confidants Clark Clifford and Supreme Court Justice Arthur Goldberg. Clifford and Goldberg represented another aspect of Johnson's complex—indeed, convoluted—persona: the anointed heir of Franklin D. Roosevelt. Johnson saw his expensive and ambitious Great Society program as the monument on which his presidency would stand shining in the spotlight of historical judgment. Now his most trusted advisers noted that wresting a national emergency and reserve mobilization from Congress would fatally undercut his plans for the Great Society. Johnson faced the dilemma of a classic "guns or butter" policy choice. The tragedy of his eventual decision was his self-delusion—abetted by Robert McNamara—that the country could have both effective guns in Vietnam and the ample butter of the Great Society. But on this summer weekend he had not quite reached that point of self-delusion.[29]

To bolster their argument, Clifford and Goldberg emphasized McGeorge Bundy's position that mobilization was tantamount to a declaration of war; no one could predict how Communist China or the Soviet Union would react. The specter of the Red Chinese hordes sweeping across the frozen mountains of Korea was still very much alive. Apparently, no one at the meeting had bothered to consult the CIA, which had been reporting for months that China's descent into the chaos of the Great Cultural Revolution had all but paralyzed the Communist leadership. China was involved in its second civil war; it was doubtful they would undertake a military intervention in Indochina.[30]

This situation represented a dubious "intelligence failure" similar to the events in the spring of 1950, when Truman's cabinet rejected explicit CIA warnings about the pending North Korean invasion. In mid-1965, however, the Johnson White House was actively hostile to the CIA. Lyndon Johnson had never trusted Kennedy's director of Central Intelligence, John McCone. The President instinctively rejected Agency estimates that North Vietnamese aggression could only be countered through a massive military intervention. By the time Johnson replaced McCone with Admiral William F. Raborn in April 1965, the President was already well entrenched within a circle of advisers who took little counsel from the CIA. Raborn himself was a high-technology submarine expert with no geopolitical background. Senior Agency officers were shocked at his ignorance of world events. He made a docile token presence at National Security Council meetings where key decisions on our Vietnam policy were made.[31]

Johnson was soon swayed by his advisers' arguments. He now reversed himself, and leaned toward the worst possible compromise. Up to 200,000 American combat troops would still be deployed; the armed forces would still be expanded. But this would be accomplished without mobilization of the reserves or an extension of terms of service.[32]

McNamara, ever the nimble statistician, blithely agreed to this disastrously illogical policy. As historian George McT. Kahin has noted, McNamara suddenly reversed field, abandoning the JCS, and assured Johnson "that an overall expansion of American armed forces could be managed without calling up the reserves." McNamara further advised the President that "his senior military advisers" were willing to accept the obvious pitfalls of this policy: the slow buildup rate, the debasing of the officer and noncommissioned officer ranks, and all the rest of it.[33] Given this advice, Johnson's decision is more understandable.

On Monday July 26, Johnson met again at the White House with his key military and civil advisers. He announced he now favored a graduated military escalation that fell short of a decisive mobilization and proclamation of an emergency. McNamara made it clear he backed the President. General Harold Johnson and his JCS colleagues sat through this meeting in shocked silence. Their civilian superior, Robert McNamara, had abandoned them.[34]

I was wrapping up my workday on that Monday afternoon when General Paul Phillips, the new director for Plans and Programs, sent me to see Major General Michael Davison, the deputy ACSFOR.

Davison came right to the point. "Okay, Jack," he said, his face grave, "we've got a new requirement for the Army Buildup Plan and your office is going to have to write it."

General Davison explained that Chill Wills's staff was exhausted by their long efforts over the previous weeks. My people were to prepare the revised plan. "The first phase calls for adding one division and three brigades as soon as possible," Davison said, consulting his notes.

"That's no problem, General," I said. "We've been working on a plan to add from one to six divisions, so all we have to do is adjust the numbers and the reserve call-up."

Davison shook his head. "Jack," he said, "there've been a few changes." McNamara, he said, had just ordered the Army to develop a plan to deploy these units to Vietnam with *no* call-up of reserve forces and *no* extension of terms of service. This first stage of the Army's Vietnam expansion would also include combat support units such as Engineers, and many more helicopter companies.

Mike Davison and I looked at each other silently for a moment. Every officer with combat experience would have shared our emotions. There are certain times in all wars when a man is asked to implement stupid, indeed disastrous, orders. This was one of them.

"Sir," I protested, "all our plans call for using reserve units to staff the training centers that we're going to need for all the new draftees." I began enumerating the obvious objections, and Davison nodded grimly. "The construction engineer battalions are all in the reserves. We're going to need them for building bases over there. And what about finding qualified officers for the new units?"

Davison cut me off. "You crank out the plan, Jack, and make a list of all these points." He paused a moment, then spoke bluntly, one soldier to another. "If you ask me, this plan is so dumb it'll never fly."

But, he added, we had to go through the exercise. I was to have the revised plan letter-perfect in multiple copies to brief General Johnson at 0700 the next morning. Johnson and I would then brief Secretary of the Army Stanley Resor at 0730, and he would brief McNamara at 0800. In turn, McNamara would carry the plan to the White House, where, we hoped, it would be quickly rejected.

☆   ☆

IT was after six when I got my staff assembled. General Davison had already alerted all our points of contact in the Army Staff to stand by for all-night duty. I explained what we had to do, told the officers to get on with their work, despite their obvious distaste for the exercise, and established a series of deadlines throughout the night by which I needed their various inputs. Somehow, they were going to have to find qualified personnel in active-duty units to staff the expanded training centers, to provide construction-engineer battalions, and of course to staff all the NCO and officer slots in the expanded units. And this would have to be accomplished with no reserve call-up and no extension of duty tours.

General Davison had some mandatory social event he had to attend, but he promised to stop in later that night to check on our progress.

My first major concern was the impact this expansion would have on our combat units in Europe. During my earlier force-structure reviews, I'd discovered the units assigned to NATO were in pretty fair shape, adequately staffed and equipped to perform their missions, but with no deadwood. Moreover, many of the Army's best officers and NCOs were assigned to Europe. This sudden Army expansion without a reserve call-up would obviously draw down hard on Europe, depleting the combat battalions' officers and NCOs.

As the frantic night continued, the dimensions of the problem grew more ominous. The proposed expansion called for an increased monthly draft of 20,000 recruits. But the Army was then losing 20,000 men a month through retirement and completion of service. Therefore, at best, the new draft was a dubious way to fill out the ranks of the expanded units. We would have to push thousands of NCOs through Officer Candidate School to have adequate second lieutenants, and replace them with "instant" NCOs. This would occur while the Reserves and National Guard had several thousand qualified junior officers who had already requested active duty but would be denied the opportunity.

Looking downstream a year or two, it became obvious that many career officers and NCOs would serve a year in the Vietnam combat zone, return for a few months' duty in the States, then be eligible for combat duty again. The negative potential of all this on Army morale was terrible. As my section leaders reported in with their figures that night, I realized the plan was actually worse than I had originally thought, but that, regrettably, it was statistically possible. And we all knew Assistant Secretary Enthoven and his systems analysts saw only numbers, not flesh-and-blood soldiers. To them, "morale" was just as invalid a concept as "the principles of war."

However, after midnight, I saw that one of the most fundamental military principles was being disregarded here. Basic doctrine held that any offensive (including an intervention such as this with offensive combat troops) be conducted in "mass." A wise commander conducted a maximum-effort offensive, not the minimum deployment proposed by McNamara and the White House.[35] In so doing, the commander improved his chances for success and also limited casualties.

The Communists in Hanoi would interpret no mobilization and no extension of duty tours as an obvious sign of muddled policy. If America intended to subdue Ho Chi Minh and turn him away from aggression in the South, we had to seriously threaten his war-making capability. The French never mobilized reserves in their strategically flawed war (they consistently underestimated Ho and General Giap), and they paid the price at Dienbienphu. And Lyndon Johnson was reputed to consider Vietnam a "pissant" country, hardly worthy of serious American contempt.[36] He was dead wrong. North Vietnam's population in 1965 was over 16 million (there were almost 15 million people in South Vietnam) and it had one of the largest per-capita military establishments in the world. The Communists were mobilized for war; we were not.

And they could readily take advantage of *their* mobilization. Without a reserve call-up or service extensions, the U.S. Army would need nine months to deploy the projected 200,000 troops to Vietnam. In that period, the NVA could easily match our numbers through infiltration south along the Trail. These problems became blatant as we struggled with the revised plan that night.

By dawn, my staff had a new Army Buildup Plan that met McNamara's requirements, at least on paper. But I had a list of serious objections to it when I entered General Johnson's office at 0700. As always, the Chief of Staff was gravely courteous. He was a man of deep inner strength and quiet dignity, attributes that probably sprang from his years of harsh captivity during World War II. Just as I began my briefing, Army Secretary Resor entered from his adjoining office. General Johnson told me to continue, and his manner signified I was to withhold nothing.

After noting the complex personnel shifts and unit juggling of the plan, I cited the major objections. With no reserve call-up or extension of service, the Army would be obliged to commit troops to Vietnam piecemeal; I pointed out that the nine-month delay in deployment gave the NVA ample time to counter our buildup. Both General Johnson and Resor were well aware that a lack of mobilization signified an obvious lack of resolve. But they were troubled when I explained this plan's impact on the officer corps. Regular officers and NCOs would draw an unfair share of combat duty and their junior ranks would soon be filled with unqualified people. The drawdown on our best units in Europe would quickly leave them "hollow," a specter feared by every commander. This impact would be hardest on the combat arms, as well as on certain support elements such as the Engineers, the Signal Corps, and Army Aviation. Furthermore, the training centers would not be able to cope with the enlarged draft without the reserve units specifically assigned to staff them. Without the mobilization of reserve construction battalions, we would have to convert combat engineers to building base areas, further weakening the Army in Europe.

Finally, I noted that our best-trained and most important combat units, such as the Air Cav, would be deployed badly understrength unless their troops' terms of service were extended.

General Johnson shook his head, his face a somber mask. "You make your point well, Colonel," he finally said.

Secretary Resor agreed. He asked me to continue briefing him on the way down to McNamara's office. No doubt we presented an unusual picture in the long corridors: a tired colonel with a sheaf of papers and an ashen-faced Army secretary. Resor went in to brief McNamara carrying a copy of my notes at 0810. I went back upstairs to finish briefing the ACSFOR staff.

At 1130, the word came down that McNamara was back from the White House. If President Johnson had even bothered to listen to our objections, he had quickly dismissed them. We were to execute this tragically flawed plan.

☆   ☆

AT noon on Wednesday, July 28, Lyndon Johnson addressed the nation on television. The United States had increased its commitment of combat troops in Vietnam to 125,000 men, and more troops would be deployed as needed. The draft would be doubled. But there would be no mobilization of reserves. Terms of service would not be extended. Most of the men in my office watching the speech had served in combat in two wars. We listened in bitter silence.

Down the hall, General Harold Johnson changed into his best summer uniform, the blouse replete with combat decorations. He told his driver to take him to the White House. He intended to resign in protest at the criminal folly just announced by his commander in chief. As the black Ford sedan approached the tall wrought-iron gates of the White House, Johnson un-pinned the four silver stars from his epaulets and jingled them lightly in his brawny hand. He had been appointed chief of staff as a lieutenant general, passing over more than a dozen men of four-star rank. Now he was about to throw away those four stars. Even a man of his deep convictions and integrity was not capable of this act. In any event, there were several generals over whom he had jumped who would gladly step in to replace him. General Johnson pinned his stars back on and told the driver to return to the Pentagon.

Years later, he told Colonel Harry Summers that he had rationalized the moment, convincing himself he could do more by staying with the Army's system than by resigning. "And now," he told Summers, "I will go to my death with that lapse in moral courage."[37]

CHAPTER TEN

Indochina

1965–1968

☆　　　☆

I WATCHED THE situation in Vietnam with mounting anxiety. My vantage point in ACSFOR gave me a good perspective to observe the predictable problems inherent to the ill-conceived, gradualist intervention policy.

I learned there was turmoil in many of the units preparing to embark for Vietnam.[1] Elite regular outfits such as the 101st Airborne, which were deploying only a single brigade, had not been seriously affected by the foolish decision not to extend terms of service. But even such a well-disciplined outfit suffered from the logistics muddle and unrealistic budget constraints of the Johnson-McNamara policy. Without a call-up of the reserve construction battalions, the pace of airfield and port building in Vietnam was slow and frustrating, further delaying the arrival of American combat troops. And the units that were deployed in 1965 were often short of vital supplies. The men of the 101st found themselves in combat without cleaning equipment for their weapons, jungle fatigues, or jungle boots.[2]

By September, the 1st Cavalry Division (Airmobile) had completed its move from Fort Benning to the II Corps area of Vietnam, the central highlands. Unfortunately, the Air Cav didn't have as high a proportion of regulars as the Airborne; when the Cav set up their new division base camp on the grassy plateau at An Khe, many battalions were badly understrength. Some of the Cav's units had lost a third of their strength when they were deployed without an extension of terms of service. This was ironic; the Air Cav was reputed to be our high-technology answer to the insurgents' favored habitat—the roadless mountain jungles. But the 1st Cav was poised to fight in these jungles with many of its troops hardly more than recruits completely untrained in airmobile tactics. At the same time, well-trained young soldiers reassigned from the division were doing make-work jobs back in holding companies in Fort Benning because their enlistments were due to expire within sixty days.[3]

American and ARVN forces were also spread too thin to effectively counter the new influx of NVA regulars. South Vietnam was divided into four military regions or tactical zones, commonly called "corps." I Corps was in the north, occupying the foothills and coastal regions east of the Annamite Mountains. The II Corps tactical zone encompassed the rugged central highlands and central plateau, the country's least populated region. But III Corps, on the alluvial plain surrounding Saigon, was densely populated, as was IV Corps, the Mekong delta, the richest agricultural region. This nomenclature was deceptive. It would have been fine if the ARVN could have fielded at least two full-strength, combat-ready divisions for each "corps." In reality, however, the only dependable ARVN combat units were the Ranger and Airborne battalions, but the paratroopers were usually kept in reserve as an anti-coup force.[4]

American intelligence had long predicted that North Vietnamese strategy would be to cut South Vietnam in half with large NVA units entering the Central Highlands through valleys from Laos and Cambodia. A multidivision NVA thrust through the highlands to the rich rice bowl of the coastal plain would probably have destroyed the Saigon government's will to fight. Equally, NVA regiment-strength assaults from sanctuaries in the Parrot's Beak region of Cambodia, which thrust like a dagger only thirty miles from Saigon, posed a similar hazard.

Westmoreland concluded that it would be better to fight these units in the underpopulated highlands and in the forest of War Zone C northwest of Saigon than in the villages and towns of the densely populated coast. My old mentor Major General Bill Depuy, Westmoreland's operations officer (J-3), developed tactics that acquired the notorious—and badly misunderstood—epithet of "search-and-destroy" operations. But Westy understood there was another small-unit guerrilla insurgency being fought each night in rural hamlets. His strategic priority, however, was the big NVA units because, unlike the small guerrilla bands, the enemy regiments and divisions had the power to destroy the ARVN.[5]

Even before Westmoreland could begin operations, American news media began a campaign of unjust criticism that ultimately rose to a crescendo. The American public had been conditioned to view the Vietnam War up to that point as an insurgency—that is, a struggle between local guerrillas and government forces for the famous "hearts and minds" of the peasantry. The fact that the guerrillas were often not local boys discontent with Saigon corruption, but rather northern regulars dressed in the ubiquitous black pajamas of the rice farmer, had not yet been accepted. American reporters often saw the destruction of enemy-controlled hamlets and the deportation of their population to secure areas as needlessly cruel scorched-earth tactics.

The most notorious case of this occurred in 1965, when a relatively unknown CBS television correspondent named Morley Safer reported on a Marine operation in the village of Cam Ne in a traditional Vietcong bastion near Danang. Safer's cameraman captured Marines setting fire to the thatched roofs of village huts with their Zippo lighters. Although he had relatively little experience in Vietnam, Safer proclaimed the incident to be an example of flawed American strategy. "Today's operation is the frustration of Vietnam in miniature," he intoned from the lurid setting of burning huts, and concluded that President Johnson had just lost potential allies among the villagers.[6] Somehow, the burning of the Vietcong rice caches in Cam Ne became symbolic of ostensibly inherent destructiveness of Westmoreland's "search-and-destroy" tactics.

This was simply not true. Westmoreland and Bill Depuy were too experienced to risk alienating the uncommitted rural people through needless destruction. Depuy understood, though, that American combat troops had to be used aggressively—that they had to seek out the NVA in their hidden jungle base camps, engage them, and then bring to bear our superior artillery and tactical air power. This was probably the only means we had to spoil the building NVA offensive in late 1965 and early 1966.

All these factors came together in America's first major engagement of the war, the battle of the Ia Drang valley. In October 1965, our Special Forces camp at Plei Me was surrounded by three regiments of NVA. Plei Me was in the highlands south of Pleiku, near the Cambodian border, just east of a rugged jungle ridge known as Chu Pong Mountain. The Ia Drang valley ran across the border into Cambodia and offered a logical infiltration route from the NVA base camps along the Trail.[7]

The newly arrived Air Cav's 1st Brigade fought a series of short firefights for several days, pursuing an enemy regiment through the valley. Division Commander Major General Harry Kinnard was frustrated; the NVA was obviously slipping behind the Chu Pong Mountain into Cambodia to evade the CAV's helicopter gunships and reconnaissance choppers. The Air Cav's leaders were further frustrated by the high proportion of untrained troops who had filled the ranks at Fort Benning before deployment.[8]

The 1st Battalion, 7th Cavalry Regiment, commanded by Lieutenant Colonel Harold G. Moore, was airlifted into the Ia Drang valley. No sooner had this battalion set down at Landing Zone (LZ) X-Ray in the tall plateau grass beneath Chu Pong Mountain than it was assaulted by several full battalions of NVA regulars from the 66th and 33rd Regiments. For three days and two nights—between November 14 and 16, 1965—the 1st Battalion, 7th Cavalry, supported by elements of the 2nd Battalion, 7th Cavalry, held out against a greatly superior enemy force.

Moore's troopers dug into the baked laterite soil as well as they could, using blasted tree trunks for cover. Air Force Skyraiders, Phantom jets, and Navy A-4s rolled in out of the blinding sun to pound the NVA with cluster bombs and high explosives. This air support was so close to Moore's position that the few trees remaining in the LZ were splintered by shrapnel. Once napalm landed only twenty meters from Moore's command post, burning several of his own men.[9]

The NVA was obviously testing the mettle of the Air Cav, trying to develop tactics to neutralize the Americans' overwhelming firepower superiority. At dawn on the last morning of the engagement, Hal Moore sensed an enemy assault and had his battalion and supporting artillery cut loose with all their weapons. They broke up a company-size NVA attack that was forming in the shattered jungle just outside their outposts.[10]

Before departing the smoking, blasted LZ, Moore's men counted 634 enemy bodies among the shattered trees and shell craters.[11] But the Air Cav had suffered terrible losses: 79 Killed in Action and 121 wounded from a force of 431 men, a casualty rate of 50 percent. Moore's unit, however, had gone to Vietnam badly weakened. Their normal TO&E complement should have been 610 officers and men. In July, Moore recalls, the White House decision not to extend terms of service had sent a "shock wave" through his battalion, then preparing for overseas deployment at Fort Benning. He'd had to release 150 of his best-trained men who had sixty days or less to serve. They included machine-gun teams who had trained together, fire-team leaders, radio men, medics, and squad leaders from each of his companies. A few were replaced by infantrymen from Fort Benning who lacked training in air-assault tactics and techniques. When the Air Cav set up its base camp at An Khe and prepared for its first combat operations, the division lost additional large groups of men whose enlistments were due to expire.[12]

The division commander, Major General Harry Kinnard, has bitterly cited the effect of this policy. "The net impact of all this on the division," he told Air Cav historian J. D. Coleman, "was that we had to strip out a great many highly trained men at exactly the worst time, namely, just as we were preparing to go to war." Coleman notes that the division's aviation units alone had to "turn loose" 500 men, including well-trained air crews and mechanics.[13]

After replacing Moore's unit, the 2nd Battalion, 7th Cavalry, became badly strung-out for almost a kilometer along a tributary of the Ia Drang as they hiked toward a clearing called LZ Albany. They collided with a full-strength NVA battalion of the 66th NVA Regiment. The U.S. forces were too dispersed to form an effective perimeter. So it was impossible to defend them with tactical air and artillery. Over the next twenty-four hours, the Air Cav battalion was decimated. One of its companies was almost wiped out. Many wounded troopers were shot by the Communists as they lay moaning in the elephant grass. Nevertheless, the battalion inflicted severe losses on the NVA, killing 403. But the ratio of American and enemy casualties was simply not acceptable. The battalion column had left LZ X-Ray with just over 500; at the end of the engagement 151 Americans were dead and 121 wounded.[14]

By MACV accounts, the NVA had lost 1,300 killed during the four weeks of fighting around Plei Me, now called the Battle of the Ia Drang Valley, but the Air Cav suffered 304 KIA.[15]

It was not an auspicious start to America's combat involvement.

As later documented by former 1st Cavalry Division officer J. D. Coleman, the NVA's 66th Regiment that inflicted so many casualties on the Air Cav was "fresh off the trail and spoiling for a fight."[16] It is now estimated that the 66th Regiment took two months to transit the Trail from North Vietnam, and arrived in their Cambodian staging base west of Chu Pong Mountain in early November, 1965. In other words, those troops were probably dispatched south in August, only days after President Johnson announced America's ill-fated piecemeal deployment of U.S. combat troops to Vietnam. As I had feared, the White House had given Ho Chi Minh ample time to counter our buildup.

☆   ☆

IF ONE traces the Ia Drang engagement on a map of Indochina, the folly of our limited, gradualist commitment becomes apparent. I could well understand Westmoreland's and Kinnard's frustrations at not being able to outmaneuver the NVA by pursuing them into their Cambodian sanctuary. It was lunacy to squander valuable troops like the Air Cav by denying them the fast freedom of maneuver the division's helicopters provided. But the White House, McNamara, and the State Department were adamant that MACV not "widen the war" by attacking NVA sanctuaries in the unpopulated jungle hills across the Cambodian border from II and III Corps. This policy, no doubt, evolved naturally from our civilian leadership's initial decision to fight the war on the cheap.

But it soon reached ludicrous proportions. In fact, the State Department became obsessed with Cambodia, probably because this country represented the defeat of diplomacy similar to that suffered by the American Foreign Service in postwar China. Cambodia's leader, Prince Norodom Sihanouk, ostensibly neutral—but actually sympathetic to Ho Chi Minh—had shut down the American embassy in Phnompenh over alleged ARVN border intrusions. Now Secretary of State Dean Rusk had convinced the White House of the need to "woo Sihanouk" back to the Western fold. To career diplomats, the specter of an important country without a functioning American embassy was anathema. In order to regain Sihanouk's good graces, the State Department ignored clear evidence that Cambodia was a major infiltration route and staging area for the NVA. American officers were forbidden to publicly discuss NVA operations in Cambodia. The word "sanctuary" was proscribed. Poor General Stanley "Swede" Larsen, one of our best field commanders in Vietnam, made the mistake of mentioning the Cambodian sanctuary at a news conference during a trip to Washington. McNamara had him on the carpet and Larsen was forced to retract at another news conference with the statement, "I stand corrected."[17]

These intrigues would have been amusing if they hadn't represented the tragic reality on the battlefield. The Air Cav's high casualties in the Ia Drang might well have been prevented if American superiority in firepower and maneuver had been properly exploited within the actual theater of operations, which included all of Indochina, not simply the countries of North and South Vietnam. As I watched our strategy evolve that winter and spring, my alarm increased. Even during the constraints of the limited war in Korea, America's civil and military leaders conducted operations within a theater context. My CIA paramilitary operations with JACK had targeted objectives in the Communists' Manchurian sanctuaries, and my seaborne teams had disrupted enemy lines of communication between China and Korea. Toward the end of the war, the Air Force was also flying regular combat missions north of the Yalu River. But now America's key civilian leaders had stuck their collective head deep in the sand and refused to realistically consider the strategic impact of the North Vietnamese sanctuary in Cambodia and their supply lines through the Laotian panhandle.

But a theater perspective was a fundamental principle of strategy. I have fought in three wars and have yet to see international borders printed on the shattered terrain of a battlefield with neat dashed lines as they are on maps. Yet Secretaries Rusk and McNamara were convinced the war could somehow be contained within the international borders of South Vietnam. This single-country perspective stemmed from the trendy counterinsurgency mentality of the Kennedy years. That had been all well and good when the Communist aggression in South Vietnam had been limited to guerrilla tactics. But the well-fed, well-armed, and damn well-led NVA regulars in khaki uniforms that assaulted Hal Moore's Air Cav troops in the smoking scrub jungle on the Cambodian border had certainly not been *insurgents*. They were an invading army.

It was criminal folly for civilian leaders to forbid our field commanders from engaging this invasion force in its base areas, ordering Westmoreland to wait until the NVA infiltrated South Vietnam, where the Communist commanders could pick the time and place of attack. Under this policy, the NVA often escaped our search-and-destroy sweeps and struck ARVN or American units with the advantage of tactical surprise.[18]

North Vietnam was quick to exploit the shortsightedness of America's leaders. The NVA made maximum use of its Cambodian sanctuaries. Speaking after the war, Nguyen Tuong Lai, an NVA regimental commander, admitted that the Communists knew American commanders had strict orders to respect the Cambodian border. "Whenever we were chased by the enemy," he said, "we knew we could retreat across the frontier demarcation into the safe zone and get some rest."[19]

Without freedom to outmaneuver the enemy in a theater of operations, American generals were obliged to compromise their tactics. Civilian leaders in the Pentagon and State Department also obliged MACV to quantify the success of American combat operations within PPBS cost-effectiveness formulas. For example, early in 1966 Westmoreland was presented a formal memorandum that had been drafted by John McNaughton, McNamara's assistant secretary for international security affairs, and McGeorge Bundy's brother William, the assistant secretary of state for Southeast Asia. They directed MACV to pursue certain highly structured objectives in 1966, which included opening a specific percentage of roads, securing and pacifying certain regions, and defending all major population and rice-growing areas. American combat units were to kill the enemy faster than North Vietnam could replace them.

Naturally, all these "objectives" were further subdivided in worthy PPBS spreadsheet fashion, so that the cost effectiveness of such expenditures as artillery ammunition, machine-gun bullets, and helicopter fuel could be weighed against accomplishments. This approach was a formula for a self-defeating war of attrition. But the Bundy brothers, McNamara, McNaughton, and their cost-effectiveness whiz kids were not military men.

They scoffed at the principles of war. They were convinced the ground war could be confined within the borders of South Vietnam, neatly wrapped in their computer spreadsheets. They were also convinced that if Westmoreland followed their directives faithfully, all the little boxes could be checked, the graph lines would run true, and victory would be inevitable.[20]

☆   ☆

IN THE FALL of 1965 I saw Bill Depuy, who was home on a brief leave before taking over as commanding officer of the 1st Infantry Division, which was being deployed in Tay Ninh Province northwest of Saigon. I sought his advice about my own best course of action in getting a worthwhile Vietnam assignment. I wanted to go to the conflict in Vietnam, even if it wasn't officially a war, because fighting and winning battles is what a professional is paid to do. I hoped to use my combat experience in two wars to the best advantage for our effort there. As I've noted, Bill was one of the smartest generals in the Army, a short, lean officer with a certain WASPish elegance. He always saw through to the heart of any problem and did not suffer fools around him.

"Jack," he said, "the best thing you can do is take an assignment as adviser to an ARVN division for a year. After that, I'll help you get your own brigade."

That would mean spending at least two years in the war zone, but I saw at once that Bill's advice was correct. As an adviser to a division, I could share my hard-earned combat knowledge with the South Vietnamese officers, and they could teach me something of the country and its people and, most important, the tactics and habits of the enemy. Armed with this new knowledge, I'd be able to effectively lead an American brigade in combat.

Bill returned overseas, promising to grease the skids in Vietnam, while I did the same with my contacts in Army Personnel.

About this time, I was called in by my former boss in ACSFOR, Brigadier General Paul Phillips. He'd become the co-director of the new Force Planning Analysis Office (FPAO) that McNamara had ordered established in the Office of the Chief of Staff. McNamara's cost-effectiveness wizards weren't satisfied that the Army was playing the PPBS game with the proper degree of enthusiasm. So they directed the Army to create a new office to improve the "interface" between the Army and the Office of the Secretary of Defense (OSD), as concerned future force structures. Phillips insisted I become deputy to him and his civilian co-director, Bill Brehm, an amazingly flexible and practical bureaucrat from Enthoven's analysis staff.

I told Paul Phillips I was due to leave for Vietnam soon as senior adviser to the ARVN 5th Division, but he convinced me to get the office organized and running, then pick my own replacement.

We were authorized forty action officers, some of whom were "tasked" to shunt PPBS cost-effectiveness requirements by the boxcarload out to Southeast Asia, then plug the predictably rosy progress data into Mc-Namara's five-year plan for winning the war.

This was staff work at its most demanding, but it was made palatable by the knowledge that I was en route to a combat assignment. One of the officers assigned to FPAO, however, did not have that consolation. Colonel George S. Patton III was a close likeness to his famous father in both appearance and temperament. He did *not* take well to Pentagon staff work. Patton wanted a combat assignment in a bad way, but he was an Armor officer and we hadn't yet committed any tank outfits to the war. Strapping a natural warrior like him to a Pentagon desk was cruel and unusual punishment. He just couldn't put up with the "bullshit" paperwork. After a short stint in the office, Phillips had Colonel Patton reassigned so he wouldn't have to write a bad efficiency rating on the son of one of our greatest generals.

One afternoon I was called in to see Major General Ray Peers, the Special Assistant for Counterinsurgency and Special Activities (SACSA) to the chairman of the Joint Chiefs of Staff. He asked how I'd feel about an "interesting" Special Operations job in Indochina. I told him of my plans to parlay an ARVN division assignment into a brigade command. He did not pursue the matter.

Several weeks later, while I was working hard to organize FPAO, I was summoned one afternoon to the Office of the Chief of Staff. General Johnson had visibly aged in the seven months since the President's flawed deployment decision. It was said the Chief personally wrote letters of condolence to the families of American soldiers killed in Vietnam, but that he had been forced to give up the practice after the heavy U.S. casualties that fall.[21]

General Johnson kindly inquired about my family, then came to the point of the visit. "Jack," he said, "I understand you told Ray Peers you're not interested in a Special Operations assignment."

"Yes, sir," I replied. "I served in Special Ops in two wars, and I'd like a conventional command in this one."

"Well," the General said, "I've reviewed your records and I've decided you're the logical choice for this assignment. I'm sending you out to Vietnam to take over MACV/SOG."

I was disappointed, but tried not to show it. MACV's Studies and Observations Group (SOG) was the Indochina equivalent of JACK in the Korean War, an unconventional-warfare, sabotage, and covert-action organization that reported directly to the SACSA.

Johnson briefly outlined the nature of the job and the size of the responsibility. SOG had been in existence almost two years, but was due for rapid expansion. Indeed, it had been SOG operations supported by the U.S. Navy that had triggered the original Tonkin Gulf incident in 1964. Now, working as a Joint Unconventional Warfare Task Force with participants from all four services plus the ARVN, SOG conducted operations in both North and South Vietnam as well as along the Ho Chi Minh Trail in Laos. The man who commanded the unit would have the equivalent of an unconventional-warfare division. He would lead a staff of field-grade Army, Navy, Air Force, and Marine Corps officers, who in turn would be responsible for large contingents from the Army's Special Forces, the Air Force's 14th Special Operations Wing, the Marine's Recon Battalion, the Navy SEALs (named for their sea/air/land capability), as well as a virtual melting pot of Indochinese mercenary troops, including Montagnards and fierce Nungs, ethnic Chinese hillsmen.

General Johnson's assignment would be interesting and challenging. But my career was at a watershed. Like any Infantry officer, I wanted the chance to command a large unit in combat. By definition, SOG was a small-unit, clandestine operation, despite its overall size.

"General," I said, "I'm already on orders for an ARVN division adviser job, then I was hoping Bill Depuy could get me an American brigade on my second tour."

I felt I might as well lay my cards on the table. Maybe the Chief would see the logic of my plans and facilitate things. But that was not to be.

Johnson's face was set in an expression of tempered impatience. "Jack," he replied, "perhaps I didn't make myself clear. General Westmoreland specifically requested *you* as the new MACV/SOG commander. That *will* be your assignment."

A colonel did not debate such matters with the Chief of Staff of the Army.

"Sir," I said, "I am now developing a great deal of enthusiasm for my new assignment."

That night I broke the news to Mary. I could tell she was relieved. Knowing my predilection for commanding combat troops from forward positions, she hadn't been overjoyed at my previous Vietnam plans.

"This is more of a staff assignment than an operational job," she asked, "isn't it?"

I was noncommittal.

"Sure," I finally said, "I suppose so."

"Jack," she chided, "I hate to say this, but you're getting a little old for the actual cloak-and-dagger stuff."

I nodded agreement. There was no sense upsetting her. But we both knew the true situation. When an Army colonel commands hard-charging young Green Berets, SEALs, and Air Commandos, he damn well better lead by example, not try to dictate with a fast-firing mimeograph machine spitting out formal orders. Without discussing the matter, we both knew what my style would be as SOG commander.

☆　　　　☆

I ARRIVED in Saigon in April 1966, having stopped en route to visit the Special Forces, Air Force, and Navy support facilities in the States, as well as SOG's Counter-Insurgency Support Office (CISO) in Okinawa. The city was hot and crowded with troops and refugees at the end of the dusty dry season. But the wide boulevards shaded by flamboyant banyan trees retained the charm of France's colonial pearl. At this point in the war there were still more pedicabs than Japanese motorbikes. In the sudden cool of the tropic dusk you still saw Vietnamese women pedaling their bicycles home from shop and office, their graceful split-skirt *ao dai* dresses turning the heads of the GIs lining the sidewalks.

I was lucky in my assigned housing billet. In order to protect my sensitive command from prying media scrutiny and overcurious junior MACV officers, I was officially just another anonymous staff colonel, conducting routine "studies" on American operations.[22] In this capacity, I shared a pleasant villa in a quiet shady neighborhood near the old French Cercle Sportif with Deputy MACV Commander Lieutenant General John Heintges. He had an interesting background, being the son of a regular German officer killed during the First World War. His mother then married an American officer and Johnny Heintges went to West Point before serving in the 3rd Infantry Division during World War II. We got along well and General Heintges was sincerely interested in Special Operations. He continually traveled around South Vietnam and frequently took me on his trips. This lent considerable prestige to SOG operations, because it showed the American and ARVN field commanders that my people were supported by the highest echelons in Saigon.

My headquarters was in the old MACV II compound in the primarily Chinese suburb of Cholon. We had ARVN and MP guards, and our offices themselves were behind locked doors. Our intelligence and operations centers were actually inside sealed air-conditioned vaults, and we maintained strict need-to-know security: agents' identities were known only to case officers; the location of intelligence teams was marked on single-copy transparent overlays, never on permanent maps.

Our Vietnamese counterpart was the *Nha-Ky-Thuat,* the Strategic and Technical Directorate (STD), commanded by Colonel Tran Van Ho, a politically savvy and notably uncorrupt veteran of the French army. Unlike many senior ARVN officers, Colonel Ho was a native of Saigon. He had been thoroughly trained in intelligence and covert operations by the CIA. His operational officer, who actually commanded the Vietnamese Special Ops troops assigned to SOG, was Colonel Ho Thieu, a very tough leader with years of combat experience in the ARVN airborne. They had close relations with General Cao Van Vien, the chairman of the Joint General Staff, the Vietnamese equivalent of our JCS.[23]

I reported directly to the SACSA in the Pentagon, General Ray Peers, but always kept General Westmoreland well briefed on our past operations and future plans. The General had veto authority, but approval for operations came from Washington. We were also required to inform the Commander in Chief, U.S. Forces in the Pacific (CINCPAC), Admiral U.S. Grant Sharp (later Admiral John McCain). Westy was very supportive of my work. And I was proud that he had chosen me to command the expansion of Special Operations in the Indochina theater. In the spring of 1966, of course, the official myth that the war was a single-country insurgency still prevailed. But we were preparing to fight the enemy throughout Indochina, where he then operated relatively unscathed within sanctuaries in Laos and Cambodia.

Taking the war directly to the enemy's home and into his sanctuaries was the essence of my assignment. To accomplish this, I had available a rich variety of personnel and technical assets that made my resources in JACK and Manchuria seem quaint in comparison. Our mission was similar to that of the OSS or British SOE during World War II: strategic and tactical intelligence, resistance operations, guerrilla warfare, sabotage, and covert "black" psychological operations. SOG had been organized by Colonel Clyde Russell, then was commanded by Colonel Don Blackburn, whom I replaced. Don had served in the Philippines during World War II, fighting several years as a guerrilla leader after the islands were overrun by the Japanese. It was under his leadership that SOG was structured.

The unit's functional arm, the Operations Staff Directorate, was divided into five numbered divisions: Op-31 through Op-35. This was Navy nomenclature because MACV had originally been organized and supported by CINCPAC, a Navy-dominated unified command.

Op-31 was the staff division that supervised our maritime operations, conducted by the Naval Advisory Detachment (NAD) at Danang. This group ran a variety of seaborne operations, including the training and support for the Vietnamese Coastal Survey Service, which was actually a raiding, sabotage, and intelligence force. NAD had a small fleet of high-speed, low-slung Norwegian-built wooden torpedo boats, hard to detect on radar.

Op-32 was the staff division that supervised our private air force, which was based on the central coast at Nhatrang, but which also had staging bases at two airfields in Thailand: Udorn and Nakhon Phanom (NKP). We had a flight of four custom-modified C-130s for agent and supply drops, and four "black" twin-engine C-123s that had been stripped of all identifying marks linking them to the United States. They were flown by Chinese air force pilots from Taiwan, who rotated regularly in and out of Vietnam. Our helicopter force was sizable, made up of both UH-1 Huey troop carriers and supporting gunships, as well as a squadron of Vietnamese air force (VNAF) CH-34s, which had also been rendered "black." We even had our own separate airfield, Long Thanh (known as "Bear Cat"), an asphalt strip big enough to accommodate C-130s, located inside a well-guarded barbed-wire compound just past the sprawling American air base at Bienhoa, northeast of Saigon.

Psychological warfare operations were supervised by Op-33. Actual operations were conducted by the Psy Ops group commanded by Lieutenant Colonel Tom Bowen. He was on his second tour and knew the country well. His shop specialized in ingenious deceptions that ranged from counterfeit North Vietnamese currency to the construction of an elaborate "notional" sham resistance movement known as the Sacred Sword of the Patriot. The primary mission of Op-33 was to foster and exploit discontent among the North Vietnamese military and civilians. We approached this task in several ways. From debriefing NVA prisoners and "ralliers" who had come over to the ARVN as part of the Chieu Hoi Program, we learned considerable detailed information about corrupt Communist officials in the North. Even though we didn't have a viable resistance movement up there, we used our Sacred Sword deception to create one.

A "black" radio transmitter near Hué broadcast a realistically clandestine program to northerners, which was often disrupted when the "resistance" operators had to shut down to evade Communist patrols. Besides broadcasting realistic enemy casualty figures, the "Patriot" station pounded relentlessly at venal and immoral Communist cadres who not only diverted funds, but also seduced the young wives of NVA soldiers in the South. As a variation on this theme, we sometimes attacked Communist officials of whom we had no knowledge of corruption, in order to undercut their effectiveness. Our few reliable agents in the North then confirmed that those targeted by the clandestine radio were often relieved of their duties. This radio was reinforced by an airborne station, which further confused Soviet radio-tracking technicians helping the North Vietnamese.[24]

Another interesting Op-33 program was called Paradise Island and depended on the Op-31 maritime group. South Vietnamese commandos would abduct North Vietnamese fishermen or peasants from coastal villages and take them by boat to an island near Danang. Our camp was a fortified hamlet facing the sea with no view toward the mainland. All the personnel were Vietnamese and the buildings were constructed in the distinctive style of northern coastal villages. But the similarity to North Vietnam stopped there. The hamlet was disguised as a "liberated zone" in the North held by the Patriots, who proudly flew their own flag above the bamboo stockade. The villagers were treated with great kindness. Already by this point in the war, the Communists' ruthless demands for troops had disrupted agriculture and commerce in the North, resulting in near famine. So the visitors were treated to as many as four meals a day, including banquet dishes, rich with pork and seafood. They received first-class medical and dental attention, and were gently indoctrinated in the beliefs of the sham resistance. Some villagers were kept for only a few weeks, others several months. They were all sent back with a generous gift package, stuffed with luxuries impossible to obtain in the North: medicines, cloth, sewing supplies, and a radio pre-tuned to the Patriots' frequency. We fully expected, of course, that the Communist security forces would confiscate these luxuries. But we also realized the villagers' testimony would be so convincing that a belief in an illusive Liberated Zone Shangri-la would spread, even among low-level Communist cadres. Later, we gave the returnees two gift packages, one to hide, one for the Communist cadres.

To make sure our clandestine radio signals were reaching the North, Tom Bowen's shop also had the pre-tuned radio sets distributed by landing teams from our patrol boats. They relied on such devices as *lost* soldiers' packs and *misplaced* travelers' bundles on trucks and buses. These radios were produced in Japan by the CIA. They were quite effective because the only signal that came through clearly was the Patriots' station, while Radio Hanoi always came through garbled with static. This gave the impression that the resistance was better equipped than the government.[25]

Our primary agent-training site was at Long Thanh. This was the working center of Operation-34, our resistance and intelligence operations against North Vietnam. Again, in another parallel to the Korean War, the resistance potential in North Vietnam was dismal. Just as practically every anti-Communist in North Korea had been evacuated during the American retreat in early 1951, almost all of North Vietnam's anti-Communists—including entire clans and villages of Roman Catholics—had been evacuated by the U.S. Navy following the 1954 cease-fire. Even if we didn't have much hope of organizing anti-Communist partisans in the North, however, we had no shortage of brave young Vietnamese (most of northern origin) willing to be parachuted into the North to conduct intelligence and sabotage missions.

Probably our biggest and most interesting activity was the cross-border Reconnaissance Teams, supervised by Op-35. This group was led by one of the toughest officers in the U.S. Army, Colonel Arthur D. "Bull" Simons, a founding member of the Green Berets. Bull Simons was a giant warrior, with close-cropped iron-gray hair and hands easily twice as big as mine. He'd been a mule skinner in the Pacific during World War II when his pack artillery outfit was selected to become the 6th Ranger Battalion. He had a vocabulary that would make a drill sergeant blush. I'd known him at the Ranger Training Center during the Korean War, where (much to my chagrin) he'd been the only man able to outshoot me on the pistol range. He was certainly the right man to head Op-35, having conducted the Special Forces' White Star program in Laos for the CIA for several years. When I took over SOG, Op-35's Recon Teams were controlled from a small base at Danang in I Corps. During my first few months in command, we expanded the cross-border teams and they were eventually staged out of Forward Operating Bases at Hué in the north, Dakto in the highlands, and Ban-methuot on the central plateau near the Cambodian border.

I made a point of traveling around the country with Bull Simons, meeting the Recon Teams at their bases and debriefing the men after extraction. As expected, Bull was running a good operation, which produced a valuable harvest of intelligence and prisoners. The only initial improvement I ordered concerned weapons. Many of the American team members carried 9mm Swedish-K submachine guns, which were light and had a very quiet report. But the clacking, metallic noise of the gun was so distinctive that the Americans were easily located in firefights. I ordered all the team members to carry high-quality Russian-made AK-47s loaded with NVA ammunition, including their trademark dull-green tracer rounds. I had ambitious plans for Op-35 and hoped that the prohibition against using teams in Cambodia would soon be lifted.

The Ho Chi Minh Trail infiltration route was the teams' target. The "Trail" was not a single route, but rather a maze of old colonial roads, Montagnard paths, and recently bulldozed truck tracks beneath the cover of the triple-canopy rain forest. The Trail was also a major enemy staging area, equipped with permanent bivouac areas, supply dumps, training centers, communication relay stations, and field hospitals. Given official U.S. policy, American ground combat forces were forbidden to operate in these areas of "neutral" Laos and Cambodia. It would be over a year after my arrival before we finally got permission to commit the teams to Cambodia. But our operations along the Trail in Laos were a going concern.

Teams were usually inserted by "black" VNAF helicopters, which landed at isolated clearings in the last light of dusk. The men quickly dispersed from the LZ and set up a night ambush position to hit any NVA Trail security troops that might have been attracted by the chopper. It was impossible to move silently in the jungle at night, so the teams could hear any approaching enemy patrols. Missions could last between one and two days all the way up to several weeks, depending on the assignment and the team's success in evading enemy patrols. When it was time to extract the team, we often used so-called McGuire rigs, slings attached to a long line dangled through the rain forest canopy from the hovering chopper. After some trial and error, this system was modified to include the STABO harness, which was easier to use and allowed team members to fire their weapons as they were lifted from the forest floor.[26]

As Op-35 expanded, I reinforced the launch sites close to the Laotian border in I Corps and II Corps. Isolated camps near Dakto and Kham Duc (the former emperor Bao Dai's summer palace) became mini-fortresses, with airstrips, deep bunkers, and their own contingents of Montagnard Civilian Irregular Defense Group (CIDG) guards. The cross-border Recon Teams using these bases developed their own specialties. Some were expert in photography and wiretapping—using state-of-the-art induction technology that allowed us to eavesdrop on NVA field telephones without actually splicing into the line. Other teams became our champion prisoner snatchers. The team led by Master Sergeant Dick Meadows, for example, held the record of thirteen successful NVA prisoner snatches. As a group, the Recon Teams became known as Spike Teams under the Op-35 program originally code-named Shining Brass, then changed to Prairie Fire for security reasons.

A separate branch of Prairie Fire were the Hatchet Teams. These were platoon- and company-size indigenous mercenary units (originally mostly Nung, later Montagnard), commanded by American NCOs, that were kept on alert to intervene across the border when a Spike Team needed help or encountered an especially lucrative target. By late 1967, Op-35 had an amazing record of almost 300 successful cross-border operations in Laos. Some were actually protracted battles, during which NVA units on routes south were ambushed, then pummeled by air attack. Our missions had a definite strategic objective. Harassing the enemy along the Trail deprived him of a sense of sanctuary. NVA units had to keep on the move or risk ambush; thus their troops were weakened by fatigue. And if they stopped to fight or maneuver around our Spike and Hatchet Teams, the enemy became easy targets for our Air Commando "slow-mover" A-1E Skyraiders.

Almost twenty-five years later, one former Communist has paid SOG's Recon Teams a real compliment. Nguyen Tuong Lai, an NVA officer operating along the Trail, recently commented on the Recon Teams: "They effectively attacked and captured our soldiers and disrupted our supply lines. This weakened our forces and hurt our morale. Because we could not stop these attacks. We understood that these American soldiers were very skillful and very brave in their tactics to disrupt infiltration from the north."[27]

Each Spike Team was a composite of American Green Berets and Indochinese soldiers, who might include ARVN Rangers, Nungs, or mercenaries from several different Montagnard tribes. Specific team missions varied. Often a team was inserted into a busy sector of the Trail with orders to maintain radio silence and avoid detection. Their job might be simply to identify particular NVA units moving south, and to accomplish this they might have to crawl through the thorns and brush to the very edge of an NVA bivouac, photograph the enemy troops and equipment, then silently extract themselves.

Other Recon Team missions weren't so passive. A team might go in with orders to ambush NVA command parties, taking out every officer, then capturing the stragglers. Often teams would tap NVA field telephone lines, mine busy Trail intersections, booby-trap weapons caches, or serve as clandestine forward observers, directing air strikes against especially lucrative targets such as truck convoys, ammunition dumps, or large supply caches. On any mission other than a silent recon, taking prisoners was a priority. But the prisoners taken after an ambush were often unarmed coolies who had hidden in the brush during the fighting. Such people were of limited intelligence value. The period following such a snatch was usually hectic. The prisoner was sometimes trussed up and carried a safe distance from the enemy camp, then the team would set up to ambush any pursuers. On reaching a prearranged extraction point, the NVA prisoner was often the first man on the STABO rig line. His fear and amazement at being plucked from the jungle like a fish from the sea usually shocked him sufficiently into becoming a very cooperative informant for our intelligence officers.

☆　　　　☆

AFTER several trips around the country to meet my local commanders and inspect their units, I still didn't have a good feel for the nature of the enemy. It was one thing to sit in my air-conditioned office reviewing stacks of sparsely written Recon Team reports, and quite another to observe the enemy first-hand on the battlefield. I jumped at the opportunity when Bill Depuy invited me up to his unit that spring. He had taken command of the 1st Infantry Division after it was deployed in III Corps Tactical Zone northeast of Saigon. Their area of operations included War Zone C in Tay Ninh Province and a hard-core Vietcong bastion, laced by tunnels and a warren of underground positions, called the Iron Triangle.

Westy had taken Depuy from his job as MACV operations officer to command the 1st Division when the outfit performed poorly after its deployment in Vietnam. Like many American units, the Big Red One had come overseas at full strength, but most of its battalions were rounded out with untrained men. The unit had also lost additional men whose terms of enlistment expired soon after the division's arrival. Their task was complicated by the hostile local population and difficult terrain, in which densely populated paddy and orchard belts were punctuated by thick jungle. Maneuvering in this country either exposed the troops to booby traps and ambushes on the jungle trails or presented the dilemma of using heavy firepower in the crowded villages. Consequently, casualties were high and the troops of this proud division had yet to inflict real damage on the enemy.

Bill Depuy was not an officer to permit such a situation to fester. He fired most of the battalion commanders, replacing them with combat-experienced young officers who shared his aggressive spirit. From his background in intelligence, Depuy knew that his enemy—main-force Vietcong battalions, reinforced by NVA regulars—operated from jungle bases on both sides of the Cambodian border. He couldn't attack into Cambodia, but he sure as hell could go after the enemy bases in Vietnam. Bill's strategy was brutally simple: aggressively push units into enemy base areas until contact was made, then "pile on" with heavy firepower, seeking to maintain contact until the Communist forces had had enough and retreated. One of his refinements of this tactic was the use of huge Rome plow bulldozers to rip wide, open fire lanes through the jungle where the retreating enemy forces could be pounded by American artillery and tactical air.

He knew the main American responsibility at this stage in the war was to destroy large enemy units, and he also knew the only way to do this was to get the Communists to fight. But it was not enough to dispatch his battalions from the comfort of an air-conditioned command trailer. Depuy believed in using his own command and control (C&C) helicopter as the bait to flush out the Vietcong from their jungle bastions.

The first day I flew with him, we left division headquarters just after dawn in the relative cool of a late dry-season morning. I sat beside Depuy on a canvas sling seat in the Huey's rear compartment. Both doors had been removed to give the two door gunners, perched on little bicycle-type saddles, freedom of fire. The chopper was modified with a command communication console between us and the cockpit, which was manned by Depuy's artillery and tactical air coordinators.

We swept over dry brown paddies where peasants in black pajamas and conical straw hats fed skinny water buffalo the last of the season's dry fodder. Out here, however, an old lady in a paddy with betel-nut-stained teeth could well be a VC major. A hot wind smelling of mildew, charcoal, and the faint overripe stench of the jungle wafted through the open doors. Depuy stared at the mapboard on his lap and spoke patiently into his helmet mike, directing the pilot deeper into the jungle.

"We ought to make contact soon, Jack," he shouted over the thumping rotor.

Only moments after he spoke, lazy green tracers floated up from an abandoned banana grove strangled by jungle brush and vines. I lurched forward against my seat belt as the young pilot expertly slowed the chopper into a banking hover. Depuy already had a compass bearing on the hidden VC machine gun. But instead of climbing to a safe altitude to wait for reinforcements, we swooped lower. Depuy was hoping to provoke other guns in order to get a better idea of the entrenched enemy position. He always told his commanders that they couldn't find the enemy unless they made contact. And he practiced what he preached. The first of several small-arms rounds clanged into the belly of the helicopter below the engine compartment. It sounded like someone had hit the hood of a car with a crowbar.

General Depuy was grinning broadly.

He spoke calmly to his artillery coordinator, who leaned back to carefully consult the mapboard. They could have been two history professors discussing some ancient battle. More tracers rose from the jungle below. Finally, the artilleryman nodded sharply and transmitted his precisely worded fire mission.

The chopper dropped fast to the left and swung back along our approach line to hover 200 feet above the forest roof. The first rounds of 155mm fire arched above us to drop close to the enemy positions. Within a minute, the jungle was spouting smoking, dusty geysers as a coordinated barrage moved toward us.

Depuy was talking on the radio now, ordering up his Rome plows, followed by armored personnel carriers. By the end of the day, there'd be one less secure base area for the Communists. As we wheeled away into the hot morning, I turned to watch the artillery still falling on the splintered trees. I'd taken fire in my third war (fourth, I guess, counting Manchuria), but I still hadn't seen the enemy in this one.

☆   ☆

I SOON discovered that the intelligence and sabotage operations against the North run by Op-34 were badly compromised. Although SOG had a steady supply of adventurous young Vietnamese volunteers willing to go north as agents, there simply wasn't a good human matrix to support them in North Vietnam. Not only had the mass evacuation of anti-Communists in the mid-1950s stripped away potential resistance, the Communists had built a typical totalitarian control system, replete with cells of informants and agents provocateurs right down to the hamlet level.

The original division chiefs for Op-34 relied on classic military intelligence (MI) doctrine when they trained and dispatched their agent teams north. Once on the ground, the agents were supposed to make contact with relatives, develop an intelligence-gathering network and a security system of safe houses, then begin reporting. Our link to the agents was through Colonel Tran Van Ho's STD, which had numerous clandestine offices in Saigon. They translated our messages into Vietnamese, then transmitted them by CW (international Morse code), encrypted, using One Time pads. The agents reported to us back through this channel. In principle, there was little danger of compromise because Colonel Ho's STD was staunchly anti-Communist and very security conscious.

But I wasn't convinced that the ARVN had done adequate security checks on our agent recruits. Soon after arriving in Vietnam, I had a team of American officers conduct a rigorous, detailed analysis of the message traffic between SOG and our Op-34 agents. At that time we had approximately fifteen teams in North Vietnam, ranging in size from one-man "singletons" to large sabotage units of twenty-eight men. When Op-34 had selected agent radio operators, they'd picked the brightest and most dedicated young volunteers. These agents were carefully trained and rehearsed in transmission security procedures by which they could easily reveal if they were under duress while transmitting. In addition, of course, each radio operator was "fist printed," which meant his unique touch on the code key was carefully tape recorded to be compared against future transmissions.

Our message-traffic analysis revealed an interesting pattern, amazingly similar to that of our compromised JACK agents in North Korea twelve years earlier. In the first few days after insertion, the messages were brief and frequent, practical housekeeping matters such as moving from one checkpoint to another. Then there would be a period of silence, followed by some type of excuse (usually equipment problems) to explain the silence. About this time requests for special supplies and equipment, often including luxury items needed to "bribe" local officials, became common. Cartons of Salem cigarettes, Seiko watches, and French colonial silver piasters (or even gold Hong Kong dollars) were typical of the resupply items requested. Interestingly enough, so were pistol silencers, threaded to fit Soviet-issued guns.

In addition to these unusual requests, the agent teams also revealed another obvious pattern of compromise. They always had excuses why they could not conduct certain critical intelligence or sabotage missions. But they were consistently able to carry out minor tasks, the results of which could not be detected by aerial reconnaissance photography.

I was convinced that most of our teams in the North had been rolled up by Communist security. Their key members, especially the radio operators, had been broken under torture and forced to act as double agents. This probably meant there were leaks somewhere in the agent pipeline, either within our own shop or on the Vietnamese side. Only later did I learn from Colonel Ho that he often informed the prime minister's office of certain politically sensitive agent operations in the North. And years afterward, it was revealed that that office had at least one resident North Vietnamese spy.

At the time, however, I only knew I must improve security and also try to exploit the compromised agents. I kept very close counsel on this matter. One of the people with a true need to know was my operations director, Colonel Benton M. "Mac" Austin, whom I'd known as a Jedburgh and served with in the 82nd Airborne Division, in JACK, and on the faculty at Fort Leavenworth. Mac Austin was rock solid. We briefed Op-34's Lieutenant Colonel Bob Kingston, also a veteran of JACK, on the problem. Fortunately, he had recruited a remarkable young American Special Forces officer, First Lieutenant Fred Caristo, as a case officer on the project. Caristo would prove to be one of our most effective SOG officers, not only in exploiting the compromised agents, but in preventing future compromises.

Fred Caristo had been a bright young ROTC cadet at Boston University who answered Kennedy's romantic challenge to "Bear any burden. . . ." He trained as a Green Beret, then in 1965 served as an adviser to the 37th ARVN Ranger Battalion. His original intention had been to get a taste of war, see some of the world, then have the Army send him through medical school. But he got more than just a taste of war. In a series of bitter engagements with the NVA, Caristo's ARVN Ranger unit was decimated, but defeated superior NVA forces. Caristo learned fluent Vietnamese and Cambodian—his battalion commander was a Cambodian Foreign Legion veteran—and acquired a good knowledge of Nung and Montagnard dialects. His teachers were the prostitute camp followers who traveled with the battalion, so he originally learned to speak using feminine pronouns, which his Vietnamese colleagues found hilarious coming from a stocky, barrel-chested American with a permanent five-o'clock shadow. By the time Caristo came to SOG, he had been wounded three times and had fought in more firefights than he could remember.

Most important for us, Fred had an excellent network of ARVN Ranger veterans who considered him family and among whom he could develop a hermetically sealed agent recruitment and training unit.

Mac Austin and our intelligence shop prepared a program of counter-counterespionage disinformation to be fed back to the doubled agents in the North, thus "tripling" them. We surmised that our doubled agents were being handled by senior NVA intelligence officers, probably assisted by Soviet Military Intelligence (GRU) or East German advisers. So we carefully tailored our requests for information to establish bogus analysis patterns, which, for example, might indicate a potential amphibious invasion north of Vinh or an airborne attack on surface-to-air missile (SAM) sites above the DMZ.

Caristo concentrated on a more direct approach. When he was certain a team had been compromised, he prepared booby-trapped "gift packages" for their resupply drops. We used our sterile C-123s to drop in low-threat areas; our C-130s dropped in the thinly populated mountains of the northwest and the Laotian panhandle. In areas where air defenses were heavier, we dropped supply canisters from Air Force fighter-bombers, using modified fuel tanks as canisters. Fred went to work on our standard bundles and canisters. Some were rigged to explode as soon as they were opened on the drop zone. Others contained time bombs or demolition charges set to explode when a carton of cigarettes was opened. The logic here was to inflict casualties at as high a level as possible in NVA intelligence.

This was nerve-racking work. Although Caristo handled explosives with perfect confidence, he couldn't be absolutely certain the recipients of the booby-trapped supply canisters would be the NVA. After the first such drop, however, aerial reconnaissance photos clearly revealed truck tracks leading into the isolated drop zone. The photos also showed a quite respectable crater where the canister had exploded.

"Sir," Caristo told me, "one thing I know for damn sure, a deuce-and-a-half truck wasn't part of that team's TO&E. Whoever came in a truck to make that pickup got what he deserved."

As the true nature of my SOG assignment became evident, I understood why Westy and General Johnson had insisted I take the job as commander. We were combating a skilled, dedicated, and devious enemy. The North Vietnamese Communists conducted a massive assassination and terror program in the South. They sabotaged American-backed development programs in the countryside, sometimes going so far as booby-trapping health clinics and mutilating agricultural extension workers, whose decapitated heads were mounted on poles to discourage peasant cooperation with the government. Lies, agit-prop campaigns, and disinformation were standard enemy procedures. As respected historian and journalist Stanley Karnow has pointed out, the Vietnamese were "inured to duplicity."[28] Karnow has also documented the ghastly massacres of innocent civilians following the Communist occupation of Hué, during the Tet offensive of 1968, which he correctly calls "the worst bloodbath of the conflict." Communist political cadres had a list of teachers, intellectuals, clergymen, and government functionaries, as well as "uncooperative merchants," slated for execution. When Hué was recaptured, the government unearthed the bodies of over 3,000 of these victims, who had been beaten to death, shot, or simply buried alive.[29]

When you engaged such a foe, terror and deception were legitimate weapons. But any American unit employing these tactics had to be very carefully supervised so that its members would not be contaminated. Civilians often don't realize that the military officers conducting special operations must maintain a high level of personal honesty and integrity. On the surface this seems contradictory. Indeed, the recent history of unconventional warfare yields a fair share of "rogues" who became so enamored of covert methods that their own careers were tainted with dishonesty and, eventually, criminal activity. We only need consider the case of Ed Wilson, the CIA renegade who trained Libyan dictator Khaddafi's terrorists in the early 1980s, to see this point. Wilson, now serving a long sentence in the maximum-security federal prison at Marion, Illinois, peddled the covert and clandestine operations skills that he had acquired in Southeast Asia to Libya's Colonel Moammar Khaddafi. Wilson went so far as to dupe American Special Forces soldiers into helping Khaddafi train and equip terrorists. But, when I ran SOG, I insisted that all my officers deal with each other with absolute honesty and integrity. All our funds had to be accounted for down to the last silver piaster. I made sure that we treated prisoners humanely. Sadism is bad for morale, and, in the long run, humane treatment yields more information than brutality. By having mature, professional officers, well grounded in professional ethics, commanding SOG, we were able to maintain the unit's integrity.

☆   ☆

With a practical program under way to exploit the compromised teams through disinformation and use them as a conduit to physically attack the enemy intelligence service, Caristo and his colleagues in Op-34 set about re-creating a trustworthy agent network in the North. But he encountered resistance among the traditional military intelligence types, who, lacking his language skills and combat experience, wanted to let the ARVN and the STD do the recruiting and training. In addition, there were CIA officer "advisers" in the section, whom Caristo saw as watchdogs to make certain our networks did not poach on the Agency's traditional turf in Laos. Fred Caristo had no time for such bureaucratic rivalries.

Using his ARVN Ranger connections, he trained new agent recruits responsible directly to him. His communications now bypassed the STD; Fred was his own translator. He was also his own parachute-training officer. Because Caristo's agents would be dropped into rain forest country of western North Vietnam, they needed tree-jumping suits. Caristo flew on every agent drop up north with his group. These were hairy rides. Due to the SAM threat along the Trail, the C-130s had to stay under 750 feet above ground level (AGL) and only 350 feet above the highest terrain feature. At that altitude, there was no need for a reserve chute; if your main canopy didn't open, you were dead.

Caristo developed the concept of fast, hit-and-run intel and sabotage operations in the North that was dubbed STRATA: Short-Term Recon and Tactical Teams. The idea was to parachute in, do the job, and extract by Air Commando helicopter or, for small teams, by Fulton Recovery System (a sky-hook device suspended by a balloon and snatched by a low-flying aircraft). We no longer tried to win any hearts and minds up there; we intended to get specific information, then ambush the enemy and get the hell out, leaving behind the lingering fear that we would come again.[30]

An interesting variant of the STRATA program involved another Vietnamese double agent, whom Caristo discovered. Fred planned a unique insertion for that guy. On the night of the drop, the double agent was issued a tree-jumping suit with a modified helmet that blocked his peripheral vision. Fred had been rehearsing this for weeks. The C-130's cargo hold was partitioned with canvas cubicles, ostensibly to protect the identities of other agents. In reality—after much trial and error—Fred had rigged four big blocks of ice to parachutes. These would be the double agent's "teammates." The double was tapped out, quickly followed by the four ice blocks.

The next morning, of course, the enemy agent led an NVA patrol back to the drop zone where they found four empty parachutes hanging in the tree canopy. They immediately set to work combing the forest for the man's phantom teammates What they found instead was a series of airdropped booby traps laid down overnight from Air Commando planes.

Caristo's most gallant action was not a SOG operation. My senior Air Force officer, Colonel Harry C. "Heinie" Aderholt, ran Escape and Evasion as part of the overall Joint Personnel Recovery Center (JPRC) for Southeast Asia. The JPRC's task was to rescue American air crew downed in enemy territory. When an enemy deserter reported two American pilots held prisoner just inside Cambodia, the 25th Division helicopter rescue force Heinie helped organize needed an American who spoke both Cambodian and Vietnamese to accompany them.

Aderholt had no one who met these qualifications. I only had one such man, Caristo. I called him in from Bear Cat. "You just volunteered," I told him, then explained the mission.

"Yes, sir," Caristo replied, "I guess I did."

The initial assault worked flawlessly, with the lead helicopter touching down unopposed, a hundred meters from the edge of the fortified enemy village. Unfortunately, the pilot landed on the wrong side of the mine field that protected the NVA stronghold. Caristo knew from experience to get away from the helicopter quickly. What he did not know was that the pilot did not intend to discharge his passengers on this paddy. Caristo dropped from five feet high to the baked mud paddy only to find the helicopter climbing away behind him. He was the sole American on the ground. The NVA cut loose with automatic weapons, recoilless rifles, and anti-aircraft machine guns.

Like the good Airborne Ranger that he was, Caristo decided to conduct a one-man attack. His CAR-15 rifle blazing, he dashed through the mine field straight to the prison hut that had been pointed out by the NVA soldier.

Caristo burst head-first through the side of the hut, only to discover an old Cambodian man and two terrified children. They pointed to a hardwood frame with rope lashings, where they said the two Americans had been bound until the night before. The prisoners had been removed only twelve hours before their rescue force arrived.

But Caristo was still alone in the middle of an NVA battalion's fortified camp. He charged out the front of the hut and dashed between the banana trees to assault the enemy recoilless rifle team from the rear. After he killed the crew, he attacked an NVA machine-gun team that was firing on the American assault force from the tree line. He killed the gunner. Caristo dodged through the mine field back toward the advancing American infantrymen.

He bobbed and weaved, keeping low in the crossfire, and was blown off his feet when the Americans detonated a Bangalore torpedo to clear the mine field. The American platoon leader was amazed to see Caristo alive and to learn that he could guide their force through a safe sector to the village.

Fred had been alone on the ground for most of the fighting, but his action had been observed by several helicopter pilots. Years later, he was awarded America's second-highest decoration for valor, the Distinguished Service Cross, for his actions that day.

Fred's gallantry was not unique among SOG personnel. One of my bravest soldiers was the expert prisoner snatcher, Master Sergeant Dick Meadows. His Recon Team, which also had JPRC responsibilities, was alerted to go after a Navy pilot downed in the jungle hills of North Vietnam. A Navy chopper had just deployed them near the pilot's last reported location when they heard the man's stricken voice on the emergency Guard frequency, announcing he was about to be captured. So the rescue mission was unsuccessful. A cautious soldier would have taken his men to the nearest extraction point and departed enemy territory.

But Meadows was not overly cautious. He staked out a well-worn trail and set up an ambush. When a full platoon of heavily armed NVA troops ambled along the trail an hour later, Meadows stepped out from the dense foliage, leveled his AK-47, and called a cheerful "good morning." The ambush was sprung.

His performance on this mission was typical of his many previous assignments. I decided to reward such courageous leadership by requesting a battlefield commission. But the Department of the Army bureaucrats promptly informed me that Meadows, at age twenty-eight, was too old to become a second lieutenant. I went right to Westmoreland, requesting Meadows be made a captain. Westy readily agreed, and his prestige, plus some push from Secretary of the Army Stan Resor, overwhelmed the renewed objections of the Washington bureaucrats.

Dick Meadows fought for many more years in Indochina, including the raid on the POW camp at Son Tay in North Vietnam in 1970. He later helped found the Army's Delta Force counterterrorism unit at Fort Bragg. Never one to shirk a dangerous assignment, he was the lead man on the ground inside Tehran during the ill-fated Desert One hostage-rescue attempt in 1980.

☆   ☆

As our STRATA and JPRC responsibilities increased, I realized we couldn't always rely on brave helicopter crews to extract our agents or downed pilots from high-threat areas. But there was a better system. Skip Sadler, my airborne specialist in JACK, had helped test a rudimentary ground snatch system by which specially equipped aircraft could snare a line suspended between two poles attached to a harnessed agent on the ground. Over the intervening years this rig was replaced by the sophisticated Fulton Recovery System. All four of our C-130s were equipped with complex V-jaw snares mounted on the aircraft nose that could snag a thick nylon rope suspended by a miniature blimp. The agent (or downed pilot) at the other end of the line would then be swooped up to dangle behind the lumbering four-engine transport. Next, a winch on the open tailgate would snare the line and pull the recovered man inside the aircraft.

It was a good system that we needed to have operational as soon as possible. But the Air Force squadron commander in charge seemed to be dragging his feet in training his crews. In early 1967, they had yet to test a live pickup. Like some career officers, he was reluctant to risk a training accident in which someone might be hurt or killed and a valuable aircraft lost. But this was a war, not peacetime garrison duty. I called the man into my office for a little chat.

"Colonel," I said, "you will make your first live pickup with that Fulton System by the end of February. Do I make myself clear?"

"Sir," he began.

"Colonel," I continued, "your rating officer will be the first person you recover. Do you know who he is?"

"Yes, sir," the man answered, visibly agitated. "It's you, sir."

"I'm glad you get the picture," I replied, dismissing him.

On the last day of February, I found myself sitting on the stiff cane grass alongside the shimmering asphalt runway at Bear Cat. I was bound in a rigid web harness. Above me, a white nylon line curved upward 500 feet to a balloon, which had just been inflated from two tanks of helium in the airdropped Fulton rig kit. Nervous Air Force officers and NCOs crouched nearby, anxiously scanning the sky. The C-130 approached out of the sun, its engines throttled back and whistling softly. I watched the aircraft slam into the line at the appropriate marker and rip the line away from the balloon. The little dull white blimp was twisted like a carnival balloon just before it broke free from the line and floated away.

The actual liftoff was gentler than I had imagined, something like a fast elevator ride—but without the floor or walls. Before I knew it, I was flying backwards in the hot, windy sunshine, face to the sky, as the plane droned north around the busy landing pattern at Bienhoa. Obviously, the crew were doing things by the numbers, acutely aware they had a full colonel dangling like a fish behind their aircraft. We had not discussed the flight pattern in detail, and I'd assumed the aircraft commander would have enough sense to orbit in the general area of Bear Cat, which was a low-threat zone. But I guess he was more concerned with avoiding other aircraft, so he proceeded to fly northeast, right toward the Iron Triangle and War Zone D. I tried to flip over, using skydiving maneuvers, but every time the line flopped me back. I could see we hadn't climbed much above a thousand feet, and I could also see where the hell we were going.

I remembered those green tracers that had smacked into Bill Depuy's chopper. In my eagerness to motivate my Air Force people, I had become a target drone for the NVA.

After what seemed like a long time, I felt a series of twanging jerks and the huge tail of the aircraft loomed overhead to block the sun. A moment later they had me up on the tailgate.

"How'd it go, sir?" the crew chief shouted above the whistling prop blast.

"Piece of cake," I lied.

☆   ☆

I WOULDN'T have minded if all of my responsibilities had been so simple. However, trying to run special-warfare operations on a theater level when U.S. policy stubbornly avoided fighting a theater war was a constant frustration. By mid-1967, the United States had almost 500,000 troops in South Vietnam, about half of them in combat units. There had been a series of heavy clashes between our forces and the NVA, during which the enemy had taken severe casualties. But the North Vietnamese still pushed a steady stream of replacements down the Trail.

Westmoreland continued to agitate for freedom of operation in Cambodia, which had become the NVA's main staging area. But he was continually stymied by the State Department, which still hoped to somehow "woo" Prince Sihanouk to our side.[31] It wasn't until the middle of the year that I received grudging authorization to employ cross-border Recon Teams in Cambodia.

But by that time, my operations in Laos were continually running afoul of the American ambassador in Vientiane, Bill Sullivan. Good diplomat that he was, he believed in upholding the much-abused international agreements guaranteeing the "neutrality" of Laos, even though the embassy's own CIA station headed by my friend Ted Shackley actively conducted a guerrilla war against the NVA and its Pathet Lao allies. The core of the problem was civilian-military turf jealousy. In reality, the Trail area of the lower Laotian panhandle was geographically separated from the rest of the country and contiguous to Vietnam. But—contrary to good security procedure—I had to submit detailed plans of all my Recon Team operations for approval by Sullivan's staff. And every time one of my teams took out a lucrative target on the Trail a few kilometers from their approved area of operations, we'd get a rocket of a telegram from the embassy in Vientiane. Sullivan usually prefaced his criticism by stating that "once more, the SOG commander has blatantly disregarded. . . ." He'd wallpaper the entire U.S. government with information copies as an ass-saving precaution, in case there was some squawk of protest from the Pathet Lao.

When I'd see Sullivan at regional meetings, however, he was always friendly enough. And he would apologize for his excesses, when we were washing our hands in the officers' club men's room and no one could hear him.

The ambassadors had a myopic view of the Indochina war. Whereas the North Vietnamese were definitely fighting on a theater scale, each American embassy tended to view enemy operations in parochial, political terms. For example, when an NVA regiment maneuvered close to Thailand, to evade American air attacks along the Trail, Ambassador Graham Martin might shoot off a long "Immediate" telegram to the State Department proclaiming the North Vietnamese were trying to influence the appointment of a particular cabinet minister in Bangkok. If Westmoreland tried to put the action in proper military perspective, he was chided by the diplomats. On the other hand, they constantly intervened in MACV business with gratuitous, amateur strategic advice.

Poor Westy not only had Ho Chi Minh and General Giap as adversaries, but he also had strong-minded American ambassadors with Napoleonic ambitions in Indochina to contend with. Sullivan and Westmoreland bumped heads on a regular basis, and Ambasasdor Martin in Bangkok was intensely protective of his bureaucratic turf. The logical place for Westmoreland to confer with the region's American military and civilian leaders was our large air base at Udorn in Thailand. But Westy couldn't officially host a meeting there because protocol demanded that Ambassador Martin, as the President's representative, be the host. To my knowledge, this was one of the few times in the history of warfare where protocol took priority over strategy.

Once I was at one such strategic conference at Udorn in 1967, when Westmoreland left the headquarters building flanked on either side by Sullivan and Martin. A crowd of airmen out front gathered with their Instamatics to snap Westy's picture for the folks back home.

Sullivan leaned toward the General and snickered, "Well, Westy, looks like you got quite a few fans over here."

Westmoreland's manner of humor was sparse and sardonic. He smiled back at Ambassador Sullivan, then at Martin. "Oh, no, Bill," he said. "This is just the first time they've ever seen a four-star general escorted by two field marshals."

The honorable ambassadors were not overly amused.

☆   ☆

ANOTHER of Westmoreland's chronic nemeses was Robert McNamara. The Secretary of Defense and his cold-blooded systems analysts believed with almost religious fervor that South Vietnam could be quarantined, protected from Communist infiltration by a high-technology barrier. The first effort to achieve this involved an ill-conceived electronic "wall" along the Demilitarized Zone (DMZ), stretching from the marshy coast near Gio Linh inland to Conthien. This was a bulldozed strip, 600 meters wide, sown with sonic sensors, alarms, and land mines. It looked great on the map. Unfortunately, the "McNamara Line" terminated in the steep Annamite foothills cut by streams and rivers, which offered a simple, zero-technology alternative to the expensive and useless barrier.

Along the Trail itself, McNamara was convinced we could stop enemy infiltration in a cost-effective manner by lacing the area with thousands of high-technology sensors. In 1968, the effort began, using primitive seismic and sonic listening devices, either embedded in the ground to detect trucks or dropped by parachute to dangle from the trees and transmit the sound of enemy troops. My Recon Teams were required to collect a variety of leaves, twigs, and seed pods from the Trail, to serve as models for sensor antennas and for explosive noisemakers, which when stepped on would sound an alarm through the sensor network.

We watched in amazement as this project grew inexorably, eventually siphoning off badly needed personnel and aircraft, not to mention funding. With the money spent on the high-tech sensors, I could have hired and equipped battalions of Nungs whose human *sensors* would have led them to the enemy on the Trail with greater efficiency.

But McNamara's zeal was all-consuming. The Pentagon spent billions on research and development contracts for an ultra-high-technology sensor network. By the time I left Indochina in late 1968, Task Force Alpha, a huge computer center to support this network, was under construction at Nakhon Phanom. Interestingly enough, this boondoggle was the only part of American military operations in Indochina that was *not* subjected to PPBS cost-effectiveness scrutiny.

On several occasions during their repeated visits to Indochina, I stressed to McNamara's staff that the problem was not locating the enemy on the Trail, it was killing him there. But they never listened.

They couldn't seem to grasp that high-speed jet fighter-bombers, operating in steep gorges or in featureless rolling foothills of triple-canopy rain forest, were simply not an effective weapon. In the absence of ground troops supported by artillery on the Trail, we needed more "slow-mover" propeller bombers like the A-1 Skyraiders and the World War II–vintage B-26s, as well as lumbering prop-driven gunships like the converted C-123s and C-130s. These planes could loiter for hours over choke points on the Trail and bring to bear direct-fire weapons like the devastating 20mm Vulcan automatic cannon that could blast through the forest canopy to destroy truck convoys.

But the Seventh Air Force commander, General William M. "Spike" Momeyer, wanted to command the first all-jet air force in history. He chafed at the idea of de-mothballing more Skyraiders for use on the Trail and converting old Flying Boxcars and C-47s into gunships. When Heinie Aderholt eventually took over the 1st Air Commando Wing at Nakhon Phanom, he ran afoul of Momeyer on this issue. The General did not take criticism lightly from a mere colonel. Aderholt was forced to retire, but then was called back to active duty and promoted to brigadier general after Momeyer himself retired. Heinie Aderholt ended the war commanding our military assistance group in Thailand.

☆   ☆

IN May 1967, I received limited authorization to deploy my cross-border teams against the NVA sanctuaries in Cambodia. I set up a new staging post, Command and Control, South (CCS), at Banmethuot. As always, the teams had mixed assignments, which included pure reconnaissance, ambushing, and prisoner snatches. As in I and II Corps, we beefed them up with platoon- and company-size Hatchet force reaction units made up of Cambodians and Montagnards. If a team found a vulnerable enemy bivouac, the Hatchet force would attack. In this manner, we could bloody the NVA units in their Cambodian rest areas so that they would arrive in-country understrength and demoralized.

The more I considered the problem of hitting the enemy in his Laotian and Cambodian sanctuaries, the clearer it became that we had to deprive the NVA not only of a physical sanctuary, but also of the psychological security that came with knowing they could retreat and regroup unmolested after sharp combat. SOG teams were finding incredibly rich munitions caches in remote jungle areas of Cambodia. At first, we either destroyed the guns and ammunition as best we could on the ground or called in an air strike.

Then I thought of an alternative. I received authorization for "Eldest Son," a project that combined the resources of Op-33 and Op-35. Drawing on our devious wizards at CISO, we developed booby-trapped ammunition for small arms, automatic weapons, and mortars. These bullets and shells exploded with devastating effect when they were fired. Now, when our teams discovered an NVA arms cache, they substituted our CISO ammo for the original. Within weeks, we received reports from American infantry units noting NVA casualties found beside exploded machine guns and AK-47s. Troops from the 25th Division found a battery of four burst 82mm mortars near Cu Chi with their dead crews beside them, victims of our ammo sabotage. Psy Ops began to spread the rumor that the NVA had received large quantities of dangerously faulty ammunition.

But Washington refused permission for two equally interesting Trail projects. Our Recon Teams were uncovering huge enemy rice caches in Cambodia—one holding over ninety tons. Destroying this rice was not easy and often exposed our men to enemy pursuit. Our scientific support unit suggested a better alternative: spraying NVA rice with a food contaminant called Bitrex, an odorless chemical that made rice so bitter it was virtually impossible to swallow. Our request to use Bitrex was denied because Washington feared we would be accused of "chemical warfare." They also denied permission to use tranquilizer darts to incapacitate enemy prisoners ambushed on the Trail. They said such darts were risky because, without knowing the subject's exact body weight, we might administer a fatal overdose. Therefore, the darts were unnecessarily "cruel." I futilely tried to convince the Pentagon that a bullet from one of our team member's AK-47s was infinitely crueler than a tranquilizer dart, and that, given a choice, the NVA soldiers in question would no doubt vote for the dart. But they held their ground.

As our operations along the Trail expanded, we felt the need for improved communications with our teams. Sometimes we missed the opportunity to hit a valuable target because the team leader spotting it could not get through to us with his small radio. Normally we depended on orbiting O-1 radio-relay planes, not a very satisfactory situation. One day Ken Sisler, an eager young lieutenant from the teams, came in to announce he'd discovered an "absolutely beautiful" limestone pinnacle in the middle of a high-traffic zone of the tri-border region of Laos.[32]

I gave him permission to occupy the pinnacle, but I felt obliged to do a personal recon before committing more men and equipment. After Sisler established the relay station, I took a handful of Montagnard bodyguards and flew out to the limestone peak, which Ken had aptly dubbed the "Eagle's Nest." The gaunt stone column fell almost vertically several hundred feet to the green jungle valley below. On top, a few hardy hardwood trees and some scrub brush had clawed their roots among chest-deep crevices. As our VNAF chopper touched down, NVA guns cut loose from the surrounding valley. Orange 37mm anti-aircraft tracers sailed by harmlessly fifty feet overhead. Heavy machine-gun rounds thudded into the limestone cliff face. We were protected by the steep angle of the pinnacle. I saw how easy it was to defend this site. Over the coming years, the NVA repeatedly assaulted the Eagle's Nest, only to be driven back on each attempt.

When I reported to General Westmoreland on the new outpost, he asked me how I could be so sure it was defensible.

"I did a recon myself, sir," I said, forgetting my pledge that, as SOG commander, I would not expose myself to capture, especially in Laos.

Westmoreland frowned for a moment, seemingly about to rebuke me. Then he grinned. "I should have guessed as much, Jack."

☆   ☆

AT MY regular weekly briefing for General Westmoreland and his deputy, General Creighton Abrams, on Monday, January 22, 1968, Westy was particularly interested in enemy order of battle details on several sectors of the Trail.[33] He confirmed something that MACV's intelligence, the CIA, and their South Vietnamese counterparts had been predicting for months: The NVA and Vietcong were about to unleash a massive, countrywide offensive, born of desperation. They had been so battered by American forces over the previous year that they were about to gamble on an all-or-nothing attack designed to inflict maximum casualties on the Americans and ARVN and to trigger a popular uprising against the government.

"Everything points to Tet," General Westmoreland noted.

The Buddhist lunar new year, Tet, was Vietnam's most important holiday. There would be a general cease-fire throughout Indochina, and easily half the ARVN would be on holiday leave. The coming attack was hardly secret. American newspaper and television reporters were already filing stories predicting an offensive. I left the briefing to spread the word among our far-flung units, ordering them to keep their indigenous forces on alert during the holiday.

For the Recon Teams in I Corps, this wasn't necessary. They had been fully deployed inside Laos for over a month. Earlier that year, my SOG launch site near the old French Legion fort at Khesanh had come under increasing pressure from NVA regulars. I'd had to tie down too many of our Trail reaction forces defending the place, so I asked the Marines to lend us a company. With the Marines' typical ponderous fashion, however, they dispatched a full battalion. Instead of digging in well, they set up shop on the exposed plateau, bivouacking in squad tents and exposing their mortars and artillery to enemy fire. Our own team based at Khesanh was dug in deeply with interlocking bunkers protected by heavy timbers, a setup reminiscent of Outpost Harry. But despite my several trips up there to plead with the Marines, they refused my offers of timber and other construction material.

That fall, the famous "Siege" of Khesanh began in earnest. Reluctantly, the Marines began to dig. By January, the upgraded Khesanh Combat Base was being compared in the press to the doomed French positions at Dienbienphu. Marines were taking a lot of needless casualties—which seemed to be a point of honor for them—but that was the only valid similarity to the 1954 battle. SOG and Special Forces teams were active in the enemy approach routes, targeting scores of enemy battalions for air strikes, including the devastating Arc Light saturation raids by B-52s. The NVA was squandering two divisions of regulars up there and my people were fully committed.

Elsewhere in the country, however, a deceptive calm had descended, a good indicator of a pending attack. For the next week, I did everything I could to make sure all of my units were well stocked with weapons, ammunition, and extra communications equipment, and would be ready to deploy in pursuit of retreating enemy units after the offensive began.

By this time, I shared a villa with Major General Walter T. "Dutch" Kerwin, Westmoreland's chief of staff. Our house was not far from the main gate of Tan Son Nhut Air Base, MACV's sprawling new headquarters compound. Around 3 A.M. on Wednesday, January 31, 1968, we were shaken out of bed by exploding rockets and incoming mortar rounds straddling the road between our house and the base. We had expected the attack to come on the actual New Year's holiday, the day before. In preparation, Westy had Kerwin alert all American military forces throughout the country to be at the highest state of readiness. But all we'd heard the night before were New Year's firecrackers. I pulled on my boots and ran out my bedroom door, almost colliding with Dutch Kerwin.

"This is it, sir," I yelled.

Kerwin nodded, buttoning his fatigue blouse. "You're right, Jack," he said. "They've finally started it."

The night sky was ripped by gliding, candy-pink tracers and fainter streams of green NVA tracer rounds. A rocket must have hit a fuel tanker on the base, because rolling orange flames lit up the pre-dawn sky. Kerwin sped across the road in his sedan while I climbed into mine. I suppose I should have waited for some guards from my downtown headquarters, but, like Kerwin, I was impatient. I had a CAR-15 on the front seat with me that wouldn't have been much help against a concerted Vietcong or NVA ambush, so I decided to avoid the main roads in from Tan Son Nhut. No sooner had I turned off the highway than I saw an ARVN MP jeep ahead of me come under fire from a VC roadblock near a truck garage.

I sped down rutted side lanes paralleling a canal. Off to my left, there were firefights and more VC roadblocks. Once I had to stop while two American armored personnel carriers (APCs) shot it out with some VC sappers attacking a local police station. By the time I reached SOG headquarters on Rue Pasteur, it was dawn.

My duty officer reported that the VC had attacked the American embassy with a small sapper unit, but that the embassy's Marine security guard had repelled them. I got on my single-sideband command radio and checked in with my units throughout the country. Almost everywhere the pattern was the same: massed attacks by Vietcong and NVA regulars, all dressed in civilian clothes, assaulting under mortar and rocket barrages. The targets seemed to be police stations, ARVN barracks, and other government facilities. While we talked there were tens of thousands of American and Vietnamese forces engaged, but our superior firepower was taking a horrible toll of the enemy.

Over the next hour or so the sounds of firing and incoming rockets petered out and stopped completely. If the NVA was trying to provoke an uprising in Saigon, they had failed miserably. Bill Donnett, my senior liaison officer with the U.S. embassy, arrived to give me a report on what he saw in the city as he came from the embassy. The fight there was over, he said; the VC had never even gotten in the building. An American Airborne platoon had just landed on the roof and had secured the entire compound.[34] The only damage, he added, was a hole blown in the outside wall and a lot of bullet-pocked concrete around the front door. I dismissed the action as a minor footnote to the countrywide battle then raging.

But at 8:15 I got a call from Westmoreland himself about the embassy.

"Jack," he said, "there've been some reports that VC have taken the embassy. I can't get through on the phone. What's the situation down there?"

"I just talked to my senior liaison officer who came from the embassy five minutes ago," I explained. "The VC never got into the building. They blew a hole in the outside wall of the compound and started a firefight in the garden. That's as far as they got."

Westmoreland listened, and I heard him sigh over the crackling Saigon telephone line. "Well," he said, "I better come down myself to have a look. They have an entirely different picture of things in Washington."

Westmoreland had been called at his headquarters by Secretary of Defense Robert McNamara, who had just seen a Chet Huntley report on the NBC Evening News (Tuesday, January 30, 1968, Washington time) that the Vietcong had captured the embassy chancery. Westy choppered in to central Saigon, landing on the embassy roof helipad. He made a personal inspection of the entire embassy, receiving a direct briefing from the Marine security guards. Satisfied that the situation was as I'd reported it to him, he called McNamara as soon as he returned to MACV headquarters to reassure him that the VC had never "captured" the chancery.

As Westy later told me, McNamara was not convinced. "That's all right, General," McNamara said in a condescending tone. "We have our own sources on that."

Obviously, the ill-informed opinions of news commentators, snatched from fragmentary and contradictory wire-service reports, were more convincing than the firsthand account of the American field commander on the scene. This exchange epitomized the gap between our political and military leaders. Over the next several days, the *capture* of the embassy became a symbol of America's military setback.[35]

☆　　　　☆

IN THE coming weeks and months, we watched bitterly as the Communists' military defeat was transformed by the news media into a victory. Beginning with the first wire-service reports the morning of the attack, the American news media almost consistently chose to interpret the Tet Offensive as a Communist triumph. Television and magazine photojournalists focused on the human devastation and physical destruction. The fact that the fighting had been centered on perhaps twenty key locations was ignored. As Peter Braestrup has sagely noted, "All Vietnam, it appeared on film at home, was in flames or being battered into ruins, and all Vietnamese civilians were homeless refugees. . . . Indeed, there were virtually no films shown or photographs published during this period of *undamaged* portions of Saigon, Hué, or other cities."[36] Braestrup was a veteran working reporter in Vietnam. His classic analysis of the news media there, *Big Story,* is required reading for anyone looking for a balanced history of the Vietnam War.

In a similar manner, the American media emphasized American casualties. The absolutely stunning enemy casualty rate was downplayed. But we in MACV knew the Communists had suffered a near-fatal blow. By the time the Tet fighting petered out in the last week of February, the enemy had suffered an incredible 37,000 killed out of a committed combat force of approximately 84,000. Worse, from the Communist perspective, most of those casualties had been among resident Vietcong forces that had answered Hanoi's call for a nationwide armed uprising. But as General Westmoreland noted, "Nothing remotely resembling a general uprising of the people had occurred." Indeed, by as early as February 1, Vietcong headquarters was conceding defeat. An intercepted enemy message noted, "We failed to seize a number of primary objectives and to completely destroy mobile defensive units of the enemy. We also failed to hold the occupied areas. In the political field we failed to motivate the people to stage uprisings and break the enemy's oppressive control."[37] Years later, Tran Van Tra, one of the NVA's senior commanders in the South, admitted the Tet offensive had been a disastrous blunder: "We suffered large loses in matériel and manpower . . . which clearly weakened us."[38]

But, despite this overwhelming evidence of enemy failure and the shocking Communist casualty rate, the news media had convinced the American people that the Tet Offensive was an enemy victory. No doubt the fact that the NVA had been able to infiltrate large numbers of troops and huge quantities of munitions from sanctuaries in Laos and Cambodia for use in South Vietnam's urban centers was a shock to the American public. In a way, we were paying the price of trying to live the myth that the Vietnam War was an insurgency that could be isolated within a single country. Tet marked the watershed in American public opinion. Before the offensive, most Americans believed that our military might could prevail; after Tet, the public became convinced we were doomed to failure.

Instead of pursuing the enemy vigorously into his sanctuaries and destroying him with our firepower, we allowed the NVA and the remnants of the decimated Vietcong to pull back and regroup.

This was an election year. Anti-administration Democratic candidates led by Senator Robert Kennedy assailed America's "failed" policy in Indochina. On March 31, 1968, less than three years after he had addressed the nation to announce our combat deployment to Vietnam, President Lyndon Johnson again spoke to his fellow Americans on nationwide television. He announced the suspension of bombing raids on North Vietnam, offered his willingness to negotiate with the leaders in Hanoi, and then announced his decision that he would not run for reelection.

We had gone into the fight with too little, too late. And now, with hard-won victory almost in sight, we were pulling out. As I watched Johnson's speech on Armed Forces Television, I realized that continuing our present policy would condemn us to defeat.

CHAPTER ELEVEN

General Officer

1968–1973

☆   ☆

EN ROUTE HOME from Saigon in August 1968, I stopped in Honolulu to brief the Commander in Chief, Pacific, and key members of his staff on MACV/SOG. The conference room of Admiral John McCain's Pacific Command headquarters was in a handsome old building at Camp Smith, on a hill overlooking Pearl Harbor. As I stood at the map of Indochina, I could look past the conference table out the window at the smooth lawns and bougainvillea. The distant gray slab of an aircraft carrier and a line of destroyers marked the naval harbor.

I had been a college student construction worker on this very building the summer of 1941, when the facility was built as a naval hospital in the middle of a hilltop pineapple plantation. That summer before Pearl Harbor had been America's last period of true peace in almost thirty years. And there was no real prospect for peace that I could see.

The small group of admirals and generals at the table were somberly attentive. Like most senior American military men, they were resigned to the fact that, for a variety of political reasons, our country had not followed up on the Communist defeat in the Tet Offensive. Now I had to report that SOG Recon Teams had sighted a steady flow of enemy reinforcements on the Ho Chi Minh Trail.

This was one of my final duties as SOG commander. I was on orders to the 8th Infantry Division in Europe, as Assistant Division Commander for Maneuver. That summer, I'd been selected for promotion to brigadier general. So, in many ways, going "home" to the 8th Division knowing I'd made general—even though I wouldn't officially wear the rank until the next year—was a very pleasant prospect. But I was troubled by the situation in Indochina, and uneasy about the future of our efforts there. Our muddled strategy meant the war would probably stretch on indefinitely, and ultimately end in defeat.

After the meeting, Admiral McCain asked to see me alone. I sat beside the Admiral's desk as he silently wrestled with some inner problem. Then he spoke.

"Jack," he said, clenching his wiry hands, "you know my son is a POW?"

"Yes, sir," I nodded. Lieutenant Commander John McCain, Jr., had been shot down over North Vietnam, reportedly badly injured during his bailout, and was now officially listed as a prisoner of the North Vietnamese.

"You've had a lot of experience with Communists in the Far East, Jack," the Admiral continued. "Do you believe they'll try to . . . well, exploit the fact that they have John?"

It was a question any father would ask. Admiral McCain was a tough professional, a combat veteran who had seen close friends die in two wars. His son had followed his profession. But now that relationship was a threat to them both. I had no choice but to be frank.

"Sir," I said, "if you give *any* indication whatsoever that his captivity is a personal burden for you or your family, if you even publicly acknowledge that your son's a prisoner, they will make every effort to exploit his position. They'll definitely try to get to you personally."

Admiral McCain stared at me for a long moment, his lips pursed. "Thank you, Jack," he said, rising from his chair. "I suspected as much, but I needed some confirmation."

As I walked across the beautifully kept grounds of Camp Smith, I was haunted by McCain's dilemma. The war had dragged on far too long. And I knew that the issue of American POWs would be cynically manipulated during any negotiations, just as it had been in Korea.

I recalled a story told by a Spanish army officer in Germany several years before about his country's civil war. During the struggle for the Fortaleza in Toledo, the commander of Franco's besieged troops received a telephone call from his enemy counterpart, a colonel. We have your son, the Colonel said, and we'll execute him if you don't surrender. The Fortaleza commander demanded proof that his son was still alive, and the younger officer was allowed to speak on the telephone. "Son," the father said, "prepare to meet your maker. I can do nothing to save you." The enemy headquarters was furious. They later executed their young prisoner.[1]

As the staff car took me from the gardens of Camp Smith into the bustle of civilian traffic en route to the airport, I wondered if Admiral McCain would face similar cruel pressure.

On the commercial flight to Seattle, I noticed a vague but perceptible coolness toward me by some of the civilian passengers. Most were middle-age vacationing couples returning to the mainland, but a few younger men and women gazed with open contempt at my uniform and the rows of campaign ribbons I wore. It was my first indication that the mood in America had shifted since my last trip home the year before.

Nineteen sixty-eight had been a year of chaotic change around the world. After the shock of the Tet Offensive, there'd been the assassinations of Martin Luther King and Bobby Kennedy. Europe had been rocked by the student uprisings in France and the Soviet suppression of the new and more liberal Czech government. In both Europe and the States the growing anti-war movement was reaching a crescendo. And the war in Vietnam was mirrored by a conflict in our streets. Whole sections of black ghetto neighborhoods in our major cities had been destroyed in bloody rioting.

Some of my fellow citizens obviously found the military a convenient scapegoat on which to focus their confused anger generated by this turmoil. It was no wonder. Every night the screens of the new color television sets around the country blazed with napalm and American artillery. The images of dead and wounded GIs and Vietnamese civilian casualties seemed endless. Footage of enemy casualties or captured weapons was rarely shown.[2]

The media's portrayal of the situation in Vietnam bore little resemblance to the reality I had experienced only days before. One interesting outcome of the failed Tet Offensive was the overall excellent performance of the ARVN and the Regional and Popular Forces auxiliary troops in the countryside. But the press accounts I read dwelt on ARVN inefficiency, poor leadership, and that old standby "corruption."

I was reminded of an earlier incident in Saigon. Bill Donnett, my senior embassy adviser who knew the country well, angrily dropped a copy of a news magazine on my desk one morning. The story in question concerned ARVN officers who were more concerned with procuring prostitutes for GIs than fighting the enemy. This ludicrous charge came directly from Vietcong propaganda leaflets. That evening, Bill and I encountered the reporter who wrote the article on the terrace of the Caravel Hotel. Bill lit into him over the piece. The reporter, an honest, old-school newspaperman, was chagrined.

"I filed my story citing that as VC propaganda," he complained. "But my editors rewrote it the way they wanted."[3]

☆   ☆

MARY met me at the Seattle airport. We were going to have a few days together in the Northwest before returning to Washington to complete plans for the move to Germany. I was tired after crossing nine time zones, but it was wonderful to be home again with my wife. She reminded me that this was my fifth return from duty in foreign war zones.

Waiting for my bags to arrive, however, I met hostility even stronger than I had encountered on the plane. One long-haired young man glared and scowled as he strolled by, his exaggerated bell-bottom jeans flapping. "Oh, wow," he said in a stage whisper to his girlfriend, "check out the *war* hero."

Maybe that type of anger was understandable, coming from a boy of draft age. But I wasn't prepared for his girl, a young woman in miniskirt and granny glasses, the age of my own daughters, who mouthed a truly foul obscenity when she turned to examine my uniform.

☆   ☆

IN Washington, a strange mood of limbo prevailed. The Democrats fought an internecine battle while the Republicans uneasily coalesced around Richard Nixon, who hinted vaguely he had a secret plan to win the war. McNamara and most of his cost-effectiveness whiz kids had left the Pentagon for high-paying positions in the private sector. Clark Clifford, an old Democratic workhorse, was the caretaker at Defense. General Westmoreland was now Army chief of staff, and Creighton Abrams, the cigar chomping tanker, ran MACV.

Naturally, it was great to be reunited with Mary and the family. Our older girl, Elisabeth, was established in college and struggling to survive the social chaos around her. Mary Ann, the youngest of the three children, was doing well academically and was about to enter high school. But I felt sorry for my son, John. Since childhood, he had hoped to attend the U.S. Military Academy at West Point and follow me in a career as a professional officer. But during a brief leave the previous winter, when he and I had gone skiing in New England, he'd told me he'd decided against applying to West Point.

"Dad," he'd said, riding the lift on Mt. Snow, "I just don't think it's a good idea."

I didn't pursue the matter, half hoping he'd change his mind. Then, after a few days, I learned what had shaped his decision. For almost a year, John explained, teachers at his high school in suburban northern Virginia had viciously harassed the children of career servicemen serving in Vietnam, sometimes going so far as to label them "killers' kids." Although John certainly didn't share their sentiments, he had come to believe the military no longer had the "respect of the public," and anyone launching on a military career could expect to serve without the support of the American people. To an officer who had fought for his country in three wars, this was a bitter pill to swallow.

Before flying to Germany, I briefed the Joint Chiefs of Staff on SOG in the "Tank," their Pentagon conference center. This windowless, light-green room was the inner sanctum of the American military. The Tank was dominated by a highly polished round table with room for the four service chiefs and the chairman. There was a handsome oak rostrum at one end of the room, surrounded by an impressive array of audiovisual screens and projectors of various calibers that could display maps, electronic situation charts, and the amazingly detailed photographs from our new reconnaissance satellites.

Just before I began my briefing, General Earle Wheeler, the chairman, received an urgent summons to Secretary Clifford's office. I continued in his absence. The service chiefs were especially interested in enemy strength and infrastructure along the Trail in the southern Laotian panhandle. They asked about NVA reaction to SOG helicopter insertions of Recon Teams, and they wanted my opinion on the ability of SOG teams to capture valuable NVA officers on the Trail. I pointed out the Pentagon's previous refusal to authorize tranquilizer darts for this very purpose. Westy made it clear the matter would be reconsidered. While I had their attention, I suggested the Chiefs also overrule the bureaucrats on using Bitrex to sabotage NVA rice caches along the Trail. I couldn't be certain, but it seemed to me the Joint Chiefs were planning for a serious land operation to cut the Trail in Laos, should the next administration take that logical course.

On my way back from four-star territory on the D-ring, I ran into General Wheeler just returning from the Secretary's office. He had that expression of calm, unruffled precision senior officers usually adopted during times of crisis.

"Jack," he said, shaking hands, "as you know, Soviet forces just invaded Czechoslovakia. It looks like you're going from the frying pan into the fire."

Upon arrival in Germany, I had a chance to debrief Chuck MacCrone, who was the Chief of Delegation of the U.S. Parachute Team at the World Championship Parachute Meet in Graz, Austria. He told me that their Russian counterparts had begun the meet with their usual strained conviviality, but then had become quite "nervous." On the third day of the competition, the airport was closed to accommodate a Soviet military Ilyushin jet transport. The head of the Soviet delegation, General Lisov, commander of the Red Army's airborne forces, had boarded the transport for a mysterious errand. A few hours later, the plane returned. But MacCrone had snooped around and discovered that the transport never left Austrian airspace. Apparently, Lisov used the airborne command post for a secret briefing. Toward the end of the parachute meet, Soviet airborne troops seized the airfield at Prague and East German forces rolled into Czechoslovakia to crush the "socialism with a human face" that had had the audacity to encourage non-Communist participation in the government of Alexander Dubcek.[4]

To give the devil his due, the Soviet invasion was preceded by a classic special-warfare operation. Red Army Spetsnaz troops commandeered a Polish airliner on a regular flight from Warsaw, then declared an emergency and requested immediate landing clearance at Prague. Instead of stopping at the terminal, the jetliner rolled up to the control tower, and the troops seized the building and called in the reinforcements on the Soviet military airlift.

By the time I took up my new assignment in 8th Division headquarters in Bad Kreuznach, the Soviet Red Army had almost ten divisions in Czechoslovakia and NATO forces along the frontier were on a high state of alert. Major General George L. Mabry, Jr., the division commander, was a short, wiry South Carolinian. He was a lively and dynamic speaker, but I sometimes had trouble understanding his strong southern accent. General Mabry was pure infantry. In World War II, he had earned an impressive array of combat decorations, including the Medal of Honor, which he won while commanding the 2nd Battalion of the 8th Infantry in the Huertgen Forest. Mabry stressed the need to keep up high unit standards, despite our critical shortage of experienced officers and NCOs.

Our primary area of responsibility was defending the Fulda Gap, about a hundred miles to the east, on the other side of the Rhine. The 8th Division was divided into three brigades, each with three to four maneuver battalions. The Pentomic organization with its impractical battle groups had been abandoned years before. And we were back to normal battalions, which seemed to be the most sensible structure for infantry troops. In turn, using battalions as building blocks, we could tailor our brigades as task forces for particular assignments. The division was well suited for such flexibility because our brigade in Mainz, commanded by my old friend from JACK, Colonel Skip Sadler, was both Airborne and mechanized, and the other brigades were mechanized infantry, one being tank heavy.

As Assistant Division Commander, Maneuver, I was responsible for close and direct supervision of these brigades' operations, training, and combat readiness. In addition, I was the designated commander for the NATO Airborne task force, which was tasked for emergency deployment anyplace in the NATO area of interest. We had the full gamut of mandatory Annual Training Tests and Operational Readiness Tests, which were the bread and butter of the American Army in NATO. Given the diverse structure of the division, this meant I had to become expert in tank operations and gunnery, mechanized infantry operations, as well as making sure Skip Sadler's brigade was current on the latest Airborne doctrine. I also supervised the division's Airborne school and noncommissioned officer academy.

The job was normally held by a brigadier general. But given the congressional limitations on the numbers of generals authorized for the Army, I would not actually wear my new rank until a vacancy occurred sometime during the next year.

Instead, all my official documents were signed "Colonel (P)," which indicated I'd been selected for promotion. I was kept so busy by all these responsibilities that I didn't have time to worry about whether I wore eagles or stars on my shoulders.

The division's shortage of officers and NCOs was common to most Army units outside Vietnam. When the decision had been made three years before to expand the Army by several hundred thousand men without activating the reserves or extending terms of service, a dangerous process was set in motion. The U.S. Military Academy, embattled ROTC programs, and the overextended Officer Candidate School (OCS) system simply couldn't keep up with the demand as more and more units were formed and deployed to Vietnam.

The reluctance of many well-qualified young Americans to serve in the Army exacerbated the shortage. As the war dragged on, anti-military sentiment grew among our best-educated youth. The college draft deferment fed this process. Graduate schools were jammed with young men earning master's degrees and Ph.D.s simply to maintain student deferment status.[5] The need for company commanders in Vietnam siphoned off most skilled West Point and ROTC graduates. So in order to encourage junior officers to stay in the Army, first lieutenants were often promoted to captain after only two years in the service. But still the Army could not retain adequate numbers of junior officers. In retrospect, it's hard to blame these young men; they faced the prospect of repeated combat tours in Vietnam, interspersed with assignments at training bases where disgruntled draftees and the swelling anti-war movement poisoned the atmosphere.

After inspecting the brigades, I was shocked to discover that *every* company in the division was commanded by a first lieutenant, most with only two years' experience. The battalions were all commanded by seasoned professional lieutenant colonels, combat veterans of Vietnam and Korea. But the battalion staffs, normally composed of field-grade officers, were also made up of green first lieutenants. A similar situation prevailed among the NCOs, who when all is said and done, are the heart of any unit, especially the infantry. As with junior officers, career NCOs were leaving the Army in record numbers. The combat units in Vietnam also absorbed the majority of experienced infantry NCOs. So we had a number of draftee sergeant squad leaders, who were constantly rotating back to the States as their two-year terms of service ended.

During our first large training exercises that fall, I observed firsthand the terrible level of inexperience among our officers and NCOs. Standard procedures such as organizing combat formations and establishing effective perimeter defense on night bivouacs—setting outposts, registering defensive artillery fires—were only vaguely familiar concepts to our young lieutenants. Visiting the units in the field, I saw harried battalion commanders tromping through the snowy woods to make sure individual machine-gun and anti-tank teams were correctly positioned, a task normally conducted by second lieutenants twenty-one years old and verified by captains and majors of the battalion staff. These battalion commanders worked sixteen hours a day back in the garrison; on field exercises, they simply went without sleep.[6]

I couldn't help but compare the plight of these battalion commanders with my own situation leading an infantry battalion in combat in Korea. There my company commanders had also been first lieutenants, but several had been West Pointers, and they all had had at least three years' experience before taking command. Equally important, my battalion staff officers were experienced pros; several were combat veteran reservists recalled for Korea. The mobilization of reserve and National Guard units during the Korean War had in fact guaranteed the quality of our commissioned officer and NCO corps. But we didn't have this critical support during the Vietnam War.

When General Westmoreland inspected the division that winter, he was also deeply troubled by the chronic shortage of officers and NCOs.

"General," I told him as we watched a company of APCs maneuvering across frozen rye fields, "commanding a battalion in Europe today is a far greater challenge than commanding one in Vietnam."

Westy cocked an eyebrow. Obviously he doubted my assertion.

"Sir," I continued, "the entire burden of command is on one man. These battalions are completely lacking qualified subordinates."

Westmoreland personally questioned several young lieutenant colonels and verified my statement. The specter of the "hollow" Army that had haunted the Pentagon in 1965 was now a reality.

We were just beginning to see organized assaults on troop morale by American anti-war activists manning off-post "coffee houses," where drugs and advice on desertion were available in equal quantities.[7] But there were well-organized European "peace" movements urging our young GIs to question orders, to disrupt training, and to evade combat duty in Vietnam by deserting to Sweden, which offered unquestioning sanctuary to any American serviceman. Our military intelligence learned from German authorities that some of these local peace organizations were financed by the Soviets and East Germans, which should have come as no surprise.[8] What was surprising, however, was how few of our troops caved in under this pressure. While I was with the 8th Division, only a handful of Americans deserted to

Sweden. And in each case, there were factors other than sincere anti-war feelings behind the action. Some soldiers and airmen had committed offenses and were fleeing military or local civilian prosecution. Others got involved with drugs or were convinced by their local girlfriends to leave.

But from my perspective as an officer who had managed psychological operations, I could see that the large, expensive Soviet effort was an overall failure. If anything, NATO was growing stronger as the Soviets brutally suppressed freedom movements in their East European satellite colonies.

Spain was not yet a member of the European alliance, but NATO leaders hoped the country could eventually be brought into the fold of democratic nations. It had been thirty years since the bitter Spanish Civil War. Dictator General Francisco Franco was an old man. Although there were American Navy and Air Force bases in Spain, our two armies had little contact. The year before, 8th Division troops had participated in a brief field training exercise, which had opened valuable contacts between the Spanish and American officers.

This year we planned to expand the exercise to include the 8th Division's Airborne brigade. From previous visits to Spain, I knew there were sparsely populated areas that would make excellent training grounds. I took a small advance party to Madrid in November to meet with the commanders of the Spanish army's parachute brigade. Their base was in a former medieval monastery near Torrejon. At first, the Spaniards were disappointed that the American delegation was led by a colonel; they'd made complex protocol arrangements for an exchange of greetings between generals. I did the best I could to assure them I was indeed the senior officer in charge of our Airborne brigade, and that I would soon be wearing a general's star.

Behind their aloof formality, I sensed feelings of inferiority. Compared to a modern Western army, the Spanish forces were poorly equipped and inadequately funded. On the nearby air base our big turboprop C-130 stood beside a row of ancient JU-52 tri-motor transports, relics of Franco's alliance with Nazi Germany. A squadron of equally venerable Messerschmidt 109s was parked across the runway. Many of the soldiers I saw at the base carried vintage bolt-action Mausers.[9]

During our initial discussions, it became clear the Spanish simply didn't have the budget or the equipment to participate in the exercise as equal partners with the NATO units. So I suggested a face-saving compromise. The Spanish forces could be deployed as lightly armed guerrillas, who would harass and attack the NATO airborne troops. This worked out quite well as far as the parachute brigade and the Army GHQ were concerned. The critical issue then was where the exercise would be run. GHQ informed me that I would have to work out the details of the location with the captain general who exercised control of all military activity in the area where I thought the maneuver should be conducted. I went to call on him at his headquarters in Valencia. Luckily, the Captain General's aide had been an observer in my battle group in the 16th Infantry seven years before. He smoothed the way and we soon had plans for Pathfinder Express, the largest training operation to date of American troops in Spain.

I flew back to Germany, where I got down to work with Colonel Skip Sadler preparing the brigade for the exercise. The original contingency plans for the deployment of Airborne forces in the Mediterranean area called for the unit to stage through Italy, departing Germany on a piecemeal, non-tactical airlift, then loading up for the drop at an Italian air base. When the principal tactical transport aircraft was the small C-119, this was not un-realistic. But in the current situation using the longer-legged C-130s and with Soviet missiles aimed at all NATO airfields, an actual combat drop would not allow us the luxury of such a leisurely deployment. I shook things up by insisting the entire task force, with its vehicles and support equipment, be loaded aboard Air Force C-130s at Wiesbaden and fly directly to the drop zone near Albacete in southeastern Spain. We had to get special per-mission to overfly France, which had withdrawn from NATO's joint military command several years before. This was not received until the very last moment, reflecting an anti-American attitude of the French government which was typical of this period.

As a gesture of gratitude to the Spanish airborne commander, General Crespe del Castillo, I had him join my headquarters unit aboard our C-130 in Germany for the mass drop. He had never jumped from a C-130 before and was clearly impressed by the aircraft. We put on a good show, dropping my command jeep by parachute-extracted pallet, then jumping right behind it from the "tailgate" of the C-130. We landed near an olive grove almost on top of the jeep. Within minutes, I had a command post set up and was able to take over control from the exercise headquarters at Torrejon. We were now involved in a ground sweep of troops dropped across the valley. When an operation like this worked well, it was quite impressive.

After weeks of practically round-the-clock work, the training exercise went off perfectly. Our Airborne units were dropped in realistic fashion, escorted by U.S. Air Force fighters from bases in Germany and Spain. The Spanish parachute brigade made worthy adversaries as guerrillas. And all my unit commanders reported excellent training results.[10]

The Spanish paratroopers repaid our hospitality by letting us jump from their historic old JU-52. They even allowed me to jumpmaster the mixed load of U.S. and Spanish officers. The interior of the plane reminded me of the RAF Stirlings I'd trained in as a Jed. But the small oval door near the tail seemed too narrow to accommodate a jumper wearing the bulky American T-10 parachute and reserve. After a little trial and error, I figured out a good exit position. The plane rumbled down the runway, sounding like a cement mixer with stripped gears. Takeoff speed was only about eighty knots and cruise was around seventy. From my narrow sling seat, I could look straight down to the olive groves through cracks between the rattling corrugated aluminum fuselage panels. Inside, I noticed Lieutenant Colonel Al Hall, my exercise deputy and division provost marshal, anxiously fingering his reserve as the old JU-52 bucked and staggered in some turbulence.

When it came time to lead the stick, I was a little nervous. Spotting the drop zone from an unfamiliar aircraft wasn't easy, and I sure as hell didn't want to sour all the good relations we'd cultivated by putting the Spanish airborne commander, who was to jump right after me, down on a village or into olive trees. But the jump went well, and the seven Americans who were lucky enough to make the jump had earned a unique entry in their parachute logbooks.

Pathfinder Express, however, was not without a nasty hitch. Several months after the exercise had been declared an outstanding success, two American reporters came to Europe from Washington and began interviewing our troops and the Spanish paratroopers, trying to uncover the sinister *real* purpose behind the exercise. When they struck a dry well with the Airborne and those who planned and conducted the exercise, they shifted to our air base at Maron, where they found a talkative officer (who didn't know much about the exercise at all). They worded their questions in such a way as to imply that Pathfinder Express was actually a rehearsal for an American intervention to aid Franco in suppressing a rebellion. They cited as proof the fact that the exercise involved suppressing "guerrillas." This provoked an unnecessary, time-consuming controversy within NATO.

☆　　　　☆

PRESIDENT Nixon's plan to end the war turned out to be "Vietnamization," the long-term expansion and support of South Vietnamese forces until they supposedly would be strong enough to face the NVA alone. The gradual reduction of American troops in Vietnam would accompany this buildup. And the sporadic Paris peace negotiations had now been expanded to include the government of South Vietnam and representatives of the Vietcong's ostensibly independent National Liberation Front. For the officers of my generation who had commanded troops in combat during the frustrating cease-fire negotiations in Korea, this policy seemed doomed to failure. For the Army's young officers and draftees, the policy offered the prospect of fighting in a war that the government had no intention of winning.

I took the time to personally interview every new officer assigned to the division. For me, these interviews were quite revealing of the social corrosion caused by the protracted war of attrition in Vietnam and our bankrupt strategy. Most of the young lieutenants had become officers almost by accident. They seemed to lack a sense of direction in their lives. It was a time of limbo, of waiting for the war to be over. Several of these new Infantry lieutenants had spent four or more years in college majoring in subjects like animal husbandry or sociology, simply to keep up their student deferments. Now, however, they found themselves dressed in the starched fatigues of an Infantry second lieutenant. For many, the situation was confusing, even bizarre.

I sensed that some of them had the makings of good professional officers and that, with a little encouragement, they might stay in the Army. An officer had to have two fundamentally important traits, I told them: integrity and courage, both physical and moral. If an officer lacked those qualities, no amount of careful planning or help from influential connections would bring him a successful career. Don't worry about your "career," I said. Solve the Army's problems and your career will take care of itself. If they felt at all inclined to become professional officers, they should "follow the sound of the cannon," go to Vietnam, lead men in battle, and, if they survived, then decide if they had a future in the Army.

For most of them this was unusual advice. Their college professors had often encouraged them to avoid hard decisions. I advised them to stand up and be counted, to test their individual mettle. Not surprisingly, some of these young officers took my advice and decided to follow the profession of arms.

That fall, as I was still busy preparing the division for the annual winter training exercises, I received a real shock: immediate orders assigning me to Fort Hood, Texas, to be Director of Plans and Evaluation for the secret new Mobile Army Sensor Systems Test Evaluation and Review, Project MASSTER. I made a few phone calls and discovered that, once again, my unofficial godfather, Lieutenant General Bill Depuy, then the assistant to the Vice Chief of Staff, had personally recommended me for this job. The project's commander was Major General Jack Norton, who had replaced Harry Kinnard as commanding general of the 1st Cavalry Division in Vietnam.

Professional officers become accustomed to sudden disruptions, but this unexpected move was especially upsetting for the family. I'd more or less been promised two uninterrupted years in Europe after thirty straight months in Vietnam. The move would be rough on Mary, who had finally gotten our quarters in Bad Kreuznach comfortably organized. And two of our children, Elisabeth and John, were enrolled in German universities. Moving back to the States meant leaving them in Europe for the rest of the academic year.

On the professional side, the MASSTER job was a real challenge. Once more, I was ordered to staff, organize, and supervise the rapid expansion of a brand-new priority project. I again faced the prospect of thankless months of sixty- and seventy-hour weeks.

Even though Robert McNamara and his high-technology zealots were long gone from the Pentagon, his strategy of interdicting the Ho Chi Minh Trail through air power alone was still intact. And it was believed that the only effective way to implement this strategy was through a massive use of sensors. So the Defense Department had pulled out the stops, wallpapering American industry and academic research labs with "Requests for Proposal" for innovative sensor technology. The Army realized that new sensor systems might not be the most effective way to find the enemy on the Trail, but many senior officers also realized that electronic sensors could play a real role on the modern battlefield. More to the point, these sensors could help protect American firebases in Vietnam, keeping casualties down while we slowly withdrew our combat forces and shifted our resources to Vietnamization.

Jack Norton was a big, cigar-smoking paratrooper with extensive combat experience in three wars. His dramatic physical presence often obscured his lively intelligence and deep tactical expertise.

We set up shop at West Fort Hood, an isolated former Strategic Air Command base in the arid juniper scrub of central Texas. The Fort Hood reservation had been opened during World War II as a camp to train newly developed tank destroyer units, and had been an Armor post ever since. The area was supposedly too dry for cattle, but supported marginal goat ranching. To the GIs and Army brats stranded in this wasteland, the local people were known as "goat ropers."

I knew from my experience in the Pentagon that you could get more from a staff on a new project if you imposed a set of rigorous but not impossible deadlines and requirements, then subdivided the goals and deadlines into much smaller milestones. This process infused a sense of urgency that kept people working without overpowering them with impossibly complex tasks. Once we had our people together, I met with our chief scientist, a brilliant young physicist, Dr. Phil Dickenson. His job was to choose candidate technology for our initial field tests. My job was to take these gadgets and thoroughly test them using individual soldiers and units to make sure the equipment not only worked, but, just as important, that it was "soldier proof."

I told Phil Dickenson I wanted to begin extensive material and troop tests within a hundred days. He wasn't sure we could pull this off, but I told him to concentrate on the science side and I would organize the Army to support him. Jack Norton made it clear that the Army gave this project high priority.

In Indochina, the Air Force had finally deployed effective interdiction gunships along the Ho Chi Minh Trail. The AC-130 Spectre was the armed variant of the workhorse Hercules turboprop transport. The Spectre carried massive side-firing ordnance: 7.62mm mini-guns, 20mm Vulcan automatic cannons, and even a long-barreled 105mm howitzer that could knock out a truck or a tank day or night with precisely aimed high-explosive shells. But more sensitive ground sensors were needed to optimize the performance of these gunships. And such sensor technology would also be put to good use by our ground troops in Vietnam.

Our first priority was to develop the Surveillance, Target Acquisition, and Night Observation (STANO) system. Industrial and university labs had presented the Army with a bewildering selection of competitive technology. We had to quickly evaluate these offerings, build practical prototypes, then put them to field tests that would hopefully replicate conditions in Indochina.[11]

I learned that scientific researchers are inveterate tinkerers, many with perfectionist qualities. If left to themselves, they'd still be fine-tuning their gadgets ten years later. But the Army needed effective combat systems, not brilliant inventions. There was a natural horizontal division between scientists on the one hand and soldiers on the other. I saw that the best way to combat this was to establish four functionally oriented directorates, each of which would combine science staff and Army personnel. This system worked well, but we still faced the challenge of adapting new technology to practical hardware.

The problem of night surveillance, for example, could be approached from many directions. Radar had long been used to detect aircraft and ships. We now had exotic new radar technology, which tuned the search beam with computer-assisted electronics to such precision that a battlefield radar aboard a helicopter or at a ground site sweeping a valley could detect troops moving along a hidden trail many kilometers away. But the first such system we were offered was too cumbersome for practical use. So we set about reducing the radar size on a crash program basis.

Another approach to surveillance was through sophisticated infrared equipment. Warm-blooded creatures such as soldiers or water buffalo radiated heat. So did truck engines and field kitchens. With the right equipment this heat could be detected day or night, even through the forest canopy. One of our sections worked around the clock on this approach. They began with clumsy gear that worked well on a laboratory bench, but was too fragile for the field. Some of it required precisely calibrated optics chilled with liquid nitrogen to detect distant ambient heat. It was difficult to imagine such equipment operating on a jungle mountaintop in the central highlands. But once more, the process of assembling the right combination of scientific, technical, and military staff and focusing them on the objective paid dividends. Practical infrared target acquisition equipment was one of our first effective combat systems.

An interesting sidelight to testing this infrared equipment was the discovery of several illegal stills in the woods of east Texas, Arkansas, and Louisiana. Helicopters equipped with the new sensors picked up unusual heat sources in isolated forests. On close investigation, these turned out to be moonshine operations. I had my aviators plot the exact locations, then turned the information over to Fort Hood's provost marshal for transmission to federal authorities. But the word quickly came back from the judge advocate's office that we couldn't transmit this evidence to civilians. The posse comitatus laws prohibited the military from assisting in civil law enforcement. It would be years before American immigration and drug enforcement officials had access to the sensor technology we developed at considerable cost to the taxpayer.

Once the project was rolling, we encountered a shortage of skilled technical personnel, especially in applied physics and advanced electrical engineering. This was surprising because there was a deep employment slump just then in aerospace companies, which had been working full bore on the Apollo moon program and defense contracts from the Vietnam buildup. Phil Dickenson told me there was no actual shortage of skilled people, but they apparently preferred to live on unemployment compensation in northern California and Florida rather than come to the barrens of central Texas. But I knew there were plenty of young draftee enlisted men with advanced science degrees, even physics doctorates, who had finally exhausted their student deferments and were now serving as clerks and radio technicians. I put out a dragnet through the Army personnel bureaucracy and soon was able to staff our technical directorates with PFC scientists and engineers.

Within a few months, we had the 163rd Military Intelligence Battalion set up as one of the Army's first combat Electronic Warfare Intelligence units to field-test our new equipment. This battalion had several former Special Forces officers and NCOs with extensive Vietnam experience, some of whom had served on cross-border operations. Their practical, hands-on approach was invaluable as we modified our prototypes.

And practicality was certainly needed. One of our proposed sensors, for example, was a "people sniffer" based on the principle that the Mexican bedbug had the unusual ability of sensing his food source, *Homo sapiens,* as far as a kilometer away and crawling in that direction. This little biological homing device had promise, but eventually proved impossible to adapt to practical hardware. Another, similar biotechnology involved the photoplankton found in seawater, which produced brilliant phosphorescence when agitated by the passage of a large sea creature. The idea here was to somehow place sealed containers with these plankton along enemy infiltration routes; the plankton would phosphoresce when enemy vehicles or troops disturbed the container. Photo-sensitive detectors would activate an alarm circuit and broadcast a warning.

This kind of exotic technology delighted the scientists, but never went very far. However, the micro-miniaturized automated electronics required for automated sensor circuits advanced with amazing speed. By early spring of 1970, we had a variety of sensors ready for deployment along the Ho Chi Minh Trail and in South Vietnam. I traveled to Indochina to see firsthand how the equipment was being used. To my utter amazement, the rudimentary sonobuoy network along the Trail had grown inexorably in size and complexity. The Task Force Alpha monitoring center at Nakhon Phanom air base in Thailand, bordering the Laotian panhandle, was housed in a huge prefab steel building almost as big as MACV headquarters near Saigon. The windowless structure was air-conditioned to a frigid chill to protect the banks of big IBM computers from the dusty heat of Thailand. One wall was taken up with electronic visual displays reminiscent of the North American Air Defense Command Center in Colorado. As sensor nets along the Trail automatically responded, their coded signals were captured by orbiting C-130s, which were jammed with computers and radio-relay equipment. Sensors damaged in air attacks or knocked out by the enemy were replaced by SOG teams or airdropped. This approach to interdiction was still far inferior to ground operations, but, with the new gunships, the NVA was finally beginning to pay an unacceptable price to move men and matériel south.

Despite this impressive technological effort, the NVA supply line remained intact. As I studied the reports of Recon Teams at the local SOG detachment, I became more convinced than ever that our failure to attack the enemy on the ground in "neutral" Laos back in 1965 had doomed our overall military effort in Indochina. The North Vietnamese would be a threat to South Vietnam as long as they could move troops and supplies down the Trail through Laos.[12]

☆   ☆

I THEN returned to the combat zone in Vietnam to inspect one of Project MASSTER's new Fire Support Surveillance Bases (FSSB). One base I visited was on a hilltop in southern I Corps. It had a clear view across two scrub-jungle valleys that were known NVA attack routes from the mountains to the coast. The base was connected to sensor networks implanted along these enemy approach routes in the surrounding jungle. Strings of hidden seismic, acoustic, and magnetic sensors at precisely registered locations alerted base operators to NVA troop movements. ARVN intelligence personnel verified through the acoustic channel that the voices heard were enemy soldiers. The NVA columns could then be tracked with the new sensitive battlefield radar and positively identified even on the darkest monsoon night with our new infrared and light-amplification night-vision systems.

In the middle of the hot, drizzly night I spent at the base, I stood on a squat observation tower of shrapnel-pocked timbers, watching the young GI at his big Night Observation Device (NOD). This was a composite instrument we'd perfected at Fort Hood. The NOD combined high-powered Navy gunnery binoculars with electronic light-amplification equipment and a precise laser range finder. The sensor network had alerted us to suspected enemy movement, three kilometers to the northwest, up a dark valley. The young soldier patiently swung the NOD on its mount, adjusted several focus nobs, then turned toward me.

"We got 'em, sir," he whispered. "Take a look."

I crouched at the binocular eyepieces. There in chalky green detail, like phantom figures on a badly tuned television, I saw a fully equipped NVA platoon, hiking in a well-dispersed column along a trail through low cane grass. An enemy platoon leader was shadowed by his radio operator, and NVA machine gunners led their ammo bearers. The formation was straight out of a North Vietnamese field manual.

The GI slid in beside me and took over the instrument. With an unseen burst, the laser range finder pinpointed the enemy column. We now had the *exact* range and azimuth. The fire-control computer at a nearby American artillery base instantly solved the necessary trigonometry equation. The fire mission was on its way. This was a Fire-for-Effect, Variable-Time (VT) barrage. The sensor system and NOD allowed the artilleryman to fire without preliminary aiming rounds that always drove the enemy to cover.

"Watch this, sir," the soldier said, turning over the NOD to me.

I gazed at the enemy column, still trudging through the cane grass up the valley. Then the familiar freight-car rumble of howitzer rounds passed overhead. The NVA soldiers heard the incoming shells. They looked up in unison, then began diving for cover. But it was too late. The VT rounds exploded with overlapping incandescent orange fire. When the smoke cleared, the ground was littered with enemy dead. Five minutes later, our observation helicopter reported no NVA survivors. Forty enemy troops had been killed without risking a single American life. I had the grim satisfaction of knowing our work at Fort Hood was paying off on the battlefield.[13]

☆   ☆

UNFORTUNATELY, managing such technology in a combat zone was too complex for our ARVN allies. As I learned from friends at MACV, Vietnamization—the process of expanding and upgrading the ARVN so that they could take over the fight as American troops progressively withdrew—was making slow, uneven progress at best. Advanced American equipment and adequate supplies of munitions were finally available to the new ARVN units. And the new crop of American advisers to these units included savvy young professional officers and NCOs with valuable experience fighting— and defeating—the NVA. As I flew back to the States, however, I knew American combat units would be needed in Vietnam for at least two more years. And I had serious doubts that the country had the political or moral will to sustain this effort.

☆   ☆

ONE brutal incident more than any other in the long war helped sour the American public on Vietnam. The event became known as the My Lai massacre. On March 16, 1968, a battalion-size task force of the Army's Americal Division conducted a sweep through the sprawling coastal village of Son My, searching for the 48th Vietcong Local Force Battalion.

Company C, 1st Battalion, 20th Infantry, was typical of the brigade, poorly trained draftee soldiers led by inexperienced nonprofessional officers. The company commander was Captain Ernest L. Medina, a former sergeant in his early thirties, who had been among the thousands of NCOs pushed through training courses and commissioned following the decision to deploy units to Vietnam without a reserve call-up or extension of terms of service.

The commander of his 1st Platoon, Second Lieutenant William L. Calley, was almost a parody of the weak, unqualified junior officer. Calley had to be recycled through Officer Candidate School because of ineptitude. The fact that he commanded a rifle platoon of the U.S. Army in 1968 was tragic proof that our officer corps had become seriously debased, just as General Johnson and I had feared in July 1965.[14]

Lieutenant Colonel Frank Barker, the task force commander, had told his company commanders that most of the population of Son My village were either "VC or VC sympathizers."[15]

Calley's platoon of approximately thirty men led the sweep through the hamlet designated My Lai 4 on the maps and known as "Pinkville" to the troops. His men immediately opened fire on old men, women, and children. Thatched huts were set ablaze, pigs and water buffalo slaughtered. The villagers not immediately killed were rounded up into groups, taken to ditches on the edge of the hamlet, and machine-gunned. When one of the platoon machine gunners refused to shoot, Calley seized the weapon and fired into a crowd of defenseless women and children himself. At least 400 Vietnamese civilians, almost all old men, women, and children, had been murdered.[16]

In my opinion, the murders at My Lai were worse than the SS slaughter at Oradour-sur-Glane. Such bestiality was to be expected from thoroughly indoctrinated Nazi troops, who committed hundreds of similar massacres in Eastern Europe and the Balkans. But, having served in three wars with American infantrymen, I knew the murder of unarmed women and children, no matter how sympathetic they might have been to the enemy, was a gross aberration. In World War II and in Korea I'd seen GIs risk their lives to spare civilians. And in Vietnam most American units often took avoidable casualties by adhering to strict rules of engagement. But the stigma of My Lai grew to unjustly taint the record of the entire American Army in Vietnam. My Lai became a metaphor for the supposed uncontrolled brutality of America's military.[17]

☆   ☆

THE shame of the My Lai massacre was only one factor eroding Army morale as the Vietnam War dragged on with little serious prospect for victory. By mid-1970, the radical counterculture and the mainstream anti-war movement had coalesced to foster a pervasive national anti-military mood. Soldiers on passes were taunted and heckled by their peers. The retention rate of skilled personnel was at an all-time low. I was chief of staff of a much expanded Project MASSTER now, and decided to do what I could to improve the troops' confidence and spirits by instilling pride. From my experience with the 16th Infantry in Germany, I knew sport parachuting brought the kind of military esprit de corps I wanted to see in the men.

But there was a problem. An earlier attempt to set up a sport parachuting club at Fort Hood was a disaster. The clubhouse, replete with bar, had been on the main post, right next to the dependents' Teen Club. The mix of skydivers, beer, and teenage girls meant trouble. Within a few months, several girls were pregnant and the club was shut down by the MPs. However, Fort Hood was a sprawling post, with plenty of room for a clubhouse and competitive drop zone away from the built-up areas.

One day that spring I called in Major Jim Hanke, operations officer for the 163rd Military Intelligence Battalion. Hanke was a former Special Forces officer who had served on Project Delta, the original cross-border Recon Teams in Laos that had evolved into SOG's Prairie Fire. He was a consummate parachutist, having trained one of the Green Berets' first high altitude–low opening (HALO) Airborne detachments.

"Hanke," I told him, "this post needs a skydiving club, and you're going to start it."

Like many Green Berets with extensive combat experience, Hanke thought for himself and was not a ticket-punching yes-man. "Sir," he said, considering my order, "I'll need authorization for a building, an FAA certification . . ."

"Just get the job done," I told him. Special Forces officers were known for their innovative skills.

"What kind of timing did you have in mind, sir?"

"Hanke," I said, in my best gruff-general manner, "that club *will* be operational in thirty days."

On receiving such instructions from a brigadier, most majors would salute smartly and depart. Not Hanke.

"Yes, sir," he replied. "I only have one condition."

"Condition?"

"Yes, sir," he continued. "The club will have its first jump within thirty days." He suppressed a grin. "And you will be the first club member to jump."

He had me there. And he also had a valid point. With a general officer involved in the project, Hanke could cut through the bureaucratic tangle. I nodded, trying hard not to smile myself. "Hanke, get the hell out of here."

He snapped off a crisp salute and was gone.

On a warm spring Sunday twenty-six days later, I sat in the open door of a Huey 4,500 feet above the mesquite and juniper of our new drop zone. Hanke, the first jumpmaster of the Fort Hood Sport Parachute Club, crouched beside me.

"Go!" he shouted above the thump of the rotors.

I slid forward and dropped into the dazzling sunlight, arched, then reached a stable position in the hot wind, falling parallel to the ground. I opened a little above 2,500 feet to get a nice ride down and managed to pull off a respectable landing within the cleared sandy oval of the drop zone.

By that fall, club membership had grown to several hundred. Fort Hood skydivers now jumped at almost every parade and local sporting event, often spiraling down, trailing red, white, and blue smoke, to land on the fifty-yard line at football stadiums. The American military in general might not have been held in very high esteem in some parts of Texas at that time, but our skydivers were a popular act in great demand.

☆   ☆

WE had a major test of Project MASSTER technology scheduled at Fort Hood for early 1971, using the Air Cavalry Combat Brigade's helicopters as platforms for a variety of our new STANO devices. As I laid down the requirements for this exercise, I encountered a familiar, subtle resistance from the Army aviators involved. Helicopter men had a natural reluctance to taking orders from non-helicopter pilots. For this reason, officers like Jack Norton were all helicopter-qualified. I realized that my future in the Army would probably involve Air Mobile troops and without being a qualified helicopter pilot, I would be the equivalent of a "straight-leg" to the Airborne.

So I bit the bullet and volunteered for helicopter flight school that fall. I was accepted into a special general officers' flight course offered at the Army Aviation School at Fort Rucker, Alabama. The only other student in my section was Major General Edward M. "Flywheel" Flanagan, Jr., the commander of the John F. Kennedy Special Warfare Center at Fort Bragg. I'd known Fly Flanagan since Korea, where he was the artillery commander of the 187th Airborne Regimental Combat Team. In Vietnam, he was the senior training adviser to the ARVN. Like me, Flanagan had decided the only way to gain the respect of the Air Mobile people was to become a helicopter pilot himself.

Going back to school at age fifty is never easy. Going to helicopter ground and flight school at that age is a lesson in humility and diligence. I'd had some flying experience in light civilian aircraft during World War II. But learning how to fly a Piper Cub and UH-1 Huey helicopter was an entirely different matter.

A fixed-wing aircraft, be it a single-engine Cessna or a Boeing jet, was designed for lift; left to itself it will glide. Fixed-wing planes have inherent aerodynamic stability; it is often said that they *want* to fly. Helicopters, on the other hand, are rotary-wing. They have as much inherent lift as a cinder block. There also is absolutely nothing inherently stable in their design. The pilot has to force a helicopter to fly. Left to itself, even for a moment, it will become unstable and crash.

Flying a light plane doesn't require much more hand-eye coordination than driving a car. You set the throttle and propeller pitch, then move the control yoke with your hands and rudder pedals with your feet. Flying a helicopter requires simultaneously manipulating two hand controls—one of which has two functions—as well as foot pedals. The cyclic control stick in your right hand tilts the rotor disk, which governs flight direction. The collective throttle, rotor-pitch control in your left hand governs engine rpm and airspeed. Your feet control movements of the tail rotor, which acts like a rudder. Each control "input" has to be smoothly integrated with the others. If not, the helicopter becomes unstable, bucking and twisting dangerously.

Someone once said that flying a helicopter was much harder than simultaneously patting your head and rubbing your belly. After four weeks of ground school and a few days in the right-hand seat of a Huey cockpit, I learned that flying a helicopter actually wasn't harder than the head-patting, belly-rubbing exercise—providing you could do it while riding a unicycle on a tightwire.

Fly Flanagan and I also learned that there was a good reason most Army helicopter pilot trainees were nineteen- and twenty-year-old warrant officers. Manual and visual dexterity are supposedly optimal at that age. I can attest they are not at age fifty.[18]

But we persevered.

The week before Christmas, 1970, I had amassed a total of sixty-seven hours of flight time in Hueys. And to my instructors' collective relief, I had survived a required solo flight. Back at Fort Hood, my instruction continued on a part-time basis. The 55th Aviation Battalion (Combat) was full of experienced Vietnam veteran gunship, troop carrier ("slick"), and medevac pilots. The battalion assigned me a young chief warrant officer with two Vietnam tours behind him. With his guidance, I learned to actually *fly* the Huey.

From my instructor's point of view, Fort Hood's fine, dry weather was a handicap. He wanted low overcast and thunderstorms, which would offer more realistic conditions. So on many of our flights we took off from Fort Hood and flew toward bad weather up around Dallas or down toward the Gulf. Once in the clouds and turbulence, he would direct me along a complex flight plan. This required absolute, white-knuckle concentration. Losing visual orientation—vertigo—was every helicopter pilot's nightmare. One minute you could be flying along straight and level, the next you might be slipping upside down into fatal instability.

"Sir," my instructor repeated on every flight, "you can't rely on instinct. You've got to learn to trust those dials because, in the soup, they're all you've got."

In mid-April 1971, I was able to pin on my Army Aviator's wings. To me they were as hard earned as any combat decoration.

☆   ☆

IN THE summer of 1971, the Army was preparing to leave Indochina, and the White House ordered the Defense Department to examine the shape of the post-Vietnam military.

Three major cross-border ground operations (two in Cambodia and one on the Laotian panhandle) had battered enemy sanctuaries. The NVA, however, had quickly recouped and reinforced their logistical bases in Laos, actually moving Soviet SAM missiles down the Trail to discourage further ARVN spoiling attacks.[19] But the tactic wasn't even necessary. The high casualty rate and the political cost of these "invasions" precluded similar operations. The U.S. Congress went so far as to pass legislation forbidding American ground forces from fighting in Cambodia or Laos.[20] So we were locked into Vietnamization as our sole strategy.

The repercussions of this for the Army meant a drastically smaller peacetime service within eighteen months. The White House also envisioned the new military as an all-volunteer force, a political expedient to disarm the controversial issue of the draft before the 1972 election.[21]

I became enmeshed in this process when I was ordered to the Pentagon to become the Director for Plans, Studies, and Budget in the Office of the Army's Deputy Chief of Staff for Personnel (DCSPER). My boss was Lieutenant General Walter T. "Dutch" Kerwin, who'd been my last housemate in Saigon.

Dutch Kerwin gave me a familiar task: organizing yet another new Army staff to meet an unusual challenge. The Vietnam emergency had come along just as the Army was hoping to rationalize its personnel system so that recruitment and training of regular NCOs and officers could be tailored to fit planned future needs, as detailed in our Force Development Plan. Now that the worst of the emergency was behind us, General Kerwin wanted me to develop a rational plan that would match our skilled manpower pool with the needs of a leaner—and hopefully meaner—volunteer Army.

I enjoyed the challenge. But I was not sure a volunteer Army would work. At several meetings with Generals Kerwin and Westmoreland I laid out my apprehensions in detail. I knew the Army of the future would need skilled technicians, capable of manning computerized battlefield equipment. But given the all-pervasive anti-military mood among young people, as well as the robust and prosperous civilian economy, I was afraid the Army would not be able to attract volunteers with the education level and intelligence of our present draftees. The draftee scientists I had used so effectively at Project MASSTER were fresh in my mind. I warned that the Army, which couldn't offer as much attractive technical training as the Air Force or the Navy, would be a job of last resort.

Westmoreland listened patiently to my arguments, then replied. "Well, Jack," he said, "I raised these same issues with the President. He told me, 'Westy, you're either going to have an all-volunteer Army or no Army at all.' "

The message couldn't have been any clearer.[22]

☆   ☆

BEFORE I had a chance to influence the shape of the officer corps of this new Army, I was shifted to yet another assignment.

The drug problem in the military, particulary among our troops in Vietnam, had reached crisis proportions.[23] Cheap, very pure heroin was flooding South Vietnam, and spilling over to our bases in Thailand and the Philippines. Increasing numbers of young servicemen in Indochina were becoming addicted to heroin and running afoul of the military justice system. And if they weren't picked up in Asia, some of these young men were being discharged back in the States with heroin habits.

The White House decided that major action was required. Whereas drug use had traditionally been a matter for military justice authorities, with each service making its own policy, President Nixon now required the Defense Department to develop a single comprehensive policy to fight drug and alcohol abuse throughout the military on a global basis. Defense Secretary Mel Laird created the position of Deputy Assistant Secretary of Defense (Drug and Alcohol Abuse) in the Office of the Assistant Secretary of Defense (Health and Environment). The new man would be responsible for creating and implementing the military's drug-abuse policy.

General Westmoreland and the other service chiefs were obliged to send the names of two general or flag-rank officers to Dr. Richard S. Wilbur, the Assistant Secretary for Health and Environment. My name was one of the Army's two, the other being Brigadier General Bob Gard, a specialist in drug-abuse prevention. Westy told me Gard was the prime candidate for the job and that I probably would be able to continue with my work for the DCSPER. Things didn't work out that way. In September, I was introduced to the public at a Pentagon press conference as the new Deputy Assistant Secretary of Defense (Drug and Alcohol Abuse). Since the job title was a mouthful that didn't easily compress to a Pentagonese acronym, I became known as the general in charge of "Drugs and Drunks."

My new assignment was in the Pentagon's inner sanctum, the Office of the Secretary of Defense (OSD). Our section was on the E-ring, on the south side of the building. We even had a window. But all I could see were the concrete walls and windows of the D-ring. Dr. Richard Wilbur was a talented physician and skilled administrator. He was similar in age to McNamara's whiz kids, but Dick Wilbur had considerable practical experience as opposed to academic expertise. A grandson of the founder of the Stanford Medical School, Wilbur had been a Navy flight surgeon and had run the California State Medical Society before Nixon brought him to Washington. He made it clear from the outset he wanted a new drug policy that would be both humane and conducive to restoring military discipline.

As I found out, combining humane treatment and discipline was not easy.

Before I could develop a new policy, I had to have a clear idea of the scope and nature of the drug problem. I had some definite ideas about alcohol abuse and treatment in the armed services, but for the moment the heroin situation took priority.

A group of Army generals had just returned from Indochina after carefully analyzing the military drug problem there. Heroin as pure as 95 percent was flowing from the Golden Triangle region of the Burma-China border, much of it under the control of the Communist Chinese. This heroin was very effectively marketed in South Vietnam, where local dealers cultivated combat GIs on in-country R&R and soldiers in the sprawling base areas. The heroin was sold in small plastic vials containing about a gram of white powder. At one dollar a vial, the drug was cheaper than black-market stateside beer in the bars and massage parlors around our bases.

The unusual purity of the heroin made it easy to use. In the States, heroin was cut many times over with powdered milk or sugar and had to be injected by needle to produce a high. GIs in Vietnam could lace a cigarette or a marijuana joint with heroin or simply snort the drug. Because they did not have to use needles, drug overdoses were not a problem. But widespread use certainly was.

I was able to quickly dispel one of the pervasive myths about GI heroin use, a myth being advanced by the anti-war left. They charged that our GIs were driven to use heroin by the brutal nature of their service in Vietnam, where, supposedly, massacres like that in My Lai were commonplace. A careful survey of GI drug users in the Far East, however, revealed that 91 percent of the men on heroin had used other drugs, usually marijuana and hallucinogens, before they were old enough to enter the service. They were now using heroin because of its cheap price and ready availability. One GI undergoing treatment wrote on his survey questionnaire: "At that price, I couldn't afford *not* to use it."

An initial drug-testing survey in Vietnam using random urinalysis as well as the mandatory pre-departure drug urinalysis revealed some fascinating data. There were proportionally far fewer men testing positive for heroin on their departure dates than among similar groups of GIs with most of their tours still to serve. This could only mean one thing: that men who had been "addicted" to heroin for many months had somehow been able to kick the habit in order to come up clean to climb on board the Freedom Bird for home.

I kept this fact in mind as I toured America's leading civilian and Veterans Administration drug treatment centers and met with our nationally recognized addiction experts. In Atlanta, I conferred with Dr. Peter Bourne, a psychiatrist who was firmly convinced that heroin addiction was an unsolvable medical problem. His approach certainly did not have much to offer the military. Dr. Bourne mentioned that he sometimes had his clients substitute marijuana for heroin.

"General," the Doctor told me gravely, "if we can just get these people off heroin and back onto marijuana, that's all we can ask for."

(A few years later, I wasn't surprised to learn that Dr. Bourne, an official in the Carter White House, had been disciplined for writing illegal prescriptions for his colleagues.)

A treatment center I visited in New York City was run by a tougher-minded psychiatrist, Dr. Judianne Densen-Gerber, wife of the Manhattan coroner. She was a large, dynamic woman with positive views. Her philosophy was the opposite of Dr. Bourne's. She felt drug addiction was nurtured by a permissive, unstructured environment. Many young people, she said, had been encouraged to seek undisciplined gratification. They had low self-esteem, and drugs or alcohol gave them an excuse for dropping out of competitive society.

"You've got a real advantage in the military, General Singlaub," she told me. "In the armed services you can structure environment and insist on discipline. We can't do it as well in civil life."

But she certainly did better than Dr. Bourne and the others who followed his permissive approach. In treatment programs like his, methadone was readily available and its dosage was poorly controlled. Dr. Densen-Gerber's program administered methadone sparingly, under tight control, and, most important, as a device to instill structure and discipline in the addict's life.

Before proposing the Pentagon's new drug policy, I conferred closely with Dr. Jerome Jaffe in the White House. He was the President's Special Action Officer for Drug Abuse Prevention. Jaffe was a hard-working, dedicated professional, an expert on heroin addiction, who had established effective treatment programs in Chicago. He encouraged my effort to create a world-wide Defense Department drug-testing and treatment program.

With this high-level support, we got down to work on a practical policy. The first priority was a more effective testing and treatment program in Vietnam. Up to that point, the mandatory pre-departure urinalysis had been unevenly conducted, and men testing positive were treated arbitrarily. Some were court-martialed, while others were given a pep talk and sent home. A few were offered effective treatment. We first worked with civilian laboratories to improve the accuracy and speed of our field test units. Next, the pre-departure urinalysis was standardized in Vietnam, eliminating loopholes that had allowed some men to evade the system.

In Saigon, I conferred with an energetic young Regular Army psychiatrist, a Medical Corps lieutenant colonel. He was convinced that withdrawal from heroin addiction was more a psychological problem than a physical ordeal. To test his theory, the doctor proposed an unorthodox experiment, which, given the exigencies of the heroin problem in Vietnam, I approved.

We met with the staff of the Cam Rahn Bay drug treatment center to prepare them for this experiment. Patients testing positive for heroin would be carefully coached through their detoxification. All the doctors, nurses, and medical orderlies involved were to be warm and supportive—above all, positive in their attitude toward heroin withdrawal. The GIs were counseled that kicking a Vietnamese heroin habit was not difficult because the drug was not adulterated with "impurities," as was stateside heroin. The overall mood of the Center was upbeat, and patients were encouraged to talk about their drug-free futures in America.

With this system in place, the average patient at Cam Rahn Bay spent less than a month at the Center. And very few needed medications to ease their withdrawal.

We used a different process at the other drug treatment center located in the military stockade compound at Long Binh, a grim place known to GIs as the "LBJ," the Long Binh Jail. There, the staff allowed all the usual rumors about the nightmare of heroin withdrawal to circulate through the ward. Some men were so convinced they would experience harsh withdrawal symptoms that they actually writhed on the floor of the ward.

The staff at the LBJ center now completed our two-part experiment. They divided their patients into three groups, and informed them they would be given one of three effective anti-withdrawal treatments. The first group was treated with Valium during a three-week period. At the end of treatment, 70 percent reported the drug had eased their withdrawal. The second group was given a stronger tranquilizer. After three weeks, 80 percent reported they had needed the medication during their withdrawal. The third group was administered intramuscular injections of distilled water, which, although the needle certainly looked impressive and the injections were painful, had no direct medical effect. A startling 90 percent of this group reported that they definitely could not have survived withdrawal without the placebo "medication."

At one of the urinalysis centers in Saigon, a humorist had tacked up the following sign on the latrine door: "The Pee House of the August Moon."

☆   ☆

ONCE I was satisfied that the testing and treatment program in Vietnam was up and running, I turned my efforts to the education side of the drug problem. I was shocked to discover that most of the drug users in the service had begun experimenting *before* high school. Clearly we had a long way to go. After visiting several innovative drug education programs at schools around the country, I got permission to begin similar programs in all Department of Defense schools, both in the States and overseas. The key, I learned at an especially effective anti-drug school program in Phoenix called "Dope Stop," was to use older students, not authority figures like policemen or teachers, as role models to go into the lower grades and work with the younger kids. And I also discovered that scare tactics and abstract medical or psychological theory had little impact on these kids. They needed to learn practical techniques for combating the relentless peer pressure toward drug use.[24]

In Vietnam, all members of the service, from four-star general to private, had to be tested before departing the country. By July 1, 1972, we were ready to implement a universal drug-testing and treatment policy throughout the armed services. Following the lead of both Dr. Wilbur and Dr. Jaffe, I stressed to my staff and to the chiefs of the four services and their senior medical officers that we needed a policy that was humane and that fostered military discipline. All the services were not equally convinced; some traditional Marine Corps generals and Navy admirals, for example, still felt the problem should be handled as a criminal matter. We made sure that they understood our approach: Criminal activity by a drug user, such as drug dealing or theft, would still be a court-martial offense. But simple drug use per se would lead to treatment, not a court-martial.

The Pentagon's new drug policy relied on servicewide random, mandatory, carefully controlled drug testing by urinalysis. Subjects were selected by a lottery method based on their Social Security number. Initially, any member of the armed services was subject to random testing. Later we concentrated our testing, education, and treatment on younger people where the drug problem was most acute. Anyone testing positive was placed in a treatment program. If drug use was discovered at the end of a man's term of service, he received a thirty-day detoxification and treatment program prior to release. If he needed more time, he was transferred to a similar program administered by the Veterans Administration.[25]

In a break with previous policy, drug use would not be automatic grounds for separation from the service with a bad-conduct discharge. Moreover, successful completion of drug treatment would be considered a medical matter, which would not reflect on a regular serviceman's career.[26]

Over the next three years, almost 5,300,000 members of the armed services were screened for drug use by random urinalysis or pre-departure tests from Southeast Asia. Seventy thousand of them tested positive for drugs, mainly heroin. They were all put into treatment, and 62,000 former drug users were returned to duty. Of the remainder who were discharged, 7,000 continued treatment at VA facilities. In July 1974, the Defense Department offered this forecast for the drug problem in the armed services: "Long-range view regarding drug and alcohol abuse is encouraging. Armed services may never be totally free of substance abuse, but the rate of abuse should continue to decline below that of similar age groups in civilian sector."[27]

Not a single one of those servicemen testing positive was charged with a criminal offense stemming solely from his drug use. This is a record I am very proud of.

During the same period, almost 27,000 service members were treated for alcohol abuse. Unfortunately, the traditional prejudices against alcoholics, even those in successful recovery, often prevailed. In one particular fight I took all the way up to Dr. Jaffe's office in the White House, a recovering alcoholic Air Force pilot was still denied his return to flight status. This wrongheaded approach was dangerous. By definition, pilots wanted to fly, but they were also human, and as a group were equally vulnerable to alcoholism as the rest of humankind. If a man faced permanent grounding for seeking alcoholism treatment, his career was jeopardized. He would therefore avoid treatment. I'm happy to say that our support of the particular Air Force colonel in question got him back on flight status and helped put the Air Force policy on the right track.

Dr. Wilbur and I traveled around the world several times on this program visiting service facilities. He always required that no tobacco be used at meetings or alcoholic drinks be consumed at working lunches. But at one luncheon in the Philippines hosted by an admiral, the white-clad mess stewards passed trays of frosty Bloody Marys. The first man to drink one was our admiral host, his hand actually shaking until he swallowed the vodka. This confirmed a suspicion I'd long held. Uncontrollable drinking among some senior officers was just as dangerous a problem as heroin use among bored and homesick GIs in Danang or Bienhoa. The incident in the Philippines spurred Dr. Wilbur to establish a confidential alcohol abuse counseling and treatment program for flag rank and general officers. In this new program a number of senior officers were successfully treated; both their health and their careers remained intact.

☆   ☆

IN THE summer of 1972, I was promoted to major general. The year before I received the Distinguished Service Medal for my work with MASSTER and a second oak-leaf cluster to my Legion of Merit for my efforts on the new drug policy. I certainly had never tried to punch the right tickets for my career advancement; rather, as I had tried to convince those young lieutenants in Germany, taking the hard, often unrewarding jobs was the best way for an officer to achieve success. But I knew the Army was in for troubled times in the immediate future. America was about to lose its first war.

President Nixon had shown real moral courage in December 1972 by finally using America's military force effectively to convince the North Vietnamese we were serious. The port of Haiphong was mined and B-52 bombers pounded military targets and lines of communication in and around Hanoi, day and night, for eleven days.[28] Although few liberals would admit it, this action finally convinced the Communist government to negotiate seriously at the Paris Peace Talks.[29] A cease-fire agreement was reached and the Hanoi government began releasing American and South Vietnamese prisoners of war.

Although the resulting cease-fire agreement allowed the Americans to withdraw the last of their troops with a semblance of honor intact, the future of South Vietnam depended to a large degree on the *honor* of the Com-

munists. For example, the cease-fire was overseen by an International Commission of Control and Supervision (ICCS) that included a military
delegation from Communist Hungary. This was obviously placing a fox in
a henhouse. Within a year, American intelligence discovered that Hungarian
ICCS commissioners were conducting detailed military reconnaissance for
the NVA.[30] This treachery did not surprise me. Having seen Communists
at work in Asia for almost forty years, I was not sanguine about the future.
To me, the conflict had entered an obvious "Fight-Talk, Talk-Fight" phase
similar to that I'd seen both in Manchuria in the 1940s and in Korea in 1953.
Hanoi had absolutely no intention of ending its aggression.

What was amazing was the overall public gullibility, tinged with apathy.
American troops were home from Vietnam and people wanted to believe
the war was won. Somehow, those in Congress and the administration who
should have known better were willing to describe the cease-fire as a victory.
Again, they were ignoring the true nature of the North Vietnamese. Their
massive Easter offensive of 1972, for example, had been a blatant example
of duplicity. While their diplomats earnestly negotiated in Paris, the North
Vietnamese high command unleashed a major, coordinated offensive, committing over 120,000 NVA regulars in a three-prong operation planned to
overwhelm I Corps, cut the central highlands, and capture Saigon itself. The
NVA was equipped with Soviet tanks, artillery, rockets, and, most ominously, with shoulder-fired anti-aircraft missiles.[31] They were successful in
the northern provinces of South Vietnam, capturing and holding the capital
of Quangtri Province for four months. Although the NVA suffered horrible
casualties (50,000 dead), they pressed their conventional ground assault for
several months.[32]

The only thing that stopped them was U.S. air power. American B-52s,
Air Force and Navy tactical air support, and the superb use of our new AC-
130 Spectre gunships finally tipped the balance in the ARVN's favor. In
several desperate night actions, U.S. Army helicopter gunships equipped
with new night-vision equipment broke up NVA tank attacks. I was proud
that STANO technology developed in Project MASSTER made this Army
air support more effective.

To me the relevance of the 1972 Easter offensive for the 1973 cease-fire
was obvious. Unless the United States was prepared to support the ARVN
indefinitely with air power, South Vietnam would ultimately fall to the
Communists.

☆   ☆

In February 1973, I was at Clark Air Force Base in the Philippines, where
I visited the first American POWs flown out of Hanoi. These were the "old
hands," some of whom had been in captivity for eight years. Most had been

savagely tortured, not for military information, but in order to extract propaganda messages. Some had broken physically, but all had kept their spirits
intact. As I went from ward to ward chatting with these scarred, gaunt men,
each group had the same question: Is Jane Fonda in jail? Several of the
men who had been subjected to inhuman torture for years were badly beaten
for refusing to appear with Fonda and her anti-war delegation in Hanoi, the
same visit during which she was photographed gleefully seated at an NVA
anti-aircraft gun. The POWs had gone so far as to draft formal complaints
against her for treasonable action. But they were convinced by civilian
debriefing teams at Clark to give up their grievances.[33]

Like the rest of the military, these POWs were learning that America's
traditional standards of honor and integrity had been eroded almost beyond
recognition.

Meanwhile, America had a demoralized, unjustly vilified Army to rebuild.
In May 1973, I learned I would have a major role in this rebuilding. My old
commanding officer from Korea, Dick Stilwell, now a three-star general in
command of the Sixth Army, with headquarters at the historic Presidio in
San Francisco, requested me to take command of the U.S. Army's new
Readiness Region VIII.

Of America's armed services, the Army had been most affected by the
long war in Vietnam. Beyond combat casualties, hundreds of thousands of
career officers and NCOs had quit. Draftees rarely reenlisted during this
period. Overall competence and experience were at a low ebb. Traditionally,
the reserve component—Army Reserve and National Guard—had served
with distinction by providing a reservoir of skills and experience the active-
duty force could call on in time of war. But the ill-fated decision to keep
the reserves out of Vietnam meant that many Army Reserve and National
Guard units had become havens for men evading combat and were filled
with *soldiers* who proved to be no better than draft dodgers.

In short, the Army's overall readiness state, the ability to fight and win
a war, had not been so low since the depression of the 1930s. And it would
be my job to help correct this situation.

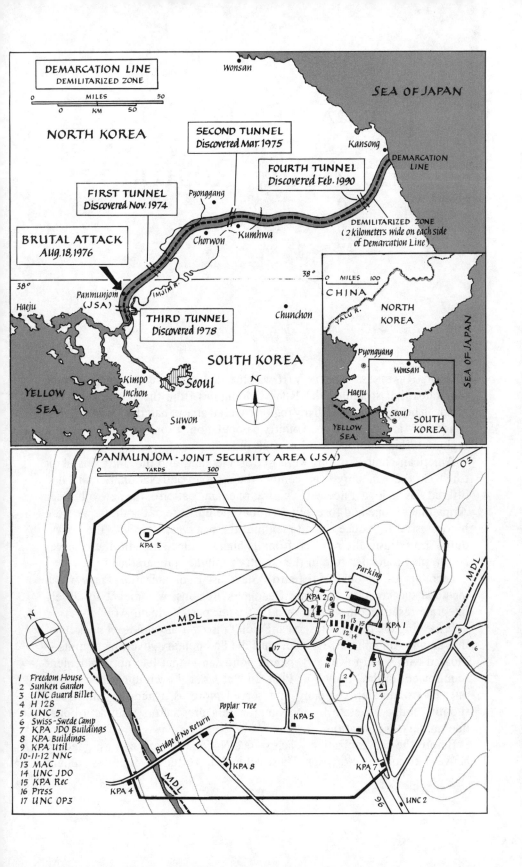

DEMARCATION LINE
DEMILITARIZED ZONE

MILES 50
KM 50

NORTH KOREA

Wonsan

SEA OF JAPAN

SECOND TUNNEL
Discovered Mar. 1975

Kansong

DEMARCATION
LINE

FOURTH TUNNEL
Discovered Feb. 1990

FIRST TUNNEL
Discovered Nov. 1974

Pyonggang

DEMILITARIZED ZONE
(2 kilometers wide on each side
of Demarcation Line)

BRUTAL ATTACK
Aug. 18, 1976

Chorwon   Kumhwa

38°

38°

Panmunjom
(JSA)

IMJIN R.

MILES 100

CHINA

YALU R.

NORTH
KOREA

Haeju

Chunchon

THIRD TUNNEL
Discovered 1978

SOUTH KOREA

N

Pyongyang

Wonsan

SEA OF JAPAN

Kimpo
Inchon

Seoul

Haeju

YELLOW
SEA

Suwon

Seoul

SOUTH
KOREA

YELLOW
SEA

PANMUNJOM - JOINT SECURITY AREA (JSA)

YARDS   300

O3

KPA 3

MDL

Parking

KPA 2

7

KPA 1

8   9   11 13 15
10 12 14

MDL

5

6

N

17

1

16

3

2

4

1   Freedom House
2   Sunken Garden
3   UNC Guard Billet
4   H 128
5   UNC 5
6   Swiss-Swede Camp
7   KPA JDO Buildings
8   KPA Buildings
9   KPA Util
10-11-12 NNC
13 MAC
14 UNC JDO
15 KPA Rec
16 Press
17 UNC OP3

Poplar Tree

KPA 5

Bridge of No Return

MDL

KPA 8

KPA 4

MDL

96

KPA 7

UNC 2

CHAPTER TWELVE
The Army Regroups
1973–1976

☆   ☆

Aʀᴍʏ Rᴇᴀᴅɪɴᴇss Rᴇɢɪᴏɴ VIII was the largest in the country, covering ten states that straddled the Rocky Mountains from the Canadian to the Mexican borders. Although my region covered almost half the United States, it had only a fraction of the country's population. I told my staff we had a region of "high altitude and low multitude."

American combat troops were out of Vietnam, and the draft was abolished. So the sanctuary from combat the reserves and National Guard had offered was no longer needed. This was one ramification of the new volunteer Army that no one had foreseen. Without the pressure of the draft, we were hard pressed to induce skilled men into the reserves. Yet, with the active-duty Army drastically reduced from its high wartime strength, the reserves had to play a greater role in the country's military preparedness.[1]

Secretary of Defense Mel Laird's Steadfast Reorganization Plan, which included the creation of Army Readiness Regions, was meant to closely integrate reserve components into the leaner post-Vietnam Army.

Inspecting the region's reserves, I didn't discover any hold-out pockets of the famous Amphibious Brigade, but I did find military government units— bloated with small-town lawyers and politicians—that had no deployment requirement in the Army War Plan. In Nebraska, I even unearthed a prisoner-of-war holding company that served more as a hunting and skeet-shooting lodge for state troopers and county prosecutors than as a bona-fide military organization.

Before the reorganization, each state's National Guard was assigned an active-duty colonel as adviser. These colonels too often saw their assignment as "OJR," on-the-job retirement. As my deputy, Colonel Arch Carpenter quipped, paraphrasing Churchill: "Never in the history of human conflict have so few been advised by so many." One of the first jobs was to convince these dignified old colonels that they were still on active duty and that they now had a regular army major general very interested in their performance.

Once I had pruned the deadwood among the advisers, I set about cutting the unnecessary reserve units. There were howls of protest from many a small-town courthouse. And no wonder: A county prosecutor in the Dakotas could drift along for years as a reservist, attending annual summer camp and slowly accruing rank. These gentlemen usually retired as full colonels after twenty-five years of "duty," and enjoyed a pension, plus full veterans' benefits.

We implemented the Army's new Command Tenure Limitation Program that broke the senior-officer promotion logjam in the reserves. There were reserve generals who had led Army readiness commands or brigades for fifteen years. This reminded me of the Spanish army. After "finding a home" in the Army, these venerable gentlemen stubbornly refused to just fade away as old soldiers were supposed to do. Henceforth, a senior command in the reserves had a fixed tenure of three years. To complete this process, I chaired the Sixth Army's promotion boards, at which, for the first time, the Army, not local cronies, selected bright younger officers for senior rank.

I had just completed the paperwork abolishing the POW company in Nebraska when General Creighton Abrams, now Army Chief of Staff, visited my Denver headquarters. "Are you sure about this POW outfit, Jack?" he asked, cocking his eye above his ubiquitous cigar. "It could attract a lot of recruits."

"Sir?" I knew he was setting me up for a ribbing.

"Damn right, Jack," he continued. "You've been overseas too long. Don't you watch 'Hogan's Heroes'?"

I had to admit that that was one TV show I normally avoided.

"Well, General," Abrams admonished, seemingly every bit the stern chief, "you've got to stay in touch with the young people. They're the future of the Army."

It's amusing to recall that hair length was a real recruitment obstacle at that time. The generation gap was so wide that most young men were under peer pressure to wear their hair longer than military regulations permitted. Some commanders—veterans of World War II—insisted on truly short "STRAC" hair. In so doing, they were forcing good men from the ranks. The hair crisis in some parts of the country had even reached the point where reservists had purchased expensive wigs. These came in two types: long or short. The long-haired wig permitted a reservist with short hair to satisfy the requirements of a demanding unit commander on weekend drill and the pressure of his peers during the week. More ingenious, the short-haired wig was worn over tucked-up tresses, allowing a hip young man to convince the drill sergeant he was actually a dedicated reservist.

During my Jedburgh training at Milton Hall, Jacques and Tony swore they wouldn't jump into occupied France with me until I let my short Airborne haircut grow out, and then be trimmed by an SOE chap who fancied himself a suitably French barber. So I passed the word down to my reserve commanders that, within reason, a man's attitude and performance were more important than the length of his hair. "After all," I told my staff, "Alexander the Great looked like a hippie, but he was a hell of a soldier." As an afterthought, I added, "So was Custer."

"Well, General," Arch Carpenter commented, "look what happened to Custer."

"Never mind that, Arch," I said. "This time around the Sioux are in the Montana National Guard."

I made a point of observing training, both to make a personal assessment of unit competence and to demonstrate the Army's concern for readiness. One of my favorite units was a cavalry regiment in the Montana National Guard. They had an Air Cav troop flying Huey helicopter gunships, so I always took the opportunity of racking up flight hours with them.

Their gunnery range southeast of Helena had two parallel hogback ridges above a narrow sagebrush valley where hulks of car and truck bodies were arranged as targets. Single gunships flew the range, south to north, exited left around the western hogback, and returned for another run, protected by the ridge. The unit's young warrant officer pilots were all cocky Vietnam vets, who wore distinctive black Stetsons.

One breezy August afternoon I was asked by the commander if I wanted to fly the course. I'm confident that he expected me to decline his offer, but I accepted immediately. The lanky CW2, whose bird I was about to fly, did not seem enthusiastic about turning over his cockpit to me. And, like most gunship pilots, he was not overly impressed by rank.

"Hey, Larry," he called to a friend about to lift off the armorers' pad, "put my hat on the hood of that pickup in the middle of the valley. With the general shooting the range, that'll be a safe place for it."

His gunship was scheduled for a single-fire rocket run, the most demanding gunnery exercise. But I couldn't back down now that the challenge had been issued. If I missed the target, however, and his hat emerged unscathed, I'd buy the gunship pilots beer that night, and drink mine washing down a mouthful of crow.

To make things more difficult, this run had to be flown at maximum speed, at an altitude of only about thirty feet, which meant I couldn't link my turns in smooth banks, but had to yaw hard right and left in clumsy lurches and snap-fire each rocket as soon as the target appeared.

My first three rockets missed the battered vehicle hulks, wide right, wide left, and ten yards short. The kid flying in the left seat was almost chewing his mustache to keep from grinning. He could taste the free beer.

"Bad luck, sir," he said. "These flat turns are tricky."

I didn't have time to reply. At a hundred knots the next target was almost on us. Just as I squeezed the weapons button on my cyclic stick, I saw the proud black Stetson on the shredded hood of the old ranch truck. The rocket screamed away with a smoking trail. I watched it, transfixed, as the missile flew with geometrical precision straight at the target. We were off to the left when the rocket exploded, right beneath the grill of the target vehicle. I saw the black Stetson career through the sunlight above the geyser of smoking clods.

When the hat was recovered, it was a felt sieve with over a hundred shrapnel holes. That night when the gunship pilots bought my beer, I made a point of ordering Lowenbrau, the most expensive brand in the club.

☆　　　　☆

Two years into my command, the war in Vietnam had entered its final, most critical phase. When Henry Kissinger had finally convinced South Vietnam's President Nguyen Van Thieu to accept the 1973 cease-fire agreement, which blatantly favored the North Vietnamese, the White House had also made a solemn promise that America would intervene with its full military might should the Communists attempt to parlay the truce into a new invasion of the South. Nixon assured Thieu that the Communists faced "the most serious consequences" if they broke the truce.[2] Bolstered by these assurances, Thieu had reluctantly signed a cease-fire agreement that allowed the North Vietnamese to maintain 150,000 regular troops in the South, while requiring the United States to remove the last combat forces still in the country.

The agreement placed no restrictions whatsoever on military assistance to North Vietnam from the Soviet bloc and China. I'd been stunned to read Defense Intelligence Agency (DIA) reports on massive Soviet- and East Bloc military aid pouring into North Vietnam. As soon as the American Navy had cleared the mines from Haiphong harbor, East Bloc ships were lined up three deep at the docks disgorging massive quantities of military hardware.[3]

The only shield South Vietnam had against this building Communist offensive was American air power. But Nixon had not foreseen the Watergate debacle or the resurgence of Congress against the "imperial presidency."

Even as Communist tanks were rumbling off the docks in Haiphong, historian Stanley Karnow noted, "Congress now began to disengage America totally from Southeast Asia." By August, Congress had reduced funding for South Vietnam and taken away White House authority to bomb NVA sanctuaries in Cambodia. It was clear that the "serious consequences" the Communists faced in breaking the truce were empty threats.[4]

We had turned our backs on South Vietnam, a loyal ally, at the time of its greatest need. The initial NVA probes of the final 1975 offensive, launched from Cambodian sanctuaries against ARVN positions in Tri Tam and Tay Ninh provinces, were tentative because the NVA leaders were afraid to expose their armor to destruction by American B-52s. But Congress reassured them. On March 12, 1975, a House caucus voted a special resolution against any additional military aid to Vietnam until the next fiscal year. The NVA occupation of the central highlands was completed and the offensive in the old III Corps tactical region began in earnest.[5]

In mid-April, I received a call from a CIA friend. He had been contacted by the Agency station chief in Kuala Lumpur, who was relaying an urgent personal message to me from Colonel Tran Van Ho. Colonel Ho had been the head of South Vietnam's Strategic Technical Directorate. In 1974, he had been assigned as defense attaché in Malaysia but had left his wife, Kim, and two sons behind in Saigon. Ho had learned that his family was on the Communist blood list, slated for execution after Saigon fell. The South Vietnamese government had refused his request to return to Saigon to rescue his family. Because Mrs. Ho was not a U.S. government employee, she was not entitled to evacuation by the Americans.

I immediately sent a message to Major General Homer Smith, the senior military officer remaining in Vietnam, requesting he expedite the evacuation of Colonel Ho's wife and sons. I received no response. The news reports were grim; Saigon was already under artillery attack. Although Mrs. Ho had run a travel agency in Saigon, she didn't have proper connections with the few airlines still operating. Had Colonel Ho been a corrupt ARVN officer, he might have bribed his family's way out of besieged Saigon.

Hearing nothing through American military channels, I contacted the CIA, finally reaching a senior officer at Langley.

"Look," I said bluntly, "there's not much time. You guys owe me a few favors and you sure as hell owe Colonel Ho something, too."

The man explained how difficult things were in Saigon at that moment.

"That's your problem, not mine," I said. "I consider this an absolutely essential matter. Colonel Ho's family won't survive one week after Saigon falls. You've got to get them out."

The official promised to do what he could.

On April 29, 1975, I watched television news coverage of Saigon's fall. Crowds of panicked Vietnamese civilians, many of whom had worked closely with the Americans, overran the American embassy, clamoring all the way to the helipad on the roof, only to be kicked away. The next day, I saw the grim news broadcast of the NVA tanks crashing through the gate of Saigon's Independence Palace. The war was over.

A week passed with no news of Mrs. Ho. I contacted Colonel Ho in Kuala Lumpur. He was shattered by grief. A few days later, I received a telegram from the Red Cross in the Philippines, notifying me that a Vietnamese refugee, Madame Ho, and her two sons were en route to a holding camp on Guam. I sent an urgent message through Navy channels to have the Ho family sent to Camp Pendleton, California, where my sister could meet them, but again there was no response. Another week passed. Then I got a late-night phone call from Fort Chaffee, Arkansas. Mrs. Ho and her sons were safely in America.

I immediately wired them plane tickets to Denver. The next night Mary and I met Mrs. Ho and her boys. They were weary from the long journey, but their spirits were high. While Mary and my daughter Mary Ann made plans to drive them to southern California, I requested the State Department notify the embassy in Kuala Lumpur to grant Colonel Ho an immediate refugee visa to join his family in America. State was not cooperative. "We have no indication Colonel Ho is in harm's way," I was informed by an officious young man in Washington. I went over his head. After another delay, the visa was granted and I wired Colonel Ho an air ticket. He and his family were finally reunited at my sister Anita's home near Los Angeles.

With fluency in four languages, Kim Ho found work at a Beverly Hills travel agency immediately. The family rented a small bungalow and the boys were enrolled in Hollywood High School that September. Colonel Ho became a volunteer worker among the swelling refugee community. Within a few months, he was hired by Los Angeles County as a full-time refugee worker.

As I read reports of thousands of South Vietnamese officials and ARVN prisoners marched off to "reeducation" camps in the malarial swamps of the delta and desolate highland regions, I could take some comfort knowing we had not abandoned a few of our loyal allies. But the final Communist domination of Indochina did not provide much comfort to our other Asian allies. For years American presidents had told the Thais, Filipinos, Malaysians, Nationalist Chinese, and South Koreans that America would stand by them in the face of Communist aggression. But now these allies learned that the word of an American president could be undercut by political intrigues in Congress.

The Asians also recognized that a subtle but unmistakable racism influenced American foreign policy. When Israel, another staunch ally of America, was threatened with extinction in the Yom Kippur War of October 1973, Congress urged the Nixon White House to conduct the most massive military resupply airlift in history. And the White House, with congressional concurrence, even went so far as to place the Strategic Air Command on full alert as a warning to the Soviet Union, which was too actively aiding Israel's enemy, Syria. Had America done as much for South Vietnam in 1975, the country could have survived.

Israel was a culturally European democracy with a predominantly white population. Israel had supporters throughout the Congress. South Vietnam was an Asian country struggling to form a democracy.

The message was not lost on South Korea, America's Asian ally that faced the most immediate Communist military threat. After the Communist takeover in Indochina, the South Koreans began a concerted effort to gain influence in Congress. Unfortunately, this campaign quickly degenerated into illegal lobbying and influence peddling that eventually boomeranged in the scandal the news media named "Koreagate."

☆   ☆

IN THE spring of 1976, the military situation in Korea became more than an abstract matter to me when I was assigned as Chief of Staff of the United Nations Command (UNC) and U.S. Forces, Korea (USFK). The job's third responsibility was Chief of Staff and Deputy Commander of the Eighth Army. Dick Stilwell, now a four-star general, had become the commander in chief of U.N. and American forces in Korea in late 1974.

I had great respect for Stilwell, having served under him in a variety of assignments, beginning in 1951 in the CIA job in Korea, then commanding one of his battalions in the 15th Infantry. Most recently, he had been my commanding officer in the Sixth Army. I was proud that he had selected me to be his chief of staff in Korea.

Mary and I arrived at Kimpo Airport in Seoul on July 1, 1976. Driving from the airport northeast to the U.N. Command headquarters at the Yongson Post, I was impressed by the Seoul skyline. I'd last seen the city in 1973, on a brief visit with Dr. Wilbur. Then, I had been stunned by Seoul's transformation from the shell-pocked ruin I'd known during the Korean War. In the early 1970s Seoul was already a handsome, prosperous capital. Now it was a boomtown. Elevated freeways curved among high-rise banks and hotels. There were towering T-head construction cranes everywhere. On the outskirts new industrial parks were surrounded by workers' apartment blocks, parks, and athletic complexes. The roads were congested with shiny new cars.

But the bustling glitter of Seoul was deceptive. Korea was not at peace. Only twenty-five miles north of the city, the Demilitarized Zone (DMZ) still divided the Korean peninsula, just as it had since 1953. The "demilitarized" frontier between Communist North Korea and the South marked one of the most heavily fortified regions in the world. The same United Nations Command, led by American officers, still met regularly with the North Koreans at the site of the original cease-fire negotiations known to the world as Panmunjom. As UNC chief of staff, one of the hats I wore was that of the senior allied representative at Panmunjom.

By 1976, the earlier collection of tents and quonset huts had evolved into an elaborate Joint Security Area (JSA), an 800-square-meter trapezoid of neutral territory, replete with permanent meeting rooms and guard outposts. The JSA, and the meeting rooms themselves, were bisected by the Military Demarcation Line (MDL) at the middle of the four-kilometer-wide DMZ frontier. In theory, this was the site of dispassionate professional contact between the two sides, a place where potentially serious confrontational incidents could be defused before they erupted into open conflict along the DMZ. In reality, the JSA itself had become a site of angry confrontation.

Later that year, when I became the senior UNC representative to the Military Armistice Commission, I decided to have some fun needling the senior North Korean, General Han, whom I faced across the negotiation table. He was a political commissar, not a combat soldier. Han had been military attaché in Egypt during the Yom Kippur War and had arranged for North Korean pilots to fly MiG-21s against Israel. Many of those pilots were shot down by U.S.-supplied Sidewinder missiles. He hated America. Eventually President Sadat declared Han persona non grata when he was caught spying on the Egyptian military. Whenever Han would raise hell about one of our legitimate exercises, I would pull his chain.

"General Han," I'd say, "if you had any military service in a combat unit, you'd realize our training exercise is perfectly normal."

The senior Communist in Panmunjom was not pleased with my observations.

But when I took over as UNC chief of staff that summer, nobody was joking in Panmunjom. The tension in Korea was at a dangerous level. In 1971, the Nixon administration had arbitrarily decided to remove the 7th Infantry Division, one of the two large American combat units stationed in South Korea. The action was part of the Nixon Doctrine, by which America tried to instill military independence in its Asian allies—and save money in the process. This left the 2nd Infantry Division the only major American combat force in Korea. The South Korean government had been stunned because we took this step unilaterally, without consulting them, even though there were still ROK troops in South Vietnam, fighting and dying beside Americans and the ARVN. The next year, North Korea's Communist dictator, Kim Il-Sung, began an unprecedented buildup of his armed forces.

Following the American pullout from Indochina in 1975, Kim accelerated the enlargement and modernization of his military, and for the first time since the 1950s dramatically shifted his force structure from a defensive posture to preparations for a full-scale invasion of the South.

The discovery of the offensive North Korean buildup entailed one of the most successful intelligence operations in history. The process was not easy. And I arrived in Korea just as the first clear evidence of North Korea's intentions was being revealed. Until the collapse of Vietnam the year before, photo interpreters and analysts at the CIA and the Defense Intelligence Agency (DIA) had been preoccupied with satellite and aerial reconnaissance imagery from Indochina. They simply hadn't devoted the resources to properly analyze the thousands of reconnaissance-flight and satellite pictures of North Korea that had stacked up in the archives for years. So, in the mid-1970s, the U.S. intelligence community still accepted the 1970 estimate of a general parity in military forces between North and South Korea. The community assumed that neither side could successfully invade the other. Indeed, it had been this assumption that permitted the withdrawal of the 7th Infantry Division.[6]

But in 1974, civilian analysts noted that North Korea's huge production of steel and concrete was apparently being channeled into unspecified military projects. The next year, the interagency Intelligence Board began to take a closer look at North Korea. John Armstrong, a young civilian who had served with distinction as an infantry officer in Vietnam, was assigned to the Army's Special Research Detachment at the National Security Agency, which manages our reconnaissance satellites. Armstrong was given free rein to dig into the enigma of North Korea's military capabilities and intentions. He scrutinized thousands of satellite and aerial reconnaissance images that had accumulated over the previous five years. Drawing upon his West Point education, Armstrong began his work with a detailed analysis of North Korea's actual strength in tanks and artillery, as well as the deployment of these forces.

What Armstrong discovered was, in his words, "horrifying." North Korean armor forces were a full eighty percent larger than the 1970 estimate. He found a previously undetected armored division with 270 tanks and 100 armored personnel carriers deployed close to the DMZ. Armstrong then applied his rigorous scrutiny to every region of North Korea. Over the next fourteen months, he "nailed down every gun in the country." The overall picture that emerged was shocking. North Korea's military was much larger than earlier estimates indicated. The force structure was weighted toward "heavy" divisions: armor, artillery, and mechanized infantry. And most of these units were massed well forward near the DMZ.

Armstrong's growing team of analysts found evidence that North Korean armor and artillery had been completely modernized. The North Korean People's Army (NKPA) armored force had doubled to 2,000 battle tanks, most of them improved Soviet-design T-62s. The NKPA had 12,400 artillery pieces. In December 1975, Armstrong briefed the UNC staff on these ominous developments. The new estimates showed that most of this artillery had been moved forward and emplaced in heavily fortified mountain positions to fire across the DMZ. A basic principle of analysis held that pushing artillery forward was a preparation for an offensive, while staggering artillery support in depth toward the rear was a good defense. The NKPA had practically stripped the rear of artillery to mass thousands of new guns just north of the DMZ.

In mid-1976, Armstrong briefed General John W. Vessey, Jr., who was scheduled to replace General Richard Stilwell as UNC commander in chief in Seoul.

I read the detailed reports of North Korea's buildup of offensive forces during my first weeks back in Korea. In 1970, American intelligence could identify twenty-one North Korean divisions, each with about 10,000 combat troops. By mid-1976, ongoing analysis produced evidence of *forty-one* North Korean divisions. It was estimated that overall North Korean force levels had almost doubled in four years, and totaled 560,000 regulars in combat units and an incredible 2,350,000 reservists. But these numbers were deceptive. North Korea was a society totally mobilized for war. Whereas many South Korean troops were assigned to support units, almost all of the North Korean forces were in the combat arms. Their transportation and supply services were manned by civilian "volunteers."[7]

From mid-1976 to the spring of 1977, Armstrong's team worked tirelessly to construct an airtight, multi-source estimate of North Korea's new offensively structured military forces. It would not be until eighteen months later, however, that the public learned the shocking truth about the North Korean military.[8]

This buildup completely upset the balance of military power in Korea. The Republic of Korea Army (ROKA) had a total of twenty-two divisions deployed in depth along the DMZ. American ground forces included the 2nd Infantry Division, which was kept in mobile strategic reserve below the DMZ, with one brigade blocking the Munsan-Seoul corridor, the open invasion route to South Korea's capital. The 2nd Infantry Division's "slice" also included artillery, aviation, signal, and logistical-support units shared with the ROK forces. Overall, United Nations military forces in Korea totaled around 600,000, including the logistical support forces. The combat elements of this force represented about one-half of the total. (The U.S. Congress had actually mandated this absolute South Korean force ceiling of 600,000.) If the new intelligence estimates were accurate, the Communists now outnumbered us two to one. Therefore, the firepower and mechanized mobility of American ground troops had become *the* key component to an effective defense of the South.

When Armstrong's team shifted to North Korean airpower, they discovered that Kim Il-Sung's generals had moved most of their attack aircraft to forward bases. Fighter-bomber squadrons were now hidden in elaborate cave hangars hacked from the granite mountains just north of the DMZ (which accounted for the earlier "missing" steel and concrete). Anti-aircraft missile and radar sites protecting these forward airfields had been hardened with concrete emplacements.

Equally ominous, the NKPA had created the VIIIth Special Corps, a Spetsnaz-type, special-forces unit of 80,000 men. This was an airborne force supported by a new fleet of 250 Soviet-supplied AN-2 paradrop transports, which were also deployed in forward positions. Again, fundamental military principles dictated that such a force was an offensive spearhead, which had no defensive function.

And North Korea had doubled its submarine force to twelve attack boats. This factor was extremely interesting. With the DMZ dividing the Korean peninsula, South Korea was virtually an island. Most of the country's trade and military supplies moved by sea. The function of a submarine is to sink enemy combat ships and supply transports, often through a coastal blockade. Since South Korea had only limited amphibious capability, the North Korean submarines were obviously meant to support a large-scale offensive.[9]

Month by month, as the true size of the North Korean buildup and the evidence of their forward deployment posture became obvious, the U.N. Command was being forced to accept a troubling, seemingly unbelievable conclusion: Kim Il-Sung was poised to invade South Korea.[10] This conclusion made sense when weighed against CIA reports that North Korea was racked by internal problems and economic difficulties. A multibillion-dollar foreign debt was crippling the already stagnant economy. There was a power struggle within the North Korean Communist Party between more moderate elements and hard-liners led by Kim Il-Sung's son and appointed heir, Kim Jong-Il. The military buildup and increased North Korean provocations along the DMZ were obviously intended to divert domestic discontent toward supporting a new patriotic war. As improbable as this might seem to people in the West, intelligence experts judged dictator Kim perfectly capable of such action.[11]

The discovery of an elaborate tunnel network under the DMZ provided the final proof of North Korea's aggressive intentions. In November 1974, an ROK patrol in the western DMZ noticed steam rising from the ground on the southern side of the MDL in the area of some abandoned rice paddies.

The soldiers dug into the frozen earth and discovered a concealed concrete hatch. They pried it open to reveal a shallow, rectangular, concrete-reinforced tunnel, replete with narrow-gauge railway, which ran beneath the ground straight back into North Korea. As they enlarged the excavation, they came under sniper fire from North Korean army troops across the MDL. Later that day, ROK troops cautiously explored the tunnel. It was cut through relatively soft black soil, reinforced with concrete pillars, and strung with electric lights. A thorough investigation of the tunnel proved it was just large enough (122 centimeters high, 90 centimeters wide, approximately four by three feet) to allow passage of several hundred infiltrators an hour, lying prone on narrow-gauge rail cars.

The initial estimate was that the tunnel was a clever—if somewhat elaborate—conduit for inserting North Korean saboteurs and assassins into the South. Within a few months, however, we learned that the tunnel was part of a far more serious operation.

In March 1975, two North Korean defectors, Kim Pu-Song, an engineer, and Yu Tae-Yon, revealed that they had worked for years on an ambitious system of tunnels beneath the DMZ, which were designed as major invasion routes, not simply ingress paths for agents. The tunneling had begun in 1972, Kim disclosed, only months after America decided to remove our first combat division and shortly after the North Koreans had agreed for the first time to allow "humanitarian" North-South Red Cross meetings on reuniting dispersed families. While these meetings progressed, the North Korean military buildup and tunneling increased. Engineer Kim stated that he had personally seen the construction of nine tunnels, all larger and deeper than the one first discovered.

ROK troops along the DMZ searched for additional tunnels. In the old Iron Triangle sector near Chorwon, Korean infantrymen reported faint rumbling, like distant artillery, which seemed to be coming from directly beneath their positions. Well drills were moved up and a series of bore holes sunk. They struck pay dirt. A full-scale U.N. Command Tunnel Neutralization Team (TNT), led by Korean and combat engineers, went to work on an interception tunnel. Finally, on March 24, 1975, their 800-meter interception tunnel broke through the solid granite into a large North Korean invasion tunnel fifty meters beneath the old Greek battalion lines.[12]

This second tunnel was twice as big as the first. Arc-shaped, with a flat floor, the tunnel stood two meters high and two meters wide. The deep granite needed no concrete reinforcement. The tunnel could provide passage for a full combat division, including their field artillery drawn by prime movers. ROK patrols cautiously probed the tunnel that originated someplace north of the DMZ and was drilled due south across the DMZ for three and a half kilometers. As they worked their way north through a series of hastily constructed barriers booby-trapped with mines, they encountered a freshly constructed reinforced concrete wall, which effectively halted further north-ward movement through this particular tunnel.

The TNT efforts were intensified all along the DMZ. Defector Kim had informed the South Korean Defense Ministry that there were probably two such large tunnels dug for each of the ten North Korean infantry divisions then deployed along the immediate northern edge of the DMZ.[13]

The United Nations Command angrily confronted the North Koreans during a regular Military Armistice Commission meeting at Panmunjom. The Communists refused to acknowledge their role in this audacious scheme, even though a banner recovered from one tunnel was emblazoned with the slogan "Down with American Imperialist Aggressors." Either the tunnels were an elaborate smear effort by the imperialists, the North Korean del-egate stated, or they were simply abandoned coal mines from the years of the Japanese occupation of Korea. When it was pointed out that coal deposits are never found in granite, the Communists did not respond. The U.N. Command conducted a tunnel press tour in 1976, in which reporters were shown evidence of drilling traces that proceeded from the North toward the South. Since this literally rock-solid evidence could not be faked, the North Korean explanation was exposed as a transparent lie.

(Two more tunnels were eventually found, one in 1978 near the Joint Security Area, and one in 1990 in the eastern Demilitarized Zone.[14])

☆　　　☆

I WENT back to the Iron Triangle to inspect the second tunnel soon after returning to Korea. Flying the Huey northeast into those familiar hills was a surprisingly emotional experience. The shantytown corps rear area of the wartime front had been replaced by neat ROK camps of quonset huts and prefab buildings. The roads were well graded and some even paved. Ap-proaching the DMZ the scene appeared almost peaceful. Farming and other civilian activities are still prohibited in the area immediately south of the DMZ. But then I saw the multiple rows of fencing and land mines that mark the southern boundary of the DMZ.

We landed near the old mountaintop artillery Observation Post where I had placed the M-48 tank to eliminate the Chinese artillery OP for the battery that had wounded me. My old battalion command bunkers and the trench line of the MLR had disappeared beneath two decades of scrub brush and low pine. I studied the smooth hump of Outpost Harry, which now marked the exact center of the DMZ, the Military Demarcation Line. The overlapping shell craters and black fougasse scars were also hidden by the new growth of brush and trees. There was nothing to indicate that hundreds of men had died for that unassuming green hilltop. But I could still see the faces of those brave young soldiers who had died on Outpost Harry.

To the north, the familiar humped mountains of Korea rolled away into the summer haze. Even through powerful ROK artillery-spotter glasses, it was impossible to detect the massed fortifications of the North Korean army. But I had studied the satellite and SR-71 Blackbird reconnaissance photos only that morning. There were at least 50,000 Communist troops poised to advance south in those innocent piney mountains. In the past few months, North Korean troops had increased their provocations along the DMZ—sniping at ROK patrols and placing booby traps in the southern DMZ. At the flashpoint of the Panmunjom Joint Security Area, North Korean guards had stepped up their verbal and physical assaults on the UNC security detachment. Our best intelligence estimate was that the Communists were planning to trigger a major provocation to serve as the rationale for a new invasion, just as they had in 1950.

(Proof of the original June 1950 provocation finally emerged forty years later. A former North Korean ambassador to the Soviet Union, Li San-Cho, now living in exile in Moscow, confirmed to Reuters that Communist dictator Kim Il-Sung consulted with Joseph Stalin before the 1950 invasion, and the two agreed to fabricate a South Korean military incursion as a pretext for the massive, Soviet-backed invasion of the South.[15])

☆   ☆

THE Communists unleashed their provocation with brutal efficiency on the morning of Wednesday, August 18, 1976.

Tension in the JSA neutral zone had been high all summer, with North Korean soldiers screaming obscenities and death threats at American security guards from the U.S. Army Support Group (USASG). The Americans had been trained to ignore these antics and to extract themselves from more serious scuffles, which had escalated from shoving matches to karate assaults on isolated American guards.

Our USASG unit was a company of three composite platoons with both American and ROK officers and enlisted men, based at nearby Camp Kitty Hawk. They were selected for strength, intelligence, and emotional stability. The unit's task was to represent United Nations' interests in the JSA, where the Military Armistice Commission met regularly. Because the North Koreans consistently provoked the U.N. security guards, they had orders to use their .45 handguns only in self-defense during a clearly life-threatening attack.

But our troops also had orders to protect U.N. interests in the JSA, which included the right to maintain guard posts and to freely patrol the area.

Each side maintained small observation posts, similar to road checkpoints or police kiosks found elsewhere in Asia. Over the twenty-three years since the fighting had stopped the JSA had become progressively covered with brush and trees. By that August, a forty-foot Normandy poplar near the so-called Bridge of No Return on the southwest side of the JSA had become so bushy that its foliage blocked the view between UNC Checkpoint No. 3 and UNC Observation Post No. 5. American and South Korean security guards surveyed the tree on August 6, and decided to cut it down. When their six-man Korean Service Corps (KSC) work team arrived with saws, however, a large North Korean guard unit intervened, ordering them to leave the tree alone.

The UNC detachment decided the bullying was unacceptable. Lieutenant Colonel Victor S. Vierra developed a plan that would satisfy legitimate security needs without provoking the Communists. On August 18, he dispatched a ten-man security force to guard five KSC workers equipped with axes, ladders, and saws, who planned to trim the poplar's lower branches but leave the tree standing. The unit was commanded by U.S. Army Captain Arthur G. Bonifas and his deputy, First Lieutenant Mark T. Barrett. They were accompanied by the interpreter, ROK Captain Kim Moon-Hwan. As a precaution, a twenty-man Quick Reaction Force was moved up to U.N. Checkpoint No. 2, just inside the JSA, ready to intervene if the tree-cutting detail was harassed by the North Koreans. The work party also placed pick handles in the back of their deuce-and-a-half truck, but following the Armistice Agreement, carried no weapons other than their sidearms.

At 10:30 that morning, the KSC workers set up two ladders and started pruning branches. Five minutes later, a North Korean truck rolled up and disgorged two North Korean officers and nine enlisted men. The senior Communist officer was First Lieutenant Pak Chol, a veteran JSA guard known to have provoked scuffles with UNC personnel in the past. He asked Captain Kim what work was in progress and was told that the KSC team was only pruning branches. Lieutenant Pak muttered, "That is good." In their normally officious manner, the North Koreans began to coach the South Korean workers on the proper method of branch pruning. This was an obvious attempt to usurp the authority of the American officers, so Captain Bonifas told the men to simply get on with their work. Twenty minutes passed, and then, for no reason, Lieutenant Pak marched up to Captain Bonifas and ordered him to halt the trimming.

Bonifas refused, adding that his men would complete their job and leave. Lieutenant Pak shouted that any more branch trimming would bring "serious trouble." Captain Bonifas and Lieutenant Barrett had heard such threats before. They ignored the Communists. Still strutting and shouting, Lieutenant Pak sent away for reinforcements. Ten more Communist guards arrived by truck, and six more came trotting up from nearby guard posts. There were now almost thirty North Koreans surrounding the thirteen UNC soldiers and five KSC workmen. Lieutenant Pak was screaming now that any additional trimming would mean "death."

The UNC Quick Reaction Force was monitoring the situation by radio and photographing the scene with a telephoto surveillance camera.

Captain Bonifas turned his back on the angry Communist officer to make sure the workers continued the pruning. He did not see Lieutenant Pak remove his watch, wrap it in a handkerchief, and stick it into the pocket of his trousers. Nor did he see the other North Korean officer rolling up the sleeves of his jacket. An American NCO strode forward to warn Captain Bonifas.

At that moment Lieutenant Pak screamed, "*Chookyo!* Kill!"

It was later established that this command was a formal military order, not a spontaneous outburst. The command meant, "Attack the enemy and kill them!"[16]

Lieutenant Pak kicked Captain Bonifas in the groin and the American went down, surrounded by three Communists. Suddenly the North Koreans had crowbars, metal pipes, and heavy clubs. Communist soldiers seized the KSC workers' axes and attacked the UNC guards, concentrating on the American officers and NCOs. Captain Bonifas was on the ground, trying to deflect kicks and blows, when a Communist soldier bludgeoned him to death with the blunt head of an ax. First Lieutenant Barrett was chased around the truck and over a low retaining wall, followed by six Communists armed with axes, clubs, and steel pipes.

The North Korean troops had divided into efficient attack teams who scattered the UNC guard formation. Individual Americans were chased and beaten. While at least one Communist guard pinned an American's arms to prevent him using his weapon, the other members of the attack team struck with clubs and steel pipes. The U.N. soldiers depended on their officers to order the use of weapons, but the officers were killed in the first seconds of the attack. Fortunately, one American soldier broke free and was able to drive the UNC truck through the melee, forcing back the Communists, while the KSC workers clambered aboard. The diversion allowed the other UNC guards to help their battered comrades.

By now the Quick Reaction Force had arrived in their own truck, and the North Koreans fled across the bridge into the North Korean part of the DMZ. The whole incident was over in about four minutes. When Lieutenant Barrett was not accounted for, a search was made. His body was found in a shallow ditch just off the road. Like Captain Bonifas, his skull had been crushed by the blunt end of an ax head. The pattern of the Communist attack was now obvious: The American officers had been singled out for murder and the American NCOs for severe beatings. This was not a spontaneous fracas, but a carefully contrived provocation.[17]

☆   ☆

I WAS in a staff meeting at UNC headquarters when I got a call from the Camp Kitty Hawk duty officer. His report was confused, indicating a "fight" had broken out between members of the UNC security guard and the North Koreans. He reported UNC casualties, but no deaths.

I left my office for the War Room, located in a concrete basement next door. As luck would have it, UNC Commander in Chief General Richard Stilwell was in Kyoto, Japan, paying a farewell call on the commander of the Japanese Self-Defense Forces, after having just announced his upcoming retirement. Deputy Commander Air Force Lieutenant General John Burns was somewhere over the Yellow Sea getting in his monthly flying time. And the American ambassador to Korea, Richard Sneider, was in the States on home leave. The senior American in Korea was Lieutenant General John H. Cushman, the combined ROK/US I Corps commander. But his headquarters was up at Uijonbu and didn't have access to the UNC staff. So I was the man on the spot.

Within minutes, I received updated messages announcing that Captain Bonifas and Lieutenant Barrett had been murdered, and that several members of the security guard detachment were seriously injured. USASG officers confirmed that the North Korean attack had been carefully coordinated and the brutality focused on American targets. This was the major Communist provocation we'd been expecting.

I called Air Force Major General Don Pittman, the commander of U.S. Air Forces, Korea, and had him dispatch a jet to Japan to fetch General Stilwell. I also told Pittman to get General Burns back ASAP. Then I talked to General Cushman and briefed him on the situation in the JSA as we knew it. I also discussed with him what levels of increased readiness could be taken without an official increase in the defense condition, "DEFCON," the war-fighting readiness status of our forces. The normal DEFCON in Korea was "4," ("5" being the lowest, "1" being "attack imminent,"), but I foresaw the possibility that we might be directed by the National Military Command Center in Washington to go to DEFCON-3 within hours. It was important not to run off half-cocked and play into Communist hands by giving them the "aggressive" response they wanted. Increasing the DEFCON level kicked off a lot of telltale activity, including radio traffic and aircraft and vehicle repositioning, which the Communists would surely observe. But we certainly couldn't carry on business as usual with an invasion possible.

When I was sure General Burns was en route to Seoul, I officially activated the War Room, but at a reduced manning level. Both Intelligence (J-2) and Operations (J-3) sent staff to man communications consoles in the underground center. UNC headquarters was no longer just a diffuse collection of offices. It was now a command preparing to go on a war footing.

In the meantime, I had had the communicators track down General Stilwell in Japan. I gave him a situation report as best I could on the nonsecure phone. He agreed with my assessment that the attack was deliberate North Korean policy, not an aberration.

"Sir," I said, "I think you should return to Seoul immediately. I have sent your aircraft to pick you up as soon as you think you can get away. Should I do anything about our DEFCON status? Are there any other instructions?"

Stilwell thought a moment. Our response to the murders had to combine forcefulness with prudence. Obviously, the North Koreans were testing our resolve. This was the middle of an election year, with a self-proclaimed reconciliation candidate, Georgia governor Jimmy Carter, doing well in the polls against President Jerry Ford, whose White House had been powerless when Congress scuttled the Vietnamese. The North Koreans were gambling Ford would not react forcefully now. The next forty-eight hours in Korea could either trigger a war or deter a new Communist invasion.

"Okay, Jack," General Stilwell finally answered. "Make sure you keep our higher headquarters, the ROK, and the U.N. allies informed of the situation. Request a MAC meeting for tomorrow, get the units ready for an increase in DEFCON, and have the staff stand by for an all-nighter."

☆   ☆

WHILE I was busy organizing headquarters staff for the late-night conference to prepare the Operations Plan (OPLAN) of our response, I got a call from the American embassy. The Political Section had just received news on the motives for the North Korean attack. North Korea had sent a large delegation to the Conference of Non-Aligned Nations in Colombo, Sri Lanka. This was the first such meeting since the fall of Vietnam and the North Korean Communists were eager to gain support for their ongoing effort to force a U.S. troop withdrawal from Korea. That afternoon, less than four hours after the murders in the JSA, the chief North Korean delegate, Kim Jong-Il, the dictator's son, addressed the conference. He distributed a document describing the incident as an unprovoked attack on North Korean guards, led by American officers. He then introduced a resolution asking the conference to condemn that day's grave U.S. provocation and calling on participants to endorse both the withdrawal of U.S. forces from Korea and the dissolution of the United Nations Command. Seconded by such *nonaligned* stalwarts as Cuba, the resolution passed.[18]

This was clear confirmation that the murders had been part of a carefully planned campaign designed to force American troops out of Korea.

☆   ☆

I briefed General Stilwell in his sedan en route to his office from the airport. We discussed what he called three possible "military school solution" options to the North Korean provocation. The first was doing nothing. The second, a massive military punitive raid, he scornfully dismissed as "starting World War III." The third option was doing something "meaningful," which he said would have to be our course of action.

That night General Stilwell met with his senior officers to begin work on the OPLAN. As chief of staff I was responsible for coordinating all the hundreds of details of the plan. So I listened intently as Stilwell spoke. He directed the senior UNC Military Armistice member, Rear Admiral Mark P. Frudden, to deliver a firm protest letter from Stilwell to Kim Il-Sung at the next day's scheduled MAC meeting. Then we got to work on the preliminary plan, which had as its key objective the removal of the poplar tree in the JSA. This was a deceptively simple goal. But within it, the operation would contain all the elements necessary to forcefully reassert UNC rights in the DMZ while simultaneously intimidating the North Koreans.[19]

We had to focus our response on the JSA itself, while also signaling the North Korean Communists that such aggression had truly serious consequences. In short, we had to punish them for their action and also demonstrate American and South Korean resolve in order to discourage future incidents.

And the UNC response to the murders had to be extremely focused, so as not to trigger any North Korean spoiling attack across the DMZ. Thus we planned our reaction on two levels: resasserting UNC rights in the Joint Security Area, and massing American air, ground, and sea power to remind the North Koreans of the nature of their opponent.

However the plan evolves, Stilwell added, "that damned tree must come down!" The poplar had become a symbol of authority in the JSA. We had allowed the North Koreans to bully us into not felling the tree earlier, and they had obviously construed this as a sign of weakness. Now we were going to go into the JSA and cut it down, employing a force large enough to intimidate the Communists. Stilwell's plan displayed the subtlety of an old Asia hand. He realized the poplar had no intrinsic value, but that our destroying the disputed tree would mean a great loss of face to the North Koreans. He also understood the massing of overwhelming American fire-

power on and around the Korean peninsula would be even more psychologically devastating. The Communists had hoped for either craven inaction
or brash overreaction on our part. Instead, they were about to learn a lesson
in the controlled application of military power from one of the world's master
practitioners.

☆　　　　　☆

THE next morning we received the JCS order to increase the alert level of
American forces in Korea to DEFCON-3. This was the first increase in the
DEFCON due to the local situation since the 1953 armistice. Thirty minutes
later, the ROK Minister of National Defense issued a similar order for all
South Korean forces. The American Armed Forces Korea Radio and Tele-
vision Network began a public recall of all U.S. personnel on pass and leave.

High-altitude supersonic SR-71 reconnaissance flights were stepped up,
with the Blackbirds screaming east and west, miles above the DMZ, their
cameras and sensors recording frantic military preparations deep inside
North Korea. A valuable benefit of these recon flights was the "illumination"
of anti-aircraft tracking radar in North Korea. The SR-71s' sensors recorded
the exact coordinates of these radars. We then ordered our long-range Nike-
Hercules missile batteries switched to their ground-to-ground mode, with
conventional warheads targeted on the enemy radar sites. Had the North
Koreans been foolish enough to fling a missile at the Blackbirds, they would
have found their fire-control radars destroyed only minutes later.

Air Force Major General Don Pittman reported by mid-morning that
flights of RF-4D reconnaissance aircraft and Wild Weasel air-defense
suppression jets were arriving at our Korean air bases at Osan, Kunsan, and
Taegu at regular intervals from Japan and the Philippines. The flight plans
of these squadrons brought them within the range of North Korean radar.
We had begun a war of nerves and proceeded to ratchet up the tension.
Nuclear-capable F-111 strategic bombers were en route nonstop from Mountain Home Air Force Base, Idaho. As I watched the bright plastic aircraft
symbols concentrate on our situation plotting chart in the War Room that
afternoon, I could imagine the emotions of my Communist counterpart in
the North. By now he had to realize that his country risked annihilation
from one of the greatest concentrations of destructive force ever assembled
in the region.

I checked with our ground commanders to be certain that the DEFCON-
3 preparations were moving forward. Lieutenant General Cushman and
Major General Morris Brady assured me that his 2nd Infantry Division and
the First ROK Army troops were proceeding to their outpost positions along
the DMZ. Nuclear and conventional artillery and missiles of various calibers

were carried forward by road and helicopter to prepared concrete bunkers. Listening posts just south of the DMZ were activated and reconnaissance patrols were mounted.

Previous readiness exercises had practiced an increase in DEFCON, including simulated ammunition movement. But we now used many more vehicles and troops than in any past exercise. The evidence of the UNC military activity was obvious. Convoys of trucks and armored personnel carriers moved steadily north. Cargo helicopters shuttled back and forth, carrying nets and pallets of munitions. A quick scan of the tactical radio net produced a multi-band cacophony of Korean and American voices. This was obviously not a training exercise. To the North Koreans, the UNC activity must have seemed ominous. That was our intention.

By the night of August 19, we had formal confirmation that North Korean forces were on a "wartime posture" all across their country. Moreover, our J-2 reported that the North Korean alert was "reactive, urgent and defensive in character," indicative of a "genuine apprehension over possible UNC retaliatory military actions."[20] This was exactly the result we had hoped to achieve. Our massive show of force had undercut previous North Korean offensive preparations and forced their military back to a defensive posture.

In the War Room, we now had multiple secure-voice and teletype links directly to the National Command Authority in the Pentagon. But General Stilwell was too savvy to prematurely bring these senior officials directly into our planning process. Every general officer in the War Room had served in Vietnam and was familiar with the regrettable tendency of civilian "field marshals" on the other side of the planet to act as local commanders via satellite telephone. Before actually implementing our plan, of course, we had to obtain formal authorization from Washington. But the longer the Pentagon had to scrutinize our OPLAN, the more likely they would want to second-guess us.

Now I joined a small group of senior officers in General Stilwell's office to complete our detailed OPLAN. We had to demonstrate to the North Koreans that the UNC, under American leadership, would not tolerate any erosion of its rights in the JSA or along the DMZ. Therefore, the task force we would deploy to cut down the poplar would also destroy two illegal swing-pipe road barriers the North Koreans had erected in the JSA in 1965. The composition of our task force would also demonstrate allied resolve and be equally balanced between American and ROK troops. But it certainly would not rise to the Communists' bait by breaking Armistice Agreement rules on actually introducing heavy firepower into the JSA. One of the most important staff officers in General Stilwell's planning group was Colonel Zane Finkelstein, the Staff Judge Advocate. He knew more about the content and the intent of the Military Armistice Agreement than any American I have ever known. More important was the fact that Colonel Finkelstein had the intellect and integrity to think positively about what was best for his country rather than what was safest for his career. His input was essential.

Every operation needs a name and General Stilwell's was appropriate: Operation PAUL BUNYAN. The key elements were surprise, speed of execution and withdrawal, and avoidance of direct engagement with North Korean troops. Our forces would include soldiers from the 2nd Infantry Division, as well as ROK Special Forces and Recon troopers of the 1st ROK Division. Altogether, a force of 813 men would be involved. Task Force VIERRA (named for Lieutenant Colonel Victor Vierra, commander of the USASG) would conduct the actual tree cutting. The unit would include sixty American and ROK guards, divided in two platoons, armed with sidearms and pickax handles. The ROK men were Special Forces; each man was a Black Belt in Tae Kwon Do. They would guard two eight-man engineer teams who would actually cut down the tree with chain saws. A truck-borne ROK reconnaissance company, armed with M-16 rifles, mortars, and machine guns, would be prominently deployed just outside the JSA: crack South Korean troops defending their own soil. They would be beefed up with American tube-launched, optically tracked, wire-guided (TOW) anti-tank–missile teams.

Vierra's troops were backed up by other elements of the division, including a reinforced composite rifle company from the 9th Infantry Regiment, which would be orbiting aboard twenty Huey helicopters a few hundred meters south of the DMZ, supported by twelve AH-1G Cobra gunships. Tank-busting F-4 Phantoms would be prowling at a slightly higher orbit. F-111 medium strategic bombers would orbit still higher, and be clearly visible to North Korean radar.

To complete the demonstration of firepower, three batteries of American 105mm howitzers were to be moved across the Freedom Bridge north of the Imjin River. Another three batteries of ROK heavy artillery would be positioned just south of the river in clear view of North Korean positions. The gunners, Stilwell said, would have "rounds in the tube and hands on the lanyards."

Operation PAUL BUNYAN was scheduled to begin at exactly 0700, the morning of Saturday, August 21, 1976.

At that precise moment, a massive flight of B-52 bombers from Guam would be moving ominously north up the Yellow Sea on a vector directly to the North Korean capital, Pyongyang. In the Sea of Japan, Task Force 77.4's aircraft carrier, U.S.S. *Midway,* would launch forty combat aircraft that would vector north above international waters.

As chief of staff, I supervised the writing of this OPLAN, which soon became a thick document, replete with detailed schedules of troop and aircraft movements. General Stilwell composed the actual transmission message to the Pentagon. He told the Pentagon this was the plan we intended to implement; he did *not* ask for their comments or suggestions, but instead made it clear that PAUL BUNYAN was a carefully coordinated operation that did not lend itself to remote-control fine-tuning from Washington. All he wanted was approval to execute the plan.

We didn't submit the detailed OPLAN to the National Command Authority until almost midnight of Thursday, August 19, which was Thursday morning in Washington.

After a quick dinner at home, I returned to the War Room Friday night. My station was at the command table, next to General Stilwell, who was away from the headquarters giving final instructions and inspiring confidence in the hearts of the U.S. and ROK soldiers and airmen who were about to face the Communist enemy eyeball-to-eyeball. The senior staff assembled at midnight to monitor the assembly of the PAUL BUNYAN task force and supporting units. We couldn't proceed with the operation, of course, until approval came from Washington. But in anticipation of Pentagon authorization, we took certain unorthodox, but vital, actions concerning communications.

Stilwell's deputy, Lieutenant General John Burns, had been the Seventh Air Force commander in Thailand during the ill-fated *Mayaguez* hijacking the year before. After the civilian ship was seized by Cambodian Communists in the Gulf of Siam, the rescue attempt had been micro-managed from Washington. At one point, Air Force fighter-bomber pilots orbiting the island where the *Mayaguez* crew was held by the Khmer Rouge were startled to hear the distinctive, Mittel-Europa murmur of Henry Kissinger in their earphones. The White House had used a command override channel to deal directly with the operation's air support. In so doing, Kissinger bypassed the entire local command structure and fouled up the operation. General Burns had been about to order the Marine helicopters not to land on an island held by the Khmer Rouge, but his radio channel to the operational aircraft was blocked by the Flash Override from Washington. The Marines landed and suffered heavy casualties. We were determined this would not happen to us.

General Stilwell routed the only secure phone lines to the Pentagon and CINCPAC in Hawaii directly to his desk in the War Room. He directed me to make sure the lines terminated there. To be certain Washington could not bypass this headquarters, we left the phone receivers off the hook, in the "open" position. To "hang up," we simply shoved a disposable Styrofoam coffee cup over the receiver mouthpieces.

To double-check this system, I called in the UNC Communications Officer

(J-6), Colonel James L. Young. "Colonel," I said sternly, "your entire future in the U.S. Army depends on how carefully you follow the orders I'm about to give you."

"Yes, sir," the J-6 said. I had his attention.

"Under absolutely no circumstances whatsoever," I continued, "will you allow any direct communication from a higher headquarters to bypass this room and contact the corps, division, or the task force itself."

The man nervously licked his lips, grasping that he was about to be squeezed between the rock of my authority and the hard place of the Pentagon. "Yes, sir."

"I don't care if the Chairman of the Joint Chiefs of Staff or President Ford himself is on the line." I had to give the Colonel some ammunition. In a situation this tense, it would be disastrous if the Pentagon War Room or the White House itself began issuing and then countermanding orders to American and Korean ground and air units. "Tell them our communications system out here is incompatible with theirs. Tell them they've got a four channel and we've got a two channel . . . whatever. Just don't allow any contact with our field forces other than from this headquarters."

The Colonel departed quickly to relay my orders to his staff.

At 2345 hours Friday night, fifteen minutes before the deadline established by General Stilwell, we received authorization to implement PAUL BUN-YAN. The OPLAN became an Operational Order. Admiral James Holloway, the acting chairman of the Joint Chiefs of Staff, had done an absolutely brilliant job of "selling" General Stilwell's plan to the Washington leadership without the typical nit-picking modifications and changes.

Less than thirty minutes later, the J-6 returned. He had received the first message from the Pentagon requesting direct communication with our task force commander, now assembling his forces below the DMZ.

"I told them the systems were incompatible," the Colonel explained, "but I assured them that you could probably answer any questions about what was going on in the command."

Soon he received another Washington query directed to the task force commander at Camp Kitty Hawk. "They want to know how old the tree is," the J-6 said, shaking his head.

"That's none of their damn business," I snapped.[21]

Twenty-five minutes later the Colonel returned. Now the Pentagon lieutenant general in charge of worldwide military communications was personally demanding the J-6 open channels to the task force. "I told the General to talk to you, sir," the Colonel said. "He was not exactly pleased."

"Don't worry, Colonel," I said, "I'm your rating officer, not him."

Less than fifteen minutes after that, the J-6 received another call, this one directly from the senior civilian engineer who had designed the secure-voice communications system. He had all kinds of good advice on how to link the supposedly incompatible channels. But the J-6 held his ground.

At around 0400, Ambassador Dick Sneider appeared in the War Room, having flown for almost twenty-four hours from the States. He took my chair beside Stilwell, and I moved down the table. General Stilwell was on the phone to Morris Brady, the task force commander. The Ambassador reached up to take the phone from Stilwell's hand, obviously eager to speak to Brady himself. I saw the muscles in Stilwell's arm clench, then go rigid. The harder Sneider tugged, the more firmly Stilwell gripped the phone. Finally, the General won this ludicrous tug-of-war with the Ambassador.

Stilwell replaced the receiver and smiled at the Ambassador. "Dick," Stilwell said, "was there something you wanted me to ask General Brady?"

Sneider was visibly ruffled. "Well," he muttered, "the *President* asked me to be his personal representative in this operation. And I . . ."

"Certainly," Stilwell said, still smiling. "I'll be happy to relay any of the President's questions to *my* field commanders."

The Ambassador got the message.

☆   ☆

JUST before dawn, I received confirmation that all the units were at their lines of departure. I got up and went to the end of the room where I could be alone to say a prayer. It was my estimate, shared by many of the staff, that the operation stood a fifty-fifty chance of starting a war. In less than an hour, several hundred thousand men might very well be fighting and dying in those steep, blood-soaked mountains.

If the murderous North Korean assault on our forces had been part of an elaborate plot to trigger an American military response, which in turn would provoke a North Korean invasion, we might be teetering on the brink of a holocaust. If North Korea unleashed a massive armored assault against Seoul, we would have no choice but to request authorization for the first use of nuclear weapons since World War II. But there was no backing down now.

☆   ☆

AT 0648, the large task force truck convoy left Camp Kitty Hawk and rolled toward the Joint Security Area. Near the head of the column was a jeep carrying an American major. As the trucks rumbled past Checkpoint No. 2 on the southern edge of the JSA, the Major's jeep, which had pulled out of the convoy just before entering the JSA, sped to the nearby quarters of the Neutral Nations Supervisory Commission, where Swiss Major General

Claude Van Muyden and Swedish Major General Lage Wernstedt were billeted. The Major presented my compliments to the European generals and informed them that the operation, which was currently under way, was limited in scope and that the actual task force in the JSA was armed with only pistols and pickax handles. The task force would simply cut down the poplar tree, remove two illegally constructed barriers, and then withdraw. He asked the neutral officers to so inform their Polish and Czech counterparts located a few hundred meters away just north of the JSA in North Korean territory. The generals were furious that I had not informed them in advance of the operation. Some weeks later, however, they admitted that it was best for their credibility as neutral observers that they did not know about PAUL BUNYAN in advance.

The lead elements of the task force convoy roared into the JSA just as twenty troop-carrier Hueys and their hovering gunship escorts clattered over the southern horizon and swung into their orbit north of the Imjin River. While one joint U.S.-ROK security platoon formed a cordon around the poplar tree, the other platoon's truck drove to the east end of the Bridge of No Return to block the North Koreans' most obvious reinforcement route.

Surprise was complete. The few North Koreans at their guard billet scurried around, then retreated north of the JSA. Our engineers' chain saws were already slashing into the tree trunk. Now an ROK Special Forces unit double-timed into the security zone and secured the road junction that was the other possible North Korean reinforcement route. Moments later, our second engineer team rolled up to the North Korean pipe barrier and ripped it from the ground with a tow chain attached to their truck frame. The second barrier was quickly removed in the same way.

By now, the North Korean security guards were dashing around and shouting into their field telephones. They grew noticeably quiet as the heavily armed ROK reconnaissance company deployed along the low ridge just south of the JSA. From the North Koreans' viewpoint, the picture must have been ominous: sixty American and South Korean security guards carrying pickax handles in the front rank, supported by the ROK recon unit armed for bear, who were in turn covered by a full company of American troops in orbiting helicopters with gunship escort.

Ten minutes later, as the felled poplar trunk was on the ground being sawed into smaller sections, a makeshift North Korean convoy, including a bus, two trucks, and a clanking East German sedan, sped toward the JSA along the main road from the north, which was built on a riverside dike. When the lead driver spotted the ranks of Korean and American troops, he stopped. One hundred and fifty North Korean soldiers, carrying AK-47s, scurried from the convoy and took cover beside the dike. The Communist officers appeared uncertain whether to proceed, hold their ground, or retreat. Our local commander sensed this confusion and ordered A Company, 2/9th Infantry, forward by truck. These troops, in full battle gear, piled from their vehicles and deployed along the road within easy small-arms range of the North Koreans. The enemy company remained hidden and withdrew later in the day.

By 0745, the remains of the poplar tree were loaded aboard the trucks and the task force began its withdrawal. The pullback was carefully coordinated not to expose any isolated UNC troops to sudden North Korean foray. At 0830, all the units were south of the DMZ and rolling toward Camp Kitty Hawk, escorted by Cobra gunships. The normal United Nations security platoon had taken their post within the JSA. North Korean guards cautiously ventured forward to examine the tree stump and the shattered ruins of their illegal roadblocks.

The only serious incident that morning occurred at 1015, when General Brady's Command and Control helicopter was hit by North Korean automatic-weapon fire as the helicopter hovered just south of the JSA. The fire stopped abruptly when six Cobras banked line-abreast and swung into firing position, their twinkling laser sights directly on the enemy gun position. As a reminder to the Communists what kind of force they faced, we kept our heavily armed infantry along the southern ridge until well into the afternoon.

We heard nothing from the North Koreans until noon, when they requested an impromptu meeting of the Military Armistice Commission. The senior North Korean army officer glumly read a message from his Supreme Commander, Kim Il-Sung. The Communist dictator expressed "regret" over the August 18 incident and hoped that both sides would make efforts to prevent similar unfortunate outbreaks. This was the first time in the twenty-three-year history of the Armistice Commission that the North Koreans had acknowledged even partial responsibility for violence along the DMZ.

Over the next several days, satellite and aerial reconnaissance revealed that the North Koreans were still on a defensive posture. Slowly they reduced the high-level alert, still obviously wary of American forces in the region. We scaled back at the same pace, again reminding the Communists of the size and flexibility of our ground, air, and naval forces. In early September, the Communists agreed to remove their remaining guard posts from the southern sector of the JSA. We then extracted a further concession by requiring they construct their own bridge into the neutral zone.

In the JSA, the net result of the operation was the physical separation of the UNC and North Korean guards. We were careful to coordinate our negotiations with military operations. The slow reduction of augmented naval and air forces followed each North Korean concession. On September

8, when the North Koreans agreed to virtually all of our demands, the JCS gave the order to reduce alert level back to DEFCON-4, and the U.S.S. *Midway* departed Korean waters for Japan.

Operation PAUL BUNYAN was a valuable reminder that North Korea's ruthless and increasingly desperate Communist leaders could be effectively dealt with only from a position of strength. They viewed our earlier reconciliation attempts as weakness to be further exploited. The only reason Kim Il-Sung finally backed down was that we made him understand the danger he faced. Despite our retreat from Southeast Asia, America stood solidly beside our South Korean ally.

☆   ☆

THE events in Korea were the first serious test of the volunteer Army. Overall, the troops performed with a high level of professionalism. But there were some notable exceptions. As soon as we increased alert status to DEFCON-3, my personnel officer reported that hundreds of Department of Army civilians who—in an austerity measure—had replaced soldiers in maintenance and supply depots began requesting immediate transportation out of Korea. Like the rest of us they were afraid a war was imminent. But unlike soldiers, they couldn't be ordered to stay. "Colonel," I told the personnel officer, "you will not spend a single U.S. government dollar on plane tickets for these people. If they want to go so badly, they can pay for the trip themselves."

Civilian workers were not my main worry, however. We had a high proportion of women enlisted personnel among the American support units. In several cases, otherwise exemplary NCOs went AWOL during the first hours of the alert, trying to locate their soldier wives or girlfriends and take them to safe areas in the rear.

Although no dependents were allowed in combat units and in the forward division areas, many of our women soldiers in rear areas had small children. Some soldier mothers were married to other GIs; some were divorced; and some had simply never bothered to marry. They normally left their children in the care of Korean women during the duty day.

But DEFCON-3 was hardly normal duty. Some support units were deployed well forward, close to the DMZ. All troops had to report in full combat gear, draw weapons and C-rations, and be prepared for twenty-four-hour duty for the duration of the alert.

At a meeting I held with command sergeants major after the crisis, I was given many troubling reports. A few women soldiers had requested immediate transfers to the rear as soon as the alert was declared. Others showed up in formation wearing helmets and flak jackets and carrying babies.

One tough old black sergeant major with a chestful of combat decorations shook his head sadly as he told his story.

"Sir," he said, "I saw a sergeant and his wife standing in formation *each* holding on to a little kid." He seemed more bewildered than angry. "That's just not a good way to go to war, sir."

I had to agree.

CHAPTER THIRTEEN

No Parade

1976–1978

☆   ☆

THAT FALL, THE U.N. Command slowly drew down the augmentation forces massed for the operation. For the moment at least, the new conciliatory tone of the North Koreans at the Military Armistice Commission meetings was matched by their tactics elsewhere along the DMZ. There were no sniping or booby-trap incidents for several months. It appeared our show of force had instilled sober caution in the Communist command.[1]

General Richard Stilwell retired that fall and was replaced by General John W. Vessey, Jr. The new commander in chief was a soldier's soldier, having risen through the ranks as a rifleman in World War II to gain a battlefield commission on the Anzio beachhead. Jack Vessey was a man of calm demeanor and absolutely rock-solid integrity. He was the perfect man for the U.N. Command in Korea.

Vessey's leadership was quickly put to the test. As the American presidential campaign wound down, senior Korean military and government leaders voiced alarm and concern to their American counterparts in Seoul. One of the planks of Democratic candidate Jimmy Carter's foreign policy platform was the withdrawal of all American ground combat troops from Korea. Some of Carter's speeches stressed the need to avoid entanglement in another Asian ground war; others described the withdrawal as an economy measure. He didn't seem to grasp that basing the 2nd Infantry Division in Korea was cheaper than maintaining the unit in the States.

To the Koreans, such a withdrawal would be another betrayal, plain and simple. They had sent 50,000 combat troops to South Vietnam and kept them there, despite heavy casualties, as a gesture of allied solidarity. In

1971, we had shown our gratitude by arbitrarily withdrawing the 7th Infantry Division from Korea without even consulting the Seoul government. Now the leading presidential candidate proposed pulling out the remaining American combat unit. The 2nd Infantry Division was the only mobile strategic reserve unit equipped with high-technology communications and firepower in South Korea. American combat troops were the major deterrent to a new North Korean invasion.

After Carter's election, I had the occasion to meet with General Lee Sae-Ho, chief of staff of the ROK army, and later with Lieutenant General Lew Byong-Hion, director of the Joint Staff. *Why,* they asked, did the President-elect still propose withdrawing American combat troops from Korea? Hadn't he received proper intelligence briefings on the North Korean buildup? They reminded me that the abrupt pullout of American troops in 1949 had triggered the 1950 North Korean invasion. Their human intelligence sources in the North—which were frankly better than ours—all indicated that a new pullout would have the same result.

"If your troops leave," General Lew told me, "Kim Il-Sung will invade again."

I assured the generals that our Joint Chiefs of Staff would set the new president straight on this matter soon after the inauguration. They were not convinced. Their Washington embassy had received ominous reports that Carter's military advisers came from liberal think tanks and left-leaning pacifist groups. I tried to reassure them, but I wasn't optimistic myself.[2]

Then, in December 1976, we received a revised intelligence estimate on the probable warning time we would have in the event of a North Korean invasion. Previous estimates had given us several days to a week to prepare for an assault. Given the North Korean forward deployment of artillery, armor, and aircraft in underground facilities, the new joint CIA-DIA estimate was less than twelve hours. The UNC staff was stunned.

The pessimism in Seoul increased on January 21, 1977, when, as his first official act, President Carter pardoned 10,000 Vietnam War draft dodgers. The symbolism was clear to my Korean colleagues: Our allies in Asia were not worth defending.

Less than two weeks later, General Vessey received a back-channel message from General George Brown, chairman of the Joint Chiefs of Staff. The President had given the JCS Presidential Review Memorandum (PRM) 13, a draft plan for the troop withdrawal, and asked their opinion on which of three schedule options was preferable. Pointedly, Carter did not solicit the Joint Chiefs' opinion on the overall merits of the pullout. It's interesting to note that PRM-13 was dated January 27, 1977; it had obviously been quickly drafted and released for interagency review within the first week of the new administration. President Carter, therefore, could not have had time to adequately review the sensitive new intelligence on the North Korean buildup before issuing the document.[3]

The first option was immediate withdrawal; the second called for pulling out a battalion every two months, with a total draw-down in two years. The final option was a phased pullout over four or five years, which included transfer of modern weapons and equipment to the South Koreans and training in their use. The White House had specifically requested that the Joint Chiefs not consult with the U.N. Command in Seoul on this matter. The Joint Chiefs informed Carter that all of these options entailed "grave risk," and therefore were unacceptable, given the North Korean military buildup. When pressed by Defense Secretary Harold Brown, the Chiefs stated the last option was the least objectionable.[4]

General Vessey assured the staff that Carter hadn't been properly "read in" on the latest intelligence estimates of the North Korean military threat and offensive intentions. Indeed, we had evidence that the North Koreans had resumed their full offensive posture after the limited, temporary defensive redeployment of the previous fall. The General noted that the White House request that the Joint Chiefs not consult Seoul was a clear indication that the matter was still being debated in Washington. He intended to forcefully present our opinion on this vital issue.

Vessey flew to Washington in March for some meetings. While there, he had the opportunity to confer with President Carter on the proposed withdrawal. At their White House meeting, the General carefully outlined the latest intelligence estimates, emphasizing the unmistakable evidence of North Korean offensive intentions. The President, Vessey later told me, remained inexpressive during the General's presentation. Vessey was not given to hyperbole; he had more combat command experience than almost any other general in the armed services. When he made such a presentation, people had to listen.

Finally, Carter responded. "General," he said, "you've made some very good points that I was not aware of. I promise that I will not reach my final decision on this matter until I've consulted you again." That was exactly what General Vessey had hoped to achieve.

A few days later in Seoul, General Vessey told me, "Jack, I think I shook up the President when I briefed him on the scale of the North Korean buildup."[5]

"I certainly hope so, sir," I replied.

☆　　　　☆

ON MARCH 9, 1977, President Carter held a press conference. He did not mention Korea in his opening statement. But a reporter asked him to reconcile his campaign promise to withdraw combat troops with the recently submitted fiscal 1978 budget, which included hundreds of millions of dollars to support those very troops in Korea. Carter explained his "commitment" to withdraw U.S. ground troops from Korea. He outlined an "appropriate" four- or five-year withdrawal schedule, which, he added, "would have to be worked out very carefully with the South Korean government."[6]

☆   ☆

THE matter did not emerge again until late April, when Army Chief of Staff General Bernard Rogers came to Seoul. I attended a luncheon in his honor at Ambassador Richard Sneider's residence.

"General," I told him, "we're just having one hell of a time trying to explain the reasons for this withdrawal to the Koreans."

Rogers nodded in grim resignation. "Jack," he said, "I sympathize with you. But you've just got to realize the President is serious about this." He shook his head sadly. "He intends to go through with it."

"Well, sir," I added, pressing Rogers, "can you at least explain his rationale for the plans?"

Rogers shook his head. "No, General," he said, "I cannot."

Senior officers around the table were frowning now. The United Nations Command certainly had not received any formal indication that the withdrawal decision had been made. Indeed, the President's assurance to consult with General Vessey before reaching the final decision was the basis for our optimism that Washington would soon come to its senses.

That optimism increased in early May, when the embassy and U.S. Forces, Korea, received a joint State/Defense Department telegram detailing plans for the visit of a senior American consultation team. The group was headed by Chairman of the Joint Chiefs of Staff General George Brown and Undersecretary of State Philip Habib, and was due in Seoul later that month to discuss the withdrawal issue with the Korean government. The telegram ordered us to stress to the South Koreans that no final decision on the withdrawal had been made and that none would be reached without "thorough consultation" with all parties involved, including the civilian and military leaders of both Korea and Japan.[7] To the officers of UNC headquarters, this message was clear evidence that wisdom was beginning to prevail in Washington.

But then the situation became badly muddled again. We received word that the Congressional Budget Office was about to release a study claiming that withdrawing American ground troops from Korea would save billions of dollars over the next five years.[8] This was ridiculous. Unless the 2nd Infantry Division was disbanded, it was much cheaper to keep the unit in

Korea where KATUSA and Korean Service Corps personnel cost us nothing and we paid no rent for valuable training areas. General Vessey was beginning to get uneasy that the White House might be staging an end run, sliding into the decision without consulting him again as Carter had promised.

Presidential Review Memorandum 13, we learned, was being hotly debated in Washington intelligence circles. The intelligence community would not yet state conclusively either way whether South Korea would be able to stop a new North Korean invasion without the support of American ground troops. But Pentagon analyst John Armstrong's group was now working literally night and day to evaluate the masses of new evidence depicting the North Korean buildup. Above all, Armstrong expected that the new information would prove North Korea's offensive intentions, which validated the role of the 2nd Infantry Division as a "trip-wire" deterrent.[9]

When I was sure our own Intelligence and Operations staffs were assembling the latest field estimates on North Korean strength and intentions, as well as our own war plans, for the consultation team, I put the withdrawal question aside and got on to more pressing business. Running a joint staff in a large command entailed a series of long working days, punctuated by tightly scheduled meetings.

☆   ☆

I WAS in the middle of just such a schedule on Wednesday, May 18, 1977, when I got a call from Jim Hausman, General Vessey's civilian special adviser. Hausman was an old Korea-hand, having served in Seoul as adviser to Korean and American officials since 1946. His office was right down the hall from mine, on the other side of General Vessey's conference room. Jim explained he was with John Saar, the *Washington Post* Tokyo bureau chief, who was in Korea to report on the upcoming consultations. I felt a twinge of wariness. American embassy officials had warned me about Saar, who they said had a bad attitude about the government of Korea, which might have been nurtured by his contacts with Korean exile leftists in Tokyo. In any event, Ambassador Sneider no longer allowed his staff to brief Saar.

But Jim explained that the U.N. Command had agreed to give Saar an on-the-record interview with the UNC Deputy Commander, Air Force Lieutenant General John Burns, concerning the role of U.S. air power in the future defense of South Korea. The Burns interview was followed by a strictly background, off-the-record briefing by Jim Hausman on the current political and military situation in Korea, so that Saar could write from a knowledgeable position. Hausman added that Saar had always honored his requests for anonymity and seemed sincerely interested in a thorough background briefing.

"Chief," Jim Hausman said, "Mr. Saar's asking some technical military questions about the role of the 2nd Infantry Division, which I frankly don't feel comfortable answering. Have you got a couple of minutes to answer his questions as part of the backgrounder we're giving him?"

"Hell, Jim," I said, "this guy hasn't done any good by us in the past. We should probably stay away from him."

"Jack," Jim Hausman said, "he's sitting right in my office and promised he'll follow all the ground rules we've laid down. He seems sincerely interested."[10]

I looked at my appointment schedule. "I've got twenty minutes free. If you can bring him over right now, I'll try to answer his questions."

I pulled the cover across the classified military situation map of Korea and closed my classified reading file. Even in a background briefing I didn't intend to inadvertently reveal any secrets.

Jim introduced the reporter and left us alone. John Saar was a slight, intense young man in his thirties. From his questions about the role of the 2nd Infantry Division, I saw he was unfamiliar with certain military principles, such as air mobility and massed firepower. I outlined the division's strength in tank-busting helicopters and TOW missiles, armored personnel carriers, and modern communications, all advanced systems the ROKA did not possess.

Saar asked why we simply couldn't sell these systems to the South Koreans.

I patiently explained that the 2nd Infantry Division needed this equipment, wherever it was stationed, and that the ROKA simply was not yet trained to operate such modern hardware as the Dragon anti-tank missile, the Cobra gunship, or the battlefield radars that made American combat troops in South Korea a formidable deterrent force.

Saar probed me about the nature of this deterrence.

I noted that U.S. combat troops provided a "double" deterrent. First, given the firepower and mobility of the 2nd Infantry Division, the North Koreans would have to concentrate their forces to successfully attack our troops. This concentration would increase the chances of our detecting their attack. Second, I added, China and the Soviet Union would restrain Kim Il-Sung from stepping on the American "trip wire" and escalating a regional conflict to global proportions. Without this constraint, I emphasized, the North Koreans might be encouraged to act recklessly.

Saar pressed me for a military evaluation of the pros and cons of withdrawing this force.

"Are you saying that you think President Carter's plan to withdraw all ground forces from Korea is likely to encourage Kim Il-Sung and lead to war?"

I carefully considered my words because I didn't know what General Burns had already told him. Moreover, this question clearly went beyond the technical explanation I'd agreed to provide.

"Well," I answered, "I think that the senior ROK officers would give you a very definite yes to that question. They're convinced of it. From a purely military point of view, I agree with them." This was a sensitive area, and I wanted to make sure Saar understood my position. "However," I added, "President Carter had many other factors to consider. Since he has available to him the same military intelligence that we have, we assume that other, non-military factors are overriding."

Saar nodded, but did not reply. He was jotting notes furiously. I hope he keeps those notes confidential, I thought. Colonel Don Gelke, the public affairs officer, had set up the briefing by Jim Hausman as an off-the-record backgrounder.

"If the decision *is* made," I continued, "we will execute it with enthusiasm and a high level of professional skill. But, since a decision has not been made and since the ROK expect a full discussion of the subject, it's imperative that the military provide their best judgment and advice. We feel it's our obligation to do so until a decision is announced."[11]

I couldn't discuss the Armstrong group's efforts or detail the shocking evidence they'd uncovered of the North Korean buildup and offensive deployment. But I wanted the reporter to know this matter was serious. "An intensive intelligence effort over the last twelve months has revealed that North Korea is much stronger than we thought." The problem as I saw it, I added, was that "people who are making the decisions are basing them on information that's two years old."

As my ROK colleagues had stressed, the situation was similar to 1949. It was also similar to 1947, when America decided to undercut the Chinese Nationalists.

After the fall of China and Vietnam, I told Saar, the specter of an intelligence failure was raised and the question was asked, " 'Did the military people in the know express themselves loudly and clearly enough that the decision-makers understood?' We want to make sure this time."

I then reminded him of the American pullout in 1949, which triggered the North Korean invasion of June 1950. I felt it was important that this young reporter understand that the men on General Vessey's staff intended to raise these vital issues during the consultations the next week.

Saar thanked me, then left, just as my next appointment arrived in the outer office. Before starting the meeting, however, I called the UNC public affairs officer, Colonel Don Gelke. "Don," I said, "why didn't you come up here to sit in with me and that reporter?" He'd always insisted on being present at other briefings I'd given.

"General," Don Gelke answered, "I didn't think it was necessary. I sat in for a few minutes with Jim Hausman, and that was going fine, so I left Saar with him." Gelke paused. "Sir, you did remind Saar that was an off-the-record backgrounder, didn't you?"

"No," I said. "Jim Hausman did that already. Was I supposed to do it, too?"

"Technically speaking. . . ." He paused again. "Did Hausman accompany Saar to your office?"

"Sure. You always tell us not to allow reporters to wander around UNC headquarters unescorted."

"Well . . ." Don Gelke was obviously uneasy.

"Look, Don," I said, "get hold of Saar and remind him that was a background briefing. And try to get a copy of what he writes."

Late that afternoon, I got a call from Saar. "General," he said, "I want to confirm that our interview was on the record."

I frowned, but resisted the urge to lash out. Arguing with the press was a no-win situation. "John," I said, as calmly as I could, "that's not the way I understand it. It's my clear understanding that our discussion was part of the background briefing you were receiving from Jim Hausman." There was silence from Saar's end. "Hausman called me in the middle of his briefing," I added, as reasonably as I could, "and asked if I had time to answer some specific military questions. This was all part of the same briefing."

Finally Saar replied, his voice edged with defiance. "You know what the rules are, General. If you don't specifically tell *me* at the beginning of the interview it's off the record, I have to consider that I'm authorized to print your comments."

I sighed with frustration. He was conveniently forgetting that Jim Hausman had escorted him to my office, thus keeping the background briefing "chain" unbroken. But such civilian intrigues were alien to my world. When you dealt with military men in either war or peace, confidences were kept. "Well, I understand the rules you're explaining now," I said, "but you certainly didn't explain them when Jim Hausman brought you to my office."

"Unless you want to retract or change what you said," Saar added, "I'm entitled to print it."

"What was your interview with General Burns, background or on the record?"

"On the record, General."

I reviewed in my mind exactly what we had discussed. The information about the vital role of the 2nd Infantry Division was valid. And all my Korean and American colleagues shared my concern about the proposed withdrawal. I was not divulging any secrets. After all, in January General Vessey himself had given Saar an interview on the same subject in which Vessey had emphasized that the troop withdrawal would "increase considerably" the risk of war with North Korea.[12] And Vessey had also recently given an on-the-record interview to United Press International, in which he'd noted, "In my view, the withdrawal of all the American ground troops would raise the possibility of war in Korea."[13] As I recalled my Saar briefing, I hadn't gone beyond anything General Vessey had already said to the press.

And I didn't have time to conduct a debate with Saar. "Well, John," I said, "I guess you've got me. I'm not going to retract anything I said because I don't believe in changing what I consider to be the truth."

We left it like that, and I made a mental note to avoid smooth-talking young reporters in the future.[14]

☆   ☆

It was around ten o'clock the next night when General Vessey phoned my quarters. I took the call in the living room where Mary was pouring coffee for our dinner guests.

"Jack," he said, chuckling warmly, "I just got a call from George Brown. It looks like John Saar's story made the front page of the *Washington Post.* George said to tell you he appreciates your taking the media heat off him."

General Brown, the chairman of the Joint Chiefs of Staff, had been pilloried over statements attributed to him that Israel's influence with American news media was out of proportion to the country's strategic importance. It was still Thursday morning in Washington and Brown had just read the *Post.*

"I hope this isn't serious, sir," I said.

"No, don't worry, Jack," General Vessey said, "George was laughing about it."

At 12:30, General Vessey phoned back. "General Brown just called again," he said. "This time he wasn't laughing."

"What happened, sir?"

"The President is furious. You are ordered to fly to Washington on the first available transportation and report to General Brown who will escort you to see President Carter. The President wants to see you personally on this matter."

"Am I being disciplined?"

Our last dinner guest, Malaysian ambassador John Denis de Silva, looked up sharply as he heard my question.

"I don't know, Jack," General Vessey answered. "You are to write a report on the incident and deliver it to General Brown ASAP."

My immediate reaction was that Jack Vessey was playing a practical joke on me. To clarify the matter, I called the headquarters public affairs office and asked them to get a copy of the *Post* story from Washington and have it at my quarters by 0600.

"What's all this about, Jack?" Ambassador de Silva asked.

"I'm not sure," I answered honestly, "but I've been ordered to report to the President by the first available means."

"Excellent," he said. "This way the whole bloody stupid withdrawal issue will get a proper airing." Everyone in the Seoul diplomatic corps was concerned about Carter's plans for the troop pullout. So the Ambassador was pleased I'd have the chance to discuss the matter directly with the President.

But I didn't share his enthusiasm.

When I read Saar's story at dawn, I understood better what the flap was all about. The telegraphic text sent by the Pentagon public affairs office noted that the article had appeared in a separate, highlighted box on the front page. "U.S. General: Korea Pullout Risks War" read the headline. This was an obvious echo of Saar's earlier interview with General Vessey. Saar's article had quoted me as calling President Carter's plan to withdraw American troops "a mistake." He had made the assessment of my ROK colleagues that the troop pullout "will lead to war" appear to be my unsolicited opinion. Instead of reporting my summary of the Korean generals' views, Saar quoted me as saying, " 'Many other senior military people' challenge the wisdom of Carter's plan." To make things worse, Saar noted, "The unusual situation of serving generals openly differing with the President's declared policy arises on the eve of talks to implement that policy."

I put down my coffee cup, my hands clenched on the telegram form. This was nonsense. I certainly had not "openly" differed with President Carter's "declared policy." Only a week earlier, the U.N. Command had been specifically instructed by Washington that the President had not yet *declared* a final policy. Besides, the briefing had been background only. But either Saar or his editors had structured my words to raise the specter of a cabal of "serving generals" publicly defying their commander in chief.

Army regulations and traditions were very clear on this matter. An officer was free to voice his opinion on pending policy matters up to the moment the civilian leadership made a decision. Once the President or the Secretary of Defense announced that a policy had been decided, however, an officer could no longer criticize it. But John Saar had ambushed me on two counts. He published our background conversation, and then distorted my words to make me appear the spokesman for a group of disgruntled, defiant generals.

Saar did note that I wanted to avoid repeating events during the fall of China and Vietnam when military leaders did not express themselves clearly enough to Washington policy-makers. He also correctly quoted me as stating, "If the decision is made, we will execute it with enthusiasm and a high level of professional skill." And he accurately summarized my statement that I was "deeply concerned that decision-makers may be working from outdated intelligence that substantially underestimates current North Korean strength."

But my assessment that "an intensive intelligence effort over the last 12 months has discovered North Korea to be much, much stronger than we thought"—which was the whole basis of my concern—was tacked on as an afterthought in the article's last paragraph.[15]

The article's overall tone left the impression I was a disgruntled malcontent at best, and a dangerous loose cannon at worst.

☆　　　　☆

THE next morning on the Korean Airline flight to Tokyo, I received another lesson in devious journalistic ethics. Jim Hausman happened to be on the same plane with his wife and daughter, and he came up to the front of the jumbo jet cabin where I was seated to chat with me. I noticed earlier that he had been talking to a young woman who I assumed was the daughter traveling with him. She sat behind us, leaning forward to listen as he and I reviewed the exact sequence of the Saar interview. When Jim left the no-smoking section to go back for a cigarette, the young woman took his seat and began asking me questions. Her line of inquiry seemed unusual for Jim's daughter. Finally, I asked her name.

"Melinda Nix," she said, removing a tape recorder from her shoulder bag. "I'm with CBS and I'd like to conduct an interview."

"Well, I certainly would not have talked to you, had I known you were a reporter," I said. "And I sure don't have any intention of granting an interview."

When Jim returned, he told me the young woman was John Saar's wife. Apparently, ambush journalism ran in the family. She got off the plane in Tokyo and filed an "exclusive interview" story on the eavesdropped opinions I had shared with Jim Hausman.[16]

But that was the least of my worries. At the Tokyo airport, I was mobbed by reporters who shouted questions in my face while prodding me with microphones and blinding me with their camera lights. It seemed the press had simplistically transformed the affair into an analog of the 1951 Truman-MacArthur confrontation.

I spent most of my time working on the report I was to deliver to General George Brown as the big jet droned northeast through the endless blue spring twilight of the Arctic. It was an exceptionally long flight from Tokyo to New York. When the report was finished, I did my best to get some sleep.

The media mob at Kennedy Airport was larger but better disciplined than their colleagues in Tokyo, thanks to the intervention of the Army public affairs officer in New York. If I hadn't been so groggy with jet lag, I would have found the situation amusing. What did these people expect me to say? I was a two-star general who had been minding his own business twenty-four hours before. Now they portrayed me as some kind of rogue out of *Dr. Strangelove.*

Luckily, airport security guards met the flight at National Airport. Given the international dateline, I had just eaten my second Friday dinner of cardboard airline rations and I wasn't eager to see more camera lights. The Army public affairs lieutenant colonel who met me had arranged a room in the general officers' quarters at Wainwright Hall at Fort Myer. He explained that General Brown had been unexpectedly called to Europe and couldn't receive me the next morning. Instead, I was to report to the Army Protocol Office in the Pentagon at 1000 Saturday morning and wait for a call from the Secretary of Defense, Harold Brown, who would escort me to the White House. I didn't like the sound of this. The new schedule completely bypassed the military chain of command.

"Colonel," I said, "this is unacceptable. Please tell your boss that I consider it vital I meet with someone in the military chain of command before talking to the political appointee civilians."

He promised to contact Major General Gordon Hill, chief of Army public affairs, at once.

The next morning, Dick Stilwell, who had retired in the Washington area, joined me for breakfast at Wainwright Hall. He carefully read my report on the Saar interview, and agreed that I had stated my case accurately and succinctly. Although retired, Stilwell retained considerable influence in the Pentagon. It was obvious, he said, that even if I had been imprudent enough to have granted Saar an on-the-record interview, my comments certainly did not breach Army regulations.

But the situation had escalated far beyond the Department of the Army. Follow-up stories in the Friday and Saturday *Washington Post* described President Carter as "distressed and angered" by my "public" criticism of his policy. Everybody seemed to assume that the troop withdrawal plan was formal policy, even though U.S. Forces, Korea, and our Seoul embassy had been specifically instructed that no decision would be made until the consultation team met with the Korean government. But unnamed White House officials, obviously trying to stay ahead of the embarrassing situation, were portraying the Carter withdrawal plan as formally established policy. Had this been true, I would have been insubordinate. But everyone knowledgeable about the situation—including the self-proclaimed open and honest Carter White House—knew this was not the case. Worse, the White House had decided to cloud the issue further by circulating the ridiculous statement that my remarks would somehow "encourage North Korea to consider another invasion of South Korea."

"I don't know where the hell they got *that* idea," Dick Stilwell said, tossing aside the *Post.* "The whole thing's gotten political in a big hurry, Jack." He noted that Senate Democrats were praising Carter for showing strong civilian control over the military.[17]

I was to learn from a Judge Advocate friend that Carter had first wanted to have me court-martialed and reduced a grade in rank. But the Army's Judge Advocate General had told the White House there was no legal grounds for this. I did not know this at the time, so I was approaching the day's activities with some apprehension. Dick Stilwell did report, however, that word in the Pentagon corridors was that Carter intended to salvage the embarrassing situation by playing the Harry Truman to my Douglas MacArthur. I wondered how far he would go.

To exacerbate the political tension, a new John Saar story from Seoul in the Saturday *Washington Post* reported that my UNC colleagues, from General Vessey down, were "saying privately" that they agreed with my view that the Carter withdrawal plan would lead to war. Saar summarized Vessey's April United Press International interview, in which the General stated that American troop withdrawal "would raise the possibility of war in Korea." The article also quoted Vessey's assessment of me as a "professional soldier with a distinguished combat record," who "will carry out faithfully and fully the policies assigned by superiors." There was a picture of General Vessey captioned "Possibility of War."[18]

I looked across the breakfast table at Dick Stilwell. We had served together in dangerous and sensitive assignments over the previous twenty-seven years. During that service, we had each luckily avoided public controversy and entanglement in politics. Dick was now safely retired. I was still a serving general. And my luck had just run out.

☆   ☆

ARMY Chief of Staff General Bernard Rogers called me to his office from the Army Protocol section. His manner was cold and abrupt.

"General," he said, "your conduct has not brought credit to the Army." It was clear that Rogers had made no effort to defend me.

"General Rogers," I said, trying to be reasonable, "all of us in Seoul believed the troop withdrawal decision had not yet been made. And I thought it was important that the reporter be familiar with all the issues involved."

Rogers glared at me, his face clouded red. "Damn it, Jack. I *told* you in April that Carter had already made his decision."

I saw the reason for General Rogers's angry posture now. He was not about to become caught in a political controversy about the President's deception over when the decision had been made.

But this was a vital issue to me. "General Rogers," I reasoned, "at that luncheon in Seoul, you certainly weren't specific about the President's decision."

Rogers continued to glare without speaking.

"And subsequent to that meeting," I continued, "our command received a specific message stating that the decision had *not* been made."

General Rogers did not comment on this. Instead, he informed me that New York congressman Samuel S. Stratton, chairman of the Investigations Subcommittee of the House Armed Services Committee, had requested that I be permitted to testify on the troop withdrawal question the next week. Pentagon Public Affairs would help me prepare an opening statement and Major General Jim Lee, the Army Chief of Legislative Liaison, would work out the details and accompany me to the hearing.

Having determined what I was going to do next week, I was now anxious to get General Rogers's estimate of what was going to happen to me in the next several hours. I asked him if he had any idea what the President and Secretary Brown were planning to do in retaliation for what they seemed to think was a challenge to their civilian authority.

"I have no idea what the President will decide to do with you. I suspect that will depend upon how you react with him during the interview and what Secretary Brown recommends. I also suspect that he'll insist, as a minimum, that you be reassigned from Korea," General Rogers responded.

I asked the Chief of Staff if he had any idea about where I might be reassigned.

Bernie Rogers stared at me coolly, playing the gruff combat commander. "You'll be told of your new assignment after your testimony."

I assumed that was a not-so-subtle hint that, if I was too honest before the House committee, I'd find myself PX officer in Greenland.

After we finished our discussion, General Rogers had me pay my respects to the new Secretary of the Army, Clifford Alexander. The Secretary was an amiable black politician from Washington, whom Carter might have selected more to demonstrate his racial tolerance than as a measure of Alexander's qualifications for the job.

"I sympathize somewhat with you, General Singlaub," Secretary Alexander said. "When I ran for mayor of Washington some years ago, that same reporter misquoted me."

I did not correct the Secretary by explaining that Saar had not misquoted my strongly held views, but had only distorted the context in which I had expressed them.

I returned to the Protocol Office to await my summons to meet with Harold Brown in his office on the E-ring of the Pentagon, just above the River entrance.

Secretary of Defense Harold Brown had a broad face with large glasses that gave him a somewhat owlish appearance. He carefully considered his words before speaking, almost as if individual sentences were sections of mathematical formulas, which had to be verified before presentation. I suppose he wished I had been as circuitous in my dealings with John Saar. I learned later that Secretary Brown was privately opposed to the troop pullout, but that he was too loyal to Carter to make his views public.[19]

He patiently listened as I explained the sequence of events that had led to the original Saar article.

In the course of the conversation, the Secretary suggested that things would go much better for me with the President if I would just explain to Carter that the reporter misquoted me. Like Secretary Alexander, Brown implied reporters had misquoted him in the past.

He was suggesting I lie on an important matter to save my skin. But I had not worn this uniform for thirty-four years just to start compromising my principles at this point.

"Well, Mr. Secretary," I said, "you obviously don't understand. I was not misquoted. John Saar distorted a few things, but his report was basically accurate. In addition to that, I believe very strongly in what I said or I wouldn't have said it."

While I spoke, Brown's special assistant, a young man named John G. Kester, came in and listened to the conversation.

Secretary Brown proceeded to give me President Carter's view on the matter. The President considered I had shown bad judgment by going public to speak in opposition to the decision he had already made to withdraw U.S. ground forces from Korea.

I couldn't let this point go unchallenged. "Sir," I interrupted, trying to keep my voice even, "every senior American in Seoul, in the embassy and UNC headquarters, was informed that the withdrawal decision would *not* be made until after there'd been consultations with the governments of South Korea and Japan." Brown and his assistant stared at me, expressionless. "I would have never spoken to a reporter on the record or off about this had I believed the withdrawal was already actual policy." Brown continued to gaze at me passively. I was frustrated now. "Mr. Secretary," I added, "we had orders to inform the Koreans the decision had *not* been made."

Now Kester spoke. "Tell me, General," he said, "if you had been told that the decision was made, but you were instructed to tell the Koreans otherwise, would that have made any difference?"

"I'm not sure I understand what you mean, John," I said. "Are you asking, would I have been willing to lie to the Koreans?"

Kester looked uncomfortable. He shook his head. "No, no, that's not exactly what I mean."

Secretary Brown and Kester exchanged glances. I sensed there was something important they were not sharing with me.

The controversy over exactly when and how President Jimmy Carter had transformed his vague plans on the troop withdrawal into a formal presidential decision was to continue for years. The closest Carter ever came to publicly announcing a final decision on the troop withdrawal policy was the vaguely worded statements during his March press conference. A few months after I was recalled, it was revealed that he had privately signed a decision memorandum in early May, *before* we had received the Joint State-DoD message that no decision had been reached.[20] But Carter certainly had not informed his chief negotiators, Philip Habib and General George Brown, of his decision. Years later, Habib was adamant that he felt he had been sent to Seoul to negotiate, not dictate policy.[21]

Jimmy Carter, who as a candidate had promised the American people he would never lie to them, had as president obviously decided to lie not only to our Korean and Japanese allies, but also to the professional diplomats and military officers serving their country in Korea. The White House smoke screen covering this duplicity was unusually thick. Historians such as Richard Stubbing and Mark Perry have found it almost impossible to pin down when Carter signed his presidential decision paper on the troop withdrawal. And the National Security Council has kept the document classified Secret into 1990.[22]

☆   ☆

THE Secretary's driver took us through the southwest gate of the White House and dropped us at the West Wing. It was a warm Saturday afternoon in late May, and the aides in the West Wing offices were dressed in slacks and polo shirts. A few wore blue jeans. As we walked toward the Oval Office, I was struck by the extreme youth and casual banter of the presidential aides in the offices we passed. Most seemed to be in their twenties or early thirties. Their animated conversation was apparently about an important White House tennis tournament, not vital matters of state. The last time I'd been in the West Wing was for a drug policy meeting during the second Nixon administration. His White House staff had been well-groomed, seasoned veterans of Washington's bureaucratic wars. President Carter's staff looked like summer interns.

We waited in a small anteroom off the Oval Office. A sense of surreal weirdness rose in me. Just down the hall, young voices whooped and hollered mock warnings of the slaughter about to be unleashed on the White House tennis courts. And I was about to confront the most powerful man in the world.

One of the President's aides came in and announced, "The President will see you in a few minutes," then motioned us to follow him into the Oval Office.

The room was empty. The Secretary and I stood together admiring a handsome painting of a Revolutionary War naval battle. Glancing around the room, my eye fell on the President's desk. On the forward edge stood a small mahogany rectangle. "The Buck Stops Here" read the inscription. Carter had prevailed on the Truman family to lend him Harry Truman's famous desk plaque, a tangible symbol of resolute decisiveness. I swallowed the irony silently.

The President cleared his throat behind us and we spun to face him. Jimmy Carter was smoothing a wide paisley tie inside his crisp blue sportcoat. I had the unmistakable impression the President had dressed quickly to receive us, which probably accounted for the delay. This too was ironic. He had apparently intended to relieve a senior Army officer dressed in slacks and a polo shirt, then thought the situation merited at least a coat and tie.

As the President approached, I was disconcerted by his relentless jack-o'-lantern grin. He continued to smile widely as we were seated at a coffee table. I waited tensely for him to speak.

"You know, General Singlaub," the President said, still grinning, "I am accustomed to making difficult decisions. After all, I served in the Navy for eight years."

He leaned toward me, as if expecting some comment. I remained silent. Carter's campaign statements that he had been a "nuclear physicist" in the Navy had rankled many senior Navy officers. President Carter had actually served just less than eight years after graduating from Annapolis in 1946. His highest rank had been lieutenant. And I knew junior officers were rarely burdened with difficult decisions.

"And I also had to make a lot of tough decisions as governor of Georgia," the President continued. "Before I even became the official presidential candidate of the Democratic Party, my military advisers recommended we withdraw our combat forces from Korea." He leaned toward Harold Brown, evoking confirmation.

Secretary Brown remained silent, his face expressionless.

Now the President turned his grin back toward me. "Since taking this office, General," he continued, "this policy has been endorsed by the Joint Chiefs of Staff."

I had to restrain myself from speaking. The Joint Chiefs had been given a fait-accompli policy to rubber-stamp, but they declared that all three withdrawal-schedule options were unsatisfactory. They stressed that even the slowest troop withdrawal would entail "grave risks." That was hardly endorsement. I looked pointedly at Harold Brown. But he still remained silent, staring out toward the Rose Garden.

"General Singlaub," Carter continued, "your boss, General John Vessey, sat right where you're sitting today and presented his case, and I considered his arguments very carefully before reaching my decision."

Again, I had to restrain myself. The President was ignoring the promise he'd made to General Vessey not to reach a decision without further consultation.

"General," the President concluded, "I've lost confidence in your ability to carry out my instructions. So I've asked the Secretary of Defense to have you reassigned."

The President nodded, indicating I could reply.

"Sir," I began, "it certainly was not my intention to embarrass you in any way by my statements. As I told that reporter, once the decision is made, I'm prepared to carry out that decision in a very professional manner." I looked at him intently, but he would not stop grinning. "But in the meantime, sir, I felt obliged to make sure all the decision-makers benefited from the best military advice possible. Those of us responsible for the defense of the Republic of Korea believe that withdrawing U.S. troops would send the wrong signal to the North Koreans, in view of their current massive buildup, just as our withdrawal did in 1949."

"General," Carter said, "as I indicated, I'm used to making hard decisions. I have already directed the Secretary of Defense to have you reassigned."

"Sir," I persisted, "I wish you would reconsider. There's been a very high turnover of general officers in Korea this year. Most of the replacements have had no previous experience in Northeast Asia. General Vessey needs someone experienced to run the UNC staff, especially if we are going to withdraw forces. I believe that my experience in the area and my knowledge of the geography and people can be a big help to him at this time."

Jimmy Carter shook his head. "No, you will be reassigned. I have decided, however, not to have you disciplined."

I stared silently back at him. I'd already learned that Carter had, indeed, wanted to have me court-martialed and reduced a grade in rank. But I was a permanent major general and that was not possible without an act of Congress. So much for yet another firm, sincere presidential decision.

We shook hands quickly and Brown led the way out of the Oval Office. Driving back to the Pentagon, the Secretary told me to consult very closely with his public affairs advisers on my congressional testimony. Like Bernie Rogers, he didn't come flat out and say my future assignment depended on good behavior up on the Hill, but the message was obvious.

☆   ☆

THE next morning, the front page of the *Washington Post* led with a banner headline, "President Fires Gen. Singlaub as Korea Staff Chief." The story quoted Secretary Brown as stating that "public statements by General Singlaub inconsistent with announced national security policy" made it difficult for me to carry out my duties in Korea. As I read the story, I realized that

I could do nothing at this point to correct the White House distortion that my statements had been public and that the withdrawal plans were firm national security policy. Once again, the President intended to use me to bolster his image as a decisive leader. And the *Post* rose to this bait by noting the President's action was the "first such disciplining of an American general since President Truman recalled and fired General Douglas MacArthur." The article also noted that Carter had originally been angry enough to have me face "stronger action," but that the remorse I showed during our meeting had evoked the President's "sympathy."[23]

This was a firsthand lesson in Washington political intrigue. Many in the Pentagon knew that Carter had wanted me court-martialed, and now he was pandering after public support by showing the benevolent side of his decisive personality.

Over the next several days, the true nature of President Carter's leniency was revealed. The White House had ordered that I not be allowed to return to Korea to close my office, prepare my staff for the new man, and help Mary pack up the house. But Jack Vessey put his foot down, insisting that I be allowed to return to Seoul. The White House gave in, but demanded I take military transport to avoid any further encounters with reporters. This posed a problem as our daughter Mary Ann, who had just graduated from the University of Colorado, wanted to join us in Korea and we'd already bought her a ticket to coincide with my travel by commercial airline. The Army Vice Chief of Staff, General Dutch Kerwin, understood and directed the transportation people to issue an invitational travel order which allowed Mary Ann to fly with me on a military plane after my congressional testimony.

As I prepared the opening statement of my congressional testimony, the Pentagon public affairs people carefully reviewed my draft comments. Above all, they said, I must leave no impression of disrespect toward the President or military insubordination to civilian leadership.

Meanwhile, both the Pentagon and the White House were engaged in a damage-control operation through the news media. Word came down that Army Chief of Staff General Bernie Rogers's official position was now that he had explained President Carter's decision to top American generals in Seoul, including me, during his April visit. This was nonsense. Casual conversation at the Ambassador's lunch table, at which General Vessey was not present, was hardly official notification of a major policy change. The Defense Department used formal, detailed documents to make such announcements. But in the bizarre world of Washington politics, perception, not reality, prevailed. And apparently General Rogers had manipulated plausible perception to cover himself.[24]

There was a major flaw in General Rogers's maneuver, however. By insisting that he had told me of the President's "decision" during the Seoul luncheon in late April, Rogers inadvertently focused congressional scrutiny on exactly when that formal decision had been made. The ostensibly open Carter White House stonewalled, refusing to reveal the date. But eventually congressional investigators uncovered the paper trail of the inept and abortive policy-decision process. Presidential Review Memorandum (PRM) 13 of January 26, 1977, was the basic decision document. It requested the Joint Chiefs of Staff to comment on the best schedule for a possible troop withdrawal. On March 7, 1977, the Joint Chiefs sent Secretary Brown their recommendation that any withdrawal be limited to a total of 7,000 troops over a five-year period and that these troops not include certain critical combat units of the 2nd Infantry Division. An interagency Policy Review Committee considered PRM-13 on April 27, 1977, and the Joint Chiefs' views went forward unchanged. Later that day, President Carter met with the National Security Council and heard arguments pro and con. On May 5, 1977 (eight days *after* the Seoul luncheon), Carter signed a Presidential Decision on the U.S. troop withdrawal. He rejected the Joint Chiefs' recommendation.[25] Although he had finally formalized his decision, Carter failed to implement it in a formal manner by instructing America's diplomatic and military leaders in Korea. Indeed, the instructions we received on preparing the South Korean military and government for the consultation team were downright duplicitous.

Carter was no doubt embarrassed by the troop-withdrawal fiasco. In fact the scandalous episode is not even mentioned in his official memoir. In *Keeping Faith: Memoirs of a President,* the only thing the reader learns about Korea is that President Park Chung Hee had a bad human rights record. I am not mentioned in the book; neither is General Vessey.[26] Jimmy Carter promised the American people that he would never lie to them. But he apparently didn't promise that he would tell the complete truth.

By the time I testified, many members of Congress, including influential Democrats, were openly critical of Carter's withdrawal scheme. And White House attempts to cast my recall in the heroic light of the Truman-MacArthur confrontation were beginning to evoke ridicule. The *Washington Post* itself lampooned this "high White House drama" in an editorial, which also criticized Carter's assertion that my statements could have provoked North Korea to invade the South. The matter would have been much better handled quietly within the Pentagon, the *Post* concluded.[27]

Across the country, columnists and editorial writers were beginning to give Carter's ill-advised troop-withdrawal plans the close scrutiny they deserved. Political cartoonists had a field day. Although it certainly had not been my intention to become a lightning rod on this issue, my very public recall, and the White House's own clumsy damage-control efforts, made this inevitable. There were even members of the intelligence community who speculated that my session with John Saar had been contrived to bring the issue to a head. This scenario held that Jack Vessey and I had flipped coins, and I had lost, so it would be my career that was sacrificed to expose Carter's flawed policy.[28]

For the next two days, the Pentagon made sure I was insulated from the press. On Wednesday, May 25, I went with a legislative affairs escort to the Rayburn House Office Building to testify before Congressman Sam Stratton's Investigations Subcommittee of the House Armed Services Committee. This fourteen-man subcommittee was basically a friendly panel, being composed for the most part of moderate and conservative Democrats and Republicans. There were a couple of liberals, however, and one outright radical, Ronald Dellums, whose California district included Oakland and Berkeley. He was an outspoken critic of the military.

Congressman Stratton prepared the ground for my testimony in his opening remarks. He noted that the President's withdrawal plan had been an ill-defined "proposal" that had been widely reported in the press. But, he added, Congress "has never been officially advised of that plan, nor has it ever considered or debated it."[29] Stratton said that the proposed withdrawal involved a grave risk of war, and that I would therefore be required to testify in both public and closed session, so that I could share with the members the most recent classified intelligence estimates of North Korean strength and intentions. He reiterated that Pentagon policy allowed me to state my personal views on policy without fear of retribution. And he hoped that I would do so sincerely.

As I sat staring up at the rostrum, I understood fully for the first time that the probable sacrifice of my military career would not be in vain. The President's impulsive action the previous Thursday had not only jerked me into the limelight, it had exposed his muddled policy to the full glare of congressional scrutiny. I saw that Congress intended to investigate the North Korean buildup and to act on the evidence our intelligence community had assembled. In so doing, I was sure, they would probably make it politically impossible for Carter to complete the withdrawal.

In my opening statement I told the panel that I was a professional soldier who firmly believed in following orders and supporting my civilian superiors' policy no matter how hard I had previously argued against that policy. I outlined my encounter with Saar and emphasized that my remarks concerned the attitudes of my South Korean colleagues. Finally, I stated that the U.N. Command and U.S. Forces Korea Command "accept and support the President's decision to withdraw ground combat forces from Korea." There was nothing else I could say; Carter's ill-defined proposal had been elevated by default into a national policy.

Congressman Stratton's questioning was friendly and supportive. He allowed me to reiterate publicly that U.S. Forces, Korea, had been ordered to inform the South Koreans that a final decision on the withdrawal would not be made until after consultations, which were taking place in Seoul that very week. I was also able to review the absolutely vital role of the 2nd Infantry Division as a deterrent to North Korean aggression.

As the questioning proceeded, I managed to enter into the public record the key aspects of the North Korean military buildup, including the fact that they had increased their inventory of tanks from 500 to 2,000 in the previous five years, and that they had deployed their forces well forward in an offensive posture. The congressmen were obviously eager to hear more of this, and I promised to go into detail in executive session.

Most of the questioning, from both Democrats and Republicans, was friendly. Clearly, they were displeased with the Carter White House, not just for its muddled policy, but for the administration's stubborn refusal to consult with Congress on such vital issues. But Congressman Ron Dellums was anything but friendly. He accused me of intentionally sabotaging the President's policy and belittled my supposition that the President might not have access to the most recent intelligence estimates of North Korean strength. And Dellums added, echoing his radical beliefs, that somehow the military was using vague estimates of a North Korean buildup to justify the wasteful deployment of 40,000 American troops in Korea. Dellums concluded by lambasting the subcommittee for holding these hearings, which, he said, were an "untimely and wholly inappropriate public spectacle" that could only further embarrass the President.

Colorado congresswoman Patricia Schroeder, although not a member of the subcommittee, dropped in to lambaste me for conducting a "kangaroo court" on Jimmy Carter. Then, much to Chairman Stratton's displeasure, she left without giving me an opportunity to respond.[30]

After two more hours of questioning, the room was cleared and we went into executive session. Several members of the full House Armed Services Committee joined us. Now the gloves were off, and I could reveal the shocking details of the North Korean buildup.

I elaborated on the findings of the new intelligence estimates, which proved that North Korea had deployed its tactical air power forward in underground hangars and had shifted the bulk of its artillery into similar reinforced underground positions just above the DMZ. I then noted that recent war games conducted by Lieutenant General John Cushman, our I Corps group commander in Korea, revealed a "very, very depressing" estimate of ROK defense capabilities, even given the presence of the U.S. 2nd Infantry Division. In March, I added, General Cushman had specifically briefed the Secretary of Defense on these findings and emphasized that the

North Koreans had the ability to overrun Seoul within one day of an invasion. Clearly, I stressed, the only true deterrent on the Korean peninsula was in the tactical nuclear weapons of American ground and air forces. If we removed the ground component of these weapons, I said, our deterrent was no longer credible.

Congressman Stratton pressed me to clarify that the worst-case scenario of our March war games included the assumption that the 2nd Infantry Division was still in place.

"That is correct, yes, sir."

"My God!" Stratton said, noting that the administration had never bothered to share this information with the House Armed Services Committee.

By the time the executive session ended around five-thirty that afternoon, I had been testifying for almost seven straight hours. It was obvious that the key members of the House Armed Services Committee were shocked by my statements. Congressman Stratton made it clear that the President's obstinate decision to continue with the Korean troop withdrawal—despite overwhelming evidence of North Korean military superiority and offensive intent in the new intelligence estimates—would not go unchallenged by Congress.[31]

The next morning's *Washington Post* ran a large front-page story announcing a "frontal assault" on Carter's Korea policy. Congressman Stratton was quoted as saying that his subcommittee would conduct intensive follow-up hearings and that the Joint Chiefs of Staff would be the next to testify.

The White House was quick to counterattack. While I'd been testifying, Defense Secretary Harold Brown told the National Press Club that Army Chief of Staff Bernie Rogers had "informed" me about Carter's decision before I briefed John Saar. This, Brown said, was the reason for my recall.[32]

I was under formal orders not to talk to the press about any aspect of the Korean troop policy. By late Wednesday afternoon, no one had informed me what my new assignment would be. General Rogers was out of town, but General Dutch Kerwin, the Vice Chief of Staff, said General Rogers would contact me that evening. I was due to fly back to Korea the next morning, stopping at a military air base in Colorado to pick up Mary Ann. So I left word that General Rogers could reach me at my son's Arlington apartment. Late that night, Bernie Rogers called.

"Jack," he said, "has anyone told you about your new assignment?"

"No, sir, they haven't."

"Well," Rogers said, "I'm down in Atlanta with Fritz Kroesen. He's agreed to take you as FORSCOM chief of staff."

I was astonished. U.S. Forces Command (FORSCOM) at Fort McPherson, Georgia, in Atlanta, was the largest of the Army's twelve commands and had control over all the active-duty and reserve components in the continental United States, including the major combat divisions. The headquarters staff was over 2,000 strong. General Fritz Kroesen, an old friend from days on the Army general staff, was now FORSCOM commander. Instead of being relegated to a backwater, Fritz and the Army had shown their faith in me—at the risk of further antagonizing President Carter—by offering this prized assignment.

"Sir," I said, "I'd completely ruled out that job. I don't imagine President Carter will be that pleased to have me in his backyard."

"Well," Rogers said, "you got the job."

I was just telling my son and his wife, Melitta, the good news when the phone rang again. It was Bernie Rogers. "Singlaub," he said harshly, "you're damn lucky to get this assignment and I don't appreciate the wisecrack about the President's backyard."

"Sir," I said, as earnestly as I could, "I understand just how fortunate I am and it wasn't my intention to be sarcastic."

"Well, dammit, General," Rogers grunted, "you'd better learn to keep your comments about the President to yourself."

"That is exactly my intention, sir."[33]

But the White House itself insisted on keeping the issue alive. While I was en route back to pack up in Seoul, President Carter called a news conference to defend what had now become official U.S. policy. He said I had committed a "very serious breach" of discipline by publicly criticizing his troop withdrawal. And he proceeded to reiterate the unlikely assertion that somehow my warning of North Korea's offensive intentions would encourage Kim Il-Sung to invade South Korea and was "an invitation to the world to expect an inevitable war."[34] Carter alluded to South Korea's poor human rights record, but made no mention of North Korea's ruthless totalitarian repression. It was well known by now in Washington that Jimmy Carter found several allied governments headed by former military leaders morally repugnant. And this sense of outraged morality seemed to prevent him from allowing the Korean blunder to disappear from the public eye. Rather than letting the issue cool off during the upcoming Memorial Day congressional recess, the front-page coverage of Carter's nationally televised news conference gave his critics in the House and Senate more ammunition.

I was glad to be aboard the noisy C-141 with my daughter while this storm raged in Washington.

☆   ☆

I TOOK leave en route back to the States that summer, and Mary and I had a chance to visit other parts of Asia, including Hong Kong, Taiwan, and Thailand. I was heartened by the reception given me by Chinese and Thai civilian officials and military officers. To them, Kim Il-Sung was one of the most dangerous men in Asia. The net result of my recall had been to focus increased American scrutiny on the North Koreans. And my Asian colleagues were certain America would reverse its policy when Kim's true intentions were revealed.

☆   ☆

THE brouhaha over Carter's Korea policy continued unabated that summer.[35] In July, General Rogers testified to the full House Armed Services Committee that the JCS had recommended against the withdrawal of our ground forces on March 17, while PRM-13 was still under consideration. Subsequent testimony revealed that President Carter had not signed a Decision Memorandum on the withdrawal until May 5. Congressman Sam Stratton announced that his committee had been unable to obtain any record of the President's decision and that it was uncertain who if anyone in the Army chain of command had been informed of that decision. Rogers made public that the Joint Chiefs had offered their own compromise withdrawal of 7,000 Army spaces in Korea, mainly through normal rotation, without the pullout of any particular unit. And he added that the Chiefs had stressed the "risks" involved in any withdrawal. This was the clearest public indication to date that Carter had overruled his military advisers.[36]

☆   ☆

FORT McPherson was a stately old post dating from just after the Civil War. The senior officers' quarters were handsome, well-shaded brick houses facing a wide green parade ground. I got down to work on my new assignment, reassured that I had survived my first real scrape with politics. My main concern now was no longer Communist divisions poised above the DMZ, but the readiness of the underfunded volunteer Army. Unfortunately, my duties soon put me on another collision course with the Carter administration.

Candidate Jimmy Carter had campaigned for a quick resolution to the stalled negotiations on a new Panama Canal treaty. As president, one of his first actions had been to issue Presidential Review Memorandum 1, which ordered Secretary of State Cyrus Vance to speed up the negotiation process "with regard to concluding new Canal treaties with Panama." As veteran journalist John Dinges correctly noted, "Perhaps it took a president with Jimmy Carter's quixotic tendencies to place Panama finally at the top of the U.S. foreign policy agenda."[37] Once more, Carter was mixing his personal (and selective) sense of morality with vital policy issues.

Panamanian sovereignty over the Canal was the key issue at dispute. Many American congressional leaders, including Senators James Eastland and Jesse Helms and Congressman Daniel Flood, held that Panama had no claim whatsoever on the Canal Zone because the country itself had gained its independence from Colombia in 1903 in a U.S.-backed and -financed coup, specifically launched to give America "perpetual" control of the land through which the Canal would be built. Issues such as greater Panamanian control over the administration of the waterway and higher royalties might be negotiable, these congressmen stressed, but sovereignty was not.

The Nixon administration had negotiated with General Omar Torrijos off and on for years over Panamanian sovereignty and the delicate issue of America's right to defend the Canal militarily. As elsewhere in Latin America, money carried a lot more weight than patriotic rhetoric and the short-lived Ford administration had reached the point of serious horse trading with Torrijos.

One of the main stumbling blocks, however, was the criminal activity of the Torrijos government, which was known to be involved in narcotics and arms trafficking. Torrijos's trusted ally and key operative in these criminal enterprises was Colonel Manuel Noriega, the General's chief of intelligence (G-2).[38] Noriega was thoroughly corrupt and viewed by many to be the real power behind Torrijos.

The Panamanian leader sought support from Cuba's Communist dictator, Fidel Castro, who was eager to help in this popular anti-imperialist struggle. Castro dispatched civil and military advisers to Panama to aid Torrijos and Noriega in psychological and sabotage operations against American interests there. This was the situation when President Carter decided to accelerate the treaty negotiations to a rapid conclusion that would demonstrate American morality and benevolence. Carter apparently did not stop to consider that such concepts were alien to Torrijos and Noriega.

That summer I was sent to Panama by the Department of the Army to assess the actual cost to the U.S. government of transferring military assets in the Canal Zone to the Panamanian government under the terms of the draft treaties then nearing completion. One treaty covered the future role of the U.S. military in Panama and had a provision for turning over to Panama hundreds of large and small American buildings and installations in the Zone. Jimmy Carter had assured the American people that the treaties would not cost taxpayers a cent. I discovered that that was a ridiculous claim. Panama insisted that all the assets we gave them be upgraded to working condition. Some of the small airstrips, barracks, and fortifications hadn't been used since World War II and had reverted to the jungle.

As I discussed these matters with my colleagues in Southern Command, high atop Ancon Hill overlooking the wide blue Pacific Canal entrance, it became clear that Torrijos and Noriega were taking America for a ride. Several officers hinted darkly that there was much more to Noriega than the public knew. If I wanted to assess the true cost to America of eventually transferring the Canal to Panama, I should get an intelligence briefing on Noriega's criminal activities.

The next afternoon I went down to Fort Amador, the stately old military post on the narrow peninsula beside the Canal entrance. The 470th Military Intelligence Group was situated in a separate fenced compound, surrounded by graceful coconut palms and mango trees. The young Hispanic officer who briefed me got right to the point. Noriega, he said, was a man of many talents. He had been on the payroll of the CIA and Army Intelligence for several years, but many of his reports on Torrijos's Cuban connections had proven to be disinformation. Noriega's criminal activities were growing.

The officer went to a large wall map of the Caribbean and read from a Classified report. Over the previous six months, several American yachts had been hijacked in the Gulf of Mexico. Their crews, including families with young children, had been murdered by the hijackers. Then the boats were loaded with bales of marijuana and boldly sailed back to their home marinas in Texas and Louisiana.

"Sir," the officer said, "we have proof that this operation is conducted by Noriega's men."

I held back my anger. "With his knowledge?"

"On his orders, sir."

"Does General Torrijos know about this?"

"Sir," the officer said, "General Torrijos gives Tony Noriega a free rein as long as the Colonel provides a steady flow of cash."[39]

In other words, the Carter administration was hell-bent on turning over the Canal to a government headed by murderous thugs. I could certainly see no morality in this. The next day, at a luncheon hosted by the faculty of the School of the Americas, a military school in the Canal Zone run by the U.S. Army for Latin American officers, I was questioned by a South American major general seated across from me.

"Sir," he said, speaking for his colleagues, "we cannot understand how the United States can justify giving the *most* strategic facility in the entire hemisphere to Panama." He looked around the room, making sure that no Panama Defense Force officers were nearby. "This government has the *least* effective and professional armed forces in the hemisphere."

I had learned that this general's own president planned to attend the treaty-signing ceremony in Washington in a few weeks. "General," I said, "if these treaties are so bad, why is your president supporting them?"

The man smiled, revealing a nice array of gold teeth, then rubbed his thumb and forefinger together in the universal Latin gesture for bribery. "General Singlaub," he said, "my president is willing to go anywhere and say anything if your president gives him eight helicopters." Other officers at the table chimed in. It seemed the upcoming show of hemispheric solidarity in Washington had been purchased through spreading costly military largess throughout Latin America, much of it among repressive governments that Carter publicly condemned for their human rights violations.

Carter's military pork barrel in South America was hardly moral, but it certainly was effective.

☆   ☆

IN JANUARY 1978, I attended a Department of the Army conference in Washington on the future role of women in the Army. The Carter administration advocated greatly expanding the number of Military Occupational Specialties (MOSs) to include jobs in combat support units, and, it was rumored, eventually combat units themselves. I prepared for the conference by making a visit to Fort Jackson, South Carolina, which was one of our larger basic training centers. I wanted to see firsthand how well women recruits were doing.

Basic training was meant to be tough, but not anywhere near as difficult as more advanced combat training, such as Airborne Jump School or Ranger training. But the sergeants and young captains I talked to at Fort Jackson frankly admitted that they had to lower physical performance standards considerably to keep up the unofficial quotas of women soldiers they were required to train.

This in itself did not alarm me, because I'd known for years the volunteer Army would entail compromises. I knew there were plenty of jobs that didn't demand great strength, beyond traditional medical and clerical work, that women could fill just as well as men. In England during World War II, I'd encountered women military truck drivers, parachute riggers, train operators, and instructor pilots. By the late 1970s, the whole range of electronic warfare MOSs was open to women. But I personally drew the line at opening up combat support and combat assignments to women soldiers.

I knew there were a lot of *men* who were unsuited for these jobs, because they lacked the strength and temperament. And my experience in Korea during Operation PAUL BUNYAN had taught me that allowing women soldiers with small children in frontline support units could be a real disaster during times of alert, not to mention actual fighting.

So, armed with this experience and these convictions, I flew to Washington. Unfortunately the President's advocates, led by a senior Department of the Army lawyer and several other outspoken feminists, arrived armed for bear themselves. We quickly clashed.

"General," the lawyer said, glaring at me across the conference table, "you are nothing but a male chauvinist." She was tactful enough to leave the epithet "pig" unspoken.

I stated my case as best I could, granting the need for a greatly increased number of MOSs open to women soldiers. But I added, "Putting a woman into a combat support or combat MOS is insane."

One of the lawyer's feminist colleagues counterattacked. "The Soviet army used women in combat to great advantage in World War II, General," she said. "You should read your history more closely."

I was taken aback by her vituperation. "I served in combat in two theaters in that war, ma'am," I answered. "I believe I'm adequately familiar with its history."

"The Israeli army has women in all its combat units," the lawyer persisted. "I see no good reason why we shouldn't either."

They had a point to make, but I couldn't accept their arguments. Traditionally, high rank in the Army came to those who had successfully commanded troops in combat. But there were many exceptions to this tradition. General Eisenhower had never commanded troops in a frontline unit, nor had General Earle Wheeler. And I recognized the need to open senior rank to women career officers. But I simply could not accept a ground combat role for women.

When the conference adjourned, I decided to do some research of my own. My friend William Craig had written one of the best histories of the Soviet army in World War II, focused on the battle of Stalingrad. I contacted him to find out more about Soviet women in combat.

"It was a disaster, Jack," he said. "Men soldiers' loyalties were badly divided between their duty to their commander and loyalty to their paramours. The Red Army learned a lesson. Today, there are absolutely no Soviet women in combat assignments. In fact, they've got a smaller percentage of women soldiers than we do."

I next called the defense attaché at the Israeli embassy to ask about women combat soldiers in his country.

"Never, General," he said. "We would never put our women in a position where they could be captured by the enemy."

I explained the lawyer's insistence that women soldiers served in every Israeli combat unit.

"They hold administrative and signal positions in these units," the Israeli brigadier explained. "But whenever the unit goes on alert they are replaced by a male reservist, who is also trained for that position."

I tried to present this information on the final day of the conference, but my views were dismissed as irrelevant. I got the distinct impression that some civilians in the Department of the Army saw my effort as another criticism of the President's announced policies.

☆ ☆

ON APRIL 27, 1978, I was invited to address ROTC cadets at Georgia Tech as part of an ongoing Perspective Building Series. These lectures were meant to bring the cadets in contact with senior civilian officials and military officers for frank and open exchanges, in order to widen the young people's frame of reference. As busy as I was in the FORSCOM chief-of-staff job, I relished the opportunity to address the cadets. I was a product of the ROTC myself, and I saw the corps as a vital component of the new volunteer Army.

So I fine-tuned my standard talk on integrity and discipline and sent the revised text for approval to my public affairs officer. At the auditorium on the day of the lecture, I was surprised to find microphones on the podium and a TV camera nearby, because the organizers had assured me that the question-and-answer period following my talk would be off the record, in order to allow both me and the cadets to speak frankly. But my escort officer told me the mikes and camera were simply part of the Georgia Tech audio-visual group that regularly recorded these lectures.

The talk went well and I enjoyed the question period. Not all of the cadets were in uniform. In fact, many were in civilian clothes, so I couldn't tell which were Navy, Air Force, or Army. But Georgia Tech attracted sharp young men and women and I wasn't surprised by the relevance of their questions.

When the question period began, I emphasized that my answers were my personal views only and did not reflect official FORSCOM policy.

During the course of the long and thought-provoking question-and-answer period, there were four questions, of the twenty or so asked, which dealt with policy decisions already made by the Carter administration. The first of these requested my personal views concerning the cancellation of the B-I bomber. I stated that I thought it was not in the best interests of the security of the United States to unilaterally cancel such an important strategic weapons system without getting any compensating concessions from the Soviets.

Another young man asked me about the recent decision to cancel development of the so-called neutron bomb, which was actually meant to be an enhanced-radiation short-range missile warhead or artillery shell. The warhead's only role was as an anti-tank weapon designed to kill Soviet or Chinese tank crews as they massed for an offensive. But the news media, responding to Soviet disinformation, had portrayed this tactical nuclear weapon as a diabolical capitalist invention designed to kill people and leave property intact. This was hogwash. The neutron warhead was meant to penetrate the hulls of enemy tanks, which standard battlefield nuclear weapons could not do.

I explained this and noted that from a military point of view, again, the cancellation had been a mistake. Above all, I said, it was illogical to give up such a trump card without demanding a reciprocal concession from the Soviets.

The third critical question concerned my views on the Panama Canal treaties. I stated frankly that giving the Canal to an unpredictable Panamanian government might mean that one day we would have to fight to have access to it. And I added that there probably had been ways to satisfy the aspirations of the Panamanian people for sovereignty over the Canal without giving away the valuable asset as we had.

A final question concerned the Strategic Arms Limitation Talks (SALT) then under way. I stated frankly that I thought our chief U.S. delegate, Paul Warnke, was a poor choice, because he had a long tradition of advocating what I considered to be unilateral American nuclear disarmament. I suggested it might be better to send a tough American labor leader such as George Meany to the SALT talks, someone who had bare-knuckle negotiation experience.

I left the lecture hall to attend a private luncheon with faculty and student leaders, where, I'd been told, there'd be another off-the-record question period. I asked my military host, Lieutenant Colonel Wayne B. Davis, the head of the Military Science department, about the ground rules for this luncheon. I wanted to make sure we'd still be off the record. After all, the theme of my address had been the integrity of a professional officer and I hated to have to start hedging my answers. Colonel Davis said he would double-check. A few minutes later, he returned looking troubled and confused. Apparently, he hadn't been well informed on the ground rules for my visit. No one had told the lecture audience that the question-and-answer period was off the record.

I didn't think too much of it at the time, however, because I'd prefaced all my answers by stating they were my "personal opinion," not official. But the slip-up was annoying; had I known the session was for attribution, I would have declined to answer questions about official policy. In the middle of the lunch I got a call from the FORSCOM public affairs officer, Colonel Harry Heath.

"General," Heath said, obviously shaken, "we've just seen a story on the AP wire saying you have again criticized President Carter's policies."

I shook my head. Once more, I'd been sideswiped by the press. Colonel Heath read me the pertinent parts of the story. The reporter made it sound like I had conducted a carefully prepared personal attack on the President, instead of answering cadets' questions. I could well imagine the reaction in Washington. I immediately called General Fritz Kroesen to explain the situation. He asked to be kept informed.

Before the lunch was over, I received another call, this one from my staff relaying an order from General Rogers that I be at his office in the Pentagon at ten the next morning to explain my actions. Fritz Kroesen was flying up for a Pentagon meeting and offered me a ride in his plane.

I met with a grim General Bernie Rogers in the Chief of Staff Office on the E-ring precisely at 10 A.M., April 28, 1978. While I was explaining the circumstances behind the press story, Army Secretary Clifford Alexander came through the private door between the Chief's and the Secretary's offices. He was absolutely quivering with rage, gripping a sheaf of yellow teleprinter wire copy.

"Did you say canceling the B-1 bomber was a mistake?" He thumped the sheet with his open palm.

"Yes, sir," I said, "but you have to understand the context in which I answered the student's question. I—"

He wasn't about to hear my explanation. "Did you say that Paul Warnke is a disarmament advocate?" the Secretary demanded.

"Sir," I explained, "I was more specific than that. I said he was a *unilateral* disarmament advocate. But that was an answer to—"

Again he interrupted, his face swollen with anger. "And did you say canceling the neutron bomb is like throwing a trump card away?"

"Yes, sir, I did." I tried to explain the context of my remarks. "I'd been told the question period was off the record, and the topic of my lecture was integrity. So when they asked my personal opinions, I had no intention of lying to those cadets."

But Alexander shook his head. "How on earth could you say such things in *public?*" He seemed about to fly into a real frenzy.

I knew Secretary Alexander was under a lot of pressure, as was Bernie Rogers. President Carter's badly muddled Korea withdrawal policy had just been torpedoed in Congress. Two days before, the House Armed Services Committee, led by Democrats, had voted an amendment requiring Carter to keep at least 26,000 American ground combat troops in Korea until a true peace agreement was signed. In other words, the 2nd Infantry Division would be in place for the duration. Carter had lost his first major foreign policy initiative only four months into his presidency.[40] Obviously, my comments in Atlanta had come at a bad time.

"Mr. Secretary," I added, "I certainly had no intention of embarrassing the Army."

At this point, Bernie Rogers intervened. "Sir," he said, "I'd like to keep this within the Army chain of command. And I'd like to get General Kroesen's recommendation on this matter."

I went back to the Pentagon FORSCOM section where General Kroesen kept an office. After all my years in the Pentagon, I finally had the use of a room with adequate space. It was a lovely spring morning in Washington.

"Well, General," I said, "I really ripped my knickers this time. I think the only honorable thing I can do now is request voluntary retirement."

We both knew fighting for my rights was a no-win proposition. I had no friends among the Department of the Army's political appointee legal staff after the disastrous confrontations over women soldiers.

Fritz shook his head. "Well, Jack," he said, "I think I agree with you."

He went back to Rogers and the Secretary to recommend I be permitted to submit a request for voluntary retirement effective May 31, 1978. The Secretary considered the matter for about two seconds and said he wanted me out of the Army by the 30th of April, which was only two days away. Fritz reminded them that I couldn't be processed out over a weekend. The Secretary graciously conceded that I be permitted to close down my office over the next week, then complete my retirement physical exams and paperwork as quickly as possible.

☆   ☆

THE next Monday I formally submitted my retirement, citing the "inadvertent public disclosure of my personal opposition to some of the policies of the current administration."

When Fritz Kroesen and I discussed the actual mechanics of my retirement, we agreed the Army wanted me kept under wraps during my final three weeks in limbo. Normally, I would have been entitled to a key place on the reviewing stand in a monthly retirement parade to which all the officers retiring at the post on the same date could invite friends and colleagues. Soldiers are sentimental about such parades. It's the last time they wear their uniforms for an official function. But I told Fritz attending a parade would draw unwanted media scrutiny and spoil the day for the other men. I would be leaving the Army after thirty-five years with no parade and no regrets.

☆   ☆

DURING my final flight physical examination at the Eisenhower Medical Center at Fort Gordon, Georgia, the medical officer colonel conducting the exam seemed uncomfortable. I asked him what the problem was.

"Sir," he said, "you've obviously got a number of service-connected disabilities." He listed my shrapnel wound and several back injuries. He then reminded me that the Army was cracking down on granting official disability status to senior officers.

There had been a certain amount of abuse of disability status. A serviceman's pension became nontaxable in proportion to the percentage of his disability on retirement. And the Colonel had been informed, he said, by the "highest authority," that I was to be released from the Army without disability.

The man looked away, embarrassed. Somebody in Washington was sending me a nasty retirement present.

Then the Colonel turned back to face me. "But, General," he added, "it's my duty to inform you that you are required to repeat this examination as soon as possible at a Veterans Administration hospital near your home. You may wish to know that they are authorized to grant disability status."

We grinned at each other, two old soldiers.

24

Panmunjom, Korea. Maj. Gen. Singlaub, senior United Nations Command representative, leads the other representatives leaving a meeting of the Armistice Commission.

Singlaub receives his second star from Dr. Wilbur (left) and Mary Singlaub (right).

Korea, 1976. Lt. Gen. John Cushman, commanding officer of the I Corps Group, briefs Maj. Gen. Singlaub on plans for Operation PAUL BUNYAN.

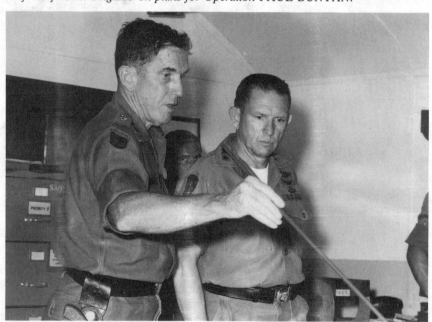

Cartoonist Bob Englehart's version of Gen. Singlaub's treatment by President Jimmy Carter.

Maj. Gen. Singlaub addresses the press at Fort McPherson, July 1977.

Fort McPherson, 1978. Maj. Gen. Singlaub accepts his army retirement certificate from Gen. Frederick Kroesen.

On the public speaking trail: Retired Generals Singlaub (left), George Patton III (center), and Daniel Graham (right).

Inside Nicaragua with Eden Pastora (second from left).

Las Vegas, Honduras, 1985. Singlaub with Col. Enrique Bermudez (center).

33

1985. Singlaub with Adolfo Calero (left) and Calero's brother Mario.

1986. Gen. Singlaub with CIA director Bill Casey.

34

PART IV

☆   ☆

Hazardous Duty

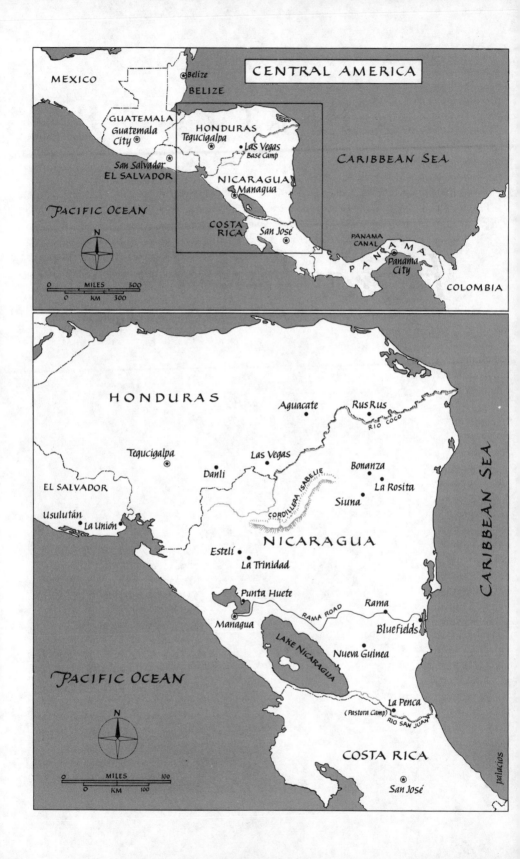

CHAPTER FOURTEEN

Counterattack

1978–1984

☆   ☆

DURING MY FINAL days at Fort McPherson, Army colleagues called to offer their moral support. They felt I had been treated unfairly, but no one put his views in writing. Speaking out on Carter's disastrous defense policy blunders might get them "Singlaubed" by Jimmy Carter, a fate few would risk.

I also received job offers from business and industry. But I wasn't ready to trade in my uniform for a pair of plaid golf pants. I still considered myself bound by my officer's oath to "support and defend the Constitution of the United States against all enemies, foreign and domestic."

So I welcomed the visit of John Fisher, president of the American Security Council (ASC), and retired Army Lieutenant General Danny Graham. Fisher had begun the ASC in the 1950s as a conservative organization dedicated to educating Congress and the American people on national security issues. One of his main activities was organizing speaking tours by academic and military experts. Danny Graham had already signed on the ASC speakers circuit and urged me to do the same.

I'd known Dan Graham for over ten years. He'd been an intelligence officer on Westmoreland's J-2 staff in Saigon. Danny was a short, feisty soldier with a ready grin and flashing blue eyes that belied a probing intellect. He had resigned as a three-star general rather than continue supporting the détente policies of the Ford White House. Danny's specialty was strategic issues, including advanced weapons systems.

I knew the defense issues that had precipitated my early retirement would continue to be critical well into the future. Carter's mishandling of the

Korean troop withdrawal, his decision to abandon new strategic weapons without demanding a compensating Soviet reduction, and his simplistic belief that the military dictators of Panama could be trusted to stably manage that vital American asset prompted me to accept John Fisher's offer.

☆   ☆

A DAY after my official retirement, the ASC hosted a press luncheon for me and Lieutenant General Gordon Sumner, who had retired on the same day I did.

General Sumner had a distinguished combat record and had held important positions in the Army and Joint Staffs. He had been president of the Inter-American Defense Board, the military arm of the Organization of American States. Sumner was the best-informed American officer on Western Hemisphere security issues. The Senate Armed Services Committee asked Sumner how his colleagues on the Inter-American Defense Board viewed the Panama Canal treaties. Unlike the Joint Chiefs of Staff, whom Carter had ordered to testify in favor of the treaties, Gordon Sumner had received no such admonition. He honestly stated that most military officers on the Board favored continued U.S. military control over the Canal.

He then stated frankly his personal opposition to the treaties and giving up American sovereignty over the Panama Canal. When he did so, he realized that Carter's retribution would be swift. Indeed, he was soon "Singlaubed."

Our press luncheon was invigorating. For the first time since my encounter with John Saar, I was free to speak publicly with complete candor. I set the record straight as to Carter's Korean troop withdrawal policy, detailing the "diplomatic sham" in sending Undersecretary of State Habib and General Brown to South Korea to consult with our allies, after the President had already secretly approved the withdrawal.

I also predicted that the Soviet Union would cynically exploit Carter's olive branch approach to stabilizing the nuclear weapons race through the SALT process. "The Soviets are not born-again Christians," I told the assembled press. "They are in fact born-again Bolsheviks. And they have no Judeo-Christian ethic guiding them to grant us the same concessions we are making in the hope they will reciprocate."[1]

Press reaction to my comments was favorable. I looked forward to my speaking tour.

☆   ☆

OVER the next two years, I spoke often to civic organizations, veterans groups, and university audiences all across the country on national security issues. The focus of my speeches was the need for America to reestablish its national defenses and strategic position as the leader of the free world, following the military debacle in Indochina and the political disaster of Watergate.

After stressing the vital principle of civilian leadership over the military, I took advantage of my retired status to speak for my active-duty colleagues whom Carter had muzzled.

This was important because Carter had repeatedly bypassed the Joint Chiefs of Staff when making key decisions.[2] Indeed, among my senior Army officer colleagues, it was widely believed that Jimmy Carter had selected Air Force General David Jones to be chairman of the Joint Chiefs of Staff because he was one of the few senior officers who publicly supported Carter's Panama Canal treaties.

Carter demanded unquestioned loyalty, but did not reciprocate by consulting senior officers. And as many of these officers learned, he was prone to use the Singlaub option. General John Vessey was also stung by Carter's vindictiveness. Carter refused to approve General Vessey's nomination to be the Army's chief of staff when his Korea assignment ended. This was because Vessey had publicly supported me. Carter instructed Army Secretary Clifford Alexander to offer Vessey the job of Vice Chief of Staff, under his former subordinate, General Edward "Shy" Meyer. Alexander and Carter assumed Vessey would rather retire. They were wrong. He served with distinction under Meyer, and was eventually selected by President Reagan to be chairman of the Joint Chiefs of Staff.

President Carter believed that the Soviet Union was a country similar to our own, which had suffered grievously during World War II and had been isolated by the West's containment policy. To Carter, the "chronic United States–Soviet confrontation mentality" was "shortsighted and counterproductive."[3]

One of his advisers on arms control negotiations with the Soviet Union was W. Averell Harriman, who assured the President that Soviet leaders had "great respect" for him and that President Brezhnev saw personally meeting Carter as "one of the great events" in his life. During the critical SALT II arms negotiations Harriman cautioned Carter that, above all, Brezhnev and his government believed in supporting socialist liberation movements around the world "just as deeply as Americans believe in human rights."[4] Therefore Carter refused to even consider using the leverage of the negotiations to extract a reduction of Soviet-sponsored subversion in the Third World.

No doubt the President sincerely held these beliefs—at least until December 1979, when the Soviet army rolled over Afghanistan. I sometimes recounted for my audiences a telling anecdote I'd heard while at Fort McPherson. After Carter's first successful gubernatorial election, but before he took office in 1971, the Greek Orthodox Primate visited Atlanta on a State Department tour. A prominent local Greek-American hosted a reception for the Primate, which Carter attended. Afterwards he told his host how much he enjoyed being present. This event was, he said, his first "international experience." Less than six years later, he was elected president of the United States and was leading our negotiations with the Soviet Union.

But I knew that the Soviet Union had used the years of the détente period for an unprecedented military buildup. By the late 1970s, the Soviets vastly outnumbered the West in ground forces, tactical air forces, submarines, and, above all, intercontinental ballistic missiles (ICBM). And their superiority in numbers was rapidly matched in qualitative parity and even superiority in certain key technologies. For example, the SALT agreements had allowed both sides to deploy 1,320 heavy ICBMs capable of carrying multiple warheads—Multiple Independently Targeted Reentry Vehicles (MIRVs). But we permitted the Soviets the exclusive right to retain 300 additional large launchers; these they quickly converted to carry accurate new ten-warhead MIRVs, in obvious disregard for the spirit, if not the letter, of the SALT I agreement. Yet the administration's chief arms control negotiator, Paul Warnke, sincerely believed the Soviets could somehow be convinced not to bend future agreements to their own advantage in a similar manner.

I was not so sanguine. America had been bogged down in Indochina during the years of the Soviet military buildup. The Soviets correctly saw us in the most vulnerable political and military position we'd been in since World War II.

I stressed to my audiences the critical need to modernize our strategic nuclear forces. For the first time since the advent of the ICBM, the United States was in a position of true vulnerability to a crippling Soviet first strike. An attack by only 300 Soviet SS-18 MIRV'd missiles—less than a third of their total ICBMs—could destroy our entire land-based ICBM force.

But the Carter administration proceeded blithely along the SALT II arms negotiation path.

Our logical response to these Soviet moves was the deployment of enough heavy MIRV'd missiles to survive a first strike with a viable deterrent. But the administration was against developing the ten-warhead MX missile. There was a chilling implication to this policy, which few in the public understood. Without a survivable ICBM force, a future president might face the terrible decision of firing our land-based missiles before an incoming Soviet strike could destroy them. This so-called launch-on-warning scenario was certainly enough to scare an old soldier like me.

In my lectures, I proposed an alternative concept that we called "peace through strength." This was the reversal of America's gradual unilateral disarmament of the détente period. The policy was predicated on the belief that the Soviets would use their growing military superiority over the West to achieve geopolitical goals.

I also proposed that the United States conduct serious research on a practical missile defense system, incorporating possibly both space- and land-based technology. From what I understood of the Soviets, they would keep building missiles far beyond their legitimate defense needs (just as they built tanks), until they were convinced we had developed a practical defense against ICBMs.

In this regard, I emphasized, America had to draw upon the vast advanced-technology resources found in our academic and industrial laboratories to counter the massive weight of the modernized Soviet armed forces. It was certainly not *immoral* for a country to defend itself, as many in the administration seemed to imply.

But in my speeches I always stressed that I did not "believe that the answer to our military decline is to be found in support of *every* program emanating from the Pentagon." I knew there were generals and admirals (supported by greedy contractors and pork-barreling congressmen) perfectly willing to bankrupt the country to see their pet weapon systems deployed.

America, I added, had to rebuild its intelligence capabilities. President Carter's director of Central Intelligence, his Annapolis classmate Admiral Stansfield Turner, had presided over the dismantling of the Human Intelligence and Covert Operations facilities of the CIA. Carter wanted to rely on reconnaissance satellites and electronic surveillance, which served little purpose in combating the growing Soviet-sponsored subversion in the Third World.

I also emphasized the need to use positive, non-military means to roll back the spread of communism, beginning with the captive nations of the Soviet empire. The Czechs, Poles, and Hungarians had been almost completely abandoned under the détente policy, which accepted Soviet control over hundreds of millions of people who had been "liberated" by the Red Army during World War II.

Finally, I believed the United States had to continue military and economic aid to our strategically located allies, even if their governments did not currently meet our high standards of democracy and stringent human rights requirements. This was the only way we could continue to influence their internal reforms. Abandoning them out of some misguided sense of moral superiority would only increase their social upheaval and invite Soviet subversion, which always found fertile ground in periods of chaos.

☆   ☆

BETWEEN my marathon road trips on the Styrofoam-coffee/cardboard-chicken circuit, I found refuge at our new home high in the Fraser Valley of Colorado. Mary and I had first visited the area when I commanded the Army Readiness Region in Denver.

Early in that tour we had purchased a small condo in Fraser, which had a great view of the Continental Divide and the Winter Park Ski Area. We spent our spare time enjoying the clean air and magnificent mountains. I could fish and hike in the summer, hunt in the fall, ski in the winter, and smell the wild columbines and snowdrops in the spring. It was a great place to relax and clear my head of bureaucratic drudgery. Mary knew the name of every flower and plant we encountered any place in Grand County. The year-round population was less than 7,000 and we did not have one traffic light in the entire valley.

We had stopped in for a few days as we traveled from Korea to Fort McPherson. During that brief visit, I located and purchased eight acres on top of a ridge overlooking the Fraser Valley and offering an even better view of the western slope of the Continental Divide. From the property, which was 9,200 feet above sea level, we faced a series of peaks over 13,000 feet high. I knew them all in detail, having climbed them all in past summers.

After my retirement we moved to the condominium, from which Mary designed and I supervised the construction of our retirement home on "the high ground." The house made generous use of local fir and granite. Its design and orientation were such as to maximize the effectiveness of the solar panels which provided its primary heating, but coincidentally gave it a truly breathtaking view.

☆　　　☆

GENERAL Danny Graham quickly became the chief public proponent of the modernization of America's strategic posture with his advocacy of a space-based missile defense system called "High Frontier." I shifted my efforts toward the other end of what I called the "spectrum of conflict," to unconventional warfare, insurgency, and low-intensity conflict.

The Soviet experience in Indochina had been exactly the opposite of our own. By supporting a Communist surrogate with massive military aid, the Soviet Union had acquired valuable strategic assets in Vietnam, including huge, well-stocked naval and air bases at Cam Rahn Bay and Danang.

The significance of these new bases was that the Soviets had achieved geopolitical prominence by supporting a surrogate's "war of national liberation." The Kremlin had learned that military expansion was a profitable business.

The Soviets were pumping arms, equipment, and military advisers into troubled regions of Africa and Latin America. Their principal military surrogate, Cuba, played an increasing role. Tens of thousands of Cuban combat troops, supported by Soviet and East German advisers, propped up the Marxist MPLA government in Angola. The new Marxist dictatorship in Ethiopia, led by a brutal military dictator named Haile Merriam Mengistu, provided the Soviets a strategic foothold in the Horn of Africa, which dominated the maritime approaches to Mideast oil ports, just as Angola dominated the tanker route around Africa.

When Soviet military support began flowing into the new Marxist government of Mozambique on the east coast of Africa, it became obvious that there was a clear geopolitical strategy unfolding. If the Soviet Union could establish a global system of strategic bases to separate Western Europe, the United States, and Japan from their sources of petroleum and vital raw materials, the policy of containment would have been finally defeated.

They deliberately targeted countries with strategic potential for subversion, while ignoring repressive governments in nonstrategic areas. Thus Angola, Mozambique, and Ethiopia received the full brunt of the Soviet-surrogate military "support," while remote brutal dictatorships such as Idi Amin's Uganda were ignored. Soviet leader Leonid Brezhnev made this abundantly clear in a confidential conversation with the president of Somalia in the mid-1970s. "Our goal," Brezhnev said, "is to gain control of the two great treasure houses on which the West depends, the energy treasure house of the Persian Gulf and the mineral treasure house of Central and Southern Africa."[5]

In Central America, Soviet-Cuban attention was focused on the three most socially dislocated countries: Guatemala, El Salvador, and Nicaragua. And it was in Nicaragua that the Soviet Union and its surrogates would make their most concerted, and successful, effort to establish a strategic foothold on the North American continent.

By the 1960s, economic domination by traditional oligarchs (usually of European ancestry) over the impoverished masses of *mestizos* and Indians was already crumbling. In the late 1970s, the dynasty of the Somoza family in Nicaragua, led by the corrupt and repressive President Anastasio Somoza, came under attack from a broad-based revolutionary movement that included labor leaders, professionals and businessmen, the Roman Catholic and Protestant churches, and *campesinos*. The Carter administration stopped military assistance to Somoza and encouraged the Organization of American States to isolate Nicaragua and promote a truly democratic, pluralistic, and nonaligned revolution.[6]

The Somoza government and its small National Guard were no match for the revolutionaries, who had joined forces under the banner of the Sandinista National Liberation Front, a coalition named for Augusto Cesar Sandino, a national hero of the 1930s. The revolutionaries toppled Somoza in 1979, and the Sandinista coalition took power in the capital Managua. The Carter administration immediately extended aid to the revolutionary government, including over $100 million in outright grants and 100,000 tons of food. Clearly the intention of the United States was to support a broad-based, nonideological revolution in Central America. President Carter invited Sandinista Comandante Daniel Ortega to Washington to discuss American support.[7]

But as both the White House and members of the Sandinista coalition soon discovered, Comandante Ortega and his brother Humberto, the Front's military leader, had little interest in Western support. Cuban military advisers had fought alongside the Sandinistas in the final offensive. Within a month of Somoza's fall, hundreds of Cuban intelligence officers from Castro's Directorate General of Intelligence (DGI), supported by a large Soviet KGB contingent and East German military officers, were already in Managua. The broad-based Front quickly became a secretive junta where power was jealously restricted to those Sandinistas such as the Ortega brothers who had been trained in guerrilla warfare by Cubans and indoctrinated in Marxist-Leninist ideology. Indeed, many of the new leaders in Managua had done relatively little of the anti-Somoza fighting, but had solid revolutionary credentials based on years of training in the Soviet Union.[8] It was these hard-core Communists who quickly organized the General Directorate of State Security (modeled on the Soviet KGB), a repressive secret police force that soon dominated Nicaraguan society.

According to historian John Norton Moore, the purpose for the sudden transformation of Nicaragua into a police state quickly became obvious. "The Comandantes," Moore has written, "began a massive secret military build-up even as the United States poured in economic assistance for their regime."[9] Over the next eighteen months, the Sandinistas increased the size of their conscript army to more than six times that of the former National Guard. Cuban and Soviet advisers trained this force, which was soon equipped with modern Soviet-bloc weapons. While the Sandinistas were still consolidating their power, Soviet, Cuban, and East European military engineers conducted surveys for large new military bases, including an airfield at remote Punta Huete (hardly the "tourist" airport proclaimed by the Sandinistas), capable of handling Soviet Backfire strategic bombers and the Bear maritime patrol bomber. The new Sandinista government described these construction activities as "disinterested help" from friendly socialist powers.[10]

It is important to note that this Soviet buildup in Nicaragua began a full two years before there was any external resistance to Sandinista rule.[11]

Faced with this blatant Communist takeover, many members of the original Sandinista coalition, including legitimate military heroes like Eden Pastora, the legendary Comandante Zero, tried to protest, but were soon imprisoned or forced into exile.

I viewed these events in Central America with increasing anxiety. Obviously, much of Latin America, including our populous southern neighbor, Mexico, was a ripe target for similar Soviet-sponsored "liberation." This subversion would clearly begin with terrorism and ostensibly broad-based revolutionary struggles, as was exactly the case in Guatemala and El Salvador.

During this period, Soviet-trained and -funded terrorist groups in the Middle East, Western Europe, and South America increased their activities. Even the decimated CIA was belatedly forced to concede that the Soviet Union had embarked on a global campaign of terrorist subversion designed to destabilize fragile Third World governments, to intimidate Israel, and to confound NATO. It was no accident that the German Red Army Faction and the Italian Red Brigades targeted their countries' key military leaders and senior executives of important defense contractors. But as veteran journalist Claire Sterling has noted, no international terrorist group ever targeted a government or military official within the Soviet empire. The reason for this was obvious: All effective international terrorist groups were under the direction or control of the KGB, its East European subordinate services, or the intelligence services of Soviet surrogates, such as Cuba or North Korea.[12]

(Although the Soviet Union consistently stonewalled for decades, denying accusations that it sponsored terrorist groups, the recent collapse of East Germany provided a bonanza of documentary evidence of Soviet and East Bloc sponsorship that included massive funding, arming, training, and logistic support. For example, a recent raid by West German police of a terrorist safe house in Frankfurt-am-Main unearthed detailed maps of the NATO fuel-pipeline system, with instructions for its sabotage. West German terrorists had used these plans for several attacks in the 1970s.[13] Many convicted West European terrorists were living in state-sponsored sanctuary when the East German Communists were overthrown.[14])

The most notorious Soviet-sponsored terrorist assassination attempt was the attack on Pope John Paul II in May 1981. One of the two assassins, a Turkish terrorist named Mehmet Ali Agca, was definitely linked to the Bulgarian secret service, which was known to be the KGB's most loyal East Bloc subordinate.[15]

☆　　　　　☆

The Sandinista takeover in Nicaragua was only one of several setbacks in 1979, the year in which the administration's foreign policy based on détente and the moral superiority of human rights ground to a complete halt.

The only positive event that year was the conclusion of the ill-fated Korean troop pullout fiasco. Representative Sam Stratton formally requested that Carter drop the withdrawal plan, which was still languishing as uncompleted White House policy. The President refused to publicly retreat, but he privately recognized his policy was dead in the water.[16]

Several congressmen went out of their way to let me know my frank testimony in 1977 had been a key factor in keeping the issue alive.

In Iran, the White House at first supported the embattled Shah, one of America's staunchest allies in the Middle East, who was under attack by domestic opponents from both the pro-Soviet left and the Muslim fundamentalist right. Once again, Carter's preoccupation with human rights eventually distorted his strategic vision. As resistance to the Shah's authoritarian, but pro-Western, government increased, his police and military suppressed rioting in Iran's cities. At this critical point, the American ambassador in Tehran, Westmoreland's old nemesis from Indochina, "Field Marshal" William Sullivan, arbitrarily tilted toward the Shah's right-wing opponent, Ayatollah Ruhollah Khomeini, a Muslim extremist with a deep hatred for America. Rather than discipline his ambassador, Carter allowed U.S. policy to be dictated from the Tehran embassy.[17]

By November 1979, the Shah was exiled, Ayatollah Khomeini was in power, and angry mobs of fundamentalist "students" had taken hostage fifty-four of our embassy staff. Ambassador Sullivan had conveniently departed before this debacle.

This image of frustrated impotence grew worse in December 1979. Two days after Christmas, the Soviet Union invaded Afghanistan, where they had been increasing their "adviser" presence for months amid growing unrest against the pro-Moscow government. The Soviets rapidly deployed large Spetsnaz detachments to secure key border passes and airports, a decisive move that opened the doors of the mountainous Asian nation to their armored and mechanized units.

Moscow claimed they had been "invited" to intervene in Afghanistan by President Hafizullah Amin. But one of the first moves by Spetsnaz troops was to capture Amin and turn him over to pro-Soviet officers who assassinated him. Within days of the invasion, a Soviet-trained Communist dictator named Babrak Karmal returned from exile in Moscow and took power.

President Carter was shocked by the invasion. His advisers had long assured him that we could do business with the Soviets if we only treated them fairly and concentrated on peaceful cooperation and détente. However, he was initially more concerned that the Soviet invasion "wiped out any chance" for Senate ratification of his SALT II treaty. But in trying to pressure the Soviets to stop their aggression in Afghanistan, Carter stubbornly refused to "link" the reward of a new arms control agreement to a Soviet pullout.[18]

Carter relied instead on the ineffectual response of an American grain embargo, which was uncoordinated with other Western grain exporters who quickly made up the Soviet shortfall. The only group hurt by this policy was the American farm community. The President next acted with typical sanctimony by leading a Western boycott of the upcoming 1980 Moscow Olympics.

Moscow was not impressed. Obviously Soviet leaders well understood the post-Vietnam syndrome in America. With the fall of Indochina and the loss of our Middle Eastern ally in Iran, America could project little military power in the region. And we also seemed deeply reluctant to again intervene in "liberation" struggles in the Third World. The country had come to view anti-terrorist activities and covert intelligence operations with bitter distaste. CIA director Stansfield Turner had encountered little resistance in Congress when he arbitrarily fired most of the Agency's veteran covert operators. In fact, Senator Frank Church, chairman of the Senate Select Committee on Intelligence, would probably have gone further, even abolishing the Agency itself—"a rogue elephant on a rampage"—and assigning its intelligence collection functions to the Pentagon and State Department.[19]

And since human rights and arms control continued to dominate the administration's foreign policy, no expanded requirement was seen for Special Operations forces. A small anti-terrorist Delta Force was finally formed within Army Special Forces, after airliner hijackings worldwide had reached epidemic proportions. And Carter approved plans to completely eliminate the Navy's SEAL units, which were our only unconventional forces trained for coastal insertion from submerged submarines. The Pentagon was being forced to severely cut back Army Special Forces, Rangers, and Air Force Special Ops units.

Later, when I asked Army Chief of Staff Shy Meyer about those cutbacks, which made no sense in light of the greatly expanded Soviet unconventional-warfare operations worldwide, he explained the prevailing attitude of the Carter White House.

"Jack," Meyer said, "we were told, 'There's no use training a Super Bowl team, if they'll never have a Super Bowl to play in.' "

That illusion was certainly shattered on April 24, 1980, when a small unit, composed of Delta Force troops, Rangers, and Air Force and Marine air crew, en route to rescue the fifty-four American diplomat hostages in Tehran met disaster on an infamous gravel airstrip in Iran known as Desert One.

I was at home in Colorado when a friend on the East Coast called with the news of the disaster early the next morning. The more I learned about the failed operation, the more obvious it became that our country had lost its well-tuned special operations capability that we had used so effectively in Indochina. The Iranian rescue mission was a Joint Task Force with combined assets of all four services. The operation was planned by Colonel Charlie Beckwith, a veteran Special Forces officer who had built up Delta Force at Fort Bragg in the 1970s. Like many of the MACV/SOG operations, Beckwith's plan combined audacity with attention to practical details.

Beckwith's small rescue force was flown by Air Force C-130s to Desert One, a gravel road in the salt desert wilderness south of Tehran. Large CH-53 Sea Stallion helicopters from the aircraft carrier *Nimitz* were to rendezvous with the rescue force and proceed to Desert Two, a mountain staging zone near Tehran. The helicopters would be hidden under camouflage nets and Beckwith's force would proceed to the Tehran embassy compound aboard trucks and vans. Late at night they would blast into the embassy compound, kill the Iranian guards, and free the hostages. AC-130 Spectre gunships would orbit overhead to suppress Iranian reinforcements. The helicopters would then land, take out the hostages and rescue team, and fly to an isolated airstrip thirty-five miles south of Tehran, which had been sealed off by Army Rangers transported from Egypt aboard C-141 Starlifters. The helicopters would then be destroyed and the entire force would extract on the C-141s.

It was a risky but well-conceived operation. Unfortunately, the White House insisted on micro-managing the tactical plans. To prevent security leaks, the entire team never trained together, and unnecessary radio silence among tactical components was ordered. But a direct satellite radio link from Desert One to the JCS Tank in the Pentagon and to the White House was required.

As often happens in war, well-laid plans unravel. No sooner had Beckwith's aircraft touched down at Desert One with the advance party than they encountered a busload of Iranian villagers and a tanker truck with gasoline smugglers. They captured the bus passengers, but the truck crew escaped. Contingency plans called for these civilians to be removed to Egypt by C-130 after the rescue force proceeded to the next phase. But only five of the six helicopters that struggled through a terrible sandstorm from the *Nimitz* were capable of flying on to Desert Two. Beckwith's plan required a minimum of six operational choppers. In different conditions he might have reduced this force, and thus his helicopter requirement, and proceeded with his mission. But Charlie Beckwith was acutely aware that the JCS and the President himself were looking right over his shoulder.[20] He opted to abort.

In the noisy confusion of blowing dust and the roar of aircraft engines, one of the helicopters collided with a C-130 and both aircraft exploded. Eight men were burned to death and several others were badly injured. Munitions began exploding and the five remaining helicopters were abandoned as the force clambered aboard the remaining C-130s.

Important Classified communications equipment and operational maps that contained the locations of safe houses in Tehran were left behind. Beckwith wanted the choppers destroyed by an air strike, but Carter personally refused to authorize the raid for fear of injuring the stranded Iranian bus passengers on the ground.[21]

I later learned that this decision had placed the four-man "ground team" of undercover CIA and Delta Force officers already in Tehran in great jeopardy. Major Dick Meadows, who had served with such distinction in MACV/SOG, had come out of retirement to volunteer for this risky assignment. He deserved better than to have the locations of his escape route safe houses revealed to the enemy. Through a combination of guts and luck, Dick Meadows and his associates eventually escaped from Tehran.

Discussing the bloody fiasco with other officers experienced in special operations, I was reinforced in my belief that the military needed a permanent, well-funded, independent Special Operations Command that would combine the assets of all four services, as well as civilian covert action personnel. This command could train together with the intensity needed for successful unconventional warfare.

☆　　　☆

As THE 1980 presidential election campaign gained momentum, I decided to support the candidacy of Ronald Reagan, who represented the principles of peace through strength that I had been advocating. I met Reagan, then an unofficial candidate, at a Senate luncheon for him the year before. He marched right up and warmly shook my hand.

"General," he said, "you give me more material for my speeches than anybody else."

Reagan had been following news accounts of my speeches and the American Security Council reports of them.

"Governor Reagan," I replied, "you're probably the only national politician who really understands what I'm talking about."

At the Republican National Convention in Detroit that August I worked with several well-known conservative politicians and leaders such as General Alexander Haig and Danny Graham to incorporate the major elements of the peace-through-strength policy into the Republican Party's national platform. I was well pleased with the nominee for president. Ronald Reagan had consistently advocated dealing with the Soviet Union from a position of military and economic strength. Unlike Jimmy Carter, Reagan was not beset by doubts about a fundamental "malaise" in American society. Reagan also recognized the difference between totalitarian states determined to undermine the West and authoritarian regimes that we could steer toward reform, using the leverage of military and economic assistance.

And George Bush, as a former CIA director and ambassador to Peking, certainly understood the realities of the global East-West struggle.

☆   ☆

SOON after the 1980 presidential election, I was invited by the Asian People's Anti-Communist League (APACL) to address their regional conference in Perth, Australia. The APACL had been founded by Chiang Kai-shek and South Korean president Syngman Rhee in 1954. In 1966, the group merged with other conservative organizations to form the World Anti-Communist League (WACL). It was a highly diverse group united by a common goal of resistance to Marxism-Leninism or any other form of totalitarianism.

My mentor and friend retired General Dick Stilwell, who was working with the Reagan transition team, assured me that, unlike Jimmy Carter, Ronald Reagan was deeply interested in America's future role in the Pacific basin and had already pledged to support our traditional allies in the region, South Korea and the Republic of China on Taiwan.

I called my address to the delegates a "Message of Hope and Optimism." I stressed that the new administration intended to strengthen the armed forces of the United States so that America would no longer be dominated by the Soviet Union. I assured the delegates that the Reagan White House would reassess the failed policy of détente. The brutal invasion of Afghanistan, I said, was one unfortunate product of détente that would not go unchallenged. Non-Communist governments in South Asia that had felt abandoned by the Americans following the Afghan invasion could expect new alliances and economic and military assistance from the United States.

Although the new administration would not punish its allies with overly rigid human rights requirements, keyed to elaborate bureaucratic ledger-keeping as a condition for military and economic assistance, human dignity would remain a major American concern. But this administration would apply the same standards to both allies and opponents. We would encourage authoritarian governments to reform, but we would not exempt totalitarian regimes from criticism.

Above all, I predicted, the new administration would conduct a realistic foreign policy, viewing the world in practical terms, not through the self-deluding idealistic prism of the Carter administration.

The conference received my message warmly. Before I left Perth, the

League's honorary chairman, Dr. Ku Cheng-kang, invited me to attend the 14th Annual Conference of WACL, which would be held in August 1981 in Taipei, Taiwan.

My speech to the Perth conference was reported in the local press, and I received a call from a former Gull Force POW, whose unit I had helped rescue on Hainan Island in 1945. This led to an invitation to Melbourne, where Major Ian Macrae, the senior surviving former Hainan prisoner, had organized a dinner in my honor.

About a dozen former POW officers and senior NCOs attended the party, held in the handsome old Navy-Army Club. I gave them a little speech about the frantic planning and execution of Mission Pigeon. They were curious about the other members of the rescue team.

When I got to the story of my Chinese interpreter, Lieutenant Peter Fong, the grizzled old veterans put down their cigars and brandy snifters and listened with silent intensity.

To me, Peter's story was both a commentary on twentieth-century realities and a monument to the human spirit. The previous year I had received a letter, carefully written in tiny Mandarin characters on a thin piece of rice paper. Among the dense ranks of characters were the English words "Mission Pigeon" and "Peter Fong." The message was accompanied by a translation from a Chinese-American lawyer in New Jersey.

Peter Fong's letter was both alarming and intriguing. Events in his life, he wrote, were then quite "difficult." He requested my help in securing an American visa for his son, Dick Kwang, who would like to visit me in the United States. Even in the translation, Peter's tone indicated he was not free to express his true situation. I contacted the American embassy in Peking offering the required guarantee that the young man would not become a ward of America and wrote to Peter, in care of his wife in Shanghai. The embassy was not convinced; Dick's visa request was refused. I sent a blistering letter to the officious young vice-consul who had refused the visa and it was finally granted.

When young Dick Kwang arrived in Colorado, he told me the true story of his father's "difficult" situation. During the chaos of the early Great People's Cultural Revolution, Mao Tse-tung had reminded his cadres that, although 95 percent of the people will support the revolution, there will always be 5 percent who are counterrevolutionaries, who must be either reeducated or eliminated. An arrest quota of 5 percent of the population—tens of millions of innocent people—was enforced in some areas.

Because Peter Fong spoke English, was a Christian, and had once worked for the Americans, he was swept up in this quota and sent to a slave labor camp on the Yangtze River, where he labored barefoot in the mud for over ten years. After the first Kissinger visit in 1972, officials wanted to learn English, so Peter was shifted from field work to teaching English to the children of camp officers. He saw a story about my encounter with President Carter and managed to smuggle the letter to me through his son during the young man's annual visit.

After learning as much as I could from Dick, I helped arrange political asylum for him and then took him to find relatives in California. The last we heard was that Peter Fong was still a prisoner, and his wife, a doctor, was forbidden to practice medicine. The former Australian POWs were outraged.

One of them, a businessman named Miskin, the ex–camp supply officer, told me his best friend had just become Australia's foreign minister and was planning a trip to China. Miskin was certain he could convince his friend to request Peter's release.

Back in the States, I worked closely with my Gull Force contacts in Australia and with the Australian embassy in Washington. At first the Peking government utterly denied there were any political prisoners or slave labor camps. But I provided the specific location of the camp and detailed descriptions that I had obtained from Dick Kwang. Then Peking admitted there were some reeducation camps for "criminals," but there was no prisoner named Peter Fong. I provided Peter's Chinese name. A few weeks later, Peking stated that Peter Fong had emigrated to the United States years before. I then provided affidavits from Peter's relatives that he was still in China.

After over six months of constant effort, Peter was released from a camp and reunited with his wife in Shanghai. He was able to buy passports from a corrupt official. Under guidelines from the Reagan State Department, the new consulate in Shanghai was favorably disposed toward anti-Communist Chinese. Peter and his wife were issued visas. In December 1981, they finally joined their son in New York. I was able to help him attain a grant of asylum and permanent resident status.

Throughout his long years in captivity, Peter Fong had never surrendered to Communist indoctrination or sought special favors from his captors. He was just as tough a soldier during those terrible years as he had been on Hainan Island.[22]

☆   ☆

In November of 1981, with the encouragement and help of Walter Chopiwskyj, I hosted a meeting in Phoenix for several conservative friends to help in the establishment of an American chapter of WACL.[23] For a few years in the 1970s, the former American WACL chapter had been headed by a notorious pseudo-scientific racist named Roger Pearson, who had successfully infiltrated the mainstream American conservative movement. He published a couple of fringe journals advocating White supremist and anti-

Semitic claptrap. It was unfortunate that Pearson used this position to second the nomination to WACL of a number of neo-Nazis and fascists, who joined several European chapters. Unable to force Pearson's resignation, the members of the board of directors voted for the disestablishment of the American WACL chapter. This took place in 1978. Until 1981, there was no recognized U.S. chapter. When I attended the WACL conference in Taipei, I was shocked to discover that a racial segregationist zealot from Mississippi, named Elmore D. Greaves, was attempting to gain recognition as the U.S. chapter.

Dr. Ku had warned me about the damage Pearson's involvement had done to the League's reputation in the United States, and had also voiced concern about the tendency of anti-democratic fanatics to flock to the League, often bringing with them their racist and anti-Semitic dogma. He hoped that an American chapter could be established around mainstream conservatives, including former military officers with distinguished records. I told him that any group I would head would be focused on national security and foreign policy and would avoid any half-baked theories of racial superiority. And I reminded Dr. Ku I had fought fascism in two theaters of World War II, and I certainly had no sympathy for strutting Nazis.

The unwelcome presence of right-wing extremists was a problem shared by many anti-Communist groups. Indeed, there were screwball zealots out there in the woodwork who were so far right that they had passed through the porous membrane separating fascist from Communist. While still at FORSCOM, I'd had my first encounter with this phenomenon. One of my old OSS Kunming associates, Mitch WerBell, ran a rather mysterious security training academy in Georgia. He went out of his way to be sociable, but I sensed he wasn't completely open about his work. Then I discovered he was on the payroll of the extremist political cult leader Lyndon LaRouche, whose deceptively named U.S. Labor Party was a collection of dangerous misfits who espoused both far-left and far-right ideology. For several months these young fanatics would telephone my office with "vital intelligence," which inevitably boiled down to their paranoid theories that the world was being dominated by an unholy alliance of Jewish bankers, the British royal family (who "controlled" global drug traffic), and their Soviet subordinates.

I warned Mitch WerBell to break off with these crazy misfits, and he said he would. Unfortunately, Mitch had become somewhat of a mercenary in his later life and kept the lucrative connection alive.

The problem of extremists is common to all political advocacy groups, not just conservatives. Liberal organizations, labor, civil rights, and "peace" groups are constantly purging their ranks of unwanted Communists and Trotskyists. And many of these organizations have been less diligent about screening their ranks than the conservatives.[24]

But I was determined that any WACL chapter I headed would be absolutely free of such racists and anti-democratic fanatics. Further, I hoped that a revitalized American branch could serve as a catalyst to purge far-right elements from other League chapters.

In November 1981, I helped create the WACL's American affiliate, the United States Council for World Freedom (USCWF), and agreed to serve as its first chairman. Lieutenant General Danny Graham became the vice-chairman. Our advisory board included a number of retired military officers, including General Lew Walt, who had commanded the Marines in I Corps during the Vietnam War. John Fisher supported the new organization by serving on its advisory board, as did Howard Phillips, chairman of the Conservative Caucus, and a bright young former combat infantry officer in Vietnam named Andy Messing, who ran an educational group called the National Defense Council. Our board included a number of mainstream conservative academics and nationally known attorneys.

☆   ☆

THE Reagan administration's first priority was to modernize America's strategic nuclear forces to achieve a better balance with the Soviet Union. The decision to build the B-1 bomber, the MX missile, and the Trident missile submarine sent an obvious message to the Soviets that they were no longer dealing with a weak, indecisive American leader.

It was in the area of strategic defense, however, that I saw Reagan making the most progress. Before his election, Ronald Reagan had voiced his opposition to continuing the doctrine of Mutually Assured Destruction. Now retired Lieutenant General Daniel Graham was able to influence the White House in exploring a practical strategic defense system. Graham's High Frontier organization worked on the premise that the United States should exploit its technological superiority to demonstrate to the Soviet Union that the MAD concept was a dead end. To do this, he proposed a "technological end run" around the Soviets by deploying a space-based missile defense system, which a panel of academic advisers assured him could be done within three years, if the administration made it a priority.

President Reagan liked Graham's ideas, and the Strategic Defense Initiative was born. Unfortunately, Dr. George Keyworth, Reagan's science adviser, was pessimistic about developing the computer capability needed to command and control an effective missile defense system. Whereas Danny Graham had stressed a practical program—akin to the "brilliant-pebbles" kinetic-kill anti-missiles now in prototype—Keyworth and other academic scientists seemed intent on using the initiative to channel R&D money into exotic basic research in lasers and charged particle beam weapons, which would have no practical application for decades. They were abetted in this by the Defense Department bureaucracy and powerful aerospace corporation contractors who had a vested interest in keeping MAD alive.

Defense Secretary Caspar Weinberger and the new JCS chairman, General John Vessey, undertook a thorough modernization of America's conventional forces, which countered the massive Soviet buildup in tanks and attack helicopters in Europe.

☆   ☆

But the Soviets were still actively exercising their "Third Option" of unconventional warfare and insurgency, using their Cuban and East European surrogates. They were, in fact, staging a strategic campaign against the West within the smoke screen of the "wars of national liberation," which Averell Harriman had convinced Jimmy Carter were legitimate Soviet foreign policy.

The fact that the West was actually at war—albeit a low-intensity conflict—became obvious to me during several trips to Central America during this period. As always, the Communist strategy was to exploit poverty and social upheaval, which was certainly to be found in abundance in Central America.

In Guatemala the Guerrilla Army of the Poor was controlled by Cuban advisers, who exploited the government's heavy-handed repression of the Indian peasant majority. Cuban agents operated with relative impunity from the traditional academic sanctuary of the national university in Guatemala City. When moderate politicians tried to reconcile the situation, they often fell victim to assassins of both the extreme right and the Communist left. During a visit to Guatemala in 1979, Danny Graham and I learned that Cuban guerrilla warfare specialists and intelligence agents were actively engaged, keeping the trouble brewing. But in the United States, the news media usually portrayed the insurgency in simplistic terms with the cruel Spanish-ancestry oligarchs brutally repressing the Indian masses.

The guerrilla war in El Salvador was different. Under U.S. pressure, the traditional ruling oligarchy had begun a program of land reform. And the army junta finally allowed a Christian Democratic Party moderate, Jose Napoleon Duarte, to take office in December 1980, eight years after his election. The small but growing Farabundo Marti National Liberation Front (FMLN) was dominated by Cuban-trained Communists and supplied by the Nicaraguan Sandinistas. There was clear evidence that the Soviet-sponsored arms buildup in Nicaragua was meant to transform that country into the central staging base for the "liberation" of Central America and eventually of Mexico.

In fact, the blatant nature of this plan was one of the proximate causes of the defection of leading non-Communists from the Sandinista government in Nicaragua. Eden Pastora, the military hero of the Sandinista victory over Somoza, was shocked by the cold-blooded approach of Sandinista leader Daniel Ortega and his brother Humberto to the insurgency in neighboring El Salvador. He later stated that the "nine top Communists" in the Sandinista government gave priority to aiding the insurrection in El Salvador over addressing critical economic problems in Nicaragua.[25] Taking a page from Ho Chi Minh's book on wars of national liberation, for years neither the Sandinistas nor the FMLN guerrillas would admit to the flow of Communist arms from Nicaragua to El Salvador. It was not until 1989 that FMLN leader Joaquin Villalobos publicly acknowledged the Sandinista aid.[26]

In August 1981, the Reagan administration's Assistant Secretary of State Thomas Enders went to Managua with an offer to renew economic assistance if the Sandinistas stopped their support for the Communist insurrection in El Salvador and cut their links to guerrilla groups elsewhere in Central America. The Sandinistas conferred with their Cuban sponsors and allowed the initiative to go unanswered while they continued their support of Communist guerrilla groups in Central America.[27]

In El Salvador itself, the army was the government's main weapon against the FMLN guerrillas. After failing to stop Nicaraguan-Cuban assistance to the rebels, the United States resumed military aid to El Salvador and the Pentagon dispatched U.S. military trainers to assist the army. But Congress was still gripped with the Vietnam syndrome, terrified of any U.S. military entanglement. They put an arbitrary limit of fifty-five U.S. trainers on our military assistance mission and severely restricted their freedom of movement in the small country to prevent any U.S. participation in combat.[28]

These restrictions limited the trainers' effectiveness. When Andy Messing and I visited El Salvador in August 1982, we found a very disturbing situation, which we both recognized from our experience in Vietnam. U.S. aid to the Salvadoran military was often inappropriate. America had equipped their air force with A-37 attack jets armed with 500-pound bombs. The army was still organized along conventional lines with clumsy battalion-size units armed with heavy-caliber weapons, including artillery. Like the ARVN of the early 1960s, this force was clearly no match for the hit-and-run attacks of the lightly armed guerrillas. Moreover, the ill-advised use of artillery and jet-attack aircraft was causing widespread civilian casualties and winning the guerrillas unearned sympathy. I couldn't believe the U.S. military was making the same kinds of mistakes we had in Indochina.[29]

Andy and I were aboard a Salvadoran army Huey helicopter returning from La Union to the capital late one afternoon when the chopper was diverted to pick up casualties from an ambush near a coffee plantation. The chopper settled down in a gritty cloud of volcanic dust. We heard the crack of small arms and the thud of automatic weapons fire nearby. Scared young soldiers trundled beneath the rotors with their wounded comrades. No sooner were the three moaning casualties dumped onto the deck than the pilot lifted off.

As we climbed away from the battlefield, one of the wounded men, a stocky kid with pronounced Indian features, began to hemorrhage bright arterial blood from a gaping wound in his thigh. The two door gunners squatting on their little bike seats simply stared at the wounded soldier as his dark face grew pale and he slipped into shock. I shouted over the roar of the engine for the gunners to administer first aid. But they stared back at me expressionless. Obviously, they didn't know what to do.

Andy Messing took charge, using the soldier's belt for a tourniquet and applying a pressure bandage to the wound. The man was still alive when we landed at Ilopango air base outside of San Salvador. When we queried the local commander about the incident, he admitted that most of his troops had never received first-aid training. And the understaffed and hard-pressed U.S. military mission could not provide that training.

This was only one of many serious deficiencies in our overly constrained military assistance program to El Salvador. In Washington I conferred with my old friend Nestor Sanchez, who had come over to the Pentagon from the CIA with Undersecretary Frank Carlucci. Nestor had been one of my captains in the JACK operation in Korea and was now a deputy assistant secretary of defense responsible for Latin America. I told him that I thought I should start a private support effort for the hard-pressed Salvadoran army. He said that as long as it was essentially humanitarian aid, there could be no objection from the U.S. government.

Over the next months I worked with concerned conservative groups in the States to fund a private military assistance effort for El Salvador, which provided volunteer American doctors and military veteran trainers in such important areas as first aid, field sanitation, and communications. We even managed to find a retired Army parachute rigger who trained a dozen counterparts in the Salvadoran airborne battalion. Lieutenant Colonel Bob Brown, the publisher of *Soldier of Fortune* magazine, was energetic in this effort. Through his vigorous activities and funding, dozens of private American non-combat trainers and advisers went to El Salvador to assist their military. By these and similar efforts elsewhere in the world, Bob Brown demonstrated true patriotism and dedication to the principles of democracy and morality which refute the image of a crass mercenary so prevalent in media reports on his activities.

But the fundamental problem in Central America, of course, remained Nicaragua, where the hard-core Communist cadre of the original Sandinista government was now firmly in control. The Soviet Union was pumping in hundreds of millions of dollars of military assistance. Thousands of Cuban and Soviet-bloc trainers were working to build an army of more than 60,000 regulars, backed by an equal number of well-armed militia: a force *ten times* larger than Somoza's National Guard. And defectors revealed that the army was intended to eventually grow to a total of 500,000 regular and reserve troops. Nicaragua's population was only 3.5 million; this meant that almost 20 percent of the population would be under arms.[30]

Although heavy weapons arrived slowly at first, within a year of the revolution Soviet T-55 battle tanks and armored personnel carriers were photographed being unloaded from Soviet and Cuban ships. Predictably, the Sandinistas conducted a vigorous disinformation campaign, claiming the huge military buildup was "exclusively for defensive" purposes.[31] But the growing Sandinista arsenal so far outstripped any force in Central America that only a fool could deny that the Soviet Union was busily constructing a major strategic base on the North American mainland.[32] And the Soviets' new Sandinista surrogates were undoubtedly destined for "internationalist" duty elsewhere in Latin America.

By this time a number of Nicaraguans who had fought to overthrow Somoza, like Adolfo Calero, a businessman and former dean at the University of Central America and a life-long opponent of the Somoza dictatorship, were living in exile and prepared to organize a democratic resistance to the growing Communist dictatorship in Nicaragua. They were joined by former Sandinista supporters, like Eden Pastora, who had become disillusioned. Naturally I was eager to meet such men, but I learned from embassy officials in Central America that the new Nicaraguan Democratic Resistance movement—the "Contras"—was already in contact with the Central Intelligence Agency, and that covert American support was being organized. My old OSS case officer, Bill Casey, was now director of Central Intelligence, so I knew the resistance was in good hands.

☆   ☆

IN VIEW of the mounting Soviet effort at the low-intensity end of the conflict spectrum, I focused my public speaking efforts on what Danny Graham christened the "Low Frontier." I pointed out to civic groups and university audiences that the high end of the conflict spectrum, full-scale nuclear war, obviously involved the highest level of violence. But it had to be recognized as having the lowest order of probability of occurrence. Conventional war, which fell in the middle of the spectrum, involved relatively moderate levels of violence. As a result of the significant improvement in our conventional forces under the Reagan defense program, the chances of America being involved in a conventional war with the Soviets, Chinese, or North Koreans were significantly reduced.

But we were *already* involved with the Soviets' surrogates at the low end of the conflict spectrum that included terrorism, subversion, and guerrilla war. The terrorism, sabotage, and assassination then sweeping much of the Third World were not simply a crime wave, but military operations in an unconventional war, which included political warfare, disinformation, and both overt and covert propaganda. Unless we recognized that our enemies were exercising their "Third Option" in the ongoing conflict, I warned, we could be defeated just as certainly as we would had we continued to ignore the Soviet threats at the upper regions of the conflict spectrum.

The United States had to increase its capability to wage unconventional warfare by supporting anti-Communist forces already engaged in the conflict in Africa, South and Southeast Asia, and Central and South America. I urged support for the President's efforts to increase the covert operations capabilities of our intelligence community, which was beginning to deliver effective support to the Mujaheddin resistance in Afghanistan, anti-Communist forces in Angola, and the new democratic resistance in Nicaragua.

But the Vietnam syndrome still crippled our efforts and dominated congressional oversight of our unconventional-warfare operations. In Angola, for example, Dr. Jonas Savimbi's anti-Communist UNITA forces were conducting a heroic resistance to the Marxist MPLA army supported by well-equipped Soviet, East German, and Cuban regulars, who outnumbered them three to one. Savimbi's tough guerrillas moved freely in all the provinces. They were inflicting heavy casualties on the 23,000 Cuban combat troops. Congress, however, through restrictive legislation known as the Clark Amendment, seriously limited the administration's freedom of action in the area, preventing us from delivering enough military aid and noncombatant advisers for UNITA to win a clear victory.

The problem there was compounded by the Gulf Oil Company, whose concession was controlled by the MPLA and guarded by Soviet and Cuban troops. Gulf's payments to the MPLA government actually subsidized this Communist occupation. And Gulf's influence in Congress was enough to keep the Clark Amendment alive.

I told my audiences that we must learn to "integrate" our economic, political, and military efforts in combined unconventional warfare just as effectively as the Soviets do. This integrated strategy entailed all the assets of covert intelligence activities, black and gray psychological operations, information campaigns, and economic warfare.

We would have to revitalize the covert action and human intelligence capabilities of the CIA that had been stripped away by Carter's CIA director, Stansfield Turner. The Special Operations forces of the Army, Navy, and Air Force had to be expanded and restructured under an effective joint command that would prevent future fiascoes like that of Desert One. Unnecessary legislative restraints like the Clark Amendment that limited assistance to anti-Communist forces in the Third World had to be abolished. And finally, we had to increase the government information activities of the Voice of America, Radio Free Europe, and Radio Liberty, and establish Radio Marti to broadcast into Cuba. We had to recognize that the Soviet Union had successfully exploited the failed policy of détente. We could turn the tables on them by encouraging resistance to Soviet rule in the captive nations of Eastern Europe and by actively aiding freedom fighters in Central America, Africa, and Afghanistan.

Those of us who had studied patterns of Soviet aggression for decades realized that their system had to expand militarily or it would implode. And we were determined to fight that expansion at the low end of the conflict spectrum. In effect, our new unconventional-warfare effort would go beyond the traditional policy of containment, which had thwarted Communist expansion since World War II, to a policy of "rollback" by providing encouragement and support to dissidents inside the Soviet empire.

As part of my Third Option information campaign, I was invited to address Reagan administration defense policy officials. National Security Adviser Dick Allen asked me to present the concept of fully integrated unconventional warfare to a group of National Security Council officers concerned with special operations. I flew to Washington and met the group at the NSC offices in the Old Executive Office Building (OEOB) next to the White House. My coordinator for this project was a friendly young Marine major named Oliver North. We hit it off very well. I heard he had a fine combat record in Vietnam and friends mentioned his seemingly limitless energy and appetite for hard work.

Over the coming months I made my presentation on the Third Option and our unconventional-warfare strategy to several of the service chiefs and secretaries. Navy Secretary John Lehman was especially enthusiastic. When Andy Messing and I mentioned to Lehman the still-current plans to eliminate the Navy SEALs, the Secretary was flabbergasted. He immediately took action to rescind the order. To my great satisfaction, I was able to watch the organization of an expanded and reinvigorated Special Operations Command during the first Reagan administration.

During my Washington visits I sometimes stopped in to brief CIA director Bill Casey in his office at the OEOB or out at the Langley headquarters. I made a point of keeping him informed on my speaking campaign and our private support efforts in Central America.

"Jack," Casey said, one sleety winter afternoon, "I want you to know that the President is aware of and pleased with your work."

He added that the emerging policy known as the Reagan Doctrine had been partially inspired by my Low Frontier speeches. The policy did indeed combine many of my fundamental concepts, including assistance to anti-

Communist rebels in the Third World and economic and psychological support for the captive nations of the Soviet empire.

I gazed past his desk, out the window to the traffic on Pennsylvania Avenue. It was a nasty evening and thousands of government workers were streaming home to the suburbs. I realized that I probably had more influence as a private citizen than I would have had as a mid-level defense official struggling in the bureaucratic trenches.

☆   ☆

MY RESPONSIBILITIES within WACL continued. One of my main concerns was still purging the League of neo-Nazis, racists, and other non-democratic elements. I was greatly helped in this effort by retired Major General Robert Close, a senator in the Belgian parliament and a representative to the European parliament. Bob Close headed the Belgian WACL chapter. He had fought in the anti-Nazi resistance during World War II, was captured, brutally treated, and spent the remainder of the war as a concentration camp prisoner. No one could accuse him of being a fascist. He came to my home in Colorado to work on the problem of expelling neo-Nazis, anti-Semites, racists, and anti-Catholics from the League. We researched the backgrounds of hundreds of League members and dozens of organizations which had applied for memberships. It became obvious that one contingent of delegates dominated by a Mexican neo-Nazi group called the Tecos would have to go, as would several British and European groups who had infiltrated League chapters.

On May 10, 1983, Bob Close and I released the so-called Tabernash Report demanding the expulsion of "extremist, neo-Nazi, neo-fascist, racist, or similar organizations" from the League. Henceforth, we would refuse to invite any extremists to attend WACL conferences we hosted. Bob Close would host the 1983 League conference in Luxembourg and I planned to host the 1984 conference in San Diego. To ensure the word got out that the League had no use for fascists, racists, and anti-Semites, I invited Irwin A. Suall, director of fact finding for the Anti-Defamation League of B'nai B'rith, to send observers to upcoming conferences. He appreciated my invitation, and we appreciated the presence of his observer teams.[33]

☆   ☆

THAT fall two events occurred that reminded the world of the true nature of the Communist powers aligned against the West. On September 1, 1983, Korean Air Lines flight 007 from New York to Seoul, via Anchorage, a Boeing jumbo jet with 269 people on board, was blasted out of the sky by a Soviet air force interceptor near Sakhalin Island. The plane was hit by at least one air-to-air rocket and exploded, its debris and innocent passengers raining down over a wide area of the Sea of Okhotsk, north of the Japanese island of Hokkaido. There were no survivors.

The Soviets tried to blunt world outrage by implying that the airliner was flying without aerial navigation lights and did not respond to repeated calls from Soviet air traffic control centers. But the American government used tape recordings from one of our electronic intelligence Ferret satellites to reveal that no attempt had been made to contact the plane or to request Japanese air controllers to do so. The truth was that the airliner had strayed from the normal Anchorage-to-Seoul air corridor, probably because of an incorrectly calibrated inertial navigation system.

For me and many of my associates the tragedy was compounded by the loss of our close friend Congressman Larry McDonald, who had been flying to Seoul to participate in ceremonies marking the thirtieth anniversary of the U.S.-Korea Defense Treaty. Larry had asked me to be a part of the delegation and travel with him. I had just returned from Korea one month earlier, so I decided against it. I did not want to wear out my welcome in Korea. I'd known Larry McDonald since I'd served in FORSCOM, when he was a conservative Democratic congressman from Georgia's 7th District. He was one of the most knowledgeable people about the U.S. Constitution and American history I'd ever met.

Even under the supposed openness of Glasnost, it's never been revealed whether the Soviet pilot knew the Boeing 747 was a civilian airliner or if he mistook it for an American RC-135 electronic intelligence aircraft that had been flying in international air space well offshore that same morning. In either case, the cruelty of the act underscored the fundamental brutality of the Soviet system. It was inconceivable that any Western air force would have committed a similar outrage, even if an unarmed Soviet spy plane were intercepted by a fighter.[34]

A month later, the South Koreans suffered another blow. A delegation of high-ranking government ministers from Seoul was in Rangoon, Burma, attending a wreath-laying ceremony at a war memorial pavilion. The group was waiting for South Korean president Chun Doo-Hwan, whose car was delayed in traffic, when a massive bomb exploded, killing sixteen of the Korean delegation and three Burmese. Local police later confronted a North Korean saboteur agent, who killed himself with a hand grenade rather than surrender. Within a week, South Korean intelligence assembled firm evidence that the bomb had been planted by the North Korean secret service.[35] Friends in the American intelligence community confirmed that the assassination attempt had been a North Korean operation, and they stressed that Kim Il-Sung's agents probably received Soviet cooperation in staging the attack.

☆ ☆

IN MAY 1984, Undersecretary of Defense for Policy Dr. Fred Ikle invited me to head a panel of outside experts to reassess our military assistance policy to El Salvador and to recommend changes. I was more than happy to do so, because I believed the effort to date was badly flawed by lack of direction, incompetence, as well as crippling congressional restrictions. There wasn't much we could do about the Congress, but I knew the Pentagon had to improve its performance or we could anticipate a prolonged bloody conflict, ending in a Communist victory.

The so-called Singlaub Panel I assembled were all recognized experts in unconventional warfare. Retired Major General Ed Lansdale had decades of experience in counterinsurgency in both the Philippines and Indochina. My old friend Brigadier General Heinie Aderholt was probably the most knowledgeable retired officer on the use of air power in counterinsurgency. And Dr. Edward Luttwak had written brilliantly on light infantry and special operations.[36]

In our discussions the panel concurred that the Salvadoran military effort to date had been clumsy, heavy-handed, and often brutal. The FMLN guerrillas operated in close proximity to the civilian population, employing small-scale terrorism, assassination, and sabotage. Even as the guerrilla forces became larger, it was basic error to combat them with regular forces, including jet aircraft and field artillery.

We unanimously agreed that the fundamental priority in any new American policy had to be de-escalating the level of violence. El Salvador was a small, poor country; waging the kind of war currently under way might well destroy it.

Ed Lansdale sagely pointed out that military assistance groups often became informal arms vendors, in effect brokering the sale of surplus weapons such as the inappropriate A-37 ground-attack jets. In order to keep these jets flying in bad weather conditions, the Americans had convinced the Salvadorans to squander part of their limited military aid budget on a sophisticated radar installation at the Ilopango air base. We resolved that future American assistance should include "slow-mover" AC-47 gunships, rather than more jets. These gunships had been used to great effect in breaking up guerrilla attacks in Vietnam and they could do the same in El Salvador without the massive collateral damage of bombing.

The list of blunders went on. We discovered that the Americans were selling the Salvadoran army extremely expensive lightweight 105mm howitzers that could be transported by helicopter. Ed Luttwak offered to find out the background of the requirement for this exotic hardware. An hour later he came back to our Pentagon conference room with the full story. In order to keep the lightweight howitzer production line open, some obscure Pentagon bureaucrat had launched the ploy of selling one per month to the hapless Salvadorans. At the price they were paying, they could have had three conventional artillery pieces for every lightweight gun we made them purchase.

But I was convinced that all this emphasis on high-caliber hardware was completely out of line. El Salvador needed a well-equipped and well-trained national police force, not a large conventional army to combat the insurgency. Their unwieldy infantry battalions conducting clumsy search-and-destroy operations only alienated the rural population. It was my strong recommendation that America concentrate its efforts in building up an effective paramilitary rural constabulary in El Salvador, an organization made up of local residents familiar with the geography and people of each village.

But here we were stymied. Over the previous decade liberals in Congress had prohibited American foreign aid being used for police training. Police in Third World countries were viewed as agents of the repressive oligarchy. But without adequate training in counterinsurgency, police often fought assassination and kidnapping through illegal means. El Salvador's notorious death squads were typical of this reaction. But the most vociferous congressional opponents of these "fascist" police refused to vote funds for American aid to reform and train the needed counterinsurgency constabulary. Nevertheless, we recommended the establishment of such a professional police force under strict control of the civilian government. We also recommended the thorough retraining of the Salvadoran army for small-unit night operations deep in traditional rebel sanctuaries. Finally, the Singlaub Panel stressed that the combined government forces in El Salvador had to undertake much greater responsibility for civic action projects in the countryside and that the thrust of our truncated military training effort should be in those directions.

I was pleased to see that every one of our recommendations was implemented in the next few years. It was especially heartening that the U.S. government was finally permitted to join an international effort to retrain El Salvador's police forces. The earlier hypocrisy of chiding the Salvadoran government over the death squads while withholding aid for professional police training had finally ended.[37]

By the summer of 1984 it seemed that America had reversed the stagnant drift of the post-Vietnam years and was set on a course to defend freedom and support democracy in our own hemisphere and throughout the world. But in all my marathon travel and public speaking, I had overlooked the obvious fact that 1984 was a presidential election year. And I had underestimated the power of congressional liberals to politicize national security.

CHAPTER FIFTEEN
Sandinistas and Contras
1984–1986

☆   ☆

In May 1984, I attended the Jedburgh's fortieth reunion in Paris. Like all gatherings of old soldiers who had been thrown into battle together as young men, it was a mixture of frivolity and introspection. No one wanted to believe he was forty years older, or that his most vital decades had slipped away in an endless blur of days and nights, sunshine and snow, and all the forgotten punctuations of a lifetime.

Meeting men like George Thompson and Phil Chadburn in the bustling lobby of the Etape St. Honore was a pleasure tinged with sadness. It was strange to see the lively eyes of a cocky young paratroop lieutenant set in the craggy face of a man in his sixties. But there weren't only men at the reunion. Several British First Aid Nursing Yeomanry (FANY), veterans who had packed our parachutes and taught us code attended. In fact, Daphne Mundinger Friele, widow of American Jed Bob Mundinger, had helped organize the festivities. We all looked for the men who were not there. The list of "Deceased U.S. Jedburghs" on the reunion bulletin board was longer than we had expected. Tony Denneau, my Jed radio operator, did not make it. He had died several years before. Stew Alsop was gone, as were Bill Dreux and Larry Swank. Cy Manierre was among the dead; Bill Colby told me that Cy had never really recovered from the brutal treatment at the hands of his Gestapo interrogators.

Like me, several American Jeds, including Mac Austin and Bill Pietsch, had stayed in the Army after the war and had fought in Korea and Indochina. The British contingent at the reunion was smaller than either the American or French. My close friend Adrian Wise had gone on to a fine career in the

British army and had retired as a brigadier. But he had died suddenly in 1962. The Brits who did attend, however, were in good form. Tommy MacPherson, one of the legends of unconventional warfare, who had escaped from a Nazi POW camp to lead one of the first Jed teams into France, was just as self-effacing as always. The miniature Military Cross on the lapel of his tweed jacket was so tiny it could have been mistaken for a flaw in the weave.

The third day of the reunion we all piled on tour buses and drove out to the handsome Resistance Memorial on Mont Valerien. It was one of those ripe spring mornings in the Ile de France, with chestnuts in flower and the sky a deep, aching blue. Under the direction of a photographer from *Le Figaro,* we donned our green Commando berets and assembled on the broad flagstone pavement before the memorial wall. The photographer climbed a tall ladder, then coaxed and chided until we had lined up in the pattern of an open parachute, with columns of Jeds forming the suspension lines converging at the base of the ladder and two curved lines of Jeds forming the canopy.

While the pictures were snapped, I gazed up at the white pencil lines of jet contrails high above. I remembered the French sky that summer of 1944. But the airliners approaching Orly and Charles de Gaulle airports carried tourists and business executives, not bombs. Those contrails were not from Eighth Air Force B-17s en route to the Saar or Berlin. That war was long over. We had fought against the totalitarian dictators, and we had won. Young men like Adrian, Tony, Stew, and all the others had volunteered to risk capture, torture, and death to help defeat fascism, one of the great evils of this century. Others of us standing on this pavement with our jaunty green berets had continued the fight against the twentieth century's other great evil, totalitarian communism.

Ours had only been the first of several generations asked to face hazardous duty in the long battle against the dictators. I remembered the rows of fresh graves, each marked by a simple wooden stake in a shell-blasted Brittany pasture. I saw again the columns of young Chinese soldiers trudging across a frozen river in Manchuria. Then I saw the faces of my men, tense but determined in the yellow flarelight, as we ran up the slope toward the inferno of Outpost Harry. I could picture young ARVN Rangers, slinging their packs into a chopper as the red dust of the Highlands swirled around some long-forgotten LZ, leaving on yet another operation on the Trail. I remembered General Stilwell's face at Kimpo Airport, a mask of controlled outrage, as we saluted the departing coffins of the two American officers murdered in the DMZ. And I could see again the stoic peasant face of that Salvadoran soldier, bleeding on the lurching deck of the Huey.

The picture session ended, and we adjourned for a festive luncheon, hosted by Jacques Chirac, the mayor of Paris, at the Hôtel de Ville. That night, the celebration continued late. Bill Casey was there, as was Bill Colby. And the reunion was probably the first time a serving and former director of Central Intelligence got a snootful of champagne and cognac and joined their raucous colleagues in a posh hotel bar to chant, "*Quarante-huit, quarante-neuf . . . quelle merde!*"

Amid the hustle of meetings, luncheons, and formal dinners at the British and American embassies, I did manage some time with Jacques de Penguilly, Jacques Martin, and Michel de Bourbon. They had all finished the war with more dangerous covert assignments while I was training guerrillas in southern China. Now Jacques Martin was the number-two man in the Direction Politique of the French Foreign Ministry.

We had a quiet breakfast one morning discussing the current strategic balance in the world. Like many educated Europeans, Jacques had originally been wary of Ronald Reagan. But Jacques now admitted that the first Reagan administration had restored the global strategic balance by blunting the most flagrant and dangerous Soviet military expansion since World War II. This being an election year, Jacques and his French colleagues wanted my opinion on Reagan's chances for reelection.

"The Democrats will probably pick Carter's vice-president, Fritz Mondale," I said. "And he's got about as much chance as a snowball in hell."

Jacques Martin tilted his face in a classic expression of Gallic skepticism. "*Eh bien,* Jack," he said, "but what about this business in Nicaragua?"

I had to admit Jacques had a point. Congressional Democrats, under the leadership of House Speaker Tip O'Neill and his close friend Massachusetts congressman Edward Boland, were determined to transform covert American support for anti-Communist Nicaraguan "Contra" resistance groups into a major election-year issue. Press accounts that spring had exposed CIA involvement in the mining of two Nicaraguan Pacific coast ports used for transshipping weapons and supplies to FMLN guerrillas in neighboring El Salvador. The White House was forced to admit the Agency's role in the operation. The news media stressed the "illegality" of the mining, but downplayed the role of Nicaragua in the arms flow to the Salvadoran Communists. Democrats were publicly outraged that the House and Senate intelligence committees had not been properly informed on the operation. But these politicians refused to admit that their staffers had repeatedly leaked details of sensitive covert operations in the past.[1]

At Boland's behest, the House had already greatly restricted American covert aid to the Contras. His 1982 amendment attached to the Defense appropriations bill barred the CIA and the Pentagon from providing any aid that might be used for "the purpose of overthrowing" the Sandinista government. The next year, Boland managed to limit American military aid to the Contras to $24 million. And by the summer of 1984, he and O'Neill were determined to stop all aid to the Nicaraguan Democratic Resistance, thus giving the Reagan administration its first major foreign policy defeat at the height of the presidential election campaign. Boland evolved a legislative strategy that skirted direct debate on the issue. His "amendments" were exactly that, last-minute tag-on additions to important legislation that usually had nothing to do with Central America. Unless the House was prepared to vote down vital appropriations bills, the members had to pass Boland's amendments.[2]

So the entire CIA covert operation funding the Contras was threatened with defeat, not in the jungle mountains of Central America, but in the back rooms of Capitol Hill. The last night of the Jed reunion, I managed to get Bill Casey alone for a few moments at the British embassy reception.

"What the hell's going to happen, Bill?" I asked. I'd heard there was a shortfall of over $20 million that summer alone and the prospects for continued aid in fiscal year 1985, which began on October 1, 1984, were exceedingly dim.

Bill Casey was normally one of the world's great optimists, who always managed to see beyond the immediate emergency to the long-term prospects of any operation. But that night in Paris, among the liveried footmen and crystal chandeliers of the embassy, he was subdued. He gazed down at his wine glass. "It's bad, Jack," he said, "and it's just going to get worse."

Neither of us, of course, realized he was voicing prophecy, not simply the understandable pessimism of a tired bureaucrat under siege.

☆　　　☆

BY LATE summer, I was also pessimistic about American aid to the Nicaraguan resistance. The CIA program had been a successful example of the Third Option. But now its future was in doubt. It was clear the Democratic majority in Congress was determined to completely eliminate American support for the Nicaraguan resistance. And, once again, this funding cut would be a unilateral American action that required no concession from the Sandinistas or their Soviet sponsors. Indeed, Soviet and Cuban military aid to Nicaragua had reached alarming proportions. Regular Cuban troops were now deployed in Nicaragua. Hundreds of Cuban advisers were training the Sandinistas in the use of 150 Soviet T-55 battle tanks, 200 armored personnel carriers, and multi-barrel mobile rocket launchers. More ominously, the Soviets had begun shipping their Mi-24 Hind attack helicopters, the so-called flying tank that carried a devastating array of rockets and automatic cannons. Any second lieutenant at Fort Benning could tell you these weapons were hardly "defensive," as the Sandinistas had claimed two years before when the buildup began.[3]

Knowledgeable conservatives I dealt with were convinced any cutoff of official American aid to the Contras would be an election-year aberration that the Congress would surely reverse during the next session.

I had already renewed my efforts to secure medical aid for the Salvadoran army. The program that Bob Brown and I had helped organize to send volunteer American veterans to train Salvadoran counterparts was running well. But I drew the line at encouraging free-lance soldiers to Central America. Some private groups were sending well-intentioned volunteers of sometimes questionable skills to fight alongside the Contras. Tom Posey of the Alabama-based Civilian Military Assistance was one of the most active. In fact, two of his men were killed that summer when their helicopter was shot down inside Nicaragua. As brave as these volunteers were, their presence gave the Sandinistas grist for their propaganda mill. After the shootdown, Managua stepped up its shrill campaign against American "mercenaries."[4]

In August, I attended the Dallas meeting of a conservative group that gathered regularly to discuss important national security issues. One of the government officials addressing the meeting was Ollie North. He'd been the National Security Council (NSC) officer who had organized my Third Option lectures several years before as a young Marine major on the NSC staff. Ollie was now a lieutenant colonel and one of the NSC's key officials, with geographic responsibility for Central America and functional responsibility for counterterrorism.

I'd had several dealings with Ollie in connection with organizing private humanitarian aid for the Salvadoran army. Over the previous months, it had become clear that North was now the administration's semi-public point man on aid to the Contras. I had no idea what his relationship was to the CIA on this issue, but he was becoming increasingly active as CIA funding for the Contra operation dried up. North had always impressed me as an intense, bright young officer willing to make hard decisions and work long hours to implement them.

Yet there was something about Ollie North's new responsibilities that bothered me. For one thing, he was only a Marine lieutenant colonel on loan to the NSC. And, as admirable as his gung-ho volunteer attitude was, he might be exposing himself out on a weak policy limb, which might suddenly break. North's superiors, National Security Adviser Robert "Bud" McFarlane and his deputy Rear-Admiral John Poindexter, were obviously aware of North's efforts. But by using a relatively junior officer as their point man, they were insulating themselves from any political flak his activities might draw from Congress. I was uneasy that North was playing in the big leagues lacking a minor league apprenticeship.

In Dallas, North brought me together with Adolfo Calero, one of the leaders of the Nicaraguan Resistance Directorate, whom I had met six months earlier in Scottsdale, Arizona, and with Rob Owen, a young American public relations specialist and dedicated Contra supporter who would serve as a private liaison channel between the Contras and American government officials.

We met at my hotel to discuss the problem of continued unofficial American support for the Contras should the Democrats actually manage to cut off all funding that fall. Calero was aware of my work raising private funds and in-kind contributions of medical supplies, boots, and uniforms for the Afghan Mujaheddin and the Lao resistance. He also knew of my success in organizing medical volunteers to work in El Salvador.

If the Contras were to survive as a fighting force through the pending funding cut, Calero said, they would need such medical volunteers as well as in-kind contributions of medicine, uniforms, and other clothing.

The current tragedy, he said, was that the Contra ranks were swelling just as American aid was about to be cut. "We are getting fifty or a hundred new volunteers into our base camps every day," Calero said. "They come in from the Nueva Segovia and Zeleya regions, and as far south as Managua itself."

He spoke earnestly, with deep conviction. Almost all these new Contra volunteers were *campesinos* who had been forced by repressive Sandinista policies to take sides in the conflict. Most of them had left their homes with few possessions and had trekked over the mountainous jungle for days or weeks. When they arrived in the Contra base camps in southern Honduras, their shoes and clothing were often shredded and they were riddled with dysentery and malaria. Yet they were perfectly willing to turn around and head back into the hills of Nicaragua to fight the Sandinistas.

"The clothes," Adolfo added, "do not have to be new. Old blue jeans and tennis shoes are better than what they have."

As long as we were being frank, I asked Adolfo and Ollie North how well the Contras were supplied with munitions.

"Someone else," Ollie said, "is handling that end."

Adolfo Calero nodded.

"At least for the moment," Ollie continued. "Their weapon supply line is intact. But they'll be short of ammunition within a few months."

This was an area I preferred avoiding, especially if the Agency had been wise enough to establish an efficient munitions supply for the Contras and to stockpile weapons and ammunition while the program was still officially funded.

I promised Calero I would do my best to provide the Contras private contributions of clothing and medical supplies. I also offered to help recruit volunteer doctors and corpsmen to come to their Honduran base camps and help train their own medics.

But the most pressing problem as I saw it was on Capitol Hill, not in the

Contra base camps. "We have to make a much better presentation to Congress," I told them. "And for that we need grass-roots support. Once people in this country know what's at stake in Central America, they'll put pressure on Congress to resume aid."

Ollie North nodded enthusiastically, but Adolfo Calero remained silent, his lips pursed, obviously uncertain of the support he might expect from his American ally.

☆   ☆

THAT fall, Calero's doubts certainly seemed justified. Led by Edward Boland, congressional Democrats managed to attach the divisive issue of renewed Contra aid to an omnibus federal spending bill. Bitter infighting over the issue in the House had delayed important appropriations bills past the beginning of fiscal year 1985 on October 1. And liberal Democrats threatened to continue their foot dragging as long as Republicans and conservative Democrats held out for any Contra funding. As in all presidential election years, the entire House of Representatives was also up for reelection. Members—especially moderate and conservative Republicans who had come into office with the Reagan administration—were anxious to return to the campaign trail.

Late on October 12, 1984, the overdue spending bill was finally passed with the latest Boland Amendment tagged on almost as an afterthought. The amendment prohibited the CIA, the Defense Department, "or any other agency or entity of the U.S. government involved in intelligence activity" from spending any funds to support, "directly or indirectly, military or paramilitary operations in Nicaragua by any nation, group or organization, movement or individual."[5]

Two days later, congressional foes of Contra aid consolidated their victory by using one of the dirtiest weapons in the Washington political arsenal: the selective leak of sensitive information. Unnamed congressional staffers gave the Associated Press a copy of a Spanish-language guerrilla warfare training manual the CIA was preparing for the Contras. The booklet was a hastily assembled hodgepodge of unconventional-warfare techniques, including psychological operations. One section encouraged guerrillas to "neutralize" Sandinista leaders through the "selective use of violence." There was an immediate firestorm of scandal in the news media and Congress. Assassination programs, either direct or indirect, led by the CIA were officially forbidden. And the instant interpretation of the manual was that it contained CIA-inspired assassination methods. A front-page story in the *New York Times* led with the headline "CIA Primer Tells Nicaraguan Rebels How to Kill."[6]

The net result of this leak was a barrage of self-righteous protest that served to pin down any congressional candidates attempting to criticize the liberal Democrats for abandoning the Contras. As in all such scandals, the facts of the issue were soon obscure. But Bill Casey's internal investigation revealed that none of the Agency's senior officials had reviewed or approved the manual, that it had been hastily drafted in the field—a cut-and-paste job from guerrilla warfare manuals dating back to World War II—and that fewer than a dozen copies were ever distributed. The fact that most of them were never even read because the information was a gibberish of often contradictory instruction delivered in a clumsy Spanish 101 translation, however, never made it to the front pages. The "Assassination Manual" controversy served as the Democrats' principal weapon for the remainder of the election campaign. Democrats accused the CIA of sponsoring terrorism and called for a special prosecutor to investigate the matter. Reagan was forced into an awkward defensive position over the training manual during a televised debate with Walter Mondale. The well-timed congressional leak was paying dividends.[7]

But the political ploy hardly affected the outcome of the presidential election. The Mondale-Ferraro ticket carried Minnesota and the District of Columbia. Reagan and Bush carried the rest of the country. But the Democrats knew the emotional issue of aid to the Contras could be an effective weapon in congressional races. And powerful House Democrats like Tip O'Neill, Boland, and Jim Wright were confident the issue could eventually do real damage to the Republican White House.

☆   ☆

As I campaigned for private support of the Nicaraguan resistance that fall, I began to grasp the dimensions of the Sandinistas' international propaganda program. It was now widely accepted in Western Europe and the United States that the Sandinista government was a coalition of moderate-left reformers struggling to eliminate the legacy of ignorance and poverty left by the Somoza dictatorship. The Contras were seen as right-wing "Somocistas," malcontents composed mainly of brutal ex-National Guardsmen, absentee landlords, and Christian fundamentalists, led by CIA-officer veterans of covert operations in Indochina. The Reagan administration was accused of distorting Soviet, Cuban, and East Bloc military involvement in Nicaragua, as well as Sandinista aid to the FMLN guerrillas in El Salvador. To a greater or lesser degree, this simplistic picture of the situation in Central America was espoused by leading American liberals, including veteran "peace" activists such as Noam Chomsky and William Sloane Coffin.[8]

It did not take much effort, however, to discover the real situation. The Nicaraguan government in 1984 was controlled by a nine-member Directorate of dedicated Sandinista National Liberation Front (FSLN) Marxist-Leninist zealots. They were supported by a ten-member FSLN security and defense committee, also composed of Communists. The fact that these key Sandinista leaders were internationalist Communists rather than home-grown socialist reformers was obvious to anyone not blinded by Sandinista propaganda. Two of the inner circle were not even Nicaraguan. Directorate member Victor Manuel Tirado was a Mexican Communist trained in Cuba. His defense and security committee colleague "Renan Montero" was actually a Cuban named Andres Barahona, a member of the Central Committee of the Cuban Communist Party and *former* Cuban intelligence case officer in charge of Castro's aid to the Sandinistas. He was the key adviser to powerful Sandinista interior minister Tomas Borge, a former Nicaraguan law student who had joined the Moscow-line Communist Party in the 1950s.[9]

The Sandinistas successfully disguised their Communist leadership for several years. But once the harbor-mining political scandal broke in 1984, and they were confident American support for the Contras was in jeopardy, they were able to indulge themselves in discussions of the country's promising Communist future. Bayardo Arce, the Directorate's political coordinator, made a secret speech to the Nicaraguan Communist Party. He acknowledged that the Sandinistas had never truly intended to build a pluralistic society with a mixed economy and a nonaligned foreign policy. Promises to that effect, he said, had been politically expedient. The true goals of the FSLN, he concluded, were building a "dictatorship of the proletariat" within a Nicaragua aligned with Cuba and Moscow.[10]

The small cadre of nine Communist Sandinista leaders shared power with an FSLN assembly, composed of their handpicked representatives. This group of 103 Sandinista officers held multiple positions in the government and military, controlling over 200 of the key assignments in the Defense and Interior ministries, mass communication, and education. They were almost an exact parallel to the Cuban power structure, which in turn closely resembled the Central Committee of the Communist Party of the Soviet Union. This was a totalitarian power structure that allowed the Sandinista government token non-Communist officials, who, although visible, lacked any real power. The formation of this government was managed closely by Cuban advisers following the overthrow of Somoza. In effect, the Sandinistas had stolen the revolution and had forced out most of the non-Communists—including military heroes like Eden Pastora and conservative anti-Somoza leaders like Adolfo Calero—during the first years of the revolution. Now the Sandinistas were poised to reveal their true colors.[11]

Unfortunately for them, a Spanish reporter tape-recorded the speech and published Arce's text verbatim in the Barcelona newspaper *La Vanguardia.*[12]

The true face of the Contra was far different from that shown in Sandinista propaganda. Adolfo Calero, for example, was hardly a right-wing Somocista. He was a thoughtful, urbane professional, a graduate of the University of Notre Dame, with a law degree from the University of Central America in Managua, where he later taught and served as a dean. Calero had been active in the anti-Somoza conservative party since 1958. As chairman of the local Coca-Cola franchise, he helped organize a managerial strike coordinated with a nationwide anti-Somoza insurrection, led by Pedro Chamorro, editor of the opposition newspaper *La Prensa*. Calero was jailed by Somoza in 1978 for helping lead a general strike, which was considered the real onset of the revolution. When Somoza fell, Calero resumed his business and teaching career and joined the new Democratic Conservative Party. But Interior Minister Tomas Borge soon forced him into exile in Honduras, where he organized the Nicaraguan Democratic Resistance (FDN) Directorate, and became its president and commander in chief.

In Costa Rica, the Contras were known as the Democratic Revolutionary Alliance (ARDE), which was mainly composed of former Sandinistas like Eden Pastora. ARDE leaders included Alfredo Cesar, a Social Democrat who had been president of the central bank under the Sandinistas, but was forced into exile when he protested the growing Communist control of the economy and the squandering of the nation's meager resources on the military buildup. Like Calero, Cesar had been a vigorous opponent of Somoza; he had joined the Sandinista ranks in 1977.

Colonel Enrique Bermudez, the commander of the Contras' northern front, had been a career army officer. He had graduated from the U.S. Army's Command and General Staff College at Fort Leavenworth and the School of the Americas. In 1965, he had been the deputy commander of the Nicaraguan contingent serving under Organization of American States leadership in the Dominican Republic. His highest position in Somoza's National Guard was as administrator of Managua's transit police. Because of his anti-Somoza sentiment, he was sent out of the country to first attend the Inter-American Defense College in Washington, then to serve as Nicaragua's defense attaché in the United States. He was well respected by the Carter administration as a professional soldier, untainted by the atrocities associated with Somoza's handpicked National Guard leaders. In 1978, when the Carter White House suggested to Somoza he should invite Bermudez back to take over the National Guard and thus prevent further human rights abuses, the dictator rejected the proposal. Bermudez was too professional for Somoza's liking.[13] In fact, the Sandinistas did actually invite Bermudez back to help organize their army in the early 1980s, and a Sandinista Defense Ministry official publicly noted that Colonel Bermudez had never been associated with the "war crimes" of the Somoza regime, which had occurred during his long tenure in Washington.[14]

Other Contra leaders came from the Miskito Indian groups and Creole communities of the Atlantic coast. These ethnic groups had been brutalized by the Cuban-led Sandinista cadres, who were hell-bent on organizing them into collective "cooperative brigades." Religious values were important to the Creoles and they rebelled early against the state-imposed atheism and the political indoctrination of their children in the Sandinista schools. When the Miskitos resisted similar Sandinista interference, they were brutally suppressed. As early as January 1980, anti-Sandinista Miskito and Creole refugees were gathering in isolated camps in southern Honduras.

Over the next two years they were joined by thousands of Spanish-stock *campesinos*. These small-hold farmers were not the downtrodden rural proletariat that the Sandinistas had learned about in Cuba. The peasants bitterly resisted the seizure of their small plots of corn and beans by Sandinista cooperatives, which took title of the farms in the name of land reform. And the peasants resented the forced mobilization of the rural population into work brigades of twenty to forty people, under the leadership of a Sandinista cadre, who was often a young city-bred zealot who knew nothing of farming.

These farmers had been used to working in family groups, who voluntarily shared resources and meager profits and protected each other during lean years. Now the Sandinistas were forcing them to band together in arbitrarily chosen work brigades that often cut across family lines. And the much-touted rural cooperatives became the monopoly buyer of all the crops, which were purchased at artificially low prices set by Managua. The peasants were outraged that the proceeds from their crop sales went directly to the political cadres in charge of the cooperatives, who distributed earnings among their favorites.

This collectivization of agriculture resulted in food shortages, and the Sandinistas used food rationing as yet another tool to spread their totalitarian control from the city to the countryside. But the stoic peasants, who had a deep attachment to their land, probably would have never fled to join the Contra resistance if the Sandinista military draft had not been so ruthlessly enforced. The Sandinista army began abducting young *campesinos*, some boys of twelve and thirteen, for military service. Those who resisted or helped hide youth were arrested, and many were executed. When traditional village leaders protested the land seizures and the arbitrarily enforced conscription, the urban Sandinista leaders simply harangued them with political cant.

By 1984, as Adolfo Calero told me, thousands of desperate young *campesinos* were streaming across the Honduran border and into the Contra base camps. An independent sociological study of the Contra soldiers commissioned by the U.S. government several years later concluded that the typical Contra fighter was "predominately a peasant who has voted with his feet to flee what is essentially an urban-based, upper-class-led revolution." Forced collectivization of agriculture in the name of land reform, arbitrary Sandinista political control in the villages, and brutally enforced military conscription (*servico militar patriotico*) were the main factors driving the thousands of *campesinos* from their land.[15]

So the myth that the Contras were basically vengeful National Guardsmen and disgruntled right-wing oligarchs was simply disinformation spread by the Sandinistas. In fact, when I looked into the makeup of the Contra military leadership, I found that less than a third had served in the National Guard. Almost a quarter of these Contra military leaders were actually former Sandinistas, and over a half had no military experience at all.[16]

Skillful Sandinista disinformation efforts, however, often convinced the American news media—and the U.S. Congress—that the Sandinistas were moderate socialist reformers, forced against their will to seek Soviet and Cuban military aid by vicious right-wing rebels supported by the CIA. As I traveled around the country that winter speaking out for private support of the Contras, I increasingly encountered well-organized Sandinista apologists in the town halls and school auditoriums where I spoke. They were often members of local "solidarity committees" whose members had visited Nicaragua on Sandinista-sponsored tours and were convinced beyond any reasoning that Nicaragua was being led by a broad-based democratic coalition that protected the interests of downtrodden peasants and workers.

The Sandinistas had begun their American propaganda campaign early, and by the mid-1980s the Network in Solidarity with the People of Nicaragua had chapters in hundreds of American cities and on college campuses nationwide. Few local chapter members realized the group could trace its lineage back to the American Communist Party's U.S. Peace Council. Nor did they realize the network had been started by two Nicaraguans, acting for the Sandinistas.[17] And perhaps this information would not have altered the impact of the "fact-finding" tours of Nicaragua on which they eagerly embarked, often led by an enthusiastic clergyman or academic guide who had been cultivated by the Sandinistas.

The brief tours of Nicaragua were centered on ministry offices and showplace factories and schools in Managua, followed by day trips out to selected nearby model agricultural cooperatives. Because of "security problems," the American pilgrims were rarely allowed to travel unescorted.

Sandinista defectors, however, revealed that these tours were actually carefully staged propaganda shows. For example, Interior Minister Tomas Borge, a dedicated Communist, prepared himself for visits by foreign religious organizations by studying the Bible and extracting relevant passages to salt his conversation and informal speeches. While foreign groups were in his office, he also provided *spontaneous* visits to the ministry by selected impoverished workers or sick peasants, during which he would personally arrange financial or medical assistance for the unfortunate supplicant.[18] But one of the most cynical and revealing devices Borge used to delude credulous foreign delegations was the decor of his own office. This was how Sandinista defector Alvaro Jose Baldizon described Borge's deception:

> To impress foreign religious groups that visit Nicaragua, Borge has decorated his Ministry of the Interior office with large pictures of poor children and prominently displayed religious objects such as crucifixes, tapestries with religious motifs, a large wooden statue of Christ carved by local artisans, and a Bible. Borge has another office, his favorite, in the Reparto Bello Horizonte where he conducts most ministerial business and where he also lives. This office contains pictures of Marx, Engels, Lenin, Augusto Cesar Sandino, and Carlos Fonseca and there are no religious objects to be seen. Copies of the *Communist Manifesto, Das Kapital, The State and the Law,* and various volumes of Marxist/Leninist philosophy are in evidence.[19]

Faced with such skillful manipulation, it was easy to understand how well-meaning and gullible young Americans would believe Sandinista propaganda. But I had a hard time grasping how experienced members of Congress like Ron Dellums of California and Pat Schroeder of Colorado could campaign for financial aid for the *good works* conducted by men like Tomas Borge. The Sandinistas took full advantage of their powerful American allies. In Comandante Bayardo Arce's secret speech, he stressed the importance of winning public opinion in the United States and bragged that the Sandinista propaganda campaign there was achieving "some degree of domestic neutralization."[20]

All this, of course, was reminiscent of the well-orchestrated peace campaign against American involvement in the Vietnam War. But I could only hope the American people had matured enough not to be deceived again.

☆   ☆

I MET with Adolfo Calero several times that winter during trips around the country. Although he never revealed details of the earlier CIA support for the Contras, he made it clear that Agency funding had been adequate, but that the actual management of the Contra operations and training of their troops had often been clumsy and ineffective. I'd heard rumors about inept CIA trainers and covert operations officers working with the Contras and ascribed the problem to the previous gutting of the Agency's covert action staff by Stansfield Turner. Now, Adolfo said, the problem of funding was critical. The Contras had been able to make up some of the shortfall at the end of fiscal year 1984 by soliciting funding from anti-Communist governments elsewhere in Latin America and private American individuals and corporations. In fact, Adolfo revealed, the FDN's accounts in overseas banks had received over $10 million from foreign governments and private individuals.[21] Because I had good contacts in the Republic of China on Taiwan and in South Korea, I offered to consult with those governments about a possible contribution to the Contra cause. Adolfo gave me the number of the FDN Directorate's account in a Panama bank, which, he said, was used to purchase military supplies.

Before I undertook the mission, I carefully read the U.S. Neutrality Act and the complete text of the latest Boland Amendment. The Neutrality Act prevented private citizens from buying war matériel in the United States and shipping it from America to an overseas conflict. But there was nothing in the act preventing private citizens from making contributions overseas that the Contras could use to purchase needed supplies. And it also seemed clear to me that the Boland Amendment certainly did not apply to private individuals like myself.

As for the authority of the Boland Amendment within the U.S. government, it seemed ludicrous that its proscriptions should apply to the National Security Council, a branch of the Executive Office of the President. I met with Ollie North in his OEOB office that winter and told him my views on the matter.

"If the intent of the amendment," I said, "is to prevent the President from carrying out his responsibilities to conduct foreign policy, it's definitely unconstitutional."

Ollie had acquired the sunken-eyed pallor of an overworked and harassed bureaucrat. His boyish face was creased now and his dark eyes were somewhat furtive, as if his responsibilities were becoming intolerable.

"Believe me, General," he said, "we've looked into it. But we can't get two lawyers to agree one way or the other. So we just have to assume the amendment does apply to the NSC, and conduct ourselves accordingly."

The Boland Amendment, he reminded me, stated that during fiscal 1985 no CIA or DoD funds or funds available to any other government intelligence "entity" could be used to support the Contras. As Ollie North read the law, the NSC was not prevented from helping others assist the Contras.

I decided that I could best help the Contras raise funds for weapons by trying to solicit government funds from Taiwan and Seoul. In Washington, I paid a call on the South Korean ambassador and on Freddy Chien, the director of the Taiwan government's Coordination Council for North American Affairs, who represented Taiwan in Washington after Jimmy Carter had cut diplomatic relations at the demand of Peking. They were both interested in helping, but they urged me to raise the matter directly with their governments during my upcoming trip to the Far East.

I didn't have any U.S. government guidance on this initiative, but I knew

I wasn't breaking or even bending any American law. And after the Boland Amendment went into effect, I certainly couldn't get my activities approved by the CIA. Bill Casey had made his position on the Boland Amendment very clear. There could be no doubt whatsoever that the law applied to the CIA. I dropped in to see him at his Langley office that winter to bring him up to date on USCWF efforts in support of anti-Communist resistance groups overseas. Casey listened to my presentation, nodding and voicing approval with his distinctive growl. But when I brought up private contributions to the Contras, Casey raised his big hand like a traffic cop.

"Jack," he said sternly, "if you even mention the word 'Nicaragua' again, I'll throw your ass out of my office."

☆   ☆

IN TAIWAN, I met with Foreign Minister Hsu Fu-shun to discuss a Taiwan government contribution to the Contras. Minister Hsu had been the Republic of China's ambassador in Seoul when I had served there. And I knew him to be a staunch friend of the United States. I explained that the FDN needed an immediate $10 million to purchase arms and equipment for the thousands of *campesino* recruits streaming across the Honduran border.

The Minister said he understood the predicament, but he stressed that this was a sensitive matter. Nicaragua was one of the few countries retaining full diplomatic relations with the Republic of China on Taiwan, a matter of great importance to Hsu's government. Any leak of a contribution to the Contras would jeopardize those relations. Nevertheless, he asked specifically what the Republic of China could do to help.

I suggested a $5 million contribution. The donation, I said, could be a confidential matter. His government could make a direct deposit into the Contra bank account in Panama. I placed a three-by-five card on Hsu's desk that listed the account number. If that was unacceptable, I said, I would be willing to meet his representative any place in the free world and personally receive a letter of credit, which I would then have deposited in the Contras' account. I added that the Contras would provide an exact independent audit account of how the funds were spent down to the last penny. There was no question here of "commissions" or profits for middlemen. A third alternative that would completely conceal Taiwan involvement would be to structure the contribution within a pending Taiwan purchase of supplies or equipment from a major U.S. or multinational corporation. I was naively hopeful that we could arrange to package part of a Taiwan payment and channel it to the Contra bank account.

"Minister Hsu," I said, "you may want to determine that I am not acting totally independent of U.S. policy."

Hsu was silent, but his smooth, ageless face acquired an expression of calm intensity that betrayed the concern that Asian politesse had prevented him from voicing. I had to prove to him I wasn't just a con man.

"I believe I can arrange some kind of signal from an official of the administration in Washington that will indicate knowledge of my visit to you and that they support my efforts on behalf of the Contras."

"General," the Minister said, "that might become necessary." The faintest of smiles crossed his seamless face. That was about as close to a commitment as I was going to get. "I will raise this matter with my government," Minister Hsu replied.

In Seoul, I met with a senior ROK general, now a key official in the Korean Central Intelligence Agency, who I knew had a direct channel to President Chun Doo-Hwan. Again I made the case for a $5 million emergency contribution. Again, I was assured the matter would be considered.[22]

Upon my return from the Far East in January 1985, I flew on to Washington where I briefed Ollie North on the trip. As always, he listened intently, but did not reveal very much. I had the feeling he was becoming a more experienced covert operator, at least in regard to sensitive transactions of this type. But as his responsibilities increased, he also had become something of a name dropper, often alluding to his direct access to the President. I knew he was working impossibly long hours, trying to keep the Contra cause alive until congressional funding might resume, so I could excuse a little bit of self-aggrandizement. I told him about my meetings in Taipei and Seoul, and said that an appropriate signal from the administration might be required before either government would make a contribution.

"Thank you, General," Ollie said, with his habitual courtesy. "I will take care of it."

Later I learned that he had in fact sent Gaston Sigur, an NSC officer with good contacts in the Far East, to assure Freddy Chien that the White House had no objections to my fund-raising for the Contras.

☆   ☆

A FEW weeks later, I made my first trip to inspect the Contras' military forces in their Honduran base camps. Before the Boland Amendment, the CIA had established operating procedures with the Honduran government that gave the Contras a base camp area in the jungle mountains of the Cordillera Entre Rios, about 120 miles east of Tegucigalpa, the capital. The Contras had cut timber and set up their camps along uninhabited ridges they named Las Vegas for the cleared garden plots of the refugee families accompanying the Contra fighters.

One of Enrique Bermudez's officers met me at the airport, and we left for the base camps in a mud-splattered Toyota Land Cruiser. Tegucigalpa is on a high plateau surrounded by extinct volcanoes. The paved highway out of the city was good by Third World standards, but beyond Danli we left the asphalt road. For the next leg, we climbed up a reasonably good gravel track wide enough to handle careening timber trucks and overcrowded buses jammed with *campesinos* bound for village markets. After a few miles on this road, we turned off onto a rutted dirt washboard that snaked even higher into the hills of scrub jungle. At a flyblown little town on the Rio Guayambera, we took a break for one last cold beer, then crossed a shaky log bridge and began the climb up the steep ridge toward Las Vegas.

Now the road was little more than a bulldozed track through increasingly dense brush. Luckily, it was dry season, because I saw the combination of washboard and deep chuck holes would have been impassable in a good rain. As it was, the jolting ride was about as bad as any I'd experienced in three wars. After three straight hours of this punishment, we swung along a relatively straight stretch of deforested ridgeline. I noticed mud-crusted concrete markers at regular intervals and shouted over the engine roar to ask my escort what they were.

"Nicaragua," he yelled, grinning. He pointed past me out the open right window toward several sandbagged bunkers poorly hidden with dead brush 100 meters to the south. "Sandinistas," he added.

Here the road marked the actual border between Nicaragua and Honduras. And the Sandinistas had set up machine-gun bunkers to cover the road.

"Do they ever shoot?" I felt an urge to tell him to speed up.

"Some days, yes," he said, grinning again. "Some days, no."

I didn't feel like asking him about the last time the Sandinistas had fired on a Contra vehicle.

We reached Enrique Bermudez's headquarters camp just before sundown. I had met Bermudez on several occasions at fund-raisers in the States, and he had encouraged me to visit his troops. Now he seemed inordinately pleased that I was actually there. No doubt a lot of well-meaning Americans had promised to come but never managed to actually make the trip.

Bermudez was dressed in reasonably clean fatigues, and his two body-guards toting Uzi submachine guns appeared alert and well disciplined. He apologized that he couldn't offer a decent dinner. His troops were down to two meals a day: rice and beans mid-morning, and beans and rice mid-afternoon. Enrique and his staff ate the same fare, except as it was occasionally augmented by gifts brought in by visitors who knew how a few cans of meat or some fresh vegetables could enhance the menu. Luckily, Bermudez could offer a mosquito net in the small bunk room adjoining his hut. His operations center and commo room had the only electric lights in the camp, powered by a small chugging generator. But their fuel supply was low. By the time I lay down to sleep, the entire camp was in darkness. Here and there, sputtering fires marked the rows of plastic-tarp squad huts scattered among the trees.

I'd seen no trenches, bunkers, or sandbagged guard posts, only a few sentries on the perimeters. The bunk room I slept in smelled of mildew and wood smoke. I could see stars through the cracks in the corrugated roofing. As I fell asleep, I hoped the sentries at the checkpoints we'd passed through on the road in were still awake.

The next morning, Enrique took me on an inspection tour of his camps and showed me some of his troops. His units were divided into task forces of 500 to 1,000 men, each with its own base camp. The camps were well placed along the ridges. But there was a dirty, rundown feel to them, more like refugee settlements than military installations. The setup was the same in each of the three camps I visited. There were long, corrugated-plastic and tin-roofed sheds of rough local lumber housing a mess hall and dispensary, a headquarters hut with a commo room, an armory hut, and a supply hut. The troops were housed in the small, ubiquitous thatched squad shelters with plastic roofs, which had obviously seen better days. About a third of the men I saw had complete uniforms with jungle boots, fatigues, web gear, and hats. Others wore fatigue trousers and T-shirts, while newly arrived recruits were dressed in threadbare shirts and jeans and wore sandals.

Enrique showed me the disposition of his forces inside Nicaragua. At that time he had about ten task forces operating in the mountains to the north and east of Managua. Some were fairly close to the border with Honduras, but many were about a ten-day trek to the southeast. They were all in contact with Sandinista patrols and one had recently ambushed and defeated a large Sandinista relief convoy bound for a besieged village near Siuna.

Despite this limited success, the overall mood in his headquarters was confused pessimism. It had been six months since the Boland Amendment. And the CIA officers managing the Contras' military operations were sorely missed. During this period, the Contras' ranks had been swollen with new volunteers, and several shipments of assorted weapons and ammunition had arrived. But the Contra forces lacked the discipline and cohesiveness of an effective combat unit.

As Enrique and I discussed the situation late that afternoon, I began to see a familiar syndrome. The CIA personnel, who included American Army and Marine veterans on contract, had taken too much operational responsibility. They had provided armorers, mechanics, commo men, and medics. They had trained Contra troops in these base camps, but had not prepared any Contra counterparts to take over training when the Americans packed up their bags and left. To be fair, however, how could anyone have anticipated such irrational behavior by the Congress?

Equally unfortunate, the CIA operation had relied too heavily on air resupply of Contra forces inside Nicaragua. The Agency had established an air base at Aguacate in a valley north of Las Vegas. While the Agency ran the operations, they functioned well, with contract civilian pilots flying helicopters and fixed-wing cargo planes into the Nicaraguan mountains to keep the Contra task forces supplied and to provide them medevac for their sick and wounded. And the vital secure radio communication links that made this operation possible were all managed by the Agency. Now the Americans were gone and the Contras were orphans, unable to manage the equipment. Nevertheless, fresh volunteers still took the dangerous trek across the Honduran border to Las Vegas. Enrique had over 6,000 troops in these camps, and most were eager to fight the Sandinistas. For many the motive was revenge; special troops of the Sandinista Interior Ministry (MINT) had executed their fathers or brothers for resisting conscription or protesting forced collectivization of farmland.[23]

The earlier overdependence on air resupply was obviously a fundamental flaw. Apparently the Agency had simply dusted off their operational plans from the long years of the war in Laos, during which the CIA's Air America had maintained aerial bridges from Udorn air base to the scattered islands of Hmong and Meo resistance forces operating in the NVA-controlled North. But the CIA in Laos had never had a Boland Amendment to contend with.[24]

Enrique went to his large operations map and showed me his supply drop zones in Nicaragua. One task force, he said, would have to be extracted within a week, because the one operating Contra airdrop plane was down with mechanical trouble in Aguacate. Without aerial resupply, he added, what was left of the dry season offensive would have to be canceled.

I thought for a long time before I commented. In a way, the funding hiatus of the Boland Amendment might prove to be a godsend for the Contras, weaning them from too strict American control. From what I had gathered, the CIA advisers had been inflexible, often doctrinaire, and above all patronizing. They had not encouraged initiative among the Contras. In effect, they were treating these Central Americans much as they had treated Montagnard mercenaries in Indochina, like "native" troops. But there were other lessons of Indochina that were more germane.

"Enrique," I said, going to the map, "the Vietcong and the North Vietnamese army did *not* have air resupply. They carried everything they used on their backs or on bicycles down the Ho Chi Minh Trail." I was ignoring, of course, the massive use of trucks by the NVA, but I had a point to make. "Driving up here I saw peasants carrying supplies on mules. I remember years ago in Burma when entire Allied divisions in the jungle were supplied by mule train. If you need mules or mule skinners, we can get them."

Enrique Bermudez smiled and shook his head. "My men do not need to be taught how to handle mules," he said.

"The war you are fighting now," I told him, "can be supplied with men carrying packs and with mules. If you need ammunition, there's plenty of it available in the Sandinista camps and on *their* supply convoys."

Enrique Bermudez nodded agreement. He realized there were many Americans willing to help, but the burden of leadership was now on his own shoulders.

When we discussed the issue of weapons, I saw that the CIA had given little consideration to equipping the Contras to perform specific tactical objectives. In other words, serious mission planning to establish objectives and tactics had not preceded the equipping and training phases of the operation. Now the Contras were armed with a hodgepodge of different weapons, including American 5.56mm M-16s and 7.62mm M-14s, NATO-standard FALs, FNs, and G-3 automatic rifles, American M-60 machine guns, and some 40mm American M-79 grenade launchers. The Sandinistas, of course, had 100 percent Soviet-bloc arms, AK-47s and RPD and RPK light machine guns, as well as RPG rocket-propelled grenade launchers. Their ammunition supply problems were simple, whereas the Contras had the logistical equivalent of the Tower of Babel.

And, as I had learned commanding SOG teams on the Trail, the distinctive sound of a weapon was a critical factor in small-unit jungle warfare. The AK-47 and RPK machine gun certainly had a characteristic report no one could mistake, as did the M-16. Tactically, it was important for Contra ambush teams not to expose their position to enemy mortar and rocket fire using weapons with distinctive sounds. I therefore convinced Enrique he had to think through the tactics of small-unit warfare and build his future arsenal accordingly. We spent many hours in his command hut working on these requirements.

First, the cumbersome task force unit had to be broken down into basic hundred-man companies, and then to ten-man squads. Naturally, each man would have an AK-47. And each squad would need an RPD light machine gun that fired the same ammunition as the AK. Each squad would also be supported by a Soviet-designed RPG grenade launcher. Each company would have at least one 82mm mortar. Using mobile squads and companies that carried their own basic ammo loads as building blocks, he could assemble strike units specifically tailored for particular objectives. Best of all, these units could resupply from captured Sandinista armories, thus reducing their dependence on airdrops. The Sandinistas were developing a good radar network and were known to have SAM-7 anti-aircraft missiles, which made the future of airdrops risky even when congressional funding was resumed.

Bermudez told me that unnamed "Americans"—his euphemism for Ollie North's contacts—had promised a large supply of Soviet-designed weapons several months before, but that these guns had never arrived. He was clearly discouraged. When I left Enrique's base camps, I took with me a basic list of his future weapons requirements to discuss with Adolfo Calero in Florida.

But before departing Honduras, I flew aboard a small Contra plane from Tegucigalpa to Rus Rus on the savannah of eastern Honduras where the Miskito Indian resistance had their base camps. The Miskitos had combined forces with the Suma and Rama Indian tribes, who felt similar hatred toward the Sandinistas and their Cuban advisers. The acronym of this coalition was appropriately MISURA. The conditions in the MISURA camps made Enrique's Las Vegas encampment seem like Fort Benning. Many of the Miskito troops were poorly dressed; few had boots. When the CIA left, they were in even worse shape than the FDN fighters because very few Indians had served in the military under Somoza. Yet their morale was high, fueled to a large degree by bitter hatred of the Sandinistas. More than any other ethnic group inside Nicaragua, the Miskitos had received especially brutal treatment from the Sandinista "land reformers," who had descended on their territory soon after the revolution. Over the next two years, the Miskitos had been singled out for collectivization. When they resisted, MINT troops had introduced "special measures." Hundreds of Miskito Indians had been abducted, tortured, and executed; hundreds more had been shipped to a penal colony in the south. Miskito villages were raided by MINT troops and women and girls raped in front of their families. In some cases, men had been buried alive as an example of what happened to those who resisted Sandinista control.[25]

The night I spent in the Rus Rus camp was memorable. These savannah plains, especially along the rivers, were the haunt of Central America's notorious vampire bats. The local Miskito commander, whose nom de guerre was Chico, kindly gave me the only mosquito net in the sleeping hut we shared. When he rolled out of his hammock at dawn, his feet were streaming blood. Vampire bats had visited in the night; their saliva contained a natural anesthetic and anti-coagulant. Sleeping prey never felt the bite of the clinging bat, and the blood continued to flow hours after the bats had fluttered off.

I made a note to add mosquito nets to the supplies the MISURA needed.

☆　　　☆

I DECIDED to see what I could do about a reliable source of Soviet-design munitions for the FDN. The year before, I had agreed to serve on the advisory board of GeoMiliTech Consultants Corporation (GMT), a Washington-based consulting firm specializing in the sale of military equipment.

GMT's president, Barbara Studley, had for several years run her own radio talk show in southern Florida. Her conservative views led her into covering the Central American wars, organizing medical relief for El Salvador, and, in turn, coordinating the delivery of transportation equipment. As a consultant to GMT I was able to introduce the firm to my military contacts around the world and to bring into GMT some truly outstanding retired general officers to expand its areas of expertise.

In 1983, Barbara Studley had been in Lebanon with the Israeli Defense Forces (IDF) and knew of the enormous quantities of Soviet weapons captured by the IDF. She arranged for me to go to Israel in April 1985 to raise the issue of an Israeli arms contribution to the Contras. Israel had good reason to help defeat the Sandinistas, who had allied themselves with Libya and radical factions of the Palestine Liberation Organization, and who had launched a virulent pogrom against Nicaragua's small Jewish community soon after the Somoza overthrow. The case of the Oscar Kellerman family was well known in Israel. Kellerman, a small businessman, like many Nicaraguan Jews, had been a refugee from the Nazis. He had almost died when a Sandinista mob had barricaded a Managua synagogue and set it afire. Later Sandinistas looted his home and his family was forced into exile beside hundreds of other Nicaraguan Jews.[26]

Through Barbara Studley's friend General Ephraim "Froika" Poran, I asked Israeli Defense Ministry officials to give the Contras some of the mountain of munitions they had captured in Lebanon two years earlier. They replied that they already had made such a contribution and that they now considered these weapons a national asset that they would sell but not give away.

Any Soviet-bloc arms I helped acquire for the FDN would have to be paid for, cash on the barrel head. Retired Lieutenant General Dan Graham was also a consultant to GMT. Since he had once been a deputy director of the CIA and had retired as the director of the Defense Intelligence Agency, Barbara approached him with the problem of locating an honest international arms broker who could provide the Soviet-bloc equipment the Contras needed. Dan came back with the name of "Sam," a Western European who had provided high-quality Soviet-design weapons of East European origin to the Defense Department and our intelligence agencies in the past. Dan agreed to introduce Barbara to Sam the next time he came to town. Before Barbara met with Sam and without mentioning the forbidden word "Nicaragua," I asked Bill Casey to check Sam's background. Some days later, he called to say that Sam was indeed a man of high integrity with no shady dealings on his record.

In order to comply with the Neutrality Act, any weapons purchase would have to be arranged overseas, using only foreign banks and transportation.

Barbara Studley had agreed to do the necessary traveling to handle that part of the transaction if Sam were able to get the munitions we needed.

When Sam next came to Washington, Danny Graham introduced him to Barbara. She, in turn, arranged for him to meet with Adolfo Calero and me in the Palm Court of the Sheraton Carlton Hotel. Sam was a suave, open-faced man with a calm demeanor and a good sense of humor. As he perused the shopping list I had drawn up with Enrique Bermudez, Sam nodded calmly and made notes on a pad with a gold mechanical pencil. He might as well have been pricing out a plumbing job. Sam looked up and said he could procure brand-new, high-quality Polish AKMS-47 assault rifles in quantity for only $135 each. If we purchased more than 200 RPK light machine guns, he could get them for $250 each. As for RPG-7 grenade launchers, he could get them from the same source for $1,650 each. Replacement rocket grenades would cost $185 apiece. Ammunition for the assault rifles and machine guns would be $110 per thousand rounds. Finally, he said, he could procure brand-new SAM-7 Mark-2 shoulder-fired anti-aircraft rockets at $164,000 per set, which included a launcher and three missiles.

Barbara and I looked at each other. We had learned that AK-47s normally retailed for between $200 and $300 on the international arms market. These were the lowest prices we had ever heard quoted.

"This *is* new equipment?" I asked.

"New from the factory," Sam assured us. "This is even better than Soviet manufacture."

"Why are the prices so low?" Barbara asked.

Sam shrugged. "I'm a good client." He didn't have to elaborate.

"But what about profit?" I asked. "Is your commission in these figures?"

"In this case," Sam said, "I keep my profits at the minimum, just to cover costs."

Adolfo Calero explained that he had roughly $5 million remaining in his overseas banks to procure weapons. He, too, was astounded at the low cost and high quality that Sam had promised to deliver. The price of $135 per AK-47, he said, shaking his his head, was indeed less than half what he had paid in the past. "We'd better talk to Ollie North about this," he said.

That afternoon, we went to North's office in the OEOB. I was surprised that Ollie invited retired Air Force Major General Richard Secord to attend the meeting. Over the past few months I had heard reports that Secord had been brought in to manage the Contras' air resupply system after the CIA pulled out. His presence at this meeting was confirmation that he was directly involved with more than just buying some surplus airplanes.

Secord was a stocky, fireplug of a guy, a former fighter pilot with the worldly confidence of an international businessman. Judging from his easy and friendly manner, Secord was obviously familiar with Adolfo. And he was certainly affable toward me. But I was uneasy. I had met him years before at a coordination meeting at a Thai air base when I commanded MACV/SOG. Secord had been a major serving as the liaison officer between the CIA and the U.S. Air Force involved with the war in northern Laos, which was not part of my operational responsibility. Since then he had served in our military assistance mission in Iran, and had held a variety of Pentagon assignments, before retiring under a cloud of scandal. In the intelligence community, Dick Secord had the reputation of being something of a rogue, a mercenary agent available to the highest bidder. This all stemmed from his association with Ed Wilson, the former CIA officer now serving a life sentence in federal prison for aiding Libya's Moammar Khaddafi by establishing and operating a terrorist training center for him. Wilson's firm had also supplied tons of C-4 plastic explosives to Khaddafi's terrorists to enable them to conduct their attacks using the best U.S. technology. A minor Wilson conviction involved his attempt to murder the federal prosecutor investigating him. Secord had been one of several Pentagon and serving and former CIA officials tainted by association with Wilson.

Although Secord was never indicted, his close dealings with the so-called Ed Wilson Gang may have been responsible for Secord's early retirement from the Air Force. His last position had been a deputy assistant secretary of defense, responsible for the Middle East and Southern Africa. In this capacity, he was reputed to have taken kickbacks from Wilson for helping to arrange lucrative arms shipments to Egypt. Anyone who dealt with Ed Wilson was suspect in my book. And I hated to see the Contras involved with someone like Secord.[27]

But I kept my opinion to myself. Ollie North was in charge of the operation and I assumed he had vetted Secord with his superiors.

Adolfo spread out our cost estimate sheet and cited the price and quantity of the weapons Sam could supply. North and Secord were obviously impressed.

Like Barbara Studley, North found it hard to believe these were factory-new, high-quality weapons. I assured him they were. And I also passed on Sam's guarantee that the weapons could be delivered to Honduras within two months of order.

Secord seemed uneasy now. He repeatedly told North that there was no way that we could provide these weapons for the costs we were quoting. He zeroed in on the SAM-7 anti-aircraft missiles, which we could provide for only $164,000 a set, including launcher and three missiles. "Those prices are hard to believe, Jack," he said.

I assured him that Sam's reputation for integrity was high, and that he promised to deliver.

At this point, Ollie intervened. "Well," he said, "Dick can provide the SAMs for $180,000 per set and he can also provide men to train the troops in their use for that price."

I didn't ask the origin of his equipment or his trainers. In this business you didn't ask unnecessary questions. "Fine," I said, "that frees up quite a bit of money for other weapons."

Before we left the office, we agreed that Secord would handle the anti-aircraft missile purchase, and that we would concentrate on small arms, automatic weapons, ammunition, and rocket grenades. With the approximately $5 million that Adolfo had available, we planned to buy 10,000 AKMS-47s, 250 RPK machine guns, 200 PRG rocket grenade launchers with 5,000 grenades, and 15 million rounds of 7.62mm ammunition. This would be enough to supply all of Bermudez's combat troops with high-quality, Soviet-bloc weapons.

Adolfo and I left the OEOB with Secord, who offered to give Adolfo a ride to National Airport. I came along because I wanted to work out the details of the arms order. We crossed Pennsylvania Avenue and strolled through Lafayette Square to a nearby hotel, where Secord had a shiny new sedan waiting. The man driving the car was Secord's business partner, Albert Hakim, a naturalized American whom Secord had met while serving in Iran. More silent alarm bells sounded in my head. I knew that Hakim had also been involved with people who were members of the Ed Wilson Gang. As we drove out 14th Street past the Mall, I noted casually to Secord that he seemed to be doing quite well in his retirement.

Yes, he noted, he and Albert had been very lucky in their overseas business dealings. At present, they had several contracts to provide aircraft revetments at air bases in the Middle East. There was a pretty good profit margin in that, he added.

"Yeah," I agreed, "I'm sure there is."

☆   ☆

BARBARA Studley traveled to Europe and arranged the bank transfer, shipping agents, and insurance, making sure no U.S. bank or shipping company, or any other American firm, was involved in the transaction. Sam took care of his end of the business with amazing efficiency. Within six weeks, a Greek freighter in an East European port loaded almost 500 tons of weapons and ammunition, being exported under an End User Certificate Sam had obtained from a well-placed Arab military official. Unfortunately, the perennial fighting in Lebanon flared up at that moment and the Greek crew almost staged a mutiny. Then Sam's agent aboard assured them that their true destination was Honduras, not the Middle East.[28]

While the weapons were en route, I received a frantic call from Ollie North. He stated that General Secord wanted to have the ship diverted to Portugal to pick up a load of munitions for the Contras that was stuck there. This was impossible. The Portuguese government would never have allowed a ship loaded with weapons from the East Bloc to land for any reason. Secord's request was troubling. Either he was so inept that he was unable to arrange transport for the arms he was assigned to acquire, or he was actually trying to sabotage our low-cost, high-quality shipment because it was too competitive.

The more I thought about the matter, the more convinced I was that probably both cases were true. Adolfo had recently complained bitterly that the earlier arms shipment Secord had arranged from Communist China had still not arrived. This "slow boat from China" had become a grim joke among the Contra leadership. And the question of Secord's profit was beginning to trouble several of us. Rob Owen, who had been Ollie North's unofficial liaison to the Contras, confided that he was deeply worried that the Contras "were being ripped off" and defrauded by Secord and his people.[29]

My suspicions about Secord's profits were confirmed that summer when I mentioned to North the issue of procuring light aircraft for the Contras. I was raising funds to purchase Heliocourier Short Take Off and Landing (STOL) airplanes for the FDN and hoped to get some supplementary money from North's sources. But he discouraged me, explaining that Secord had already arranged for the delivery of similar Maule aircraft, built in Georgia.

"Ollie," I said, "I don't know too much about the Maule, but I can tell you the Heliocourier is a superior plane." I explained that the Heliocourier had been combat-tested in Indochina; it was rugged, all metal (the Maule was partially fabric covered), and carried a heavier load than the Maule.

Ollie seemed uncomfortable. "Sir," he finally said, "my air adviser General Secord assures me the Maule is the better plane. And it's a lot easier to fly than that Heliocourier."

North said Secord had several Maules ready for delivery, and Ollie was looking for private donors to buy them. That was the end of the discussion. But I wasn't satisfied. I asked my friend Heinie Aderholt to look into the Maules. He went to the plant in Georgia and discovered the plane was available for $40,000. But Ollie North was participating in the solicitation of wealthy conservatives like my friend brewer Joe Coors to contribute $65,000 for each plane.

That meant Secord was making a profit of more than 50 percent. It was then that I began to suspect that Ollie North's motives in these complex transactions might not be as pure as he would have me believe.

☆   ☆

OUR arms shipment arrived in Honduras in early July. Adolfo Calero and the FDN had an arrangement with the Honduran military, who officially took possession of arms shipments and arranged their transport upcountry to the Contra base camps. Adolfo informed me that the 500 tons of munitions had arrived in perfect condition and invited me down to the Las Vegas camp later that summer.

Meanwhile, I intensified my fund-raising efforts. For direct and in-kind contributions we concentrated on humanitarian "non-lethal" aid—canned food, clothing (especially boots), and medical supplies and equipment. Moving up the contribution scale, I was able to raise funds for boats and outboard motors, which made the Contras' food-distribution system a lot more efficient, especially during the rainy season. Remembering the hungry vampire bats of Rus Rus, I made sure the MISURA fighters got some mosquito nets. Mario Calero, Adolfo's brother, managed FDN logistics in New Orleans. He had warehouses there to which we shipped food, medicine, and clothing, which was often carried south by rickety Honduran charter DC-4s.

Addressing small grass-roots audiences across the country, I urged them to prepare Freedom Fighter Friendship Kits, cloth ditty bags containing soap, toothbrushes, razors, insect repellent, and inexpensive personal sundries. These goods certainly would not win a battle, but the thousands of kits that came in from individual donors went a long way toward raising the morale of the Contra troops in the field. They were a tangible symbol that the American people had not turned their backs on the Contra cause, even if the Congress had.

At the highest end of the contribution scale, one of our largest individual contributors was Mrs. Ellen Garwood, a wealthy conservative from Austin, Texas. She contributed $65,000 toward purchasing a used Huey UH-1 helicopter, which we had reconditioned as a medevac aircraft. When the chopper was ready for delivery, we made sure the name "Lady Ellen" was painted prominently on the nose. All of this successful fund-raising, of course, did not go unnoticed by the news media. By late summer, my name and picture were appearing almost daily in the press. And there were ominous media rumblings that unnamed White House officials were supervising the effort.[30]

That summer, Ollie North expressed concern about the amount of publicity my fund-raising for the Contras was generating. He was worried that my links to the NSC might be revealed. I told him that you couldn't raise money without publicity and that every time I gave a fund-raising speech I had to grant interviews to local TV and newspaper reporters. And the humanitarian aid and transportation equipment I was sending them were vitally needed. In fact, Adolfo Calero had told me that my highly visible fund-raising efforts had helped raise morale among the Contras.

"Besides," I said, "having me so visible actually makes the rest of the fund-raisers a lot *less* visible." They could conduct their work out of the media spotlight.[31]

I had in mind men like former treasury secretary William Simon, Richard Viguerie, and *Soldier of Fortune* publisher retired Lieutenant Colonel Bob Brown. Bob was leading training missions to the Contra base camps—surviving barrages of Sandinista Katusha rockets in the process—and he didn't need extra publicity.

But there were other, less savory people raising funds for the Contras with whom Ollie North unwisely chose to associate, who would reflect badly on the cause if they became better known. Carl R. "Spitz" Channell was a conservative fund-raiser who ran an outfit called the National Endowment for the Preservation of Liberty. Because Channell and several of his close associates were supposedly homosexuals, media wags had already named them the "Lavender Bund" or Ollie North's "Fruit Loop." They were teamed up with Washington public relations executive Richard R. Miller to make huge profits by helping "aid" the Contras. To circumvent the Boland Amendment, Ollie North would attend lavish Washington fund-raising dinners they hosted, give an emotional presentation about the plight of the Contras, then leave. Channell and his colleagues would then put the bite on the wealthy guests. I heard disturbing reports that a lot of the money they were raising did not end up buying ponchos and jungle boots for the Contras, but supported an extravagant life-style for Channell and his dubious band of patriots.[32]

As a matter of fact, Spitz Channell later testified that he raised approximately $10 million. Adolfo Calero claims that no more than $1 million of that was ever made available to support the Contras. Considering the obvious and very painful need of the Freedom Fighters, who were dying for lack of food, medicine, and clothing, it has been very difficult to be charitable to this group.

☆   ☆

DURING a brief visit to the Contra base camps in August, I found conditions and morale vastly improved. Adolfo Calero and Enrique Bermudez proudly showed me the shiny new weapons from the shipment Sam had arranged. The AKMS had a folding metal stock, which made it very handy to carry in the deep brush. And the RPK machine guns were lighter and more reliable than the M-60s the Contras had used earlier.

But training the swelling ranks of new recruits was still a problem. Because of Sandinista propaganda that Somoza's National Guard was entirely made up of "war criminals," the CIA and State Department had forbidden the FDN from actively recruiting former National Guardsmen. And now, even though the U.S. government no longer had direct supervision of the Contras, Adolfo and Enrique were leery of antagonizing the State Department by inviting former National Guardsmen now in exile in Florida to join the ranks of the FDN. I found this situation deplorable. I had been in contact with these exiles, who were eager to join the Contra ranks. They guaranteed that their group, made up of professional NCOs and officers like Enrique, had never taken part in the atrocities attributed to Somoza's Guard. I had to accept their word on this matter.

But it was obvious that the more than sixty pilots, air crew, and mechanics of the former Nicaraguan air force in the exile group called the Nicaraguan Aeronautical Organization were not war criminals. They were experienced military aviators willing and ready to fly for the Contras. Above all, they knew local flying conditions and had the skills needed to keep the small Contra air wing operating effectively. But the FDN leadership was too intimidated by its American mentors to accept the group into its ranks.

This reluctance was very unfortunate because the Contras needed all the military help they could get at that moment. With the Boland Amendment in effect, the Sandinistas were determined to wipe out the Contras. They had already attacked the Las Vegas base camps with rocket barrages that spring, using helicopters to transport multi-barrel 122mm rocket launchers right up to the Honduran border. More ominously, their Mi-24 Hind helicopter gunships were now deployed throughout the northern provinces. This was one hell of a weapon against the Contras' light infantry. It carried a fast-firing automatic cannon and a machine gun in the nose and over a hundred 57mm rockets slung in four pods. The Hind's heavy armor made it relatively invulnerable to small arms and light automatic weapons fire. And the Hinds were flown by Cuban pilots with combat experience in Angola. These gunships now protected the Sandinista outposts in the northern mountains and had forced the Contra task forces inside Nicaragua to move out of the open agricultural areas, where the *campesinos* provided them good support, into the heavily forested areas, where there was adequate concealment from aerial observation and attack. The area around La Trinidad north of Managua was an example of Contra territory lost to the Hind-D helicopter attacks.[33]

But by late summer, Secord's promised SAM-7 anti-aircraft missiles and the men to train the Contras in their use had not yet arrived. Privately, Adolfo expressed his doubts that he had made the right decision in ordering the vital missiles through Secord. In any event, he said, it was too late to order more because the funds he controlled were exhausted and Richard Secord was now in charge of weapons procurement.

The situation in the field soon became desperate. Sandinista helicopter gunships were effectively strangling the Contras' new ground supply lines into their mountain outposts in northern Nicaragua. But the American news media scoffed at those of us sounding the alarm about the growing Cuban combat role. We were called crazy right-wingers who saw Cubans under every bed. Then the Contras shot down an armed Sandinista Mi-8 helicopter, killing its two Cuban pilots, and brought their ID cards back into the base camps. The media could no longer continue the myth that the Sandinistas were not Soviet surrogates.[34]

☆　　　☆

THAT fall, I learned something about the kind of dirty hardball certain international arms dealers were willing to play in order to capture the lucrative Contra business. I was in Los Angeles, giving lectures at a conservative conference, when I received a call from a man in Miami named Mario Del'Amico, who said he had to speak to me urgently on a matter of great importance concerning the Contras. I arranged to meet him at my airport hotel at Los Angeles International.

He turned out to be a Cuban-American, almost a parody of a shady Graham Greene character, squat and paunchy, thick, dark glasses, and a sinister grin half-hidden by the smoke of his giant Honduran cigar. Mario said he represented certain interests in the United States and Honduras who wanted to "help" the Contras' cause of freedom by supplying them arms.

I cut his phony bromides short by explaining I knew he worked for Ron Martin, a Miami arms merchant with a somewhat unsavory reputation, including the unsubstantiated rumor, circulated by Ollie North, that some of his funding came from drug merchants.

Del'Amico explained that Ron Martin had established a huge arms "supermarket" in Honduras that contained every type of Soviet-bloc weapon and munition the Contras could possibly need. Sam had told me that Martin had a bankroll of unknown origin and was combing the arms bazaars of Europe and the Middle East for Soviet weapons. Del'Amico explained that their contacts with the Honduran government were so tight that there would be absolutely no problem with any arms transaction involving the Contras. Their prices, he said, were "very competitive."

"General," he said, "I'm here to get your assurance that any future arms you purchase for the Contras will come from us."

I stared at him without answering.

He reiterated how close his organization was to Honduran authorities and added that it was unlikely any arms we might try to bring in from the outside would make it through customs. This was obviously a threat.

"I'm more interested in bringing firepower to bear on the Sandinistas," I finally told him, "than in saving money." I didn't add that his prices were in fact *not* very competitive, when compared to Sam's. "But," I said, ending the conversation, "if your prices are competitive, we'll certainly keep you in mind."

Del'Amico gave me his most sinister "Miami Vice" frown and said it was regrettable I could not give him the assurances he needed.

It was obvious from this effort that Ron Martin was desperate. At one time, he probably had a good working arrangement with the CIA to provide arms to selected groups. In the case of the Contras, Martin may have been told that he would be the one to provide the weapons and ammunition for the whole Nicaraguan resistance program. Why else would a businessman tie up nearly $20 million in inventory of Communist-bloc weapons? The only group that needed these arms was the Contras. The Sandinistas and the Cuban-supported FMLN guerrillas in El Salvador and Guatemala had their own sources. What Martin and probably the CIA did not count on was that Ollie North would turn over this lucrative business to his friend Richard Secord when Congress cut off Contra funding to the CIA. Martin probably concluded that I was the only other possible source of funding, so he wanted me as an ally, not a competitor in the provision of arms to the Contras.

Two weeks later, Mario Del'Amico went to an Eastern-bloc embassy in Washington and demanded that this government sell Ron Martin's company arms for the Contras at the same prices Sam had obtained. The diplomat he spoke with said this was illegal. At that point, Del'Amico handed over a full set of Xeroxed documents tracing our June arms shipment from the East European port to Honduras.

Twenty-four hours later, Sam was summoned by furious East European authorities in Switzerland. They were outraged that Del'Amico or Ron Martin might leak this information to the press, thus exposing internal procedures that, at best, were somewhat irregular. It took all of Sam's considerable diplomatic finesse (and probably a fair amount of hush money) to calm down the offended government officials.

We later discovered that Del'Amico had actually met our shipment at the Honduran port that July posing as the representative of the Honduran colonel to whom the shipment was consigned. Although he hadn't delayed the arms delivery to the Contras, he had obtained the file of documents to use in threatening those involved.

Despite his sinister bravado, however, Del'Amico was no warrior. Here's how Bob Brown described his encounter with Del'Amico the day Brown's training group returned from the Las Vegas base camps to Tegucigalpa: "This guy was something else: coke bottle sunglasses, some type of black

'Death from Above' T-shirt covering a belly that protruded over his belt, fat cigar and .45 auto in a fast-draw holster. A 'Mr. Combat'—arrogant, pompous, and fat. Bermudez told him to provide security for us back to Tegucigalpa, but he took off never to be seen again."[35]

It was unfortunate that sleazy parasites like this were in the picture, and that Ollie North's effort to force them out was more pecuniary than patriotic.

CHAPTER SIXTEEN

Hazardous Duty

1986–1989

☆   ☆

In December 1986, National Security Adviser Bud McFarlane suddenly resigned. It was rumored that he'd had an emotional breakdown. I wondered what the hell was going on to cause him that degree of stress.

My contacts with Ollie North were now constrained. Because media scrutiny made it impossible for me to come to his OEOB office, we would occasionally meet at local hotels when I was in Washington. But I got the definite feeling that either he was preoccupied with other matters or Secord had convinced him to cut his dealings with me and others working without profit to help the Contras.

One issue I did raise with both Ollie and the CIA was support for the non-Communist Iranian resistance. I had been contacted by Lieutenant Colonel Shapoor Ardalan, an exiled Iranian army officer with an excellent channel into military forces willing to help topple the Ayatollah Khomeini and provide information on the U.S. hostages in Lebanon. When I suggested Ollie meet with Shapoor, he was uncharacteristically vague on the matter, and suggested I contact the CIA. So I went to see Bill Casey. I explained that if nothing else, Shapoor could provide additional intelligence on the true situation inside Iran, which was now involved in a prolonged and bloody war with Iraq. Shapoor had gone back inside Iran on several occasions. As usual, Casey was enthusiastic about this potential contact.

Casey put me in touch with an Agency officer whose cover name was Bob Court, and I introduced him to Shapoor. Over the next several months I received disturbing reports about the Agency from Shapoor. Court was handling him like a walk-in street agent, instead of exploiting Shapoor for his top-level channel to discontented senior Iranian military officers. At one point, Bob Court demanded that Shapoor somehow extract the most important of these officers from Iran to a third country where they could be polygraphed by Agency handlers. This was an impossible demand which disappointed and frustrated Shapoor.

Then he became convinced there was a leak within the CIA funneling back information on his organization to the Ayatollah's men. The final straw for Shapoor was the apparent CIA naïveté about Iranian government leaders like parliament speaker Hashemi Rafsanjani, whom they told Shapoor were "moderates" the West could deal with. Shapoor knew these men to be rabidly anti-Western. That winter he broke off his contacts with the CIA.

He told me that the Agency was getting some very bad advice on Iran. I had to agree with him.

☆   ☆   ☆

IN EARLY 1986, Barbara Studley invited me to have dinner with Eden Pastora in Washington. While initially reluctant to waste time on someone considered by the State Department—and according to Ollie North, the CIA, and the Defense Department—to be more of a liability than an asset to the Democratic Resistance in Nicaragua, I agreed to the social meeting. During the next few weeks, I had several long discussions with Pastora, reviewing his failures and his past successes. Eden invited me, Barbara Studley, and some staff members to visit him inside Nicaragua.

I had first met the legendary Comandante Zero the year before in Miami. Pastora was a complex, charismatic guerrilla leader, and certainly the best-known person in Nicaragua. In August 1978, Pastora led a small guerrilla unit that captured Somoza's National Assembly building in Managua, where he took hundreds of Somoza government officials hostage. These he bargained for the safe conduct out of Nicaragua for his team and the release of fifty-nine Sandinista prisoners, including the notorious Tomas Borge. His daring, handsome demeanor and obvious sangfroid captured the imagination of all Latin America. Pastora ended the anti-Somoza war fighting on the southern front from base camps in Costa Rica.

After the Sandinista takeover, he was named vice-minister of the interior and vice-minister of defense, serving under two powerful but shadowy Marxist comandantes, Tomas Borge and Humberto Ortega, brother of Daniel Ortega, the leader of the Sandinista Directorate. When the Communist nature of the Sandinista government became obvious, Pastora resigned his positions and eventually took over his old Costa Rican base camps to wage another guerrilla war, this time against the Sandinistas.[1]

He called his particular Contra formation the Sandino Revolutionary Front (FRS), which he incorporated within the forces of the Democratic

Revolutionary Alliance (ARDE). This alliance was led by Alfonso Robelo, who had led middle-class resistance to Somoza, and had been one of the five members of the Sandinistas' initial junta. A few months after *La Prensa* publisher Violeta Chamorro resigned from the junta, Robelo concluded that he had absolutely no power or influence within the Marxist Directorate, so he also resigned, then left Nicaragua for Costa Rica. Like the FDN Contras operating in the north, Pastora's and Robelo's forces were supported by the CIA. And, unfortunately, like the Contras in the north, the ARDE fighters were badly mishandled by their Agency case officers.

Pastora was one of those extraordinary characters who believed fervently in his own public image. He was a *guerrillo* par excellence, a romantic Latin warrior who evoked intense loyalty among his troops. The Agency treated him like a native mercenary. Worse, Pastora's CIA handlers included bureaucratic bean counters who required all supply requisition forms completed in English, in triplicate. The cultural barriers between Pastora and the CIA were insurmountable.

In short, the Agency ruined the only chance they had of exploiting the most famous military leader in Central America. Enrique Bermudez was a well-educated professional soldier, but Comandante Zero was a national hero troops could rally around.

That didn't mean he was easy to get along with. On the contrary, he was constantly sniping at his colleagues and jealously protecting his own turf and supply lines. He was especially jealous of the better-equipped Northern Front Contras, whom he often accused of being dominated by Somocista former National Guardsmen. Pastora resisted efforts to combine the Northern and Southern Contra Fronts and conducted his own offensive into the sparsely populated hills around Nueva Guinea, where he had a small following among the local *campesinos*.

On May 29, 1984, Pastora assembled a press conference at his river camp of La Penca, just inside southern Nicaragua. The purpose of the gathering was to demonstrate he could operate independent of CIA-supplied base camps in Costa Rica. Pastora never had the chance to address the small group of assembled Latin American and international journalists. A powerful bomb exploded in his headquarters shed, killing several ARDE fighters and two journalists, maiming several others, and badly wounding Pastora.

ARDE leaders accused the Sandinistas of planting the bomb, noting that the year before a Basque ETA terrorist had been caught drawing plans to Pastora's safe house in Costa Rica in order to booby-trap it, and that two Sandinista agents had died when a briefcase bomb meant to kill ARDE leaders in Costa Rica had exploded. Other ARDE leaders blamed the CIA.[2] Pastora himself, undergoing medical treatment in Venezuela, refused to blame the CIA.[3]

When I met him the next year in Washington, Pastora certainly wasn't blaming the CIA because he was actively lobbying Congress and conservative groups for a share of CIA funding, when and if the Boland Amendment restrictions were lifted. He often expressed his bitterness about Agency mismanagement of his funding and supplies, but he never told me he suspected the Agency had tried to kill him. We were quite frank with each other, and an initial grudging mutual respect developed into a genuine friendship. I passed on complaints I had heard from Agency officers that Pastora was hopelessly disorganized, completely inept at managing more than a small ragtag band of guerrilla fighters. Eden rejected the criticism, showing me actual "supply requisitions" that he said the Agency had rejected. These epitomized the cultural gap in the operation. Eden's idea of a supply request was to pin a handwritten note, replete with his rubber headquarters stamp, onto an uncompleted computerized resupply form: "I need everything for 2,000 men for two months."

"You're just not a good commander," I had chided him. "An effective officer does whatever he has to, in order to see that his men are fed and supplied with ammunition."

Eden Pastora's big dark face always clouded when I brought up such practicalities. "The CIA stole my supplies" was his usual rejoinder.

By the spring of 1986, Pastora was back in Costa Rica, operating on a virtual shoestring, but still retaining the loyalty of his ill-equipped ARDE troops. Senator Jesse Helms of North Carolina, the minority leader of the Senate Foreign Relations Committee, was a firm advocate of Pastora. Through one of his staff aides, he asked us to make one last effort at bringing Pastora's group into the new United Nicaraguan Opposition (UNO) then being formed. Earlier I had checked with Bill Casey, who still refused to discuss operational matters dealing with Nicaragua. Casey had simply told me that Pastora was a very "difficult" man to work with, but had agreed that he was the most famous man in Nicaragua.

Before going to see Pastora in March 1986, I discussed the matter with Elliott Abrams, Assistant Secretary of State for Inter-American Affairs. He agreed with my basic premise that Pastora was a resource we ought to have working for us rather than against us. I explained that Pastora was bitter about the way he'd been handled by the CIA. But I explained my hope to get him to agree to join the other Contras under the umbrella of UNO. The situation, I said, was similar to the problem of aiding the French resistance. The OSS and SOE had not been overjoyed supplying the Communist FTP, but we had done so because they were willing to fight Nazis. And now I was certain Eden Pastora would fight Sandinistas.

Abrams wished me luck, but expressed doubt that I would have any success.[4]

In March 1986, I had a trip planned to El Salvador to introduce Barbara

Studley to Salvadoran air force chief General Juan Bustillo. Her company was hoping to arrange the sale of several surplus prop-driven T-28 ground-attack planes much better suited to anti-guerrilla warfare than the A-37 jets America had provided. We decided to stop first in Costa Rica so that I could meet with Pastora.

The GMT team consisted of Barbara, myself, her son Michael Marks, and Mike Timpani, a former Army helicopter pilot who had flown for Pastora under a CIA contract after leaving the Army. Our original plan called for Timpani to fly Pastora and me to make a brief helicopter inspection of his forces south of the Rama Road near Nueva Guinea in Nicaragua. This was probably a risky endeavor, but I knew actually going into Nicaragua with Pastora would bolster his confidence in me, thus giving weight to my argument that he should join the United Resistance. It would also be a signal to his troops that they had not been completely abandoned.

Unfortunately, our flight to San Jose was diverted by weather to Panama City, and it was many hours later when we finally landed in Costa Rica. Eden Pastora had waited at the airport, then returned to his safe house in the outskirts of San Jose.

We found hotel rooms, and the next morning I went to see the American ambassador, Lew Tambs. He received me in his office together with Joe Fernandez, the CIA station chief who used the cover name of Tomas Castillo, and the American defense attaché. I told them I was meeting with Pastora and that I knew he was not very popular with the embassy staff. I had known Lew Tambs when he was a professor at Arizona State University and later when he was working on the NSC staff. I trusted him to be frank with me.

"I'd like to know specifically what Eden is doing that is causing you problems," I told him.

Tambs and Castillo exchanged a look of frustration. Obviously, Pastora had been a burden on the embassy. "To begin with," Tambs said, "Eden Pastora simply will not take advice from his advisers." The Ambassador began ticking off items on his fingers. "His troops are much too open here in Costa Rica. They don't carry out the operations they promise to. . . . The guy is simply hopeless, a loser."

"Well, Lew," I said, reiterating what I had told Elliott Abrams, "I believe Pastora could be an asset that we ought to have on our side. If we continue to treat him the way we have, he'll definitely become a liability."[5]

The Ambassador and his men looked skeptical, but said nothing to discourage me.

We met Pastora and began the long drive north from San Jose to his border camp with Eden, wearing one of his disguises, at the wheel. The Costa Rican capital is a handsome colonial city in the green volcanic highlands. The road north soon left the plateau and descended to a muddy plain of scrub jungle cut at odd intervals by the steep ravines of small rivers. It began to rain. Now the track became almost impassable. We had to winch the Toyota Land Cruiser up each ravine face, a process that took at least half an hour per ravine. Then after a few hundred meters, we would slide out of control down the next gully, splash across the muddy torrent, and start the winching process all over again. It was 3 A.M. when we finally arrived at a primitive farmhouse belonging to one of Pastora's supporters a short distance from the Rio San Juan. Barbara and Michael Marks had never experienced anything like this. In fact, Mike Timpani and I had difficulty recalling when we had walked, pulled, and pushed so long in such deep mud and so much rain.

Eden was greeted with big smiles and *embrasos* on the steps of an open-sided farm shed that was to be our shelter for the next day or so. We were battered and jolted, soaked to the skin, and covered with a layer of slimy red mud. The only food the farm family could offer was some small ears of dried corn, which a peasant woman had soaked in hot water, but which was now only tepid. As we attempted to chew the corn, Eden told us that we should not worry about the occasional gunfire we could hear coming from the direction of the river. At least there were no vampire bats.

Pastora's plan was for all of us to cross the river into Nicaragua in the morning, visit several of his base camps there, for me to inspect his troops, and move back to the river to rendezvous with a helicopter from Panama that would carry us up to his Nueva Guinea base camp sixty miles north in Nicaragua.

In the morning, the GMT team, Eden, and two Costa Rican friends boarded three big dugout canoes and headed across the island-studded San Juan River into Nicaragua. After a few hours' walk, we came to one of Eden's camps where he had assembled some troops for us to inspect.

They were a brave, cheerful, and pathetic lot. One young boy no more than twelve had walked for eighty miles to join Eden after his parents had been killed by the Sandinistas two years earlier. He was obviously malnourished, but carried his AK-47 with pride. His feet were a mass of infected blisters from his oversize rubber farm boots. Other soldiers looked close to starvation. But their weapons were clean. On checking their web gear, however, I found that no one had more than twenty rounds of ammunition for his AK-47. Looking around the camp, I saw a junkyard of broken and discarded equipment, including more outboard motors, a field generator, and gasoline lamps. One hut contained a stack of radios, useless without batteries, and a stack of captured weapons, useless without soldiers.

Looking around the poorly tended banana grove and the riverbank of featureless scrub jungle, I suddenly realized what an isolated spot this was.

We were miles inside Nicaragua. Had Eden Pastora actually been a secret Sandinista agent as some people claimed, this would have been the ideal spot for him to have arranged an ambush. Certainly the Sandinistas would have taken pleasure in killing a notorious Contra supporter like me. But I knew Eden was nothing more than he claimed to be, an authentic warrior caught up in his own romantic myth.

Eden and I sat down over tin cups of strong black coffee and talked frankly about his needs. What would it take, I asked, for him to move these troops north to their Nueva Guinea base area and start operations against the Rama Road?

By now, Eden knew I would not accept a vague answer about "everything" his men might need. For once he was specific. He wanted 6,000 rounds of AK-47 ammunition, 300 pairs of boots, batteries for his radios, malaria suppressants, vitamins and antibiotics to keep the men healthy, and some antiseptic solutions and field dressings for his wounded. He explained that food was available from his supporters up in Nueva Guinea, and that he could supply the rest of his troops from captured Sandinista truck convoys.

"Nada mas?" I asked. Nothing more?

Pastora shook his head. *"Nada mas."*

I told him I was confident Adolfo Calero could provide the ammunition, boots, and radio batteries, and that I could have the medical supplies shipped from the States within days. I also promised him a few American volunteer trainers and technicians to repair his broken commo gear and outboard motors.

Once he received a promise of these supplies, Eden agreed he would go back into Nicaragua and set up a drop zone to receive them from his own plane and pilots. He could then begin operations. He wanted badly to reopen the Southern Front, he said, and was willing to do so under the UNO banner.

Back at the river crossing site on the Costa Rican side, we were amazed to see a Hughes 500 helicopter sitting on the bank. His Panamanian pilot had somehow beat the weather to get there. But the weather to the north was right on the ground. So we scrubbed our planned trip to Nueva Guinea and set out again for San Jose, with Eden driving again.

While the others collapsed at the hotel, I called Ambassador Tambs and told him that I had just returned from my visit with Eden. He suggested that I come down to the embassy and brief him on the trip. I reported to essentially the same group of officials what I had learned. The bottom line, I said, was that Eden Pastora, in exchange for a few supplies and a small amount of ammunition, was willing to finally move all of his troops out of Costa Rica and resume the fight in Nicaragua.

"Would he put that in writing?" Tambs asked.

"I'm confident that he will," I replied.

I rousted Barbara, Marks, and Timpani and we joined Eden and a young woman translator at his San Jose safe house. There was a dusty old manual typewriter and some flimsy stationery available. Eden and I talked out the details of an agreement, specifying what he would do in exchange for the supplies he needed. Barbara took notes during the discussion. Once we had an agreement, Barbara dictated while Michael typed up the final document. Unfortunately, we were all so groggy from the trip that no one noticed the words "The United States agrees to provide . . ." until Michael had laboriously typed out the whole document. This was ambiguous language and might imply U.S. government involvement, which was certainly not the case. It would have been better if this wording was "Private American interests . . ." I explained this to Eden and he understood. But we were reluctant to retype the document, so we both signed the agreement, understanding its true intent.

We returned to the hotel very late in the afternoon. I called the Ambassador at his office to report that I had a signed agreement with Eden Pastora along the lines we had discussed. He suggested that Barbara and I come to his home that evening and have a quiet, informal dinner with him and his family.

When we delivered the document to Lew Tambs that evening at the embassy residence, he was effusive with his praise. "Jack," he said, shaking my hand, "you've no idea what a great service you have done for your country." Costa Rican authorities had been planning to arrest Pastora because of his flagrant violation of their country's neutrality. Now that he promised to take his troops back into Nicaragua, the Costa Ricans would be mollified. Lew Tambs promised to send the text of the document to Elliott Abrams by back channel message.

Eden Pastora's value transcended his limited military potential. He was a legend in Europe, especially among moderate to left-wing Socialists. If he could be shepherded through one successful, newsworthy military operation, he could then be pulled out to hit the triumphant speaker's circuit in Europe and his troops given to a more competent field commander. I knew we had to wage the war against the Sandinistas on the psychological front, not just in the field.

Before leaving San Jose, I arranged with Eden to dispatch one of his few operable airplanes to Ilopango air base in El Salvador, where I planned to have the munitions from the FDN and the medical supplies from the States delivered.

The GMT team of Studley, Singlaub, Marks, and Timpani flew on to El Salvador, where we had our scheduled meeting with General Bustillo, the commander of the Salvadoran Air Force. We were surprised to find that General Bustillo had invited his friend and close personal adviser Felix Rodriguez, who was introduced by his nom de guerre, Max Gomez. U.S.

Army Colonel Jim Steele, the commander of the U.S. Military Assistance Group in El Salvador, also attended. While some GMT business was discussed, General Bustillo was most anxious to learn about our visit with Eden Pastora, who was a longtime friend of the General. He made it clear that he would help Pastora's pilot in any way he could.

An interesting sidelight to the trip from Costa Rica to El Salvador was an unscheduled stop in Managua, Nicaragua. The four GMT members stared in shocked disbelief when the announcement came over the P.A. system. After I determined that we did not have to disembark and that no Sandinista security people would come aboard, we positioned ourselves in vacant window seats to photograph the recently arrived Mi-24 helicopters which were dispersed around the main Managua airport.

In Tegucigalpa, Barbara and I had dinner with Adolfo Calero, who was pleased but skeptical that Eden planned to rejoin the battle. Adolfo made careful note of the ammunition and other equipment Pastora required. "This will be no problem," he said, and promised to prepare the goods for shipment within a few days.

I flew up to the Las Vegas base camp area by helicopter to inspect the troops after their latest encounter with the Sandinistas. The day before Easter, several thousand well-armed Sandinistas, led by Cuban advisers and covered by helicopter gunships, had attacked across the Honduran border in a well-planned assault designed to inflict maximum casualties. But it was the Sandinistas who had suffered most.

Although a number of the base camps were shattered by rocket fire, the Contras had formed into small, disciplined ambush teams and fanned out through the hills to pound the advancing Sandinista columns. The weapons requirements and tactics Enrique had worked out the year before had certainly paid off. Using coordinated machine-gun and RPG fire, Contra units had completely demoralized the advancing Sandinistas, who, I learned from several prisoners, had been briefed to expect a rabble of poorly armed Contras hiding in their camps.

I was in high spirits when I returned to Washington. But Elliott Abrams quickly shattered my good mood. He chided me for drawing up the document without his approval, and said coldly that I as a private citizen had no right to commit the "United States" to any agreement. I explained the circumstances and assured him that Eden Pastora understood the aid would come from the FDN and private American donors. Abrams seemed mollified and indicated he would do nothing to block the transaction.

☆   ☆

My optimistic mood was tempered somewhat by news out of Lebanon. The Palestinian terrorist Abu Nidal had just announced that I was at the top of his assassination list. His spokesman, known as Atef Abu Bakr, gave CBS TV an interview, taped in the Bekaa valley. In retaliation for the recent American air strike on Libya, he said, Abu Nidal had decided to "execute" three prominent Americans: NSC officer Oliver North; Dr. Edward Luttwak, who served as a consultant to the Defense Department; and retired Major General John K. Singlaub. Just in case Abu Nidal's men didn't know what I looked like, CBS featured my picture prominently. I was alarmed, but not surprised. There were close relations between the Sandinistas and Marxist Arab terrorist groups like Abu Nidal's. The FBI assured me that the threat was not a bluff. Abu Nidal's group was responsible for slaughtering innocent travelers in the Rome and Vienna airport massacres. They would certainly have no qualms about killing me if their Sandinista friends asked for a little fraternal help.[6]

This threat was certainly going to make international travel more interesting.

☆   ☆

BEFORE leaving for the Far East on a GMT trip a few weeks later, I made sure all the players were in place to resupply Eden Pastora. In State, Elliott Abrams and his deputy Bill Walker assured me that they would not interfere. Adolfo confirmed that everything was ready in Honduras. Mario Calero in New Orleans indicated that he would be able to replace the non-lethal supplies being transshipped to Ilopango for Pastora.

I also discussed with Abrams the issue of trying to raise more money for the Contras in the Far East during a trip to Taipei and Seoul to celebrate Captive Nations Week, an annual WACL event. I told him that, as far as I was aware, my earlier effort had not been successful and that this time I'd take the case right to the top of both governments. But I explained I'd definitely need a signal from the U.S. government that I wasn't just some "crazy con man" out to defraud the Chinese and Koreans. Don't worry, General, Elliott said, I'll send the signal myself.

So in Taipei, again armed with my trusty three-by-five cards listing a Contra bank account, I contacted Generals Tan Ying and Chiang Wego, requesting an appointment to see Wego's brother, Republic of China President Chiang Ching-kuo. Wego had been one of my classmates at Command and General Staff College years earlier, and we had maintained contact ever since. He jumped the protocol fence to secure a meeting with President Chiang at short notice.

But late that night I received a frantic call from one of Pastora's officers in San Jose, Costa Rica. He verified that Eden had indeed dispatched his light cargo plane to Ilopango, then moved with his troops north into Nicaragua to await the air drop of the promised supplies. Two weeks had gone by and no cargo had arrived at Ilopango. Now, the man said, Pastora was completely disheartened. He planned to trek back into Costa Rica and surrender to the local authorities. I pleaded with the officer to radio Pastora to wait. I was sure there had been some misunderstanding, that a logistics logjam, not a change of heart, had delayed the supplies. Adolfo had given me his word, and I had never known him to go back on it.

Unable to contact either Calero or Pastora, I called Elliott Abrams. He claimed to be completely ignorant of the situation.

"I have no idea what could have gone wrong," he said. Then he abruptly changed the subject. "As long as I have you on the phone," Abrams said, "don't hold that meeting, General." From his strained tone, there was obviously something wrong.

"Why?" I asked. "What's happened?"

He paused, and finally answered. "The approach, ah . . . will be made at the highest possible level."

"What about Seoul?"

"Don't do anything there either," he said.

I hung up, troubled and confused. Ollie North seemed oblivious to the Contra needs. Now Abrams had just cut me out of the effort, yet I knew from Adolfo that the situation in the field had become desperate. I couldn't imagine who would have a better connection to President Chiang at that moment than I had.

Only later did I discover that President Reagan himself had been convinced to personally intervene and appeal to the Republic of China government.[7]

Barbara Studley agreed to interrupt her trip to fly to San Jose to try to break up the supply bottleneck. But she arrived in Costa Rica too late. Eden Pastora had come out and surrendered to the Costa Rican authorities. He declared that his fight against the Sandinistas had finally ended. He asked for asylum in Costa Rica, and was formally placed under arrest for violating the country's laws against armed political groups. Comandante Zero's war was, indeed, over.

Months later, back in the States, I learned what had happened. While I had been acting in good faith to arrange the logistics of Pastora's resupply operation, Pastora had been ordered back to Washington to consult with Ollie North and Elliott Abrams. But once there, he found it impossible to make an appointment with either official. Meanwhile in Costa Rica, CIA officers had "invited" his four best commanders to a safe house, where they were given the typical Agency carrot-and-stick treatment to convince them to abandon Pastora. This was part of a secret official "denigration" campaign that North and Abrams were obviously party to, but which they had never revealed to me. While Pastora was waiting in limbo, he received a frantic call from an aide in Costa Rica who told him his commanders had been "kidnapped." Eden immediately returned to Central America and went back into Nicaragua, hoping to find the commanders. He discovered that they had succumbed to CIA pressures and had taken their troops to join El Negro Chammoro, the Southern Front Contra leader supported by the Agency. He then waited near the assigned drop zone for the promised supply flight. When it, too, failed to materialize, he concluded that the betrayal was total. He came back to Costa Rica, turned himself in, and was arrested.

When Barbara, accompanied by Peter Collins of ABC, found Pastora at the prison in San Jose, the warden gave them his own office for their meeting. Pastora said he now understood that North, Abrams, and the CIA had set him up. Barbara's whole purpose of going to Costa Rica was to tell Eden the truth, so he would know we had not been part of this conspiracy. Because of his legendary name, she still hoped he would rejoin the Contras. One sign of Pastora's popularity in Central America was the stream of important visitors to the prison. While Barbara and Collins were there, former Costa Rican president Rodrigo Carazo Odio arrived to visit Pastora and warmly embraced the imprisoned hero.[8]

Peter Collins, who had covered Eden Pastora for years, was amazed at Eden's story. Pastora even gave Collins a copy of the signed agreement, and Collins arranged an on-camera interview with Ambassador Lewis Tambs. During the interview, the Ambassador denied that he had seen me in over two years. When Peter showed Tambs a copy of the agreement, he became flustered and tried to trivialize our meetings as a single social event. He denied that he'd known in advance that I was going into Nicaragua, or that he had in any way encouraged me in my efforts to bring Pastora back into the resistance fold.

Ambassador Tambs's behavior seemed so bizarre to Peter Collins that he brought his videotape to the Los Angeles International Airport and showed it to me upon my return from Korea. I had to confirm to Peter that most of what Tambs had said on camera was absolutely false. Fortunately for Lew Tambs, ABC decided not to air that interview.

The episode reminded me of the old adage that an ambassador is an honorable man sent abroad to lie for his country.

☆   ☆

ON MAY 29, 1986, a civil damage lawsuit was filed in the United States District Court, Southern District of Florida, and placed on the docket of respected federal judge James Lawrence King. The plaintiffs were two American free-lance journalists, Tony Avirgan and his wife, Martha Honey, who had a long history of espousing left-wing causes and were reputed to be pro-Sandinista. They were represented by attorney Daniel P. Sheehan, the general counsel of a strange Washington-based "interfaith center for law and public policy" called the Christic Institute. On the day he filed suit in Miami, the Christics staged a news conference at the National Press Club in Washington, apparently to make sure the case received the media attention Sheehan felt that it deserved. As I was to learn, Sheehan was not shy about publicity.

The plaintiffs' complaint, he explained to the assembled reporters, was filed under the civil provisions of the Racketeer Influenced and Corrupt Organizations Act (RICO). Avirgan and Honey's lawsuit claimed damages of $23.8 million for physical and psychological injuries, pain and suffering, and punitive sanctions resulting from the assassination-attempt bombing against Eden Pastora at his La Penca camp in southern Nicaragua on May 30, 1984. Avirgan had been an ABC stringer cameraman at the ill-fated news conference. Although eight men and women had died in the blast and many more were seriously wounded, Avirgan escaped with a few bruises and lacerations to the middle finger of his left hand.[9] His wife was nowhere near the camp, but nevertheless joined the suit, claiming, among other things, loss of consortium and loss of income during the period of her husband's recovery.

The size of the damage claim was only one of many bizarre features of the suit. The list of defendants was even more unusual. My name was among the thirty defendants, who also included Contra leader Adolfo Calero, Americans Andy Messing, Richard Secord, Albert Hakim, Rob Owen, former CIA officer Theodore Shackley, arms dealer Ron Martin, and his sidekick Mario Del'Amico, a couple of fugitive Central American cocaine traffickers, an American ranch property developer in Nicaragua named John Hull, and, finally, Medellín Cartel cocaine barons Pablo Escobar and Jorge Ochoa.

To round out the Alice in Wonderland weirdness of this legal action, the plaintiffs alleged that the La Penca bombing was engineered by the defendants acting as part of an ongoing conspiracy involving a criminal RICO enterprise that relied on drug smuggling to finance arms supplies to the Contras. Just to make things interesting, Sheehan accused us of conspiring to assassinate Ambassador Lewis Tambs in San Jose, Costa Rica.

Sheehan breathlessly explained he would call unnamed witnesses who had attended a 1984 Miami meeting at which Adolfo Calero plotted Pastora's murder. The actual attempt, Sheehan said, was made by a renegade Libyan of no known address.[10]

These charges were so outrageous that I was initially amused by Sheehan's paranoid grumblings. I told the press the charges were "transparently scurrilous, cynical, and duplicitous."

On checking into the Christics, I discovered, predictably enough, that they were a remnant of the 1960s radical left, founded in Washington in 1981 by a Jesuit priest named William J. Davis. According to Dr. Susan Huck, who has studied the Christics closely, Davis was an acolyte of Marxist "liberation" theology, as were several Sandinista Jesuit government officials. The new "interfaith" legal and public policy center was granted tax-exempt status. Davis's literature explained that the name of his center derived from early twentieth century Jesuit Pierre Teilhard de Chardin, who theorized a "Christic" force that would mystically spread to unite long-suffering mankind—no doubt led by radical priests like Davis—to do "battle against evil."[11]

In Daniel Sheehan, Davis found a natural ally. Sheehan was a curly-headed Irishman from upstate New York, who was radicalized as a student in the sixties, supposedly when his ruthless ROTC instructors at Northeastern University forced him to learn how to garrote innocent Vietnamese women. He left the ROTC program and went on to get a Harvard law degree, enjoying a student draft deferment. Years later, Sheehan reportedly liked to tell the story that he forced the draft board to continue his deferment by threatening to expose the evil ways of his sinister "Green Beret" trainers.[12]

Sheehan bounced from a minor position at a Wall Street law firm back to Harvard, where he studied ethics at the Divinity School, then dropped out to work on the legal defense of the American Indians involved in the murder of federal officers at Wounded Knee. He reportedly used "unorthodox methods" working on the notorious Karen Silkwood case for the National Organization for Women. Sheehan alleged Silkwood had been murdered by evil corporate conspirators because she had been about to blow the whistle on the theft of nuclear fuel at the Kerr-McGee Corporation nuclear plant where she worked. Although only a helper on the case, Sheehan later claimed credit for the out-of-court settlement for Silkwood's family. With this taste for conspiracy, Sheehan found a home in the Christics. Writing in the liberal magazine *Mother Jones,* journalist James Traub aptly described Sheehan as "a brilliant publicist with more than a shadow of the huckster, a charismatic personality who magnetizes others by the force of his certainty, a spiritual figure who sometimes stops to adjust his halo in the mirror."[13]

During my two years of fund-raising for the Contras, I had often encountered such hecklers from the ranks of true believers of radical groups camouflaged by religious cover. So I was ready to dismiss the Christics as "just another wacky, moribund left-wing hive," as they were later so aptly described by journalist David Brock.[14]

And when Judge King threw the suit back to Daniel Sheehan as unacceptable, it was easy enough to forget a posturing self-promoter like Daniel Sheehan.

☆   ☆

I FELT morally obligated to try one final time to convince Eden Pastora to return to the Contra ranks. Barring his decision to do so, I at least wanted to help him with his local debts in Costa Rica, which had to be paid off before he was released from custody. So I flew to San Jose and met with him briefly. There was no convincing him to take up the Contra cause again after what he correctly saw as the latest of many CIA betrayals. I used several thousand dollars of USCWF funds to help settle his local debts. He told me he would probably try for a bank loan to begin a fishing cooperative on the Pacific coast of Costa Rica.

But the other ARDE forces on the southern front and the FDN in the north were still in the battle. However, they were almost out of funds. When I met with Adolfo Calero in Miami, he was desperate. Although he was certain several million dollars from foreign donor governments had been channeled through Ollie North, earmarked for Contras' weapons purchases, the FDN had not received any substantial arms for months. And he was unable to contact Dick Secord to discuss the matter. Adolfo begged me to help free a few million dollars from the Contra bank accounts controlled by North and call on Sam to arrange a quick shipment of AK-47s and ammunition at the same prices we had offered him the year before.

In Washington, Ollie North made it clear that my arms procurement efforts for the Contras were no longer welcome. Through intermediaries he assured me there were arms in the "pipeline" that would soon reach the Contras. I was not so sanguine. Neither was Rob Owen. He told me of his concerns about Secord and Hakim reaping large profits, while the Contras were stalled in their base camps for want of munitions. Ollie had grown unusually secretive and distant. And more than once I caught him in lies. This troubled me. In clandestine operations, which by their very nature rely on public deception, the last thing you wanted to hear from a colleague was a lie. But I had to remind myself that Ollie North was actually not a veteran clandestine operator, no matter how much he liked to play at the cloak-and-dagger swashbuckler.

I was especially frustrated with Secord. From what I saw in Central America and heard from Adolfo, Secord's air resupply of the Contra groups inside Nicaragua depended on obsolete, poorly maintained aircraft that spent more time down for repairs than in the air. I told Ollie I could purchase a turboprop C-130 on the international market for $1 million with only a $250,000 down payment. The plane could meet all of the Contras' airdrop requirements, and also ferry donated humanitarian supplies from the States. Ollie was not interested. Dick Secord, he said, was handling the air operation quite well.

☆   ☆

My attention was unexpectedly diverted from Central America to Southeast Asia. An American treasure-salvage group called Nippon Star, whose chief investors included a reputable couple named Harrigan from Memphis, contacted me concerning their work to uncover hidden Japanese war booty in the Philippines. Normally, I would not have been interested in buried-treasure schemes, but the Nippon Star group were not naive beachcombers. And I knew from past experience that stories of buried Japanese gold in the Philippines were legitimate. Before offering me a consultancy as a security adviser, the Harrigans outlined the situation.

General Tomoyuki Yamashita had been the Japanese commander in chief in the Philippines. He was later executed by the Filipinos for war crimes. In 1942, the Japanese hoped to formally annex the Philippines, then sue the United States for peace, offering to withdraw from other Japanese-occupied areas of Asia. Their field commanders looted the national treasuries, private banks, and temple complexes in Hong Kong, Burma, Indochina, and the Dutch East Indies, and shipped hundreds of tons of gold bullion and golden temple artifacts for safekeeping in their proposed future colony, the Philippines. The Harrigans produced credible documents that estimated upwards of 300 tons of bullion and other gold had reached the Philippines by 1943.

But the Japanese plan to annex the islands failed. The advancing American forces cut off the Philippines before the Japanese could ship their gold back to Japan. Faced with these Allied victories, General Yamashita dispersed the assembled treasure around the islands, where it was buried in 172 carefully chosen sites. The Japanese trained an elite team of geologists and engineers to perform the actual burials. All the sites were disguised and all were protected by several layers of booby traps, both manmade and natural. One underwater site in Calatagan Bay south of Manila was a shaft blasted seventy feet deep into a coral reef. Japanese records indicated five tons of gold bullion and several barrels of precious stones had been deposited there.

The entire treasure-burial operation was carefully documented by General Yamashita's staff, who used coded maps and ledgers, which were flown back to Japan before the capitulation.

By the 1970s, some Filipinos had allied themselves with both bogus and authentic Japanese treasure hunters, and the secret digging began. But neither side figured on the shrewdness of Philippine dictator Ferdinand Marcos. His spies kept the treasure hunters under close surveillance. When they literally struck pay dirt, the Marcos forces moved in to arrest the treasure hunters and confiscate their gold. Marcos's $12 billion fortune actually came from confiscated treasure, not skimmed-off U.S. aid.

But Marcos had only managed to rake off a dozen or so of the biggest sites. That left well over a hundred untouched. With the Marcos overthrow and the advent of the Cory Aquino government, there was renewed interest in the so-called "Yamashita Treasure."

The only problem in the summer of 1986, however, was that several of the most promising sites Nippon Star had staked out were in remote provinces where the Communist New People's Army or bandit groups were in control. The group needed a qualified security adviser and offered me the job. What made the offer attractive was their promise to provide several percent of the eventual profit directly to the U.S. Council for World Freedom. I agreed to help them.

The situation I found in Manila was intriguing, but confused. The Harrigans' partner, Allan Forringer, was the chief of operations. Ill-advisedly, he had concentrated all their efforts on the reef site in Calatagan Bay. Not only was the Japanese concrete shaft cover too hard for their drilling equipment, the site itself was exposed to treacherous tides and currents that repeatedly swept away the Nippon Star work platform.

After close scrutiny of their Japanese maps and coded ledgers, I was convinced they had some exciting leads. But squandering their resources on the Calatagan Bay site was a tactical error. There was one promising site beneath a modern house in Cavite Province sixty miles south of Manila. From partial deciphering of the ledgers, it was clear that this site, and several others nearby at Los Banos, offered the best hope of immediate return.

On my second visit to the Philippines, I agreed to take charge of the Nippon Star operation and to staff it with competent retired American military officers familiar with the area and known to the Aquino government. Although treasure hunting has a romantic aura, the work we did that summer in the Philippines was basically a no-nonsense logistics and construction effort. Unfortunately, Nippon Star ran into funding problems before we could exploit our best sites.

☆   ☆

ALTHOUGH the Christic lawsuit remained a minor irritant that summer, I had not even bothered to hire a lawyer. I was confident that Judge King would reject the revised RICO suit the Christics were preparing for Avirgan and Honey, just as he had the first. When I mentioned this to Bill Casey at a dinner for former OSS officers, however, he advised caution.

"These people could be dangerous, Jack," he said. "They're more than just a nuisance."

"What do you think I ought to do, Bill?" Casey was a veteran attorney with a first-rate legal mind.

"I'll find you a lawyer," he said.

Casey put me in touch with John Sears, a Washington attorney with whom he had worked on the first Reagan campaign. Sears agreed to handle my case on an expenses-only basis. Neither of us realized the head of steam the Christics suit was gathering. And neither of us could predict the ruthless and unethical methods Sheehan and the Christics would employ.

In a series of revised RICO complaints, Honey, Avirgan, and the Christic Institute alleged that the plaintiffs were the victims of a massive conspiracy that spanned three decades and involved the devious activities of a cabal of former American government officials, ex-CIA and ex-military officers, Colombian drug lords, Cuban exile mercenaries, and arms dealers. This group Sheehan dubbed the "Secret Team," which, he proclaimed, had actually taken over American foreign policy from the democratically elected government. I was supposedly involved in this illegal conspiracy by dint of my nefarious activities in Southeast Asia during the Vietnam War and later during my activities in support of the Contras.[15]

Sheehan was also juggling the defendant list to suit his political goals. But I recognized a pattern in his tactics. Certainly drug barons like Pablo Escobar and Jorge Ochoa would not be expected to defend themselves. And the Christics had not named a single active-duty military or intelligence agency officer or serving government official as members of the alleged conspiracy.

Ted Shackley, Rob Owen, Richard Secord, and I were all private citizens. Had any of us been serving government officials, we would have had access to Department of Justice resources in our defense. And no doubt the Christics understood that a massive counterattack by Justice would have quickly blown them out of the water. Once the Christics refiled their RICO complaint, and Judge King accepted Sheehan's written assurance he had evidence to back his wild claims, the Christics had subpoena powers during the discovery process. This meant they could require the defendants to give depositions under oath, and they would have access to our personal files. I certainly had nothing illegal to conceal. But I did have a lot of sensitive information about anti-Communist resistance groups. I would naturally have to resist wholesale snooping. John Sears could not continue representing me *pro bono* during a protracted discovery process. This meant I would have to retain counsel and would accumulate substantial legal bills.

So Tom Spencer, a brilliant Miami attorney with years of federal litigation experience, took over my case. Like all top-drawer lawyers, he did not come cheap. The clock of my eventually crippling attorney fees was now running, and there was no end in sight.[16]

And it was clear that the Christics would indeed drag out the pretrial process of discovery. They were using the lawsuit as an extremely effective fund-raising tool. According to one of their solicitation pamphlets:

> A shadow government run by a "Secret Team" has been operating for the last 25 years carrying out covert actions without Congressional approval and at times even without Presidential approval.
> They have financed their operations by stealing from the U.S. Government and by trafficking in DRUGS.
> During the Viet Nam War Richard Secord, John Singlaub and others in the C.I.A. imported heroin from S.E. Asia into the United States. Today these same people are importing cocaine from South America.[17]

Over the coming months, the Christics raised millions of dollars in widespread fund-raising activities. They held countless fund-raisers on college campuses, where credulous academics and gullible students lined up to hear Sheehan expound his bizarre conspiracy theory, which explained all American foreign policy for the past thirty years, and even included a convenient explanation for the Kennedy assassination. Clever marketers, the Christics pedaled video and audio cassettes, books, pamphlets, and bumper stickers at these sessions. They even sold bound copies of Sheehan's exciting but legally dubious complaints and affidavits, which were ballyhooed as shocking "evidence."[18]

Their small Washington staff swelled to over sixty, including ten lawyers and eight full-time investigators. And they managed to recruit forty-six volunteer members of the Trial Lawyers for Public Justice to work on the case. I came to realize my legal fees in defending myself against this frivolous lawsuit might well ruin me financially.

At one point during the suit, Sheehan told an audience of his supporters that I and the other defendants were "going to get fined $20 million and lose everything they have."[19] Ted Shackley aptly described the Christic's tactics as "legal terrorism," which has as its objective setting "a political agenda via the courts."[20]

Sheehan made his intentions very clear that fall when he submitted a sensational revised affidavit alleging details on the thirty-year global conspiracy of the "Secret Team." He claimed to have legally acceptable evidence that the defendants were responsible for the bomb that caused the plaintiffs' injuries. This affidavit was written in the first person and read more like a cheap spy thriller than a legal document.[21] It alleged the members of the Secret Team had been conspiring to control American foreign policy for decades and had resorted to assassination, drug trafficking, and sundry other corrupt practices to achieve their evil goals. He claimed to have legally admissible depositions and statements of his seventy-nine witnesses to prove these charges.

People began comparing the Christics to the Lyndon LaRouche political cult; indeed, Jonathan Kwitny, a *Wall Street Journal* reporter, was later harassed by "glassy-eyed" Christic followers during a book promotion tour. They demanded to know why he disagreed with Sheehan's bizarre claims of a global conspiracy led by the Secret Team.[22]

But others wondered why Judge King was obliged to listen to Sheehan's crazy charges. When an attorney in good standing like Sheehan makes such claims, ostensibly backed by evidence, a judge is required to take him seriously. Mutual trust is the foundation of our legal system.

Unfortunately, Sheehan refused to divulge the identity of his witnesses, whom he listed only by number. When Judge King ordered him to do so, Sheehan and the Christics appealed, stating that revealing the witnesses' names would expose them to possible assassination by the evil crew of conspirators being sued. This reminded many people of Senator Joe McCarthy's famous list of Communists in the State Department. Judge King was not amused by the Christics' maneuvers.[23]

And I certainly was not amused by my mounting legal bills.

☆   ☆

BACK in the Philippines, I tried to bring some semblance of organized discipline to the Nippon Star field operations. John Harrigan in Memphis and John Voss in Denver had secured better funding through an investment consortium. I was able to obtain the services of some well-qualified retired Army personnel to assist in running the several scattered work sites. I set out to build better bridges to the Philippine government by giving periodic and detailed reports of our activities to Teodoro "Teddy" Locsin, Jr., a key adviser to President Cory Aquino.

We concentrated on the Cavite site, but unfortunately ran into more water problems. Several meters down the shaft we struck one of the subterranean streams the Japanese had successfully dammed during the initial excavation. The men digging were almost drowned in liquid mud. We had to start again, reinforcing the shaft with expensive shoring. At this point, funds became a problem. And Forringer was obliged to hustle for more investors overseas.

Natural and financial obstacles were not the only problems we encountered. The local *cavitano* Mafia, who controlled everything from the colorfully painted jitney buses to the cockfights of the sugarcane workers, wanted a part of our action as well. They threatened us with all manner of mayhem, but I managed to thwart their attempts at extortion.

I wasn't so fortunate with the Communist New People's Army. The NPA must have gotten word of the Abu Nidal death threat against me. That autumn, they made it clear I was on their hit list. I began to move about cautiously, using real tradecraft, not the James Bond movie nonsense the earlier Nippon Star crew had employed.

I was immersed in these problems that September when I got a call from friends in the States. Both houses of Congress had just signed a continuing-resolution budget bill that included $100 million in aid to the Nicaraguan Contras. The President was specifically authorized to use these funds for both lethal and non-lethal aid. Congress had finally come to its senses. The two-year hiatus of the Boland Amendment was over.

But my euphoria over this news was short-lived. On October 6, 1986, I heard a BBC radio report that a C-123K cargo plane had been shot down over southern Nicaragua while on an airdrop supply mission to the Contras. Three crewmen had been killed, but a fourth, an American named Eugene Hasenfus, had parachuted to safety and was taken prisoner by the Sandinistas. As more details were revealed over the next few days, I became incensed. Apparently the aircraft had been flying in broad daylight and at a low altitude and had been shot down by a Sandinista SAM-7 missile. A C-123 is an aircraft very vulnerable to ground fire. Only a fool would dispatch such a plane on a clandestine airdrop during daylight. To make matters worse, Hasenfus and the three dead crewmen had been carrying their wallets with identity cards linking them to Southern Air Transport, a known CIA proprietary company. The final straw in this foul-up was the fact that the plane's logbooks were on board, which also linked the operation back to the CIA.

I recalled how Ollie North had smugly insisted that his "air adviser," Dick Secord, knew more about running clandestine aerial resupply operations than I did. For almost two and a half years as commander of MACV/SOG, I had run very similar resupply flights into North Vietnam, the most hostile anti-aircraft environment in history. And I had never lost a plane. But if one of my aircraft *had* been shot down, the crew sure as hell would not have been carrying their wallets and ID cards. Once more, Ollie North's grandiose self-image as a master covert operator had come back to harm the Contra cause.

This incident could not have come at a worse time. There was bound to be bad reaction in Congress, especially among the disgruntled liberals who had just had their precious Boland Amendment voted down. This was another election year and, once more, politics would interfere with sound foreign policy.

Two days later I left for the States to attend an IRS hearing on the tax-exempt status of USCWF. Before boarding my flight in Manila, I called the Nippon Star office in town to check on last-minute messages. They told me Elliott Abrams of the State Department had just phoned, urgently trying to reach me, but they had explained I was on a trip. I thought no more about this until I reached the States and called Barbara Studley in Washington.

"General," she said, "have you heard the news?"

I was groggy from yet another trans-Pacific flight. "What news?"

"Someone in the government told the press that the Hasenfus plane was part of your operation. They're blaming you."

This was outrageous. Not only had North and Secord fouled up the Contra resupply operation, they apparently now had the gall to foist the blame onto me.[24]

When I reached National Airport late that afternoon, there was a news media ambush even bigger than the one that had hit me at Kennedy Airport in 1977. But Michael Marks had outfoxed them. Posing as an airport security guard, he had ordered the camera crews away from the passenger gate. As I trudged down the corridor, he stepped forward unobtrusively and guided me into a private airline club, from which we escaped by a side exit to a waiting limousine with smoked-glass windows. Unfortunately, the media had posted a motorcycle scout in the taxi rank at the National terminal who trailed us all the way in to the Sheraton Carlton Hotel. But the hotel staff kept the hungry reporters at bay that night.

The staff of the Sheraton Carlton were really magnificent. When it was necessary for me to leave the hotel, they would arrange to sneak me out to a waiting car through the labyrinth of hotel laundry and other subterranean tunnels.

I immediately called Elliott. He denied that either he or Ollie North had made the scandalous leak to the press. But to me his assurances were transparent lies. Why else would he have called me urgently in Manila? I had come to realize that Elliott Abrams was one of those ambitious political creatures for whom lying simply came more naturally than honesty.

The next day, rested up from my trip, I held a press conference. "I wish I *had* been in charge of that flight," I told the reporters. "I would have done it right."[25]

Despite my public denials during the news conference, at which *New York Times* reporter Richard Halloran was present, the *Times* again charged that I was responsible for the Hasenfus flight when it was shot down. Halloran claimed that "Administration officials privately" confirmed the earlier information. A personal telephone complaint to the *New York Times* editor produced a promise of a public retraction, which never came.[26]

A few days later, Abrams assured Congress that there had been no U.S. government involvement with the ill-fated Hasenfus flight.

☆　　　　☆

THAT November I was back in Manila, trying to keep the Filipino laborers paid and safe from the *cavitanos,* the American supervisors talking to each other, and the Philippine government happy—when the Iran-Contra story broke.

The news initially arrived in driblets. A pro-Iranian magazine in Beirut called *Al-Shiraa* ran a story that former national security adviser Bud McFarlane had traveled secretly to Tehran to negotiate with the Ayatollah Khomenei. Rumors of ill-advised bartering for American hostages held in Lebanon by pro-Iranian Shiites abounded in the international press. The President denied them.

Then came the deluge. On November 19, President Reagan announced a "secret initiative" to Iran that had supposedly been designed to better relations between the two countries. He confirmed that America had sold arms to the government of Ayatollah Khomeini in full defiance of our announced policy and in complete breach of agreements with allied governments to prevent arms from reaching Iran. Over the next few days, an official government investigation revealed that thousands of TOW anti-tank missiles and a score of HAWK anti-aircraft missiles had been delivered to Tehran, some in an elaborate three-way transaction involving Israel.

By November 21, it was clear that Ollie North had been the administration point man in this endeavor. Attorney General Ed Meese led an investigative team into the role of the NSC. It was soon revealed that a "diversion" of funds accruing from the profit of these arms sales had occurred. The Attorney General announced that some of these proceeds had been used to support the Nicaraguan Contras while the Boland Amendment was in effect. Meese then announced the resignation of Admiral John Poindexter and the firing of Lieutenant Colonel Oliver North.

Former senator John Tower led a commission of inquiry convened by the President. Ostensibly the operation was begun to secure the release of William Buckley, the former CIA Beirut station chief kidnapped by the Iranians in 1984. But the true nature of the failed policy soon became evident. Although three American hostages were eventually released during the course of the arms-for-hostages barter, *five* more were eventually kidnapped to take their places. I was absolutely outraged by these revelations.

Not only were American citizens abroad placed at much greater risk by the administration's actions, our government had lost whatever moral authority it had in trying to dissuade other countries from negotiations with terrorists. The White House had gone blindly into the cruel and devious bazaar of the Middle East hoping to save the lives of a few citizens, and instead we had allowed our nation's foreign policy to become a hostage. In the future, I knew, any tin-horn dictator or terrorist would target Americans for kidnapping knowing the leverage he could extract.

President Reagan was the commander in chief of the American armed forces. In that capacity he should have had the moral courage to sacrifice the lives of others, if need be, in order to protect our national integrity. I knew from personal experience that the hardest decision a commander could make was to risk a few men to protect the majority of his command. Reading about Ronald Reagan's failed policy, I couldn't help but remember all those long nights on the Main Line of Resistance when a handful of gallant men in my command defended Outpost Harry. Being a commander forced cruel choices on a man.

But the revelations of convoluted profit "diversions," ostensibly to the Contras, were even more disturbing than the hostage bartering. It was eventually revealed that Richard Secord and Albert Hakim, through a holding company called Lake Resources, were the repositories of those profits. Yet I knew from discussions with Adolfo Calero and Enrique Bermudez that the Contra troops had been going hungry, without needed ammunition and medicines for months, when the millions in profits had been supposedly *diverted* to them.

In February, I was contacted by the FBI, who were conducting preliminary investigations for both Judge Lawrence Walsh, the special prosecutor—now called the independent counsel—and the Joint Select Congressional Committees investigating the Iran-Contra fiasco. They told me I was not the subject of a criminal investigation, but that they would definitely appreciate interviewing me. I flew home from the Philippines.

The week I arrived in Washington, Bud McFarlane took an overdose of Valium and nearly died the night before he was scheduled to testify before the Tower Inquiry Board. The next week, President Reagan conceded, "What began as a strategic opening to Iran deteriorated into trading arms for hostages."[27]

☆　　　☆

THAT winter and spring, I spent hours testifying and giving depositions on my role in aiding the Contras. At no time was I ever accused of criminal wrongdoing or unethical behavior. Since I had absolutely nothing to hide, I testified with complete openness.

I did not see Oliver North, Richard Secord, Bud McFarlane, or any other of the Iran-Contra notables during this period. Unfortunately, I did not have a chance to discuss the issue with Bill Casey. He had undergone emergency surgery for a brain tumor in December, and was in critical condition and rapidly deteriorating.

On April 29, 1987, I spent most of the day on Capitol Hill giving a sworn deposition to Kenneth Ballen, staff counsel of the House committee, and

Charles Kerr, his counterpart of the Senate committee. Since I was not facing criminal charges, I appeared voluntarily, requested no immunity whatsoever, and answered almost six straight hours of questions with complete candor. I detailed the role I had played in securing private funds for the Contras. I carefully documented my part in helping Adolfo Calero buy high-quality weapons at bargain prices. I delivered to the attorneys my complete file on the arms transaction. I discussed my relationship with Oliver North, Richard Secord, and Elliott Abrams.

Obviously, the two committees, each controlled by partisan Democrats, were trying to trace a smoking gun of causality back to the desk of Ronald Reagan. Congressional Democrats clearly wanted to discover an impeachable high crime or misdemeanor that would cripple the Republican presidency and sow the ground for a Democratic victory in the next year's election. I had no knowledge of any action or event that would help them. When I finished my deposition, Ken Ballen told me I had probably been the most honest and forthcoming of any witness he had interviewed. It was only later that I discovered Richard Secord, who gave deposition under subpoena on February 6, 1987, had repeatedly pleaded the Fifth Amendment when asked even relatively innocuous questions.[28]

The Joint Congressional Iran-Contra Select Committees hearings began on May 5, 1987. Richard Secord was the first witness. His testimony was less than forthright. He testified for three days, detailing a skein of private individuals, bank accounts, and front companies he called the "Enterprise" that sold missiles to Iran and supposedly diverted the millions of dollars of proceeds from the profits back to the Contras, all with the aid of his trusty Middle Eastern companion, Albert Hakim. But Secord was elusive about the amount of money actually returned to the Contras. The Congressional committees investigating the Iran-Contra affair found from the Swiss bank accounts that Secord had purchased a Porsche sports car and a personal airplane from the proceeds.[29] He contended that his relationship with Oliver North had been made at the suggestion of CIA director William Casey, who, apparently, had been looking for just such an upright citizen to help Oliver North manage aid to the Contras during the term of the Boland Amendments.

This was a very convenient contention. Bill Casey died the day Richard Secord began his testimony.

☆   ☆

I BEGAN my own testimony on the afternoon of May 20, following that of Adolfo Calero. I was proud of Adolfo. Far from being the toady of the CIA that the left had portrayed him, Adolfo correctly labeled the Agency as "more snoopers than helpers," who had managed the Contra operation inefficiently. He spoke well of Ollie North, but complained of his secretiveness once Secord had been put in charge of the Contra resupply in 1986. Calero was especially bitter about profiteering by arms dealers, like Secord, whom he had been shocked to learn had made profits of 20 to 30 percent on weapons delivered to the Contras. He conceded that he had handed over Contra funds in the form of traveler's checks to Ollie North, who used the money for expenses not related directly to the FDN.[30]

When I was sworn in on the witness stand, I couldn't help noting the intentionally theatrical atmosphere in the Senate Caucus Room, the same room that had been used fourteen years earlier in the Watergate hearings. Congressional aides, of course, had been obliged to enlarge the raised dais to accommodate the Joint Committee, but they managed to keep the same appearance as the Senate Watergate panel. This time, Senator Daniel Inouye was in the middle of the dais.

In my opening remarks, I emphasized that all the funds I raised for the Contras here in the United States had been used for non-lethal humanitarian aid. My decision to help the Contras obtain weapons overseas, I said, had been based on the conditions I personally witnessed in the Contra base camps in March 1985. Our methods of operation had been the subject of a written ruling by the Department of Justice, in which it was concluded that all of my actions were legal.[31] I ended these remarks with an appeal for continuing support for the Nicaraguan Democratic Resistance. Quoting Winston Churchill's comments on his country's lone struggle against the Nazis in 1940, I said the Contras "fight *by* themselves alone, but they do not fight *for* themselves alone."

The questioning was surprisingly even-handed. Obviously the congressmen had been briefed on my deposition and saw there was nothing for me to hide.

☆ ☆

ONE of the most interesting witnesses to appear in the coming weeks was Stanley Sporkin, former general counsel of the CIA. He testified that he had denied Richard Secord a security clearance in 1983, because of a Justice Department investigation of Secord's alleged ties to renegade former CIA officer Edwin P. Wilson.[32] This investigation of Secord never resulted in formal prosecution. Sporkin's testimony was little noticed in the press, but carefully noted by former associates of Bill Casey who had witnessed his outrage at Ollie North's employment of Secord and members of the "Ed Wilson Gang."

Another interesting witness was Albert Hakim. He completely refuted

Richard Secord's testimony that Secord had worked on the operation almost as a "philanthropic" hobby. Hakim detailed the obscene profits the Enterprise had reaped on the arms transactions. Hakim also testified that he had tried to channel a secret payment of $200,000 into a bank account set up for Ollie North's wife, Betsy.

Hakim testified that his Enterprise had grossed almost $48 million in proceeds between December 1984 and December 1986. The Enterprise's profits from the sale to Iran of U.S. missiles, which included the Hawk surface-to-air missile, amounted to just over $18 million, not including such minor items as private airplanes and Porsche sports cars. But only $7.8 million could be accounted for, and was then frozen in Swiss bank accounts. Less than $5 million had actually been "diverted" to the Contras.

The true *diversion* of funds had not been to the hard-pressed Contra troops, fighting for survival in the Nicaraguan mountains, but to Secord's and Hakim's secret Swiss bank accounts. Foreign governments, acting in good faith, had contributed millions of dollars to the Contras, but—contrary to the media's interpretation of the complex affair—much of this money, not just the profits from arms sales to Iran, had never reached the Nicaraguan resistance.[33]

☆　　　☆

THE star witness in this long televised spectacle, of course, was Marine Lieutenant Colonel Oliver North. He was a serving officer and entitled to wear his uniform, complete with his combat decorations. He did so. The televised image of his earnest young face juxtaposed with the multiple rows of decorations was powerful. He exuded patriotism and sincerity. Within a day of his first televised appearance on July 7, 1987, young men across the country were asking their barbers for close-cropped "Ollie North" haircuts.

North testified with apparent sincerity that in 1984, as the Boland Amendments loomed on the horizon, it had been William Casey who "had suggested General Secord to me as a person who had a background in covert operations." According to Ollie, Bill Casey had told him that Secord was a man who "got things done, and had been poorly treated."

Naturally, Bill Casey was not there to challenge that testimony. Later, former CIA official Clair George testified that it was very doubtful Casey had introduced Secord to North. Casey, George said, was aware of Secord's reputation and would not have willingly brought such a person into the Contra supply operation.[34] Throughout his subsequent testimony, Ollie North repeatedly relied on the ghost of William Casey as his moral, tactical, and political compass.

North also testified that it had been Bill Casey—whom I had known for forty years as a strict legalist—who had proposed establishing a "full-service covert operation" that would conduct "off-the-shelf operations" while preserving "plausible deniability" in order to protect the CIA. Again, Bill Casey was not there to refute this charge.

☆   ☆

BUT other senior CIA officers have done so. Clair George's public testimony has been augmented by a confidential interview I had with a former senior CIA executive, who wishes to remain anonymous. I asked this official a series of specific questions about the Casey-Secord-North relationship. He was emphatic that Bill Casey was "very leery" of Secord's previous involvement with Ed Wilson. Casey, the officer told me, had endorsed General Counsel Sporkin's refusal to grant Secord a security clearance that would have given him access to Agency premises. The officer also stated that it was extremely doubtful that Casey would have introduced Secord to North. "Casey would have never personally brought Secord into a secret operation," the officer stated, "and Casey would not have acted on Ollie North's word alone." This was because North had a bad reputation among the senior Agency staff and was known for "going off half-cocked on most occasions."

When asked if Casey would have encouraged North to turn the private Contra support organization into a profit-making commercial concern, the officer stated: "This is absurd." He categorically denied that Casey wanted North to create a "stand-alone" covert action organization, as North had testified. "This is bullshit," the officer answered angrily. "Casey was a lawyer. Before he did anything, he always consulted his legal staff." Such an organization, he added, would have been illegal, and Casey was always conscious of legalities.

I could certainly attest to that because every time I tried to mention Nicaragua during the tenure of the Boland Amendments, Casey had threatened to throw me out of his office. And Bill Casey was not a man to make idle threats.

This former official concluded his interview by stating, "The North-Secord-Casey relationship was grossly exaggerated. . . . [Casey] would never have colluded with the likes of Secord. He listened on occasion to reports from North, in my view, only because North forced himself on the Director and because someone had to keep tabs on what North was up to."[35]

☆   ☆

ON ANOTHER day of testimony, when North was pressed by congressional counsel to explain why he had stopped ordering high-quality, low-cost arms through my channel with Sam and had shifted all the lucrative business to Secord's high-profit Enterprise, he gazed at the television cameras with his most sincere expression and proceeded to stab me in the back. He stated that there had been three possible sources. One was Ron Martin's arms supermarket, which, he said, was tainted by a questionable funding. The second source was my group. Director Casey, Ollie North said, had warned him against conducting another multimillion-dollar transaction with this broker, because the firm "had been involved in reverse technology transfer to the Eastern Bloc, and he [Casey] told me to do everything possible to discourage further purchases."[36]

Watching North's televised testimony that afternoon, I felt as if he had crept up behind me and delivered a sucker punch. "Reverse technology transfer" was a euphemism for espionage. North's slander had probably been a spontaneous lie to cover his own involvement with Secord, but it unjustly tarnished the reputations of several people, including Sam and me. Sam, after all, had worked his contacts in Eastern Europe in order to provide Soviet-bloc military technology to the United States, not the other way around. Ollie North's lie was therefore especially outrageous.

For two years I had been willing to take public scorn and harassment in order to shield individuals like Ollie North who were delivering vital aid to the Contras. Now, North had the audacity to evoke Bill Casey's name to justify his dealings with Secord and Hakim, which, I now suspected and it was later confirmed in North's trial, had involved illegal "gratuities" to North himself.

By this point in the hearings circus, however, Ollie North had so endeared himself with the American people as a sincere young war hero that this slander almost went unchallenged. But in the sensitive world of international commercial military technology, the accusation that a company and its officers had been involved in reverse technology transfer to the Soviet bloc was poisonous. It was analogous to accusing an auditor of embezzlement. Integrity was the most precious attribute a person possessed in this professional arena, and North had just blithely committed character assassination on me and my colleagues in order to protect himself. I was furious, but not actually surprised.

I later learned from a former staffer on the Congressional Select Committee that most of the investigators considered North a consummate liar. As for North's testimony that Bill Casey had warned him against us because of our involvement in reverse technology transfers to the Eastern Bloc, the staffer said Committee investigators had found "absolutely no evidence whatsoever that this was true. In fact, the opposite was true." North, the staff member added, was known to be "perfectly capable of lying on the witness stand in order to bolster his own cause, and was willing to impugn the reputation of others to do so."[37]

☆   ☆

THE hearings finally ended. Congressional investigators had found no smoking gun linking President Reagan or Vice-President Bush with Ollie North and the Secord-Hakim Enterprise.

☆   ☆

IRONICALLY, it was during the bitterest internecine political warfare of the Iran-Contra scandal that President Reagan's support for the United Nicaraguan Opposition paid its biggest dividends. While scores of congressmen, supported by hundreds of publicly funded attorneys and staff members, scrutinized every detail of the aid given the Contras during the period of the Boland Amendments, the Contras themselves were quietly regrouping into an effective combat force.

With renewed American military aid and revitalized CIA training and logistical assistance, the Contras were able to maintain hard-hitting mobile task forces deep inside Nicaragua. The Sandinistas undoubtedly hoped the Iran-Contra scandal would spell the final end to American Contra aid. They were mistaken.

Faced by new military pressure, the Sandinista Directorate reluctantly accepted the Central American peace plan put forward by Costa Rican president Oscar Arias Sanchez. In Guatemala that August, all five Central American presidents signed the Arias Plan, which called for cease-fires in Nicaragua and El Salvador, negotiations between the combatants, the release of political prisoners, and amnesties on both sides in the two countries. The new pressure from the revitalized Contra deep-strike forces was Sandinista president Daniel Ortega's strongest impetus for signing the agreement. But the Sandinistas also hoped to sway the pending congressional vote against renewed fiscal year 1988 Contra funding.

In 1987, when it became obvious that Congress would not support the White House request for $270 million in new Contra aid, the Sandinistas felt they had scored another victory in the predictable Marxist Talk-Fight, Fight-Talk war. Despite the Arias Peace Plan, Comandante Bayardo Arce stated: "There will never, at any time or in any place, be any direct or indirect political dialogue with the counterrevolutionary leadership." And in another rejection of the Guatemala agreement, Sandinista hardliners stubbornly refused to release the more than 5,000 political prisoners held in their jails.

The true intentions of the Sandinista comandantes were revealed in December when Major Roger Miranda, a key subordinate of Defense Minister Humberto Ortega, defected. Miranda carried documents that showed the Soviet Union and Cuba intended to build a Sandinista army of 80,000 regulars, supported by well-armed reserves of 520,000. This force of 600,000 would be in place by 1995 and would be equipped with heavy weapons and jet attack aircraft. Rather than deny Miranda's assertions, Daniel Ortega himself confirmed that the Sandinistas planned to build their forces to 600,000 men, under "agreements with the Soviet Union." This military buildup, he said, would continue, even if relations with the United States were "normalized."[38] In other words, the Sandinistas had given lip service to the agreement simply to again influence Congress and to prevent the Contras from consolidating their growing battlefield advantage.[39]

But the Contras showed they could wage Talk-Fight warfare as well as the Marxists. They used the cease-fire to reinforce their guerrilla enclaves inside Nicaragua. When Ortega staged a publicity blitz in Washington, directly lobbying House Speaker Jim Wright to undercut the new Contra aid plan, Enrique Bermudez and the UNO political leadership decided the Sandinistas needed additional pressure to force them into serious negotiations.

In late December, the UNO Contra forces staged their most effective operation of the seven-year war. For over a month they had been moving troops from southern and central enclaves and the Honduran base camps along the Rio Coco. Over 8,000 combat-hardened Contras massed in the jungle mountains of the Cordillera Isabelia, surrounding the fortified Sandinista gold-mining towns of Siuna, Bonanza, and La Rosita. What made this deployment remarkable was the fact that thousands of Contras from the southern and central region had trekked undetected for almost a month, in formation, carrying their arms and equipment, to join the attack in the northeast. Obviously, they could not have made this march without the full support of the rural population. In the words of Mao, they were, in fact, guerrilla "fish" in an ocean of *campesino* supporters. This fact was not lost on the urban-based Sandinista comandantes.

The Contras struck the week before Christmas. In two days of sharp fighting, they captured all three fortified towns. At Siuna, a thousand Contras routed 750 heavily armed Sandinista regulars, who abandoned artillery and automatic weapons in their flight. The Contras captured a large ordnance supply depot and liberated enough Soviet-made weapons and munitions to supply a thousand troops. They blew up the runway at the Siuna air base and destroyed the Soviet GCI radar site that had threatened their resupply flights. At La Rosita, two battalions of Contras overran a brigade headquarters under a devastating mortar and rocket barrage. They cut all the bridges in the area and destroyed Sandinista bunker complexes guarding the roads.[40]

The weather was bad, with clouds and mist choking the mountain valleys. This effectively grounded the Sandinistas' Hind attack helicopters. Contras firing American Red Eye and Soviet-made SAM-7 anti-aircraft missiles kept Sandinista resupply helicopters and attack planes at bay. But the bad weather also made flying very difficult for the Contras' medevac helicopter. The Lady Ellen, however, did manage to evacuate seriously wounded Contras to field hospitals north of the Rio Coco. When the Contras withdrew to their base camps in the south and in Honduras, their pack mules carried over fifty tons of weapons and food. This was Third Option unconventional warfare at its most devastating.

At the indirect peace talks in the Dominican Republic, the Sandinistas quickly agreed to a new cease-fire, but stubbornly refused the Contra demands for direct, face-to-face negotiations. Congress responded by granting an administration request for stopgap, non-lethal aid for the Contras. This aid, together with the munitions they had captured inside Nicaragua, would keep the Contras a viable fighting force for months.[41]

Under battlefield pressure, the Sandinista comandantes now agreed to meet important terms of the Arias Peace Plan. They announced the pending release of all political prisoners and promised to suspend the six-year state of emergency under which they exercised their harshest totalitarian control. But they still refused direct negotiations with the Contras. Then, when they saw congressional support shifting back to the Contras, the Sandinistas agreed to face-to-face peace talks. But this was more Talk-Fight. With the peace talks under way in Costa Rica, the Sandinistas launched a repeat of their Easter 1986 offensive across the Rio Coco. Several thousand Sandinista regulars attacked the Contra base camps inside Honduras, trying to capture the arms depots where the CIA had stockpiled over 300 tons of supplies, paid for with the last of the fiscal 1987 military aid funding. Again the Contras employed guerrilla tactics effectively to slip away from the Sandinista advance and harass their flanks.

The Reagan administration response was swift. Four battalions of the 82nd Airborne Division parachuted onto a Honduran air base in a "readiness exercise" that sent a clear message to the Sandinistas. The Honduran air force, flying U.S.-supplied F-5 jets, attacked Sandinista positions just inside Nicaragua. The politically clumsy Sandinista invasion aroused Congress, which quickly voted an emergency Contra aid package of $48 million, including several million for new weapons.[42]

Despite the political bloodletting of the Iran-Contra affair, the Sandinistas and their Soviet sponsors had been unable to cripple American foreign policy. Over the coming months, the Sandinistas reluctantly conceded to serious peace talks, which would eventually lead to the first free and open election in Nicaragua's history.

☆   ☆

JUDGE Walsh and his independent counsel staff took over after the congressional hearings. Carl "Spitz" Channell and his associate Richard Miller had already pleaded guilty to felony fraud charges involving tax evasion in the Lavender Bund scam. In March 1988, Bud McFarlane pleaded guilty to four misdemeanor charges that he had withheld information from Congress about Iran-Contra.

The attorneys for Richard Secord, Albert Hakim, and Ollie North sparred with and successfully evaded Judge Walsh's prosecutors during the new election year of 1988.

☆   ☆

IN JUNE 1988, the ludicrous Christic lawsuit finally sputtered to a conclusion. For fifteen months, the Christics had managed to delay revealing their witness list, eventually taking their appeal all the way to the Supreme Court, which rejected it. During this time, my Florida lawyer, Tom Spencer, was unable to depose any of the plaintiffs' witnesses.

But once the list was revealed, the true nature of the Christics' case was exposed. Opening up Sheehan's bag of *evidence* was like turning over a rotten log: The squirmy critters underneath quickly disappeared in the harsh light of day. According to Sheehan, the major accusations linking the defendants to the La Penca bombing came from a *source* known only as "David," who had revealed his story to associates of Avirgan and Honey, and who had then been conveniently murdered. Other sources on the list were now identified by Sheehan as "unknown." As Tom Spencer and his staff of hard-working attorneys went through Sheehan's witness list, one source after another failed to substantiate the wild claims of his explosive affidavit. One of Sheehan's key "Secret Team" witnesses, a former Army warrant officer named Gene Wheaton, who Sheehan falsely claimed had been an intelligence officer—and whom the Christics had paid $20,000 in cash for expenses—failed to provide any substantiation for the major claims about me that Sheehan had attributed to him.[43]

In short, when held up to the rigorous scrutiny of a sworn deposition, those of Daniel Sheehan's witnesses who actually existed in the real world—and not simply in the mystic ectoplasm of his imagination—completely refuted his allegations.[44]

But there were people who obviously resented Spencer's success in putting the federal legal system back on a constitutional track. His Miami law firm began receiving threatening phone calls and poison-pen mail. At one point a scorpion fell out of an envelope his receptionist was opening. Rosie Gonzalez, who handled press relations for his firm, received several death threats, which she managed to shrug off. Then one day a caller claimed to have just kidnapped her young son, who would be killed unless Spencer's firm stopped defending Singlaub. Even though the threat was bogus, she quit her job.

Tom Spencer received most of the death threats. But he was a tough trial lawyer who kept a careful log of these illegal harassments for future action. One afternoon when he was in Washington taking a deposition, his son was called by a "hospital emergency room," which told the young man that Spencer had been shot and critically wounded. This was merely another cruel fabrication.[45]

I was outraged by these tactics, but not surprised. Like followers of Lyndon LaRouche, the mindless disciples of the Christics were perfectly capable of such illegal action in the name of doing mystical battle against the evil Secret Team.[46]

On June 23, 1988, five days before the case would have gone to trial, Judge James Lawrence King issued a summary judgment dismissing the notorious Christic lawsuit against me and the twenty-eight other defendants. Avirgan, Honey, and their Christic attorneys, he said, had completely failed to prove any conspiracy or secret enterprise had ever existed.

Sheehan quickly appealed.

On February 2, 1989, Judge King granted me and several other defendants sanctions against the plaintiffs in the Christic lawsuit amounting to $1,034,381 to cover some of the attorneys fees and expenses we had accrued over thirty-one months of legal terrorism. Since Tom Spencer had led the battle exposing Sheehan's secret list of bogus witnesses and sources, he was awarded almost $300,000 in fees, the highest of any of the defendants' attorneys. In granting our motion for sanctions under Rule 11 of the Federal Code, which prohibits frivolous lawsuits, Judge King noted, "The Christic Institute must have known prior to suing that they had no competent evidence to substantiate the theories alleged in their complaint." He added that the Christics' wild claims of a wide-ranging conspiracy spanning thirty years (the infamous Secret Team nonsense) "were based upon unsubstantiated rumor and speculation from unidentified sources with no first-hand knowledge."[47]

When the Christics tried to appeal this ruling, Judge King quite rightly obliged them to post a bond for 125 percent of the Rule 11 sanctions awarded to us. The Christics went to one of their prime funding areas, the wealthy liberal enclaves of Santa Monica and Bel Air, where the Hollywood left had been active in raising financial support for the original Christic lawsuit. But apparently the leftist glitterati's passion for leftist causes did not extend as far as writing checks for $1.25 million. The Institute found a sugar-daddy in one Aris Anagnos, a Greek-American known to have supported a number of liberal causes. He provided credit for most of the funds required to post the bond while yet another Christic appeal crept ahead, and, of course, Sheehan and his colleagues continued their own fund-raising.[48]

Despite Judge King's firm action, the Christics' legal terrorism continues.

☆   ☆

ON MARCH 1, 1989, I testified for several hours at the federal felony trial of former Marine lieutenant colonel Oliver North. Once more, I repeated the details of our relationship during the frustrating months that the Boland Amendment had been in effect. The prosecutor, David Zornow, asked me about my relationship to William Casey. I looked away from Ollie North when I talked about the exciting, dangerous months in the summer of 1944 when Bill Casey had been my OSS case officer.

Among men who have been in combat together, there are times when you later encounter someone who, through normal human weakness or perhaps basic character flaw, has dishonored himself by showing moral or physical cowardice. At those times, be they social occasions or chance encounters, you always feel uncomfortable, embarrassed for the other man. Ollie, like other cowards, had faced a hard choice and had made his decision. And now he had to live with it.

I certainly had no reason to doubt Ollie North's bravery on the I Corps battlefield in Vietnam. But I felt the familiar embarrassment here at his trial. I had learned too much about his moral courage to ever respect him again.

On May 4, 1989, Ollie North was convicted of destroying federal documents, accepting illegal gratuities, and obstructing Congress. Judge Gesell sentenced him to a suspended prison term and a fine of $150,000. Ollie North began his appeal.

Epilogue:
After-Action Report

1990

☆   ☆

I LEAVE THE general officers' guest quarters at Fort Myer's Wainwright Hall on a cool fall morning and stroll through the falling maple leaves of Arlington National Cemetery. I often come here to think before the start of another hectic day chasing telephone and fax messages around the planet. The cemetery is so large that I can usually find a new path among the rows of white headstones.

The green hills and mature hardwoods of Arlington mute the drone of the nearby parkway and the growl of jets from National Airport. Among the old soldiers of this troubled century's wars, I find a peace and harmony lacking in the city. Here I can reflect on the battles of my own life.

☆   ☆

I ATTENDED the annual conference of the World Anti-Communist League in Brussels during the fiftieth anniversary of the Nazi occupation in July. For more than half a century, Western Europe had been threatened by totalitarian enemies, first Nazi Germany, then the Soviet Union. But there is now reason to hope that Soviet totalitarianism is mortally wounded and in retreat.

The world has changed more in the previous twelve months than in the past five decades. Fifty years after Hitler's armies swept through Belgium, the captive nations of Eastern Europe are struggling to throw off the yoke of the Communist dictatorships. In the Soviet Union, the Communist Party faces the first true challenge to its autocratic power. The centralized Soviet economy is in ruins, and the old ruling triumvirate of Party, KGB, and Red Army is scrambling to retrench.

A year ago Communist China brutally crushed a massive popular revolt against repression, nepotism, and corruption, but, in so doing, the absolute authority of the Party has been shattered. Communist surrogate forces worldwide have suffered defeats. In Nicaragua, UNO's landslide election victory swept the Sandinistas from formal power, although they quickly regrouped.

The news media and government leaders worldwide announced the "end of the Cold War."

In view of these cataclysmic changes, General Bob Close and I were pleased to see corresponding changes within the League. We had long advocated reorganizing and renaming the organization to reflect a more positive, activist role. At the Brussels conference, WACL officially became the World League for Freedom and Democracy. This new title eliminated any negative, obstructionist image, and enhanced the League's endorsement of worldwide democratic values and free economies.

Following the conference, I visited my daughter Elisabeth and her family in West Germany where she teaches. The mood in Germany is an odd mixture of elation, apprehension, and somber reflection. East Germany has to confront the realities of its totalitarian past.

The truth has emerged after forty-five years of silence. Independent investigators have revealed that the Soviet occupation forces made ample use of the Nazi infrastructure. The Soviet NKVD (predecessor of the KGB) took over the infamous Nazi concentration camps such as Buchenwald and Sachsenhausen. Almost half a century after the 1945 "Liberation" by the Red Army, East Germans are digging up secret mass graves around the Soviet-run Nazi camps where as many as 50,000 political opponents of the new regime were buried. These included thousands of Social Democrats who had survived the Nazi years and had refused to join the new German Communist Party.[1]

And as similar investigations are conducted in Poland, Czechoslovakia, Hungary, and Romania, similar secret graveyards—the true *memorials* to Communist liberation—are discovered. For decades, anti-Communists in the West had denounced the Soviet enslavement of Eastern Europe as a genocide rivaling that of the Nazis. But Western liberals ridiculed us. In the summer of 1990, the ghosts of 1945 can finally speak. At ceremonies consecrating one Stalinist graveyard, Cardinal Jozef Glemp, Roman Catholic Primate of Poland, noted that the postwar liberation by the Communists had been a time of "terrifying evil that raged, unmindful of any violation of morality, capable of the utmost contempt of humanity."[2]

☆   ☆

IN THE Soviet Union itself, the process of political disintegration and retrenchment continues. One after another, Soviet republics have announced their sovereignty from the centralized Soviet government. And Boris Yeltsin, the leading anti-Gorbachev political figure, became the president of the Russian Republic after renouncing his Communist Party membership.

As the Soviet Union's Warsaw Pact allies freed themselves from Communism, Soviet president Gorbachev announced a new, "defensive" Soviet military posture. Soviet forces, he said, would be cut by hundreds of thousands of troops, and some defense industries would be shifted to the consumer economy. This was seemingly Perestroika taken to its most extreme. From all appearances, the Soviet Union was no longer a totalitarian state that sponsored destabilizing global wars of national liberation.

This is certainly the image put forward by the Soviet government. But what are the realities? In January 1990, high-level active and former American and Soviet military officials and academics met near Moscow to discuss "The Changing U.S.-Soviet Strategic Balance." The conference was sponsored by the Soviet Academy of Sciences and the Washington-based International Security Council. The Soviet delegation made an impressive presentation. They acknowledged past Soviet "errors," which might have seemed "provocative." (I imagine they had in mind such minor irritants as the bloody suppression of liberty in Eastern Europe and the invasion of Afghanistan.) But the Soviets stressed their military posture had been changed by "new thinking." Offensive formations based in Eastern Europe, such as the Red Army's powerful Operational Maneuver Groups, as well as multiple airborne divisions and huge Spetsnaz special-forces units, would all be removed to within the boundaries of the Soviet Union. This, they said, was clear proof that the massive Soviet military was only intended for defensive purposes. If more proof were needed, the Soviets offered a list of twenty-two new major military doctrine manuals that had been rewritten along defensive lines. This evidence of new military thinking, the Soviet delegation emphasized, was presented with complete frankness and candor, more tangible proof of Glasnost.

Therefore, Western prohibitions on high-technology exports to the Soviet Union, the Russian delegates stressed, were outmoded Cold War relics.

But the candor suddenly stopped when the American delegation began asking hard questions. Highly publicized troop withdrawals from Hungary and East Germany had nothing to do with political changes in Eastern

Europe, the Russian delegates insisted. And the Soviets refused to discuss continued arms transfers to Afghanistan, Angola, and Cuba. Mi-17 troop-carrying helicopters then being unloaded in Nicaraguan ports, they claimed, were for "agricultural" purposes. They denied outright that the Soviet Union was pursuing military space programs and a ballistic missile defense system similar to America's Strategic Defense Initiative. And Soviet delegates insisted that the huge anti-missile radar complex at Krasnoyarsk was actually a civilian space research project. Apparently these delegates had not been informed that their own government had already acknowledged that the Krasnoyarsk radar was a violation of the anti-ballistic missile treaty and would be dismantled. When probed on this, the Soviet delegation retreated behind the familiar Cold War stonewall.[3]

Predictably, the Western news media were hesitant to challenge the image of the new, peaceful Soviet Union that it had helped create. But historian Edward Jay Epstein offers one of the most cogent interpretations of this ongoing Soviet duplicity in his recent book, *Deception: The Invisible War between the KGB and the CIA*. Epstein traces the erratic progress of Glasnost from its earliest manifestations soon after the Bolshevik Revolution. There have been at least six "openness" campaigns since 1921, he notes, and all were consciously directed policy, not spontaneous political or social phenomena.[4]

The Soviet leaders, Epstein reveals, have always resorted to Glasnost-type bridges to the West—beginning with Lenin's New Economic Policy—when driven by overriding economic or military need.

The pattern has continued through various détentes up to the present day. Whenever the Soviet Union had desperate needs that could only be met in the West, the Soviet totalitarian state became miraculously "Western." When these needs were met, the Soviet government reverted to repression. But is this historic pattern still valid, or has the country undergone such sweeping changes that it can never return to totalitarian rule? The answer lies in the actual nature of the changes.

Although a new Congress of People's Deputies parliament has been seated, control of the economy, the military, and the infamous "Organs of State Security" (KGB and GRU) still rests with the *nomenklatura* elite of the Communist Party. And senior KGB officers, who have resigned in disgust, reveal that their former organization has no intention of relinquishing its grip on Soviet society.[5]

As Epstein correctly indicates, international adulation for Gorbachev's Glasnost is "all the more impressive because the underlying control structure of the Soviet Union has not substantially changed."[6] Major Soviet news media remain a state enterprise. Private publications depend on the state for paper, printing equipment, and renewable permits. Free labor unions have not yet been authorized. The internal passport, a relic of Stalinist totalitarian control, is still a burden imposed on all Soviet citizens. The list goes on.

When specially trained Soviet Interior Ministry troops (the spiritual mentors of Nicaragua's MINT forces) massacred dozens of men, women, and children in Tbilisi, Georgia, in April 1989, Gorbachev promised a thorough investigation. The initial inquiry confirmed what Radio Liberty had broadcast the day after the massacre: Soviet troops had used poison gas and sharpened engineers' shovels to slaughter the unarmed citizens, who were peacefully demanding greater autonomy from Moscow. Eighteen months after the massacre, no Soviet official has been charged.

☆   ☆

GIVEN this picture of Glasnost and Perestroika in the Soviet Union, the obvious question emerges as to how far we should lower our national defenses now that the Cold War is "over." As a professional soldier for more than thirty-five years, I had to deal with the world as it really was, not as I wished it to be. I follow those same principles today. I think that we can reduce our defenses commensurate with those of our potential enemies— which include the Soviet Union and its surrogates, Communist China, and highly armed dictatorships such as Iraq, Iran, and North Korea—no more, no less.

And to date, according to the Defense Intelligence Agency, the Soviet Union has only modernized, not actually reduced, its armed forces. Despite a near-bankrupt economy, the Soviet Union still produces hundreds of high-technology fighters like the MiG-29 and Su-27 (superior to many in the Western arsenal) each year. Their T-80 battle tank assemblyline recently increased production, even as Western television networks broadcast the withdrawal of obsolete T-64s from Hungary. The production lines for advanced ICBMs are still open. All across the board, the Soviet military is cutting flab and sharpening its technological edge. If anything, the proportion of the Soviet gross national product taken up by the military has increased, not decreased, since Gorbachev's Glasnost and Perestroika. This is hardly an indication of an enfeebled state.[7]

Soviet support for surrogate Communist nations in the Third World has remained steady. More than a year after the pullout of uniformed Soviet forces from Afghanistan, the Soviets continue to prop up their surrogate government in Kabul with hundreds of millions of dollars of military aid each month. Soviet military support of the Marxist government in Angola continues unabated. Although the Soviet economic crutch under Castro's Communist dictatorship in Cuba has grown weak, the Soviet Union still pumps military matériel and personnel into Cuba.

In turn, the Cubans continue to aid Marxist rebels in Latin America, particularly the FMLN in El Salvador. This support has become so blatant that the *Washington Post,* which has long turned a blind eye to Soviet-sponsored Cuban subversion in Central America, recently warned in an editorial against the continued aid. The *Post* predicted a new Communist offensive just as peace negotiations have a chance at success. This offensive, the *Post* says, will involve "new troops trained in Cuba and the deployment of the Cuban-provided surface-to-air missiles," which the Sandinistas shipped into El Salvador during the last guerrilla offensive in November 1989. The editorial ended with a plea to Congress not to abandon the democratically elected Salvadoran government.[8] The erosion of traditional American support that the FMLN previously enjoyed coincides with revelations by the liberal human rights group Americas Watch that the Marxist guerrillas have engaged in summary executions of captured civilian opponents.[9]

There was little need for the Soviets and Cubans to continue massive overt aid to Nicaragua. According to Enrique Bermudez and to Adolfo Calero (who has just returned from Managua), the situation there is bleak. Despite the landslide victory of the anti-Communist UNO candidate Violeta Chamorro in February 1990, the Sandinistas have stubbornly refused to relinquish real power. And their stockpile of military matériel is massive.

Before the election, I was frustrated by the attitude of the Bush administration. When I contacted people in the White House about their plans for assistance to the UNO government, it was obvious they anticipated a Sandinista victory. They weren't alone. All the smart money in the liberal think tanks inside the Beltway was betting on Ortega and the Sandinistas. But I knew from Contra soldiers that their fellow *campesinos* would vote out the Sandinista comandantes, given a free election.

Obviously, the Ortega brothers, Tomas Borge, and their comrades had similar fears. They began consolidating power through a series of secret decrees even before the February vote. The Sandinistas proceeded to steal through edict what they soon lost at the polling place. In December 1989, President Daniel Ortega had secretly passed a sweeping decree: the "Law of Military Organization of the Sandinista People's Army." This stripped the defense minister of power and gave the army commander—his brother, General Humberto Ortega—virtual dictatorial control over all aspects of the Nicaraguan military. Then, after the election, the comandantes went further by transferring the powers of Tomas Borge's hated Interior Ministry to the army. With this combined internal and external security establishment firmly in the hands of the Sandinistas and their Cuban advisers, they retain de facto control of Nicaragua, despite the titular authority of Violeta Chamorro's government.[10]

Even more ominous, the Contra forces that have returned to Nicaragua under the terms of the Arias Peace Plan have been completely disarmed, leaving the hard-core Sandinista military and their brutal Ministry of Interior forces the only armed group in the country. Cruelly repressive members of the Sandinista secret police, such as Lenin Cerna, the Cuban-trained son of a Communist activist, have simply moved their offices from the Interior Ministry to heavily armed Sandinista army camps. This has created a bizarre situation. For example, the Chamorro government's new education minister, Sofonias Cisneros, recently encountered Cerna at an official reception and recognized the former MINT officer as the man who had tortured him for protesting Communist orientation of the schools under the Sandinistas. Cerna laughed in his face.[11] Given this situation, it is doubtful that the widespread massacres of Miskito Indians or the murders of thousands of anti-Sandinista draft resisters will soon be investigated and those responsible brought to justice.[12]

A tragic example of this continuing Sandinista power was the assassination of Enrique Bermudez. On February 18, 1991, the former Contra military commander was lured to the Intercontinental Hotel in Managua by a spurious telephone call. He was shot and killed in the hotel parking lot. Because the Sandinistas still control Nicaragua's security forces and courts, it is unlikely that Enrique Bermudez's killers will ever be found.

As the Soviet Union maneuvers along the track of Glasnost and Perestroika in order to accrue needed Western financial support and high technology, Communist regimes in Asia have simply stood fast. I was amazed at the shock and outrage expressed by so many American liberals when the People's Army tanks rolled over the unarmed demonstrators in Tiananmen Square. And these same liberals voiced disbelief when it was revealed that the troops who had brutally suppressed the pro-democracy movement were personally loyal to a corrupt warlord, Marshal Yang Shang-kun. I explained to those who would listen that the Chinese Communist leaders were just being good Chinese Communists; like all despots, they jealously guarded their power and cruelly eliminated anyone who challenged it. These were the agrarian reformers America had backed to replace Chiang Kai-shek's "corrupt" generals.[13]

To guarantee the unquestioning obedience of young people in the future, the Politburo in Peking has introduced a mandatory year of military indoctrination prior to the commencement of university study. But this may well boomerang. As one university student put it, the year was not a complete waste; at least he and his friends had learned how to handle weapons.

On the Korean peninsula, the four-decade stalemate continues. South Korea has become a world economic power. Democracy is progressing slowly, with South Korean president Roh Tae-Woo gradually relaxing control as the military threat from the North seems to diminish. But the Communist dictator of North Korea, Kim Il-Sung, remains unpredictable. He has placed a full 5 percent of his population under arms. The North Korean military now numbers more than a million troops on active duty, making it the world's fourth largest army.[14] And Western intelligence and diplomatic experts predict that this military establishment will seize power as soon as the elder Kim dies and passes on the Party chairmanship to his son Kim Jong-Il in what has been called the Communist world's "first dynastic succession."[15]

American combat troops remain on duty below the DMZ thirteen years after President Carter unwisely attempted to remove them. They are still the trip-wire deterrent to Communist aggression. Recently, yet another North Korean tunnel was discovered beneath the DMZ, a reminder that the Korean peninsula is still a potential flashpoint in the continuing East-West confrontation.[16]

In Indochina, the Communist governments brought into power by the North Vietnamese victory remain steadfastly doctrinaire. Although there are ripples of home-grown Glasnost and Perestroika in Ho Chi Minh City (formerly Saigon), the rest of the territory controlled by the North Vietnamese appears almost Stalinist. With an army of over 2 million regulars and reservists, Vietnam is nearly as much a militarized society as North Korea. A steady flow of boat people refugees continues.[17]

Meanwhile, in the Philippines, the Communist New People's Army makes steady strides, while Cory Aquino's government is undercut by nepotism and corruption.[18]

From the Asian perspective, the Cold War is hardly over, and the West certainly has not "won" the struggle.

☆   ☆

As I travel in Asia and Europe and discuss these developments with colleagues and former comrades-in-arms, they often ask me to predict America's future policies in this realigned but still dangerous world. This is a difficult question to answer. Our leadership of the West through four decades of the containment policy, including eight years of the Reagan Doctrine, is widely recognized as the decisive factor in the rollback of communism. But I am worried about our continued resolve.

I am convinced that the Reagan Doctrine of matching the Soviet military buildup of the past twenty years, while exercising the Third Option of supporting anti-Communist resistance movements, blunted the most dangerous Soviet challenge since the Vietnam War. Equally important, the Reagan administration's decision to initiate the Strategic Defense Initiative research program that retired Lieutenant General Daniel Graham long advocated made it clear to the Soviet military that they could never successfully intimidate the West through the nuclear blackmail of their modernized strategic missile arsenal.

Through great expense and sacrifice, we forced the Soviet dictatorship to retreat from military conquest. But I wonder if we will have the stamina to continue during this dangerous period of Glasnost and Perestroika, during which the Soviet Union is regrouping. I don't know the answer. I do know that Congress is already abandoning support for the successful Third Option resistance to Soviet surrogates in Angola and Afghanistan. Over 40,000 Cuban troops remain in Angola, yet it is likely that Congress, prodded by leftists like Berkeley's Ron Dellums, will cut funding to Jonas Savimbi's UNITA resistance. Although the Soviet Union continues to provide major military aid to the Marxist Afghan government, Congress is likely to stop support to the anti-Communist Mujaheddin.[19]

But at least the political bloodletting of Iran-Contra has finally ended in a predictable anticlimax. Only weeks after Admiral John Poindexter, the last major criminal defendant prosecuted by Judge Walsh, was convicted of obstructing Congress, Ollie North won his first appeal, reversing a major count of his 1989 conviction. The successful appeal process might well continue for each defendant. In the end, they will probably all be legally, if not ethically, exonerated.[20] In my opinion, Admiral Poindexter was the least guilty of those prosecuted; he simply relinquished too much power to Ollie North.

But Poindexter certainly never received illegal "gratuities" from Secord or Hakim, as Ollie North was convicted of having done. A former Congressional investigation committee attorney has told me that, in his opinion, North was probably never prosecuted for what were probably his most serious offenses: allowing Secord and Hakim to gain leverage over him through financial favors. Certainly North's congressional and criminal trial testimony that he bought his daughter an $8,000 horse and managed to buy a van with small change the family dropped in a closet piggy bank did not ring true with my former congressional counsel source.[21] And I can attest that this testimony rang false with me, too.

Maybe not one red cent of the millions in "diverted" funds for the Contras ever stuck to Ollie North's fingers. All I know for certain is that while today the disarmed Contras struggle to survive under the Sandinista's shadow government, Ollie North is reportedly earning both his Marine Corps pension and substantial fees as a public speaker. And apparently only Secord and Hakim know the whereabouts of several million dollars of Iran-Contra profits that were never diverted to the Nicaraguan resistance, but which seem to have disappeared into the labyrinth of Swiss bank accounts.[22]

One of the saddest legacies of the Iran-Contra affair is Bill Casey's tarnished reputation. Casey always wished to be remembered as the patriot he was.

☆   ☆

DESPITE the harassment and financial battering of the past decade, there is much I can take pride in. I was able to help guide the Reagan administration in the modernization of America's military forces and the restructuring of our war-fighting doctrine. These were among the finest achievements of Reagan's presidency. I am especially pleased that our unconventional-warfare units and Airborne were given the support they deserved. The success of our military intervention in Panama, during which the Noriega dictatorship was finally toppled with minimum military and civilian casualties, is a tribute to this modernization.

And the rapid deployment of American forces to Saudi Arabia in response to the Iraqi invasion of Kuwait is another achievement Americans can take pride in. President Bush, Defense Secretary Dick Cheney, and JCS chairman General Colin Powell acted with decisiveness. The reserves were mobilized and terms of service were extended for the duration of the emergency. Unlike our faltering deployment to Vietnam in 1965, Operation Desert Shield was a clear demonstration of power that certainly got the attention of the Iraqi dictator, Saddam Hussein. And I consider for a moment how the West would have reacted to such aggression ten years earlier, during the "malaise" of the Carter administration. Then we did not have the troops, the tactical and naval air power, the air and sea lift, and certainly not the national resolve for such action.

☆   ☆

WALKING among the graves, I read the pitted headstone of a young sergeant who fell with Colonel Wild Bill Donovan's 69th Infantry during the Meuse-Argonne offensive of 1918. Nearby is the grave of a twenty-year-old private who died on D-Day 1944, fighting with the 1st Infantry Division on Omaha Beach. There are many graves from Korea, marking the three years of bloody combat on all those steep, shell-scarred ridges. The young men who went to Vietnam lie among their fathers and older brothers. Off to the left, I even find the gleaming new limestone grave marker of a young 82nd Airborne trooper named Manrique-Lozano who was killed in Panama.

I look around the hills of Arlington, hoping I won't see more new headstones here next year marking the graves of the dead from the Persian Gulf. But the young Americans facing their own hazardous duty in the Arabian desert are following a long tradition of sacrifice. Perhaps these graves are the inevitable price we pay for our free and prosperous society.

As a soldier, I will continue to take pride that America is willing to defend the West's principles in the face of militaristic aggression, just as we did five decades ago.

Sitting down on the hillside in the morning sun, I feel a familiar coolness on my chest. I reach down and untangle my Army dog tags. In 1985, when I began to travel the dangerous roads of Central America with the Contras, I decided that I had, in fact, returned to war and that if I were ambushed or my vehicle struck a mine, I'd better put my dog tags back on. That would be one way to at least identify my body. Then I understood that the gesture was also symbolic of my commitment. Once I put those worn old steel tags back around my neck, I decided to keep them on until the war was over.

I am still wearing them today.

Notes

☆   ☆

1 • OSS: The Jedburghs

1. For a colorful and informative account of OSS training in the United States, see William B. Dreux, *No Bridges Blown* (Notre Dame, IN: University of Notre Dame Press, 1971), Chap. 2, "The Congressional Country Club and Raleigh Manhattans," pp. 11–19. Bill Dreux was a good friend and a brave soldier. His laconic wit helped ease the strain of many tense months of training before our eventual combat deployment.

2. In reconstructing official briefings, orders, and training instructions, the authors have relied on both documentary sources and the personal recollections of the participants. It is important to note that OSS Special Operations officers were selected in part for their good memories, and during their exhaustive training before combat they were encouraged to hone their memories to sharp-edged precision. These officers were obliged to memorize detailed tactical information on field exercises, without the benefit of written notes, then to transmit this information in encrypted form. Therefore, it is not surprising that many former OSS officers have retained detailed recollections of events during this exciting period, which they generously shared with the authors.

3. Anthony Cave Brown, *The Last Hero* (New York: Times Books, 1982), p. 236.

4. William Colby and Peter Forbath, *Honorable Men: My Life in the CIA* (New York: Simon & Schuster, 1978), pp. 36–37. It is interesting to note that my Jedburgh colleague Bill Colby was one of the best young American officers at "living" a cover story. He later went on to become director of the Central Intelligence Agency.

5. Captain Coombe-Tennant also had a colorful postwar career. He served with the Welsh Guards in Palestine, joined the British Foreign Service, and finally became a Benedictine monk. As Dom Joseph, he died at Downside Abbey in November 1989, at the age of seventy-six.

2 • Team James

1. M. R. D. Foot, *SOE in France: An Account of the Work of the British Special Operations Executive in France, 1940–1944* (London: Her Majesty's Stationery Office, 1966), pp. 32–35. Like many successful SOE officers, Flight Lieutenant André Simon had lived in France before the war and spoke fluent French.

2. It is interesting to note that my team's area of operations was not far from the famous limestone caves near Lascaux, where Cro-Magnon Man decorated cave walls with the famous, evocative paintings of hunting scenes.

3. Unlike regular British or American Army units, the Jedburghs tried to follow Free French military procedures and use French nomenclatures. We were encouraged in this by General Donovan himself, who was a renowned francophile. My former colleague Colonel Aaron Bank details these aspects of Jedburgh procedures in his excellent book *From OSS to Green Berets: The Birth of Special Forces* (Novato, CA: Presidio, 1986).

4. The widespread use of supply airdrops to OSS-sponsored guerrillas in World War II has an interesting origin. On the last day of World War I, November 11, 1918, Colonel William Donovan, who was recuperating from his wounds, witnessed an experimental airdrop of men and equipment at Orly field in Paris. Donovan had fought nonstop in the trenches for almost nine months; he immediately saw the potential of the airplane and parachute as a means to leapfrog standard defenses and penetrate deep into enemy territory. See Anthony Cave Brown, *The Last Hero: Wild Bill Donovan* (New York: Times Books, 1983), p. 164.

5. For an excellent account of the FTP–Armée Secrète rivalry in the Corrèze see Max Hastings, *Das Reich: The March of the 2nd SS Panzer Division through France* (New York: Holt, Rinehart and Winston, 1981), pp. 28–31.

6. For a more complete description of the massacres at Tulle and Oradour-sur-Glane, see the Office of Strategic Services' Directors' Cables (OSSDC), National Archives, Washington, DC. Telegraphic field report from Allen Dulles, Bern, Switzerland, to General William Donovan, OSS Headquarters, Washington, DC, July 5, 1944. The best history of these massacres is Max Hastings's *Das Reich: The March of the 2nd SS Panzer Division through France,* Chap. 9, " '. . . A Rapid and Lasting Clean-up . . .': Oradour," pp. 161–79.

7. For further information, see William J. Casey, *The Secret War Against Hitler* (New York: Berkley Books, 1988), pp. 181–82. The delicate issue of trying to reconcile the Gaullist and Communist resistance units under Jedburgh leadership is treated in *A War Diary, SO Branch, OSS London,* Vol. 9, *Training,* declassified August 9, 1984, National Archives, Washington, DC, pp. 15–18.

8. Letter, Jacques Le Bel de Penguilly to John K. Singlaub, January 14, 1990, p. 7. Jacques has preserved his war diary, which proved to be an excellent resource in reconstructing the events of this often chaotic battle.

9. A total of twenty-one Jedburgh officers and men were killed during the summer and fall of 1944, making the units' casualties proportionally similar to those of frontline infantry companies. In my opinion, the best published account of the Jedburgh campaign is Bill Dreux's *No Bridges Blown.* Dreux has written a gripping and vivid account of our selection and training, and has brought alive

many of the colorful characters attracted to this unique organization. His account of his own team's battles in Brittany is one of the most vivid combat memoirs of the Second World War.

3 · OSS China

1. An excellent source on these political/military intrigues is R. Harris Smith, *OSS: The Secret History of America's First Central Intelligence Agency* (Berkeley, CA: University of California Press, 1972). For a more personal account from the field soldier's perspective, see Aaron Bank, *From OSS to Green Berets: The Birth of Special Forces* (Novato, CA: Presidio, 1986).
2. Letter from William McAfee to John K. Singlaub, January 23, 1990, p. 1.
3. OSS support for Ho's guerrillas became the source of much misinformation over the intervening decades since World War II. For the clearest historical interpretation of this period see Ronald H. Spector, *United States Army in Vietnam, Advice and Support: The Early Years, 1941–1960* (Washington, DC: Center of Military History, United States Army, 1983), Vol. 1, Chap. 3, "From the Japanese Coup to V-J Day," pp. 37–43.
4. Office of Strategic Services, China Theater, Secret Field Memorandum, October 4, 1945; subject: Prisoner of War Humanitarian Teams. National Archives, Washington, DC, declassified December 18, 1989.
5. See William Craig, *The Fall of Japan* (New York: The Dial Press, 1967), pp. 141–43, 284.
6. Mission Dove was a six-man team sent to Mukden, Manchuria, to liberate the large POW camp there. One of the members, Staff Sergeant Hal Leith, later served with me in the CIA in Manchuria. His team liberated a number of Allied general officers, including Lieutenant General Jonathan Wainwright, former American commander in the Philippines. Letter from H. B. Leith to John K. Singlaub, April 9, 1990, p. 4.
7. Ralph Yempuku's courageous sangfroid during this operation earned him several well-deserved decorations, and the praise of the Australian Department of the Army; see letter from Commonwealth of Australia, Department of the Army, to Captain Ralph Yempuku, January 3, 1946, Strategic Services Unit Records, National Archives, Washington, DC.
8. For a detailed, gripping account of the deprivations suffered by the Allied POWs on Hainan see Courtney T. Harrison, *Ambon, Island of Mist, 2/21st Battalion AIF (Gull Force), Prisoners of War, 1941–45* (North Geelong, Australia: T. W. and C. T. Harrison, 1988), Chap. 8, pp. 186–259.
9. Ibid., p. 229.
10. Letter from James McGuire to John K. Singlaub, December 4, 1989, p. 2. Also, letter from Benjamin T. Muller to John K. Singlaub, January 2, 1990, p. 3. I am especially grateful to former captain Merritt Lawlis, now a professor at the University of Indiana, for sharing with me his vivid memoir of captivity on Hainan: "POW," an unpublished manuscript.
11. For a detailed account of the captivity of these men see Lawrence J. Hickey, *Warpath across the Pacific: The Illustrated History of the 345th Bombardment*

Group during World War II, 2nd ed., rev. (Boulder, CO: International Research and Publishing Corp., 1982), pp. 289–300.

12. These atrocities were carefully documented by Lieutenant John Bradley, and appear in his mission diary, which he generously shared with me: memorandum from John Bradley to John Singlaub, December 27, 1989, author's archives. Also see Harrison, *Ambon, Island of Mist,* pp. 240–41.

13. See the memorandum "Report on OSS Team on Hainan Island" to Colonel Paul L. E. Helliwell, Chief, Intelligence Division, from Captain John K. Singlaub, Commander, Mission Pigeon, October 6, 1945; also see Mission Pigeon Report, Strategic Services Unit Records, National Archives, Washington, DC. Colonel Andrus's objectional behavior was detailed at the time by First Lieutenant John Bradley, whose handwritten mission log is available through the author's personal archives.

4 • CIA Manchuria

1. Letter from E. Howard Hunt to John K. Singlaub, February 12, 1990, p. 3.

2. Whenever possible, throughout the text, Chinese proper nouns will be rendered in the Wade-Giles romanization system, which was the most widely accepted during the period in question.

3. See "Seven High Chinese Officials Protest to Foreign Office Against Crimea Agreement; Ask Foreign Office to Hold Decision Affecting China and Made Without China's Approval Not Binding," *New York Times,* February 24, 1946, pp. 1, 2, 24.

4. For an interesting and informative firsthand view of the Marshall mission to China see Albert C. Wedemeyer, *Wedemeyer Reports!* (New York: Devin-Adair Company, 1958), pp. 362–99.

5. The term "officer" is correctly applied to both civilian and military personnel serving in executive capacities in intelligence organizations. The misnomer "agent" should never be given such a person; agents are generally foreign nationals serving under the "control" of intelligence officers, often in "networks." Unfortunately, since World War II, the popular media have dulled the distinction, often referring to CIA officers as American "agents."

6. "Transport Difficulties Continue to Delay USSR Evacuation," *New York Times,* January 30, 1946, p. 4.

7. Chiang Kai-shek, *Soviet Russia in China: A Summing Up at Seventy,* trans. by Madame Chiang Kai-shek (Taipei, Republic of China: China Publishing Co., 1969), p. 151.

8. For a reasonably accurate description of this tense period see O. Edmund Clubb, *20th Century China* (New York: Columbia University Press, 1964), pp. 260–67. Ed Clubb was American consul general in Mukden when I served there. Although we differed sharply in our assessments of the Nationalists and Communists, Clubb's book is a valuable contribution to modern Chinese history.

9. When we observed the Soviet military trains leaving southern Manchuria, we were amazed to see flatcars carrying armor and artillery as well as beds, overstuffed furniture, armoires, dressers, and mirrors looted from the homes of

Japanese civilians. The Red Army presented a strange spectacle: a hybrid of Blitzkrieg and gypsy caravan. Over the years of my Army career, I often invoked that spectacle when the units I commanded appeared less than military: "You look like the Soviets withdrawing from Manchuria," I'd always say.

10. An American war reparations team led by President Truman's personal representative, Ambassador Edwin Pauley, toured Manchuria. His classified "Pauley Report" summarized the Russian looting: "The methods employed by the Soviets in their removals were essentially the same in all areas. The Soviets were apparently following a plan which called for the removals to start in early September and to be completed by 3 December 1945, the date first set for the withdrawal of Soviet forces from Manchuria. In many instances specially trained Soviet engineering officers were in charge while in others the local military commander directed the removals. In each locality the Japanese head of the industrial installation was called by the Soviet Command and directed to furnish detailed plans of the plant. The equipment to be removed was then designated and the Japanese were ordered to dismantle and load the equipment within a given time. Chinese and Japanese labor, including prisoners of war, was used under overall Soviet direction. . . . After the removals the Soviet forces permitted and even encouraged Chinese mobs to pillage. In the process thousands of buildings and homes were destroyed. Motion pictures of the pillaging mobs in action were taken by the Soviets." These films were part of a propaganda campaign designed to lay blame for all the looting in Manchuria on spontaneous anti-Japanese mobs. See "Report on Japanese Assets in Manchuria to the President of the United States," 2 volumes, the report of the U.S. government reparations team led by Edwin W. Pauley, U.S. ambassador and personal representative of the President on reparations (hereafter: "Pauley Report"), July 1946. This passage is from pp. 23–26.

11. Library of Congress Reference Service: Research Query Response, February 27, 1990.

12. For an informed and lively discussion of these diplomats' attitudes see Wedemeyer, *Wedemeyer Reports!*, Chap. 21, pp. 302–20. Summarizing the Foreign Service position, Wedemeyer states, "Their sympathy for the Chinese Communists is obvious in their reports and in their recommendations that we back the Communists instead of the Nationalist Government. . . . It seems obvious not only that their sympathies lay with the Chinese Communists, but also that they were either consciously or unwittingly disseminating exaggerated or false, Communist-inspired, reports concerning the Nationalist Government designed to stir up all manner of Sino-American distrust" (pp. 312–13).

13. The fact that the Communists' New Democracy system in the liberated areas was a sham apparently never occurred to these diplomats. But as British historian Henry McAleavy has noted about this system: "The Communists ensured that one-third of the people elected at any level should be members of the Party, and that this third should have complete direction of affairs." See Henry McAleavy, *The Modern History of China* (New York: Frederick A. Praeger, 1967), pp. 317–18.

14. Wedemeyer, *Wedemeyer Reports!*, p. 315.

15. "Pauley Report," p. 12, p. 35.
16. The Central Intelligence Group became the Central Intelligence Agency in September 1947. All of us serving in CIG field assignments were automatically assigned to the CIA.
17. Letter from Fitzhugh H. Chandler to John K. Singlaub, June 18, 1990, pp. 5–6.
18. *New York Times*, June 22, 1946, p. 2; June 23, 1946, p. 1.
19. *New York Times*, May 13, 1946, p. 1.
20. Wedemeyer, *Wedemeyer Reports!*, p. 363.
21. *New York Times*, February 7, 1947, p. 11.
22. Letter from John W. Collins III to John K. Singlaub, February 12, 1990; enclosure: "Preliminary Report by Captain John W. Collins III: Capture and Detention of Rigg and Collins," May 3, 1947, pp. 1–26.
23. See John King Fairbank, *The Great Chinese Revolution: 1800–1985* (New York: Harper & Row, 1986), pp. 265–66. Historian Fairbank notes that recent research indicates Lin Piao shifted back to guerrilla tactics in mid-1947 and concentrated "with feverish energy" on converting the rural population in government-held regions to the Communist cause. To accomplish this, Fairbank states, the Communists employed the techniques of "village indoctrination, land reform, thought reform [and] social engineering under forced draft." These tactics worked, he writes, because villagers believed the Communists' claims of nationalism and social revolution.
24. Letter from Scott Miler to John K. Singlaub, February 3, 1990; enclosure III, pp. 1–2.
25. "Government Military Source Says USSR Aid to Communists Exceeds Aid to Government 'During or Since World War II,' " *New York Times*, December 17, 1947, p. 23. "TASS Denies USSR Aids Communists," *New York Times*, January 6, 1947, p. 11.
26. Letter from Scott Miler to John K. Singlaub, February 3, 1990, p. 5.

5 · CIA and U.S. Army, China and Korea

1. General Wei Li-huang was arrested in Canton later that month for "failure to carry out orders" on the withdrawal from Manchuria. See *New York Times*, November 21, 1948, p. 37, and December 5, 1948, p. 44. In 1951, when I was serving with the CIA in Korea, I received an urgent letter from General Wei, asking me to meet him in Hong Kong to discuss a matter of great importance. I was too busy at the time to make the trip. The next we heard of General Wei, he had returned to mainland China to join the Communists. He disappeared during the chaos of the Cultural Revolution. General Fu kept his forces intact until Mao's Red armies overran his area. He reluctantly threw in his lot with the Communists and was rewarded with a minor ministerial position in their government.
2. Author's interviews with Walter Pforzheimer, former legislative counsel, Central Intelligence Agency, January and February 1990. Mr. Pforzheimer was a key executive in the early CIA and served under the Agency's first four directors.

He confirms that MacArthur's refusal to help the CIA recover after the collapse of Nationalist China had a major bearing on our intelligence operations in Asia in the 1950s.

3. After more than twenty-five years in prison and much notoriety about his case, Hugh Redmond committed suicide in prison. He should have never been allowed to attempt "transformation" to stay-behind agent status. But, I later learned, he had insisted he could accomplish his mission. I blame our own counterespionage people for allowing it. They seemed to believe that the Chinese Communists were as unsophisticated in counterintelligence and counterespionage as the Japanese had been. Many foreign agents had survived for years under Japanese occupation in the huge city of Shanghai. But, whereas the Japanese had been ruthless, they had not been as unremittedly totalitarian as the Chinese Communists.

4. Chiang Kai-shek, *Soviet Russia in China: A Summing Up at Seventy* (Taipei, Republic of China: China Publishing Co., 1969), pp. 64–66; also see "Creation of Class Conflicts," Appendix, pp. 382–83.

5. Confidential letter to Major John K. Singlaub from Colonel Robert A. Schow, Assistant Director, Central Intelligence Agency, July 29, 1949, author's archives. An Army officer serving with the CIA in those days did not receive normal efficiency ratings; therefore, "departure" letters from your superiors were critical. In mine, Colonel Schow noted that I had "displayed outstanding diplomacy, tact, judgment and discretion in the handling of numerous problems of critical interest both to this organization and to the United States Army and Navy." The letter also noted my "diligence, perseverance and constant alertness to opportunity," which furthered the goals of U.S. intelligence in a "critical area." Even though America's Nationalist ally had suffered defeat, my station had been able to establish a practical intelligence network in Manchuria and Soviet Siberia. The fruits of that network would be enjoyed in the coming year with the onset of the Korean War.

6. Walter G. Hermes, *Truce Tent and Fighting Front: United States Army and the Korean War,* Vol. 2 (Washington, DC: Office of the Chief of Military History, United States Army, 1966), pp. 3–7, 9.

7. Major Robert K. Sawyer, *Military Advisors in Korea: KMAG in Peace and War* (Washington, DC: U.S. Army Publication, 1962), Chap. 1.

8. Although it took forty years, the Communists have finally acknowledged the role of Joseph Stalin in the 1950 invasion of South Korea. In July 1990, Li San-cho, North Korea's ambassador to Moscow in the 1950s, told Reuters that Joseph Stalin approved Kim Il Sung's plans for the invasion and provided the necessary military support. See the Reuters dispatch from Moscow quoted in the *Washington Times,* July 5, 1990, p. A-9.

9. T. R. Fehrenbach, *This Kind of War: A Study in Unpreparedness* (New York: Macmillan, 1963), p. 54.

10. The authors are indebted to Mr. Walter Pforzheimer, a longtime executive of the Central Intelligence Agency, for the information he provided on the congressional inquiry on the role of U.S. intelligence in Korea in June 1950. Other CIA officers still serving have provided additional information on this matter.

11. Harold P. Ford, *Estimative Intelligence: The Purposes and Problems of Intelligence Estimating* (Washington, D.C.: Defense Intelligence College, School of Strategic Intelligence, 1989), pp. 60–65. More information on the CIA estimate of North Korean intentions was obtained from Walter Pforzheimer in an interview on February 13, 1990.

12. "War No Surprise, Intelligence Says," *New York Times,* June 27, 1950, p. 3.

13. "Rightist Attack Repelled in Korea," *The Daily Worker,* June 26, 1950, p. 1.

14. In 1759, the first American Ranger commander, Major Robert Rogers, made his largely illiterate troops memorize a set of nineteen Standing Orders. Order No. 1 was, "Don't forget nothing." Another order was, "When you're on the march, act the way you would if you was sneaking up on a deer. See the enemy first." Order No. 14 was a rule that saved my own life on more than one occasion: "Don't sit down to eat without posting sentries." The final order was one that the descendants of Rogers' Rangers followed in one way or another in many wars: "Let the enemy come 'til he's almost close enough to touch. Then let him have it and jump out and finish him up with your hatchet."

15. Max Hastings, *The Korean War* (New York: Simon and Schuster, 1987), p. 121.

16. Ibid., p. 115.

17. Ibid., pp. 125–26.

18. Fehrenbach, *This Kind of War,* p. 282.

19. Billy C. Mossman, *Ebb and Flow, November 1950–July 1951* (Washington, DC: Center of Military History, 1990).

20. Ibid., pp. 96–101.

21. Hastings, *The Korean War,* p. 159.

22. Letter, with enclosures from Colonel James Harvey Short, USA (ret.), to John K. Singlaub, February 8, 1990.

23. For further reading see Steve A. Fondacaro, *A Strategic Analysis of U.S. Special Operations during the Korean Conflict, 1950–1953* (Fort Leavenworth, KS: U.S. Army Command and General Staff College, 1988), pp. 80–110.

24. Setting up this operation was not without hazard. In January 1951, a Navy PBM patrol bomber out of Okinawa with a twenty-five-man American team on board was downed in the East China Sea, killing twenty. My friend Dave Longacre survived with a broken back. Letter from Colonel David Longacre, USA (ret.), to John K. Singlaub, February 26, 1990, p. 6.

25. "U.N. Partisan Forces in the Korean Conflict," by Military History Detachment Three, Army Forces, Far East, 1953. U.S. Army Military History Institute Collection, Army History Office, Washington, DC.

26. For a good concise history of the Ranger companies in Korea see Gordon L. Rottman, *US Army Rangers & LRRP Units, 1942–87* (London: Osprey Publishing, 1987), "The Korean War," pp. 23–26.

27. Letter from Colonel John F. "Skip" Sadler, USA (ret.), to John K. Singlaub, June 28, 1990. Skip Sadler makes the point that many of the later successful techniques of unconventional warfare were pioneered by JACK improvisers like us.

28. Colonel Richard G. Stilwell was no relation to General Joseph Stilwell, American commander of the China/Burma/India theater in World War II.

6 • 15th Infantry, Korea

1. Anna Rosenberg was the Defense Department official who instituted this policy in 1951.
2. Walter G. Hermes, *Truce Tent and Fighting Front: United States Army and the Korean War,* Vol. 2 (Washington, DC: Office of the Chief of Military History, United States Army, 1966), pp. 309–10. Also see "One Officer and 87 Men of 3d Div 65th Regt Convicted of Refusing Action Against Enemy," *New York Times,* January 25, 1953, p. 1.
3. Command Report Number 27, 1 November–30 November 1952, 15th Infantry Regiment, 3rd Infantry Division, Enclosure 2: 2nd Battalion Staff Journal, National Archives, Military Collection, Suitland, Maryland. This Battalion Staff Journal cites several instances of heavy casualties among battalion patrols due to their inability to efficiently call in artillery fire support after contacting enemy patrols at night forward of the MLR.
4. Max Hastings, *The Korean War* (New York: Simon and Schuster, 1987), p. 273.
5. Command Report Number 29, 1 February–28 February 1953, 15th Infantry Regiment, 3rd Infantry Division, Enclosure 2: 2nd Battalion Staff Journal, National Archives, Military Collection, Suitland, Maryland.
6. Ibid.
7. Hermes, *Truce Tent and Fighting Front,* p. 459.
8. Memorandum to John K. Singlaub from George A. Meighen; subject: recollections of 2nd BN, 15th Inf. Reg., 3rd Inf. Div.—Korea, 1952–53, p. 7. According to Meighen, the sight of me clomping around the MLR with my arm in a sling and my leg in a cast was a real morale booster for the troops; it showed them that professional soldiers were willing to literally risk life and limb for the well-being of their men.
9. Author's interview with Colonel Dan Foldberg, USA (ret.), March 2, 1990.
10. Command Report Number 31: 1 April–30 April 1953, 15th Infantry Regiment, 3rd Infantry Division, Enclosure 2: 2nd Battalion Staff Journal, National Archives, Military Collection, Suitland, Maryland. The Battalion Journal entry for 3 April 1953 makes exciting reading. The communications clerks of Headquarters Company obviously sensed the drama of the battle for Outpost Harry. They logged the exact communications exchanges between battalion headquarters, the outpost, and supporting artillery organizations.

7 • The Profession of Arms

1. "New Red Attacks Hit Central Front," *New York Times,* June 19, 1953, p. 3. Also see Walter G. Hermes, *Truce Tent and Fighting Front: United States Army and the Korean War,* Vol. 2 (Washington, DC: Office of the Chief of Military History, United States Army, 1966), Chap. 21, "The Last Offensive," pp. 459–473.
2. John Miller, Jr., et al., *Korea 1951–1953* (Washington, DC: Department of the Army, Office of the Chief of Military History, 1956), pp. 282–84.
3. Miller, *Korea 1951–1953,* p. 283.

4. Lieutenant Colonel Winant Sidle, USA, "The College Role in the Army School System," *Military Review,* Vol. 36, No. 2, May 1956, pp. 5–15.

5. Walter A. McDougall, . . . *The Heavens and the Earth: A Political History of the Space Age* (New York: Basic Books, 1985), pp. 55–56. McDougall notes that the Soviet response to America's "resolve" in resisting Communist aggression in Korea was to double the Red Army to 5.8 million men by 1955, "and, without pausing to admire their atomic bombs, pushed on at once for their huskier offspring. In August 1953, they exploded the first thermonuclear device and tested a deliverable H-bomb in November 1955."

6. Ibid., pp. 105–6.

7. Edmund Beard, *Developing the ICBM: A Study in Bureaucratic Politics* (New York: Columbia University Press, 1976), pp. 133–34.

8. One of the best studies of this situation is General Maxwell D. Taylor's *The Uncertain Trumpet* (New York: Harper & Brothers, 1960).

9. General William C. Westmoreland, *A Soldier Reports* (Garden City, NY: Doubleday, 1976), pp. 38–40.

10. Ronald H. Spector, *United States Army in Vietnam, Advice and Support: The Early Years, 1941–1960,* Vol. 1 (Washington, DC: Center of Military History, United States Army, 1983), Chap. 4, "The Chinese Occupation of North Vietnam, August–October 1945," pp. 51–73.

11. For more background on Ho Chi Minh see John T. McAlister and Paul Mus, *The Vietnamese and Their Revolution* (New York: Harper & Row, 1970), and John T. McAlister, *Vietnam: The Origins of Revolution* (Garden City, NY: Doubleday, 1971).

12. Spector, *United States Army in Vietnam,* pp. 37–40.

13. For a description of this almost forgotten incident see Joseph Buttinger, *Vietnam: A Dragon Embattled,* Vol. 2, and *Vietnam at War* (New York: Praeger, 1967), pp. 424–30.

14. My friend "Earthquake" McGoon, an American contract pilot with China Air Transport, who had often flown into the besieged Mukden airport, was killed in this operation, one of the first American casualties in our long involvement in Indochina.

15. Spector, *United States Army in Vietnam,* pp. 182–90.

16. Ibid., Chap. 11, "The Question of Intervention," pp. 191–214.

17. Ibid., p. 209.

18. For a more complete discussion of tactical nuclear weapons see "Tactical Nuclear Operations," U.S. Army Field Manual FM 100-5, Chap. 10, pp. 10-1 to 10-9, Department of the Army, Washington, DC, July 1976.

19. Andrew F. Krepinevich, Jr., *The Army and Vietnam* (Baltimore: Johns Hopkins University Press, 1986), "Background of the Airmobile Concept," pp. 112–15. The author cites the pioneering work done by the Aviation Department of the College on this concept.

20. Colonels Raymond L. Shoemaker and Peter L. Urban, Lieutenant Colonels John Clapper, William D. McDowell, Daniel A. Raymond, John K. Singlaub, and Cecil C. Helena, and Major John H. Cushman, "Readiness for the Little War: Optimum Integrated Strategy," *Military Review,* Vol. 37, No. 1, April

1957, pp. 15–26; Shoemaker et al., "Readiness for the Little War: A Strategic Security Force," *Military Review*, Vol. 37, No. 2, May 1957, pp. 14–21. By the time the articles were published, Winant Sidle was a speechwriter on General Maxwell Taylor's staff and requested that his name not be included among the authors.

21. A. J. Bacevich, *The Pentomic Era: The U.S. Army between Korean and Vietnam* (Washington, DC: National Defense University Press, 1986), pp. 54–57, 64–66, 92–96, 118–19, passim. General Maxwell D. Taylor, *Swords and Plowshares* (New York: W. W. Norton & Co., 1972), pp. 170–71. Also see Maxwell D. Taylor, *The Uncertain Trumpet* (New York: Harper & Brothers, 1960), pp. 169–70, 173–75.

22. For a good discussion of this problem see Westmoreland, *A Soldier Reports*, pp. 31–32.

23. Retired Army Lieutenant General John H. Hay bitterly remembers this period. He calls Hallock and Cushman McGarr's "henchmen." Letter from Lieutenant General John H. Hay, USA (ret.), to John K. Singlaub, March 24, 1990.

24. Letter from Colonel Harvey Short, USA (ret.), to John K. Singlaub, February 2, 1990.

8 · Cold War

1. General William C. Westmoreland, *A Soldier Reports* (Garden City, NY: Doubleday, 1976), p. 30.

2. *New York Times*, May 14, 1958, p. 1.

3. "Eisenhower Sends Marines and Paratroopers to Cuban and Puerto Rican Bases," *New York Times*, May 14, 1958, p. 1.

4. "USSR Hints 'Volunteers' Might Reinforce Rebels," *New York Times*, June 20, 1958, p. 1.

5. Dr. Gene L. Curtis, the young commander of my Combat Support Company in Baumholder, recently reminded me that my habit of running *behind* some formations that had been accustomed to "losing" a few troops as they passed the mess hall—rather than leading the column—had a definite "inspirational" effect on the men. Letter from Dr. Gene L. Curtis to John K. Singlaub, April 11, 1990.

6. "USSR, Charging Threatening Western Stand on Berlin, Announces Plan to Resume Nuclear Testing," *New York Times*, August 31, 1961, p. 1.

7. For a thoughtful examination of the Walker case and resignation as a means of voicing dissent see Colonel Lloyd J. Mathews, USA (ret.), "Resignation in Protest," *Army*, Vol. 40, No. 1, January 1990, pp. 12–23.

8. Letter from Lieutenant General Robert C. Taber, USA (ret.), to John K. Singlaub, June 27, 1990.

9. Letter from Powell Moore to John K. Singlaub, April 4, 1990.

10. "U.S. Battle Group Reaches West Berlin Without Incident," *New York Times*, August 21, 1961, p. 1.

11. "USSR and US Tanks Face Each Other 100 Yards Apart," *New York Times*,

October 28, 1961, p. 1. "USSR and US Pull Tanks Back from Border after 16-Hour Confrontation," *New York Times,* October 29, 1961, p. 1.
12. "Readiness of US Forces Unclear," *New York Times,* October 18, 1962, p. 1.

9 · The Pentagon

1. Walter A. McDougall, . . . *The Heavens and the Earth: A Political History of the Space Age* (New York: Basic Books, 1985), pp. 127–29.
2. A. J. Bacevich, *The Pentomic Era: The U.S. Army between Korea and Vietnam* (Washington, DC: National Defense University Press, 1986), pp. 93–95.
3. Mark Perry, *Four Stars: The Inside Story of the Forty-Year Battle between the Joint Chiefs of Staff and America's Civilian Leaders* (Boston: Houghton Mifflin Company, 1989), pp. 111, 114–15.
4. Alain C. Enthoven and K. Wayne Smith, *How Much Is Enough: Shaping the Defense Program 1961–1969* (New York: Harper & Row, 1971), pp. 89–92; as quoted in Colonel Harry G. Summers, Jr., *On Strategy: A Critical Analysis of the Vietnam War* (Novato, CA: Presidio, 1982), p. 47. Harry Summers's analysis of the impact of the McNamara Defense Department on America's Vietnam policy is absolutely essential reading for any serious student of this period.
5. Perry, *Four Stars,* pp. 169–71.
6. Letter from General Frederick J. Kroesen, USA (ret.), to John K. Singlaub, July 16, 1990.
7. Although the Army was prepared to fight a tactical nuclear war in Europe as a last resort, NATO forces would never initiate one. Therefore, our training plans centered around repulsing a conventional Warsaw Pact attack. Had such a Communist offensive "gone nuc," casualties, equipment losses, and disruption of lines of communication would have overwhelmed even the ambitious plans of the Medical Corps.
8. The air- and sea-lift assets that accrued out of STRATMOVE 69 were not fully tested for twenty-five years. But when they were, the system functioned well. It was this logistics bridge that allowed America to deploy 100,000 combat troops to Saudi Arabia in less than a month in August 1990.
9. General William C. Westmoreland, *A Soldier Reports* (Garden City, NY: Doubleday, 1976), pp. 136–39.
10. Ronald H. Spector, *United States Army in Vietnam, Advice and Support: The Early Years, 1941–1960,* Vol. 1 (Washington, DC: Center of Military History, United States Army, 1983), p. 219.
11. Ibid., p. 303.
12. Ibid., pp. 234–46.
13. Ibid., p. 312. Spector cites William R. Andrews, *The Village War: Vietnam Communist Revolutionary Activities in Dinh Tuong Province, 1960–1964* (Columbia, MO: University of Missouri Press, 1973), p. 59. It is interesting to note that this brutal campaign of terror on the village level comes straight from Mao's textbook on revolutionary guerrilla warfare.
14. Spector, *United States Army in Vietnam,* p. 313. Spector cites declassified intelligence reports, based on debriefing of Communist defectors, that note the

"effective infiltration" of most of South Vietnam's rebellious religious sects, including the influential (and very telegenic) Vietnam-Cambodian Buddhist Association.

15. David Halberstam, *The Best and the Brightest* (New York: Random House, 1969), pp. 286–91.

16. William Colby and Peter Forbath, *Honorable Men: My Life in the CIA* (New York: Simon and Schuster, 1978), pp. 209–17.

17. Jeffrey J. Clarke, *United States Army in Vietnam, Advice and Support: The Final Years, 1965–1973,* Vol. 3 (Washington, DC: Center of Military History, United States Army, 1988), p. 81.

18. Walter Hermes, "The United States Army in Vietnam, the Buildup: 1965–1968" (Washington, DC: Center of Military History, U.S. Army, unpublished manuscript), pp. 1-30, 1-31, 2-18, 2-23.

19. Hermes, "The United States Army in Vietnam," p. 4-16.

20. Westmoreland, *A Soldier Reports*, p. 139.

21. Ibid., pp. 138–40.

22. Hermes, "The United States Army in Vietnam," p. 4-16.

23. The best study of the Dominican Republic affair, known throughout the military since then as "the Dom Rep," is General Bruce Palmer, Jr., *Intervention in the Caribbean: The Dominican Crisis of 1965* (Lexington, KY: The University Press of Kentucky, 1989). An especially interesting examination of the U.S. decision process is found in Chap. 2, pp. 30–50.

24. Hermes, "The United States Army in Vietnam," p. 4-20.

25. *New York Times,* July 10, 1965, p. 1.

26. Memorandum from the Secretary of Defense for the President, 20 July 1965; Subject: Recommendations of Additional Deployments to Vietnam, Top Secret; declassified 1979, in archives of Center of Military History, Washington, DC, quoted in Hermes, "The United States Army in Vietnam," p. 4-19.

27. Perry, *Four Stars*, p. 153.

28. Ibid., p. 153.

29. George McT. Kahin, *Intervention: How America Became Involved in Vietnam* (New York: Alfred A. Knopf, 1986), pp. 378–89.

30. For an insightful discussion of Lyndon Johnson's fears of Soviet and Chinese reaction see Larry Berman, *Planning a Tragedy: The Americanization of the War in Vietnam* (New York: W.W. Norton & Co., 1982), pp. 121–29.

31. Authors' interview with Walter Pforzheimer, veteran CIA executive, May 26, 1990. For these insights, the authors also relied on a former high-ranking intelligence official who noted that effective Chinese control of its military was deeply eroded by the ill-conceived Great Leap Forward of the early sixties, the failure of which spawned the Great People's Cultural Revolution. By the mid-1960s, this official notes, "millions of teenagers marched throughout China destroying, beating, killing, and imprisoning all Chinese related directly or even indirectly with education, wealth, or one of the professions such as medicine or engineering." Given this situation, it was unlikely the Chinese could sustain a massive military intervention in Indochina.

32. Perry, *Four Stars*, p. 155. Also see Martin Binkin and William W. Kaufmann,

U.S. Army Guard & Reserve: Rhetoric, Realities, Risks (Washington, DC: The Brookings Institution, 1989), "The Vietnam War," pp. 48–59.

33. Kahin, *Intervention*, p. 390. For this information on McNamara, Professor Kahin cites William Bundy's unpublished 1972 Vietnam study, Chap. 30, pp. 10–11.

34. The best sources for this pivotal meeting are Perry, *Four Stars*, pp. 155–56 (who in turn relies on Kahin, *Intervention*, pp. 366, 367, 390, 394), and Hermes, "The United States Army in Vietnam," pp. 4-40, 4-41, who quotes a Secret (declassified 1979 archives of the Center of Military History) policy statement by Secretary of the Army Stanley Resor to the Army Policy Council on March 30, 1966.

35. As that most thoughtful analyst of America's strategic failure in Indochina Colonel Harry Summers has pointed out, however, McNamara's systems analysts found maximum efforts untidy; they preferred minimum numbers that fit nicely into their cost-effectiveness formulas. See Summers, *On Strategy*, p. 50.

36. Halberstam, *The Best and the Brightest*, p. 594.

37. Colonel Harry G. Summers, Jr., *The Parameters of Military Ethics: Introduction,* ed. by Lloyd J. Mathews and Dale E. Brown (Washington, DC: Pergamon-Brassey's International Defense Publishers, 1989), p. XVII. Also see Perry, *Four Stars*, p. 156. In the mid-1970s, when I was a major general, I attended an Army Reserve banquet at which General Johnson, then retired, was an honored guest. I mentioned that fateful morning in July, and told the General frankly that I had been disappointed that he did not object more strenuously to the execution of that terribly flawed Buildup Plan. The General smiled thinly and nodded, allowing how he had mistakenly hoped to accomplish more by staying within the system than by acting on his principles and resigning.

10 · Indochina

1. Walter Hermes, "The United States Army in Vietnam, the Buildup: 1965–1968" (Washington, DC: Center of Military History, U.S. Army, unpublished manuscript), pp. v-20, v-36.

2. Colonel David Hackworth, *About Face* (New York: Simon and Schuster, 1989), pp. 481–82.

3. Interview with Lieutenant General Harold G. Moore, USA (ret.), June 5, 1990. As a lieutenant colonel, Hal Moore commanded the division's 1st Battalion, 7th Cavalry Regiment, in 1965.

4. Interview with Lieutenant Colonel Frederick Caristo, USA (ret.), June 4, 1990. Caristo, then a Special Forces lieutenant, was an adviser to the gallant 37th ARVN Ranger Battalion in 1964–1965.

5. Message, COMUSMACV, to CINCPAC et al., June 7, 1965, Department of the Army IN 6783316, Top Secret (declassified 1979, in Center of Military History Archives). Also see General William C. Westmoreland, *A Soldier Reports* (Garden City, NY: Doubleday, 1976), pp. 146–47.

6. Peter Braestrup, *Big Story: How the American Press and Television Reported and Interpreted the Crisis of Tet 1968 in Vietnam and Washington* (New Haven, CT: Yale University Press, abridged ed., 1977), p. 39. Braestrup's book is a

monument to professionalism. Anyone wishing to understand the role of the news media in the Vietnam War should read it.

7. Westmoreland, *A Soldier Reports,* p. 157.

8. Letter from Lieutenant General Harold G. Moore, USA (ret.), to John K. Singlaub, May 31, 1990, and interview with General Moore, June 5, 1990. And letter from Brigadier General Thomas W. Brown, USA (ret.), to John K. Singlaub, June 8, 1990, p. 2. Also see Al Santoli, *Everything We Had: An Oral History of the Vietnam War by Thirty-three American Soldiers Who Fought It* (New York: Ballantine Books, 1982), "Ia Drang, Thomas Bird, Rifleman, 1st Cavalry Division, An Khe, August 1965–August 1966," pp. 34–43. Bird was captured by NVA troops and held several days in the Ia Drang battle when his unit ran out of ammunition and could not be resupplied by helicopter because of enemy anti-aircraft fire. Bird comments about his own low level of training in airmobile infantry tactics.

9. Shelby L. Stanton, *Anatomy of a Division: The 1st Cav in Vietnam* (Novato, CA: Presidio, 1987), pp. 61–62. And interview with Brigadier General Thomas W. "Tim" Brown, USA (ret.), June 8, 1990; General Brown, then a colonel, commanded the 3rd Brigade in Vietnam.

10. A well-researched and graphic published account of the Ia Drang battles is J. D. Coleman, *Pleiku: The Dawn of Helicopter Warfare in Vietnam* (New York: St. Martin's Press, 1988); see pp. 189–249. Coleman served with the Air Cav in the Highlands and brings an accuracy and vividness to his book that only an eyewitness to the battle can provide.

11. Colonel John A. Cash, "Fight at Ia Drang," in *Seven Firefights in Vietnam* (Washington, DC: Office of the Chief of Military History, U.S. Army, 1970).

12. Moore letter, May 31, 1990, and Moore interview, June 5, 1990.

13. Coleman, *Pleiku,* pp. 34–35.

14. Ibid., pp. 248–49.

15. Westmoreland, *A Soldier Reports,* p. 157.

16. Coleman, *Pleiku,* p. 174.

17. Westmoreland, *A Soldier Reports,* pp. 180–83.

18. Interestingly enough, two of the NVA regiments that engaged the Air Cav in the Ia Drang valley pulled back to Cambodia to refit, then proceeded across the Central Highlands undetected to the coast. They attacked the 37th ARVN Ranger Battalion at Thach Tru. The Rangers' American adviser was 1st Lieutenant Fred Caristo, who called in naval gunfire from the American destroyer U.S.S. *O'Brien.* The morning after the attack, the Ranger battalion had been almost wiped out, but the enemy left over a thousand dead outside the barbed wire. Many of the dead NVA carried American weapons and equipment captured in the Ia Drang valley. Some had tattoos which said *San Bac Tu Nam* ("Born in the North, Die in the South"): interview with Lieutenant Colonel Frederick Caristo, June 4, 1990.

19. Al Santoli, *To Bear Any Burden: The Vietnam War and Its Aftermath in the Words of Americans and Southeast Asians* (New York: E. P. Dutton, 1985), Nguyen Tuong Lai, "Soldier of the Revolution," pp. 145–47.

20. Westmoreland, *A Soldier Reports,* pp. 160–61.

21. Mark Perry, *Four Stars: The Inside Story of the Forty-Year Battle between the Joint Chiefs of Staff and America's Civilian Leaders* (Boston: Houghton Mifflin Company, 1989), p. 150.

22. The unit had originally been called MACV/Special Operations Group, but this name was too revealing. So my predecessors changed the name to Studies and Observations Group. For an excellent brief history of MACV/SOG see Terrence Maitland, Peter McInerney, and the editors of the Boston Publishing Company, *A Contagion of War: The Vietnam Experience* (Boston: Boston Publishing Co., 1983), "Battlefield Indochina," pp. 118–35.

23. Letter from Colonel Tran Van Ho to John K. Singlaub, July 23, 1990; enclosure, pp. 1–4.

24. Letter from Brigadier General Thomas Bowen, USA (ret.), to John K. Singlaub, July 13, 1990, insert, p. 3.

25. Ibid., p. 6.

26. For an interesting description of cross-border Recon Teams' methods and equipment see Ashley Brown and Jonathan Reed, eds., *The Unique Units, the Elite, the World's Crack Fighting Men* (Harrisburg, PA: National Historical Society, 1989), Leroy Thompson, "The Secret War," pp. 108–13.

27. Santoli, *To Bear Any Burden*, p. 147.

28. Stanley Karnow, *Vietnam: A History* (New York: The Viking Press, 1983), p. 554.

29. Ibid., p. 530.

30. Letter from George W. Gaspard to John K. Singlaub, August 9, 1990, p. 2.

31. Westmoreland, *A Soldier Reports*, pp. 181–83.

32. Sisler was later posthumously awarded a Medal of Honor for his heroic defense of a SOG team on the Ho Chi Minh Trail.

33. Westmoreland, *A Soldier Reports*, p. 319. Westmoreland indicates that "late reconnaissance" by SOG on the enemy's obvious preparation of new infiltration routes in the A Shau valley convinced him that prisoner reports of a pending offensive were valid.

34. For a colorful, first-person account of this action see Colonel Jack Speedy, "Charlie Company to the Rescue," *Vietnam*, June 1990, pp. 22–28.

35. Braestrup, *Big Story*, Chap. 4, "Military Victory or Defeat for Hanoi?," pp. 117–42. Braestrup correctly notes that most American reporters in Vietnam chose to believe that the embassy had in fact been captured and, further, that the embassy—not MACV headquarters at Tan Son Nhut—was America's nerve center in Vietnam. Thus, allowing the chancery to "fall" to the VC epitomized the American military's ostensibly poor preparation for the Tet offensive.

36. Ibid., p. 179.

37. Westmoreland, *A Soldier Reports*, p. 332.

38. Karnow, *Vietnam*, p. 544.

11 • General Officer

1. Hugh Thomas, *The Spanish Civil War* (London: Michael Joseph, Ltd., 1961), p. 203.
2. Ernest W. Lefever, *TV and National Defense: An Analysis of CBS News, 1972–1973* (Boston, VA: Institute for American Strategy Press, 1974), pp. 3, 141–42. Lefever's book, a compilation of serious scholarly research, faults such "advocacy journalism" of American television networks during the Vietnam War.
3. Interview with William Donnett, June 18, 1990.
4. Interview with Charles MacCrone, June 17, 1990, and Gordon Riner, June 18, 1990. As members of the U.S. Parachute Team at the meet, both men recall the tension between the Soviet and Czechoslovak teams; at one point a Czech judge actually took a marking fléchette and pointed it like a dummy machine gun at the broad khaki back of his Soviet "comrade." Letter from Charles R. MacCrone to John K. Singlaub, June 21, 1990; enclosure: "Minutes, International Parachuting Committee, General Meeting, Paris, France, January 1969."
5. General William C. Westmoreland, *A Soldier Reports* (Garden City, NY: Doubleday, 1976), p. 297.
6. For an interesting comment on the plight of experienced young career officers during this period, see Hackworth, *About Face,* pp. 636–40, 644–45.
7. Ibid., p. 298.
8. Serge Schmemann, "Bonn, After Arrests, Checks for Honecker Link to Terrorists," *New York Times,* June 22, 1990, p. 1. After the collapse of the Communist government of East Germany, the long-time support of West German radical groups by the "Stasi" secret police has finally been made public. Also see Claire Sterling, *The Terror Network* (New York: Holt, Rinehart and Winston, 1981), pp. 221–22.
9. Aircraft and weapons were not the only ancient relics in the Spanish military. There was no mandatory retirement age for officers, and we encountered venerable colonels and generals well past eighty. It was common to see captains and majors in their fifties and sixties. Obviously, if Spain could be lured into NATO, one of the alliance's priority tasks would be to modernize the country's officer corps, which would also speed the arrival of democracy in Spain.
10. The success of this training might have been partially due to the fact that the Spanish army received generous rations of excellent brandy, which they had saved to share with their American guests. Letter from B. J. Pinkerton to John K. Singlaub, July 12, 1990, p. 3.
11. Charter Memorandum, Project Mobile Army Sensor Systems Test, Evaluation and Review (MASSTER), 27 October 1969, Department of the Army; enclosure with letter from Arthur R. Woods to John K. Singlaub, June 19, 1990, pp. 1–4.
12. Interviews with Colonel Harry G. Summers, Jr., USA (ret.), and Lieutenant General Phillip B. Davidson, USA (ret.), June 1990. Both of these distinguished officers recommended a seminal recent work on our failed Indochina strategy: Norman B. Hannah, *The Key to Failure: Laos and the Vietnam War* (Lanham, MD: Madison Books, 1987), Chap. 18, "Laos—The Dropped Stitch," pp. 217–

37. Mr. Hannah's book is mandatory reading for any serious student of the Vietnam War.

13. For a detailed account of the FSSB system in Vietnam see *A Distant Challenge: The U.S. Infantryman in Vietnam, 1967–70,* edited by the staff of *Infantry Magazine* (Birmingham, AL: Birmingham Publishing Co., 1971), Lieutenant Colonel Jack B. Farris, Jr., "The Fire Support Surveillance Base," pp. 333–38.

14. Westmoreland, *A Soldier Reports,* p. 378. Westmoreland correctly states, "Had it not been for educational draft deferments, which prevented the Army from drawing upon the intellectual segment of society for its junior officers, Calley probably never would have been an officer."

15. Department of the Army, *Report of the Department of the Army Review of the Preliminary Investigations into the My Lai Incident,* Vol. I, *The Report of the Investigation* (Washington, DC: U.S. Government Printing Office, 1970), p. 2-1. The Army's exhaustive investigation of the My Lai massacre was led by Lieutenant General W. R. "Ray" Peers, my old boss from OSS days in Burma and China and later at the SACSA. The three volumes of the investigation became known as the "Peers Report." Anyone wishing to study the My Lai massacre is well advised to read it.

16. Ibid., p. 2-3.

17. Seymour Hersh, *My Lai 4: A Report on the Massacre and Its Aftermath* (New York: Random House, 1970). *New York Times* reporter Seymour Hersh's investigation of the massacre won him a Pulitzer Prize. Unfortunately, few, if any, journalists were familiar with or bothered to investigate the underlying causes for the debasement of the officer corps. Also see Hackworth, *About Face,* p. 772. The shame of My Lai haunted many dedicated professional officers, among them Colonel David Hackworth, one of the most controversial combat commanders in Vietnam. My Lai was one of several factors that drove him from the service.

18. Letter from LTG E. M. Flanagan, Jr., USA (ret.), to John K. Singlaub, July 7, 1990, p. 2.

19. Christopher Robbins, *The Ravens: The Men Who Flew America's Secret War in Laos* (New York: Crown, 1987), p. 306.

20. Stanley Karnow, *Vietnam: A History* (New York: The Viking Press, 1983), pp. 628–30.

21. General Bruce Palmer, Jr., *The 25-Year War: America's Military Role in Vietnam* (New York: Touchstone, 1984), p. 93. In 1970, unfair student draft deferments were finally replaced by a nationwide draft lottery. But this first lottery was flawed and was itself replaced the next year by a more equitable system. Unfortunately, American combat troops were almost all gone from Vietnam by this time, 1971.

22. Westmoreland, *A Soldier Reports,* pp. 374–75.

23. Hackworth, *About Face,* p. 804. During his last tour in Vietnam, Colonel Hackworth noted an increasing number of heroin-addicted soldiers, especially in the rear areas.

24. The Office of the Deputy Assistant Secretary of Defense (Drug and Alcohol Abuse), *The Department of Defense Experience in Drug Abuse Programs* (Wash-

ington, DC: Department of Defense, 1973), Appendix A, "Report of Department of Defense Team Involvement Activities," pp. A-1 to A-9.

25. Federal Drug Strategy Council, *Federal Strategy for Drug Abuse and Drug Traffic Prevention* (Washington, DC: U.S. Government Printing Office, 1973), pp. 90–97.

26. Memorandum for the Secretaries of the Military Departments, from the Assistant Secretary of Defense (Health and Environment), 5 May 1972; subject: Department of Defense Policy Concerning Persons Identified as Drug Dependent. Archives of the Office of the Secretary of Defense, Washington, DC.

27. Memorandum, Office of the Assistant Secretary of Defense (Health and Environment), 19 July 1974; subject: DoD Drug and Alcohol Abuse Control Program, OSD Archives, Washington, DC.

28. Karnow, *Vietnam*, pp. 653–54. Historian Stanley Karnow notes that the so-called Christmas bombing of 1972 was hardly the "Hiroshima" claimed by anti-war activists. He states that the American B-52s "pinpointed their targets with extraordinary precision," sparing needless civilian casualties.

29. Martin F. Herz, *The Prestige Press and the Christmas Bombing, 1972: Images and Reality in Vietnam* (Washington, DC: Ethics and Public Policy Center, 1980), pp. 30–36.

30. Colonel William E. Le Gro, *Vietnam from Cease-fire to Capitulation* (Washington, DC: U.S. Army Center of Military History, 1981), p. 128.

31. Tony Cullen and Christopher F. Foss, eds., *Jane's Land-Based Air Defense, 1989–90* (Coulsdon, Surrey, UK: Jane's Defense Data, 1989), p. 39. Ten U.S. and South Vietnamese aircraft were shot down by shoulder-fired SAM-7s in the Easter offensive; six months later, the figure had jumped to forty-five.

32. Karnow, *Vietnam*, pp. 640–43.

33. Letter from LTG Roy Manor, USAF (ret.), to John K. Singlaub, July 12, 1990, and follow-up interview, July 17, 1990.

12 • The Army Regroups

1. Letter from Secretary of the Army Robert E. Froehlke to Brigadier General John K. Singlaub, November 1, 1971. The Secretary informed me that the Department of the Army would take sixteen separate actions in 1972 to reduce the ranks of commissioned and noncommissioned officers, "who in many cases will not desire to terminate." In other words, the regular army was shedding deadwood and would be more than ever dependent on the reserves for critical skills in the event of a national emergency.

2. Stanley Karnow, *Vietnam: A History* (New York: The Viking Press, 1983), pp. 649–50.

3. Colonel William E. Le Gro, *Vietnam from Cease-fire to Capitulation*, pp. 27–32. Colonel William E. Le Gro, a combat infantryman and military intelligence officer with wide experience in Indochina, has correctly noted that this massive Communist resupply of North Vietnam was the key factor that eventually tipped the military balance in their favor.

4. Karnow, *Vietnam: A History*, p. 656.

5. Le Gro, *Vietnam from Cease-fire to Capitulation,* p. 170.
6. Interview with John Armstrong, July 10, 1990. Armstrong, a former Army officer, was the civilian intelligence analyst who led the effort to unveil the North Korean buildup.
7. Detailed intelligence estimates are still classified. For an unclassified summary of these estimates see Richard A. Stubbing with Richard A. Mendel, *The Defense Game* (New York: Harper & Row, 1986), p. 346, and U.N. Korean War Allies Association, Inc., *Axe-Wielding Murder at Panmunjom* (Seoul, Korea: U.N. Korean War Allies Association, Inc., 1976), pp. 22–23.
8. Don Oberdorfer, "Estimate of North Korean Army Raised," *Washington Post,* January 4, 1979, p. A1. The *Post* cited the Armstrong group's 1978 study that estimated NKPA strength at forty-one divisions, instead of the maximum strength of twenty-five in the earlier intelligence estimates.
9. Memorandum, 30 August 1990, from Thomas M. Ryan, Command Historian, U.S. Forces Korea, to MG J.K. Singlaub; subject: information on NKPA buildup, extracted from the USFK/EUSA Annual Historical Report.
10. *1976 Annual Historical Report: United Nations Command/U.S. Forces, Korea/ Eighth U.S. Army,* p. 26, originally classified Secret, declassified December 31, 1985; also interview with General John W. Vessey, USA (ret.), July 3, 1990. General Vessey replaced Stilwell as Commander in Chief, U.N. Command, and Commanding General, U.S. Forces, Korea, in October 1976.
11. Interview with General Richard G. Stilwell, USA (ret.), July 1, 1990; *1976 Annual Historical Report,* p. 25.
12. Korean Overseas Information Service, *Secret Tunnel Under Panmunjom* (Seoul, Korea: Government of Korea Printing Office, 1978), pp. 26–27.
13. Don Oberdorfer, "Busy World Beneath the Surface," *Washington Post,* May 27, 1975, p. A-2. Oberdorfer notes that there were doubts that a full North Korean division could pass through tunnel number two in only one hour, "but there was no question that the passage could accommodate many men and weapons."
14. Peter Maas, "Alleged North Korean Tunnel into South Found," *Washington Post,* March 4, 1990, p. A-10.
15. Reuters, "Ex–North Korea Envoy Says Kim Started War," *New York Times,* July 5, 1990, p. A-7.
16. "Chronology of Events in Joint Security Area 18 August–22 September 1976," provided by ROK Ministry of Defense to author through ROK Defense Attaché, Washington, DC, September 7, 1990.
17. *1976 Annual Historical Report,* pp. 12–15.
18. "North Korea Gives Warning," Associated Press dispatch, Colombo, Sri Lanka, August 18, 1976. "Violence Can Flare Quickly at the Front Line in Korea," *New York Times,* August 19, 1976, p. 2. Also see Editorial, "Pick Axe Diplomacy," *New York Times,* August 19, 1976, p. 19.
19. Colonel Conrad A. DeLateur (USMC), "Murder at Panmunjom: The Role of the Theater Commander in Crisis Resolution," Twenty-ninth Session, 1986– 1987 National Defense University, Elective 178, T-4, R-b (unpublished), pp. 9– 13, National Defense University Archives.

20. *1976 Annual Historical Report*, p. 18.
21. DeLateur, "Murder at Panmunjom," p. 20.

13 • No Parade

1. *Extract: Joint Duty Officers' Log/Operation Logs of the U.S. Army Support Group—JSA/Communications Log, Armistice Affairs Division, United Nations Command*, obtained from Archives of the Command Historian, UNC Seoul.
2. Charles Hayslett, "Carter Began Korean Pullout Study as Governor," *Atlanta Journal and Constitution*, June 4, 1978, p. A-20. Investigative journalists later determined that retired rear admiral Gene LaRocque, director of the left-liberal Center for Defense Information, and the staff of the Brookings Institution advised Carter, a foreign policy neophyte, on this matter as early as 1974. I met LaRocque myself in Atlanta in 1978, when I attended a public policy symposium at Emory University at which he was giving an address. LaRocque confirmed that he had, indeed, been Carter's "military adviser" on the ill-fated troop withdrawal. He also admitted he'd given the advice because he felt American troops had simply "been there too long."
3. "Review of the Policy Decision to Withdraw United States Ground Forces from Korea," *Report of the Investigations Subcommittee of the Committee on Armed Services, House of Representatives, with Dissenting and Supplementary Views, Ninety-fifth Congress, Second Session, April 26, 1978* (Washington, DC: U.S. Government Printing Office, 1978), pp. 7–8.
4. Interview with General John W. Vessey, Jr., USA (ret.), July 3, 1990.
5. Ibid.
6. "Transcript of the President's News Conference on Foreign Policy," *New York Times*, March 10, 1977, p. 26.
7. Vessey interview, July 3, 1990. Despite repeated written requests, the State Department has been unwilling or unable to produce this telegram under the provisions of the Freedom of Information Act.
8. Richard Halloran, "U.S. Study Supports Korea Pullout," *New York Times*, May 19, 1977, p. 9.
9. Interview with John Armstrong, July 10, 1990. Armstrong's recollections of this period are supported in detail in an excellent recent academic study: Joseph Wood, "President Carter's Troop Withdrawal from Korea," Draft Case Study for the John F. Kennedy School of Government, Harvard University, November 1989 (unpublished), author's archive, pp. 7–11. Also see Don Oberdorfer, "Carter's Decision on Korea Traced to Early 1975," *Washington Post*, June 12, 1977, p. A-15; "Army Head Says Service Chiefs Opposed Plan for Korea Pullout," *New York Times*, July 14, 1977, p. 7.
10. Letter from James H. Hausman to John K. Singlaub, May 8, 1990. Jim Hausman took notes on the events of that afternoon and has retained a clear memory of our conversation.
11. Memorandum for General George Brown, Chairman, Joint Chiefs of Staff, from MG John Singlaub; subject: MG Singlaub's Interview with Mr. John Saar on 18 May 1977, memo dated 21 May 1977; author's archives and archives of the

Joint Staff, Department of Defense. On May 19, 1977, I drafted a detailed memorandum on my interview at the request of General Brown. Obviously, my recollection of the exact questions and answers was still fresh.

12. John Saar, "U.S. General: GI Pullout Would Heighten Korea War Risk," *Washington Post,* January 7, 1977, p. A-20.

13. United Press International, Tokyo, Daily News Summary, April 30, 1977.

14. Later, John Saar attempted to protect his professional reputation by describing our encounter differently. He admitted that he had been granted a background briefing by Jim Hausman, but neglected to note that Hausman had arranged for me to answer specific military questions as part of that same briefing. Instead, Saar stated: "I went to the general's office, introduced myself as a Post reporter and openly took full notes of our 30-minute conversation." John Saar, "Background on the Singlaub Affair," *Washington Post,* June 3, 1977, p. A-27.

15. John Saar, "U.S. General: Korea Pullout Risks War," *Washington Post,* May 19, 1977, p. A-1.

16. Hausman letter, May 8, 1990. CBS World News Roundup, May 20, 1977, 8 A.M. EDT, Radio TV Reports, Inc., Washington, DC: Ms. Nix quotes me in her five-paragraph "exclusive interview with CBS News" as being "baffled" by the recall order because I was not dissenting from official withdrawal policy. The gist of her report is that I voluntarily granted her an interview.

17. Edward Walsh, "President Summons General Who Criticized Korea Policy," *Washington Post,* May 20, 1977, p. A-1.

18. John Saar, "Singlaub's Colleagues Also Oppose GI Pullout," *Washington Post,* May 21, 1977, p. A-6.

19. Stubbing and Mendel, *The Defense Game,* p. 345. The authors state that Carter "overruled" Secretary Brown on the troop withdrawal issue.

20. Oberdorfer, "Carter's Decision on Korea Traced to Early 1975," *Washington Post,* June 12, 1977, p. A-15. And "Army Head Says Service Chiefs Opposed Plan for Korea Pullout," *New York Times,* July 14, 1977, p. 11. Also see Wood, "President Carter's Troop Withdrawal from Korea," pp. 12–16.

21. Interview with Philip Habib, August 16, 1990.

22. Letter from Steven D. Tilley, Director for FOIA/PA Activities, Information Policy Directorate, National Security Council, to Malcolm McConnell, July 25, 1990. Also see Stubbing and Mendel, *The Defense Game,* pp. 345–46, and Mark Perry, *Four Stars: The Inside Story of the Forty-Year Battle between the Joint Chiefs of Staff and America's Civilian Leaders* (Boston: Houghton Mifflin Company, 1989), pp. 267–68.

23. Austin Scott, "President Fires Gen. Singlaub as Korea Staff Chief," *Washington Post,* May 22, 1977, p. 1.

24. George C. Wilson, "Administration Used Singlaub Firing as Signal to South Korea," *Washington Post,* May 24, 1977, p. A-17.

25. Interview with archive official, National Security Council, August 1, 1990. Also see "Korea: The U.S. Troop Withdrawal Program," *Report of the Pacific Study Group to the Committee on Armed Services, United States Senate, January 23, 1979* (Washington, DC: U.S. Government Printing Office, 1979), p. 1.

26. Jimmy Carter, *Keeping Faith: Memoirs of a President* (New York: Bantam Books, 1982), pp. 195, 578.

27. "The Singlaub Affair," Editorial: *Washington Post,* May 24, 1977, p. A-18.

28. Armstrong interview, July 10, 1990.

29. *Hearings on Review of the Policy Decision to Withdraw United States Ground Forces from Korea Before the Investigations Subcommittee, also the Committee on Armed Services, House of Representatives, Ninety-fifth Congress, First and Second Sessions, May 25, 1977* (Washington, DC: U.S. Government Printing Office, 1978), p. 2.

30. Ibid., pp. 23, 39–41.

31. Ibid., p. 75.

32. George C. Wilson, "House Panel Begins 'Frontal Assault' on Korea Policy," *Washington Post,* May 26, 1977, p. A-1.

33. Unclassified EFTO EYES ONLY Back Channel Message, General Kroesen to MG Singlaub, 31 May 1977. Fritz Kroesen was certainly pleased to have my services and hoped that press scrutiny could be neutralized. He laid plans to have me arrive at Fort McPherson unannounced to avoid a media circus, with television crews "filming your triumphal approach to the main gate."

34. Edward Walsh and George C. Wilson, "President Defends His Korea Policy," *Washington Post,* May 27, 1977, p. A-1.

35. "Pro and Con: Should U.S. Withdraw Troops from Korea?" Interview with General Richard G. Stilwell, U.S. Army (ret.), *U.S. News & World Report,* June 20, 1977, pp. 27–28.

36. "Army Head Says Service Chiefs Opposed Plan for Korea Pullout," *New York Times,* July 14, 1977, p. 7.

37. John Dinges, *Our Man in Panama: How General Noriega Used the United States—And Made Millions in Drugs and Arms* (New York: Random House, 1990), p. 91.

38. Frederick Kempe, *Divorcing the Dictator* (New York: G. P. Putnam's Sons, 1990), pp. 76–78.

39. For an interesting commentary on Noriega's activities during this period see Seymour M. Hersh, "The Creation of a Thug: Our Man in Panama," *Life,* April 1990, p. 86. Also see M. Stanton Evans, "The Panama Cover-Up," *American Legion Magazine,* Vol. 129, No. 2, August 1990, pp. 24–25, 62–63.

40. "Hill Unit Votes to Require Carter to Leave Troops in Korea," *Washington Post,* April 27, 1978, p. B-1.

14 • Counterattack

1. "Newly Retired Singlaub, Sumner Speak Out," *Washington Report,* July 1978, American Security Council Education Foundation, p. 7.

2. Mark Perry, *Four Stars: The Inside Story of the Forty-Year Battle between the Joint Chiefs of Staff and America's Civilian Leaders* (Boston: Houghton Mifflin Company, 1989), p. 154.

3. Jimmy Carter, *Keeping Faith: Memoirs of a President* (New York: Bantam Books, 1982), p. 188.

4. Ibid., pp. 214–15, 222.

5. I first heard this quote from Howard Phillips, Chairman of the Conservative

Caucus. Its validity has been confirmed by American and allied intelligence officers.

6. John Norton Moore, *The Secret War in Central America: Sandinista Assault on World Order* (Frederick, MD: University Publications of America, Inc., 1987), pp. 9–10.

7. Ibid., p. 12.

8. J. Valenta and V. Valenta, "Sandinistas in Power," *Problems of Communism,* No. 1, September–October 1985, pp. 24–25.

9. Moore, *The Secret War in Central America,* p. 21.

10. *New York Times,* September 7, 1979, p. 3.

11. Moore, *The Secret War in Central America,* pp. 24–25.

12. Claire Sterling, *The Terror Network: The Secret War of International Terrorism* (New York: Holt, Rinehart and Winston/Reader's Digest Press, 1981), pp. 16–18.

13. Letter from Professor Geir Finne, an international relations expert at Tromso University, Norway, to John K. Singlaub, November 20, 1990.

14. Steven Emerson, "Where Have All the Spies Gone?" *New York Times Magazine,* August 12, 1990, pp. 17–20. Steven Emerson, an investigative journalist and expert on national security matters, notes that the East German "Stasi" intelligence service controlled the Red Army faction for years. He also documents how the *Stasi* itself was controlled by the Soviet KGB.

15. Embarrassing details of Bulgarian–East German cooperation on this operation are now coming to light. See Marc Fisher, "The Spy Liquidation Sale: Bargain Basement at Berlin's Secret Police," *Washington Post,* August 23, 1990, p. D-1, and John Tagliabue, "Secret Dossiers Arousing Germans," *New York Times,* September 8, 1990, p. 3.

16. Don Oberdorfer, "Estimate of North Korean Army Raised," *Washington Post,* January 4, 1979, p. A-1; Bernard Weinraub, "Opposition Growing on Korean Pullout," *New York Times,* January 21, 1979, p. 15.

17. Carter, *Keeping Faith,* pp. 443–46. Carter states that he wanted to pull Sullivan out of Tehran, but that he allowed Secretary of State Cyrus Vance to convince him to keep the Ambassador in place. This sent a clear signal to the Shah's enemies that America had lost confidence in the monarch.

18. Ibid., p. 264.

19. William Colby and Peter Forbath, *Honorable Men: My Life in the CIA* (New York: Simon and Schuster, 1978), pp. 403–5. Also see Bob Woodward, *Veil: The Secret Wars of the CIA, 1981–1987* (New York: Simon and Schuster, 1987), p. 71.

20. Colonel Charlie A. Beckwith, USA (ret.), and Donald Knox, *Delta Force* (New York: Harcourt Brace Jovanovich, 1983), p. 277.

21. Paul B. Ryan, *The Iranian Rescue Mission: Why It Failed* (Annapolis, MD: Naval Institute Press, 1985), p. 94.

22. For an interesting account of Peter Fong's courageous odyssey see John McCaslin, "The 'Hidden' China: One Man's Tragedy," *Washington Post,* May 16, 1984, p. 1-B.

23. These included Dr. David Rowe, professor emeritus from Yale University and

a genuine expert on China; Dr. Lewis Tambs, a professor of Latin American affairs at Arizona State University in nearby Tempe, Arizona; Dr. Robert Morris, former general counsel of the State Committee on Internal Security; Congressman Larry McDonald, Democratic representative from the 7th Congressional District of Georgia; Jay Parker, president of the Lincoln Institute, Washington, DC; etc.

24. Peter Collier and David Horowitz, *Destructive Generation: Second Thoughts about the Sixties* (New York: Summit Books, 1989), pp. 168–69.
25. Moore, *The Secret War in Central America*, p. 32.
26. Jill Smolowe, "Conversations with Two Foes," *Time*, October 2, 1989, p. 26.
27. Ibid., p. 37.
28. The arbitrary limit of fifty-five U.S. trainers in our El Salvador Military Group was set during congressional committee hearings when a Pentagon official explained that that was the current number. Liberal congressmen seized the opportunity to set the limit at fifty-five. Later, when these same congressmen wanted to bring Marxist Mozambiquan Frelimo officers to the United States for training, conservative congressman Mark Siljander said he would back the program "when the Soviets limit the number of their military advisers in Angola to fifty-five."
29. For a good description of American military assistance to El Salvador at this time see "U.S. Presence Looms Large on Military Front, Where U.S.-Trained and U.S.-Supplied Soldiers Fight Insurgents," *New York Times*, July 8, 1981, p. 2.
30. U.S. Department of State, *The Sandinista Military Build-Up: An Update* (Washington, DC: U.S. Government Printing Office, 1987), Publication No. 9432, rev., October 1987, p. 18.
31. "Sandinista Official Sergio Ramirez Mercado Says Military Buildup Is 'Exclusively Defensive,' " *New York Times*, March 10, 1982, p. 1.
32. *Report of the Congressional Committees Investigating the Iran-Contra Affair* (Washington, DC: U.S. Government Printing Office, 1987), pp. 483–85. Also see U.S. Departments of State and Defense, *The Challenge to Democracy in Central America* (Washington, DC: U.S. Government Printing Office, 1986), p. 20.
33. As Craig Pyes, an associate of the Center for Investigative Reporting, noted, our efforts transformed the League, winning it "new respectability." See "Private General, Mystery Man of the Reagan Doctrine," *The New Republic*, September 30, 1985, pp. 11–12.
34. One of the clearest accounts of the tragedy is Alexander Dallin, *Black Box: KAL 007 and the Superpowers* (Berkeley, CA: University of California Press, 1985).
35. Clyde Haberman, "Bomb Kills 19, Including 6 Key Koreans," *New York Times*, October 10, 1983, p. 1; also "Burma Police Search Rangoon for the Killers," *New York Times*, October 11, 1983, p. A-12.
36. Members of the Singlaub Panel, May 1984: MG John K. Singlaub, USA (ret.), Chairman; F. Andy Messing, National Defense Council, Director; members: MG Edward Lansdale, USAF (ret.); BG "Heinie" Aderholt, USAF (ret.); Dr.

Seale Doss, Professor of Philosophy, Ripon College (Col. USAR, Special Forces); Dr. Sam Sarkisian, Professor, Loyola University; Dr. Edward Luttwak, Center for Strategic and International Studies; Colonel John Wagglestein, USA; a senior representative from the CIA; observer: Cmdr. "Skip" Crane, USN.

37. Andy Messing convinced Congressman Jim Sensenbrenner to accompany him to El Salvador to inspect the national police forces. When Sensenbrenner returned to Washington, he introduced legislation to provide police-training funds.

15 • Sandinistas and Contras

1. The most politically balanced historical summary of the Iran-Contra affair is "Special Report: The Iran-Contra Affair," *Congressional Quarterly Almanac, 100th Congress, 1st Session, 1987,* Vol. XLIII (Washington, DC: Congressional Quarterly Inc., 1988), pp. 61–111. This report summarizes both the Democratic majority and the Republican minority views of the entire affair, and helps place the issue in the proper political perspective, which the commercial news media have rarely done.

2. "The Boland Amendments: A Review," *Congressional Quarterly Almanac, 100th Congress, 1st Session, 1987,* Vol. XLIII (Washington, DC: Congressional Quarterly Inc., 1988), p. 72.

3. "Nicaragua Reportedly Has Received Number of Soviet-Built Attack Helicopters Recently," *New York Times,* November 7, 1984, p. 1. Although there was ample evidence that the attack helicopters were in Nicaragua that summer, the mainstream American news media chose to ignore the issue until after the presidential election.

4. "Two Americans Killed Are Identified," *New York Times,* September 5, 1984, p. 1.

5. "The Boland Amendments: A Review," *Congressional Quarterly Almanac,* p. 72. For a complete chronology of the interrupted government funding for the Nicaraguan resistance see *Report of the Congressional Committees Investigating the Iran-Contra Affair* (Washington, DC: U.S. Government Printing Office, 1988) [Senate Report No. 100-216; House Report No. 100-433], Appendix C, *Chronology of Events.*

6. *New York Times,* October 17, 1984, p. 1.

7. Bob Woodward, *Veil: The Secret Wars of the CIA, 1981–1987* (New York: Simon and Schuster, 1987), pp. 444–49.

8. Peter Collier and David Horowitz, *Destructive Generation: Second Thoughts about the Sixties* (New York: Summit Books, 1989), pp. 150–51, 236–37.

9. U.S. Department of State, *Nicaraguan Biographies: A Resource Book* (Washington, DC: U.S. Department of State, 1988), pp. 4, 15–21.

10. *La Vanguardia,* Barcelona, Spain, July 31, 1984, p. 1.

11. U.S. Department of State, *Nicaraguan Biographies,* p. 17. This State Department study clearly shows how the small and secretive Sandinista Directorate closely controlled all key government positions, including the all-powerful Ministry of the Interior, as well as all official public information organizations and labor unions.

12. *La Vanguardia,* Barcelona, Spain, July 31, 1984, p. 1.
13. John Norton Moore, *The Secret War in Central America: Sandinista Assault on World Order* (Frederick, MD: University Publications of America, Inc., 1987), p. 44.
14. U.S. Department of State, *Nicaraguan Biographies,* pp. 39–42.
15. "A Profile of the Contra Combatant," U.S. Department of State Circular Telegraphic Message, March 14, 1989.
16. U.S. Department of State, "Misconceptions about U.S. Policy toward Nicaragua," Department of State Publication 9417, Revised April 1987, pp. 12–13.
17. Collier and Horowitz, *Destructive Generation,* p. 155.
18. Moore, *The Secret War in Central America,* p. 48.
19. U.S. Department of State, "Inside the Sandinista Regime: A Special Investigator's Perspective," Department of State Publication 9466, 1986, pp. 11–12.
20. Borge speech, *La Vanguardia,* Barcelona, Spain, July 31, 1984, p. 1.
21. "Rebels Have Raised More than $10 Million," *New York Times,* September 9, 1984, p. 1.
22. The most complete record of my fund-raising activities for the Contras is found in my deposition to the Congressional Select Committees on the Iran-Contra Affair. See *Report of the Congressional Committees Investigating the Iran-Contra Affair,* Appendix B, *Depositions,* Vol. 25, pp. 914–25. My entire deposition given on April 29, 1987, is on pp. 909–1066.
23. Evidence of widespread MINT executions has finally come to light. See Mark A. Uhlig, "Sandinistas Accused as Burial Sites Are Unearthed," *New York Times,* August 5, 1990, p. 22.
24. For an interesting discussion on this point see Harry Claflin, "SOF Trains Contras," *Soldier of Fortune,* October 1990, p. 70. Lieutenant Colonel Robert K. Brown, publisher of the magazine, includes a sidebar in the article, "Questions for the CIA," which directly addresses the issue of the Agency's overcontrol of the Contras before October 1984.
25. U.S. Department of State, "Inside the Sandinista Regime," pp. 7–10: "Special Measures—Government Assassinations of FSLN Opponents." Defector Alvaro Baldizon, a MINT inspector, documented the abuses against the Miskitos and was then ordered to suppress the evidence by Interior Minister Tomas Borge.
26. U.S. Department of State, *Nicaraguan Biographies,* p. 73.
27. For a more complete discussion of Richard Secord's relationship to Edwin Wilson see Peter Maas, *Manhunt* (New York: Random House, 1986), pp. 31–32, 58–59, 138–39, 234, 247–49, 278–79 (re Albert Hakim's relationship to Wilson see pp. 287–88). Also see Felix I. Rodriguez and John Weisman, *Shadow Warrior* (New York: Simon and Schuster, 1989), pp. 237–39.
28. For a complete discussion of my role in this arms shipment see *Report of the Congressional Committees Investigating the Iran-Contra Affair,* Appendix B, *Depositions,* Vol. 25, pp. 962–93.
29. By the next year, Owen's fears had reached the point that he wrote a memo alerting North to the possibility that Secord was defrauding the Contras. See ibid., Appendix B, *Depositions,* Vol. 20, pp. 707–9.
30. When the Associated Press interviewed me on this matter in June, I could

honestly say that I was no longer receiving guidance from Oliver North. See "White House Links Are Claimed to Private Nicaraguan Rebel Aid," Associated Press, *Denver Post,* June 10, 1985, p. A1. Also see "Who Was Helping the Contras," *Time,* May 27, 1985, p. 35; "Hearts, Minds, Money—Private U.S. Supporters Raise Millions for the Contras," *Newsweek,* August 26, 1985, pp. 20–21.

31. *Report of the Congressional Committees Investigating the Iran-Contra Affair,* Appendix B, *Depositions,* Vol. 25, pp. 951–52.

32. "Special Report: The Iran-Contra Affair," *Congressional Quarterly Almanac,* pp. 61, 96, 98.

33. U.S. Department of State, "The Sandinista Military Build-up: An Update," Department of State Publication 9432, 1987, pp. 8–9.

34. "U.S. Officials Say Cuban Advisers Engage in Combat in Nicaragua," *New York Times,* December 6, 1985, p. 1.

35. Claflin, "SOF Trains Contras," *Soldier of Fortune,* October 1990, p. 106.

16 · Hazardous Duty

1. U.S. Department of State, *Nicaraguan Biographies: A Resource Book* (Washington, DC: U.S. Department of State, 1988), p. 83.

2. John Lantigua, "Injured Nicaraguan Rebel Flies to Venezuela but Vows to Return," *Baltimore Sun,* June 2, 1984, p. A-2.

3. "Pastora Satisfactory after Surgery," *Washington Post,* June 13, 1984, p. A-13.

4. *Report of the Congressional Committees Investigating the Iran-Contra Affair* (Washington, DC: U.S. Government Printing Office, 1988) [Senate Report No. 100-216; House Report No. 100-433], Appendix B, *Depositions,* Vol. 25, pp. 1052–1053.

5. For a full description of this meeting see ibid., pp. 1056–1059.

6. "Arab Death Squad Nabbed in Israeli Shrine Murder," *New York Post,* April 29, 1986, p. 1.

7. Government Admission of Facts, U.S. District Court for the District of Columbia, Criminal Case No. 88-0080-02-GAG; *United States of America v. Oliver North,* p. 12, Point No. 32.

8. "U.S. Deal with Rebel Undercut by CIA, Retired General Says," Associated Press Washington Bureau Dispatch, *The El Paso Times,* June 1, 1986, p. 1. Also see *Report of the Congressional Committees Investigating the Iran-Contra Affair,* Appendix B, *Depositions,* Vol. 25, p. 1054. Staff counsel of the congressional committees confirmed that CIA officers had unleashed a "denigration campaign against Pastora."

9. Dr. Susan Huck, *Legal Terrorism: The Truth about the Christic Institute* (McLean, VA: New World Publishing Limited, 1989), p. 22.

10. Julia Preston, "Reporter Sues Contras for Alleged Murder Plot," *Washington Post,* May 30, 1986, p. A-26. This article described the Christics as "a Liberal, church-funded law group."

11. David Brock, "Christic Mystics and Their Drug-running Theories: An Obscure

Washington Institute Is Filling America's Head with Nonsense and Making a Killing," *The American Spectator,* May 1988, p. 22.

12. James Traub, "The Law and the Prophet," *Mother Jones,* February–March 1988, p. 25.

13. Ibid., p. 48.

14. Brock, "Christic Mystics," *The American Spectator,* May 1988, p. 22.

15. United States District Court, Southern District of Florida: *Tony Avirgan and Martha Honey, Plaintiffs, v. John Hull, Bruce Jones, Rene Corbo, et al., Defendants;* Case No. 86-1146-CIV-KING: Third Amended Complaint RICO Conspiracy, etc. Complaint for Damages and Other Relief, March 28, 1988.

16. Eventually I conferred with Ted Shackley and several other defendants in the Christic RICO suit, and we helped form Victims of the Christic Institute. This was a nonprofit legal defense fund and education effort. The group raised attorneys' fees for some defendants who had fewer financial resources than Ted or I. And the group also helped underwrite the research for *Legal Terrorism* by Dr. Susan Huck. The book is a hard-hitting exposé of the Christic's goals and methods.

17. Fund-raising material, the Christic Institute, circa 1986.

18. "Join Thousands of Americans Who Want to Learn the Whole Truth" (Order Form), *Convergence, The Christic Institute,* Spring 1988, p. 24.

19. Rod Holt, ed., *Assault on Nicaragua: The Untold Story of the U.S. 'Secret War,'* speeches by Daniel Sheehan and Daniel Ortega (San Francisco: Walnut Publishing Co., 1987), p. 76.

20. Huck, *Legal Terrorism,* p. 7; confirmed in telephone interviews with Ted Shackley on Jan. 25, 1991, and Feb. 7, 1991. Also see: Theodore G. Shackley, "Legal Terrorism," *Journal of Defense & Diplomacy,* December 1987, pp. 8–9.

21. David Corn, "Is There Really a 'Secret Team'?" *The Nation,* July 2, 1988, p. 10.

22. Traub, "The Law and the Prophet," *Mother Jones,* February–March 1988, p. 48; Brock, "Christic Mystics and Their Drug-running Theories," p. 24.

23. Order Granting Motions for Costs and Attorneys' Fees, U.S. District Court, Southern District of Florida, Case No. 86-1146-CIV-KING, February 2, 1989.

24. For an interesting explanation of the Ollie North–Elliott Abrams damage-control effort see *Report of the Congressional Committees Investigating the Iran-Contra Affair,* Appendix C, *Chronology of Events,* p. 102.

25. Doyle McManus, "Singlaub Played Double Role in Aid to Contras," *Los Angeles Times,* October 13, 1986, p. 4.

26. Richard Halloran, "A U.S. Agency Used Plane Lost in Nicaragua," *New York Times,* October 10, 1986, p. A-3. Also see "Singlaub Denies Link to Plane," *New York Times,* October 9, 1986, p. A-8.

27. *Report of the Congressional Committees Investigating the Iran-Contra Affair,* Appendix C, *Chronology of Events,* pp. 128–39.

28. Ibid., Appendix B, *Depositions,* Vol. 24, pp. 983–1137.

29. *The Report of the Congressional Committees Investigating the Iran-Contra Affair,* Senate Report No. 100-216, House Report No. 100-433, Chapter 22 (Washington, DC: U.S. Government Printing Office, 1987), p. 344.

30. Walter Pincus and Dan Morgan, "Some Apparently Went to Personal Use," *The Washington Post,* May 21, 1987, pp. A1, A42; Haynes Johnson, "Across the 'Hero' Image of Oliver North, a Shadow Starts to Fall," *The Washington Post,* May 21, 1987, p. A42.

31. Interview with former Justice Department attorney Lawrence Barcella, September 6, 1990.

32. *Report of the Congressional Committees Investigating the Iran-Contra Affair: Hearings,* Part I, Testimony June 24, 1987, p. 117, Vol. 26B. Also see: *Congressional Quarterly Almanac,* 100th Congress, 1st Session . . . 1987, Vol. XLII (Washington, DC: Congressional Quarterly, Inc., 1987), June 27, 1987, pp. 1353, 1356, 86.

33. "Special Report: The Iran-Contra Affair," *Congressional Quarterly Almanac, 100th Congress, 1st Session, 1987,* Vol. XLIII (Washington, DC: Congressional Quarterly Inc., 1988), p. 77. Also see "North Says Casey Aided Contra Project," *New York Times,* July 9, 1987, p. 1.

34. *Report of the Congressional Committees Investigating the Iran-Contra Affair:* Appendix D: Vol. 2, Testimonial Chronology: Witness Accounts, Supplemented by Documents, pp. 104–5, citing Clair George testimony of August 6, 1987.

35. Interview with a former senior executive of the Central Intelligence Agency (who wishes to remain anonymous), September 8, 1990. Also see Clair George testimony, pp. 104–5, cited in Note 34.

36. For a more complete discussion of North's testimony on this matter, see *Report of the Congressional Committees Investigating the Iran-Contra Affair with Supplemental, Minority, and Additional Views, November 17, 1987,* p. 51.

37. Background interview with former staff member of the Congressional Select Committees to Investigate Arms Transactions with Iran (person wishes to remain anonymous), August 18, 1990.

38. James LeMoyne, "Nicaragua to Keep Big Military Force, Its Leader Declares," *New York Times,* December 16, 1987, p. 1.

39. "Still Gunning for Peace," *Time,* November 9, 1987, p. 72.

40. James LeMoyne, "Raids by Contras on Three Towns Called Hard Blow," *New York Times,* December 25, 1987, p. 1.

41. "Battles of Bullets and Dollars: The Rebels Score Victories On and Off the Field," *Time,* January 4, 1988, p. 50.

42. "A Restrained Show of Force," *Time,* March 28, 1988, pp. 16–17.

43. For a scathing legal opinion of the Christic Institute's misuse of "witnesses," see *Order Granting Motions for Costs and Attorneys' Fees,* United States District Court Southern District of Florida, Case No. 86-1146-CIV-KING, February 2, 1989, pp. 1–3.

44. Affidavit of Thomas R. Spencer, Jr., Counsel for Defendant John K. Singlaub, Re: Rule 11 Sanctions, Case No. 86-1146-CIV-KING, United States District Court Southern District of Florida, July 20, 1988, pp. 2–14. Also see Speech to the Joseph Story Society, Washington, DC, July 21, 1988, by Thomas R. Spencer, Jr. (author's archive), pp. 9–10.

45. Confirmation by Tom Spencer in fax message, January 28, 1991.

46. For an amusing comparison of the Christics and LaRouchites see Mark Hosenball

and Michael Isikoff, "The Harmonic Convergence of Sleaze: One Big Scandal," *The New Republic,* April 4, 1988, p. 12.
47. *Order Granting Motions for Costs and Attorney's Fees,* Case No. 86-1146-CIV-KING, February 2, 1989, pp. 1–3.
48. "Christic Saviors," *The Nation,* April 3, 1989, p. 440.

Epilogue: After-Action Report

1. Henry Kamm, "A Haunted German Graveyard—East Germans Unlock a Murky Past: Nazi Prisons Turned into Soviet Prisons," *New York Times,* March 28, 1990, p. A-8. Also see John Tagliabue, "Secret Dossiers Arousing Germans," *New York Times,* September 8, 1990, p. 3.
2. Blaine Harden, "Warsaw Right Recalls Terrors of Stalin Era," *Washington Post,* October 31, 1989, p. A-1.
3. "What 'New' Soviet Military Thinking?" *Global Perspectives 1990,* Conference Report, International Security Council, Washington, DC, 1990.
4. Edward Jay Epstein, *Deception: The Invisible War between the KGB and the CIA* (New York: Simon and Schuster, 1989), Chap. 17, "The Sixth Glasnost," pp. 244–79.
5. Bill Keller, "Ousted KGB General Running for Parliament," *New York Times,* August 5, 1990, p. A-18. And Bill Keller, "Another KGB Officer Is Charging Incompetence and Graft," *New York Times,* September 8, 1990, p. 3.
6. Epstein, *Deception,* p. 278.
7. Department of Defense, *Soviet Military Power, 1989: Prospects for Change* (Washington, DC: Department of Defense, 1990), pp. 67–69, 108–9.
8. "An Eye on El Salvador," Editorial, *Washington Post,* August 24, 1990, p. A-26.
9. Al Kamen, "Salvadoran Leftists Accused of Killing Civilian Captives," *Washington Post,* May 31, 1990, p. A-12.
10. William Branigan, "Sandinista Hold on Army, Police Haunts Chamorro," *Washington Post,* August 7, 1990, p. A-6.
11. Ibid., p. A-8.
12. Mark A. Uhlig, "Sandinistas Accused as Burial Sites Are Unearthed," *New York Times,* August 5, 1990, p. 22.
13. "A Day in the Life of China," *Time,* October 2, 1989, p. 75.
14. Don Oberdorfer, "North Korean Armed Forces Now Put at 1 Million," *Washington Post,* January 26, 1989, p. A-20.
15. David Jackson, "Same Bed, Different Dreams," *Time,* July 2, 1990, p. 40.
16. Memorandum from Commander in Chief, United Nations Command, General Louis C. Menetrey, to General Lee Jong Koo, Chief of Staff, Republic of Korea Army, re Neutralization of North Korean Tunnels in the DMZ, 14 Feb. 1990. General Menetrey makes it clear that new or undiscovered North Korean tunnels through the DMZ continue to be a threat to security, fifteen years after the first tunnel was discovered.
17. Barbara Crossette, "If Communism Is Waning, Asia Defies the Trend," *New York Times,* June 20, 1990, p. A-10.

18. Ray Cline, "Seeds of the Next Crisis," *Washington Times,* September 5, 1990, p. G-1.

19. Carroll J. Doherty, "Covert Aid: Wars of Proxy Losing Favor as Cold War Tensions End," *Congressional Quarterly,* August 25, 1990, pp. 2721–25.

20. Walter Pincus, "North Ruling Appealed by Prosecution," *Washington Post,* September 5, 1990, p. A-14.

21. Interview with former Congressional Committee Counsel, August 14, 1990.

22. Walter Pincus, "Secord's Records Said to Be Altered; Swiss Financier Testifies Iran-Contra Evidence Had Been Changed," *Washington Post,* September 8, 1990, p. A-6; David Johnston, "Iran-Contra Data Termed Falsified," *New York Times,* September 6, 1990, p. B-8. Also see "Special Report: The Iran-Contra Affair," *Congressional Quarterly Almanac, 100th Congress, 1st Session, 1987,* Vol. XLIII (Washington, DC: Congressional Quarterly Inc., 1988), p. 77, and "North Says Casey Aided Contra Project," *New York Times,* July 9, 1987, p. 1.

Index

☆   ☆